# THE
# GOLF
# GUIDE

## —PGA—

### WHERE TO PLAY
### WHERE TO STAY

## 1993

Endorsed by
The Professional Golfers' Association

FHG Publications
Paisley

# Acknowledgements

The Publishers wish to acknowledge the assistance of the Professional Golfers' Association, their staff at the Belfry and their golfing correspondents in the preparation of THE GOLF GUIDE. Thanks are particularly due to Jane Carter, Rosemary Drake and Laraine Beeching.

For colour illustrations we wish to acknowledge the South East Tourist Board (p7), the Southern Tourist Board and Peter Titmuss Photography (p9), Jersey Tourism (p11), Bournemouth Tourism (p14), the Moray Tourist Board (pp33 & 34) and Michael Gedye (pp35 & 39). We also gratefully acknowledge the assistance of Tourist Boards, hotels and others who supplied additional information and illustrations throughout this latest edition of THE GOLF GUIDE.

Our front cover features one of the excellent greens on the championship course which is one of the many attractions of The Carlyon Bay Hotel, near St. Austell in Cornwall. Guests enjoy all the luxuries and facilities appropriate to the Cornish Riviera's leading hotel along with free golf in a spectacular setting overlooking Carlyon Bay. Further details are shown on the outside back cover and in the main Cornwall section of THE GOLF GUIDE.

Finally, our thanks to our advertisers and to the Club Secretaries, Professionals and others who have co-operated in the annual updating of the directory entries for clubs and courses which are the essential ingredient of THE GOLF GUIDE: Where To Play/Where To Stay.

*Cover design:* Ted Carden, Glasgow

*Title page picture:* Old Thorns Golf Course,
Hotel and Restaurants, Liphook, Hampshire.

ISBN 1 85055 167 7 © FHG Publications 1992-93

Published by FHG Publications, a member of the U.N. Group, Abbey Mill Business Centre, Seedhill, Paisley PA1 1TJ (041-887 0428)

*Distribution.* **Book Trade:** WLM, 117 The Hollow, Littleover, Derby DE3 7BS
(Tel: 0332 272020. Fax: 0332 774287.)
**News Trade:** UMD, 1 Benwell Road, Holloway, London N7 7AX
(Tel: 071 700 4600. Fax: 071 607 3352.)

Typeset by RD Composition Ltd., Glasgow
Printed and bound by Benham's Ltd., Colchester

PRINTED AND PUBLISHED IN BRITAIN

# Foreword

HAVING BEEN a golf professional for more than 40 years it never ceases to amaze or delight me just how the game of golf has grown in popularity. More and more people of all ages and both sexes are turning to the sport every day and long may it continue.

Among the great pleasures of this great game are the hundreds of golf courses throughout Great Britain and Ireland waiting for golfers of any ability to play and enjoy. *THE GOLF GUIDE* with its accommodation entries is the perfect companion to any golfer who wishes to explore these many fairways from John O'Groats to Land's End and across the water to the Emerald Isle.

Wherever you visit you can be sure that a PGA professional will not be far away to welcome you and make your visit as pleasant as possible.

*THE GOLF GUIDE* and the PGA through its 4,000 professionals, are dedicated towards helping you enjoy your golf and get the most from this rewarding game. On behalf of The Professional Golfers' Association I wish you many happy hours exploring the pages of this guide and even more enjoying the many courses, both old and new, which it lists.

*Ross Whitehead*
*Captain 1993*
*The Professional Golfers' Association*

# The Golf break other golfers want to keep a secret

Country Club Hotels' Short Breaks are a closely guarded secret among people who really enjoy the game of golf…and want to play it on some of Britain's finest courses.

With 10 venues located in beautiful countryside settings, Country Club Hotels offer the perfect environment to challenge friends to a rewarding game…entertain business clients or colleagues…or simply take a well-deserved break from home or office routine.

To help you relax and unwind, we provide a range of leisure activities – from tennis, swimming and squash to jacuzzis, saunas and fitness studios. So your partner is sure to enjoy a stay at Country Club Hotels as much as you do!

For details about our 2-Day and 5-Day Breaks, call Central Reservations on the number below.

*Short Break Holidays*
Weekends, Midweek & Golf

## COUNTRY CLUB HOTELS
### Experience the luxury of choice

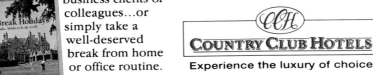

CALL FREE ☎ **0800 100 181** AND QUOTE CG901

# How to Use The Golf Guide

THE GOLF GUIDE Where to Play • Where to Stay, contains up-to-date basic information on every course (as far as we know) in Britain. Details are provided by the clubs themselves. You will also find sections on France, Majorca and Portugal. The guide also carries entries from hotels, guest-houses and other accommodation convenient to specific courses or areas. These are generally 'paid' entries and usually follow a recommendation from a club. THE GOLF GUIDE itself is endorsed by the Professional Golfers' Association and is usually available for sale in golf clubs through the Professional and/or the Secretary – as well as bookshops etc.

## Golf Course Information

For virtually every course you will find the following details, updated annually:

1. Name, address and telephone number.
2. Location.    3. Brief description.
4. Number of holes, length and Standard Scratch Score.    5. Green fees.
6. Details of facilities for visitors – individuals, groups and societies.
7. Name and telephone number of the Professional and the Secretary.

The accuracy of details published depends on the response of the clubs and to our best knowledge is correct at the time of going to press (October 1992). However, we cannot accept responsibility for errors or omissions and we recommend that you check important details with clubs before making any arrangements.

## Choosing a Course

The golf clubs and courses are listed alphabetically by nearest town or village within the appropriate county section for England, Scotland, Wales, Ireland, the Isle of Man and the Channel Islands. Courses in France, Majorca and Portugal are also listed by region. We have chosen to classify by place-name rather than club or course name since this seems more straightforward and recognisable to the majority.

If you want to find a club or course by its name, you should simply refer to the Index where you will see the page number of the listing. In each entry the name of the club or course is always shown in bold type after the place-name heading.

## Accommodation

Accommodation entries are placed as near a particular club or course as possible and there are also hotel displays in the front colour section. Most of the accommodation advertised has been recommended by the local golf club. A full index is provided.

## Maps

At the back of THE GOLF GUIDE you will find a set of maps showing cities, towns and villages in Britain with counties, motorways and main roads. Although many of the place-names under which the courses are classified are on the maps, please note that the maps are not golf course or club location maps.

The location details supplied with each entry should get you there and if you are in any doubt at all you should ask directions from the club itself.

Please mention THE GOLF GUIDE Where to Play • Where to Stay when you make a hotel booking or play at courses after using our guide.

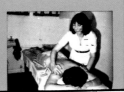

*In trouble at Royal St. George's, Sandwich, Kent.*

# Golfing Around Britain

Where to Play and Where to Stay around the Golfing Regions of Britain

BRITAIN HAS the oldest, the most varied and per head of population the greatest number of golf courses in the world. They are spread throughout the country, often in clusters, but distributed widely enough to allow any golfer to travel up and down the land without ever being far from a testing 18 holes. We've used the PGA's regions in the following brief golfing tour of Britain.

## Golf in the South

With over 300 courses and driving ranges from the Thames estuary south and westwards to the Isle of Wight and the New Forest, the South of England isn't short of courses. But with its huge population yielding almost 3 million golfers of all sorts, the pressure on teeing-off times is severe. Indeed, well over a third of all new golf developments are in the South in an attempt to satisfy the needs of the rapidly growing band of enthusiasts.

Amongst the existing golfing centres are some of the great names of British golf. Royal St George's at Sandwich in Kent has regularly hosted the Open Championship, most recently in 1985. Nearby, at Deal, the Royal Cinque Ports Golf Club celebrated its centenary year in 1992. The Ivyside Hotel at Westgate is within easy reach of these and several other courses in Kent. There's enjoyable seaside golf in Sussex, especially around

7

Bexhill, Brighton and Eastbourne, where the Lansdowne Hotel is a popular golfing base. Inland golf is well supplied also with such favourites as the Royal Ashdown and Dale Hill, and the new East Sussex National Golf Club at Little Horsted near Uckfield. Farther west at Chichester, and perhaps better known for the sounds of racing cars and horses, Goodwood Golf Club had its hundredth birthday in 1992.

On the south-west fringes of London, the 100-year-old Royal Mid-Surrey draws the golfer out towards the embarrassment of riches offered by such illustrious names as Walton Heath, Wentworth and

Sunningdale. It was at Sunningdale in 1903 that the first 'big' tournament organised by the then recently formed Professional Golfers' Association was played – the *News of the World* Matchplay, for a prize of £200! Wentworth nowadays, of course, is the internationally-known venue of the annual World Match Play Championship while Sunningdale has come to alternate with Walton Heath for the European Open.

Away from the urban sprawl the South offers many scenic attractions to accompany the pleasures of golf. Old Thorns at Liphook has all the appeal of a

*Enjoying golf amid the autumn colours of the New Forest.*

Old Thorns Golf Course, Hotel and Restaurants complex is a unique combination of old and new creating a country estate appeal with the traditional beauty of the old tile hung farmhouse providing blazing log fires in winter and terraces which overlook the magnificent 200 acres of Hampshire downs. The regal oaks, beeches and Scotch pines have been painstakingly conserved and the superb course is enhanced by the creation of water features fed from natural water springs.

Our testing 18-hole championship course provides a fine challenge for the enthusiastic golfer. The fairways wind their way through parkland, over lakes and streams and some holes cut through the pines or over the heathered slopes. A fleet of 30 golf cars has a track carefully incorporated within the contours of the fairways. Mid-week enjoyment for societies and golfing weekends is ensured by a driving range and practice green on hand for the individual golfer and adds up to perfect golf for everyone.

Our resident teaching professional will assess, encourage and monitor golfing skills. Everything needed to play is available on hire from the Pro's shop which carries a very comprehensive selection of golfing accessories. A wide range of brand name items are stocked as well as a variety of prizes for societies.

The tranquillity and peace of Old Thorns is complemented by the elegant new Japanese Centre carefully developed to blend naturally into the background of the undulating countryside thus cleverly uniting Eastern and Western culture.

Within one hour's drive of London, Heathrow and Gatwick airports, Old Thorns can provide the perfect venue for any business or social function.

*La Moye Golf Club, Jersey.*

fine country estate and whether by the Hampshire coast or around the New Forest, there are comfortable hotels like the Watersplash at Brockenhurst, Busketts' Lawn at Woodlands, The Bell Inn at Lyndhurst and Little Forest Lodge throughout this part of the country.

For those whose tastes include island golf, Hayling is a convenient overnight stop for a round before taking the ferry for the Isle of Wight and the several very pleasant courses there. Although well to the South West, and nearer France than England, the Channel Islands are nevertheless affiliated to the PGA's South Region. Guernsey and Jersey both offer excellent golf and excellent golfing accommodation and even tiny Alderney can boast its own 9-holer!

# Golf in the West and Wales

## by RICHARD CLIFFORD

FOR THE golfing enthusiast on holiday Wales and the West can cater for all tastes – from those who are looking for top quality action to those who just want peace and quiet and some spectacular scenery.

South Wales golf has long been associated with the championship courses of the coastal strip and rightly so, but now there are a number of young pretenders forcing their way into the reckoning.

Mountain Lakes, just five miles north of Cardiff, is a magnificent new championship course offering a panoramic view that is second to none. As the name suggests the course is littered with water hazards – 23 at the last count and all of them natural.

Just off the main A48 between Cardiff and Newport Peterstone Golf and Country Club straddles Gwent and Glamorgan and from the newly built

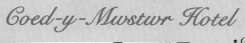

clubhouse you can take full advantage of the scene across the Bristol Channel. Peterstone is far more than a golf club and it also offers some of the finest fishing waters in Wales at the Peterstone trout lodge.

These are two courses that should continue to attract plaudits but Royal Porthcawl remains the flagship for the game in Wales. The rugged seaside links has been host to a number of professional championships as well as the European Amateur Team Championship

and the British Amateur Championship. The ever popular Seabank Hotel remains a favourite with visitors and as Porthcawl prepares to host the Walker Cup in 1995 its high profile is guaranteed to continue.

Farther west in Dyfed, Ashburnham is another familiar championship course with a view across the Loughor Estuary from the elevated sixteenth tee. Moving back east and the last but not least stop · before crossing the River Severn into England is St Pierre at Chepstow. A brace of championship courses – the Old

# BEACH BUNGALOW
## OUR WORLD BY THE SEA

Executive Beach Bungalow, in its own grounds, quiet secluded cove, with your own beach moments from your Patio door. Every comfort in an area of outstanding natural beauty. On flat coastal strip confirming Gulf Stream mild climate. Tour beautiful Snowdonia. "The Castles" and the famous Llŷn peninsula & beaches. Tastefully furnished by Parker Knoll. Modern split level lounge-dining room, overlooking lawn, beach & sea. 3 bedrooms, vanitory units, T.V.s & duvets; 1 & 2 Double & Single; 3 Single or double; 4 children's upstairs 4 singles; 2 Bathrooms en suite. Teletext colour T.V., video, compact disc tape & music centre, dish washer, microwave, fridge, freezer, washing machine, tumble dryer, electric blankets, telephone & central heating, patio furniture, parking 5 cars. P.O. & shop handy. Safe bathing and water sports, sea/river fishing. Nearby Restaurants, Bar Snacks, take-aways & most leisure activities, including golf, rambling, pony trekking, three major Leisure Centres. Featured by BBC & Wales Tourist Board (top grade 5 award). Come & inspect anytime, between Caernarfon & Nefyn on A499 (Llŷn Peninsula). Try a £49 Minibreak.

| JAN | FEB | MARCH | APRIL | MAY | JUNE | JULY | AUG | SEPT | OCT | NOV | DEC |
|---|---|---|---|---|---|---|---|---|---|---|---|
| 2...£109 | 6...£99 | 6...£129 | 3...£199 | 1BH...£199 | 5...£329 | 7...£419 | 7...£549 | 4...£415 | 2...£269 | 6...£159 | 4...£99 |
| 9...£89 | 13...£99 | 13...£139 | 10BH...£369 | 8...£219 | 12...£339 | 10...£499 | 14...£549 | 11...£389 | 9...£239 | 13...£149 | 11...£99 |
| 6...£79 | 20...£109 | 20...£149 | 17...£199 | 15...£229 | 19...£379 | 17...£529 | 21...£529 | 18...£359 | 16...£199 | 20...£129 | 17...£299 |
| 3...£79 | 27...£109 | 27...£159 | 24...£189 | 22...£259 | 26...£389 | 24...£549 | 28BH...£499 | 25...£319 | 23...£279 | 27...£119 | 24...£349 |
| 0...£89 |  |  |  | 29BH...£399 |  | 31...£549 |  |  | 30...£279 |  | 31...£259 |

*Deposit ¼ of total. Minimum £50 p.w. & Insurance £3 nightly. Sleeps 10, over 5 persons £35 each per week. Free electric allowance £7. Central Heating 70° £35 weekly. (Dogs £5 nightly. 2 only. Never left alone.) Weekend, Midweek or Week Breaks Phone 0286 660400.*

# VILLA CHALET

Your own beach moments from your lounge patio sliding door, overlooking lawn, beach & sea. Every comfort, Lounge Dinette, exclusive 3 piece suite. Teletext colour T.V. Electric fire, bed settee. 3 separate bedrooms. 1. Double, vanitory basin, en suite to bathroom, electric blanket & heater. 2. Double, or two singles, two drop-down beds for children. 3. Single with drop-down bed. Blankets and pillows provided. Bring [li]nen & towels or own duvet? Kitchen Area. Microwave, electric hob & oven, fridge-freezer, slow [coo]ker, kettle, toaster & hoover. Bathroom, Sit-down shower-bath, wash basin, toilet. Well heated, [pati]o furniture, much up market Dragon Award. Featured by the BBC & Wales Tourist Board. View [any] time. Try a £25 Minibreak.

**WALES** *It's magic*

| MARCH | APRIL | MAY | JUNE | JULY | AUG | SEPT | OCT |
|---|---|---|---|---|---|---|---|
| ...£79 | 3....£119 | 1BH...£119 | 5...£229 | 3...£269 | 7...£319 | 4...£259 | 2...£139 |
| ...£94 | 10BH...£159 | 8...£149 | 12...£239 | 10...£279 | 14...£319 | 11...£219 | 9...£119 |
|  | 17...£119 | 15...£169 | 19...£249 | 17...£299 | 21...£299 | 18...£189 | 16...£109 |
|  | 24....£99 | 22...£179 | 26...£259 | 24...£319 | 28BH...£309 | 25...£169 | 23...£159 |
|  |  | 29BH...£299 |  | 31...£319 |  |  |  |

*2 Bedroomed, Similar, Deduct £25 from above rates. Deposit ¼ of total, minimum £50 p.w. & Insurance £2 nightly. Sea view £3 nightly. Limited to 8, over 5 persons £21 each per week. (Dogs, £3 nightly, never left alone, 2 only.) Weekend, Midweek or Week Breaks Phone 0286 660400.*

# BEACH HOLIDAY HOME

BEACH MODERN LUXURY HOLIDAY HOME (Tourist Board approved caravan) Your own beach moments from your door. Top Grade 5 award. 6 berth B type 2 bedrooms: 8 berth A type 2 bedrooms limited to 6: 10 berth A type 3 bedrooms limited to 8. Lounge, Kitchen, Dinette. Bedrooms: 1st, one double; 2nd, Some have a Single with a drop down bed, or 2 Singles to make a double; 3rd, Single or Twins, some make a double. Request on phone and on white booking form. In some a double bed settee makes up in the Lounge/dinette. Blankets & pillows provided. Bring linen & towels or own duvet? Bathroom, shower, wash basin, toilet. Well heated, remote control Colour T.V. Fridge. Large Cooker. Electric Blanket, kettle & hoover. Featured by The BBC, Wales Tourist Board, and British Holiday Home Parks. Superior Dragon Award Holiday Homes with heated Bedroom. £2 nightly. View anytime. Try a £12 Minibreak.

| MARCH | | | APRIL | | | | MAY | | | | JUNE | | | | JULY | | | | AUGUST | | | | SEPTEMBER | | | | OCTOBER | | | |
|---|---|---|---|---|---|---|---|---|---|---|---|---|---|---|---|---|---|---|---|---|---|---|---|---|---|---|---|---|---|---|
| 6 berth | 8 berth | 10 berth | Date | 6 berth | 8 berth | 10 berth | Date | 6 berth | 8 berth | 10 berth | Date | 6 berth | 8 berth | 10 berth | Date | 6 berth | 8 berth | 10 berth | Date | 6 berth | 8 berth | 10 berth | Date | 6 berth | 8 berth | 10 berth | Date | 6 berth | 8 berth | 10 berth |
| £33 | £38 | £40 | 3 | £39 | £49 | £52 | 1BH | £41 | £49 | £53 | 5 | £69 | £89 | £95 | 3 | £109 | £129 | £139 | 7 | £155 | £189 | £199 | 4 | £79 | £99 | £109 | 2 | £39 | £45 | £47 |
| £34 | £39 | £42 | 10BH | £49 | £69 | £79 | 8 | £41 | £55 | £57 | 12 | £79 | £99 | £105 | 10 | £115 | £139 | £145 | 14 | £155 | £189 | £199 | 11 | £65 | £79 | £85 | 9 | £35 | £45 | £47 |
|  |  |  | 17 | £39 | £49 | £52 | 15 | £45 | £55 | £59 | 19 | £89 | £115 | £119 | 17 | £135 | £169 | £179 | 21 | £155 | £185 | £199 | 18 | £49 | £65 | £69 | 16 | £35 | £45 | £47 |
|  |  |  | 24 | £39 | £45 | £47 |  |  |  |  | 26 | £99 | £119 | £129 | 24 | £155 | £189 | £199 | 28BH | £129 | £159 | £169 | 25 | £45 | £55 | £57 | 23 | £45 | £55 | £59 |
|  |  |  |  |  |  |  | 29BH | £99 | £129 | £159 |  |  |  |  | 31 | £155 | £189 | £199 |  |  |  |  |  |  |  |  |  |  |  |  |

*[?] wide super luxury holiday homes, 20% more spacious. Add £35 to above prices. Deposit £25 p.w. & Insurance £1 nightly. Sea view £2 nightly. Twin bedded [roo]m £1 nightly. Peak & B/H £2 nightly. Microwave £1 nightly. Dragon Award, with heated bedroom £2 nightly. latest model, recent model, up market model, special etc £5 nightly. Request quotation. Over 6 persons £2 per night each. (Dogs £2 nightly.) Weekend, Midweek or Week Breaks Phone 0286 660400.*

BEACH HOLIDAY, WEST POINT, THE BEACH, PONTLLYFNI, CAERNARFON, NORTH WALES, LL54 5ET

## PERSONAL ATTENTION, BROCHURE & RESERVATIONS TEL. 0286 660400.

*Queen's Park (above) and Meyrick Park (left), two of Bournemouth's courses.*

Course and the Mathern – combined with the superb leisure facilities on offer make this another Mecca for the holidaymaker.

Into Avon and at Weston-Super-Mare the Commodore Hotel is always a favourite due to its close links with both the Worlebury and Weston Golf Clubs. Nearby Bristol also has plenty to offer including the wonderfully undulating parkland course at Long Ashton, where they celebrated their centenary last year by staging both the British Women's Open Stroke-play and the prestigious Carris Trophy.

In Somerset golfers shouldn't miss Burnham-on-Sea where the Burnham and Berrow club offers championship links golf and on-the-spot accommodation to an equally high standard. Less well-known is the Mendip Golf Club at Shepton Mallet near Bath, a distinctive downland course that is also within easy reach of the famous spa town itself.

In Devon, the Lundy House and Darnley hotels provide the ideal base for visiting any number of high quality courses including Ilfracombe, Saunton – home of the 1992 British Women's Championship – and Royal North Devon.

Not surprisingly Bournemouth is the focal point of golf in Dorset, the great seaside town boasting four courses including the excellent Knighton Heath.

Cornwall is a traditional golfing stronghold in England and St Mellion, near Saltash, home of the Benson and Hedges International, is usually the first course that springs to mind. Equally popular these days are the "Riviera" courses at St Austell and Carlyon Bay, both served by the four-star Carlyon Bay Hotel. They offer a golfing holiday that can also be combined with the more traditional family break at the seaside.

Also worthy of a mention, if only for its unusual combination of seaside and parkland, is the nine-hole Praa Sands situated between Helston and Penzance.

# MORETONHAMPSTEAD:
## a secret no longer!

"The ubiquitous motorways are not everyone's choice of road, but they have proved of benefit to holidaymakers and visitors seeking easier access to the more remote corners of the country, not least the West Country.

The M5 to Exeter has been a boon to that part of England, a green and tranquil corner where countryside on the edge of Dartmoor has remained unchanged for centuries, compelling in its beauty and serenity. Here are to be found dozens of lovely villages, all thatched roofs and flowerpots, and miles of golden beaches.

Golf here is a particular delight and nowhere is it better or more appealing than at Moretonhampstead, where the gracious old Manor House Hotel sits in regal splendour overlooking a golf course that is a sight for sore eyes at any time of year.

Only 17 miles from the ancient cathedral city of Exeter, near the village of North Bovey, the Manor House and its golf course was once the best-kept secret in British golf, the haunt for those to whom it represented all that was best in life.

Set on the edge of the Dartmoor National Park, the course provides a stunning combination of natural beauty and ideal golf terrain perhaps without peer. It is a rare mix of moor and parkland folded into the floor of a valley that winds around the 270 acre estate hidden from the eyes of the unknowing who pass the gatehouse lodge and the entrance to the mile-long driveway which splits the course and leads to the elegant hotel.

Formerly a country retreat for the rich and titled, the Manor is presently owned by 'Principal Hotels' and is currently undergoing an extensive refurbishment programme which aims to retain its former glory whilst providing the high standard of comfort and service you would expect.

Stand on the hotel's terrace and immediately below is the first tee. Down to the right, tucked into a bend of the River Bovey, lies the first green.

The river is a recurring feature of the first eight holes as it threads its way through the valley imposing its presence on virtually every shot played.

After your game relax in the recently re-opened 'Spikes Bar' with its 'pub like' atmosphere serving a selection of hot and cold snacks, plus the usual alcoholic beverages, it is the ideal spot to sit and discuss the finer points of your game.

Another bonus, and part of the formerly well-kept secret, is the elegant former country home that is now the Manor House, a hotel in the grand tradition with oak panelled lounges, lots of open fireplaces, wide sweeping staircases, superb cuisine and impeccable service.

The hotel also offers the additional sports of game and fly fishing, squash, tennis, croquet and a challenging par 3 course.

Add walks through countryside of matchless beauty where hidden villages offer a treasure trove of lovely restaurants and shops in a setting of total tranquillity, and the prospect is one of idyllic holidays you will want to re-live again and again''.

*Richard Wade writing in 'Golf Holiday Digest'.*

COME AND EXPERIENCE THE SECRET.

# Pedn-Olva

## HOTEL & RESTAURANTS

Guests are assured of a warm, friendly welcome, personal attention, comfort and good food at Pedn-Olva, situated just two minutes' walk from the harbour and the quaint, narrow streets of St. Ives.

The hotel has direct access to safe Porthminster beach for bathing, and arrangements can be made for water ski-ing, paragliding, windsurfing, fishing, clay-pigeon shooting and golf.

35 bedrooms with private facilities, tea-makers, TV and radio, telephone and baby listening. Car parking available.

* Open all year    * Fully licensed
* Heated swimming pool    * Sun terrace

AA
★★
RAC

**Porthminster Beach, St. Ives, Cornwall TR26 2EA**
**Telephone (0736) 796222    Fax (0736) 797710**

# "THE CREAM OF GOLF AT CORNWALLS FINEST..."

## "...set in 250 spectacular acres."

The Carlyon Bay Hotel Golf Course has been owned by the hotel since 1929. Even in its earliest days, this spectacular location attracted the keenest golfers including the Duke of Windsor and Sir Winston Churchill .

Improved in 1978 by golf architect Hamilton Stutt, the emphasis of continual improvement has remained to this day. The Extensive clubhouse complex includes spacious modern locker rooms, bar, restaurant, lounge and club professionals shop.

The 6,505 yard course stretches through the beautiful countryside of Cornwall. The Carlyon Bay Course proves both interesting and challenging to golfers of all handicaps. A full course layout is available from The Brend Hotels Travel Centre 0271 44496.

- Spectacular Location
- One of Cornwalls Premier Courses
- 4 star luxury at Cornwalls finest Hotel
- Professionally managed course

## The Carlyon Bay Hotel
### AND GOLF COURSE

AA ★★★★ RAC

St.Austell, South Cornwall. PL25 8RD
Telephone: St.Austell 812304

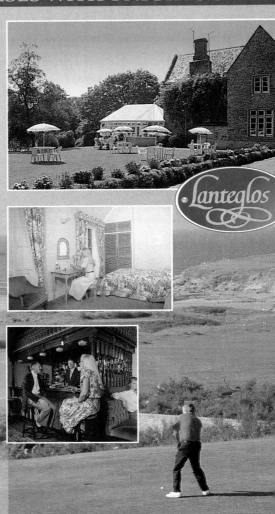

# Golf in the East

*Barnham Broom Hotel and Country Club, near Norwich.*

by BRYAN POTTER

THE EAST REGION of the PGA may not claim the most heavily populated golfing acres within the UK, but its quality and variety is beyond question. Before its reformation and extension to seven counties in 1987 the region was based essentially on the area of East Anglia. There were less than 100 courses within the combined boundaries of Suffolk, Norfolk, Bedfordshire and Cambridgeshire. Now they are linked and, some would say, reinforced with another 100 from Essex, Middlesex and Hertfordshire. This trio from the Greater London area have certainly added weight in numbers and provided a comfortable balance in character and style.

East Anglians have always been proud of their golfing heritage. It is based largely on those lovely, rolling seaside tests around the coasts of Norfolk and Suffolk and the demanding heathland tracks adorned with the heather and gorse that so characterise the game throughout the area.

Among the most glittering of these golfing jewels is Hunstanton. Stretched along the resort's northern beach its rolling fairways and lightning fast greens have attracted many professional and amateur championships over the years and is the one every golfer loves to tackle. Next door there is historic Brancaster, a place that time seems to have left behind and farther along the coast Sheringham and Royal Cromer have provided the best in clifftop golf for visitors.

Moving south there is a change of scenery at King's Lynn where immaculate fairways twist within avenues of trees to create what has been described as the Augusta of the East. The PGA Club Professional Championship was staged there in 1991 and a heavily sponsored annual regional Pro-am is further testimony to the qualities of the Castle Rising layout. Parkland golf is offered seven miles south-west of Norwich with 36 holes at the Barnham Broom Hotel and Country Club. It includes a 52-room hotel and time-sharing opportunities.

Nowhere is the colour and beauty of heathland golf better presented than in Suffolk. At Thorpeness there is the added convenience of a golf hotel and within a short driving distance are equally compelling golfing acres at Aldeburgh, Woodbridge and Purvis Heath. Hintlesham Hall, a 16th century mansion with a high class hotel and matching restaurant, has added a superb course in secluded countryside close to Ipswich.

Just off the A11 near Newmarket is famous Royal Worlington, the adopted home of Cambridge University golfers and once described as the best nine-hole course in Europe. They only allow two-ball matches. Cambridge offers the quaintly named but always immaculate Gog Magog course, built on chalk-based hills and said to be the highest point in a line from the Ural Mountains. Its superb drainage makes it one of the true year-round courses. The Moat House Hotel course three miles out of Cambridge is a fine challenge and Christy O'Connor found it to his liking, winning three of his six British Seniors' titles there.

Bedfordshire can boast one of the finest parkland courses available anywhere at the John O'Gaunt club where, apart from an additional 18 hole "Cartagena" layout, the PGA East Region headquarters are located.

Golfing tourists wishing to combine the grandeur of an 18th century mansion with Tour class golf course, should visit Moor Park near Rickmansworth where until recently the Four Stars Celebrity Tournament attracted showbusiness and sports superstars from around the world. The sumptuous, Palladian style clubhouse was used as a military HQ during World War Two. Another manor house rich in English history forms the nucleus of the Hanbury Manor Golf & Country Club near Ware. Apart from an immaculate and demanding 7000-yard course the Manor offers a health club with swimming and squash available.

Switching to styles more contemporary, Essex appears to be in line for staging future major tour events with the building of two tournament-class courses at Quietwaters near Maldon. A comprehensive multi-facility country club and a 94-room hotel are planned and the project has enormous potential.

Although the more traditional golfing areas of the region are to be found in the North and East, geography and the demands of travel generally rule them out of the 'Pro-am' circuit. It is in the more commercially-minded southernmost counties of Herts, Essex and Middlesex where most of the region's 70-odd tournaments are staged each year.

# Golf in the Midlands

by JENNIFER PRENTICE

THE MIDLANDS, the centre of England, is in good golfing heart! During 1993 the attention of the whole golfing world will be focused on the region and one of its most prestigious venues – The Belfry.

The 1993 Ryder Cup clash between Great Britain & Europe and the United States will be staged over the famed Brabazon course, with the home team going all out to regain this historic trophy, reclaimed by the Americans in that tantalisingly close encounter at Kiawah Island in 1991. Previous Ryder Cup matches at The Belfry have all produced

moments of high drama, of tension, sheer excitement and raw emotion. There is no doubt this year's tussle will provide more of the same. The dramatic closing hole in particular has been the scene of so much golfing history including celebrations or commiserations as a watery grave for plummeting hopes.

But it is a course – and a hotel – used throughout the year by many golfers of all ranges of expertise, playing over either the Brabazon or the Derby courses. Last year too it hosted the Murphy's English Open with top golfers from the European

The Belfry – hotel and Ryder Cup venue. Also the home of the PGA.

# HAWKSTONE PARK HOTEL AND GOLF COURSES

*'Where Sandy Lyle learned his game'*

New golf centre for all golfers open Spring 93.
Golf Societies welcome.
18 Hole Hawkstone course.
9 Hole Weston course (new extension to be completed 1995).
Corporate events – our speciality.
Tastefully refurbished hotel facilities.
Excellent cuisine in the Hawkstone Restaurant.

All of this is situated in idyllic natur Grade 1 listed parkland, surrounde by restored follies. This 80 acre historic park opens in Spring 93. Hawkstone is half an hour from the M54 and 40 minutes from the M6.

*Telephone today for our new brochure.*

**HAWKSTONE PARK**
HOTEL & GOLF COURSES

## HAWKSTONE PARK HOTEL
**Weston-under-Redcastle, Shrewsbury, Shropshire. SY4 5UY**
**Tel: (0939) 200611   Fax: (0939) 200311**

See ou
entry
Shre

Tour chasing the £550,000 prize fund and renewing their acquaintance with the special atmosphere.

In that field were top finishers from the Midland PGA 1991 Order of Merit – Kevin Dickens (SMC Engineering Sales), a Tour pro cardholder, and Graham Farr, the region's new captain from the spring, who is professional at the Telford Hotel Golf and Country Club in Shropshire.

Graham Farr succeeds Tim Rouse (Northants Co.) as Midland captain. An innovation by Tim Rouse was the annual dinner, staged right at the end of another busy season, at the Forest of Arden Hotel, Golf and Country Club at Meriden, near Coventry. The course there has been the setting for the Midland Professional Championship on several occasions in recent years.

Midland PGA headquarters are not very far away. Regional secretary Ray Ellis and his team are based at Kings Norton Golf Club, one of the many impressive inland courses throughout this "hidden jewel" of a region. There are 27-holes here in loops of 9 – red, blue and yellow – combining to present a tough test. Captain Graham Farr's own home base at Telford attracts many enthusiastic golfers throughout the year and there are now more bedrooms available making it another ideal spot for a golfing break.

Traditionally Hawkstone Park has been another fine Midlands venue and golfers who follow the game need no reminding that it was here that Sandy Lyle learnt to play.

In 1992 a Midland Order of Merit ranking championship – the E.C. Osborne Midland Masters – was contested at Patshull Park Hotel, Golf and Country Club. It proved highly successful and Patshull Park was used too for company days in the season, including the first ever organised for the world's leading tyre manufacturers,

# There's More than Golf at Gloucester

Excellent golfing facilities are just one reason why the Gloucester Hotel and Country Club is well worth a visit – but there are many more attractions for the whole family.

Set in over 200 acres of beautiful Cotswold countryside, this modern hotel has 117 luxury bedrooms. An investment of over £3.5 million has ensured it offers a unique combination of sporting and leisure facilities including ski-ing, snooker, swimming, squash and tennis. With so much on offer, your golfing break could well turn into a family holiday.

For the keen golfer the 6,127 yard par 70, 18 hole course features a strategically laid out bunker formation. The natural hazards – trees, copses, small lakes and a variety of hillside undulations test all golfing skills.

The 9 hole par 3 course appeals to those who don't have time for a full round of golf, and the 12 bay floodlit driving range is always available for practising your swing.

Catering for all levels of golfing skills, tailored courses and special breaks are available, with tuition from the Club's 3 resident professionals.

For those learning the game, the residential beginners golf instruction week covers basic techniques, discussion of rules and etiquette by the experts, and, for fun, concludes with a competition on the 9 hole course.

Away from the fairways, members of the whole family may wish to try out the

premier dry ski slopes in England – and the excellent "après-ski" facilities at the new Ski Lodge. Perhaps a game of tennis or squash for the more energetic, or chalk your cues for a game of snooker or pool.

Warm and welcoming water attractions include an exciting leisure pool, complete with rapids, spa pool, steam room, sauna and jacuzzi to provide that period of relaxation.

Not only catering for leisure breaks, the Hotel has extensive conference facilities ranging from rooms for select confidential business meetings to a full scale delegation of 150 people. The Redwell Restaurant, a popular venue for business lunches offers haute cuisine standards and an extensive wine cellar.

Should you wish to make the most of your stay in this most attractive area, Gloucester boasts an excellent shopping centre, many surrounding sites of historic interest and scenic walking routes in the Cotswolds. Reception staff are fully informed on all seasonal activities in the area.

The complex enjoys easy access from the M5 motorway, and is just 1½ miles from the City Centre.

The Gloucester Hotel and Country Club is a member of the Jarvis Hotel Group.

# A golfing break for people who hate golf.

Firstly, the bad news. At the Gloucester Hotel & Country Club, set among 280 acres of the Cotswolds you'll find a superb, if testing, 18-hole par 70 golf course, plus a pleasing 9-hole course, floodlit driving range and a well stocked shop.

But the good news is that this luxurious hotel also boasts a magnificent new leisure complex, complete with superb pool, whirl-pools, steam room, sauna and solarium.

Not to mention squash, twin tennis courts and a fully-equipped supervised gym.

Of course, all 117 bedrooms are appointed to the highest standards and our 'Redwell' à la carte restaurant can more than cater for the gourmet in you.

So whether golf is the love or bane of your life, call us on (0452) 525653 for more details about our great valus short stay breaks.

## GLOUCESTER HOTEL AND COUNTRY CLUB

**Robinswood Hill, Gloucester GL4 9EA. Fax (0452) 307212.**   **Jarvis▯Hotels**

Goodyear, who have their factory at Wolverhampton.

Breadsall Priory is another hotel golf course to host a company event.

A recent newcomer to the courses in the Daventry area is Hellidon Lakes which, like nearby Staverton, offers golfers the additional facilities of its Hotel and Country Club.

There is a rich wealth of venues, covering many types of terrain – heathland, parkland and, on the eastern side of the region, links which may be undulating, hilly or comparatively flat to add spice to the challenges this great game never ceases to provide.

Good surroundings and good company are the essence of any golfing occasion and Midland professionals and officials pride themselves on creating the right atmosphere for all events. Given the wide choice of appropriate venues, it is not surprising that golf in the Midlands is flourishing at every level and any visitor will find much of great appeal within its boundaries.

## Golf in the North

### by DAVID BIRTILL

TWO ISLANDS and a wedge of Britain stretching from the east to west coast, an area containing more than 400 clubs, constitutes the largest of the seven regions under the PGA umbrella.

It is debatable whether a greater variety of courses can be found elsewhere in the country. When anyone mentions the North West, for instance, they invariably wax lyrical about the magnificent Championship links at Royal Lytham and St Annes and, just across the Ribble Estuary, at Royal Birkdale.

Further down the coast is another course granted royal approval, at Hoylake, where the Great Britain and Ireland team won back the Curtis Cup from the United States on a glorious summer's day last year. It seemed appropriate that Prince Andrew, a new devotee to the royal and ancient game, witnessed the occasion as he had the Open at Birkdale the previous year.

Setting foot on any of these superb links is more awe-inspiring than treading the hallowed turf of Wembley, Twickenham or Lord's for the golfer can play on the same fairways and to the same greens as so many legendary figures have done in the past.

From Anglesey to North Wales, to Liverpool, across the sea to the Isle of Man, back to Southport and then up the Fylde coast and beyond, there is a rich seam of links to be explored. Castletown, restored in recent years to its former glory, is one of seven courses – two public – on the Isle of Man and is the home of the Bradford and Bingley Manx Classic. Jutting out to sea on the

Langness Peninsula, the holes were laid out 100 years ago by Old Tom Morris of St Andrews. He would have been proud of the work done on the course by the new owners, the Palace Group. The Links Hotel, nestling near the 18th green, offers cuisine of the highest standard in a tranquil setting where the sea laps gently on three sides.

Back on the mainland, the golfer is spoiled for choice. The Greater Manchester area, for example, claims to encompass a greater density of courses than anywhere in the world. And with membership waiting lists extending into the next millenium, new clubs and driving ranges are springing up like mushrooms! Some are still on the drawing board – most being designed by top architect Dave Thomas at Warrington – while others are already operational and, in time, will indeed justify their championship-standard claims.

Mottram Hall, near Macclesfield, with its beautifully-appointed hotel and country club, has been open for less than three years but has matured so quickly that the North Region Championship, sponsored by brewers Greenalls, is staged there. Only a short drive away is Shrigley Hall, which also affords top class accommodation, and The Tytherington which is the headquarters of the Women's European Tour. A few miles down the M6 is Mere Golf and Country

*Shrigley Hall, near Macclesfield – country house hotel and golf club.*

Club, one of the jewels in the Cheshire crown, where the Brother Winter Series is played every year.

Over in Vale Royal, the new 'pay-as-you-play' complex at Portal, Tarporley is arguably the most challenging track in the North and, while you are in the area, try the more forgiving Oaklands which is situated next door.

Across the Pennines and into Yorkshire and Humberside, there is a bewildering number of courses, from parkland to moorland, set in some of England's most spectacular countryside. Fulford, Ganton, Sand Moor, Harrogate, Moortown, Brough, Hull . . . the list appears endless. Where to play, where to stay is indeed a pleasant problem to cogitate!

The Bass Leeds Cup, the oldest in professional golf, was staged at Pannal last year while other North Region tournaments were at Lindrick and Stressholme, a public course near Darlington which puts many private ones to shame. And while in County Durham, try taming Seaton Carew!

Links abound in Cumbria. Silloth-on-Solway is one of the toughest tests of golf you are likely to find anywhere, especially when the wind blows as it often does. Seascale and Penrith are also worthy of a visit. Windermere, home of the Rayrigg Motors Lakes Autumn Classic, is a charming course with views that take your breath away. Newby Grange, near Carlisle, is the latest addition to the area.

The rugged Northumberland coastline may not be blessed with as many courses as the West but there's still plenty of choice. Alnmouth, which boasts dormy house accommodation, should not be overlooked. Neither, too, should Bedlingtonshire, a public course, which hosts the Wansbeck Classic, one of the North Region's five major tournaments.

In Tyne and Wear, Washington with its Moat House Hotel is the home of the Sunderland Masters, while Whitley Bay is as enchanting as its name implies.

# Golf in Scotland

by ELSPETH BURNSIDE

SCOTLAND, golf and superb hospitality combine to make a potent cocktail. Shake them together – and pour out a golfer's dream.

North, south, east or west, the Home of Golf has a course and a hotel to suit all tastes. The nine-hole clubs provide a welcome introduction for the holiday novice, while others can dream – "this one for the Open" – by following in the footsteps of Nick Faldo, Tom Watson, Severiano Ballesteros and Greg Norman over the renowned links of Muirfield, Royal Troon, St Andrews and Turnberry.

Edinburgh would be a 'Capital' choice to start a golfing break north of the border, and an ideal location would be Dalmahoy Golf & Country Club, host to the 1992 Solheim Cup and a member of the Country Club Hotel group that specialise in golfing clientele.

Then take a trip down the coast to East Lothian – a golfer's paradise. Longniddry, Aberlady, Gullane, North Berwick and Dunbar present a ribbon of courses along the Firth of Forth, with each one offering interesting and varied tests. The hotel accommodation is of an equally high quality with The Golf in Aberlady, The Mallard in Gullane and the Point Garry, Nether Abbey and

Brentwood in North Berwick among the select choice.

Down to the Borders, and a plethora of holiday layouts. St Boswells, Melrose, Selkirk, Innerleithen and Torwoodlee are among the picturesque nine-hole tests, while Peebles, Hawick and Kelso are 18 holes and well worth a visit. In the South-West, the often underrated Southerness stands out as a halt not to be missed,

*The Old Course, St. Andrews, and its 'new' hotel.*

# Scottish Golfing Breaks

## with Mount Charlotte Thistle Hotels

Enjoy the beauty of Scotland and guaranteed tee-off times at some of Scotland's finest golf courses. Centered around 3 top grade,5 crown hotels, Scottish Golfing Breaks are the ideal way to spend 3,5 or 7days away on a golf inclusive package.

**Choose from:**

*Hospitality Inn*
Irvine

**The Angus Thistle Hotel**
**Dundee**

**Altens Skean Dhu Hotel**
**Aberdeen**

Prices start at £165 for a 3 night "Hole in One" break, to £450 for the "Par Excellence" 7 night break, with special "Highlife" and "Weekaway" rates for non golfers.

**For a FREE leaflet & booking form contact:**

*Hospitality Inn*

**46,Annick Road, Irvine,KA11 4LD**
**Telephone: 0294 74272  Fax: 0294 77287**

---

## STOTFIELD HOTEL

**LOSSIEMOUTH, MORAY IV31 6QS**
**Tel: 0343 812011   Fax: 0343 814820**
**GROUPS AND SOCIETIES WELCOMED**
**CONFIRMED TEE TIMES ARRANGED**

Elegant Victorian Hotel overlooking Moray's premier 18-hole Championship Golf Course, also a second 18-hole course. Many fine golf courses a short drive away. The Hotel has 47 en-suite bedrooms, all with colour TV, video channel, tea and coffee making facilities, direct dial telephones, clock radio-alarms; a sauna and mini-gym are available. Excellent food. American Bar and Grill.          **Enquiries to Mike and Patricia Warnes, resident owners.**

---

## PUBLISHER'S NOTE

While every effort is made to ensure accuracy, we regret that FHG Publications cannot accept responsibility for errors, omissions or misrepresentation in our entries or any consequences thereof. Prices in particular should be checked because we go to press early. We will follow up complaints, but cannot act as arbiters or agents for either party.

while Dumfries & County and Powfoot are other attractions.

Heading north, and the golfer is spoilt for choice in Ayrshire. Old Prestwick, scene of the very first Open Championship; Troon, Barassie and Largs are all worth a visit. The Caledonian Hotel in Ayr offers golf packages, while the Marine Highland at Troon and Turnberry's Malin Court would be other chosen hotels as well as the Hospitality Inn at Irvine.

Move east and the golfer will come to Cardross on the outskirts of Glasgow, and the venue for the 1992 Scottish Professional Championship. On the other side of the former European City of Culture lies Westerwood Golf & Country Club. The course was designed by Severiano Ballesteros, and made its debut as a major championship venue in 1992 when hosting a PGA Scottish Region "major", the Sunderland of Scotland Masters.

*Beside the sea at Buckpool Golf Club, Buckie, on the Moray Firth.*

Farther north, and golf can be enjoyed to the background of Scotland's breathtaking mountain scenery. Gleneagles – spoil yourself by staying at the hotel! – is famous as the venue for the Bell's Scottish Open, while near neighbours Auchterarder, a course that celebrated its centenary in 1992, and Crieff are other delights. The Murrayshall Country House Hotel at Scone offers its own restaurant and golf facilities, while Taymouth Castle, Blairgrowrie and Pitlochry are other Perthshire gems.

Aberdeenshire offers a variety of courses – Ballater, Braemar, Aboyne and Banchory for the parkland addicts, plus the links of Cruden Bay and Murcar. Farther north, Lossiemouth, Nairn and Royal Dornoch, all regular halts on the Northern Open circuit, are others worth a visit. The far north should not be forgotten: Wick, Thurso and Reay all provide a different, and enjoyable, test while across the sea in Orkney, the Kirkwall and Stromness clubs offer the best in hospitality.

St Andrews is Fife's and Scotland's jewel in the golfing crown, but there are many other attractions including Crail, Elie and Lundin Links. Carnoustie, another famous Open Championship venue, lies just a little way farther north along with Montrose, Monifieth and Edzell. Letham Grange Hotel is another welcome Angus halt and has two golf courses to entertain guests and visitors alike.

Speyside is famous as a tourist, whisky and castle trail. But the golfing addict can also follow a path of pleasure through Newtonmore, Kingussie, Boat-of-Garten and Grantown-on-Spey – all good courses with scenery to match.

Whatever your golfing pleasure, there is no doubt that Scotland can satisfy the need. There are over 400 courses to choose from, and the history and tradition adds to the appeal. The 'apres-golf' hospitality is equally renowned – so why not head north and test the mixture? It should provide many moments to savour.

*Rothes Golf Club in the Spey Valley near Elgin; recently opened.*

*Golf at Chamonix in the Alps, near Mont Blanc.*

# Holiday Golf in France

*by Michael Gedye*

AS NEAR NEIGHBOURS, the histories of Britain and France have much in common. We respect our national differences while acknowledging our common heritage. Few would until recently, however, have considered France as a major golfing destination. This is all the more surprising since the first golf course in continental Europe (built as an extension of the expatriate British Club at Pau in south-west France) was opened in 1856 and a Basque named Arnaud Massey became the first non-British winner of the Open in 1907. From then, the game remained private, exclusive and relatively unchanged, the preserve of a few clubs near major centres with the only courses popular for holiday play by the rich and well-connected being sited along the Channel coast, near Biarritz and on the Côte d'Azur. Limited golf for a limited market.

But in recent years all this has changed. Rising domestic interest in golf (and the value of golfing tourism) has been followed by an explosion in course construction. During the past five years, France has been the fastest-growing country in the world of golf with currently more than four hundred and fifty places to play, the majority geared to a tourist market. It now has more courses than any other European country apart from England.

Such a rapid expansion has brought bonus benefits for the visitor. New clubs

are normally built to modern specifications, with a well-equipped clubhouse complete (never forget this is France) with superb restaurant and a course that is watered and manicured to high standards. Golf membership is not cheap so top quality facilities are the norm. A further benefit currently available to visitors is that, since most domestic players are beginners (such has been the speed of growth of the game), many will be hard at it on the practice ground, leaving the golf course relatively free for visitors. Combined with green fees that are highly competitive and much lower than many alternative holiday golfing countries, here is a situation where the touring golfer has it made.

This wealth of golf is a relatively new phenomenon but it provides a perfect passport to all that France has always had to offer. Few could deny the prime position it has maintained to attract the visiting historian, art lover, gourmet, wine buff or general connoisseur of culture. The lasting image of France is one of elegant chateaux, high fashion, vintage claret, noble cheese and now, a wide choice of highly playable golf.

This considerable selection of places to play is as varied as the country itself. Play cliff-top holes in Normandy, just across the Channel, or the craggy heath and farmlands of Brittany. Test your skills over the seaside or pine forest courses of Aquitaine. Wonder at green fairways dwarfed by snow-clad peaks in the Savoy Alps or just enjoy the rich ambience of sun-drenched golf across former vineyards in Provence. There are classic links from the past and modern, US-inspired designs replete with sand and water – golf for all, from debutante to champion.

A unique innovation, which will prove of considerable interest to touring golfers, was created in 1987 by the French Ministry of Tourism in collaboration with the French Golf Federation. A sizeable number of golf clubs, mainly in key resort locations, have satisfied strict criteria to be rated 'touristic golf courses' and are promoted as such under the banner of France Golf International. Visitors can have confidence that the system works. The approved courses will have a high standard of maintenance, the clubhouse will boast full facilities including a good restaurant and that there will be multi-lingual staff and a warm welcome for golfing tourists as temporary members.

Although golf courses abound in every region of France, as the selection in this guide confirms, the main areas of tourist interest are found around the coast. Brittany has a pleasant blend of old and new, most of its recent development following the south-western coast in a golfing chain that merges with the various delights of the Western Loire, where stately chateaux and crisp wine provide a background to a good selection of courses, many of high quality.

Moving south through Poitou-Charentes and Bordeaux, an equally fine choice lies waiting in a country where history and great vintages go hand in hand. This is Aquitaine, leading down to the elegant resort areas of Biarritz, close to where golf in mainland Europe began and which became a focal point for the game and its players in the early part of the century. Here you will find older courses with a pedigree and new ones with a challenge – something of a golfing feast for the enthusiast.

The recent growth of golf is best seen in the south, where the formerly exclusive fairways of the early Côte d'Azur have been surrounded by new places to play; as have other areas of Provence such as Aix and Marseille along with Nîmes and Montpellier in Languedoc-Roussillon. Here modern golf architecture has transformed rustic landscapes, coastal pine forest and marshland into fine examinations of the game.

One inland area not to be overlooked, however, is the region of Rhône Alpes, where snow-capped mountains and crystal lakes enhance some adventurous golf in superb settings. France has always had much to offer the visitor – its present wealth of golf is a welcome bonus.

FRANCE GOLF INTERNATIONAL

*Sun, sea, sand . . . and golf! Val do Lobo, near Faro in the Algarve.*

# Holiday Golf in Portugal

*by Michael Gedye*

WHEN GOLFERS dream of the ideal holiday location, a warm escape perhaps from the rigours of a northern winter, the picture can have many familiar features. Lush green fairways winding in well-watered ribbons past ranks of umbrella pine, immaculate holding greens, attractive splashes of sand and water, backed by the heady scent of wild flowers under bright, remedial sunshine. Sufficient choice, from demanding championship layouts to subtle tests demanding strategy and finesse

supported by superb views of mountain or sea – such golfing dreams do exist in Portugal.

Only a short flight away, Portugal now offers some thirty courses in a charming country full of interest and history. The game has been played there for more than a century, ever since expatriate British port wine shippers established a links course near Oporto in the north.

For the holiday golfer, the country has much to attract. Bordering the Atlantic, just north of the African continent, it has

# HOTEL PALACIO
## *Estoril*

**Rua do Parque 2765 ESTORIL/PORTUGAL (near Lisbon)**
**Tel: (010-351)-1-4680400; Telex 12757 PLAGE**
**Fax: (010-351)-1-4684867**

The HOTEL PALACIO . . . a modern symbol of luxury and comfort in the tradition of the Old World . . . 200 rooms and suites of quiet elegance . . . Conference and Meeting Rooms, plus full convention facilities . . . swimming pool in spacious garden . . . magnificent beach . . . special privileges for international championship golf course . . . 18 clay tennis courts, nearby . . . Gambling Casino.

the benefit of year-round sunshine, temperate sea breezes and a wide range of topography. From inland mountains and wooded valleys, gently rolling slopes planted with fig, pomegranate, mimosa and eucalyptus or the natural beauty of craggy cliffs and broad sandy beaches – golf has been created throughout the land and its islands to captivate the visitor. Add in some of the freshest fish and superb wines, a panoply of culture and glories past, native charm, a friendly welcome – who would ask for more.

In the north, where it all began, three courses are found near Oporto in a region famous for wines, particularly port, while inland there is a further course at the mountain spa resort of Vidago. Moving south to Lisbon, eight courses lie

*The Hotel St. Andrews, convenient for Estela Golf Club, near Oporto.*

within driving distance, with a mixture of nine and eighteen-hole courses to the west including the internationally famous test of Estoril. South across the Tagus river are three more, relatively unsung but in the Portuguese Country Club at Aroeira and the sandy links of Tróia, undoubtedly two of the best courses in the country.

Ask any player about Portuguese golf and he will automatically think of the Algarve, notably the curving stretch of southern coast running from Faro west to Cape St. Vincent. There are no less than fifteen courses – 297 holes currently in play with more to come – a veritable banquet for the golfing gourmet, with a range of choice from championship tests to relaxed layouts in beautiful settings. Golf for all tastes, with holes running along the white sandy beach, across rugged red clifftops, fairways plunging between ranks of green umbrella pine, across slopes of fig or cork oak or rising gently to manicured greens against a sea or mountain backcloth.

Further afield, two islands in the Azores offer golf while on the semi-tropical isle of Madeira, a fine new course at altitude adds a new dimension to a holiday garden location.

Historic Portugal, land of winter sunshine, superb seafood and *vinho verde*, has much to offer.

# Contents

# Publisher's Note

Like most aspects of our lives, golf has been affected by the hazards of the economic climate during 1992. Players, clubs, spectators, sponsors, promoters, manufacturers, hotels all around the world: very few have escaped some form of penalty. Despite an increased handicap, however, most play on!

The world of golf continues – indeed opportunities grow. Development has slackened but new clubs and courses appear and sleeping giants awake. France may well be one of these and we are featuring in the new edition of *THE GOLF GUIDE* an introduction to holiday golf in France in addition to revised descriptions of golf in Portugal and Majorca.

As well as new clubs and courses in Britain, we are pleased to welcome a wider range of accommodation choices for golfers, their families, friends and colleagues. Many of these advertising entries are recommended by golfers themselves and we are always happy to receive comments and new recommendations.

**Enquiries and Bookings.** It is quite normal to confirm a booking in writing and also to receive written confirmation – and a receipt for any advance payment. You should check prices and also any special requirements.

**Cancellations.** Any booking is a form of contract for both parties. If you have to cancel, try to give maximum notice. With reasonable notice the hotel should normally refund any advance payment but on short notice a full refund is not necessarily a legal entitlement.

**Complaints.** Most owners/managers are anxious to sort out problems on the spot so that you are a satisfied customer. If a problem persists you can get advice from a Citizens' Advice Bureau, Consumers' Association, Trading Standards Office, Tourist Board or indeed your own solicitor.

Serious complaints are unlikely to arise with the kind of accommodation you'll find on our pages. FHG Publications Ltd. do not inspect accommodation and an entry does not imply a firm recommendation. However, most of the advertisers have been recommended or proposed by local golf clubs and have standards which satisfy and in many cases far exceed those expected by inspecting authorities. In addition we will be pleased to hear from you if you have a serious complaint and although we cannot act as intermediaries or accept responsibility for our advertisers, we will record the complaint and follow it up with the advertiser in question.

We are grateful to all Club Secretaries and Club Professionals who assist in the supply and revision of entries and to the PGA for editorial co-operation. We also thank accommodation proprietors and managers for their support.

When you contact them with enquiries and bookings, please mention this new and revised edition of *THE GOLF GUIDE. Where to Play: Where to Stay.*

Peter Clark
*Publishing Director*

# The PGA Year

THE PROFESSIONAL GOLFERS' ASSOCIATION was formed over 91 years ago with 50 members. Perhaps its potential membership and influence was reflected by the standing of its first president, the Rt Hon. James Balfour who was shortly afterwards to become the Prime Minister! The current president is the equally distinguished Lord Derby and the membership has grown to around 4,000, including 800 working abroad.

The working club professional continues to give lessons, repair clubs and run his shop and increasingly he has to play the "business" game as well as he plays golf! His time is very much taken up with pro-ams, company days and regional tournaments which have become vital to the economics and the image of professional golf. Other competitive demands on the professional have less to do with golf than with shopkeeping – in the shape of the trading competition he faces from retail sportshop chains and large supermarkets.

However, the club professional still has prestigious national tournaments where he can put his skills on more public show and compete against the best in his business in his own selected game – golf. It is with these annual and important events that our review of the PGA year deals.

## THE TRUSTHOUSE FORTE PGA SENIORS' CHAMPIONSHIP

PLAYED AT the Royal Dublin Club in June, the Forte PGA Seniors' Championship was won by Tommy Horton, popular professional at the Royal Jersey Club in the Channel Islands. The 51-year-old Horton took on one of British golf's "old masters" Christy O'Connor and former PGA professional champion Tony Grubb (Rodway Hill) in a sudden death play-off to win the oldest title in European seniors' golf and collect a cheque for £12,500.

It was a fitting finale to the 72-hole tournament being sponsored by Forte for the 12th successive year and Horton was clearly delighted to have claimed his first seniors' title in such dramatic and memorable circumstances.

"It is fantastic that I have finally made the breakthrough into seniors' golf and to have beaten a player of the calibre of Christy to do so. The man is a magician and it was very gratifying to know I had beaten such a player to win the title," said a thrilled Horton following his victory watched by more than 1,000 people on the final day.

South African John Fourie set the standard when he shot a final round of 73 to finish at 290, six over par, over the testing Royal Dublin course which had provided a tough test for the seniors' field all week.

Horton had begun the final round tied with O'Connor at three over par, with Tony Grubb a shot further back. O'Connor was playing superbly but seemed unable to make inroads into that three shot Horton lead. It was eventually Horton himself who gave him the opening when he double bogeyed the 17th hole to move to five over and only one shot ahead playing the last. Both missed the green and Horton failed to get up and down in two leaving himself at six over and in a play-off with Grubb.

*The Hon. Rocco Forte presents the Forte Trophy to Tommy Horton (photo by Mel Fordham).*

O'Connor faced a testing 10 footer for his par to secure his place in the play-off and when it toppled into the hole you could have heard the roar in Dublin City.

So it was back to the 18th tee for the tough trio and after three good drives Grubb was the first man to fall when he knocked his second shot out of bounds. So it was down to O'Connor and Horton who both found the green with their second shots, although well away from the pin. The canny Irishman putted first to within a few feet of the hole leaving Horton to do all the work. The Royal Jersey professional who had looked a ruined man after dropping those three shots calmly addressed the putt and

rolled all of its 30 feet into the hole for a birdie and victory.

Much of the attention had been centred on O'Connor from day one, a six times past winner of the title and playing at his home club. Winner for the past two years Brian Waites (Notts) was also drawing the attention and warm wishes of his fellow competitors after making such a spectacular and hard-earned recovery following an horrific car accident a year earlier. He has still to get back to full fitness but was more than satisfied with his final round of 73 for a total of 310 and a share of 17th place.

It was Fourie who set the pace on the opening day together with Scot John

Hamilton (Brickendon Grange) who both shot a two under par 69 while Horton was disappointed with his opening 74. On the second day he made his move with a three under par 68 to take a one stroke lead over O'Connor and two over Fourie who saw a 73 become a 75 when he was penalised two shots because his ball had struck his caddy.

A 74 in the third round by Horton was pipped by a 73 from Christy to leave the two sharing the lead at three over par going into that exciting final round culminating in the play-off and Horton's first seniors' victory.

"The last putt was the longest I had holed all week and what a great time to do it. I still can't believe I have won. It is marvellous," he said.

The former European Tour winner paid tribute to O'Connor and his performance at the age of 67 years. "I hope I still have 16 years left in me. He was playing shots out there that guys on the European Tour would be proud of. It was a fantastic showcase for seniors' golf."

Forte, who put up the £55,000 prize fund for the event, also brought a smile to the faces of local children when the curtain-raising pro-am raised enough money to buy a Variety Club Sunshine Coach for a school for deaf children in Dublin.

## THE WILSON CLUB PROFESSIONAL CHAMPIONSHIP

WITH A TOTAL purse of £50,000, the Wilson Club Professional Championship took place from June 30–July 3 at the St. Pierre Hotel, Golf and Country Club at Chepstow, Gwent. In the lead from the first round, John Hoskison of West Surrey finished on 275, nine under par and six shots ahead of runner-up Chris Hall.

It was Hoskison's fourth title of the year, and the accompanying £6,000 was his biggest ever cheque. In becoming the first Englishman to take the title since

Robin Mann in 1985, the lightly built Southerner also broke Scotland's six year monopoly of the Club Professionals' dream title.

In a week of mixed conditions – scorching heat, floods and thunder and lightning – Hall also never strayed over par, and with a closing 71 held off Eyemouth's Craig Maltman by a shot to take the £4,000 runner-up prize. The 39-year-old Scot made his late charge for third spot with a best of final day, 67.

While Hoskison had most to celebrate, the top seven had similar cause to crack open the champagne as they claimed the automatic places in the European side to meet the US PGA in the Johnnie Walker PGA Cup Match staged at The K Club, Kildare, Ireland from September 18-20.

Brian Rimmer (Oaklands) and David Jones (Knockbracken), joint fourth on 283, and Peter Cowen (Lindrick) and Nick Job (Richmond), on 285, completed the lucky seven, and were later joined by Captain Paul Leonard's two "wild card" selections, Russell Weir and John Chillas.

Hoskison, a former European Tour player who played in the 1988 PGA Cup at The Belfry, came into the championship as a man in form having won the Southern Professional and Southern Club Professionals' Championships plus the Surrey Open within the past year.

He continued in the same vein with an opening four under par 67 that was only matched by Peter Allan (Ashton-in-Makerfield).

Hoskison and Allan were fortunate to post tallies before lightning and heavy rain caused a two-hour suspension, and they finished the day with a three shot lead over the Scottish pair of Alan McCloskey and Alastair Forrow, John Harrison and Paul Wesselingh.

In the second round, Hoskison equalled par and had his advantage reduced to one over Shirley Park's Hogan Stott, and two ahead of Hall, who had won the Midland Masters at Patshull Park the previous week and Gordon

*John Hoskison receives the trophy from Andy Ferguson, Managing Director, Wilson Sporting Goods (photo by Prestige Photography).*

Gray (Dumfries & County). Allan slipped back with a 76.

The day's low return, later equalled as the best of the tournament by fellow Scot Campbell Elliott, was a 66 from Maltman. The five under par score included a remarkable run of four birdies in five holes from the 13th – all from 15 feet or more – and it helped the Scot recover from a disappointing opening round of 77.

On day three, Hoskison repeated his opening 67 and moved into a commanding five shot lead over Hall and Elliott, whose 66 was a concoction of a career best nine birdies, four bogeys and five pars.

Hoskison's fear on the eve of the closing round was that he would collapse, *à la* Gil Morgan at the US Open. "What I need is a nice steady start" he said.

His prayers were answered, and the champion-elect set out with six straight

pars, followed by a bogey and two birdies to cover the front nine in one under par 34.

The 31-year-old Hall did momentarily get to within a couple of shots when, having opened with a birdie, he picked up another shot at the seventh. But with the Nottingham man dropping a shot at the ninth, Hoskison's birdie finale to the first half coupled with his level on the back nine settled the Championship.

"This is the greatest day of my career," said a delighted Hoskison. "To now hold four titles, and get back into the PGA Cup side, is very special."

For Hall, Maltman, Rimmer and Cowen the real excitement was the prospect of making their PGA Cup debuts in Ireland, while for Jones, with four appearances, and Job, who played alongside Hoskison in the 1988 side, it was a case of "welcome back!"

## PEUGEOT CUP FOR THE PGA ASSISTANTS' CHAMPIONSHIP

THE 1992 PEUGEOT CUP for the PGA Assistants' Championship was held at East Sussex National Golf Club, August 9-14. The specifically designed tournament East course provided a magnificent test which the experienced Paul Mayo from Newport conquered in exemplary fashion.

Mayo led from start to finish with rounds of 70, 71, 77 and 67 to give a three under par total of 285. His last round of 67 broke the course record by one shot. Such a performance in the last round of a National Championship is not only a testament to Mayo's experience – having competed in four Open Championships and one US Masters – but over such a demanding course in conditions of fierce wind and rain it speaks eloquently of his talent. Only three other players broke par on the last day.

Stuart Little from Minchinhampton finished runner-up, 8 shots behind, with a five over par total of 293. Little, a member of the PGA European Tour, produced consistent and improving rounds of 73, 76, 74 and 70.

Little is currently ranked no. 129 on the European Tour Order of Merit but is increasingly confident that he is "playing well enough" to maintain his card for next year.

The 16th hole on the East course, as it was for many players, proved to be Little's nemesis. He dropped five shots on the par 3 over the four rounds. Indeed, scores of 7 and 8 were not uncommon for some players on this most difficult of par 3's.

Despite the inclement weather the course was praised by all players. Many were particularly pleased to see Peugeot and the PGA showing such a commitment to once again staging the National Final on a demanding Championship course. Last year's final

*Paul Mayo with The Peugeot Cup (photo by Prestige Photography).*

was held for the new Edinburgh course at Wentworth.

Alone in third place was the former British Boys' and British Youths' Champion James Cook from Leamington and County. His four rounds of 75, 80, 71 and 69 are an appropriate symbol of Cook's recent fortunes. As an amateur playing in last year's Tillman Trophy, Cook injured his wrist barring him from competitive golf up until the beginning of this year. Prior to his injury last May, Cook had played the best golf of his life to come from behind with a closing 64 to win the Lagonda Trophy.

Cook attributed his first two rounds at East Sussex to a lack of match practice. By his own admission he was more concerned with worrying about making the cut than concentrating on the shot in hand. Yet, with the first two rounds out of the way, Cook played the last 36 holes in four under par, four shots better than even the course record breaker, Paul Mayo. Cook's 71 on the third day in the midst of the very worst of the weather displayed considerable skill.

Cook is now eagerly awaiting the qualifying school for the European Tour and hopes that he is fortunate enough to have the opportunity to qualify over the East Sussex course. Several players, besides Cook, again expressed their satisfaction that East Sussex has now been chosen as a site for prequalifying for the European Tour school.

The Zimbabwean James Loughnane finished in fourth place on 298. His four rounds of 74, 71, 79 and 74 were similar to Mayo's in highlighting the difficulty of the third day's weather conditions. Loughnane, representing Cotswold Hills, commented "I haven't ever seen so much rain. In the last two days here there has probably been more rain than in the last six years in Zimbabwe." Loughnane, perhaps unsurprisingly then, is returning to South Africa in October to compete on the Sunshine Tour.

*1992 PGA National Assistants' Champion Paul Mayo receives the keys to a 205 GTi from Peter Williams, Marketing Director of Peugeot (photo by Prestige Photography).*

Both fifth placed men, John Peters and John Mellor, held the view that East Sussex "tests your thinking far more ruthlessly" than any other course they have played.

The Tournament Director, Gary Tait, was fully satisfied with the week, commenting that the cream had risen to the top. He was moved to express a desire to see the Peugeot Cup return in the near future to such a "fantastic venue". Tait echoed Mayo's gratitude to Peugeot for their continued support of young professional golf.

In that regard Mayo was rewarded for his efforts with the use of a Peugeot 205 GTi, a cheque for £3,750, an all expenses paid trip to the US Assistants' Championship next year (courtesy of Titleist), and the possibility of competing in the Peugeot French Open and to follow in last year's winner's footsteps, Simon Wood, to compete in the Peugeot Spanish Open.

*The Rt. Hon. Lord Derby M.C. presents the trophy to Darren Panks (photo by Prestige Photography).*

## LORD DERBY'S KNOWSLEY SAFARI PARK TOURNAMENT

*Safari Shoot-out!*

DARREN PANKS, a 23-year-old assistant at Lindrick, defeated his friend Carl Robinson in a sudden-death "shoot-out" to win the Lord Derby's Knowsley Safari Park Tournament at Bolton.

The pair, who met through competing in the PGA's North Region, had matched each other when they played together for a "small wager" in the practice round and did so again in the final but, of course, for much higher stakes. Fellow Yorkshireman Robinson, who moved from Cambridge Moat House to Moortown 18 months ago, had the chance for an outright victory in the event. He charged a 10-foot putt on the final green half the distance past the hole before sinking the return for a one-under-par 69 to set up the play-off. Overnight leader Andrew Collison, of King's Lynn, should have made it a three-way tie but three-putted the last hole to share third place with Kidderminster's Neil Turley.

Panks, starting the day one behind Collison, quickly made up the leeway with birdies at the first two holes and was the sole player on the leaderboard under par until he missed the green at the 10th. He then failed from two feet at the 12th to go back to level. Another bogey at the next hole proved costly but Panks showed great resolve in parring the last when he got up and then down from 40 feet to finish on 70 for a one-over total of 141.

Earlier, 22-year-old Robinson who had

trailed by two strokes overnight, strung together 13 pars in a row before hoisting himself into contention with birdies at the 14th and 17th. Like so many players before him, Robinson missed the green with his approach to the difficult final hole and he admitted the pressure got to him when he failed to secure his par.

The end came quickly. With Panks perfectly placed down the middle of the fairway on the first play-off hole, Robinson's pushed drive landed underneath a bush and he could only chip out sideways. Panks left his wedge shot some 35 feet short but rolled up the putt to a few inches before Robinson agonisingly saw his attempt stop almost on the lip.

He was the first to congratulate Panks. "You deserved it," he told his friend graciously, also summing up the fine spirit in which the event was played. It was Panks's first major victory since turning professional five years ago and it earned him £1,000.

He received his award from the Rt Hon. The Earl of Derby MC, the PGA President and toasted his success with a double magnum of Moët and Chandon.

## THE PGA CUP

*Europe's club professionals slip to PGA Cup defeat once again against strong USA opponents.*

"WE LOST, but we lost with a lot of pride" was the verdict of Captain Paul Leonard as Europe failed to win back the Johnnie Walker PGA Cup at the K Club, Straffan, Ireland. In the end the American team proved just too strong against the valiant Europeans who matched them tee to green but failed to hole those crucial putts. The standard of golf was worthy of any Ryder Cup but some superb fourball performances by the Americans left Europe with just too much to do on the final day, needing seven points from the 10 singles matches.

"My team did everything I asked of them and I am proud to have been their

Captain. We were beaten on the greens as we were equally as good from tee to green. But that is what golf is all about – you have to hole those putts," said Leonard.

The United States took a commanding lead after the first day's play when Captain Pat Rielly's comments that his team loved the course certainly rang true.

The morning foursomes were halved two matches each with the first signs that David Jones and Peter Cowen, and Chris Hall and Nick Job, were to be formidable pairings. Jones and Cowen beat Tom Wargo and Mike San Filippo 2&1 while Hall and Job finished with two birdies to win their match against Steve Veriato and Mike Schuchart on the last. The Scottish pairing of Russell Weir and John Chillas proved unable to match what was probably the best pairing of either side, Brett Upper and Gene Fieger, and eventually lost by 6&4, while John Hoskison and Craig Maltman lost to Larry Gilbert, the reigning PGA champion, and Bob Borowicz.

With the score two-all before the first day's fourballs, Captain Paul Leonard took the decision to drop Weir and Chillas and allow Tim Giles and Brian Rimmer to make their debut. It was not a good afternoon for Europe. After their good start to the day, they could only manage a half point from the four available. That came from the previously successful Jones and Cowen who were 1-up playing the last. Sadly neither could improve on par and Schuchart snatched a halved match with a birdie four. Job and Hall lost 4&3 to Wargo and McDougal and had to contend with a barrage of birdies on the back nine.

The final scoreline for the day was US 5½ points to Europe's 2½ and Captain Paul Leonard was clearly disappointed after such a strong performance in the morning's foursomes. He said: "It could have been four down this morning but we played well to grab two points. This afternoon's difference was on the greens.

They holed a lot more putts than we did."

The Europeans were raring to go on the second day and things were looking decidedly better when they halved the opening match and won the next two. Weir and Chillas had to make do with a half after being 2-up after 15 when the Americans hit back with two birdies in the last three holes. Hoskison and Maltman romped to a 4&3 victory over Rinker and San Filippo and Hall and Job continued with their magnificent record, beating Gilbert and Veriato 2&1. Only Jones and Cowen lost but it took an eagle from Upper and Fieger at the last – Upper holing a 15-foot putt to take the point.

Europe had narrowed the deficit to two points and Leonard retained the same pairings for the afternoon fourballs. This produced the best golf of the match with all four pairings playing superb golf on both sides. The US took the first blood with Wargo and McDougal, who had proved a powerful partnership for the Americans, beating Maltman and Hoskison by 2&1. Chillas and Weir matched the Americans Rinker and Schuchart birdie for birdie and at the turn they were all square and three under par. The Americans edged ahead at the 16th with a birdie and another birdie earned them the point 2-up. It was Job and Hall who got the European flags waving again when they staged a marvellous recovery against Gilbert and Bob Borowicz. The Americans were 2-up after 15 holes but birdies from six feet and three feet by Job and a fantastic birdie at the last by Hall saw them snatch the point out of the hands of the Americans. It was to be the only point of the afternoon for Europe but only after a memorable final match between Jones and Cowen and Upper and Fieger. It was golf worthy of the Ryder Cup and both pairs launched birdie after birdie to come to the last all square and both eight under par. The end came dramatically, in keeping with the golf, as Upper made his second eagle putt of the day at the final hole from eight

Above: *The American pairing of Fieger and Uppa were unbeaten as individuals and as a partnership through the match.* Below: *The victorious US captain Pat Rielly and his British counterpart Paul Leonard with the Johnnie Walker PGA Cup.*

feet, to finish 10 under par against the Europeans' nine-under-par total.

The scoreline was 10-6 and now the Americans needed just three points from the 10 singles to retain the trophy or three and a half for a clear win. Paul Leonard had nothing but praise for his team's performance or the standard of the golf but again matches had been won and lost on the greens.

The final day brought disappointment for Brian Rimmer when the American Larry Gilbert was forced to withdraw due to illness. The "envelope" rule was invoked and Rimmer was the unlucky European who had to drop out. Each team was awarded a half point leaving the Americans needing just two and a half points to retain the Llandudno Trophy. Controversy later surrounded Gilbert's withdrawal as rumours abounded that he had been dropped because of an incident in the locker room the previous evening and that he had felt he could not win his match against the on-form Peter Cowen and so had asked not to play. PGA Executive Director Jim Awtrey firmly dismissed these rumours, insisting that

Gilbert was not fit.

Nick Job set the pace when he won his match by 5&4 against Tom Wargo. It was a fitting finale performance for the professional who was the man of the match for Europe and described by partner Chris Hall as "a tower of strength". But to overcome the 10-6 deficit was asking too much.

The Americans took their first point when Gene Fieger beat David Jones by 3&2. However, Russell Weir won his match for Europe 3&2. Chris Hall played the final hole 1 up but a birdie by Schuchart snatched a half and left the Americans needing just one point to retain the Cup. It came from Borowicz who had a comfortable victory over Scotland's Craig Maltman. The half point for an outright American win came in the Tim Giles and Mike San Filippo match where Giles avoided defeat by making a birdie at the last hole.

That half was good enough for the Americans and with the singles series finally tied at five points each the final score line read 15-11 in favour of the USA.

# THE GOLF FOUNDATION
**57 London Road, Enfield, Middlesex EN2 6DU**
**Telephone: 081-367 4404**

Established in 1952 The Golf Foundation has the specific aims of introducing more young people to the game of golf and of promoting and developing their skills and enjoyment of the game. The basis of the Foundation's work is the Coaching Scheme, whereby qualified members of the PGA give instruction to students at schools and universities. The Foundation also sponsors Open Coaching Centres during vacations, and implements a Coaching Award Scheme for teachers. A four-stage Merit Award Scheme operates successfully throughout the country, and Age Group Championships help raise the standard of junior golf by providing real competition at all levels of ability.

A newsletter "Tee to Green" is published, as well as other coaching material, visual aids and films.

The Golf Foundation is a non-profit-making organisation and a Registered Charity, relying on support from organisations within the game, commerce and industry, and individual Golf Clubs and club members. As the national body responsible for junior golf it plays a vital role in the future development of the game.

# Golfing Manners!

## by Jane Carter

ETIQUETTE, ACCORDING TO the Oxford English Dictionary, is "the customs or rules governing behaviour regarded as correct in social life". Whether golf can be regarded as social life is a moot point but there can be no doubt that there are many rules of etiquette for which the game is almost as well known as its rules of play. The sport of gentlemen (and in these times of equality, ladies) is regarded as such because of its rules of etiquette. Sportsmanship, fairness, trust and judgement are all expected of any golfer before he or she sets foot on the fairways and woe betide the player who brings them and the game into disrepute.

Turn to the opening chapter in the rules of golf and there you will find the very first word, "etiquette", followed by no less than 17 paragraphs on the subject. This is probably to ensure that even the simplest of people will realise that this is a most important subject. Courtesy on the course, care of the course and courtesy towards fellow players are drummed into the reader before he has even begun to deal with the complications of penalty drops, playing out of bunkers, lost balls and even what to do if your ball lands in the middle of a nest!

Etiquette and courtesy are never more important than when a player is visiting a club, whether as a guest of another member or simply as a green fee. There have been many stories of people who have behaved badly, abused hospitality as well as the course and returned to their own club only to find a red-faced secretary clutching a letter of complaint.

Any golf club has the standard notices asking people to repair pitch marks on the greens, rake bunkers once they have played out of them, call people through when necessary and observe any special local rules of the club at all times – but it never ceases to astound golf clubs how many people suddenly seem to suffer from temporary word blindness when confronted with such a notice.

When visiting a course it should be your first priority to have a quiet word with the PGA professional and ask him about such rules before venturing out and possibly bringing down the wrath of the club secretary when you do something you should not. It will help his ulcer and prevent you from getting one (if you have not already got one after battling with the mind-boggling rules of golf and etiquette).

Consideration for other players appears in large green type in the rule book – which is probably more to do with ensuring attention than any environmental issue! Basically, don't move, talk or even breathe if you could disturb a fellow player. And just remember when whooping with joy as you hole a 30 footer that behind that hedge someone may have just died with fright – or God forbid, missed a two-footer because of you.

Safety is important. You should remember not to swing your clubs around like a Roman gladiator in case you hit a passer-by or even yourself, which has been known. Before playing a shot, make sure the people in front are well out of range. We all hit a good shot occasionally and this could be it, so wait for them to clear.

It is standard at most courses that two-ball matches take precedence over any three- or four-ball match and a person on his own has no standing at all.

Another golden rule of etiquette which has probably been written about more than any other is "in the interest of all, players should play without delay". Now, delay seems to mean different things to different people. The most common cause of delay on a golf course is when people seem determined not to prepare for their shot until it is their turn to play. It is summed up nicely in Peter Dobereiner's "Golf Rules Explained" when he says: "Slow play is the bane of modern golf and one of the major reasons is the time-wasting convention of switching off all thoughts of our own game while others play, and then only getting down to the job in hand when all

the rest of our group are arranged in a motionless and silently admiring audience".

So remember to be thinking about that job in hand and getting ready for your shot or putt while your other partners are doing the same. It will speed up your game no end, win you friends in the match behind and above all, allow far more drinking time in the bar!

Damage to the course is another bone of contention with many golf clubs. It is amazing how many blame visitors for the many pitch marks or badly raked bunkers when really they should look closer to home. However, make sure that you are not held to blame by remembering to repair pitch marks, be careful where you are pulling your trolley, keep spike marks to a minimum and treat the tees as hallowed ground, particularly the first when half the club will probably be watching you.

The rules of etiquette, or really they should be called guidelines, are set out to make the game more enjoyable for everyone who plays it. You are not awarded a two-shot penalty or loss of hole if you choose to ignore them but do it too often and loss of friends and playing partners may result.

When visiting a course you are a guest and you should behave as you would expect its members to behave when visiting *your* club. So the next time you land in a footprint in a bunker when you need a par for the match, just remember how annoying it can be and practise what you preach!

# Golf in England
## WHERE TO PLAY • WHERE TO STAY

WITH THE long history of golf in England, it's not surprising that flourishing clubs abound in all parts of the country. From the Cape Cornwall club not far from Land's End to the North Foreland club at Broadstairs in Kent; from Ventnor on the southernmost Isle of Wight to the quaintly-named Magdalene Fields club in Berwick-on-Tweed – the golfer in England has a huge choice.

*One of England's many golf courses on the edge of Dartmoor at Roborough, near Plymouth, Devon.*

Although temporarily slackened, there is demand for still more and *THE GOLF GUIDE 1993* features new as well as revised club and course entries. As the number of entries grows, we are happy also to be able to offer a greater range of hotels and other accommodation for the travelling golfer.

# London

ASHFORD. **Ashford Manor Golf Club,** Fordbridge Road, Ashford, Middlesex (Ashford (0784) 252049). 18 holes, 6343 yards. S.S.S. 70. *Green Fees:* information not provided. *Visitors:* welcome with introduction. Professional: M. Finney (0784 255940). Secretary: B.J. Duffy.

BARNET. **North Middlesex Golf Club,** The Manor House, Friern Barnet Lane, Whetstone N20 0NL (081-445 1732). *Location:* five miles north of Finchley, A1000. 18 holes, 5611 yards. S.S.S. 67. *Green Fees:* weekday round/day £22.00; weekends and Bank Holidays £30.00. *Eating facilities:* luncheons, snacks and dining facilities. *Visitors:* welcome (with Official Handicap), weekends playing with a member and in possession of Official Handicap. Advisable to telephone Professional to book time. *Society Meetings:* catered for. Professional: A.S.R. Roberts (081-445 3060). General Manager/Secretary: M.C.N. Reding (081-445 1604).

BARNET. **Old Fold Manor Golf Club,** Hadley Green, Barnet, Herts EN5 4QN (081-440 1650). *Location:* Junction 23 M25. A1000 one mile north of Barnet. Heathland course. 18 holes, 6456 yards. S.S.S. 71. Practice nets and putting green. *Green Fees:* £27.00 per round, £30.00 per day, with a member £10.00 (Mondays and Wednesdays £7.50 per round); weekends with a member only £12.00. *Eating facilities:* restaurant and bar except Mondays and Wednesdays. *Visitors:* welcome weekdays. *Society Meetings:* catered for Thursdays and Fridays. Professional: Peter Jones (081-440 7488). Manager: D.V. Dalingwater (081-440 9185).

BEXLEY HEATH. **Barnehurst Golf Club,** Mayplace Road East, Barnehurst, Bexley Heath (Crayford (0322) 523746). 9 holes, 5320 yards. S.S.S. 66. *Green Fees:* information not provided. *Visitors:* welcome Monday, Wednesday and Friday without reservation. *Society Meetings:* not catered for. Professional: B. Finch. Secretary: J. Thomson.

BROMLEY. **Bromley Golf Club,** Magpie Hall Lane, Bromley. *Location:* off A21 Bromley to Farnborough road. Short, flat, open course with a few trees. 9 holes, 2745 yards. S.S.S. 35. Putting green and teaching facilities. *Green Fees:* information not available. *Eating facilities:* snacks available. *Visitors:* no booking required as this is public course. *Society Meetings:* by arrangement with Bromley District Council. Professional: Alan Hodgeson (081-462 7014).

CHINGFORD. **Chingford Golf Club,** 158 Station Road, Chingford E4 (081-529 2107). 18 holes, 6342 yards. S.S.S. 70. *Green Fees:* on application. *Visitors:* welcome weekdays only, an article of red must be worn. Professional: John Francis. Secretary: Bryan Sinden.

CHINGFORD. **Royal Epping Forest Golf Club,** Station Road, Chingford, London E4 7AZ (081-529 6407). *Location:* 200 yards east of Chingford (BR) Station. A private club on a public course. Wooded 18 holes, 6342 yards. S.S.S. 71. *Green Fees:* weekdays £6.00, weekends £9.00. *Eating facilities:* public snack bar. *Visitors:* may play course but may not use clubhouse. Must wear red garment (trousers or shirt/sweater). Professional: Simon Preston (081-529 5708). Secretary: Tom Flack (081-529 2195).

CHINGFORD. **West Essex Golf Club,** Bury Road, Sewardstonebury, Chingford, London E4 7QL (081-529 0928). *Location:* two miles north of Chingford BR Station. M25 (Junction 26) and Waltham Abbey follow directions to Chingford (Daws Lane on left). Parkland, wooded, hilly. 18 holes, 6289 yards. S.S.S. 70. *Green Fees:* weekdays £28.00 per round, £35.00 per day; weekends with member only. *Eating facilities:* restaurant and bar facilities. *Visitors:* welcome weekdays except Tuesday mornings and Thursday afternoons; after 3pm competition days. Phone first. *Society Meetings:* catered for by arrangement Mondays, Wednesdays and Fridays. Professional: C. Cox (081-529 6347). Secretary: P.H. Galley MBE (081-529 0928).

DULWICH. **Dulwich and Sydenham Hill Golf Club,** Grange Lane, College Road, London SE21 (081-693 3961). *Location:* off South Circular, Dulwich Common. 18 holes, 6051 yards. S.S.S. 69. *Green Fees:* £25.00 per round. *Eating facilities:* lunch every day. *Visitors:* welcome, with reservation on weekdays. *Society Meetings:* catered for, maximum 30. Professional: David Baillie. Secretary: Anne Stevens.

EDMONTON. **Leaside Golf Club,** Pickett's Lock Sports Centre, Edmonton N9 0AS (081-803 4756). *Location:* near North Circular Road. Flat parkland. 9 holes, 2496 yards. S.S.S. 32. Driving range, putting green. *Green Fees:* information not available. Reductions weekdays for Senior Citizens and Juniors. *Eating facilities:* cafe and bar. *Visitors:* booking required at weekends. *Society Meetings:* by arrangement with Sports Centre. Professional: R. Gerken.

EDMONTON. **Picketts Lock Golf Course,** Picketts Lock Centre, Edmonton, London N9 0AS (081-803 3611). *Location:* north east London, near North Circular Road and A10. River Lea borders course. 9 holes, 2600 yards. S.S.S. 32. Floodlit driving range. *Green Fees:* contact Golf Shop for details. *Eating facilities:* available. *Visitors:* open to public every day, weekend booking advisable (contact Professional). *Society Meetings:* small societies welcome weekdays. Professional: Richard Gerken. Manager: S. Welch.

ELTHAM. **Eltham Warren Golf Club,** Bexley Road, Eltham SE9 2PE (081-850 1166). *Location:* A210 Eltham. Parkland. 9 holes, 5840 yards. S.S.S. 68. *Green Fees:* £25.00 per day; with member £10.00. *Eating facilities:* two bars, diningroom. *Visitors:* welcome weekdays only, weekends with member only. *Society Meetings:* by arrangement. Professional: R.V. Taylor (081-859 7909). Secretary: D.J. Clare (081-850 4477).

ELTHAM. **Royal Blackheath Golf Club,** The Clubhouse, Court Road, Eltham SE9 5AF (081-850 1795). *Location:* off Court Road, Eltham. 18 holes, 6209 yards. S.S.S. 70. Practice area. *Green Fees:* £38.00 per day (£10.00 with member); weekends £10.00 (only with member). *Eating facilities:* excellent diningroom and two bars. *Visitors:* welcome weekdays, weekends if introduced by and playing with member. Museum. *Society Meetings:* catered for midweek, prior booking essential. Professional: Ian McGregor. Secretary: R. Barriball.

ENFIELD. **Crews Hill Golf Club,** Cattlegate Road, Crews Hill, Enfield EN2 8AZ (081-363 0787). *Location:* off Junction 24 M25, follow directions to Enfield. Parkland. 18 holes, 6230 yards. S.S.S. 70. Practice area. *Green Fees:* on application. *Eating facilities:* restaurant by arrangement, bar. *Visitors:* welcome weekdays. Handicap Certificate required. Weekends by invitation of member. *Society Meetings:* by arrangement. Professional: J.R. Reynolds (081-366 7422). General Manager: E.J. Hunt (081-363 6674).

ENFIELD. **Enfield Golf Club,** Old Park Road South, Enfield, Middlesex EN2 7DA. *Location:* off Junction 24, M25; follow directions to Enfield. Parkland. 18 holes, 6200 yards. S.S.S. 70. *Green Fees:* on request. *Eating facilities:* full bar and catering facilities. *Visitors:* welcome weekdays only, with current Handicap Certificate. *Society Meetings:* catered for Mondays, Wednesdays and Fridays by prior arrangement. Professional: Lee Fickling (081-366 4492). Secretary: Nigel Challis (081-363 3970; Fax: 081-342 0381).

ENFIELD. **Whitewebbs Golf Club,** Clay Hill, Beggars Hollow, Enfield EN2 9JN (081-363 2951). *Location:* A10 off M25, north of Enfield. Parkland course. 18 holes, 5863 yards. S.S.S. 68. Small practice area and putting green. *Green Fees:* £7.60 weekdays; £10.80 weekends. *Eating facilities:* public cafe on site. *Visitors:* welcome, public course, no restrictions. *Society Meetings:* contact the Secretary. Professional: D. Lewis (081-366 4454). Secretary: Victor Van Graan (081-363 2951).

FINCHLEY. **Finchley Golf Club,** Nether Court, Frith Lane, Finchley, London NW7 1PU (081-346 0883). *Location:* close A1/M1 Mill Hill East tube station. Wooded course. 18 holes, 6411 yards. S.S.S. 71. *Green Fees:* weekdays £28.00; weekends £37.00. *Eating facilities:* bar; diningroom open daily except Mondays. *Visitors:* welcome weekdays except Thurs-

days, weekends after mid-day. *Society Meetings:* catered for Wednesdays and Fridays. Professional: David Brown (081-346 5086). Secretary: John Pearce (081-346 2436).

GREENFORD. **Ealing Golf Club,** Perivale Lane, Greenford, Middlesex UB6 8SS (01-997 2595). *Location:* on Western Avenue A40 half a mile from Hanger Lane Gyratory System. Flat parkland. 18 holes, 6216 yards. S.S.S. 70. *Green Fees:* £30.00 weekdays; weekends with a member only. *Eating facilities:* men's bar, mixed lounge, restaurant – lunches and snacks. *Visitors:* welcome weekdays with reservation through Professional. *Society Meetings:* catered for on Monday, Wednesday and Thursday. Professional: A. Stickley (081-997 3959). Secretary: M. Scargill (081-997 0937).

GREENFORD. **Horsenden Hill Golf Club,** Whitton Avenue, Woodland Rise, Greenford UB6 0RD (081-902 4555). *Location:* off Whitton Avenue East, next door to Sudbury Golf Course. Very tough though short course. 9 holes, 1632 yards, 1490 metres. S.S.S. 55. Practice area, nets and putting green. *Green Fees:* weekdays £3.75 for 9 holes; weekends £5.60 for 9 holes. *Eating facilities:* restaurant and bar. *Visitors:* welcome at all times, unrestricted. Professional: Tony Martin. Secretary: W. Pyemont.

GREENFORD. **Perivale Park Golf Club,** Stockdove Way, Greenford, Middlesex (081-575 7116). *Location:* A40, turn off at sign for Ealing and Perivale. Flat parkland. 9 holes, 2667 yards. S.S.S. 34. Excellent practice ground. *Green Fees:* weekdays £3.75 for 9 holes; weekends £5.60 for 9 holes. *Eating facilities:* cafeteria. *Visitors:* welcome – public course. Professional: Peter Bryant. Secretary: George Taylor.

HAMPSTEAD. **Hampstead Golf Club,** Winnington Road, London N2 0TU (081-455 0203). *Location:* down Hampstead Lane adjacent to Spaniards Inn. Undulating parkland with trees. 9 holes, 5812 yards. S.S.S. 68. *Green Fees:* £25.00 (£30.00 per day) weekdays; weekends £30.00. *Eating facilities:* bar; snacks and afternoon teas; lunches bookable. *Visitors:* welcome weekdays (not Tuesdays) if members of a golf club or have Handicap Certificate. Limited at weekends. 1993 is Club's Centenary Year. *Society Meetings:* small societies catered for weekdays by prior arrangement. Professional: Peter Brown (081-455 7089). Secretary: K.F. Young (081-455 0203).

HAMPTON HILL. **Fulwell Golf Club,** Wellington Road, Hampton Hill, Middlesex TW12 1JY (081-977 3188). *Location:* opposite Fulwell Railway Station and bus garage. Flat parkland course. 18 holes, 6490 yards. S.S.S. 71. Practice ground. *Green Fees:* weekdays £25.00, weekends £35.00. £12.00 with member. *Eating facilities:* lunches and teas. *Visitors:* welcome

57

weekdays. *Society Meetings:* welcome weekdays. Professional: D. Haslam (081-977 3844). Secretary: C.A. Brown (081-977 2733).

HAMPTON WICK. **Home Park Golf Club,** Hampton Wick, Kingston-upon-Thames KT1 4AD (081-977 6645). *Location:* between Hampton Court and Kingston Bridge, entrance at Kingston Bridge roundabout. Flat parkland. 18 holes, 6598 yards. S.S.S. 71. *Green Fees:* weekdays £15.00 (£24.00 all day), weekends and Bank Holidays £20.00 (£30.00 all day). *Eating facilities:* full bar and dining facilities. *Visitors:* welcome – no advance booking. *Society Meetings:* catered for by arrangement. Professional: D.L. Roberts (081-977 2658). Secretary: Mr B.W. O'Farrell (081-977 2423).

HENDON. **Hendon Golf Club,** off Sanders Lane, Devonshire Road, Mill Hill, London NW7 1DG (081-346 8083). *Location:* leave M1 southbound at Junction 2. Turn off A1 into Holders Hill Road. 10 miles north of London. Parkland, wooded, well bunkered. 18 holes, 6266 yards. S.S.S. 70. *Green Fees:* weekdays £24.00 per round, £30.00 per day; weekends £35.00. *Eating facilities:* full bar and catering facilities. *Visitors:* welcome weekdays (limited at weekends and Bank Holidays), book through Pro Shop. *Society Meetings:* catered for by arrangement Tuesdays to Fridays, book through Secretary's office. Professional: Stuart Murray (081-346 8990). Secretary: David Cooper (081-346 6023).

HIGHGATE. **Highgate Golf Club,** Denewood Road, Highgate, London N6 4AH (081-340 1906). *Location:* near A1, turn down Sheldon Avenue, opposite Kenwood House and first left. Parkland. 18 holes, 5985 yards. S.S.S. 69. *Green Fees:* weekdays £27.00/£35.00; weekends only with member. *Eating facilities:* bar, restaurant. *Visitors:* welcome weekdays except Wednesdays before 3.30pm. *Society Meetings:* catered for Thursdays/Fridays. Professional: Robin Turner (081-340 5467). Secretary: Colin Manktelow (081-340 3745).

HILLINGDON. **Hillingdon Golf Club,** 18 Dorset Way, Hillingdon, Middlesex UB10 0JR (Uxbridge (0895) 239810). *Location:* near A40, adjacent to RAF Uxbridge. Very undulating – well wooded course, sloping down to river. 9 holes, 5459 yards, 4480 metres. S.S.S. 67. *Green Fees:* weekdays £17.50 for 18 holes, £25.00 per day. *Eating facilities:* bar meals available Tuesday to Saturday. *Visitors:* welcome Mondays, Tuesdays and Fridays; Thursdays – Ladies Day, weekends with members only. *Society Meetings:* catered for by special arrangement only with committee through club Secretary. Professional: D.J. McFadden (0895 251980). Secretary: R.G. Goodfellow (0895 233956).

HOUNSLOW. **Airlinks Golf Club,** Southall Lane, Hounslow, Middlesex TW5 9PE (081-561 1418; Fax: 081-813 6284). *Location:* Junction 3 on M4, A312 to Hayes. Same entrance as D. Lloyd Tennis Centre. Flat parkland course with water holes and doglegs. 18 holes, 5885 yards. S.S.S. 68. Floodlit driving range. *Green Fees:* weekdays £10.00 per round, £17.00 per day; weekends £12.50. *Eating facilities:* full catering and bar facilities/restaurant area. *Visitors:* weekdays no restrictions, some restrictions weekends, bookings advised seven days in advance. *Society Meetings:* catered for all week. Professionals: Bill Mylward/Ken Wickham (081-561 1418). PR Officer: P.D. Watson.

HOUNSLOW. **Hounslow Heath Municipal Golf Course,** Staines Road, Hounslow TW4 5DS (081-570 5271). *Location:* Staines Road A315 between Hounslow and Bedfont. Undulating course with water hazards. 18 holes, 5820 yards. S.S.S. 68. *Green Fees:* weekdays £7.00 per round, £11.20 per day; weekends and Bank Holidays £9.80 per round, £14.50 per day. Reduced rates for Juniors and Senior Citizens weekdays except Bank Holidays (Council Leisure Card must be held). *Eating facilities:* snacks; tea, coffee, soft drinks. *Visitors:* welcome at all times, bookings required at weekends and Bank Holidays. *Society Meetings:* by arrangement with Professional. Professional: P. Cheyney (081-570 5271). Secretary: D.J. Darby.

ISLEWORTH. **Wyke Green Golf Club,** Syon Lane, Isleworth TW7 5PT (081-560 4874). *Location:* situated half a mile north of A4 near Gillettes Corner. Fairly flat parkland. 18 holes, 6242 yards. S.S.S. 70. *Green Fees:* weekdays £28 per day; weekends £48 per day (half price with member). *Eating facilities:* catering daily except Mondays. *Visitors:* welcome with reservation weekdays; weekends only with member until after 3pm. *Society Meetings:* catered for on Tuesdays, Wednesdays and Thursdays by arrangement, minimum 20. Professional: Tony Fisher (081-847 0685). Secretary: D. Wentworth-Pollock (081-560 8777).

LONDON. **London Scottish Golf Club,** Windmill Enclosure, Wimbledon Common SW19 5NQ (081-788 0135). *Location:* just off A3 – Tibbetts Corner – just south of Putney SW15. Parkland (no bunkers). 18 holes, 5438 yards. S.S.S. 67/68. *Green Fees:* £13.50 per round, £20.00 per day. *Eating facilities:* bar and catering. *Visitors:* welcome weekdays only. Check with Professional recommended. Red top must be worn, no jeans or sweatshirts. *Society Meetings:* minimum 20 players. Professional: Matthew Barr (081-789 1207). Secretary: Jack Johnson (081-789 7517).

LONDON. **Mill Hill Golf Club,** 100 Barnet Way, Mill Hill, London NW7 3AL (081-959 2282). *Location:* A1, south half a mile before Apex Corner left into clubhouse car park – signposted. Flat wooded parkland. 18 holes, 6232 yards, 5697 metres. S.S.S. 70. Practice ground. *Green Fees:* weekdays £22.00 per round; weekends £36.00 per round. Winter societies special rates. *Eating facilities:* restaurant and bar. *Visitors:* welcome Monday to Friday; weekends and Bank Holidays bookings only. Two snooker tables. *Society Meetings:* catered for Mondays, Wednesdays and Fridays with prior booking. Professional: Mr A. Daniel (081-959 7261). Secretary: Mr F.H. Scott (081-959 2339; Fax: 081-906 0731).

LONDON. **Springfield Park Golf Club,** Burntwood Lane, London SW17 0AT (081-871 2468; Fax: 081-871 2221). *Location:* Burntwood Lane off Garrett Lane in the grounds of Springfield Hospital. Inland links course in rural setting in heart of London, beautiful feature trees. 9 holes, 4400 yards. S.S.S 62. *Green Fees:* weekdays £8.00; weekends £10.00. *Eating facilities:* fully licensed bar and catering facilities. *Visitors:* welcome except Saturday and Sunday mornings when members only. Bowling and Croquet Club, snooker and function room. *Society Meetings:* welcome weekdays only. Professional: Patrick Tallack. Secretary: Christine Morgan.

LONDON. **Trent Park Golf Club,** Bramley Road, Southgate, London N14 (081-366 7432). *Location:* opposite Oakwood Tube Station. Undulating parkland. 18 holes, 6008 yards. S.S.S. 69. Large practice area. *Green Fees:* on application. *Eating facilities:* bar and snacks. *Visitors:* open to public at all times. Bookings advised on weekdays and necessary at weekends. *Society Meetings:* welcome Monday to Thursday. Professional: Craig Easton. Secretary: F.L. Montgomery.

NORTHOLT. **The London Golf Centre,** Lime Trees Park Golf Club, Ruislip Road, Northolt, Middlesex UB5 6QZ (081-845 3180). *Location:* just off A40 at the Polish War Memorial roundabout. Undulating parkland with interesting water hazards. 9 greens, 18 tees, 5838 yards. S.S.S. 70. Floodlit driving range. *Green Fees:* weekdays £5.00 for 9 holes; £9.00 for 18 holes; weekends £6.75 for 9 holes; £12.75 for 18 holes. Concessions for Juniors and Senior Citizens. *Eating facilities:* two bars/bistro. *Visitors:* welcome at all times. Golf superstore. *Society Meetings:* welcome for. Professional: Gary Newall (081-845 3180). Secretary: Nigel Sturgess (081-842 0442; Fax: 081-842 2097).

NORTHWOOD. **Northwood Golf Club Ltd,** Rickmansworth Road, Northwood, Middlesex HA5 2QW (0923 825329). *Location:* on A404 between Pinner and Rickmansworth. Parkland/wooded course. 18 holes, 6493 yards. S.S.S. 71. *Green Fees:* weekdays £20.00. *Visitors:* welcome weekdays only. *Society Meetings:* by arrangement. Professional: C.J. Holdsworth (0923 820112). Secretary: R.A. Bond.

NORTHWOOD. **Sandy Lodge Golf Club,** Sandy Lodge Lane, Northwood, Middlesex HA6 2JD (Northwood (0923) 825429). *Location:* adjacent Moor Park Underground Station. Inland links. 18 holes, 6340 yards. S.S.S. 70. *Green Fees:* weekdays £25.00 per round. *Eating facilities:* full catering and bar service available. *Visitors:* not weekends – telephone first. Handicap Certificate required. *Society Meetings:* catered for by prior arrangement. Professional: Alex M. Fox (0923 825321). Secretary: J.N. Blair (0923 825429; Fax: 0923 824319).

ORPINGTON. **Lullingstone Park Golf Club,** Park Gate, Chelsfield, Near Orpington, Kent (Knockholt (0959) 32928). *Location:* M25 Junction 4, fifth exit on left (signposted). Undulating parkland. 18 holes, 6779 yards. S.S.S. 72. 9 holes, 2432 yards. Par 33. Pitch and putt/putting green, driving range. *Green Fees:* weekdays £6.00 per 9 holes, £9.00 per 18 holes; weekends £7.00 per 9 holes, £13.50 per 18 holes. *Eating facilities:* cafeteria and bar. *Visitors:* welcome at all times. All players on 18-holes course must have recognised golf shoes. *Society Meetings:* catered for, phone the Professional. Professional: Dave Cornford (0959 34542; Fax: 0959 34012). Secretary: G.S. Childs (0959 34297).

PINNER. **Grim's Dyke Golf Club,** Oxhey Lane, Hatch End, Pinner, Middlesex HA5 4AL (081-428 4093). *Location:* on A4008 Watford to Harrow (2 miles west of Harrow). Parkland, tree lined, testing greens. 18 holes, 5598 yards. S.S.S. 67. Practice area. *Green Fees:* weekdays £25.00. No weekend fees unless guest of a member. *Eating facilities:* lunches, teas, snacks except Monday. *Visitors:* must produce Certificate of Handicap. *Society Meetings:* catered for. Professional: Carl Williams (01-428 7484). Amateur record J. Thornton, 65. Secretary: P. Payne (081-428 4539).

PINNER. **Pinner Hill Golf Club,** Southview Road, Pinner Hill HA5 3YA (081-866 0963). *Location:* one mile west Pinner Green. 18 holes, 6280 yards. S.S.S. 70. *Green Fees:* £25.00 weekdays, £32.00 weekends by prior arrangement only; Public Days (no access to clubhouse), Wednesdays and Thursdays £7.15 per round, £9.90 per day. *Eating facilities:* light refreshments served at all times (except Wednesdays and Thursdays). *Visitors:* welcome with Handicap Certificate or letter of introduction. *Society Meetings:* Mondays, Tuesdays and Fridays. Professional: Mark Grieve (081-866 2109). Secretary: Jeremy Devitt (081-868 4817).

ROEHAMPTON. **Roehampton Club Ltd,** Roehampton Lane, London SW15 5LR (081-876 1621). *Location:* South Circular Road between Sheen and Putney. Parkland. 18 holes, 6011 yards. S.S.S. 69. *Green Fees:* weekdays £15.00, weekends £20.00. *Eating facilities:* bar and full restaurant available all week. *Visitors:*

59

welcome if introduced by member, and must play with member at weekends. *Society Meetings:* catered for by arrangement, if introduced by member. Professional: Alan L. Scott (081-876 3858). Chief Executive: Martin Yates (081-876 5505; Fax: 081-392 2318).

RUISLIP. **Ruislip Golf Club,** King's End, Ickenham Road, Ruislip, Middlesex HA4 7OQ (Ruislip (0895) 638081). *Location:* two and a half miles from Junction 1, M40, first left after M40/A40 merge, onto B467, then left at T-Junction onto B466. Parkland course. 18 holes, 5702 yards. S.S.S. 68. Driving range (40 bays). *Green Fees:* £8.00 weekdays, £11.00 weekends. *Eating facilities:* full restaurant facilities. *Visitors:* welcome mid-week, no booking; booking necessary at weekends. *Society Meetings:* welcome by arrangement. Professional: Derek Nash (0895 632004). Secretary: B.J. Channing (0895 638835).

SHEPPERTON. **Sunbury Golf Club,** Charlton Lane, Shepperton, Middlesex TW17 8QA (0932 772898). *Location:* just off Junction 1 of the M3. Flat parkland course. 9 holes, 6502 yards. S.S.S. 72. 32 bay floodlit range, green 8am to 10pm. *Green Fees:* weekdays £7.50; weekends £8.50. *Eating facilities:* two bars, restaurant. *Visitors:* welcome, no restrictions. *Society Meetings:* welcome. Professional: Alistair Hardaway. Secretary: Sally Clark.

SHOOTERS HILL. **Shooters Hill Golf Club Ltd,** "Lowood", Eaglesfield Road, Shooters Hill, London SE18 3DA (081-854 1216). *Location:* off A207 between Blackheath and Welling. Hilly wooded course. 18 holes, 5736 yards. S.S.S. 68. *Green Fees:* weekdays £27.00. *Eating facilities:* bar and dining-room. *Visitors:* members of other clubs welcome weekdays on production of letter of introduction, or official Handicap Certificate. Jacket, collar and tie required in clubhouse. *Society Meetings:* catered for Tuesdays and Thursdays only. Professional: M. Ridge (081-854 0073). Secretary: B.R. Adams (081-854 6368).

SOUTHALL. **West Middlesex Golf Club,** Greenford Road, Southall, Middlesex UB1 3EE (081-574 0166). *Location:* junction of Uxbridge Road (A4020) and Greenford Road. 18 holes, 6242 yards. S.S.S. 70. *Green Fees:* weekdays £15.00 per round (£9.00 Mondays and Wednesdays), £25.00 per day; green fees not permitted weekends. *Visitors:* welcome without reservation. *Society Meetings:* catered for by prior arrangement. Professional: L. Farmer. Secretary: P.J. Furness (081-574 3450).

SOUTHWARK. **Aquarius Golf Club,** Beachcroft Reservoir, Marmora Road, Honor Oak, Southwark SE22 0RY (081-693 1626). *Location:* nearest main road – Forest Hill Road. The course is situated on and around a reservoir, testing first and eighth holes. 9 holes, 5034 yards. S.S.S. 65. *Green Fees:* £10.00. *Eating facilities:* limited. *Visitors:* welcome with member only. Professional: F. Private. Secretary: Mrs Marilyn Moss.

STANMORE. **Stanmore Golf Club,** 29 Gordon Avenue, Stanmore, Middlesex HA7 2RL (081-954 4661). *Location:* nearest roads A41, Uxbridge Road. Wooded, undulating course. 18 holes, 5639 yards. S.S.S. 68. *Green Fees:* on application. *Eating facilities:*

lunchtime snacks, evening meals by prior arrangement. *Visitors:* welcome Tuesdays, Wednesdays and Thursdays, Handicap Certificates required on Wednesday and Thursday. *Society Meetings:* catered for Wednesday and Thursday by prior booking only. Professional: Vivian Law (081-954 2646). Secretary: L.J. Pertwee.

TOTTERIDGE. **South Herts Golf Club,** Links Drive, Totteridge N20 (081-445 0117). *Location:* off Totteridge Lane one mile from Whetstone, nearest station Totteridge. Parkland. 18 holes, 6432 yards. S.S.S. 71. *Green Fees:* on application. *Eating facilities:* lunch, high tea (Dinner served by arrangement). *Visitors:* welcome with reservation Wednesday, Thursday, Friday, lunch, high tea, dinner. Professional: R. Livingstone (081-445 4633). Secretary: P.F. Wise (081-445 2035).

TWICKENHAM. **Strawberry Hill Golf Club,** Wellesley Road, Twickenham (081-894 1246). *Location:* near Strawberry Hill Station. 9 holes, 2381 yards. S.S.S. 62. *Green Fees:* £18.00 per round, £25.00 per day. *Eating facilities:* light lunches, bar snacks. *Visitors:* welcome with reservation, only with a member at weekends. No ladies before 1.30pm at weekends. *Society Meetings:* small numbers catered for. Professional: P. Buchan (081-898 2082). Secretary: F.E. Ingoldby (081-894 0165).

TWICKENHAM. **Twickenham Golf Course,** Staines Road, Twickenham (081-783 1698). *Location:* just off A316. Parkland. 9 holes, 3050 yards. S.S.S 35. Practice area. *Green Fees:* £3.80 weekdays per round, £5.00 weekends. Senior Citizens and Juniors £2.50 weekdays. *Eating facilities:* Pavilion Bar and cafe. *Visitors:* welcome, public course. Function room available. *Society Meetings:* welcome, full banqueting facilities. Golf Director: Suzy Baggs (081-783 1698). Secretary: Norman Harnett (081-783 1748).

UPMINSTER. **Upminster Golf Club,** 114 Hall Lane, Upminster (Upminster (04022) 20249). *Location:* one mile from Upminster Station. Parkland/wooded – river runs through the course. 18 holes, 5931 yards. S.S.S. 68. *Green Fees:* £25.00 per round, £30.00 per day weekdays. *Eating facilities:* full catering at club, bookable. *Visitors:* welcome weekdays except Tuesday mornings and must produce evidence of handicap. *Society Meetings:* catered for Wednesdays, Thursdays and Fridays (max 40). Professional: Neil Carr (04022 20000). Secretary: Philip Taylor (04022 22788).

UXBRIDGE. **Uxbridge Golf Course,** The Drive, Harefield Place, Uxbridge UB10 8PA (Uxbridge (0895) 272457). *Location:* off Swalkelys Junction – M40. Undulating parkland. 18 holes, 5753 yards. S.S.S. 68. *Green Fees:* weekdays £9.00; weekends £12.00. *Eating facilities:* bars, restaurant. *Visitors:* welcome anytime, booking required at weekends. Function suite. *Society Meetings:* welcome Thursdays. Professional: Phil Howard (0895 237287; Fax: 0895 810262). Secretary: Brian Russell.

WANSTEAD. **Wanstead Golf Club,** Overton Drive, Wanstead E11 2LW (081-989 0604). *Location:* one mile from junction of A12 and A406. Parkland bordering Epping Forest with featured lake. 18 holes, 6109 yards. S.S.S. 69. *Green Fees:* £25.00 per day weekdays; weekends as members guest only. *Eating facilities:* dining room and bars. *Visitors:* welcome Mondays, Tuesdays and Fridays by prior arrangement with the Secretary. Handicap Certificate required. Weekends with member only. *Society Meetings:* welcome, apply Secretary. Professional: Gary Jacom (081-989 9876). Secretary: Keith Jones (081-989 3938).

WEMBLEY. **Sudbury Golf Club Ltd**, Bridgewater Road, Wembley, Middlesex HA0 1AL (081-902 3713). *Location:* junction of A4005 (Bridgewater Road) and A4090 (Whitton Ave East). Undulating parkland. 18 holes, 6282 yards. S.S.S. 70. Practice ground. *Green Fees:* weekdays £26.40 per round, £40.00 two rounds. *Eating facilities:* dining room and bars. *Visitors:* welcome weekdays with Handicap. *Society Meetings:* catered for. Professional: Neil Jordan (081-902 7910). Secretary: Colin Brown (081-902 3713).

WEST DRAYTON. **Holiday Inns Golf Club,** Stockley Road, West Drayton, Middlesex UB7 9NA (0895 444232). Flat parkland course. 18 holes, 3856 yards. S.S.S. 62. *Green Fees:* weekdays £5.25; weekends £6.50. *Eating facilities:* catering and bars. *Visitors:* welcome. *Society Meetings:* welcome except weekends. Professional: N. Coles. Secretary: P. Davies (081-561 3471).

WIMBLEDON. **Royal Wimbledon Golf Club,** 29 Camp Road, Wimbledon SW19 4UW. *Location:* one mile west of War Memorial in Wimbledon Village. 18 holes, 6300 yards. S.S.S. 70. *Visitors:* not permitted. *Society Meetings:* Wednesdays and Thursdays only, by arrangement. Professional: Hugh Boyle (081-946 4606). Secretary: Maj. G.E. Jones (081-946 2125). Caddiemaster (081-946 1118).

WIMBLEDON. **Wimbledon Common Golf Club,** 19 Camp Road, Wimbledon Common, Wimbledon SW19 4UW (081-946 0294). Links type wooded course. 18 holes, 5438 yards. S.S.S. 66. *Green Fees:* weekdays £13.50 per round, £20.00 per day. *Eating facilities:* light lunches available every day; bar. *Visitors:*

welcome weekdays, but only with a member at weekends. *Society Meetings:* not catered for. Professional: J.S. Jukes (081-946 0294). Secretary: B.K. Cox (081-946 7571).

WIMBLEDON. **Wimbledon Park Golf Club,** Home Park Road, Wimbledon, London SW19 7HR. *Location:* Church Road, Arthur Road and Home Park Road from Wimbledon High Street, or by District Line to Wimbledon Park Station where signposted. 18 holes, 5465 yards. *Green Fees:* £25.00 per day. *Eating facilities:* dining room and bar snacks each day except Monday. *Visitors:* welcome weekdays, occasional weekends after 3.30 pm (check with Professional). *Society Meetings:* catered for. Professional: D. Wingrove (081-946 4053). Secretary: M.K. Hale (081-946 1250).

WINCHMORE HILL. **Bush Hill Park Golf Club,** Bush Hill, Winchmore Hill, London N21 2BU (081-360 5738). *Location:* Enfield, nine miles north of City. Parkland. 18 holes, 5809 yards. S.S.S. 68. Practice ground and nets. *Green Fees:* weekdays £20.00 per round, £25.00 per day; weekends only with member. *Eating facilities:* full catering and bar facilities. *Visitors:* welcome weekdays, Handicap Certificate required. *Society Meetings:* catered for weekdays except Wednesdays (minimum of 30 required). Professional: G. Low (081-360 4103). Secretary/Manager: Keith Maplesden (081-360 5738).

WOOD GREEN. **Muswell Hill Golf Club,** Rhodes Avenue, Wood Green, London N22 4UT (081-888 2044). *Location:* one mile Bounds Green Underground Station. Parkland. 18 holes, 6491 yards. S.S.S. 71. *Green Fees:* weekdays £23.00 per round, £33 per day; weekends limited booking through Professional £35.00 per round. *Eating facilities:* available in Clubhouse. *Visitors:* welcome weekdays, weekends pre-booked by Professional. *Society Meetings:* catered for Monday, Wednesday, Thursday and Friday, charges on request. Professional: I. Roberts (081-888 8046). Secretary: J.A.B. Connors (081-888 1764).

# Avon

BATH. **Bath Golf Club,** Sham Castle, North Road, Bath BA2 6JG (Bath (0225) 425182). *Location:* off A36, one mile south-east of Bath City Centre. 18 holes, 6369 yards, 5824 metres. S.S.S. 70. *Green Fees:* weekdays £22.00; weekends and Bank Holidays £26.00. *Eating facilities:* catering every day. *Visitors:* with bona fide handicap welcome. *Society Meetings:* catered for Wednesday and Friday. Professional: Peter Hancox (0225 466953). Secretary: P.B. Edwards (0225 463834).

BATH. **Entry Hill Golf Club,** Entry Hill, Bath BA2 5AN (0225 834248). *Location:* one mile south of city centre, off A367 road to Wells. Hilly parkland course

with many young trees. 9 holes, 2103 yards, 1922 metres. S.S.S. 61 (18 holes). Practice net. *Green Fees:* weekdays £6.50; weekends £8.00. Weekdays: rounds completed before 12 noon £5.00. *Visitors:* no restrictions but pre-booking up to one week in advance essential. Well equipped Pro Shop. *Society Meetings:* as per visitors. Professional: T. Tapley (0225 834248). Secretary: J. Sercombe (0225 834248).

BATH. **Fosseway Country Club and Centurion Hotel,** Charlton Lane, Midsomer Norton, Bath BA3 4BD (0761 417711; Fax: 0761 418357). *Location:* off A367 10 miles south of Bath; midway between Bath and Wells. Flat parkland course. 9 holes, 4278 yards.

S.S.S. 65. *Green Fees:* weekdays £10.00; weekends and Bank Holidays £15.00. *Eating facilities:* table d'hôte/à la carte restaurant, full bar meals. *Visitors:* welcome except Saturday and Sunday mornings and Wednesday evenings. Outdoor bowls, squash, snooker, heated indoor pool. *Society Meetings:* welcome. Secretary: R.F. Jones (0761 412214).

BATH. **Lansdown Golf Club,** Lansdown, Bath BA1 9BT (Bath (0225) 425007). *Location:* four miles from M4 junction 18 adjoining Bath Racecourse. Flat, parkland, 800ft above sea-level, panoramic views. 18 holes, 6299 yards, 5759 metres. S.S.S. 70. *Green Fees:* weekdays £24.00, weekends £30.00. *Eating facilities:* snacks at all times, lunch or dinner by arrangement with Steward. *Visitors:* weekdays only. Professional: T. Mercer (0225 420242). Secretary: Ron Smith (0225 422138).

BRISTOL. **Bristol and Clifton Golf Club,** Beggar Bush Lane, Failand, Bristol BS8 3TH (0275 393117). *Location:* two miles west of the Suspension Bridge or three miles south of the M5-Junction 19 access. 18 holes, 6294 yards. S.S.S. 70. Parkland course. *Green Fees:* weekdays £25.00; weekends £30.00. *Eating facilities:* available. *Visitors:* welcome weekdays without reservation, must have current golf club Handicap Certificate. *Society Meetings:* welcome. Professional: Peter Mawson (0275 393031). Managing Secretary: Cdr P.A. Woollings (0275 393474).

BRISTOL. **Chipping Sodbury Golf Club,** Chipping Sodbury, Bristol BS17 6PU (Chipping Sodbury (0454) 312024). *Location:* 12 miles north of Bristol, nine miles from Junction No. 14 on M5 and three miles from Junction 18 on M4. Parkland course. 18 hole course, 6912 yards; 9 hole course, 3076 yards. S.S.S. 73. *Green Fees:* 18-hole course weekdays £20.00; weekends £25.00. 9 hole course £2.50 any day. *Eating facilities:* full catering available. *Visitors:* welcome except Saturday/Sunday morning and Bank Holidays. Must have Handicap Certificate. *Society Meetings:* catered for by prior arrangement weekdays only. Professional: Mike Watts (0454 314087). Secretary: K.G. Starr (0454 319042).

BRISTOL. **Filton Golf Club,** Golf Course Lane, Filton, Bristol BS12 7QS (Bristol (0272) 692021). *Location:* off A38 north of Bristol. Parkland, 18 holes, 6277 yards. S.S.S. 70. Two practice fields. *Green Fees:* weekdays £20.00 per round, £25.00 per day, £12.00 with member; weekends £12.00 with member only. *Eating facilities:* meals available. *Visitors:* accepted daily subject to programme. *Society Meetings:* all catered for, subject to programme – must book well in advance. Professional: J.C.N. Lumb (0272 694158). Secretary: Mr M. Burns (0272 694169).

BRISTOL. **Henbury Golf Club,** Henbury Hill, Westbury-on-Trym, Bristol BS10 7QB (Bristol (0272) 500660). *Location:* north M5 Junction 17 A4018 to Westbury-on-Trym; next to Blaise Castle. Wooded parkland, 18 holes, 6039 yards. S.S.S. 70. *Green Fees:* weekdays £20.00, £9.00 with member; weekends with member only. *Eating facilities:* dining room and bar snacks. *Visitors:* welcome, restricted at weekends and

Bank Holidays. *Society Meetings:* Tuesdays and Fridays by prior arrangement. Professional: Nick Riley (0272 502121). Managing Secretary: J.R. Leeming (0272 500044).

BRISTOL. **Knowle Golf Club,** Fairway, Bristol (Bristol (0272) 776341). *Location:* three miles south of city centre, left off Wells Road. A4 – Bath. Parkland course. 18 holes, 6100 yards. S.S.S. 69. Practice field. *Green Fees:* weekdays £21.00 for 18 holes, £26.00 for 27 holes; weekends £26.00 for 18 holes, £31.00 all day. *Eating facilities:* bar and snacks, dinners by arrangement with Stewardess. *Visitors:* welcome with Handicap Certificate. *Society Meetings:* Thursdays only with Handicap Certificate. Professional: Mr Gordon M. Brand (0272 779193). Secretary: Mrs J.D. King (0272 770660).

BRISTOL. **Mangotsfield Golf Club,** Carsons Road, Mangotsfield, Bristol (Bristol (0272) 565501). *Location:* four miles M32 via Downend, one mile Warmley A420. Parkland, hilly course. 18 holes, 5337 yards, 4877 metres. S.S.S. 66. Small practice area. *Green Fees:* weekdays £10.00; weekends £8.00. *Eating facilities:* no restriction on food and drink. *Visitors:* welcome, no restrictions. *Society Meetings:* catered for weekdays only. Professional: Craig Trewin. Secretary: Terry Bindon (0272 755432 daytime, evenings 0272 697032).

BRISTOL. **Shirehampton Park Golf Club,** Park Hill, Shirehampton, Bristol BS11 0UL (Bristol (0272) 823059). *Location:* one mile from Junction 18 on M5 on B4054 to Shirehampton. Parkland course. 18 holes, 5498 yards. S.S.S. 67. *Green Fees:* weekdays £18.00, weekends £25.00 (check with Secretary/Professional). *Eating facilities:* lunches, snacks, teas, etc available daily. *Visitors:* welcome weekdays, with reservation (check with Secretary), not weekends or Public Holidays. *Society Meetings:* catered for on Mondays, application to Secretary. Professional: Brent Ellis (0272 822488). Secretary: Piers Drew-Wilkinson (0272 822083).

BRISTOL. **Tall Pines Golf Club,** Cooks Bridle Path, Downside, Backwell, Bristol BS19 3DJ (0275 474889). *Location:* Bristol Airport half a mile. Parkland. 18 holes, 4250 yards. S.S.S. 62 (to be extended 1993). *Green Fees:* weekdays £10.00; weekends £12.50. *Eating facilities:* restaurant, bar. *Visitors:* welcome at all times, bookings at weekends. *Society Meetings:* welcome. Professional/Secretary: Terry Murray (0275 472076).

BRISTOL. **The Long Ashton Golf Club,** The Club House, Long Ashton, Bristol BS18 9DW (0275 392229). *Location:* three miles south-west of Bristol on the B3129 Clevedon/Bristol Road. Wooded parkland. 18 holes, 6219 yards, 5532 metres. S.S.S. 70. Practice ground. *Green Fees:* weekdays £22.00; weekends £30.00. *Eating facilities:* full catering daily, bar open Monday to Saturday (11am – 11pm). *Visitors:* welcome, must have current Handicap Certificate. *Society Meetings:* by arrangement with Secretary. Professional: Denis Scanlan (0275 392265). Secretary: B. Manning (0275 392316).

BRISTOL. **Tracy Park Golf and Country Club,** Bath Road, Wick, Bristol BS15 5RN (0272 372251; Fax: 0272 374288). *Location:* M4 Junction 18, A46 towards Bath, A420 towards Bristol. Turn left at bottom of steep hill for Lansdown/Bath. Wooded parkland with water hazards. 27 holes, 6800, 6800, 6200 yards. S.S.S. 73, 73, 70. Practice ground. *Green Fees:* weekdays £15/£22, weekends £20/£30. *Eating facilities:* full catering available. *Visitors:* welcome – telephone ahead. *Society Meetings:* welcome. Tennis, swimming, squash, croquet, snooker available. Professional: Grant Aitken (0272 373521). Manager: Stephen Allen.

CLEVEDON. **Clevedon Golf Club,** Castle Road, Clevedon BS21 7AA (0275 873140). *Location:* two miles from M5 Junction 20. Picturesque course, looking down onto River Severn. 18 holes, 5887 yards. S.S.S. 69. *Green Fees:* weekdays £20.00, weekends and Bank Holidays £30.00. *Eating facilities:* meals from 11am to 2pm and from 4pm to 6pm daily, Fridays and Saturdays from 11am to 11pm, Mondays light snacks only. *Visitors:* welcome (afternoons only on Wednesdays). Must be member of a Golf Club in possession of Handicap Certificate. *Society Meetings:* catered for on Tuesdays only. Professional: (0275 874704). Secretary: Capt. M. Sullivan (0275 874057).

SALTFORD. **Saltford Golf Club,** Golf Club Lane, Saltford, Bristol BS18 3AA (Saltford (0225) 873220). *Location:* off A4 between Bristol and Bath. Wooded parkland course. 18 holes, 6081 yards. S.S.S. 69. Practice ground. *Green Fees:* weekdays £20.00 single round, £24.00 more than one round; weekends £25.00

single round summer only. *Eating facilities:* restaurant bar service. *Society Meetings:* welcome. Professional: D. Millensted (0225 872043). Secretary: Valerie Radnedge (0225 873513).

WESTON-SUPER-MARE.     **Weston-Super-Mare Golf Club,** Uphill Road North, Weston-super-Mare BS23 4NQ (Weston-super-Mare (0934) 621360). *Location:* on the sea front next to Royal Hospital, M5. Seaside links course. 18 holes, 6251 yards. S.S.S. 70. Practice facilities. *Green Fees:* weekdays £20.00, weekends £28.00. *Eating facilities:* full bar and catering facilities. *Visitors:* welcome weekdays, restriction weekends to small numbers, with Handicap Certificate required. *Society Meetings:* catered for weekdays. Professional: Terence Murray (0934 633360). Secretary: D. Lee (0934 626968).

WESTON-SUPER-MARE. **Worlebury Golf Club,** Monks Hill, Weston-super-Mare BS22 9SX (Weston-Super-Mare (0934) 623214). *Location:* from the M5 then A370 main road to the town for two miles, turn right into Baytree Road and continue to top of hill. Club situated at crossroads Milton Hill/Worlebury Hill Road. Hill top with extensive views of the Severn Estuary and Wales. 18 holes, 5936 yards. S.S.S. 69. Limited practice area. *Green Fees:* weekdays £16.00 including VAT, weekends and Bank Holidays £26.00 including VAT. *Eating facilities:* bar and restaurant. *Visitors:* welcome without reservation. *Society Meetings:* catered for by arrangement with Secretary. Professional: Gary Marks (0934 418473). Secretary: Ralph Bagg (0934 625789).

# Bedfordshire

AMPTHILL. **Millbrook Golf Course,** Millbrook, Ampthill MK45 2JB (0525 840252; Fax: 0525 405669). *Location:* one mile from town centre, M1 Junction 12 from south, Junction 13 from north, towards Ampthill (A507), located on A418. Hilly tree-lined parkland, one of the longest courses in Britain. 18 holes, 6779 yards. S.S.S. 73. Practice ground and bunkers. *Green Fees:* weekdays £15.00 – £25.00; weekends £14.00 with member only. *Eating facilities:* bar snacks, meals available from 11am daily, booking required for main evening meals. *Visitors:* welcome weekdays only, not weekends or Bank Holidays. *Society Meetings:* weekdays only by arrangement with Professional or Secretary. Professional: T.K. Devine (0525 402269). Secretary: Mrs M.R. Brackley.

BEADLOW. **Beadlow Manor Hotel, Golf and Country Club,** Beadlow, Near Shefford SG17 5PH (Silsoe (0525) 860800; Fax: 0525 861345). *Location:* from M1 (J12) take A5120 east to Ampthill, then A507 to Shefford. From A1 (J10) take A507 west to Ampthill. Challenging, rolling parkland with water hazards. Established 36 hole course, 6619 yards. S.S.S. 73. Covered 25 bay floodlit driving range, practice area. *Green Fees:* from £7.00. *Eating facilities:* restaurant, two bars, snacks, refreshments. *Visitors:* welcome at all times. Integral Health Farm offers steam room, sauna, sunbeds, spa baths, beauty salon, gym. Residential Golf and Health Breaks available. Professional shop. Special mid-week and weekend Breaks for Society and Company Groups. All reservations through Sales and Marketing Office.

BEDFORD. **Bedford and County Golf Club,** Green Lane, Clapham, Bedford (Bedford (0234) 354010). *Location:* off A6 north of Bedford before Clapham Village. Parkland. 18 holes, 6290 yards. S.S.S. 70. *Green Fees:* weekdays £27.50, with member £10.00; weekends and Bank Holidays £15.00 with a member only. *Eating facilities:* full catering facilities and bar. *Visitors:* welcome without reservation except weekends. *Society Meetings:* catered for Mondays, Tuesdays, Thursdays and Fridays. Professional/Manager: Eddie Bullock (0234 359189/352617; Fax: 0234 357195).

BEDFORD. **Bedfordshire Golf Club,** Biddenham, Bedford MK40 4AF (Bedford (0234) 353241). *Location:* one mile west of Bedford town centre on the A428. Flat parkland. 18 holes, 6185 yards. S.S.S. 69. *Green Fees:* on application. *Eating facilities:* catering seven days, evenings by arrangement. *Visitors:* welcome on weekdays, must be members of registered golf clubs. Ladies' Day Tuesday. *Society Meetings:* catered for weekdays. Professional: G. Buckle (0234 353653). Secretary: T.A. Nutt (0234 261609).

BEDFORD. **Mowsbury Golf Club,** Kimbolton Road, Bedford (0234 771493). *Location:* on B660 at northern limit of city boundary. 18 holes, 6510 yards. S.S.S. 71. Driving range. *Green Fees:* on request. *Eating facilities:* meals and bar snacks until 2pm; evening meals if booked in advance. *Society Meetings:* not on Fridays or weekends. Professional: Paul Ashwell (0234 216374), for tee reservations and fees. Secretary: L.W. Allan (0234 771041).

DUNSTABLE. **Dunstable Downs Golf Club,** Whipsnade Road, Dunstable LU6 2NB (Dunstable (0582) 604472). *Location:* on B4541; from the south, leave M1 at Markyate, A5 to centre of town, turn left at roundabout into West Street, turn left into Whipsnade Road at third roundabout, club half a mile on left. Downland course, 18 holes, 6184 yards. S.S.S. 70. *Green Fees:* on application. *Eating facilities:* catering Tuesday to Sunday. *Visitors:* weekdays if members of recognised Golf Club, weekends with member only. Handicap Certificate required. *Society Meetings:* Tuesdays and Thursdays. Professional: M. Weldon (0582 662806). Secretary: P.J. Nightingale (0582 604472).

DUNSTABLE. **Tilsworth Golf Centre,** Dunstable Road, Tilsworth, Leighton Buzzard LU7 9PU (Leighton Buzzard (0525) 210721). *Location:* two miles north of Dunstable off A5, Tilsworth turn-off. Parkland. 18 holes, 5303 yards. Par 69. *Green Fees:* weekdays £7.50; weekends £9.50. *Eating facilities:* bar snacks and restaurant available. *Visitors:* welcome any time (except Sundays before 11.45 am). Bookings taken up to seven days in advance. *Society Meetings:* welcome by prior arrangement. Professional: Nick Webb (0525 210721).

LEIGHTON BUZZARD. **Aylesbury Vale Golf Club,** Stewkley Road, Wing, Leighton Buzzard LU7 0UJ (0525 240196). *Location:* four miles west of Leighton Buzzard, on the Aylesbury Road turn right at the village of Wing and then take the Stewkley Road and we are one and a half miles down this road on the left. Gently undulating course with lakes. 18 holes, 6622 yards. S.S.S. 72. Driving range. *Green Fees:* Monday to Thursday £10.00, Friday £12.00; weekends £17.50. *Eating facilities:* full catering service and bar. *Visitors:* welcome any time, no restrictions apart from correct dress. *Society Meetings:* all welcome. Professional: Lee Scarbrow (0525 240197). Secretary/Manager: Chris Wright (0525 240196).

LEIGHTON BUZZARD. **Leighton Buzzard Golf Club,** Plantation Road, Leighton Buzzard LU7 7JF (Leighton Buzzard (0525) 373812). *Location:* off A5 between Dunstable and Milton Keynes at village of Heath and Reach. Wooded parkland course. 18 holes, 6101 yards. S.S.S. 70. Practice ground. *Green Fees:* weekdays £20.00 per round; weekends with member only £15.00. *Eating facilities:* available – dining room and two bars. *Visitors:* welcome weekdays with Handicap Certificate only. (Tuesday Ladies Day). Weekends and Bank Holidays with member only. *Society Meetings:* catered for weekdays only, except Tuesdays. Professional: Lee Muncey (0525 372143). Secretary: J. Burchell (0525 373811).

LEIGHTON BUZZARD Near. **Ivinghoe Golf Club,** Ivinghoe, Near Leighton Buzzard (Cheddington (0296) 668696). *Location:* three miles from Tring and from Dunstable. 9 holes, 4602 yards. S.S.S. 62. *Green Fees:* weekdays £6.00, weekends £8.00. *Eating facilities:* bar and catering. *Visitors:* welcome without reservation. *Society Meetings:* small, catered for. Professional: P.W. Garrad. Secretary: Mrs S. Garrad.

LEIGHTON BUZZARD near. **Mentmore Golf and Country Club,** Mentmore, Near Leighton Buzzard LU7 0UA (0296 662020; Fax: 0296 662592). *Location:* half a mile south of Mentmore Village. Parkland – 10 lake features. Two courses – Rothschild and Rosebery. Practice ground. *Green Fees:* information not provided. *Eating facilities:* restaurant, bar snacks; function suite. *Visitors:* welcome. Indoor swimming pool. *Society Meetings:* welcome. Professional: Pip Elson.

LUTON. **South Beds. Golf Club,** Warden Hill Road, Luton LU2 7AA (Luton (0582) 591500). *Location:* on east side A6, two and a half miles north of Luton. Undulating downland course. 18 holes, 6342 yards. S.S.S. 71. Also 9 holes, 4914 yards. S.S.S. 64. Practice fairway, huts and chipping area. *Green Fees:* 18 holes weekdays £26.00 per day, £17.00 per round; weekends £34.50 per day, £24.00 per round (not on Competition Days). 9 holes (twice round) weekdays £8.00, weekends £11.00. *Eating facilities:* full course meals (must be booked), snacks at all times. *Visitors:* welcome weekdays with reservation. Handicap Certificate essential. Tuesday afternoon is Ladies' Day. *Society Meetings:* catered for by arrangement. Professional: Eddie Cogle (0582 591209). Secretary: S. Beaton (0582 591500).

LUTON. **Stockwood Park Golf Club,** London Road, Luton LU1 4LX (Luton (0582) 23241). *Location:* adjacent Exit 10 of M1 exit Luton Airport. Parkland. 18 holes, 5973 yards. S.S.S. 69. Driving range, mini golf course and pitch and putt. *Green Fees:* weekends £6.65; weekdays £4.55. *Eating facilities:* two bars and restaurant. *Visitors:* always welcome, municipal club. *Society Meetings:* catered for Mondays, Tuesdays and Thursdays by prior arrangement. Professional: G. McCarthy (0582 413704). Secretary: A.J. Bland.

MILTON KEYNES. **Aspley Guise and Woburn Sands Golf Club,** West Hill, Aspley Guise MK17 8DX (Milton Keynes (0908) 582264). *Location:* two miles west of Junction 13 M1, between Aspley Guise and Woburn Sands. Undulating parkland, 18 holes, 6248 yards. S.S.S. 70. *Green Fees:* weekdays £18.00 per round, £23.50 per day. *Eating facilities:* full catering except Mondays. *Visitors:* welcome weekdays with bona fide handicaps – check with Secretary; only with a member at weekends. *Society Meetings:* Wednesdays and Fridays. Professional: Glyn McCarthy (0908 583974). Secretary: T.E. Simpson (0908 583596).

SANDY. **John O'Gaunt Golf Club,** Sutton Park, Sandy SG19 2LY (0767 260360; Fax: 0767 261381). *Location:* on B1040 off A1 two miles north of Biggleswade. Parkland courses. Two 18 hole courses: John O'Gaunt Course 6513 yards, S.S.S. 71 and Carthagena Course 5869 yards, S.S.S. 68. Small practice area. *Green Fees:* weekdays £35.00, weekends £50.00. *Eating facilities:* restaurant and bar. *Visitors:* welcome. Handicap Certificate required at weekends. *Society Meetings:* welcome weekdays, with some limitations on Thursdays and Fridays. Professional: P. Round (0767 260094). Secretary: I.M. Simpson (0767 260360).

WYBOSTON. **Wyboston Lakes Golf Club,** Wyboston Lakes, Wyboston MK44 3AL (Huntingdon (0480) 218411). *Location:* one mile south of St. Neots, off A1 and A45. Parkland with play round five lakes. 18 holes, 5803 yards. S.S.S. 69. Driving range. *Green Fees:* weekdays £11.00 per 18 holes; weekends £14.00 per 18 holes. £20.00 per 36 holes weekdays only. *Eating facilities:* clubhouse catering. *Visitors:* welcome weekdays, booking times required for weekends. Motel on site. *Society Meetings:* catered for weekdays only. Professional: P. Ashwell (0480 212501). Secretary: B. Chinn (0480 219200).

---

# NOTE

All the information in this book is given in good faith in the belief that it is correct. However, the publishers cannot guarantee the facts given in these pages, neither are they responsible for changes in policy, ownership or terms that may take place after the date of going to press. Readers should always satisfy themselves that the facilities they require are available and that the terms, if quoted, still apply.

# Berkshire

ASCOT. **Berkshire Golf Club,** Swinley Road, Ascot SL5 8AY (Ascot (0344) 21495). *Location:* off A332. Heathland (wooded) course. 36 holes. Blue Course: 6260 yards, S.S.S. 70, Par 71. Red Course: 6369 yards, S.S.S. 70, Par 72. Practice facilities. *Green Fees:* £40.00 per round, £55.00 per day weekdays. *Eating facilities:* dining room open daily except Monday, snack bar open daily; bar open every day. *Visitors:* welcome weekdays by application to the Secretary only. *Society Meetings:* catered for by prior bookings. Professional: K.A. MacDonald (0344 22351). Secretary: Major P.D. Clarke (0344 21496).

ASCOT. **Lavender Park Golf Centre,** Swinley Road, Ascot (0344 884074). *Location:* Ascot Race Course A30, Bracknell/Ascot A329. Flat, semi wooded course. 9 holes, 1104 yards. S.S.S. 28. 26 bay driving range. *Green Fees:* 9 holes £2.95, 18 holes £3.95 weekdays; 9 holes £4.25, 18 holes £7.00 weekends. *Eating facilities:* Sloanes Bar and pub snacks. *Visitors:* open to public seven days a week. *Society Meetings:* welcome. Professional: Paul Slater (0344 886096).

ASCOT. **Royal Ascot Golf Club,** Winkfield Road, Ascot SL5 7LJ (Ascot (0344) 22923). *Location:* A329 Ascot High Street, Winkfield Road is off Ascot High Street. Heathland. 18 holes, 5709 yards. S.S.S. 68. *Green Fees:* weekdays £11.00 as member's guest; weekends £13.00 as member's guest. *Eating facilities:* full catering available except Mondays. *Visitors:* welcome only as guests of members. *Society Meetings:* catered for Wednesdays and Thursdays, maximum 40. Professional: Garry Malia (0344 24656). Secretary: Derek Simmonds (0344 25175).

ASCOT. **Swinley Forest Golf Club,** Coronation Road, Ascot SL5 9LE (0344 20197). *Location:* between Ascot and Bagshot. 18 holes, 6001 yards. *Green Fees:* £65.00 only on the introduction of a member. *Eating facilities:* lunches served. *Visitors:* welcome only with a member. *Society Meetings:* catered for. Professional: R.C. Parker. Secretary: I.L. Pearce.

CROWTHORNE. **East Berkshire Golf Club,** Ravenswood Avenue, Crowthorne RG11 6BD (Crowthorne (0344) 772041). *Location:* M3 Junction 3 – Bracknell turn off follow signs to Crowthorne, Ravenswood Avenue opposite Railway Station. Heathland course. 18 holes, 6344 yards. S.S.S. 70. *Green Fees:* weekdays £33.00. *Eating facilities:* meals à la carte except Monday. *Visitors:* welcome weekdays, Handicap Certificate essential. *Society Meetings:* Thursdays and Fridays only. Professional: Arthur Roe (0344 774112). Secretary: W.H. Short (0344 772041; Fax: 0344 777378).

MAIDENHEAD. **Maidenhead Golf Club,** Shoppenhangers Road, Maidenhead SL6 2PZ (Maidenhead (0628) 20545). *Location:* adjacent to Maidenhead Station (south side), one mile from M4. Flat course. 18 holes, 6360 yards. S.S.S. 70. *Green Fees:* weekdays £27.00. *Eating facilities:* bar meals Monday to Friday. *Visitors:* welcome weekdays, no visitors after 12 noon Fridays, Handicap Certificate required. *Society Meetings:* weekdays except Fridays. Professional: Clive Dell (0628 24067). Secretary: Iain Lindsay (0628 24693).

MAIDENHEAD near. **Hawthorn Hill Golf Centre,** Drift Road, Hawthorn Hill, Near Maidenhead SL6 3ST (0628 770556). *Location:* M4 Junction 8/9 to Maidenhead, A330 to Ascot. Parkland course. 18 holes. 38 bay floodlit driving range. *Green Fees:* £10.00 per round (£6.00 for 9 holes) weekdays; £12.00 per round (£7.50 for 9 holes) weekends. Juniors/Senior Citizens concessionary rates. *Eating facilities:* large clubhouse, restaurant, barbecue, private function hall. *Visitors:* always welcome, open every day except Christmas Day. Large Pro shop, Conference facilities. *Society Meetings:* always welcome. Professional: (0628 26035). Secretary: Alan Kibblewhite (0628 771030).

MAIDENHEAD. **Temple Golf Club,** Henley Road, Hurley, Near Maidenhead SL6 5LH (0628 824248). *Location:* on the A423 Maidenhead to Henley Road (exit 8/9 on M4) Parkland. 18 holes, 6206 yards. S.S.S. 70. Putting, pitching, net. *Green Fees:* £35.00 per day weekdays; £45.00 per day weekends. Society full day £55 including meals. *Eating facilities:* available. *Visitors:* welcome by arrangement with Secretary. *Society Meetings:* must book a year in advance. Professional: Alan Dobbins (0628 824254). Secretary: D.W. Kirkland (0628 824795).

MAIDENHEAD. **Winter Hill Golf Club,** Grange Lane, Cookham SL6 9RP (Bourne End (0628) 527810). *Location:* M4 Junction 8/9, four miles from Maidenhead. Parkland. 18 holes, 6408 yards. S.S.S. 71. Large practice ground. *Green Fees:* £22.00 weekdays. *Eating facilities:* lunches/snacks available daily. *Visitors:* welcome weekdays – confirmatory telephone enquiry advisable. Dress – strictly no jeans/trainers/shell suits on course or in clubhouse. *Society Meetings:* welcome, main day Wednesday. Professional: Mr. Paul Hedges (0628 527610). Secretary: Mr G.B. Charters-Rowe (0628 527613).

NEWBURY. **Newbury and Crookham Golf Club Ltd,** Bury's Bank Road, Greenham, Newbury. *Location:* on south side of Newbury off A34 opposite American Air Base. 18 holes, 5843 yards. S.S.S. 68. *Green Fees:* information not provided. No visitors weekends or Bank Holidays, unless with member. *Eating facilities:* catering available, coffee, lunch, tea, etc. *Visitors:* welcome with reservation, not weekends or Bank Holidays without member. *Society Meetings:* welcome by prior arrangement, not weekends. W. Harris (0635 31201).

NEWBURY. **West Berkshire Golf Club**, Chaddleworth, Newbury RG16 0HS. *Location:* M4 Junction 14, SP RAF Welford, OS Map Ref SU411 762. Downland. 18 holes, 7069 yards. S.S.S. 74. *Green Fees:* £23.00 weekdays. *Eating facilities:* full catering available. *Visitors:* welcome with reservation. Members and guests only at weekends. *Society Meetings:* catered for. Professional: D. Sheppard (04882 8851). Secretary: (04882 574).

NORTH ASCOT. **Mill Ride Golf Club**, Mill Ride Estate, North Ascot SL5 8LT (0344 886777). *Location:* off Junction 3 of M3 or Junction 6 of M4, one mile from Ascot Racecourse. Parkland; designed by Donald Steel. 18 holes, 6750 yards. Par 72. Putting green, chipping green, driving range. *Green Fees:* information not provided. *Eating facilities:* lounge bar/restaurant/private dining room. *Visitors:* by reservation only at specified times. Gym/saunas/steam rooms. Accommodation. Pro shop. Professional: Suzy Baggs (0344 886777). Secretary: Julian Deeming.

READING. **Calcot Park Golf Club**, Bath Road, Calcot, Reading RG3 5RN (0734 427124). *Location:* off Exit 12, M4 along A4 towards Reading, approximately one mile. Undulating wooded parkland. 18 holes, 6283 yards. S.S.S. 70. Limited practice areas. *Green Fees:* weekdays £30.00. *Eating facilities:* fully licensed restaurant, snacks available, two bars. *Visitors:* welcome on provision of Handicap Certificate. Not weekends or Bank Holidays. Advisable to ring first to check availability. *Society Meetings:* catered for Tuesday, Wednesday and Thursday. Professional: Albert MacKenzie (0734 427797). Secretary: A.L. Bray.

READING. **Hurst Golf Club**, Sandford Lane, Hurst, Reading (0734 344355). *Location:* five miles Reading towards Wokingham. Parkland by the side of a large lake. 9 holes, 3154 yards. S.S.S. 70. *Green Fees:* weekdays £5.10; weekends £5.95. Reductions for Juniors and Senior Citizens. *Eating facilities:* bar and bar snacks. *Visitors:* unrestricted, bookings accepted. *Society Meetings:* welcome. Professional: Paul Watson (0734 344355). Secretary E. Brewer (Fax: 0344 301020).

READING. **Reading Golf Club**, 17 Kidmore End Road, Emmer Green, Reading RG4 8SG (Reading (0734) 472169). *Location:* two miles north of Reading off the Peppard Road (B481). Parkland. 18 holes, 6212 yards. S.S.S. 70. Practice facilities. *Green Fees:* £26.00 per day, £12.00 with member. *Eating facilities:* available. *Visitors:* welcome Monday to Thursday if member of recognised club, with handicap of 24 or less. Friday to Sunday with member only. *Society Meetings:* catered for by arrangement Tuesdays, Wednesdays and Thursdays. Professional: Tim Morrison (0734 476115). Secretary: J. Weekes (0734 472909).

READING. **Sonning Golf Club**, Duffield Road, Sonning RG4 0GJ (Reading (0734) 693332). *Location:* left off A4 at Sonning Roundabout, then left again. Parkland. 18 holes, 6366 yards. S.S.S. 70. *Green Fees:* on application. *Eating facilities:* lunches served –

advance booking necessary. *Visitors:* welcome Monday to Friday, must be member of a recognised golf club with an official handicap. *Society Meetings:* catered for. Professional: R.T. McDougall (0734 692910). Secretary: P.F. Williams.

SINDLESHAM. **Bearwood Golf Club**, Mole Road, Sindlesham RG11 5DB (Arborfield Cross (0734) 761330). *Location:* on B3030 from Winnersh to Arborfield. Flat wooded course. 9 holes, 2802 yards. S.S.S. 68 (18 holes). 9 hole Pitch and Putt. *Green Fees:* weekdays £8.00 for 9 holes, £15.00 for 18 holes. *Eating facilities:* food available all day. *Visitors:* welcome weekdays, Handicap Certificate required. Weekends as guests of members only. *Society Meetings:* maximum of 18 catered for, Thursdays only. Professional/Manager: Barry Tustin (0734 760643). Secretary: C. Dyer OBE (0734 760060).

SLOUGH. **Datchet Golf Club**, Buccleuch Road, Datchet (Slough (0753) 543887). *Location:* within two miles of both Windsor and Slough. 9 holes, 5978 yards. S.S.S. 69. *Green Fees:* £16.00 per round, £22.00 per day. *Visitors:* welcome without reservation during week up to 3pm. Lessons and club repairs for non members. *Society Meetings:* small societies welcome. Professional: Andy Greig (0753 542755). Secretary: Anne Perkins.

STREATLEY ON THAMES. **Goring and Streatley Golf Club**, Rectory Road, Streatley on Thames RG8 9QA (Goring (0491) 872688). *Location:* 10 miles north west of Reading off A417 Wantage Road. Parkland course on Berkshire Downs. 18 holes, 6255 yards. S.S.S. 70. *Green Fees:* £27.00 per day; £18.00 per round after 4pm except Weekends. Weekends only playing with a member. *Eating facilities:* full restaurant and bar meals. *Visitors:* welcome on weekdays by telephone booking. *Society Meetings:* catered for. Professional: Roy Mason (0491 873715). Secretary: J. Menzies (0491 873229).

SUNNINGDALE. **Sunningdale Ladies' Golf Club**, Cross Road, Sunningdale SL5 9RX (0344 20507). *Location:* second left going west on A30, past Sunningdale level crossing. Heathland. 18 holes, 3622 yards. (Designed for Ladies' Golf). S.S.S. 60. *Green Fees:* £17.00/22.00 weekdays; £19.00/27.00 weekends. *Eating facilities:* snack lunches available except Sundays. *Visitors:* welcome, telephone first. Must have Handicap Certificate. *Society Meetings:* catered for (Ladies only). Secretary: John Darroch.

WOKINGHAM. **Downshire Golf Course**, Easthampstead Park, Wokingham RG11 3DH (Bracknell (0344) 424066). *Location:* between Bracknell and Crowthorne off Nine Mile Ride. Parkland. 18 holes, 6395 yards. S.S.S. 71. 9 hole pitch and putt, driving range and golf academy. *Green Fees:* weekdays £10.20; weekends £11.90. *Eating facilities:* bar meals, grills, free house bar and restaurant. *Visitors:* welcome. *Society Meetings:* welcome. Professional: Paul Watson (0344 302030; Fax: 0344 301020). Secretary: (0344 422708).

# Buckinghamshire

AYLESBURY. **Chiltern Forest Golf Club,** Aston Hill, Halton, Aylesbury (Steward: Aylesbury (0296) 630899). *Location:* five miles south-east of Aylesbury, signposted St. Leonards. Wooded, hilly course. 18 holes, 5755 yards. S.S.S. 69. *Green Fees:* £24.00 per day weekdays, £17.00 with a member weekends. *Visitors:* weekdays unrestricted, weekends with a member. *Society Meetings:* welcome, preferably Wednesdays. Professional: Christopher Skeet (0296 631817). Secretary: L.E.A. Clark (0296 631267).

AYLESBURY. **Ellesborough Golf Club,** Butlers Cross, Aylesbury HP17 0TZ (Wendover (0296) 622375). *Location:* on B4010 one and a half miles from Wendover. Chiltern Hills course. Undulating links. 18 holes, 6271 yards. S.S.S. 70. Practice net/ground. *Green Fees:* £30.00 per day, £20.00 per round weekdays (until April 1993). *Eating facilities:* available. *Visitors:* except weekends, Tuesday mornings and competition days, must provide Handicap Certificate. *Society Meetings:* catered for Wednesdays and Thursdays only by arrangement with Secretary. Professional: Paul Warner (0296 623126). Secretary: K.M. Flint (0296 622114).

AYLESBURY. **Weston Turville Golf & Squash Club,** New Road, Weston Turville, Near Aylesbury HP22 5QT (Aylesbury (0296) 24084). *Location:* two miles south east of Aylesbury off A41. Easy walking course at the foot of the Chiltern Hills. 18 holes, 6002 yards. S.S.S. 69. *Green Fees:* weekdays £15; weekends £20. *Eating facilities:* meals, snacks and visitors' bar. *Visitors:* truly welcome, booking advisable Saturday and Sundays. Squash courts available. *Society Meetings:* especially catered for. Professional: Tom Jones (0296 25949). General Manager: Mr Barry Hill (0296 24084).

BEACONSFIELD. **Beaconsfield Golf Club Ltd,** Seer Green, Near Beaconsfield HP9 2UR (Beaconsfield (0494) 676545/6). *Location:* from A40 at Beaconsfield, A355 Amersham Road, one mile turn right to Jordans, one mile signposted. Parkland course. 18 holes, 6469 metres. S.S.S. 71. Large practice ground. *Green Fees:* £40.00 per day, £33.00 per round. *Eating facilities:* dining room or bar menu; 2 bars. *Visitors:* welcome weekdays with accredited introduction – check with Pro. *Society Meetings:* catered for Tuesdays and Wednesdays. Professional: Mike Brothers (0494 676616). Secretary: P.I. Anderson (0494 676545/6; Fax: 0494 681148).

BUCKINGHAM. **Buckingham Golf Club,** Tingewick Road, Buckingham MK18 4AG (0280 813282). *Location:* one and a half miles south west of Buckingham on A421. Undulating parkland – eight holes affected by river. 18 holes, 6142 yards. S.S.S. 69. Practice ground. *Green Fees:* weekdays £26.00, weekends as members' guests only. *Eating facilities:* seven day catering – bars, lunch and evening. *Visitors:* welcome weekdays only. *Society Meetings:* pre-booked on Tuesdays or Thurs-

days. Professional: Tom Gates (0280 815210). Secretary: David Rolph (0280 815566).

BURNHAM. **Burnham Beeches Golf Club,** Green Lane, Burnham, Slough SL1 8EG (Burnham (0628) 661150). *Location:* on M4 for Slough two miles, M40 seven miles. Wooded parkland course. 18 holes, 6449 yards. S.S.S. 71. *Green Fees:* weekdays £24.00 per round, £36.00 per day; weekends with a member. *Eating facilities:* bar and restaurant, full catering available. *Visitors:* welcome weekdays, weekends only with a member. *Society Meetings:* welcome by arrangement. Professional/Secretary: A.J. Buckner (0628 661661 or 661448).

BURNHAM. **Lambourne Golf Club,** Dropmore Road, Burnham SL1 8NF (0628 666755; Fax: 0628 663301). *Location:* take M4 to Exit 7; take M40 to Exit 2. Parkland. 18 holes. S.S.S. 72. Practice facilities available. *Green Fees:* information not supplied. *Eating facilities:* full facilities in temporary clubhouse, main clubhouse opening this year. *Visitors:* welcome. Professional: R.A. Newman. Secretary: C.J. Lumley.

CHALFONT ST. GILES. **Harewood Downs Golf Club,** Cokes Lane, Chalfont St. Giles HP8 4TA (Little Chalfont (0494) 762308). *Location:* off A413, two miles east of Amersham. Rolling, tree lined. 18 holes, 5958 yards, 5448 metres. S.S.S. 69. Practice ground. *Green Fees:* weekdays £27.00 per day, weekends £30.00. *Eating facilities:* lunches served at club. *Visitors:* welcome on weekdays with current handicap, weekends by prior arrangement only. *Society Meetings:* catered for by arrangement. Professional: G. Morris (0494 764102). Secretary: M.R. Cannon (0494 762184).

CHESHAM. **Chartridge Park Golf Club,** Chartridge, Chesham HP5 2TF (0494 791772). Parkland, interesting wooded course with panoramic views. 18 holes, 5900 yards. S.S.S. 69. Practice ground. Buggies available on the John Jacobs designed course. Green Fees: weekdays £13.50; weekends £17.50. *Eating facilities:* two bars and restaurant. *Visitors:* welcome mid-week. *Society Meetings:* always welcome weekends. Professional: Peter Gibbins. Secretary: Anita Gibbins.

CHESHAM. **Chesham and Ley Hill,** Ley Hill, Chesham HP5 1UZ (Chesham (0494) 784541). *Location:* off A41 on B4504 and follow signs for Ley Hill, nearest town – Chesham. Wooded parkland. 9 holes, 5296 yards. S.S.S. 66. Putting green and practice net. *Green Fees:* weekdays £12.00 per round, £17.00 per day. *Eating facilities:* licensed bar, food available at certain times. *Visitors:* welcome Mondays and Thursdays all day; Wednesdays after 12 noon; Fridays till 1.00pm, providing no competitions being held. All other days with member only. *Society Meetings:* Thursdays only by prior arrangement. Secretary: J.R. Taylor (0494 784541).

DENHAM. **Denham Golf Club,** Tilehouse Lane, Denham UB9 5DE (Denham (0895) 832079). *Location:* one and a half miles from Uxbridge off the left hand side of the A412 on route to Watford. Parkland – undulating. 18 holes, 6451 yards, 6159 metres. S.S.S. 71. Practice ground. *Green Fees:* £30.00 per round, £44.00 per day weekdays; weekends with a member only. *Eating facilities:* diningroom, bar snacks. *Visitors:* welcome Monday to Thursday by prior arrangement only. Handicap Certificate. *Society Meetings:* catered for Tuesdays, Wednesdays and Thursdays. Professional: John Sheridan (0895 832801). Secretary: Wg Cdr D. Graham (0895 832022; Fax: 0895 835340).

GERRARDS CROSS. **Gerrards Cross Golf Club,** Chalfont Park, Gerrards Cross SL9 0QA (Gerrards Cross (0753) 883263). *Location:* alongside A413 (to Amersham) about one mile from junction with A40 (London to Oxford road). Wooded parkland course. 18 holes, 6295 yards. S.S.S. 70. *Green Fees:* weekdays £26.00 per round, £35.00 per day. *Eating facilities:* lunch available to order, bar snacks at all times. *Visitors:* welcome except at weekends and Public Holidays but must produce a letter of introduction or current Handicap Certificate. *Society Meetings:* catered for Thursdays and Fridays, maximum number 50. Professional: A.P. Barr (0753 885300). Secretary/Manager: P.H. Fisher.

HIGH WYCOMBE. **Flackwell Heath Golf Club Limited,** Treadaway Road, Flackwell Heath, High Wycombe HP10 9PE (Bourne End (0628) 520027). *Location:* M4 Exit 3 from London, Exit 4 from Oxford. 2 miles High Wycombe. Heath and woodland, some hills. 18 holes, 6207 yards. S.S.S. 70. *Green Fees:* weekdays £27.00; weekends £10.00 with member only. *Eating facilities:* restaurant and bars daily (limited catering Mondays). *Visitors:* welcome weekdays only with Handicap Certificate. Weekends with member only. *Society Meetings:* catered for by arrangement Wednesdays and Thursdays. Professional: Steven Bryan (0628 523017). Secretary: Peter Jeans (0628 520929).

HIGH WYCOMBE. **Hazlemere Golf and Country Club,** Penn Road, Hazlemere, Near High Wycombe (High Wycombe (0494) 714722). *Location:* on B474 about half a mile from junction with A404 High Wycombe/Amersham Road – three miles from High Wycombe centre. Undulating parkland course. 18 holes, 5873 yards. S.S.S. 68. *Green Fees:* weekdays £22.00; weekends £30.00. *Eating facilities:* restaurant and bar. *Visitors:* restricted at weekends. Snooker table. *Society Meetings:* by prior arrangement. Professional: Steve Morvell (0494 718298). Secretary: D. Hudson (0494 714722).

IVER. **Iver Golf Course,** Hollow Hill Lane, Off Langley Park Road, Iver SL0 0JJ (Slough (0753) 655615). *Location:* situated off Langley Park Road leaving the town of Langley heading towards Iver. Flat parkland, easy walking with natural ditches and ponds. 9 holes, 5988 yards (men), 5230 yards (ladies). S.S.S. 70 (men), 72 (ladies). Driving range and practice ground for short game. *Green Fees:* weekdays £4.90 for 9 holes, £8.00 for 18; weekends £6.50 for 9 holes, £11.00 for 18. Special rates available, please enquire. *Eating facilities:* lunch served 12 noon to 2.30pm seven

days, snacks and rolls always available. *Visitors:* always welcome, best to phone on day of play for booking. *Society Meetings:* always welcome. Professional: Geraldine Teschner (0753 655615).

LITTLE CHALFONT. **Little Chalfont Golf Club,** Lodge Lane, Little Chalfont HP8 4AJ (0494 764877). *Location:* Junction 18 M25, two miles towards Amersham on A404, first left past garden centre. Undulating parkland. 9 holes, 5852 yards. S.S.S. 68. *Green Fees:* weekdays £10.00; weekends £12.00. *Eating facilities:* full bar and eating facilities. *Visitors:* always welcome. *Society Meetings:* welcome midweek. Professional: B. Woodhouse and A. Philpott (0494 762942). Secretary: J.M. Dunne (0494 764877).

MILTON KEYNES. **Abbey Hill Golf Club,** Abbey Hill, Milton Keynes (Milton Keynes (0908) 562408). *Location:* 2 miles south of Stony Stratford. 18 holes, 5732 metres. S.S.S. 69. Short par 3 course available. Municipal green fees on application. *Eating facilities:* available. *Visitors:* welcome. *Society Meetings:* catered for, apply Professional. Professional: S. Harlock. Secretary: Mr I.D. Grieve.

MILTON KEYNES. **Three Locks Golf Club,** Partridge House, Great Brickhill, Milton Keynes MK17 9BH (0525 270470). *Location:* turn off A4146 Leighton Buzzard to Milton Keynes road. Parkland with water hazards on six holes. 9 holes, 6680 yards. S.S.S. 72. Practice ground. *Green Fees:* weekdays £5.00 9 holes, £8.00 18 holes; weekends £7.00 9 holes, £9.50 18 holes. *Eating facilities:* lounge and bar serving hot and cold bar snacks. *Visitors:* welcome every day. Accommodation available in Club's hotel, free golf for residents. Pro shop. *Society Meetings:* welcome every day. Society Days/Dinners catered for. Professional: Colin Ancsell (0525 270050). Secretary: Gordon Critchley (0525 270470).

MILTON KEYNES. **Wavendon Golf Centre,** Lower End Road, Wavendon, Milton Keynes MK17 8DA (0908 281296; Fax: 0908 281257). *Location:* two minutes from Junction 13 M1, just off A421 link road. Parkland with six small lakes as hazards. 18 holes, 5479 yards. S.S.S. 67. 9 holes, 1424 yards. S.S.S. 27. 36 bay driving range, practice green and bunker. *Green Fees:* weekdays £9.00; weekends £12.00. Senior Citizens and Juniors half price; twilight evening rates. *Eating facilities:* 65 seater carvery restaurant and downstairs bar. *Visitors:* welcome. *Society Meetings:* welcome weekdays, weekends by arrangement. Professional: Nick Elmen (0908 281811). Secretary: Cynthia Caeney (0908 281297).

MILTON KEYNES. **Windmill Hill Golf Course,** Tattenhoe Lane, Bletchley, Milton Keynes MK3 7RB (0908 648149). *Location:* A421 Milton Keynes – Buckingham. Flat parkland course, Henry Cotton layout. 18 holes, 6773 yards. S.S.S. 72. 23 bay floodlit driving range. *Green Fees:* weekdays £6.00; weekends and Bank Holidays £8.50. Reduced rates Juniors and Senior Citizens. *Eating facilities:* public bar and food available. *Visitors:* welcome at any time. Telephone Professional. *Society Meetings:* welcome at all times. All bookings through Professional. Professional: C. Clingan (0908 378623). Secretary: Pat Long.

MILTON KEYNES. **Woburn Golf and Country Club,** Bow Brickhill, Milton Keynes MK17 9LJ (Milton Keynes (0908) 370756). *Location:* M1 Junction 13. 36 holes: Duke's Course 6940 yards S.S.S. 74. Duchess' Course 6641 yards, S.S.S. 72. Two practice grounds. *Green Fees:* information on request. *Eating facilities:* two restaurants; breakfasts, lunches and dinners. *Visitors:* welcome on weekdays with prior notice. *Society Meetings:* catered for, details on application. Professional/Managing Director: Alex Hay (0908 647987 or 370756).

PRINCES RISBOROUGH. **Whiteleaf Golf Club Ltd,** The Clubhouse, Whiteleaf, Aylesbury HP17 0LY (08444 3097). *Location:* A4010 from Princes Risborough. 9 holes, 5359 yards. S.S.S. 66. *Green Fees:* weekdays £15.00 for 18 holes, £25.00 all day; members only at weekends. *Visitors:* welcome on weekdays only. *Society Meetings:* on application, Thursdays only. Professional: K.S. Ward (08444 5472). Secretary: D.G. Bullard (0844 274058).

SLOUGH. **Farnham Park Municipal Golf Course,** Park Road, Stoke Poges SL2 4PJ (0753 643335). *Location:* centrally situated between Stoke Poges and Farnham Royal, off Park Road. Parkland. 18 holes, 5847 yards. S.S.S. 68. *Green Fees:* weekdays £7.70; weekends £10.25. Reduced rates for Senior Citizens and Juniors. *Eating facilities:* available. *Visitors:* welcome. Professional: P. Harrison (0753 643332). Hon. Secretary: Maureen Brooker (0753 647065).

STOKE POGES. **Stoke Poges Golf Club,** North Drive, Park Road, Stoke Poges SL2 4PG (Slough (0753) 526385). *Location:* one mile north of Slough. 18 holes, 6654 yards. S.S.S. 72. *Green Fees:* weekdays £27.00 single round, £37.00 per day. *Eating facilities:* lunch and snack restaurant. *Visitors:* welcome weekdays only with Handicap Certificate or letter of introduction; weekends as member's guest only. *Society Meetings:* catered for. Professional: Kim Thomas. Secretary/Manager: R.C. Pickering.

STOWE. **Stowe Golf Club,** Stowe, Buckingham MK18 5EH (0280 816264). *Location:* situated at Stowe School, four miles north of Buckingham. Parkland course with follies and lakes. 9 holes, 2189 yards. S.S.S. 63. *Green Fees:* £10.00. *Visitors:* only as a guest of a member. *Society Meetings:* catered for by appointment. Secretary: Mrs S.A. Cross (0280 813650).

WEXHAM. **Wexham Park Golf Course,** Wexham Street, Slough SL3 6NB (0753 663271). *Location:* M40 to Beaconsfield, A40 to Gerrards Cross, direction to Fulmer on right hand side, near Wexham Park Hospital. Parkland. 18 holes, 5390 yards. S.S.S. 66. Also 9/18 hole course, 2851/5702 yards. S.S.S. 34/68; and 9 hole course, 2283 yards. S.S.S. 32. Driving range. *Green Fees:* weekdays £8.00 for 18 holes, £4.90 for 9 holes; weekends £11.00 for 18 holes, £6.50 for 9 holes. *Eating facilities:* clubhouse bar and full kitchen facilities. *Visitors:* welcome – Pay and Play, open to all. Hotel and sports complex. *Society Meetings:* weekdays only (except Bank Holidays), minimum 12 people. Professional: David Morgan (0753 663425). Secretary: P.J. Gale.

# Cambridgeshire

CAMBRIDGE. **Cambridgeshire Moat House Golf Club,** Bar Hill, Cambridge CB3 8EU (Craftshill (0954) 780555). *Location:* five miles from Cambridge on A604 Huntingdon Road. Undulating parkland with a lake, ditches and many trees. 18 holes, 6734 yards. S.S.S. 72. Practice grounds. *Green Fees:* weekdays £19.00; weekends and Public Holidays £25.00. Daily and weekend golf packages. *Eating facilities:* restaurant, bars, bar meals (Mon-Fri lunch). *Visitors:* welcome anytime by prior phone call. 100 Bedroom Hotel, Squash, Tennis, Residents' Health and Fitness Club and Indoor Heated Swimming Pool. *Society Meetings:* welcome weekdays. Resident Societies only at weekends. Professional and Sports Manager: Geoff Huggett (0954 780098). Secretary: (0954 780555).

CAMBRIDGE. **Girton Golf Club,** Dodford Lane, Cambridge (Cambridge (0223) 276169). *Location:* 3 miles north of Cambridge. 18 holes, 6000 yards. S.S.S. 69. *Green Fees:* £18.00 per day with Handicap Certificate, £23.00 without; weekends with a member only. *Eating facilities:* available. *Visitors:* weekdays only. *Society Meetings:* welcomed. Professional: S. Thomson. Secretary: Mrs M.A. Cornwell.

CAMBRIDGE. **Gog Magog Golf Club,** Shelford Bottom, Cambridge CB2 4AB (0223 247626; Fax: 0223 414990). *Location:* two miles from A11 – A604 roundabout. Colchester – Cambridge Road A604. Open, undulating. Two courses. 18 holes, 6386 yards. S.S.S. 70. 9 holes, 5805 yards. S.S.S. 68. *Green Fees:* Old Course £25.00 per round, £30.00 per day. 9-hole course £15.00 per day. *Eating facilities:* diningroom, bar meals, mixed and men's bar. *Visitors:* welcome, only with members at weekends and Bank Holidays, Handicap Certificates required, Handicap limit on Old Course 22 and below. *Society Meetings:* catered for Tuesdays and Thurdays. Professional: I. Bamborough (0223 246058). Secretary: John E. Riches (0223 247626).

ELY. **Ely City Golf Course Ltd,** Cambridge Road, Ely CB7 4HX (Ely (0353) 663810). *Location:* on southern outskirts of city on A10 going to Cambridge. Parkland course, slightly undulating, magnificent views of the 12th century cathedral. 18 holes, 6602 yards. S.S.S. 72. Practice area. *Green Fees:* weekdays £22.00 weekends and Bank Holidays £30.00. *Eating facilities:* bar snacks and full restaurant facilities. *Visitors:* wel come anytime with a member or if in possession of a valid Handicap Certificate. Jeans, T-shirts and trainers not allowed. *Society Meetings:* welcome Tuesday to Friday inclusive by arrangement. Professional: F.C. Rowden (0353 663317). Secretary: Mr G.A. Briggs (0353 662751).

HUNTINGDON. **Brampton Park Golf Club,** Buckden Road, Brampton, Huntingdon PE18 8NF. *Location:* three-quarters of a mile off A1, travelling north take first Huntingdon turn, south take second sign for "RAF Brampton". Picturesque parkland/meadowland with many water hazards and wooded areas. 18 holes, 6364 yards. S.S.S. 73. *Green Fees:* weekdays £24.00; weekends £36.00. *Eating facilities:* full à la carte restaurant, members bar, bar snacks. *Visitors:* welcome at all times, no restrictions save telephone for tee reservations at weekends. Accommodation and business conference facilities available. *Society Meetings:* welcome. Professional: Mike Torrens (0480 434705). Secretary: John Prout (0480 434700).

HUNTINGDON. **Ramsey Golf Club,** 4 Abbey Terrace, Ramsey, Huntingdon (Ramsey (0487) 813573). *Location:* 20 minutes from A1, 12 miles south of Peterborough, 10 miles north of Huntingdon. Parkland, 18 holes, 6145 yards. S.S.S. 70. Two practice grounds. *Green Fees:* weekdays £20.00 per round or day with Handicap Certificate. Weekends, Bank Holidays with member only. *Eating facilities:* full catering available. *Visitors:* welcome without reservation. *Society Meetings:* catered for by arrangement, weekdays only. Professional: S.J. Scott (0487 813022). Secretary: Mr R. Muirhead (0487 812600).

MARCH. **March Golf Club,** Grange Road, March (March (0354) 52364). *Location:* one mile south of town centre on west side of by-pass (A141). 9 holes, 6210 yards. S.S.S. 70. *Green Fees:* £15. *Eating facilities:* meals available in clubhouse. Professional: Richard Keys (0354 52364).

PETERBOROUGH. **Orton Meadows Golf Club,** Ham Lane, Orton Waterville, Peterborough PE2 0UU (Peterborough (0733) 237478). *Location:* four miles west of Peterborough on A605. Parkland. 18 holes, 5800 yards. S.S.S. 68. Practice ground. *Green Fees:* weekdays £6.20; weekends £8.70. Weekday reductions for Juniors and Senior Citizens. *Eating facilities:* restaurant attached to course. *Visitors:* unrestricted – public course. *Society Meetings:* welcome. Professionals: N. Grant, M.D. Booker. Secretary: K. Boyer.

PETERBOROUGH. **Peterborough Milton Golf Club,** Milton Ferry, Peterborough PE6 7AG (Peterborough (0733) 380204). *Location:* on A47 west of

Peterborough, 3 miles east of A1. Parkland. 18 holes, 6431 yards, 5856 metres. S.S.S. 71. *Green Fees:* weekdays £20.00 per round, weekends £25.00 per round. Societies £30.00 per day. Eating facilities: daily except Mondays. *Visitors:* welcome weekdays; as member's guest at weekends. *Society Meetings:* Tuesdays, Wednesdays and Thursdays by arrangement with Secretary. Professional: Nigel Bundy (0733 380793). Secretary: Mrs D.K. Adams (0733 380489).

PETERBOROUGH. **Thorpe Wood Golf Club,** Thorpe Wood, Peterborough PE3 6SE (Peterborough (0733) 267701). *Location:* three miles west of town on A47. Parkland. 18 holes, 7086 yards. S.S.S. 74. Practice ground. *Green Fees:* weekdays £6.70, weekends and Bank Holidays £9.40. Weekday reductions for Senior Citizens and Juniors. *Eating facilities:* Public House attached to course. *Visitors:* unrestricted. Public Course. *Society Meetings:* welcome - book early. Professionals: Dennis and Roger Fitton (0733 267701; Fax: 0733 332774). Secretary: R. Palmer.

ST. IVES. **St. Ives (Hunts) Golf Club,** Westwood Road, St. Ives PE17 4RS (St. Ives (0480) 64459). *Location:* B1040 off A45. 9 holes, 6052 yards. S.S.S. 69. *Green Fees:* weekdays £20.00. *Eating facilities:* lunches at club, except Mondays. Order in advance. *Visitors:* no visitors weekends or Bank Holidays. *Society Meetings:* catered for. Professional: A. Currie (0480 66067). Secretary: Ray Hill (0480 68392).

ST. NEOTS. **Abbotsley Golf and Squash Club,** Eynesbury Hardwicke, St. Neots PE19 4XN (Huntingdon (0480) 215153; Fax: 0480 403280). *Location:* two miles off A1 (M) from St. Neots, 12 miles off Junction 13 M11. Pleasantly undulating parkland. Two courses, 36 holes – Abbotsley 6311 yards. S.S.S. 71; Cromwell – 6087 yards. S.S.S 69. Driving range. *Green Fees:* weekdays Abbotsley £16.00, Cromwell £9.00; weekends Abbotsley £18.00, Cromwell £11.00. *Eating facilities:* available all day. *Visitors:* always welcome. Six squash courts. Accommodation available in 16 bedroom hotel. Residential golf schools. *Society Meetings:* always welcome, weekends on Cromwell course. Professional: Miss Vivien Saunders (0480 406463). Secretary: Miss Jenny Wisson (0480 474000/403300).

ST. NEOTS. **St. Neots Golf Club,** Cross Hall Road, St. Neots PE19 4AE (0480 74311; Fax: 0480 72363). *Location:* A45 off A1, eastwards, one mile east of Great North Road. 18 holes, 6027 yards. S.S.S. 69. *Green Fees:* on application. *Eating facilities:* full catering facilities. *Visitors:* at weekends/Bank Holidays with member only. *Society Meetings:* welcome. Professional: G. Bithrey (0480 76513). Secretary: R.J. Marsden (0480 72363).

# Cheshire

ALDERLEY EDGE.**Alderley Edge Golf Club,** Brook Lane, Alderley Edge SK9 7RU (Alderley Edge (0625) 585583). *Location:* off A34. 9 holes, 5836 yards. S.S.S. 68. *Green Fees:* weekends £20.00, weekdays £16.00. *Eating facilities:* meals served in clubhouse. *Visitors:* subject to restrictions on Tuesdays, Wednesdays and weekends. Professional: A. Sproston (0625 584493). Secretary: J.B. Page.

ALTRINCHAM. **Hale Golf Club,** Rappax Road, Hale, Altrincham WA15 0NU (061-980 4225). 9 holes (2 rounds), 5780 yards. S.S.S. 68. Pleasant undulating parkland. *Green Fees:* weekdays £15.00 per round, £20.00 per day; weekends with member only £5.00. *Eating facilities:* by arrangement with Steward. *Visitors:* welcome weekdays (except Thursday) with reservation. *Society Meetings:* by arrangement with Hon. Secretary. Professional: John Jackson (061-904 0835). Hon. Secretary: R.V. Murphy (061-980 6438).

APPLETON. **The Warrington Golf Club,** Hill Warren, London Road, Appleton, Near Warrington WA4 5HR (0925 61620). *Location:* M56 exit 11, A49 Warrington one and a half miles. Parkland course. 18 holes, 6217 yards. S.S.S. 70. *Green Fees:* information not provided. *Eating facilities:* available except Monday lunchtime. *Visitors:* welcome with reservation. *Society Meetings:* Wednesdays only. Professional: A.W. Fryer (0925 65431). Secretary: R.O. Francis (0925 61775).

CHEADLE. **Gatley Golf Club Ltd,** Waterfall Farm, Styal Road, Heald Green, Cheadle SK8 3TW (061-437 2091). *Location:* from Gatley village to South down Styal Road and follow directions into Yew Tree Grove, then Motcombe Grove to Club entrance. Parkland course. 9 holes, 5934 yards. S.S.S. 68. *Green Fees:* weekdays £15.00 and £6.00 with member, weekends only if playing with member. Special rates by arrangement. *Eating facilities:* available except Monday, bar. *Visitors:* welcome Mondays, Wednesdays and Thursdays. *Society Meetings:* as above. Professional: S. Crake (061-436 2830). Secretary: P. Hannam F.C.A.(061-437 2091).

CHESTER. **Chester Golf Club,** Curzon Park, Chester CH4 8AR (0244 675130). *Location:* one mile south west of city centre. From Chester Castle take A483 (Wrexham) to first roundabout over Grovesnor Bridge. Turn right into Curzon Park North and follow signs. Parkland on two levels overlooking the River Dee. 18 holes, 6487 yards. S.S.S. 71. *Green Fees:* weekdays £20.00 per day; weekends £25.00. Reductions if playing with a member. *Eating facilities:* full restaurant and bar facilities except Mondays, when snacks only are served except by special arrangement. *Visitors:* welcome most days but advisable to telephone first. *Society Meetings:* catered for by prior arrangement. Professional: George Parton (0244 671185). Secretary: Peter Griffiths (0244 677760).

CHESTER. **Upton-by-Chester Golf Club,** Upton Lane, Chester CH2 1EE (Chester (0244) 381183). *Location:* off A41, near Zoo turn-off traffic lights. Flat parkland course. 18 holes, 5808 yards. S.S.S. 69. *Green Fees:* £16.00 per round, £21.00 per day weekdays; £21.00 per round weekends. *Eating facilities:* large restaurant and four bars. *Visitors:* no restrictions except Competition Days. *Society Meetings:* welcome except Mondays, Tuesdays and weekends. Minimum number 16. All day package £32.00, half day £24.00. Professional: Peter Gardner (0244 381333). Secretary: John B. Durban (0244 381183).

CHESTER. **Vicars Cross Golf Club,** Tarvin Road, Great Barrow, Chester CH3 7HN (Chester (0244) 335174). *Location:* three miles from Chester on the A51 to Nantwich. Wooded parkland, undulating course. 18 holes, 6243 yards. S.S.S. 70. *Green Fees:* weekdays £20.00 day ticket only; weekends and Bank Holidays must be with a member. *Eating facilities:* full catering except Mondays, two bars. *Visitors:* welcome Monday to Thursday only, members guests on Friday, weekends and Bank Holidays. *Society Meetings:* catered for Tuesdays and Thursdays only. Professional: J.A. Forsythe (0244 335595). Secretary: A. Rogers.

CONGLETON. **Astbury Golf Club,** Peel Lane, Astbury, Near Congleton CW12 4RE (Congleton (0260) 272772). *Location:* on A34 Congleton to Newcastle-under-Lyme road. Parkland. 18 holes, 6367 yards. S.S.S. 70. Large practice area. *Green Fees:* weekdays £25.00; £8.00 with member. *Eating facilities:* diningroom and bar. *Visitors:* welcome weekdays, weekends with a member only. Must be members of recognised golf club with bona fide Handicap. *Society Meetings:* Thursdays only. £20.00 per player. Professional: Nigel Griffith (0260 272772). Secretary: Tom Williams (0260 279139).

CONGLETON. **Congleton Golf Club,** Biddulph Road, Congleton CW12 3LZ (Congleton (0260) 273540). *Location:* one mile south of Congleton Railway Station on Biddulph Road. Parkland. 9 holes, 5080 yards. S.S.S. 65. *Green Fees:* information not provided. *Eating facilities:* lunches and evening meals served if ordered in advance. Snacks available except Monday evenings. *Visitors:* welcome. *Society Meetings:* catered for, one year's notice if accepted. Professional: John Colclough (0260 271083). Secretary: T. Pegg (0260 273540).

CREWE. **Crewe Golf Club Ltd,** Fields Road, Haslington, Crewe CW1 1TB (0270 584227). *Location:* off A534 between Crewe and Sandbach. Parkland course. 18 holes, 6201 yards. S.S.S. 70. *Green Fees:* weekdays £16.00 per round, £21.00 per day; weekends with members only. *Eating facilities:* bar, diningroom. *Visitors:* welcome weekdays only, not Bank Holidays

Snooker room. *Society Meetings:* Tuesdays only. Professional: R.E. Rimmer (0270 585032). Secretary: David G. Elias B.Sc. (0270 584099).

CREWE. **Onneley Golf Club,** Barrhill Road, Onneley, Near Crewe (Stoke-on-Trent (0782) 750577). *Location:* one mile from Woore off A51, two miles from Stoke-on-Trent. Parkland on gentle slope. 9 holes, 5584 yards. S.S.S. 67. *Green Fees:* weekdays £12.50 (£6.00 with member); Saturdays and Bank Holidays with member only. Juniors half normal price. *Eating facilities:* light bar snacks when bar is open in summer. *Visitors:* welcome weekdays unrestricted. *Society Meetings:* welcome, except Tuesdays and Fridays. Hon. Secretary: L.A.C. Kennedy (0270 661842).

CREWE. **Queens Park Golf Course,** Queens Park Drive, Crewe CW2 7SB (0270 662378). *Location:* next to Queens Park, one mile from Crewe Station. Parkland. 9 holes x 2, 4920 yards. S.S.S. 64. *Green Fees:* weekdays: 18 holes £3.30; weekends: 18 holes £4.20. *Eating facilities:* bar with excellent bar snacks. *Visitors:* welcome, restrictions Sunday mornings to 11am. *Society Meetings:* welcome. Professional: (0270 666724). Secretary: K. Lear (0270 628352).

FRODSHAM. **Frodsham Golf Club,** Simons Lane, Frodsham WA6 6HE (0928 32159). *Location:* Frodsham 10 minutes M56 Junction 12 Cheshire. Parkland with views over Mersey estuary; undulating. 18 holes, 6289 yards. S.S.S. 70. Two practice areas with bunkers, putting green and nets. *Green Fees:* weekdays £18.00; weekends £22.00. *Eating facilities:* clubhouse, spike bar, lounge bar, dining areas. *Visitors:* welcome at all times, no parties at weekends though. *Society Meetings:* welcome weekdays, groups from 12 noon to 1pm. Professional: Graham Tonge (0928 39442). Secretary: Eric Roylance.

HELSBY. **Helsby Golf Club,** Towers Lane, Helsby, Warrington WA6 0JB (Helsby (0928) 723407). *Location:* Junction 14 M56 to Helsby. Through traffic lights one mile, first right into Primrose Lane, then first right into Towers Lane (200 yards). Flat parkland course. 18 holes, 6204 yards. S.S.S. 70. Practice area available. *Green Fees:* £18.00 weekdays. *Eating facilities:* full facilities, except Mondays. *Visitors:* welcome weekdays, weekends must play with a member. Snooker facilities. *Society Meetings:* welcome Tuesdays and Thursdays by arrangement. Professional: I. Wright (0928 725457). Secretary: G.A. Johnson (0928 722021).

HIGHER WALTON. **Walton Hall Golf Club,** Warrington Road, Higher Walton, Warrington WA4 5LU (Warrington (0925) 266775). *Location:* two miles south of Warrington, Exits 10 and 11 M56. Wooded

parkland. 18 holes, 6849 yards. S.S.S. 73. Practice ground. *Green Fees:* weekdays £5.40, weekends £6.80. Reduced rates 9-hole evening rounds; Juniors and Senior Citizens. *Eating facilities:* clubhouse, snack bar. *Visitors:* unrestricted. *Society Meetings:* welcome. Secretary: D. Judson (0925 266775). Professional: M.J. Slater (0925 263061). Director of Golf: B. Thomas (0925 444400).

KNUTSFORD. **Knutsford Golf Club,** Mere Heath Lane, Knutsford (Knutsford (0565) 633355). *Location:* one mile east of town centre. 9 holes, 6200 yards. S.S.S. 70. *Green Fees:* information not provided. *Eating facilities:* by prior arrangement with Steward. *Visitors:* welcome with reservation except Tuesdays and Wednesdays. To be introduced by member. *Society Meetings:* catered for by special arrangement with Hon. Secretary. Professional: A. Gillies. Secretary: D. Francis.

KNUTSFORD. **Mere Golf and Country Club,** Chester Road, Mere, Knutsford WA16 6LJ (0565 830155; Fax: 0565 830518). *Location:* two miles out of Junction 19 M6 and three miles west of Junction 7 M56. Regarded as one of the finest Parkland Championship courses in the country. 18 holes, 6817 yards. S.S.S. 73. Practice area, two 9-hole putting greens, driving range. *Green Fees:* £45.00 weekdays, £55.00 weekends. *Eating facilities:* coffee shop, à la carte restaurant, five function suites. *Visitors:* welcome by prior arrangement only. *Society Meetings:* Mondays, Tuesdays and Thursdays only by arrangement. Professional: Peter Eyre (0565 830155 extension 317). Secretary: Alf Turner (0565 830155 extension 324/328).

KNUTSFORD. **Wilmslow Golf Club,** Great Warford, Mobberley, Knutsford WA16 7AY (0565 872148). *Location:* two miles from Wilmslow off the Knutsford road. Parkland course. 18 holes, 6611 yards. S.S.S. 72. Practice facility. *Green Fees:* weekdays £25.00 per round, £35.00 per day; weekends £35.00 per round, £45.00 per day. *Eating facilities:* full catering except Monday, two bars. *Visitors:* welcome Tuesdays, Wednesdays and Thursdays and the weekends. *Society Meetings:* Tuesdays and Thursdays only. Professional: L.J. Nowicki (0565 873620). Secretary: A. Lawrence (0565 872148).

LYMM. **Lymm Golf Club,** Whitbarrow Road, Lymm WA13 9AN (0925 752177). *Location:* five miles south east of Warrington, two and a half miles from Junction 20 on M6 and Junction 9 on M56. Parkland. 18 holes, 6304 yards. S.S.S. 70. Practice ground. *Green Fees:* £18.40 weekdays. *Eating facilities:* coffee, bar snacks, lunches and dinner, bar. *Visitors:* welcome with Handicap Certificates, no visitors on Thursdays until 1.30pm, weekends or Bank Holidays. *Society Meetings:* catered

for Wednesdays with reservations. Professional: Steve McCarthy (0925 755054). Secretary: J.M. Pearson (0925 755020).

MACCLESFIELD. **Macclesfield Golf Club**, The Hollins, Macclesfield SK11 7EA (0625 423227). *Location:* turn left at Windmill Street off the A527 Leek road. Hilly course. 12 holes, 5974 yards, 5462 metres. S.S.S. 69. Extending to 18 holes May 1993. *Green Fees:* £17.00 weekdays; £20.00 weekends and Bank Holidays. *Eating facilities:* full catering and bar available except Tuesdays. *Visitors:* welcome without reservation. *Society Meetings:* welcome by arrangement. Professional: A. Taylor (0625 616952). Secretary: N.H. Edwards (0625 615845).

MACCLESFIELD. **Prestbury Golf Club**, Macclesfield Road, Prestbury, Near Macclesfield (0625 829388). *Location:* on the Macclesfield road leaving Prestbury village. 18 holes, 6359 yards. S.S.S. 71. *Green Fees:* information not provided. *Eating facilities:* lunches, teas and dinners. *Visitors:* welcome on weekdays with official club handicap; Bank Holidays and weekends only with a member. *Society Meetings:* Thursdays only. Professional: Nick Summerfield (0625 828242). Hon. Secretary: A.W.J. Wilkinson (0625 828241).

MACCLESFIELD. **Shrigley Hall Golf Club**, Pott Shrigley, Macclesfield SK10 5SB (0625 575755). *Location:* easily accessible by M56, M62/63, M6 and A523 and A6. Parkland. 18 holes, 6305 yards, 6895 metres. S.S.S. 71. Driving range. *Green Fees:*

weekdays residents £15.00, non-residents £20.00; weekends residents £23.00, non-residents £28.00. *Eating facilities:* golf clubhouse, wine bar, restaurant. *Visitors:* on availability. 156 bedroomed, four star hotel. *Society Meetings:* all welcome – £35.00 per person. Handicap preferred. Professional: Granville A. Ogden (0625 575626). Secretary: Sandra Major.

MACCLESFIELD. **The Tytherington Club**, Macclesfield SK10 2JP (0625 434562; Fax: 0625 611076). *Location:* one mile north of Macclesfield on A523. Championship course in beautiful parkland setting, Headquarters of WPGET. 18 holes, 6756 yards, 6136 metres. S.S.S. 72 (men) 74 (ladies). Practice area. *Green Fees:* £25.00 18 holes, £35.00 36 holes weekdays; £30.00 18 holes, £40.00 36 holes weekends. *Eating facilities:* bar snacks, bistro, à la carte, private rooms. *Visitors:* welcome, Handicap Certificates required, no other restrictions. Full Country Club facilities, pool, tennis. *Society Meetings:* very welcome weekdays. Professional: Sandy Wilson. Managing Director: P. Dawie.

NORTHWICH. **Delamere Forest Golf Club**, Station Road, Delamere, Northwich CW8 2JE (Sandiway (0606) 882807). *Location:* M6, A556. On Frodsham side of A556 between Chester and Northwich. Heathland course. 18 holes, 6305 yards. S.S.S. 70. Two practice grounds and two indoor nets. *Green Fees:* weekdays £20.00 per round, £30.00 per day; weekends and Bank Holidays £25.00 per round. *Eating*

*facilities:* bar snacks, diningroom for parties of 30 plus. *Visitors:* welcome any day except Competition Days. *Society Meetings:* welcome if 30 or more in number with prior booking – Tuesdays and Thursdays only. Professional: E.B. Jones (0606 883307). Secretary: L. Parkin (0606 882807).

NORTHWICH. **Sandiway Golf Club,** Chester Road, Sandiway, Northwich CW8 2DJ (Sandiway (0606) 883247). *Location:* off A556, Northwich by-pass. Undulating heavily wooded parkland. 18 holes, 6435 yards. S.S.S. 72. *Green Fees:* weekdays £30.00 per round, £35.00 per day; weekends £35.00 per round, £40.00 per day. *Eating facilities:* lunches and teas served daily, full restaurant facilities. *Visitors:* welcome on weekdays with letter of introduction and Handicap Certificate from home club. *Society Meetings:* restricted to Tuesdays, parties up to 120. Professional: William Laird (0606 883180). Secretary: V.F.C. Wood. Caterer: (0606 882606).

PRESTBURY. **Mottram Hall Golf Course,** Wilmslow Road, Mottram St. Andrew, Prestbury SK10 4QT (0625 820064). *Location:* M56 and M6. Flat parkland/woodland course. 18 holes, 6905 yards, 6250 metres. S.S.S. 72. Practice area. *Green Fees:* £30.00 weekdays; £35.00 weekends. Reduced green fees for Hotel residents. *Eating facilities:* golf centre bar and restaurant. *Visitors:* no restrictions. Accommodation in 133 bedrooms. *Society Meetings:* no restrictions. Professional: Tim Rastall.

RUNCORN. **Runcorn Golf Club,** Clifton Road, Runcorn WA7 4SU (0928 572093). *Location:* signposted The Heath, A557. High parkland course. 18 holes, 6035 yards, 5514 metres. S.S.S. 69. *Green Fees:* weekdays £18.00 per round or day, weekends and Bank Holidays £22.00 per round/day. *Eating facilities:* bar snacks; meals by arrangement. *Visitors:* welcome weekdays except Tuesday mornings. No visitors weekends or Bank Holidays except with a member. Handicap Certificate required. *Society Meetings:* by arrangement Mondays. Professional: I. Sephton (0928 564791). Secretary: W.B. Reading (0928 574214).

SANDBACH. **Malkins Bank Golf Club,** Betchton Road, Malkins Bank, Sandbach CW11 0XN (0270 767878). *Location:* M6, Junction 17 south, one mile via Sandbach. Countryside course. 18 holes, 6071 yards. S.S.S. 69. Practice area. *Green Fees:* £5.00 weekdays, £6.00 weekends. Special rates for Juniors and Senior Citizens. *Eating facilities:* bar and meals available. *Visitors:* welcome at all times, pre-booking advised weekends via club Professional. *Society Meetings:* welcome by prior arrangement. Professional: David Wheeler (0270 765931). Secretary: Ken Lea.

SANDBACH. **Sandbach Golf Club,** 117 Middlewich Road, Sandbach CW11 9EA (Crewe (0270) 762117).

*Location:* two miles from Junction 17 of M6 on Middlewich Road. Meadowland course. 9 holes, 5593 yards. S.S.S. 67. Practice field. *Green Fees:* weekdays £12.00 per day, £6.00 with member; weekends and Bank Holidays must be accompanied by a member. *Eating facilities:* available except Mondays and Thursdays. *Visitors:* welcome weekdays, weekends by invitation only. *Society Meetings:* catered for only by advance arrangement with Hon. Secretary. Secretary: A.F. Pearson.

SOUTH WIRRAL. **Ellesmere Port Golf Club,** Chester Road, Hooton, South Wirral L66 1QH (051-339 7502). *Location:* approximately six miles north of Chester on main A41 trunk road to Birkenhead. Wooded with a lot of ponds. 18 holes, 6432 yards. S.S.S. 71. *Green Fees:* weekdays £4.40, weekends £5.50. Special fees for Juniors and Senior Citizens, and concessions for unemployed during weekdays. *Eating facilities:* catering is booked through clubhouse. *Visitors:* welcome weekdays, bookable through Professional. *Society Meetings:* catered for Monday and Friday only. Professional: Mr D. Yates (051-339 7689). Secretary: Mr B. Turley (051-335 8800).

STALYBRIDGE. **Stamford Golf Club,** Oakfield House, Huddersfield Road, Heyheads, Stalybridge SK15 3PY (0457 832126). *Location:* on B6175 off A6018. Moorland course. 18 holes, 5701 yards. S.S.S. 68. *Green Fees:* weekdays £16.50; weekends after 3pm £22.00. *Eating facilities:* meals lunchtime and evening (except Monday). *Visitors:* very welcome except Tuesday (ladies day). *Society Meetings:* catered for by appointment. Professional: Brian Badger (0457 834829). Secretary: F.E. Rowles.

STOCKPORT. **Davenport Golf Club,** Middlewood Road, Poynton, near Stockport SK12 1TS (0625 877321). *Location:* A6 from Stockport, Macclesfield Road at Hazel Grove, left at Poynton Church. Undulating parkland course. 18 holes, 6065 yards. S.S.S. 69. *Green Fees:* weekdays £24.00 (£6.00 with member), weekends £30.00 (£8.00 with a member). *Eating facilities:* bar snacks daily except Mondays, full meals by arrangement. *Visitors:* welcome, tee booking in operation after consultation with Club Professional. *Society Meetings:* catered for Tuesdays and Thursdays only. Professional: Wyn Harris (0625 877319). Secretary: B. Commins (0625 876951).

STOKE-ON-TRENT. **Alsager Golf and Country Club,** Audley Road, Alsager, Stoke-on-Trent ST7 2UR (0270 875700). *Location:* off M6 at Junction 16 onto A500, first left to Alsager, course is two and a half miles on right. Parkland. 18 holes, 6192 yards. S.S.S. 70. *Green Fees:* weekdays £18.00, weekends with member. *Eating facilities:* restaurant and bar snacks. *Visitors:* welcome weekdays without reservation. Disco, conference and banqueting facilities. *Society*

*Meetings:* welcome, package available on request. Professional: Nick Rothe (0270 877432) Secretary: A.E. Moffat (0270 875700).

TARPORLEY. **Oaklands Golf Club,** Forest Road, Tarporley CW6 0JA (0829 733884; Fax: 0829 733666). *Location:* half a mile from Tarporley on A49. Undulating parkland with lovely views. 18 holes, 6169 yards. S.S.S. 72. *Green Fees:* weekdays £21.00 per round, £30.00 per day. *Eating facilities:* spike bar, bar meals. *Visitors:* welcome except weekends. Gymnasium, swimming pool, snooker. *Society Meetings:* catered for. Professionals: B. Rimmer/Miss J. Stratham (0829 733215). Secretary: Roy Hitchen (0829 733211).

WARRINGTON. **Birchwood Golf Club,** Kelvin Close, Birchwood, Warrington WA3 7PB (Warrington (0925) 818819). *Location:* Junction 11, two miles Leigh – Warrington road M62. Parkland with water. 18 holes, 6810 yards. S.S.S. 73. *Green Fees:* weekdays £22.00, weekends £30.00. *Eating facilities:* full restaurant facilities and bar snacks. Must book in advance. *Visitors:* conference and banqueting facilities for 200. *Society Meetings:* catered for weekdays except Fridays. Package deals available. Professional: Derrick Cooper. Secretary: R.G. Jones (0925 818819).

WARRINGTON. **Leigh Golf Club,** Kenyon Hall, Broseley Lane, Culcheth, Warrington WA3 4BG (0925 763130). *Location:* off A580 East Lancs Road to Culcheth Village. Parkland – tree lined fairways. 18 holes, 5876 yards. S.S.S. 68. Three practice areas, practice nets. *Green Fees:* weekdays £20.00, £7.00 playing with member; weekends and Bank Holidays £25.00. *Eating facilities:* two bars and restaurant. *Visitors:* check with Professional. *Society Meetings:* catered for Mondays (except Bank Holidays) and Tuesdays. Professional: Andrew Baguley (0925 762013). Secretary: G.D. Riley (0925 762943).

WARRINGTON. **Poulton Park Golf Club Ltd,** Dig Lane, Cinnamon Brow, Warrington (0925 812034/ 825220). *Location:* off A574 (Warrington/Leigh, Crab Lane). 9 holes, 4937 metres. S.S.S. 66. *Green Fees:*

weekdays £16.00; weekends £18.00. *Eating facilities:* available except Mondays. *Visitors:* welcome. *Society Meetings:* catered for. Golf Society Package £22.00. Professional: A. Cuppello. Secretary: J. Reekie.

WIDNES. **St. Michael's Jubilee Golf Club,** Dundalk Road, Widnes WA8 8BS (051-424 6230). *Location:* five minutes from M56 and M62. Undulating parkland. 18 holes, 5612 yards. S.S.S. 67. Putting and practice areas. *Green Fees:* information not available. *Eating facilities:* bar, meals in restaurant. *Visitors:* unrestricted. *Society Meetings:* by arrangement with Professional. Professional: B. Bilton. Secretary: W. Hughes.

WIDNES. **Widnes Golf Club,** Highfield Road, Widnes WA8 7DT (051-424 2440). *Location:* near town centre, five miles from M56 and M62. Flat course. 18 holes, 5688 yards. S.S.S. 68. *Green Fees:* weekdays £16.00, weekends £20.00. *Eating facilities:* two bars and full catering service. *Visitors:* welcome most days, subject to prior arrangement with Secretary or Professional. *Society Meetings:* catered for Wednesdays only. Professional: Mr S. Forster (051-420 7467). Secretary: Margaret M. Cresswell (051-424 2995).

WIDNES. **Widnes Municipal,** Dundalk Road, Widnes (051-424 6230). 18 holes, 5638 yards. S.S.S. 67, Par 69. *Visitors:* unrestricted. Secretary: W. Hughes. Professional: Bob Bilton.

WINSFORD. **Knights Grange Golf Course,** Sports Complex, Grange Lane, Winsford CW7 2PT (0606 552780). *Location:* signposted "Sports Complex" from traffic lights Winsford Town Centre. 6 miles from M6. Very flat but a challenging course. 9 holes, 2860 yards. S.S.S. 35/37. Practice area. *Green Fees:* £2.40 for 9 holes, £3.20 for 18 holes weekdays; £3.60 for 9 holes, £4.80 for 18 holes weekends. *Eating facilities:* snacks and hot drinks from golf shop, public house adjacent. *Visitors:* unrestricted (Municipal Course), 24 hour advance booking available 0606 552780. Bowls, tennis, football, athletics and crazy golf. *Society Meetings:* welcomed – booking in writing in advance. Professional: G. Moore.

# Cleveland

BILLINGHAM. **Billingham Golf Club,** Sandy Lane, Billingham TS22 5NA (Stockton (0642) 554494). *Location:* off A19 trunk road, one mile west of Billingham town centre. Undulating parkland. 18 holes, 6460 yards. S.S.S. 71. Practice area including pitching green and putting greens. *Green Fees:* weekdays £17.50, £10.00 with member; weekends £30.00, £15.00 with

member. *Eating facilities:* full catering Monday to Saturday. No hot meals on Mondays. *Visitors:* welcome weekdays, proof of membership of another club or Handicap Certificate required. *Society Meetings:* catered for with prior booking. Professional: P.S. Bradley (0642 557060). Secretary: D.J. Bruce OBE (0642 533816).

---

*If you are writing, a stamped, addressed envelope is always appreciated.*

---

EAGLESCLIFFE. **Eaglescliffe Golf Club Ltd,** Yarm Road, Eaglescliffe, Stockton-on-Tees TS16 0DQ (Eaglescliffe (0642) 780098). *Location:* two miles north of Yarm, A135 (Yarm road), off A19. Hilly parkland course. 18 holes, 6275 yards. S.S.S. 70. Practice area and putting green. *Green Fees:* weekdays £18.00, weekends and Bank Holidays £24.00. *Eating facilities:* full menu service except Mondays, two bars. *Visitors:* welcome weekdays, restriction on Tuesdays and Fridays. *Society Meetings:* catered for except weekends. Professional: N. Gilks (0642 790122). Secretary: A.H. Painter.

HARTLEPOOL. **Castle Eden and Peterlee Golf Club,** Castle Eden, Hartlepool TS27 4SS (Wellfield (0429) 836220). *Location:* two miles south of Peterlee, use exits from A19. Picturesque parkland course. 18 holes, 6262 yards. S.S.S. 70. Practice ground. *Green Fees:* weekdays £18.00 per day, weekends and Bank Holidays £25.00. *Eating facilities:* restaurant, lounge and bar. *Visitors:* welcome, 9.30am — 11.30am, 1.45pm — 3.30pm. Tuesday Ladies' day. *Society Meetings:* weekdays only with reservation. Professional: Graham J. Laidlaw (0429 856689). Secretary: Peter Robinson (0429 836510).

HARTLEPOOL. **Hartlepool Golf Club Ltd,** Hart Warren, Hartlepool (Hartlepool (0429) 274398). *Location:* off A1086 at Hart Station (north of town). Seaside links course, 18 holes, 6255 yards. S.S.S. 70. Practice ground. *Green Fees:* weekdays £16.00; weekends £22.00. Half green fees if playing with a member. *Eating facilities:* meals and snacks available. *Visitors:* welcome (excluding Sunday) without reservation. *Society Meetings:* catered for by prior arrangement. Professional: M. E. Cole (0492 267473). Hon. Secretary: W.E. Storrow (0492 870282).

HARTLEPOOL. **Seaton Carew Golf Club,** Tees Road, Seaton Carew, Hartlepool (Hartlepool (0429) 266249). *Location:* two miles south of Hartlepool on A178. Seaside links. 22 holes. Old Course: 6604 yards. S.S.S. 72. Brabazon Course: 6802 yards. S.S.S. 73. *Green Fees:* weekdays £20.00 per day, weekends and Bank Holidays £28.00 per day. *Eating facilities:* available. *Visitors:* welcome, some weekend restrictions. *Society Meetings:* catered for by arrangement. Professional: W. Hector (0429 266249). Secretary: P.R. Wilson (0429 261473).

MIDDLESBROUGH. **Middlesbrough Golf Club,** Brass Castle Lane, Marton, Middlesbrough TS8 9EE (0642 316430). *Location:* five miles south of Middlesbrough west of the A172. Parkland course. 18 holes, 6111 yards. S.S.S. 69. *Green Fees:* weekdays £22.00; weekends £27.50. *Eating facilities:* lunches, teas and dinners. *Visitors:* welcome with reservation. *Society Meetings:* catered for. Professional: D.J. Jones (0642 311766). Secretary: J.M. Jackson (0642 311515).

MIDDLESBROUGH. **Middlesbrough Municipal Golf Club,** Ladgate Lane, Middlesbrough TS5 7YZ (Middlesbrough (0642) 315533. Fax: 0642 300726). *Location:* two miles south of Middlesbrough on A174. Parkland course with featured streams. 18 holes, 6314 yards. Par 71. S.S.S. 70. Floodlit driving range. *Green Fees:* weekdays £6.50; weekends £8.50. *Eating facilities:* bar meals and functions. *Visitors:* welcome, but starting times must be booked in advance. *Society Meetings:* by prior arrangement. Professional: Alan Hope/David Symington. Secretary: John Dilworth.

REDCAR. **Cleveland Golf Club,** Queen Street, Redcar TS10 1BT (Redcar (0642) 483693). *Location:* south bank of River Teesmouth to A1042 into Redcar. 18 holes, 6685 yards, 6117 metres. S.S.S. 72. *Green Fees:* weekdays £14.50; weekends £25.00. Societies £25.00. *Eating facilities:* all week except Monday. *Visitors:* welcome but not on weekends or Bank Holidays. *Society Meetings:* catered for by prior arrangement weekdays only. Professional: D. Masey (0642 483462). Secretary: L.R. Manley (0642 471798).

REDCAR. **Wilton Golf Club,** Wilton Castle, Redcar (Cleveland (0642) 454626). *Location:* eight miles east of Middlesbrough A174, four miles west of Redcar. Wooded parkland course. 18 holes, 6104 yards. S.S.S. 69. Small practice area. *Green Fees:* weekdays £16.00, £8.00 with member; Sundays and Bank Holidays £22.00. *Eating facilities:* lunches, except Sundays; evening meals by arrangement. *Visitors:* not on Saturdays. *Society Meetings:* by arrangement. Secretary: Mr Elder (0642 465265).

SALTBURN BY THE SEA. **Saltburn by the Sea Golf Club Ltd,** Hob Hill, Saltburn by the Sea TS12 1NJ (Guisborough (0287) 22812). *Location:* from Saltburn take Guisborough Road, one mile out of town on left. 18 holes, 5846 yards. S.S.S. 68. *Green Fees:* weekdays £17.00 per day, weekends and Bank Holidays £20.00 per day. *Eating facilities:* available except Mondays. *Visitors:* welcome, limited Sundays and Thursdays and no visitors Saturdays. *Society Meetings:* catered for by arrangement. Professional: David Forsythe (0287 24653). Secretary: David Becker.

STOCKTON-ON-TEES. **Teesside Golf Club,** Acklam Road, Thornaby, Stockton-on-Tees TS17 7JS (Stockton (0642) 676249). *Location:* A19 — A1130 to Thornaby, seven miles on right hand side. Flat parkland, partly tree lined. 18 holes, 6498 yards. S.S.S. 71. Practice ground. *Green Fees:* weekdays £16.00; weekends £22.00. Parties over 10 £12.00. *Eating facilities:* catering except Mondays, bars 11am to 11pm. *Visitors:* welcome mid-week up to 4.30pm, weekend after 11am subject to starting sheet. *Society Meetings:* catered for midweek only. Professional: K. Hall (0642 673822). Secretary: Mr W. Allen (0642 616516).

# Cornwall

BODMIN. **Bodmin Golf Club,** Lanhydrock, Near Bodmin PL30 5AQ (0208 73600; Fax: 0208 77325). *Location:* one-and-a-half miles outside Bodmin on B3269. Moorland/parkland with brooks and natural water hazards. 18 holes, 6142 yards. S.S.S. 69. Driving range, putting green and practice area. *Green Fees:* weekdays £15.00; weekends £18.50. *Eating facilities:* bar, limited catering. *Visitors:* welcome, please book tee times. *Society Meetings:* welcome by arrangement. Secretary: K. Trahair.

BUDE. **Bude and North Cornwall Golf Club,** Burn View, Bude EX23 8BY (Bude (0288) 352006). *Location:* seaside links course situated in the centre of the town adjacent to beaches. 18 holes, 6202 yards. S.S.S. 77. Practice net and grounds. *Green Fees:* weekdays £20.00 per round or day; weekends £25.00. *Eating facilities:* catering and bar snacks. *Visitors:* welcome without reservation. Snooker, billiards and pool. *Society Meetings:* catered for by bookings. Professional: John Yeo (0288 353635). Secretary: Kevin Brown (0288 352006).

CAMBORNE. **Tehidy Park Golf Club,** Camborne TR14 0HH (Portreath (0209) 842208). *Location:* A30 via Blackwater and Camborne by-passes to sign for Portreath. Parkland, wooded, 3 new lakes. 18 holes, 6241 yards. S.S.S. 70. *Green Fees:* weekdays £20.00 per round, £25.00 per day; weekends £25.00 per round, £30.00 per day. *Eating facilities:* bar snacks, à la carte restaurant except Mondays. *Visitors:* welcome with Handicap Certificate except Tuesdays and Thursdays. *Society Meetings:* by arrangement; early booking essential. Professional: J. Dumbreck (0209 842914). Secretary: John Prosser (0209 842208).

FALMOUTH. **Budock Vean Golf and Country House Hotel,** Near Mawnan Smith, Falmouth TR11 5LG (Mawnan Smith (0326) 250281). *Location:* between Helford and Falmouth, area of Helford River. 9 holes/18 tees, 5222 yards. Par 68. S.S.S. 65. *Green Fees:* weekdays and Saturdays £14.00; Sundays and Bank Holidays £18.00 for non-residents, Hotel Guests

Free. *Eating facilities:* catering and bars available. *Visitors:* daily only for outside visitors who are most welcome, but must have Handicap Certificate. Hotel accommodation. Secretary: F.G. Benney. Golf Manager: A. Ramsden.

FALMOUTH. **Falmouth Golf Club,** Swanpool Road, Falmouth TR11 5BQ (0326 311262).*Location:* quarter-of-a- mile west of Swanpool Beach, Falmouth, on the road to Maenporth. Wooded parkland course with magnificent views. 18 holes, 5680 yards, 5192 metres. S.S.S. 67. Five acres of practice ground. *Green Fees:* on application. *Eating facilities:* catering and bar all year round. *Visitors:* welcome at all times, except during major competitions. *Society Meetings:* are always welcome, four weeks' notice required. Professional: David Short (0326 316229). Secretary: D.J. de C. Sizer (0326 40525).

HELSTON. **Mullion Golf Club,** Cury, Helston TR12 7BP (Mullion (0326) 240276). *Location:* from Helston on the A3083 past Culdrose Air Station, turn right after three miles. Cliff top and links. 18 holes, 6022 yards. S.S.S. 69. *Green Fees:* £18.00 from 1st April to 30 September; £14.00 from 1st October to 31st March. *Eating facilities:* snacks and meals available each day. Caterers: (0326 241281). *Visitors:* welcome. Golfers with handicap only. *Society Meetings:* welcome on prior booking. Professional: R. Goodway (0326 241176). Secretary/Treasurer: D. Watts, F.C.A. (0326 240685).

LAUNCESTON. **Launceston Golf Club,** St. Stephens, Launceston PL15 8HF (0556 773442). *Location:* one mile north of town on Bude road (B3254). Parkland. 18 holes, 6407 yards. S.S.S. 71. *Green Fees:* weekdays £20.00 per round, £25.00 per day. *Eating facilities:* available. *Visitors:* welcome without reservation, no visitors weekends between March 1st and October 31st. *Society Meetings:* catered for. Professional: J. Tozer (0566 775359). Secretary: B.J. Grant (0566 773442).

LOOE. **Looe Golf Club,** Bin Down, Looe PL13 1PX (Widegates (05034) 239). *Location:* three miles east of Looe on A387. Downland/parkland, fabulous views of S.E. Cornwall and beyond. 18 holes, 5940 yards. S.S.S. 68. Large practice ground. *Green Fees:* on application. Five and seven day membership available. *Eating facilities:* two bars, bar snacks and diningroom. *Visitors:* welcome, phone for tee reservations. Clubs for hire. Golf tuition available. *Society Meetings:* welcome by arrangement. Professional: Alistair MacDonald. Manager: Graham Bond.

NEWQUAY near. **Carvynick Golf and Country Club,** Carvynick, Summercourt, Near Newquay (0872 510716). *Location:* turn off the A30 at Summercourt then take B3058 towards Newquay. Half a mile on left. Parkland and wooded course. 9 holes, 1246 yards. S.S.S. 27. *Green Fees:* £6.00. *Eating facilities:* at 16th century village inn and restaurant. *Visitors:* welcome all year. Sauna, gym, indoor swimming pool and badminton court. Holiday cottages available. Secretary: Peter Barton.

NEWQUAY. **Newquay Golf Club,** Tower Road, Newquay TR7 1LT (0637 872091). *Location:* 400yards from Newquay Town Centre. Seaside links with 107 bunkers. 18 holes, 6140 yards, 5526 metres. S.S.S. 69. *Green Fees:* weekdays £17.00 per round, weekends £21.00 per round. £70.00 per week. *Eating facilities:* lunches and bar snacks. *Visitors:* welcome at all times. *Society Meetings:* catered for except Sundays (£14.00). Professional: P. Muscroft (0637 874830). Secretary: G. Binney (0637 874354).

NEWQUAY. **Treloy Golf Club,** Newquay TR7 4JN (0637 878554). *Location:* five minutes' drive from Newquay on the A3059 Newquay to St. Columb Major road. Parkland, seaside. 9 hole Executive golf course. First of its kind in Cornwall – sculptured greens, American Pencross grass, extensive mouldings and bunkers. 9 holes, 2143 yards, 1955 metres. S.S.S. 31. Practice green. *Green Fees:* 9 holes £7.50, 18 holes £11.50. *Eating facilities:* vending machines. *Visitors:* welcome. *Society Meetings:* welcome. Changing facilities, golf shop, club hire and professional tuition will be available on site. Secretary: Jim Reid.

PADSTOW. **Trevose Golf and Country Club,** Constantine Bay, Padstow PL28 8JB (0841 520208). *Location:* off B3276, four miles west of Padstow at Constantine Bay. Seaside links course. 18 holes, 6461 yards. S.S.S. 71. *Green Fees:* weekdays £20.00 to £30.00 depending on season. Weekly and fortnightly rates available. *Eating facilities:* restaurant, bar open 11am to 11pm. *Visitors:* welcome if checked by telephone beforehand; Handicap Certificate required. Tennis, summer swimming pool available, also self catering accommodation. *Society Meetings:* by application. Professional: G. Alliss (0841 520261). Secretary: L. Grindley (0841 520208).

PENZANCE. **Cape Cornwall Golf and Country Club,** Cape Cornwall, St. Just, Penzance TR19 7NL (0736 788611). *Location:* turn off onto the B3071 to St. Just from Penzance A30. Walled undulating pasture land. 18 holes, 5788 yards. S.S.S. 68. Practice putting green and golf area. *Green Fees:* information on request. *Eating facilities:* restaurant, main clubroom bar. *Visitors:* welcome every day, Saturdays and Thursdays after 10.30am, Sundays after 11.30am. *Society Meetings:* catered for, please ask for rates. Professional: Mr B. Hamilton. Secretary: Mr J. Osborne.

PENZANCE. **Praa Sands Golf Club,** Germoe Crossroads, Near Penzance TR20 9TQ (0736 763445; Fax: 0736 763399). *Location:* midway between Helston and Penzance on A394. Seaside, parkland – beautiful sea views from all holes. 9 holes, 4096 yards. S.S.S. 60 Par 62. Practice net. *Green Fees:* £11.00 per round; weekly £66.00. *Eating facilities:* restaurant, bar and bar snacks. *Visitors:* welcome every day except Sunday mornings and Friday evenings after 5pm. *Society Meetings:* catered for by arrangement. Secretary: Ray Hudson. Proprietors: Kate and David Phillips.

PERRANPORTH. **Perranporth Golf Club,** Budnick Hill, Perranporth (Truro (0872) 572454). Seaside course overlooking Perranporth and beach. 18 holes, 6208 yards. S.S.S. 70. Par 72. *Green Fees:* information on request. *Eating facilities:* lunch and dinner. *Visitors:* welcome without reservation. Concessionary rates from selected holiday accommodation. *Society Meetings:* catered for with advance notice; concessionary rates. Professional: D. Michell. Secretary: P.D.R. Barnes (0872 573701).

REDRUTH. **Radnor Golf and Ski Centre,** Radnor Road, Treleigh, Redruth TR16 5EL (Redruth (0209) 211059). *Location:* two miles north east of Redruth, signposted from A3047 at Treleigh and North Country crossroads. Purpose-built Par 3 – interesting layout. 9 holes, 1312 yards. S.S.S. 52. Covered floodlit 18-bay driving range. *Green Fees:* £4.00 for 9 holes, £6.00 for 18 holes. *Eating facilities:* available. *Visitors:* welcome. Indoor ski training machine. Professional: Gordon Wallbank.

SALTASH. **St. Mellion Golf and Country Club,** Near Saltash PL12 6SD (Liskeard (0579) 50101). *Location:* Tamar Bridge. Old Course: 18 holes, 5927 yards, par 70. S.S.S. 68. Nicklaus Course. 18 holes, 6626 yards, par 72, S.S.S. 72. *Green Fees:* on application. *Eating facilities:* many within club complex. *Visitors:* welcome, Handicap Certificate required. *Society Meetings:* welcome. Hotel accommodation: 24 rooms, full facilities (badminton, squash, swimming, tennis, sauna, solarium, multi-gym). Golf Director: D.M. Webb. Professional: Tony Moore (0579 50724).

ST. AUSTELL. **Carlyon Bay Hotel Golf Course,** Carlyon Bay, St. Austell (0726 814250). *Location:* on the coast in the centre of the Cornish Riviera. Clifftop, spectacular views, undulating. 18 holes, 6505 yards. S.S.S. 71. Two practice grounds. *Green Fees:* £20.00. *Eating facilities:* bar and restaurant open 11.30am to 11.00pm. *Visitors:* welcome, starting times bookable by phoning Professional. Accommodation available in four star hotel. *Society Meetings:* catered for, playing times bookable by phoning Professional. Professional: Nigel Sears (072681 4228; Fax: 072681 5604). Secretary: Peter Clemo.

ST. AUSTELL. **St. Austell Golf Club,** Tregongeeves, Tregongeeves Lane, St. Austell PL26 7DS (St. Austell (0726) 72649). *Location:* one mile west of St. Austell on A390 St. Austell to Truro road. Parkland course. 18 holes, 6089 yards, 5569 metres. S.S.S. 69. *Green Fees:* information on request. *Eating facilities:* full service; arrange for Hot Meals before play. *Visitors:* welcome with reservation, must be club members and hold Handicap Certificate. *Society Meetings:* catered for weekdays by arrangement. Professional: M. Rowe (0726 68621). Secretary: S.H. Davey (0726 74756).

ST. IVES. **Tregenna Castle Hotel Golf Club,** Trelyon Avenue, St. Ives TR26 2DE (0736 795254). *Location:* the Hotel is positioned just outside St. Ives on the main road to St. Ives. The golf course is situated in Tregenna Castle Hotel grounds. Tregenna is directly across from St. Ives Motors Company garage (Ford) on the left. Parkland course overlooking St. Ives, scenic views, tight fairways and undulating greens. 18 holes, 3549 yards. S.S.S. 57. *Green Fees:* £10.00. Residents and guests of members half price. *Eating facilities:* available in the Hotel. *Visitors:* tee booking is required at weekends and Bank Holidays. Hotel offers squash, badminton, tennis facilities. *Society Meetings:* are welcome on booking conditions. Professional: Miss Ingrid Knapp. Secretary: Mr Joe Goodman.

ST IVES. **West Cornwall Golf Club,** Church Lane, Lelant, St. Ives TR26 3DZ (0736 753319). *Location:* two miles from St. Ives. Seaside links – wonderful coastal views. 18 holes, 5879 yards. S.S.S. 68. Practice ground. *Green Fees:* weekdays £20.00; weekends £25.00. Five Day ticket £60.00, Seven Day ticket £80.00. *Eating facilities:* bar and restaurant. *Visitors:* must be golf club members with Handicap Certificate.

Snooker table. *Society Meetings:* on written application. Professional: P. Atherton (0736 753177). Secretary: W.S. Richards (0736 753401).

TORPOINT. **Whitsand Bay Hotel Golf Club,** Portwrinkle, Torpoint PL11 3BU (St. Germans (0503) 30276). *Location:* on coast six miles from Torpoint. Clifftop course. 18 holes, 5796 yards. S.S.S. 68. *Green Fees:* weekdays £12.50; weekends £15.00. *Eating facilities:* clubhouse and hotel. *Visitors:* welcome at all times with Handicap Certificate. Swimming/leisure complex. *Society Meetings:* catered for and hotel accommodation arranged on application to hotel. Professional: D.S. Poole (0503 30778). Secretary: G.G. Dyer (0503 30418). Hotel: (0503 30276).

TRURO. **Killiow Golf Club,** Killiow Golf Park, Kea, Truro (0872 70246). Location: take A39 from Truro directed to Falmouth, 2.75 miles. Large sign on right into park. Parkland, superb setting with lakes and church as backdrop. 18 holes, 3396 yards. S.S.S. 58. All-weather floodlit driving range and bunker/putting facilities. *Green Fees:* contact reception. *Eating facilities:* check whether available. *Visitors:* course restricted to members until 10.30am at weekends otherwise available to visitors – check with reception. Secretary: John Crowson (0872 72768).

TRURO. **Truro Golf Club,** Treliske, Truro TR1 3LG (Truro (0872) 72640). *Location:* two miles west of Truro on A390 to Redruth. Undulating parkland. 18 holes, 5357 yards. S.S.S. 66. *Green Fees:* weekdays £17.00 per day or round, weekends and Bank Holidays £22.00 per day or round. *Eating facilities:* available. *Visitors:* welcome with Handicap Certificates but restrictions on competition days, Tuesdays and weekends. *Society Meetings:* catered for on weekdays. Professional: N.K. Bicknell (0872 76595). Secretary: B.E. Heggie (0872 78684).

WADEBRIDGE. **St. Enodoc Golf Club,** Rock, Wadebridge PL27 6LB (Trebetherick (0208) 863216). *Location:* B3314 from Wadebridge. Left at St. Minver to Rock. Seaside Links. Two 18 hole courses, 6207 yards and 4165 yards. S.S.S. 70 and 61. *Green Fees:* information not provided. *Eating facilities:* bar and full dining facilities as well as sandwiches and snacks. Please phone for reservation. *Visitors:* members of recognised golf clubs welcome. Handicap Certificates will be required for main course. Starting times may be booked with the Professional up to four days in advance. *Society Meetings:* catered for by arrangement with the Secretary. Professional: N.J. Williams (0208 862402). Secretary: L. Guy.

# Isles of Scilly

ST MARY'S. **Isles of Scilly Golf Club,** St. Mary's, Isles of Scilly (0720 22692). *Location:* one mile from Hugh Town, St. Mary's. Heathland by the sea with magnificent views. 9 holes, 3025 yards, 2791 metres. S.S.S. 69. Par 73. *Green Fees:* weekdays £13.00 per day. *Eating facilities:* lunches and evening meals available. *Visitors:* welcome weekdays; Sunday play with member only. Secretary: Steve Watt (0720 22536).

# Cumbria

ALSTON. **Alston Moor Golf Club,** The Hermitage, Middleton in Teesdale Road, Alston CA9 3DB (0434 381675). *Location:* one-and-three-quarter miles from Alston on B6277 to Barnard Castle. Parkland with panoramic views (highest golf course in England). 9 holes, 5386 yards. S.S.S. 66. Practice ground. *Green Fees:* weekdays £5.00, weekends £8.00. Juniors half price. *Eating facilities:* 19th Hole bar, catering available by prior notice. *Visitors:* welcome anytime, prior notice required for groups. *Society Meetings:* welcome by arrangement. Secretary: A. Dodd (0434 381242).

APPLEBY. **Appleby Golf Club,** Brackenber Moor, Appleby-in-Westmorland (Appleby (07683) 51432). *Location:* off A66 at Coupland Beck, two miles south of Appleby. Moorland course. 18 holes, 5914 yards. S.S.S. 68.*Green Fees:* information not provided. *Eating facilities:* available except Tuesdays. *Visitors:* welcome without reservation. *Society Meetings:* catered for by prior arrangement. Secretary: B.W. Rimmer.

ASKAM-IN-FURNESS. **Dunnerholme Golf Club,** Duddon Road, Askam-in-Furness LA16 7AW (Dalton (0229) 62675). *Location:* A590 onto A595. Seaside links. 10 holes (18 tees), 6181 yards. S.S.S. 69. Practice area. *Green Fees:* as on notice board. Special rates for parties of 12 or more. *Eating facilities:* by request for parties. *Visitors:* welcome without reservation, excluding competition days. *Society Meetings:* catered for. Secretary: J.H. Mutton (0229 62979).

BARROW-IN-FURNESS. **Barrow Golf Club,** Rakesmoor, Hawcoat, Barrow-in-Furness LA14 4QB (Barrow (0229) 825444). *Location:* one mile from Barrow town centre, turn right first traffic lights into town then one mile. 18 holes, 6209 yards, 5679 metres. S.S.S. 70. *Green Fees:* weekdays £15.00 per day, £8.00 if playing with a member; weekends £20.00. *Eating facilities:* available; bar. *Visitors:* welcome without reservation, must be members of recognised golf club. *Society Meetings:* catered for up to 40. Professional: N. Hyde (0229 831212). Secretary: D. Barker (0229 821172).

BARROW-IN-FURNESS. **Furness Golf Club,** Central Drive, Walney Island, Barrow-in-Furness LA14 3LN (Barrow (0229) 471232). *Location:* A590 into Barrow, follow sign to Walney Island, over bridge, straight on at lights. Clubhouse half a mile on right hand side. Seaside links. 18 holes, 6363 yards. S.S.S. 71. Practice area. *Green Fees:* £10.00 daily, (£8.00 weekdays with member); Societies £6.00 per head for parties numbering over 12. *Eating facilities:* by arrangement with Steward. *Visitors:* parties by prior arrangement, others without reservation. Ladies' Day – Wednesdays; Competition Days – Saturdays or Sundays in summer. *Society Meetings:* welcome (tee reservation prior by arrangement). Professional: K. Bosward. Secretary: P.F. Duignan.

BRAMPTON. **Brampton Golf Club,** Talkin Tarn, Brampton CA8 1HN (Brampton (06977) 2255). *Location:* situated on the Brampton-Castle Carrock road (B6413), approximately one and a half miles from Brampton. Rolling fell countryside, excellent views. 18 holes, 6420 yards. S.S.S. 71. *Green Fees:* on application. Practice facilities available plus snooker and pool tables. *Eating facilities:* catering available every day during playing season and on most days during winter period. *Visitors:* welcome without reservation, but should avoid Sunday, Monday, Wednesday and Thursday mornings. *Society Meetings:* catered for, limited numbers at weekends. Contact for visiting societies, J.F. Swift (0228 36699). Professional: S. Harrison (06977 2000). Secretary: Ian J. Meldrum (0228 23155).

CARLISLE. **Carlisle Golf Club,** Aglionby, Carlisle CA4 8AG (Carlisle (0228) 513303). *Location:* on A69 Newcastle Road, half a mile from Junction 43 of M6. Parkland. 18 holes, 6278 yards. S.S.S. 70. Practice area. *Green Fees:* £25.00 per day weekdays; £30.00 Sundays only. *Eating facilities:* snacks, lunches, dinners and high teas. *Visitors:* welcome Mondays to Fridays and Sundays. *Society Meetings:* catered for Mondays, Wednesdays and Fridays, parties of 12 or more. Professional: John S. Moore (0228 513241). Administrator/Secretary: J. Hook.

CARLISLE. **Dalston Hall Golf Club,** Dalston Hall, Dalston, Carlisle CA5 7JX (0228 710165). *Location:* leave M6 at Exit 42, take road to Dalston; at Dalston turn onto B5299, course on the right after one mile. Scenic parkland course. 9 holes, 5294 yards. S.S.S. 67. Practice area. *Green Fees:* £4.00 9 holes, £7.00 18 holes. *Eating facilities:* full catering and bar facilities. *Visitors:* welcome, tee reservation is required at weekends and after 4pm during the week. *Society Meetings:* welcome by prior arrangement. Secretary: Jane Simpson (0228 710165).

CARLISLE. **Newby Grange Golf Club,** Newby Grange Hotel, Crosby on Eden, Carlisle (0228 573645; Fax: 0228 573420). *Location:* M6 three miles. Parkland course beside the Eden with six lakes. 18 holes, 7146 yards. S.S.S. 73. *Green Fees:* weekdays £14.00; weekends £18.00. *Eating facilities:* full hotel facilities. *Visitors:* welcome at all times. 20 bedroomed hotel, conference facilities. *Society Meetings:* welcome by prior arrangement with Professional. Professional: Phil Harrison (0228 573645 extension 221). Secretary: Denis Wiley.

CARLISLE. **Stoneyholme Municipal Golf Club,** St. Aidans Road, Carlisle (Carlisle (0228) 33208). *Location:* off A69 between M6 Junction 42 and town. Parkland course, 18 holes, 6000 yards. S.S.S. 68. Large practice area, changing rooms. *Green Fees:* information not available. *Eating facilities:* bar and restaurant. *Visitors:* welcome without reservation, but booking advisable weekends and Bank Holidays. *Society Meetings:* welcome by prior arrangement. Professional: Stephen Ling (0228 34856).

EMBLETON. **Cockermouth Golf Club,** The Clubhouse, Embleton, Near Cockermouth CA13 9SG (Bassenthwaite Lake (07687) 76223). *Location:* second exit A66 to Embleton across Old Road and up 1:5 hill. Scenic fell land course. 18 holes, 5457 yards. S.S.S. 67. *Green Fees:* weekdays £10.00; weekends and Bank Holidays £15.00. *Eating facilities:* meals by arrangement with Stewardess. *Visitors:* welcome; with members at weekends. *Society Meetings:* catered for mid week only. Secretary: R.D. Pollard (0900 822650).

GRANGE-OVER-SANDS. **Grange Fell Golf Club,** Fell Road, Grange-over-Sands LA11 6HB (05395 32536). *Location:* Cartmel Road from Grange one mile. Hillside course with panoramic views. 9 holes, 4826 metres. S.S.S. 66. *Green Fees:* weekdays £10.00, weekends and Bank Holidays £15.00. *Visitors:* welcome without reservation. *Society Meetings:* not catered for. Secretary: J.B. Asplin (05395 32021).

GRANGE-OVER-SANDS. **Grange-over-Sands Golf Club,** Meathop Road, Grange-over-Sands LA11 6QX (Grange-over-Sands (05395) 33180). *Location:* leave the A590 at roundabout signposted Grange, take the B5277 for approximately three miles. Flat parkland. 18 holes, 5912 yards, 5685 metres. S.S.S. 69. Practice area. *Green Fees:* weekdays £15.00 per round, £20.00 per day; weekends and Bank Holidays £20.00 per round, £25.00 per day. *Eating facilities:* diningroom, bar open every day except Tuesdays. *Visitors:* welcome without reservation weekdays and most weekends. *Society Meetings:* by arrangement with Secretary. Secretary: J.R. Green (05395 33754).

KENDAL. **Kendal Golf Club,** The Heights, Kendal (0539 724079). *Location:* off A6 at Town Hall, signposted. 18 holes, 5483 yards. S.S.S. 67. *Green Fees:* £16.00 (£8.00 with member), weekends £20.00 (£10.00 with member). *Eating facilities:* meals available any day except Mondays. *Visitors:* welcome without reservation. Professional: D.J. Turner. Secretary: R.E. Maunder.

KESWICK. **Keswick Golf Club,** Threlkeld Hall, Keswick CA12 4SX (Threlkeld (07687) 79013). *Location:* four miles from Keswick on A66 road to Penrith. Scenic fell and parkland course. 18 holes, 6175 yards. S.S.S. 72, Par 71. Extensive practice area. *Green Fees:* weekdays £12.00, weekends £15.00. *Eating facilities:* daily by arrangement; bar. *Visitors:* welcome, Ladies' Day Thursdays 12 noon to 1.30pm. *Society Meetings:* welcome by arrangement, unrestricted weekdays, 11.30am to 12.30pm weekends. Secretary: Richard Bell (07687 79324).

KIRKBY LONSDALE. **Kirkby Lonsdale Golf Club,** Scalebar Lane, Barbon, Kirkby Lonsdale, Carnforth (0468 36366). *Location:* three and a half miles from Kirkby Lonsdale on the A638 Sedbergh Road. Parkland, over Barbon Beck and sweeping down to the River Lune. 18 holes, 6280 yards. S.S.S. 70. Practice area. *Green Fees:* weekdays £14.00; weekends £18.00. *Eating facilities:* limited dining and bar facilities. *Visitors:* welcome. Tee reserved for members until 9.30am and between noon and 1.30pm. Accommodation and meals can be arranged at local hotels. *Society Meetings:* by arrangement. Secretary: P. Jackson (0468 36365).

MARYPORT. **Maryport Golf Club,** Bankend, Maryport (0900 812605). *Location:* adjacent to beach. Links course. 11 holes, 18 tees. 6272 yards. S.S.S. 71. *Green Fees:* weekdays £10.00 per day; weekends £15.00. *Eating facilities:* by arrangement. *Visitors:* welcome without reservation. *Society Meetings:* catered for. Secretary: N.H. Cook (0900 815652).

MILLOM. **Silecroft Golf Club,** Silecroft, Millom LA18 4NX (0229 774250). *Location:* junction of A595 and A5093, eight miles north of Broughton-in-Furness. 9 holes, 18 tees, 5712 yards. S.S.S. 68. Large practice area near 9th/18th green. *Green Fees:* £10 per day. *Visitors:* welcome without reservation except Bank Holidays. Secretary: M.O'N. Wilson (0229 774160).

PENRITH. **Penrith Golf Club,** Salkeld Road, Penrith CA11 8SG (Penrith (0768) 62217). *Location:* one mile from A6 to east of town. 18 holes, 6026 yards, 5510 metres. S.S.S. 69. *Green Fees:* weekdays £15.00, weekends and Bank Holidays £22.00. *Eating facilities:* dining facilities, excellent cuisine. *Visitors:* welcome with Handicap Certificate. Tee reservation is required at weekends and telephone enquiries advisable weekdays. No visitors to start before 9.15am or after 4pm. *Society Meetings:* catered for, restricted at weekends. Professional: C.B. Thomson. Secretary: J. Carruthers (0768) 62217).

SEASCALE. **Seascale Golf Club,** The Banks, Seascale CA20 1QL (Seascale (09467) 28202). *Location:* B5344 off A595 to north of village. Links. 18 holes, 6416 yards. S.S.S. 71. 16-acre practice ground. *Green Fees:* weekdays £18.00; weekends £22.00.

*Eating facilities:* catering limited on Mondays and Tuesdays, bar available every day. *Visitors:* welcome when no tee reservations in force. *Society Meetings:* catered for by arrangement with Secretary. Secretary: C. Taylor.

SEDBERGH. **Sedbergh Golf Club,** Catholes – Abbot Holme, Sedbergh LA10 5SS (05396 20993). *Location:* one mile out of Sedbergh on road to Dent, well signposted. Superbly scenic course in Yorkshire Dales National Park. 9 holes, 5800 yards. S.S.S. 69. Large practice area. *Green Fees:* weekdays £12.00; weekends £15.00. *Eating facilities:* by prior arrangement. *Visitors:* welcome most weekdays without booking; weekends booking essential. *Society Meetings:* very welcome by prior arrangement. Secretary: A.D. Lord (05396 20993).

SILLOTH. **Silloth on Solway Golf Club,** The Clubhouse, Silloth, Carlisle (06973 31304). *Location:* M6 Junction 41 – B5305 to Wigton, B5302 Silloth. Seaside links. 18 holes, 6357 yards. S.S.S. 72. Practice facilities. *Green Fees:* weekdays £23.00 per round; weekends and Bank Holidays £18.00 per day. Restriction, only one round allowed per day at weekends. *Eating facilities:* full bar and catering. *Visitors:* welcome without reservation. *Society Meetings:* maximum 40 catered for weekends, one round per day. Professional: John Burns. Secretary: John G. Proudlock.

SILVERDALE. **Silverdale Golf Club,** Redbridge Lane, Silverdale, Carnforth LA5 0SP (Silverdale (0524) 701300). *Location:* M6 to Carnforth, then two miles west, adjacent to railway station. Testing heathland course with rock outcrops and excellent views. 9 holes, 5256 yards. S.S.S. 67. *Green Fees:* weekdays £12.00, weekends and Bank Holidays £17.00. *Eating facilities:* not available. *Visitors:* welcome except Sundays in the Summer unless with a member. *Society Meetings:* welcome by arrangement with Secretary. Professional: S. Sumner Roberts. Secretary: P.J. Watts (0524 701307).

ULVERSTON. **Ulverston Golf Club Ltd,** Bardsea Park, Ulverston LA12 9QJ (Ulverston (0229) 52824).

*Location:* Exit 36, M6. A590 to Barrow then A5087 to Bardsea village. Wooded parkland. 18 holes, 6142 yards. S.S.S. 69. *Green Fees:* weekdays £25.00, weekends and Bank Holidays £30.00. November to February £18 and £22; Juniors half price. *Eating facilities:* lunch and bar snacks (except Mondays and Fridays after 1.45pm). *Visitors:* welcome except Saturdays (competition day), and Tuesdays (Ladies' day). Must be members of accredited golf club and have a handicap. *Society Meetings:* welcome, write with reservation to the Match Secretary. Professional: M.R. Smith (0229 52806). Secretary: I.D. Procter.

WHITEHAVEN. **St. Bees Golf Club,** Whitehaven (Whitehaven (0946) 822695). *Location:*four miles south of Whitehaven. 9 holes, 5079 yards. S.S.S. 65. *Green Fees:* information not provided. *Visitors:* unrestricted. Secretary: J.B. Campbell, Rhoda Grove, Rheda, Frizington CA26 3TE (0946 812105).

WINDERMERE. **Windermere Golf Club,** Cleabarrow, Windermere LA23 3NB (05394 43123). *Location:* one mile from Bowness-on-Windermere on Crook road, B5284. Idyllic National Park setting. 18 holes, 5006 yards. S.S.S. 65. Practice ground. *Green Fees:* weekdays £18.00, weekends £23.00. *Eating facilities:* restaurant. *Visitors:* welcome with bona fide handicaps and if members of recognised golf clubs. *Society Meetings:* catered for by prior arrangement with Secretary, numbers from twelve to 50, corporate days by arrangement. Professional: W.S.M. Rooke (05394 43550). Secretary: K.R. Moffat (05394 43123).

WORKINGTON. **Workington Golf Club Ltd,** Branthwaite Road, Workington (Workington (0900) 603460). *Location:* on A596, two miles east of town. Meadowland. 18 holes, 6252 yards. S.S.S. 70. *Green Fees:* weekdays £15.00, weekends and Bank Holidays £20.00. *Eating facilities:* lunches and dinners except Mondays and Thursdays. *Visitors:* welcome without reservation, must be members of recognised golf club. *Society Meetings:* welcome by prior arrangement. Professional: A. Drabble (0900 67828). Secretary: J.K. Walker (0900 605420).

# Derbyshire

ALFRETON. **Alfreton Golf Club,** Wingfield Road, Alfreton (Alfreton (0773) 832070). *Location:* B6024 (Matlock Road) one mile from Alfreton. 9 holes, 5012 yards. S.S.S. 65. *Green Fees:* £12.00 per round, £15.00 per day weekdays; weekends only with member. *Eating facilities:* lunches except Mondays. *Visitors:* welcome with reservation. *Society Meetings:* catered for. Secretary: F.I. Lees.

ASHBOURNE. **Ashbourne Golf Club Ltd,** Clifton, Ashbourne (Ashbourne (0335) 42078). *Location:* on A515 Ashbourne to Lichfield, one and a half miles out of Ashbourne. Undulating parkland. 9 holes, 4960 yards. S.S.S. 66. *Green Fees:* weekdays £12.00. *Eating facilities:* catering available by prior arrangement with Steward; bar. *Visitors:* welcome most times. *Society Meetings:* by arrangement. Secretary: N.P.A. James (0335 42077).

BAKEWELL. **Bakewell Golf Club,** Station Road, Bakewell (Bakewell (0629) 812307). *Location:* Sheffield Road out of Bakewell, turn right over River Bridge. Parkland, scenic hillside course. 9 holes, 5600 yards. S.S.S. 66. *Green Fees:* weekdays £12.00. *Eating facilities:* available except Mondays. *Visitors:* welcome weekdays only unless accompanied by a member. *Society Meetings:* welcome, but available weekdays only. Professional: T.E. Jones. Secretary: T.P. Turner.

BUXTON. **Buxton and High Peak Golf Club,** Town End, Buxton SK17 7EN (Buxton (0298) 23453). *Location:* A6 one mile north of Buxton. Gently undulating open Peak District countryside. 18 holes, 5980 yards. S.S.S. 69. *Green Fees:* weekdays £20.00; weekends £25.00. *Eating facilities:* full catering facilities except Thursdays. *Visitors:* welcome without reservation, ring at weekends. *Society Meetings:* up to 40 welcome. Contact Mrs S. Arnfield. Professional: A. Hoyles (0298 23112). Secretary: J.M. Williams (0298 26263).

BUXTON. **Cavendish Golf Club Ltd,** Gadley Lane, Buxton SK17 6XD (0298 23494). *Location:* three quarters of a mile west of Buxton town off A53 signposted. Parkland/moorland course, designed by Dr McEnzie who designed Augusta. 18 holes, 5833 yards. S.S.S. 68. Practice ground. *Green Fees:* £22.00 per round weekdays; £30.00 per round weekends. Juniors half price and visitors half price if playing with a member. *Eating facilities:* usual bar hours, snacks available, meals by prior booking. *Visitors:* casual visitors by arrangement with Professional. Snooker facilities. *Society Meetings:* catered for weekdays only (contact Professional). Professional: John Nolan (0298 23256). Secretary: D.N. Doyle-Davidson (0298 25052).

CHAPEL-EN-LE-FRITH. **Chapel-en-le-Frith Golf Club,** The Cockyard, Manchester Road, Chapel-en-le-Frith SK12 6UH (0298 812118). *Location:* midway between Sheffield and Manchester, 25 miles from each

on the B5470. Parkland, scenic. 18 holes, 6065 yards. S.S.S. 69. Practice ground. *Green Fees:* weekdays £15.00, weekends £20.00. *Eating facilities:* all meals daily except Mondays. *Visitors:* welcome, small numbers without reservation. *Society Meetings:* catered for by arrangement. Professional: D. Cullen (0298 812118). Secretary: J.W. Dranfield (0298 813943).

CHESTERFIELD. **Chesterfield Golf Club Ltd,** The Clubhouse, Walton, Chesterfield S42 7LA (Chesterfield (0246) 232035). *Location:* two miles from town centre on Chesterfield to Matlock road (A632). Parkland. 18 holes, 6326 yards. S.S.S. 70. Practice ground. *Green Fees:* weekdays £20.00 per round, £25.00 per day; weekends £7.00 with member only. *Eating facilities:* full catering, two bars. *Visitors:* weekdays only. *Society Meetings:* catered for on application except weekends. Professional: Michael McLean (0246 276297). Secretary: A. Bonsall (0246 279256).

CHESTERFIELD. **Stanedge Golf Club,** Walton Hay Farm, Walton, Chesterfield S45 0LW (Chesterfield (0246) 566156). *Location:* five miles south-west of Chesterfield, off B5057 near "Red Lion" public house. 9 holes, 4867 yards. S.S.S. 64. *Green Fees:* weekdays £10.00, £5.00 with member; Saturdays and Bank Holidays £10.00, must be playing with member. *Visitors:* welcome by prior arrangement. Must book in by 2pm Monday to Fridays. No visitors on Sundays until 4 p.m. and they must be with member. *Society Meetings:* catered for by prior arrangement. Secretary: W.C. Tyzack (0246 276568).

CHESTERFIELD. **Tapton Park Golf Club,** Murray House, Crow Lane, Chesterfield (0246 203960). *Location:* head for Chesterfield railway station, turn left onto Crow Lane, 250 yards on. Parkland course. 18 holes, 6025 yards. S.S.S. 69. Also 9 hole course, 2478 yards. *Green Fees:* weekdays £4.50; weekends £6.00. *Eating facilities:* meals and bar all day. *Visitors:* welcome without reservation. Coaching by qualified PGA staff. *Society Meetings:* welcome with reservations. Municipal course, open to general public. Professional: Carl Weatherleat. Secretary: G.C. Howard (0246 854588).

CODNOR. **Ormonde Fields Golf Club,** Nottingham Road, Codnor, Ripley DE5 9RG (0773 744157). *Location:* five miles M1 Junction 26 towards Ripley on A610. Parkland. 18 holes, 6011 yards. S.S.S. 69. Practice area. *Green Fees:* £15.00 weekdays, £20.00 weekends. *Eating facilities:* restaurant available. *Visitors:* unrestricted. *Society Meetings:* catered for; book through Secretary. Secretary: R.N. Walters (0773 742987).

DERBY. **Allestree Park Golf Club,** Allestree Hall, Allestree, Derby (Derby (0332) 552971). *Location:* 2 miles north of city centre on A6. Municipal course – hilly parkland. 18 holes, 5749 yards. S.S.S. 68. *Green*

*Fees:* £7.50. *Eating facilities:* full bar, catering arranged with Steward. *Visitors:* booking sheet at weekends, weekday bookings available for parties through Professional. Professional: C. Henderson (0332 550616). Secretary: G. Rawson.

DERBY. **Breadsall Priory Hotel Golf and Country Club,** Moor Road, Morley DE7 6DL (0332 832534 country club; 0332 832235 hotel). *Location:* when turning off the A61 towards Breadsall proceed on Croft Lane, turn left into Rectory Lane, then bear right onto Moor Road, continue past the Church for approximately one mile. Two courses – Priory is a parkland course and Moorland is a contrast of open moorland. Priory – 18 holes, 5844 yards. S.S.S. 68 off yellow tees; Moorland – 18 holes, 5820 yards. S.S.S. 68 off yellow tees. Practice area and putting green. *Green Fees:* £22.50 weekdays; £26.00 weekends. Golf Packages available. *Eating facilities:* restaurant and poolside grill room, bar. *Visitors:* welcome any time. *Society Meetings:* catered for by prior arrangement, rates on application. Hotel has 92 bedrooms, leisure club and conference facilities. Professional: Andrew Smith (0332 834425). Golf Manager: Pat Wolf (0332 832534).

DUFFIELD. **Chevin Golf Club,** Golf Lane, Duffield DE6 4EE (0332 840497). *Location:* five miles north of Derby on A6 at Duffield village. Hilly course. 18 holes, 6057 yards, 5451 metres. S.S.S. 69. Two practice areas. *Green Fees:* £24.00 per day. *Eating facilities:* full catering and bar. *Visitors:* welcome weekdays, Handicap Certificates required. *Society Meetings:* welcome weekdays, but never weekends. Professional: W. Bird (0332 841112). Secretary: C.P. Elliott (0332 841864).

GLOSSOP. **Glossop and District Golf Club,** Sheffield Road, Glossop SK13 9PU (0457 853117). *Location:* off A57, one mile from town centre. Moorland course. 11 holes, 5726 yards. S.S.S. 68. *Green Fees:* weekdays £15.00 per round; weekends £20.00 per round. *Eating facilities:* full catering facilities available. *Visitors:* welcome with reservation through Professional, except Saturdays during playing season. *Society Meetings:* welcome, same restrictions as visitors. Professional: P. Hunstone. Secretary: D.M. Pridham (061-339 3959).

HORSLEY. **Horsley Lodge Golf Club,** Smalley Mill Road, Horsely DE2 5BL (0332 780838). *Location:* north of Derby on A61 past Little Eaton, right turn sign posted. Parkland. 18 holes, 6432 yards, 5901 metres. S.S.S. 71. *Green Fees:* £15.00. *Eating facilities:* bar open to general public. *Visitors:* welcome weekdays except on competition days. Three bedrooms available. *Society Meetings:* acceptable if properly registered. Company Secretary: (Horsley Lodge LDT) Richard Salt; Hon. Secretary: (club) George Johnson (0332 880599).

ILKESTON. **Erewash Valley Golf Club,** Stanton-by-Dale, Near Ilkeston (Ilkeston (0602) 322984). *Location:* from M1 Junction 25 follow signs to Sandiacre. 18 holes, 6487 yards. S.S.S. 71 plus par 3 course. *Green Fees:* weekdays £20.00 per round, £25.00 per day; weekends and Bank Holidays £25.00 per day or round. *Eating facilities:* dining room service available with advance booking (0602 323258), bar snacks at all

times. *Visitors:* welcome all week. *Society Meetings:* by arrangement. Professional: Mike Ronan. Secretary: J.A. Beckett.

ILKESTON. **Ilkeston Borough Golf Club,** Peewit Municipal Golf Course, West End Drive, Ilkeston (0602 304550). *Location:* one mile west of Ilkeston market place. Slightly hilly meadowland. 9 holes, 4116 yards. S.S.S. 60. *Green Fees:* information not available. *Eating facilities:* not available. *Visitors:* welcome, no restrictions. Secretary: S.J. Rossington (0602 320304).

MATLOCK. **Matlock Golf Club Ltd,** Chesterfield Road, Matlock DE4 5LF (Matlock (0629) 582191). *Location:* Matlock-Chesterfield road, A632, one mile out of Matlock, left hand side main road. Moorland with extensive views. 18 holes, yellow tees, 5801 yards. S.S.S. 68. *Green Fees:* weekdays £25.00; weekends and Bank Holidays £12.50 with a member only. *Eating facilities:* snacks available, luncheons and evening meals by arrangement (except on Mondays). *Visitors:* welcome weekdays. *Society Meetings:* catered for Tuesday to Friday. Professional: M. Deeley (0629 584934). Secretary: A.J. Box.

MICKLEOVER. **Mickleover Golf Club,** Uttoxeter Road, Mickleover, Derby DE3 5AD (Derby (0332) 513339). *Location:* three miles west of Derby on the A516/B5020 to Uttoxeter. Undulating. 18 holes, 5708 yards, 5222 metres. S.S.S. 68. *Green Fees:* weekdays £17.00, weekends and Bank Holidays £24.00. *Eating facilities:* bar snacks available. *Visitors:* welcome, no restrictions – telephone Professional before arrival. *Society Meetings:* Tuesdays and Thursdays. Professional: Paul Wilson (0332 518662). Secretary: Doug Rodgers (0332 516011).

MICKLEOVER. **Pastures Golf Club,** Pastures Hospital, Mickleover (0332 513921 extension 419). *Location:* four miles west of Derby. Undulating meadowland. 9 holes, 5005 yards. S.S.S. 64. Practice area. *Green Fees:* £10.00 weekdays and Saturdays, no green fees Sundays. *Eating facilities:* bar facilities/snacks. *Visitors:* welcome every day except Sundays and must be with a member. *Society Meetings:* by arrangement. Secretary: S. McWilliams (0332 513921 extension 348).

QUARNDON. **Kedleston Park Golf Club,** Kedleston, Quarndon, Derby DE6 4JD. *Location:* four miles north of Derby on Kedleston Hall Estate – National Trust. Parkland with lakes. 18 holes, 6636 yards, 6068 metres. S.S.S. 72. *Green Fees:* weekdays £25.00 per round, £30.00 per day. *Eating facilities:* full catering, bars. *Visitors:* welcome Monday to Friday. *Society Meetings:* welcome Monday to Friday. Professional: J. Hetherington (0332 841685). Secretary: K. Wilson (0332 840035).

SHEFFIELD. **Renishaw Park Golf Club,** Golf House, Station Road, Renishaw, Sheffield S31 9UZ (Eckington (0246) 432044). *Location:* A616 Barlborough (Junction 30 M1) to Sheffield. Parkland/meadowland. 18 holes, 6253 yards. S.S.S. 70. Practice net. *Green Fees:* weekdays £18.00 per round, £25.00 per day; weekends £30.00 per round/day. *Eating facilities:* bar meals, full restaurant, full bar available. *Visitors:* welcome without reservation (advisable to ring

Pro prior to arrival). *Society Meetings:* by prior arrangement. Full day package available. Professional: S. Elliott (0246 435484). Secretary: G.B. Denison (0246 432044).

SHEFFIELD. **Sickleholme Golf Club,** Bamford, Sheffield S30 2BH (Hope Valley (0433) 651306). *Location:* A625 west of Sheffield, right at Marquis of Granby, Bamford. 18 holes, 6064 yards. S.S.S. 69. *Green Fees:* information not available. *Eating facilities:* by arrangement. *Visitors:* must be members of a recognised Golf Club. *Society Meetings:* catered for by arrangement. Professional/Manager: P. H. Taylor (0433 651252).

SHIRLAND. **Shirland Golf Club,** Lower Delves, Shirland DE5 6AU (Alfreton (0773) 834969/834935). *Location:* one mile north of Alfreton off A61, three miles from M1 Junction 28 via A38. Tree-lined rolling parkland, 18 holes, 6072 yards. S.S.S. 69. Par 71. Two practice grounds. *Green Fees:* £15.00 per round, £25.00 per day weekdays; £20.00 per round, £30.00 per day weekends. *Eating facilities:* full restaurant, bar meals. Conference and banquet rooms. *Visitors:* unrestricted weekdays, but must book through Pro-

fessional at weekends. County standard bowling green available. *Society Meetings:* welcome. Secretary: Mrs C.S. Fincham (0773 832515). Professional: N.B. Hallam (0773 834935).

SINFIN. **Derby Golf Club,** Shakespeare Street, Sinfin, Derby DE24 9HD (Derby (0332) 766323). *Location:* two miles town centre, access via Wilmore Road. Parkland. 18 holes, 6144 yards, 5618 metres. S.S.S. 69. *Green Fees:* on application to the Professional. *Eating facilities:* light meals and bar facilities. *Visitors:* welcome weekdays. *Society Meetings:* welcome weekdays. Professional: Colin Henderson (0332 766462). Secretary: P. Davidson.

STOCKPORT. **New Mills Golf Club,** Shaw Marsh, New Mills (New Mills (0663) 743485). *Location:* off A6015. 9 holes, 5633 yards. S.S.S. 67. *Green Fees:* £15.00 weekdays only. *Eating facilities:* catering except Thursdays. *Visitors:* welcome weekdays with reservation, weekends with members. No visitors competition days. *Society Meetings:* no catering Thursdays, catered for by appointment. Professional: Edward Litchfield. Secretary: R. Tuson.

# Devon

AXMOUTH. **Axe Cliff Golf Club,** Squires Lane, Axmouth, Seaton EX12 2BJ (0297) 20499). *Location:* A35 from Lyme Regis, turn left on to B3172 at junction with A358 Seaton. Seaside wooded course. 18 holes, 5057 yards. S.S.S. 65. *Green Fees:* weekdays £12.00; weekends £16.00. *Eating facilities:* dining room. Hot meals/snacks, etc. *Visitors:* welcome without reservation, some restrictions Wednesdays and weekends. *Society Meetings:* catered for, apply Secretary. Secretary: Mrs D. Rogers (0297 24371).

BIDEFORD near. **Clovelly Golf and Country Club,** Woolsery, Near Bideford EX39 5RA (0237 431442; Fax: 0237 431734). *Location:* between Bideford and Bude A39, signposted from main A39 road. Parkland. 18 holes, 5500 yards, 5159 metres. S.S.S. 67. *Green Fees:* £12.00. *Eating facilities:* restaurant and bar. *Visitors:* welcome at all times. 29 lodges fully equipped sleeping up to six available. *Society Meetings:* welcome. Secretary: M. Dando.

BIGBURY. **Bigbury Golf Club Ltd,** Bigbury, Kingsbridge TQ7 4BB (Bigbury on Sea (0548) 810207). *Location:* off main Plymouth to Kingsbridge road, turn right at Harraton Cross. Two courses: No 1 – 18 holes, 5902 yards. S.S.S. 68. No. 2 (Comp) – 18 holes, 6076 yards. S.S.S. 69. *Green Fees:* weekdays £20.00; weekends £24.00. *Eating facilities:* buffet catering always available: medium to full catering order in advance. *Visitors:* welcome, Handicap Certificate required. *Society Meetings:* catered for by prior arrangement. Professional: Simon Lloyd. Secretary: B.J. Perry (0548 810557).

BRAUNTON. **Saunton Golf Club,** Saunton, Braunton (0271 812436; Fax: 0271 814241). *Location:* eight miles west of Barnstaple on Linksland at north side of Barnstaple Bay. East course 18 holes, 6703 yards. S.S.S. 73. West course 18 holes, 6356 yards. S.S.S. 71. *Green Fees:* weekdays £25.00, weekends £30.00. *Eating facilities:* full catering available. *Visitors:* wel-

come with reservation, must be members of other golf club and must be able to produce Handicap Certificate. *Society Meetings:* catered for by arrangement. Professional: J.A. McGhee (0271 812013). Secretary: W.E. Geddes (0271 812436).

BRIXHAM. **Churston Golf Club Ltd,** Churston, Near Brixham TQ5 0LA (0803 842218). *Location:* Torquay – follow road signs to Brixham. Seaside course overlooking Torbay. 18 holes, 6243 yards. S.S.S. 70. *Green Fees:* weekdays £20.00, weekends £25.00. *Eating facilities:* available all day. *Visitors:* welcome, must be members of recognised club. Handicap Certificate required. *Society Meetings:* catered for by arrangement. Professional: Richard Penfold (0803 842894). Manager/Secretary: A.M. Chaundy (0803 842751).

BUDLEIGH SALTERTON. **East Devon Golf Club,** North View Road, Budleigh Salterton EX9 6DQ (Budleigh Salterton (0395) 442018). *Location:* three miles from Exmouth. Heathland, 18 holes, 6214 yards. S.S.S. 70. *Green Fees:* weekdays £22.00 per round, £26.00 per day; weekends £26.00 per round, £30.00

per day. *Eating facilities:* meals and snacks available every day except Mondays. *Visitors:* welcome with letter of introduction, Handicap Certificate or Devon County card. *Society Meetings:* catered for by arrangement. Professional: Trevor Underwood (0395 445195). Secretary: J.C. Tebbet (0395 443370).

CHULMLEIGH. **Chulmleigh Golf Course,** Leigh Road, Chulmleigh EX18 7BL (Chulmleigh (0769) 80519). *Location:* midway between Barnstaple and Crediton on A377. Undulating course. 18 holes, 1450 yards. S.S.S. 54. Mid December to end of March 9 holes x 2, 2352 yards. *Green Fees:* £5.00 per round, 2 rounds £7.50. Day ticket £10.00. Reductions for Juniors. *Eating facilities:* snacks, bar. *Visitors:* welcome. *Society Meetings:* welcome by prior arrangement. Professional: Michael Blackwell (0769 81068). Owner/Secretary: P.N. Callow.

CREDITON. **Downes Crediton Golf Club,** Hookway, Crediton (Crediton (0363) 773991). *Location:* off Crediton-Exeter road. Part flat, part hilly course featuring woods and water. 18 holes, 5917 yards. S.S.S. 68. *Green Fees:* £16.00 weekdays, £22.00 weekends.

*Eating facilities:* available from 11.30am to one hour before bar closes. *Visitors:* welcome, advisable to phone first and must produce Handicap Certificate. *Society Meetings:* by arrangement. Professional: Howard Finch (0363 774464). Secretary: W.J. Brooks (0363 773025).

CULLOMPTON. **Padbrook Park Golf Club,** Padbrook Park, Cullompton (0884 38286; Fax: 0884 38359). *Location:* Junction 28 of M5, one mile away. Parkland. 9 holes (18 tees), 6108 yards. S.S.S. 70. Nets. *Green Fees:* weekdays £5.00 9 holes, £8.00 18 holes; weekends £7.00 9 holes, £14.00 18 holes. Juniors half price. *Eating facilities:* two bars and restaurant. *Visitors:* always welcome. Handicap Certificate required. Indoor bowls, tennis, pool, fishing. *Society Meetings:* welcome by prior arrangement. Professional: Stewart Adwick. General Manager: Richard Chard.

DAWLISH. **Warren Golf Club,** Dawlish EX7 0NF (0626 862738). *Location:* 12 miles south of Exeter off A379. Links golf course lying on a spit of land between the sea and Exe Estuary. 18 holes, 5968 yards. S.S.S. 69. *Green Fees:* weekdays £19.00, weekends and Bank Holidays £21.00 (half price with a member). *Eating facilities:* bar and full catering available. *Visitors:* welcome with Handicap Certificate.*Society Meetings:* welcome by arrangement, Special Packages available. Professional: Geoff Wicks. Secretary: D.M. Beesley (0626 862255).

EXETER. **Exeter Golf and Country Club,** Countess Wear, Exeter EX2 7AE (0392 874139). *Location:* near M5, exit Junction 30. Parkland course. 18 holes, 6000 yards. S.S.S. 69. Large practice ground. *Green Fees:* £23.00. *Eating facilities:* sports bar, lounge bar, diningroom. *Visitors:* welcome except Tuesdays (Ladies' Day) and weekends (very busy with members), booking number 0392 876303). *Society Meetings:* catered for Thursdays only. Professional: Mike Rowett (0392 875028). Secretary: C.H.M. Greetham (0392 874023).

EXETER near. **Fingle Glen Golf and Leisure Complex,** Tedburn St. Mary, Near Exeter EX6 6AF (0647 61817). *Location:* A30 five miles from Exeter on the Okehampton Road. Parkland with streams and lakes. 9 holes, 2466 yards. S.S.S. 31. Par 33 (66). Undercover practice range. *Green Fees:* weekdays £3.50 9 holes, £6.50 18 holes; weekends £9.00 9 holes, £16.50 18 holes. *Eating facilities:* restaurant, bar snacks, family area, sun terrace. *Visitors:* welcome at all times. 3 star accommodation available. *Society Meetings:* welcome at all times. Professional: Stephen Gould. Secretary: Chris Wilson.

HOLSWORTHY. **Holsworthy Golf Club,** Kilatree, Holsworthy (Holsworthy (0409) 253177). *Location:* leave Holsworthy on Bude road, A3072; one mile on

left. Parkland, 18 holes, 6012 yards. S.S.S. 69. *Green Fees:* weekdays £13.00; weekends £16.00. *Eating facilities:* snacks at bar, diningroom. *Visitors:* without reservation, (after 12 noon on Sundays). *Society Meetings:* catered for by arrangement. Professional: Tim McSherry. Secretary: Barry Megson (0409 253177).

HONITON. **Honiton Golf Club,** Middlehills, Honiton EX14 8TR (0404 47167). *Location:* one mile south of town proceed from New Street to Farway. Flat parkland. 18 holes, 5940 yards. S.S.S. 68. Small practice ground. *Green Fees:* weekdays £18.00 per day, weekends and Bank Holidays £23.00. *Eating facilities:* bar and restaurant. *Visitors:* bona fide members of other clubs welcome, with restrictions on Wednesdays (ladies' day) and weekends (club competitions). *Society Meetings:* bookable on Thursdays only. Professional: Adrian Cave (0404 42943). Secretary: J.L. Carter (0404 44422).

ILFRACOMBE. **Ilfracombe Golf Club,** Hele Bay, Ilfracombe EX34 9RT (0271 862050). *Location:* on main coastal road between Ilfracombe and Combe Martin. Undulating parkland with spectacular views from every tee and green. 18 holes, 5893 yards. S.S.S. 68. Practice area and green. *Green Fees:* weekdays £16.00; weekends £18.00. *Eating facilities:* full catering available; normal club bar hours. *Visitors:* welcome (Handicap/membership Certificate preferred). Weekends until 10am and then between 12 noon and 2pm with members only. *Society Meetings:* catered for, with some time restrictions. Professional: David Hoare (0271 863328). Secretary: Rodney C. Beer (0271 862176).

MORETONHAMPSTEAD. **Manor House Hotel and Golf Course,** Moretonhampstead TR13 8RE (Moretonhampstead (0647) 40355). *Location:* Junction 31 from M5, B3212 for two miles. Parkland with rivers. 18 holes, 6016 yards. S.S.S. 69. Extensive practice facilities. Practice ground, Par 3 course. *Green Fees:* weekdays £22.50; weekends £28.00. *Eating facilities:* brunch service, cream teas, two bars. *Visitors:* welcome. Please book in advance. Accommodation (Hotel), squash courts, tennis courts. *Society Meetings:* by prior arrangement. Professional/Golf Manager: Richard Lewis (0647 40355).

NEWTON ABBOT. **Newton Abbot (Stover) Golf Club,** Bovey Road, Newton Abbot TQ12 6QQ (Newton Abbot (0626) 52460). *Location:* A382 three miles north of Newton Abbot. Wooded parkland with river. 18 holes, 5886 yards. S.S.S. 68. *Green Fees:* £21.00 weekdays, weekends and Bank Holidays. *Eating facilities:* full catering daily from 11.00am. *Visitors:* welcome if members of recognised club. *Society Meetings:*

catered for on Thursdays, parties of 24 and over. Professional: M. Craig (0626 62078). Secretary: R. Smith (0626 52460).

OKEHAMPTON. **Okehampton Golf Club,** Off Tors Road, Okehampton EX20 1EF (0837 52113) *Location:* from A30 take turning from centre of Okehampton then follow the signposts. Parkland. 18 holes, 5191 yards. S.S.S. 67. *Green Fees:* weekdays £13.00; Saturdays £20.00, Sundays £17.00. *Eating facilities:* by arrangement; bar. *Visitors:* welcome. *Society Meetings:* catered for. Professional: Philip Blundell (0837 53541). Secretary: S. Chave (0837 52113).

PLYMOUTH. **Elfordleigh Hotel, Golf and Country Club,** Near Colebrook, Plympton, Plymouth PL7 5EB (0752 336428). *Location:* one mile from Plympton. Woodland course in picturesque countryside. 9 holes, 5470 yards (twice round). S.S.S. 67. Practice area. *Green Fees:* £15.00 weekdays, £20.00 weekends. Special rates available on request. *Eating facilities:* bar meals available from Country Club bar. *Visitors:* welcome. Hotel accommodation available. *Society Meetings:* catered for by arrangement. Secretary: Mrs P. Parfitt (0752 348425; Fax: 0752 344581).

PLYMOUTH. **Staddon Heights Golf Club,** Staddon Heights, Plymstock, Plymouth PL9 9SP (0752 401998). *Location:* from Plymouth city follow signs to Plymstock. Seaside links. 18 holes, 5874 yards. S.S.S. 68. Practice area. *Green Fees:* weekdays £15.00; weekends £20.00. *Eating facilities:* diningroom open daily. *Visitors:* welcome except when tee booked for club competitions. *Society Meetings:* by arrangement with Secretary. Professional: John Cox (0752 492630). Secretary: Mike Holliday (0752 402475).

SIDMOUTH. **Sidmouth Golf Club,** Cotmaton Road, Peak Hill, Sidmouth EX10 8SX (0395 513023). *Location:* half a mile from town centre, 12 miles south east of M5 Junction 30. Parkland with breathtaking views over

Sid Valley and Lyme Bay. 18 holes, 5109 yards. S.S.S. 65. *Green Fees:* £18.00 per day. *Eating facilities:* catering available except Mondays. All day bar Saturdays. *Visitors:* welcome anytime other than club competition, tee reservations. *Society Meetings:* catered for, contact Secretary. Professional: M. Kemp (0395 516407). Secretary: I.M. Smith (0395 513451).

SOUTH BRENT. **Wrangaton Golf Club,** Golf Links Road, Wrangaton, South Brent TQ10 9HJ (South Brent (0364) 73001). *Location:* heading south take next exit off A38 after South Brent. Undulating parkland/moorland course. 18 holes, 6041 yards. S.S.S 69. Practice area and net. *Green Fees:* weekdays £16.00 per day, weekends and Bank Holidays £20.00. *Eating facilities:* full catering and bar facilities available. *Visitors:* welcome, restricted on club competition days, phoning beforehand advised during season. *Society Meetings:* all welcome, written notice required. Professional: Alistair Cardwell (0364 72161). Secretary/ Manager: Richard R. Hine (0364 73229).

TAVISTOCK. **Hurdwick Golf Club,** Tavistock Hamlets, Tavistock PL19 8PZ (0822 612746). *Location:* one mile north of Tavistock on the Brentor Road. Parkland. 18 holes, 4800 yards. S.S.S. 64. *Green Fees:* weekdays £14.00 per round, £20.00 all day; weekends £16.00 per round, £25.00 all day. *Eating facilities:* fresh sandwiches, licensed bar. *Visitors:* welcome anytime. *Society Meetings:* (10 or more) 36 holes and buffet for £20 a head. Professional: available. Secretary: Major Roger Cullen.

TAVISTOCK. **Tavistock Golf Club,** Down Road, Tavistock PL19 9AQ (0822 612049). *Location:* Whitchurch Down one mile from Tavistock. 18 holes, 6250 yards. S.S.S. 70. *Green Fees:* £17.00 weekdays, £22.00 weekends and Bank Holidays. *Eating facilities:* full catering facilities. *Visitors:* welcome with reservation. *Society Meetings:* catered for. Professional: R.M. Cade (0822 612316). Secretary: B. G. Steer (0822 612344).

TEIGNMOUTH. **Teignmouth Golf Club,** Haldon Moor, Teignmouth (0626 773614). *Location:* two miles north of Teignmouth on the Exeter Road – B3192. Level heathland course, panoramic views. 18 holes, 6227 yards. S.S.S. 71. *Green Fees:* information on application. *Eating facilities:* full catering service midday to 6pm. *Visitors:* welcome with reservation if members of another club with Handicap Certificate. *Society Meetings:* catered for weekdays only. Professional: P. Ward (0626 772894). Secretary: D. Holloway (0626 774194).

THURLESTONE. **Thurlestone Golf Club,** Thurlestone, Kingsbridge TQ7 3NZ (0548 560221). *Location:* turn off A379 near Kingsbridge. Downland with superb views. 18 holes, 6303 yards, 5818 metres. S.S.S. 70. Practice area. *Green Fees:* £22.00 per day. *Eating facilities:* catering available from 10.00am until 5.30pm daily. *Visitors:* must produce Handicap Certificate, please telephone in advance. *Society Meetings:* not catered for. Professional: Neville Whitley (0548 560715). Secretary: R.W. Marston (0548 560405).

TIVERTON. **Tiverton Golf Club,** Post Hill, Tiverton EX16 4NE (Tiverton (0884) 252114). *Location:* three miles east of Tiverton, Junction 27 of M5, proceed through Sampford Peverell and Halberton. Parkland, tree-lined fairways. 18 holes, 6263 yards. S.S.S. 71. *Green Fees:* on application. *Eating facilities:* snacks, lunches and teas; evening meals by arrangement. *Visitors:* welcome with reservation, Handicap Certificate or introduction required. Professional: R.E. Freeman (0884 254836). Secretary: M. Crouch (0884 252187).

TORQUAY. **Torquay Golf Club,** 30 Petitor Road, St Marychurch, Torquay TQ1 4QF (0803 327471). *Location:* north east of Torquay. St. Marychurch. Parkland. 18 holes, 6192 yards. S.S.S. 69. *Green Fees:* on application. *Eating facilities:* lunches, teas and evening meals available. *Visitors:* welcome if members of a golf club with Handicap Certificate. *Society Meetings:* catered for. Professional: M. Ruth (0803 329113). Secretary: B.G. Long (0803 314591).

TORRINGTON. **Torrington Golf Club,** Weare Trees, Torrington EX38 7EZ (Torrington (0805) 22229). *Location:* one mile north of Torrington on Weare Giffard road. Exposed common land with excellent views. 9 holes, 4418 yards, 4044 metres. S.S.S. 61. *Green Fees:* weekdays £10.00; weekends £14.00. *Eating facilities:* light meals and bar snacks available during bar hours. *Visitors:* welcome except on Saturday and Sunday mornings and during club and open competitions. *Society Meetings:* catered for by arrangement. Secretary: Geoffrey S.C. Green (0237 472792).

TOTNES. **Dartmouth Golf and Country Club,** Blackawton, Totnes TQ9 7DG (080-421 650; Fax: 080-421 628). *Location:* five miles from Dartmouth on the A3122. Undulating inland course with lakes, rock faces and multiple tees. 9 holes (club), 18 holes (championship). Driving range. *Green Fees:* weekdays £26.00; weekends £30.00. *Eating facilities:* bar, bar snacks and restaurant. *Visitors:* welcome at all times except weekends when restrictions will apply. Accommodation can be arranged. *Society Meetings:* details of golf packages available on request.

UMBERLEIGH. **Highbullen Hotel Golf Course,** Chittlehamholt, Umberleigh EX37 9HG (0769 540561). *Location:* M5 Tiverton Exit (27) A361 to South Molton, B3226 five miles. Right uphill to Chittlehamholt. Pleasant parkland setting amongst mature specimen trees and water hazards, spectacular views. *Green Fees:* non-residents only (free to hotel guests) £8.00 weekdays; £10.00 weekends. £2.00 reduction after 5pm. *Eating facilities:* in hotel – including snack lunches. *Visitors:* welcome anytime. *Society Meetings:* welcome, small numbers only. Professional: Paul Weston (0769 540530). Secretary: Martin Neil (hotel).

UMBERLEIGH. **Libbaton Golf Club,** High Bickington, Umberleigh EX37 9BS (0769 60269). *Location:* situated on B3217, one and a half miles south High Bickington, close to A377. Parkland, rolling countryside, NOT steep up and down slopes. 18 holes, 6428 metres. S.S.S. 72. Floodlit driving range. *Green Fees:* weekdays £12.00; weekends £15.00. *Eating facilities:* bar food served 10am to 9pm. *Visitors:* always welcome, after 9.30am weekends. Three bedroomed house to let. *Society Meetings:* welcome by prior arrangement. Special Society Packages. Professional: John N. Phillips. Secretary: Jack H. Brough.

WESTWARD HO! **Royal North Devon Golf Club,** Golf Links Road, Westward Ho!, Bideford EX39 1HD (0237 473824). *Location:* A39 Tiverton. Links course. 18 holes, 6662 yards, 6089 metres. S.S.S. 72. Practice area. *Green Fees:* weekdays £19.00 per round, £23.00 per day; weekends £23.00 per round. *Eating facilities:* full catering available. *Visitors:* welcome with Handicap Certificate. Tee reservations should be made in advance. *Society Meetings:* catered for. Professional: G. Johnston (0237 477598). General Manager/Secretary: J.E. Linaker (0237 473817).

YELVERTON. **Yelverton Golf Club,** Golf Links Road, Yelverton PL20 6BN (Yelverton (0822 853618). *Location:* eight miles north of Plymouth on A386 road. Moorland course. 18 holes, 6293 yards. S.S.S. 70. Practice ground. *Green Fees:* £20.00 per day or round. *Eating facilities:* full catering available. *Visitors:* welcome if member of a recognised golf club or golf society. Handicap Certificate required. *Society Meetings:* catered for, welcome by arrangement with Secretary. Professional: Ian Parker (0822 853593). Secretary: D.R. Bettany (0822 852824).

# Dorset

BLANDFORD. **Ashley Wood Golf Club,** Wimborne Road, Tarrant Rawston, Blandford (Blandford (0258) 452253). *Location:* one-and-a-half miles south of Blandford on B3082. 9 holes, 6227 yards, 5692 metres. S.S.S. 70. Practice ground. *Green Fees:* weekdays £17.00, £9.00 with a member; weekends £24.00, £13.00 with a member. *Eating facilities:* bar and dining area. *Visitors:* welcome without reservation except on Tuesday mornings, weekends before noon, competition and match days. *Society Meetings:* welcome by arrangement with Secretary. Professional: Spencer Taylor (0258 480379). Secretary: Peter Lillford (0258 452253).

BOURNEMOUTH. **Bournemouth & Meyrick Park Golf Club, (Playing over Municipal course),** Meyrick Park, Bournemouth BH2 6LH (Bournemouth (0202) 290307). *Location:* one mile from town centre. Beautiful woodland. 18 holes, 5663 yards. S.S.S. 68. Practice area. *Green Fees:* weekdays £8.90 (winter), £10.40 (summer). *Eating facilities:* clubhouse restaurant and bar available if signed in by member; public cafe. *Visitors:* welcome at anytime (pay as you play) but must be signed in by members. *Society Meetings:* catered for. Bookings (0202 290871). Professional: J. Waring (0202 290862). Secretary: Ms. J. Bennett (0202 290307).

BOURNEMOUTH. **Knighton Heath Golf Club,** Francis Avenue, Bournemouth BH11 8NX (Bournemouth (0202) 577870). *Location:* A348 and A3049 roundabout exit Francis Avenue. Undulating heathland, 18 holes, 6000 yards. S.S.S. 69. *Green Fees:* on application. *Eating facilities:* meals and bar snacks available daily, except Monday. *Visitors:* welcome with reservation, after 9.30am weekdays. Restrictions on competition days. Not al weekends unless with a member. Handicap Certificate required. *Society Meetings:* catered for if arranged in advance. Professional: Jane Miles (0202 578275). Secretary: R.C. Bestwick (0202 572633).

BOURNEMOUTH. **Queen's Park (Bournemouth) Golf Club,** Queens Park Golf Pavilion, Queens Park West Drive, Bournemouth BH8 9BY (0202 394466). *Location:* Wessex Way – three miles from town centre. Ringwood to Bournemouth Spur road. Play over Queens Park course. Wooded parkland course, undulating. 18 holes, 6505 yards. S.S.S. 72. Practice area. Changing rooms. *Green Fees:* information on application. *Eating facilities:* restaurant and bar. *Visitors:* unrestricted, except no play Sundays after 3pm (11am last tee time). *Society Meetings:* on application to Borough Parks Dept (0202 396198). Professional: R. Hill (0202 36817). Secretary: D.W.J. Blakeman (0202 302611).

BRIDPORT. **Bridport and West Dorset Golf Club,** East Cliff, West Bay, Bridport DT6 4EP (Bridport (0308) 22597). *Location:* one and a half miles south of Bridport, east of West Bay harbour. Clifftop links course. 18 holes, 5246 yards, 4795 metres. S.S.S. 66. Practice area. *Green Fees:* weekdays £18.00; weekends £25.00. *Eating facilities:* lounge and dining-room. *Visitors:* welcome. *Society Meetings:* catered for by prior arrangement. Professional: John Parish (0308 421491). Secretary: P.J. Ridler (0308 421095).

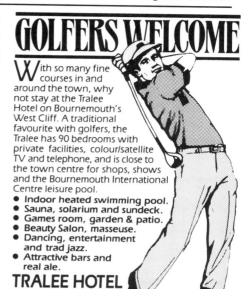

BROADSTONE. **Broadstone (Dorset) Golf Club,** Wentworth Drive, Broadstone BH18 8DQ (Broadstone (0202) 693363). *Location:* off A349 to B3072 to Broadstone. Heathland. 18 holes, 6183 yards. S.S.S. 70. *Green Fees:* weekdays £30.00. *Eating facilities:* full catering available. *Visitors:* welcome, after 9.30am weekdays by arrangement, current Handicap Certificate required. No visitors weekends. *Society Meetings:* welcome by arrangement. Professional: Nigel Tokely (0202 692835). Secretary: J.M. Cowan (0202 692595).

CHRISTCHURCH. **Christchurch Golf Club,** Iford Bridge, Barrack Road (0202 473817). *Location:* boundary of Bournemouth on road to Christchurch. 9 holes, 4654 yards. S.S.S. 63. *Green Fees:* weekdays £4.70, weekends £5.35. Driving range 50 balls £1.60. *Eating facilities:* snack bar and bar. *Visitors:* welcome (car park). Professional: P. Troth. Secretary: P.H. Miller.

CHRISTCHURCH. **Highcliffe Castle Golf Club,** 107 Lymington Road, Highcliffe on Sea, Christchurch BH23 4LA (Highcliffe (0425 272953). *Location:* on the coastal road linking Lymington and Christchurch. Flat, wooded course. 18 holes, 4686 yards, 4284 metres. S.S.S. 63. *Green Fees:* weekdays £18.00, after 4pm £11.00; weekends before noon £27.00; afternoon £22.00, after 4pm £15.00. Must be in possession of Handicap Certificate. *Eating facilities:* full catering available. *Visitors:* welcome after 9.30am if member of recognised golf club, after 3.00pm on competition days. *Society Meetings:* catered for Tuesdays only by prior arrangement, all must be members of recognised golf clubs. Professional: R.E. Crockford (0425 276640). Secretary: Mrs E. Thompson (0425 272210).

DORCHESTER. **Came Down Golf Club,** Came Down, Dorchester DT2 8NR (Dorchester (0305) 812531). *Location:* two miles south of Dorchester. Downland course. 18 holes, 6224 yards, 5914 metres. S.S.S. 71. Practice area and nets. *Green Fees:* £20.00 weekdays; £25.00 weekends and Bank Holidays. *Eating facilities:* full catering available; bar. *Visitors:* welcome without reservation except Sunday mornings and competition days – phone in advance. All visitors must have Handicap. *Society Meetings:* Wednesday only. Professional: R. Preston (0305 812670). Secretary: David E. Matthews (0305 813494).

DORCHESTER. **Lyons Gate Golf Club,** Lyons Gate, Dorchester DT2 7AZ (03005 239). *Location:* on A352 going north from Dorchester about 11 miles or south from Sherborne about seven miles. Parkland with

spectacular views, probably England's most spectacular 9 hole course, famous for its wild flowers. 9 holes, 2000 yards. S.S.S. 30. Practice nets, greens. *Green Fees:* £4.50 for 9 holes, £7.50 for 18 holes. Children under 17 years half price. *Eating facilities:* snacks in shop, vending machine. *Visitors:* welcome, no restrictions, dogs on leads. *Society Meetings:* by arrangement. Secretary: Mr F. Driver.

FERNDOWN. **Dudsbury Golf Club,** Christchurch Road, Ferndown BH22 8ST (0202 593499; Fax: 0202 594555). *Location:* Ferndown town centre. Follow signs for Poole on A348, turn left at first mini roundabout, turn left to Hurn Airport, 200 yards. Club on right hand side. Parkland course designed by Donald Steel, three lakes in beautiful Dorset countryside rolling gently down to the River Stour. 18 holes, 6208 yards. S.S.S 70. Par 71. 5 hole teaching academy practice range. *Green Fees:* weekdays £17.00 per round, £25.00 per day; weekends £25.00 per round. *Eating facilities:* two bars, spikes bar snacks, à la carte Clocktower Restaurant. *Visitors:* welcome mid week. Handicap Certificate required. *Society Meetings:* welcome Monday to Friday, Handicap required. Professional: Andy Greig (0202 594488). General Manager: Ken Heathcote.

FERNDOWN. **Ferndown Golf Club,** 119 Golf Links Road, Ferndown BH22 8BU (Ferndown (0202) 872022). *Location:* off A31. Wooded heathland. 18 holes, 6442 yards. S.S.S. 71. 9 holes, 5604 yards. S.S.S. 68. Practice ground. *Green Fees:* Old Course: £35.00 weekdays, £40.00 weekends. New Course: £15.00 weekdays, £20.00 weekends. Societies £50.00 for the day. *Eating facilities:* available. *Visitors:* welcome but prior permission recommended. Handicap Certificate required from a recognised golf club. Professional: D.N. Sewell (0202 873825). Secretary: E. Robertson (0202 874602).

LYME REGIS. **Lyme Regis Golf Club,** Timber Hill, Lyme Regis DT7 3HQ (Lyme Regis (0297) 442043). *Location:* just off A35, one mile north of town centre. Seaside links. 18 holes, 6220 yards. S.S.S. 70. *Green Fees:* weekdays £24.00 per day, £20.00 after 2pm; weekends and Bank Holidays £24.00. *Eating facilities:* restaurant and bar. *Visitors:* welcome, but not before 9.30am and restrictions Thursday and Sundays; best to check with Professional. Handicap Certificate or proof of membership of a golf club required. *Society Meetings:* minimum for Tee Booking 12. Professional: Andrew Black (0297 443822). Secretary: R.G. Fry (0297 442693).

OKEFORD FITZPAINE. **Mid-Dorset Golf Club,** Belchalwell, Okeford Fitzpaine DT11 0EW (0258 861386). *Location:* near Blandford, between Blandford and Sturminster Newton. 18 holes, 5938 yards. S.S.S. 71. Practice ground. *Green Fees:* weekdays £15.00; weekends £20.00. *Eating facilities:* lunches and evening meals. *Visitors:* welcome all week. *Society Meetings:* welcome. Reduction in green fees for groups of 30 or more. Professional: Spencer Taylor (0258 861184). Secretary: David Astill.

POOLE near. **Bulbury Woods Golf Club,** Halls Road, Lytchett Matravers, Near Poole BH16 6EP (092945 574). *Location:* Poole – Bere Regis Road. Wooded parkland. 18 holes, 6020 yards. S.S.S. 69. Practice ground. *Green Fees:* £15.00 per round. *Eating facilities:* bar and restaurant. *Visitors:* welcomed; dress requirements – recognised golf attire, no jeans, vests or training shoes. *Society Meetings:* welcome by prior arrangement. Professional: J. Sharkey. Secretary: T.I. Williams.

POOLE. **Parkstone Golf Club,** Links Road, Parkstone, Poole BH14 9JU (0202) 707138). *Location:* off A35 Bournemouth to Poole. Wooded heathland. 18 holes, 6250 yards. S.S.S. 70. *Green Fees:* £24.00 per round, £32.00 per day weekdays; £30.00 per round, £40.00 per day weekends and Bank Holidays. *Eating facilities:* catering available daily. *Visitors:* welcome with reservation and Handicap Certificate. *Society Meetings:* catered for as above. Professional: Mark Thomas (0202 708092). Secretary: A.S. Kinnear (0202 707138).

SHERBORNE. **Sherborne Golf Club,** Higher Clatcombe, Sherborne DT9 4RN (Sherborne (0935) 812475). *Location:* one mile north of town on B3145 to Wincanton. Parkland. 18 holes, 5949 yards. S.S.S. 68. Practice facilities. *Green Fees:* £20.00 weekdays, £25.00 weekends and Bank Holidays. *Eating facilities:* snacks, lunches, suppers, teas; dinners to order. *Visitors:* as commitment allows, telephone in advance. Handicap Certificates required. Thursday is Ladies' Day. *Society Meetings:* catered for Tuesdays and Wednesdays. Professional: Stewart Wright (0935 812774). Secretary/Manager: Mrs J.M.C. Guy (0935 814431).

STUDLAND. **Isle of Purbeck Golf Club,** Studland, Swanage BH19 3AB (0929 44210). *Location:* A351 towards Swanage, at Corfe Castle turn onto B3351 to Studland. Heathland courses with wonderful views. Purbeck – 18 holes, 6248 yards, 5823 metres. S.S.S. 71. Dene – 9 holes, 2022 yards. S.S.S. 30. *Green Fees:* £22.50 per round, £30.00 per two rounds weekdays; £27.50 per round, £35.00 per two rounds weekends. *Eating facilities:* bar and restaurant. *Visitors:* welcome. *Society Meetings:* catered for by arrangement, minimum 8. Professional: Kevin Spurgeon (0929 44354). Secretary: Mrs J. Robinson (0929 44361).

VERWOOD. **Crane Valley Golf Club,** Verwood BH31 6LE (0202 814088; Fax: 0202 813407). *Location:* on B3081 Verwood to Cranborne Road. Parkland featuring lakes and River Crane. 18 holes, 6400 yards. S.S.S. 71. 9 hole course, 2100 yards. Covered driving range. *Green Fees:* weekdays £18.00; weekends £24.00. *Eating facilities:* restaurant and spikes bar. *Visitors:* course opening April 1993, visitors not able to play before this date then welcome at all times except weekend mornings. Accommodation adjoining course at West Farm. *Society Meetings:* by appointment. Professional: Alan Egford. Secretary: Martin Wilson.

WAREHAM. **East Dorset Golf Club,** Hyde, Wareham BH20 7NT (0929 471706), Fax: 0929 471294). *Location:* take A352 off Wareham by-pass, enter Puddletown Road, Worgret Heath. Proceed 4 miles to ARC Blockworks, turn right immediately before Blockworks (signposted). 200 yards to clubhouse. Parkland. Lakeland Course. 18 holes, 6556 yards. S.S.S. 71. Woodland Course 18 holes, 4853 yards. S.S.S. 64. Driving range and Pro shop. *Green Fees:* Lakeland Course weekdays £25.00; weekends £32.00. Woodland Course £22.00 weekdays, £25 weekends. *Eating facilities:* excellent bar and restaurant. *Visitors:* welcome with prior tee reservation. *Society Meetings:* welcome with prior notice. Professional: G. Packer (0929 472272). General Manager: D.F.C. Thomas (0929 472244).

WAREHAM. **Wareham Golf Club,** Sandford Road, Wareham BH20 4DH (Wareham (0929) 554156). *Location:* adjoining A351 near railway station. Partly wooded course. 18 holes, 5603 yards. S.S.S. 67. *Green Fees:* weekdays £15.00 per round, £20.00 per day; weekends with a member only £8.00. *Eating facilities:* bar and restaurant. *Visitors:* welcome, after 9.30am weekdays only. *Society Meetings:* catered for by arrangement. Secretary: Major J.L. Hollaway (0929 554147).

WEYMOUTH. **Wessex Golf Centre,** Rapipole Lane, Weymouth (Weymouth (0305) 784737). *Location:* on bypass road by Weymouth Football Club. Flat public course. 9 holes, 1385 yards. Par 3. Driving range. *Green Fees:* information not available. *Visitors:* welcome; public course.

WEYMOUTH. **Weymouth Golf Club Ltd,** Links Road, Weymouth DT4 0PF (0305 784994). *Location:* A354 from Dorchester, take last exit at Manor roundabout then second left at Chafeys roundabout. Undulating parkland. 18 holes, 6009 yards, 5410 metres. S.S.S. 69 (Par 70). Practice area. *Green Fees:* weekdays £16.00, weekends and Bank Holidays £22.00. Half price playing with a member. Juniors half price. *Eating facilities:* food and drink always available. *Visitors:* welcome, but only with Handicap Certificate. *Society Meetings:* catered for weekdays only, arrange with Secretary. Professional: Mr Des Lochrie (0305 773997). Secretary: Mr Colin Robinson (0305 773981).

# County Durham

BARNARD CASTLE. **Barnard Castle Golf Club,** Harmire Road, Barnard Castle DL12 8QN (Barnard Castle (0833) 37237). *Location:* one mile north of Barnard Castle Town Centre on the B6278. Open parkland, 18 holes, 5838 yards. S.S.S. 68. *Green Fees:* weekdays £13.50, weekends and Bank Holidays £20.00. *Eating facilities:* full catering – limited on Mondays. *Visitors:* welcome, but booking system at weekends and Bank Holidays. *Society Meetings:* catered for by prior arrangement. Professional: J. Harrison (0833) 31980). Secretary: A.W. Lavender (0833 38355).

BISHOP AUCKLAND. **Bishop Auckland Golf Club,** High Plains, Durham Road, Bishop Auckland DL14 8DL (Bishop Auckland (0388) 602198). *Location:* leave Bishop Auckland Market Place on route to Spennymoor/Durham, half a mile on left. Parkland, 18 holes, 6420 yards, 6124 metres. S.S.S. 71 (Par 72). Practice fairways. *Green Fees:* weekdays £16.00 per round, £20.00 per day; weekends £22.00 per round. Visiting parties over 20 have day reduction to £16.00. *Eating facilities:* bar, full catering facilities except Mondays. *Visitors:* welcome mid-week only. Ladies' day Tuesday. Two snooker tables. *Society Meetings:* catered for on application, not weekends and Christmas period, and official Handicap required. Professional: Mr D. Skiffington (0388 661618). Secretary: Mr G. Thatcher (0388 663648).

BRANCEPETH. **Brancepeth Castle Golf Club,** Brancepeth DH7 8EA (Durham (091-378) 0075). *Location:* four miles west of Durham city on A690 Durham to Crook road. Parkland. 18 holes, 6415 yards. S.S.S. 71. Practice ground. *Green Fees:* weekdays £23.00 per day, weekends by prior booking £30.00. *Eating facilities:* available every day – limited Mondays. *Visitors:* welcome weekdays, weekends by prior arrangement. *Society Meetings:* catered for Monday to Friday only. Professional: D.C. Howdon (091-378 0183). Secretary: J.T. Ross (091378 0075).

CHESTER-LE-STREET. **Chester-le-Street Golf Club,** Lumley Park, Chester-le-Street DH3 4NS (Chester-le-Street (091-388) 3218). *Location:* Off A1 adjacent to Lumley Castle, half a mile east of Chester-le-Street. Parkland, 18 holes, 6054 yards, 5535 metres. S.S.S. 69. *Green Fees:* weekdays £20.00, weekends and Public Holidays £30.00. *Eating facilities:* lunches, snacks, dinners, bar. *Visitors:* welcome weekdays with letter of introduction or Handicap Certificate, but some restrictions weekends and Public Holidays. *Society Meetings:* catered for but not weekends and Public Holidays. Professional: A. Hartley (091-389 0157). Secretary: W.B. Dodds (091-388 3218).

CHESTER-LE-STREET. **Roseberry Grange Golf Club,** Grange Villa, Chester-le-Street DH2 3NF (091-370 0670). *Location:* three miles west of Chester-le-Street on A693. Parkland course. 18 holes, 5809 yards. S.S.S. 68. Driving range. *Green Fees:* weekdays £7.60 per round, £10.50 per day; weekends £10.30 per round, £13.00 per day ticket. Half price weekdays for Juniors and Senior Citizens. *Eating facilities:* bar meals 12 noon to 2.00pm and 7.00pm to 9.30pm. *Visitors:* welcome, no restrictions. Professional: A. Hartley (091-370 0660). Secretary: J. Turnbull (091-370 2047).

CONSETT. **Consett and District Golf Club,** Elmfield Road, Consett DH8 5NN (Consett (0207) 502186). *Location:* A691 from Durham (12 miles), A692 from Gateshead (12 miles). 18 holes, 6013 yards. S.S.S. 69. *Green Fees:* weekdays £15.00; weekends £20.00. *Eating facilities:* full catering available. *Visitors:* most welcome without reservation. *Society Meetings:* catered for by arrangement, enquiries welcomed. Professional: S. Corbally (0207 580210). Secretary: Mr J. Horrill (0207 562261).

CROOK. **Crook Golf Club,** Low Jobs Hill, Crook DL15 9AA (Bishop Auckland (0388) 762429). *Location:* six miles west of Durham City on A689. Hilly, demanding parkland course. 18 holes, 6075 yards. S.S.S. 69. Practice nets and fairway. *Green Fees:* weekdays £12.00; weekends £15.00. *Eating facilities:* full catering facilities. *Visitors:* at any time other than when club competitions are held. Caravan Club Site (5 Vans) adjacent clubhouse. *Society Meetings:* catered for by arrangement with Secretary. Secretary: R. King (0388 746400).

DARLINGTON. **Blackwell Grange Golf Club,** Briar Close, Blackwell, Darlington DL3 8QX (0325 464464). *Location:* one mile south of Darlington on A66 turn into Blackwell. Signposts to Club. Parkland course. 18 holes, 5621 yards. S.S.S. 67. *Green Fees:* weekdays £15.00 per round, £18.00 per day; weekends and Bank Holidays £20 per round. *Eating facilities:* full menu except Mondays. *Visitors:* welcome without reservation except weekends. *Society Meetings:* catered for except Wednesday and weekends. Professional: Ralph Givens (0325 462088). Secretary: F. Hewitson (0325 464458).

DARLINGTON. **Dinsdale Spa Golf Club,** Middleton-St-George, Darlington DL2 1DW (Dinsdale (0325) 332222). *Location:* Darlington to Teesside, Airport Road, right at Middleton-St-George, one mile on Neasham Road. Flat course. 18 holes, 6022 yards. S.S.S. 69. Large practice ground. *Green Fees:* weekdays £15.00; weekends with a member only. *Eating facilities:* full catering available. *Visitors:* welcome Wednesdays, Thursdays and Fridays. *Society Meetings:* catered for Monday to Friday by arrangement. Professional: D.N. Dodds (0325 332515). Secretary: Mr P.J. Wright (0325 332297).

DARLINGTON. **Stressholme Golf Club,** Snipe Lane, Darlington (0325 353073). *Location:* one mile south of Darlington town centre near junction of A66 and A167. 18 holes, 6511 yards, 5953 metres. S.S.S. 71. Practice ground. *Green Fees:* £6.35 weekdays; £7.40 weekends and Bank Holidays. Junior rates £3.70 and after 1pm weekend half price. *Eating facilities:* two bars, three course meals to snacks. *Visitors:* always welcome anytime. *Society Meetings:* all welcome any time – reserved tees available. Professional: Tim Jenkins (0325 461002). Secretary: Graham A. Patrick (0325 466587).

DARLINGTON. **The Darlington Golf Club (Members) Ltd,** Haughton Grange, Darlington DL1 3JD (0325 463936). *Location:* northern outskirts of town A1150 off A167, approximately 800 yards. Parkland, flat. 18 holes, 6271 yards. S.S.S. 70. Large practice ground. *Green Fees:* weekdays £20.00 per round/day; weekends with member only. *Eating facilities:* first class catering, Men's Bar, lounge bar available. *Visitors:* welcome weekdays with reservation, must be members of recognised golf club. *Society Meetings:* by arrangement weekdays, no more than 40 members. Professional: I. Todd (0325 462955). Secretary: Mr G.E. Callender (0325 355324).

DURHAM. **Durham City Golf Club,** Littleburn, Langley Moor, Durham DH7 8HL (Durham (091) 3780806). *Location:* from Durham City take A690 to Crook – course signposted in Langley Moor. Parkland with river. 18 holes, 6326 yards. S.S.S. 70. Large practice area. *Green Fees:* weekdays £16.00, weekends £20.00. £14.00 per person for parties of 20 or more. *Eating facilities:* no catering Mondays or Thursday evenings. *Visitors:* welcome, only restrictions when club competitions are being held – ring Professional for details. *Society Meetings:* welcome, but restricted to weekdays. Professional: S. Corbally (091 3780029). Secretary: I. Wilson (091 3780069).

DURHAM. **Mount Oswald Golf Club,** South Road, Durham DH1 3TQ (091-386 7527). *Location:* A1(M) Junction marked Bowburn. A177 Durham City A1050. Parkland, partially wooded. 18 holes, 6101 yards. S.S.S. 69. *Green Fees:* weekdays £10.00 per round, weekends and Bank Holidays £12.00 per round. *Eating facilities:* bar meals, Sunday lunches, set meals, etc. *Visitors:* welcome except Sunday mornings before 10am (members only). Bookings only at weekends and Bank Holidays. *Society Meetings:* welcome, same restrictions as visitors, must order food. General Manager: S.E. Reeve (091-386 7527).

NEWTON AYCLIFFE. **Aycliffe Golf Club,** Oak Leaf Sports Complex, School Aycliffe Lane, Newton Aycliffe TL5 6QZ. *Location:* between A167 – A68, near School Aycliffe, five minutes off A1. Rolling parkland. 9 holes (to be extended to 18), 5962 yards, 5150 metres. S.S.S. 69. Driving range. *Green Fees:* information not provided. Reduced rates for Senior Citizens and under 16's. *Eating facilities:* bar, limited eating facilities. Contact Stewardess (0325 300700). *Visitors:* welcome by prior arrangement, slight restriction Saturday and Sunday mornings for club competitions. *Society Meetings:* all welcome by prior arrangement. Professional: Robert Lister (0325 310820). Secretary: W.J. Findley (0325 312994).

NEWTON AYCLIFFE. **Woodham Golf and Country Club,** Burnhill Way, Newton Aycliffe DL5 4PN (Newton Aycliffe (0325) 320574; Fax: 0325 315254). *Location:* A167, one mile north of Newton Aycliffe on the Shildon road. Parkland, wooded with lakes. 18 holes, 6727 yards. S.S.S. 72. Practice grounds. *Green Fees:* weekdays £15.00 per round, £20.00 per day; weekends £20.00 per round, £25.00 per day. Discounts for group bookings. *Eating facilities:* bar snacks, meals and a la carte restaurant available. *Visitors:* unlimited weekdays; tee restrictions after 10.30 am weekends and Bank Holidays. *Society Meetings:* welcome by arrangement. Professional: Payl Lunson (0325 318346). Secretary: Richard Smith.

SEAHAM. **Seaham Golf Club,** Shrewsbury Street, Seaham SR7 7RD (091-5812354). *Location:* off A19 to Dawdon, Seaham. Heathland, 18 holes, 6017 yards. S.S.S. 69. Practice area. *Green Fees:* weekdays £15.00 (£7.00 playing with a member); weekends and Bank Holidays £18.00 (£9.00 playing with a member). *Eating facilities:* snacks available, meals on request. *Visitors:* welcome, unrestricted. *Society Meetings:* welcome on application. Secretary: Vincent Smith (091-5815413).

STANLEY. **Beamish Park Golf Club,** Beamish, Stanley DH9 0RH (Durham (091-370) 1382). *Location:* follow directions to Beamish Museum. Parkland, 18 holes, 6205 yards. S.S.S. 70. Two practice areas. *Green Fees:* weekdays £16.00 per round, £20.00 per day; weekends £24.00 per round, £30.00 per day. *Eating facilities:* bar and a la carte menu. *Visitors:* welcome, Monday to Friday. Professional: C. Cole (091-370 1984). Secretary: L. Gilbert (091-370 1382).

STANLEY. **South Moor Golf Club,** The Middles, Craghead, Stanley DH9 6AG (Stanley (0207) 232848). *Location:* eight miles north-west of Durham, seven miles north-west of A1 (M) from Chester-le-Street. Parkland and moorland. 18 holes, 6445 yards, 5891 metres. S.S.S. 71. *Green Fees:* weekdays £14.00 per round, £21.00 per day; weekends and Bank Holidays £25 per day. *Eating facilities:* available. *Visitors:* members only before 9.30am and 12 – 2pm. No casual visitors weekends or Bank Holidays unless with member. *Society Meetings:* catered for except Sundays. Professional: S. Cowell (0207 283525). Secretary: B. Davison (0207 239719).

# Essex

BASILDON. **Basildon Golf Club,** Clay Hill Lane, Basildon (Basildon (0268) 533297). *Location:* off A13 or A127 on A176 – Kingswood Roundabout. Undulating woodland. 18 holes, 6122 yards. S.S.S. 69. Practice area. *Green Fees:* £8.70 weekdays; £13.50 weekends. *Eating facilities:* snack meals/bar. *Visitors:* welcome anytime, booking system at weekends and Bank Holidays. *Society Meetings:* catered for – apply to Basildon Council. Professional: Mr G. Hill (0268 533352). Secretary: A. M. Burch (0268 533849).

BASILDON. **Pipps Hill Golf Club,** Pipps Hill Country Club, Cranes Farm Road, Basildon (Basildon (0268) 23456). 9 hole course, 5658 yards. *Green Fees:* on request. *Visitors:* unrestricted at all times. Golf days catered for.

BRAINTREE. **Braintree Golf Club,** Kings Lane, Stisted, Braintree CM7 8DA (Braintree (0376) 24117). *Location:* A120 to Colchester, 300 yards east of Braintree by-pass, signposted Stisted and Golf Club. Parkland, with slopes down to the river. 18 holes, 6153 yards, S.S.S. 69. Practice ground, pitching area. *Green Fees:* £20.00 weekdays, £35.00 Saturdays only. *Eating facilities:* available. *Visitors:* welcome Monday to Saturdays; Fridays and Sundays must have Handicap Certificate. *Society Meetings:* catered for Mondays, Wednesdays and Thursdays. Professional: A.K. Parcell (0376 43465). Secretary: G.J. Bardsley (0376 46079).

BRAINTREE. **Towerlands Golf Club,** Panfield Road, Braintree CM7 5BJ (Braintree (0376) 326802). *Location:* off A120 into Braintree, then B1053. Undulating course. 9 holes, 2703 yards. S.S.S. 66. Golf range. *Green Fees:* weekdays £8.50 for 9 holes, £10.50 for 18 holes; weekends and Bank Holidays £12.50 for 18 holes only after 12 noon. *Eating facilities:* full bar and restaurant. *Visitors:* welcome. Wide range of other sports facilities. *Society Meetings:* by arrangement. Professional: A. Boulter (0376 347951). Secretary: Mr K. Cooper (0376 513519).

BRENTWOOD. **Bentley Golf Club,** Ongar Road, Brentwood CM15 9SS (Coxtie Green (0277) 373179). *Location:* situated on A128 approximately five miles from Junction 28 of M25. Flat course. 18 holes, 6709 yards, 6136 metres. S.S.S. 72. Practice field. *Green Fees:* weekdays £19.00 per round, £25.00 day ticket. Reductions for Senior Citizens and Juniors. *Eating facilities:* snacks and bar available all day. *Visitors:* welcome weekdays with Handicap Certificate or letter of introduction. Restrictions Bank Holidays; weekends with member only. *Society Meetings:* welcome by prior arrangement. Professional: Keith Bridges (0277 372933). Secretary: J.A. Vivers (0277 373179).

BRENTWOOD. **Hartswood Golf Club, (Play on Brentwood Municipal),** King George's Playing Fields, Ingrave Road, Brentwood (Brentwood (0277) 217128). *Location:* one mile south of Brentwood on A128. Parkland, 18 holes, 6238 yards. S.S.S. 70. *Green Fees:* information not provided. *Eating facilities:* full catering available. *Visitors:* welcome without reservation. *Society Meetings:* limited number of society bookings. Professional: J. Stanion (0277 230474). Secretary: A.D. Jevans (0277 218850).

BRENTWOOD. **The Warley Park Golf Club,** Magpie Lane, Little Warley, Brentwood CM13 3DX (0277 224891). *Location:* leave M25 at Intersection 29. A127 towards Southend. Turn left three-quarters-of-a-mile Little Warley, Hall Lane. Turn left into Magpie Lane. Parkland, 3 Courses, (27 holes). S.S.S. 70-69. Large practice area, putting greens. *Green Fees:* weekdays £20.00 per round, £30.00 per day. *Eating facilities:* lounge bar and restaurant/spike bar. *Visitors:* welcome Monday to Friday, must produce club Handicap Certificate. *Society Meetings:* catered for, minimum 20. Professional: P. O'Connor (0277 212552). Secretary: K. Regan (0277 224891).

BRENTWOOD. **Thorndon Park Golf Club Ltd,** Thorndon Park, Ingrave, Brentwood CM13 3RH (0277 811666). *Location:* three miles south of Brentwood on A128. 18 holes, 6403 yards. S.S.S. 71. *Green Fees:* £40.00 per day, £30.00 per round weekdays, weekends with members only. *Eating facilities:* lunches served at club. *Visitors:* welcome with reservation, weekdays subject to prior permission. *Society Meetings:* catered for. Professional: Brian White (0277 810736). Secretary: J.E. Leggitt (0277 810345).

BULPHAN. **The Langdon Hills Golf Club,** Lower Dunton Road, Bulphan RM14 3TY (0268 548061; Fax: 0268 548065). *Location:* 8 miles from M25, Dartford River crossing, Basildon three miles between A127 and A13. Gently undulating parkland. 18 holes, 6485 yards. S.S.S. 71. 22 bay floodlit driving range, large shortgame practice area, 3 full practice holes making 9 hole course. *Green Fees:* weekdays £18.50 per round, £26.50 per day; weekends £25.00 per round. *Eating facilities:* restaurant, two bars and private function room. *Visitors:* welcome most times, ring for details. 42 bedroomed hotel. *Society Meetings:* welcomed. Professional: John Sunger (Golf Director). Secretary: Mrs C. Hammond.

BURNHAM-ON-CROUCH.  **Burnham-on-Crouch Golf Club Ltd,** Ferry Road, Creaksea CM0 8PQ (Maldon (0621) 782282). *Location:* one mile west of Burnham-on-Crouch, turn right off B1010. Undulating meadowland. 9 holes, 5918 yards. S.S.S. 68 (additional 9 holes due to open mid 1993). *Green Fees:* £20.00 weekdays. *Eating facilities:* teas, evening meals except Monday. *Visitors:* no visitors weekends and Bank Holidays, must commence play Mondays to Fridays (except Thursdays) 9.30am to 2pm. Thursdays 12 noon to 2pm. *Society Meetings:* catered for Tuesdays. Secretary: to be appointed.

CANVEY ISLAND. **Castle Point Golf Club,** Somnes Avenue, Canvey Island SS8 9FG (0268 511149). *Location:* just off A13, A130 to Canvey Island. Seaside links course. 18 holes, 5627 yards, 5146 metres. S.S.S.

69. Driving range. *Green Fees:* weekdays £8.40; weekends £12.50. Juniors and Senior Citizens £4.20 weekdays. *Eating facilities:* restaurant and bar available. *Visitors:* welcome anytime. Changing facilities, showers. *Society Meetings:* welcome, catered for weekdays only. Professional: John Hudson (0268 510830). Secretary: Vic Russell (0268 698909).

CHELMSFORD. **Channels Golf Club,** Belsteads Farm Lane, Little Waltham, Chelmsford CM3 3PT (0245 440003). *Location:* A12 – Chelmsford A130. Old sand and gravel quarry, incorporating water, hills, etc. 18 holes, 5980 yards. S.S.S. 69. 9 hole pitch and putt. *Green Fees:* £27.50 per day weekdays; weekends only with a member £15.00. Juniors and Senior Citizens £13 per day weekdays. *Eating facilities:* excellent restaurant and bar in 13th century clubhouse. *Visitors:* welcome weekdays only. *Society Meetings:* catered for weekdays. Professional: I.B. Sinclair (0245 441056). Secretary: Mr A.M. Squire (0245 440005).

CHELMSFORD. **Chelmsford Golf Club,** Widford Road, Chelmsford (0245 250555). *Location:* close to Widford roundabout on A1016. 18 holes, 5944 yards. S.S.S. 68. *Green Fees:* information not provided. *Eating facilities:* dining room and bar. *Visitors:* welcome Monday to Friday with reservation. Professional: D. Bailey. Manager: Wg. Cdr. B.A. Templeman-Rooke DSO, DFC, AFC, RAF (Retd.) (0245 256483).

CHIGWELL. **Chigwell Golf Club,** The Clubhouse, High Road, Chigwell IG7 5BH (081-500 2059). *Location:* On A113, 14 miles from London, seven miles Waltham Abbey exit M25. Testing undulating parkland course. 18 holes, 6279 yards. S.S.S. 70. Practice shed and ground. *Green Fees:* weekdays £28.00 per round, £35.00 per day; weekends with introduction by member only. *Eating facilities:* restaurant and bars available. *Visitors:* weekdays by prior arrangement, Handicap Certificate required and membership of authorised Golf Club. *Society Meetings:* weekdays by arrangement. Professional: R. Beard (081-500 2384). Secretary: Mr M. McL. Farnsworth (081-500 2059).

CHIGWELL. **Hainault Forest Golf Club,** Romford Road, Chigwell IG7 4QW (081-500 2097). *Location:* off A12 towards Chigwell-Hainault. Flat wooded course with several lakes. 18 holes, 6600 yards. S.S.S. 71. 18 holes, 5754 yards. S.S.S. 67. Practice field and putting green. *Green Fees:* weekdays £8.80, weekends £11.00. *Eating facilities:* course restaurant; bars in private club. *Visitors:* public course. *Society Meetings:* weekdays by arrangement with Secretary. Professional: E. Frost (081-500 2131).

CLACTON. **Clacton Golf Club,** West Road, Clacton (0255 421919). Seaside course. 18 holes, 6244 yards. S.S.S. 71. *Green Fees:* £20.00 weekdays, £30.00 weekends and Bank Holidays. *Eating facilities:* full catering by prior arrangement. *Visitors:* welcome with reservation and current Handicap Certificate. Weekends and Bank Holidays not before 11.00am. *Society Meetings:* Monday to Friday catered for by arrangement. Professional: S.J. Levermore. Secretary: H.F. Lucas.

COLCHESTER. **Birch Grove Golf Club,** Layer Road, Colchester CO2 0HS (0206 734276). *Location:*

on B1026, two miles south of town. Parkland – small but challenging. 9 holes, 4038 yards. S.S.S. 60. *Green Fees:* £10.00 weekdays, £12.00 weekends and Bank Holidays for 18 holes. *Eating facilities:* hot meals and snacks are available during opening hours. *Visitors:* welcome without reservation Monday to Saturday and after 1pm Sundays. *Society Meetings:* catered for weekdays. Secretary: Mrs M. Marston.

COLCHESTER. **Colchester Golf Club,** Braiswick, Colchester CO4 5AU (Colchester (0206) 852946). *Location:* one mile north-west of Colchester North Station, on A133. Parkland. 18 holes, 6319 yards. S.S.S. 70. *Green Fees:* £20.00 per day weekdays; £25.00 weekends. *Eating facilities:* catering available all day. *Visitors:* welcome except Saturday and Sunday mornings. *Society Meetings:* catered for by prior arrangement. Professional: Mark Angel (0206 853920). Secretary: Mrs J. Boorman (0206 853396).

COLCHESTER. **Earls Colne Golf and Leisure Centre,** Earls Colne, Colchester CO6 2NS (0787 224466; Fax: 0787 224410). *Location:* we are on the B1024 Earls Colne – Coggeshall Road, four miles A12, two miles A120 (Euro-Route), one mile A604. Flat parkland courses (3). 4 hole teaching course; The Honeywood Course – 9 holes, 3100 yards. Par 34; 18 hole course 6715 yards. Par 73. *Green Fees:* weekdays £12.00; weekends £15.00. *Eating facilities:* à la carte restaurant, poolside grill and spike bar, two bars. *Visitors:* pay and play course – visitors welcome anytime. Full leisure centre including gym, swimming pool, whirlpool spa. *Society Meetings:* welcome anytime. Professional: Owen McKenna. Secretary: Sally Blackwell.

COLD NORTON. **Three Rivers Golf and Country Club,** Stow Road, Cold Norton (Maldon (Essex) (0621) 828631). *Location:* 12 miles Chelmsford and five miles from Maldon at Cold Norton Village. 18 and 9 holes, 6609 yards. S.S.S. 72. *Green Fees:* on application. *Eating facilities:* comprehensive. *Visitors:* welcome Monday to Friday without reservation. En suite accommodation available (inc. swimming pool, snooker, saunas, sun beds, 4 squash courts, 5 tennis courts). *Society Meetings:* catered for mainly Tuesdays and Thursdays. Professional: Lionel Platts. General Manager: Stephen Evans.

EPPING. **Theydon Bois Golf Club,** Theydon Road, Epping CM16 4EH. *Location:* M25 Waltham Abbey/Epping A121 London to Cambridge, turn right at Bell Hotel. Wooded course. 18 holes, 5472 yards. S.S.S. 68. Practice area. *Green Fees:* (1992 rates) £23.00 per day, £34.00 at weekends. *Eating facilities:* restaurant and bar. *Visitors:* welcome except Wednesday and Thursday morning. Not available November to March. *Society Meetings:* Monday and Tuesday £32 per person plus catering per day. Professional: R.T. Joyce (0992 812460). Secretary: Ian McDonald (0992 813054).

FRINTON-ON-SEA. **Frinton Golf Club,** 1 Esplanade, Frinton-on-Sea CO13 9EP. *Location:* 17 miles east of Colchester, A12 – A133, B1033. Flat seaside links course, strength of wind always a feature. 18 holes, 6265 yards. S.S.S. 70. Short Course 2508 yards, no Handicap Certificate required. Practice facilities. *Green*

*Fees:* £22.00. *Eating facilities:* snack and restaurant facilities. *Visitors:* welcome, check with Secretary. Handicap Certificate required. *Society Meetings:* catered for Wednesday and Thursday by arrangement. Professional: Peter Taggert (0255 671618). Secretary: Lt Col R.W. Attrill (0255 674618).

HARLOW. **Canons Brook Golf Club,** Elizabeth Way, Harlow CM19 5BE (Harlow (0279) 25142). *Location:* A414. 18 holes, 6745 yards. S.S.S. 73. *Green Fees:* £25.00 per weekday. *Eating facilities:* full catering except Mondays. *Visitors:* welcome weekdays. *Society Meetings:* catered for except Mondays. Professional: Roger Yates (0279 418357). Secretary: G.E. Chambers (0279 421482).

HARWICH. **Harwich and Dovercourt Golf Club,** Station Road, Parkeston, Harwich CO12 4NZ (Harwich (0255) 3616). *Location:* A604 thence to sign Parkeston Quay. Course marked on left hand side of Parkeston Road. 9 holes, 5862 yards. S.S.S. 68. *Green Fees:* information not provided. No visitors Saturdays, Sundays and Bank Holidays unless playing with a member. *Eating facilities:* order before playing. *Visitors:* welcome with Handicap Certificates. *Society Meetings:* catered for. Secretary: Mr B.Q. Dunham.

ILFORD. **Fairlop Waters,** Forest Road, Barkingside, Ilford IG6 3JA (081-500 9911). *Location:* two miles north of Ilford, half a mile from A12, one and a half miles from southern end of M11. Parkland course. 18 holes, 6281 yards. S.S.S. 70. *Green Fees:* £7.00 weekdays; £10.00 weekends. *Eating facilities:* Daltons American Diner open from breakfast till late 7 days a week, lunchtime bar food. *Visitors:* welcome all week. Banqueting for 250 and conferences. Professional: Tony Bowers (081-501 1881). Manager: Keith Robson.

ILFORD. **Ilford Golf Club,** 291 Wanstead Park Road, Ilford RG1 3TR (081-554 5174). *Location:* at end of M11. Parkland with winding river. 18 holes, 5787 yards. S.S.S. 68. *Green Fees:* weekdays £13.50, weekends £16.00. *Eating facilities:* restaurant and bar. *Visitors:* welcome weekdays, restricted times at weekends. *Society Meetings:* welcome. Professional: S. Dowsett (081-554 0094). Secretary: P.H. Newson (081-554 2930).

LEIGH-ON-SEA. **Belfairs Golf Club,** Eastwood Road North, Leigh-on-Sea SS9 4LR (Southend (0702) 526911). Park front 9, heavy woodland back 9; easy walking but challenging golf. Play over Belfairs municipal course, 18 holes, 5857 yards. S.S.S. 68. *Green Fees:* weekdays £10.20, weekends and Bank Holidays £15.30 (approximately). *Visitors:* unrestricted on the course but no clubhouse facilities available to non-members. Bookings required at weekends, Bank Holidays and during school holidays. Professional: Roger Foreman (0702 520202). Secretary: J.W. Pacey (0702 520322).

LOUGHTON. **Loughton Golf Club,** Clay's Lane, Loughton IG10 2RZ (081-502 2923). *Location:* just north of Loughton, on edge of Epping Forest. Flat parkland. 9 holes, 4700 yards. S.S.S. 63. *Green Fees:* weekdays £4.00 9 holes, £6.00 18 holes; weekends £5.30 for 9 holes, £9.50 for 18 holes. *Eating facilities:* bar, snacks available. *Visitors:* welcome, telephone to

book. *Society Meetings:* welcome. Professional/Manager: Brian Davies.

MALDON. **Bunsay Downs Golf Club,** Little Baddow Road, Woodham Walter, Maldon CM9 6RW (Danbury (024 541) 2369 or 2648). *Location:* 7 miles east of Chelmsford off A414 at Woodham Walter, left onto Little Baddow Road. Undulating landscaped course. 9 holes, 2913 yards. S.S.S. 68. Par 3 course, indoor range. *Green Fees:* information not supplied. *Eating facilities:* bar/grill restaurant. *Visitors:* welcome at all times. Gift shop. *Society Meetings:* small societies welcome. Professional: Mickey Walker (024 541 2648).

MALDON. **Forrester Park Golf and Tennis Club,** Forrester Park, Beckingham Road, Great Totham, Near Maldon CM9 8EA (Maldon (0621) 891903). *Location:* three miles off A12 Rivenhall turn-off, on B1022 in Great Totham, near Witham between Compasses and Bull. Parkland course. 18 holes, 6050 yards. S.S.S. 69. *Green Fees:* weekdays £13.00; weekends £18.00. *Eating facilities:* two bars, meals or bar snacks. *Visitors:* welcome weekdays but not after 4pm Wednesdays nor Saturdays, Sundays and Bank Holidays before 1pm. *Society Meetings:* welcome with prior reservation. Secretary: Tim Forrester-Muir (0621 891406).

MALDON. **Maldon Golf Club,** Beeleigh, Langford, Maldon CM9 6LL (Maldon (0621) 853212). *Location:* B1019 two miles north west of Maldon, turn off at the Essex Waterworks. Flat parkland. 9 holes, 6197 yards, 5667 metres. S.S.S. 69. *Green Fees:* 18 holes £15.00, all day £20.00 weekdays; 18 holes £12.00, all day £17.00 with a member only weekends. *Eating facilities:* by prior arrangement only; bar. *Visitors:* welcome weekdays, Handicap Certificates required. *Society Meetings:* catered for by arrangement. Secretary: G.R. Bezant.

MALDON. **Quietwaters Hotel, Golf and Country Club,** Colchester Road, Tolleshunt Knights, Maldon CM9 8HX (Maldon (0621) 868888; Fax: 0621 869696). *Location:* eight miles from Colchester on B1026. Links type courses. (Two courses). Links Course – 18 holes, 6222 yards, 5690 metres. S.S.S. 70. Lakes Course – 18 holes, 6767 yards, 6186 metres. S.S.S. 72. *Green Fees:* Links – weekdays £18.00, weekends £22.50; Lakes – weekdays £40.00, weekends £50.00. *Eating facilities:* full catering available in hotel restaurant, bar snacks. *Visitors:* welcome at most times except Sunday mornings. *Society Meetings:* catered for. Professional: Gary Pike/Clive Tucker (0621 819540). Director of Golf: P.D. Keeble (0621 868888).

MALDON. **Warren Golf Club,** Woodham Walter, Maldon CM9 6RW (Danbury (0245) 223198/223258; Fax: 0245 223989). *Location:* close to Chelmsford. A414 turn off to Maldon. Undulating wooded course. 18 holes, 6211 yards. S.S.S. 70. Large practice area. *Green Fees:* £25.00 per round, £30.00 per day weekdays. *Eating facilities:* restaurant, bar, bar snack menu. *Visitors:* welcome with reservation weekdays except Wednesdays am. Handicap Certificate required. *Society Meetings:* catered for weekdays – up to 40 players. Professional: Mickey Walker (0245 224662). Manager: M.L.F. Durham.

OCKENDON. **Belhus Park Golf Club,** Belhus Park, Aveley By-Pass, South Ockendon RM15 4QR (0708

852248 complex, 0708 854748 office). *Location:* on A13 London – Southend Road, approximately one mile from Dartford Tunnel. Parkland. 18 holes, 5188 yards. S.S.S. 68. Driving range. *Green Fees:* £10.25. *Eating facilities:* cafe and bar. *Visitors:* welcome anytime (municipal course), but booking essential weekends and Bank Holidays. Swimming pool. *Society Meetings:* by arrangement with complex. Professional: Gary Lunn (0708 854260). Secretary: D.A. Faust (07084 46224).

ORSETT. **Orsett Golf Club,** Brentwood Road, Orsett RM16 3DS (0375 891352). *Location:* A13 junction roundabout with A128. South towards Chadwell St. Mary on A128. Heathland, parkland course. 18 holes, 6614 yards. S.S.S. 72. *Green Fees:* £30.00 per round or day. *Eating facilities:* full catering available. *Visitors:* welcome on weekdays only. Must be members of a club and have handicap. Proof must be produced. *Society Meetings:* welcome on Mondays, Tuesdays and Wednesdays. Professional: Robert Newberry (0375 891797). Secretary: P.M. Pritchard (0375 891226).

ROCHFORD near. **Ballards Gore Golf Club,** Gore Road, Canewdon, Near Rochford SS4 2DA (0702 258917). *Location:* Southend Airport three miles, London via A127, club two miles from Rochford. Parkland with lakes. 18 holes, 7062 yards. S.S.S. 74. Practice area. *Green Fees:* £20.00 weekdays. *Eating facilities:* diningroom (100 covers). *Visitors:* welcome weekdays only. *Society Meetings:* catered for by arrangement. Professional: Ian Marshall (0702 258924). Secretary: N.G. Patient (0702 258917).

ROCHFORD. **Rochford Hundred Golf Club,** Hall Lane, Rochford SS4 1NW (Southend-on-Sea (0702) 544302). *Location:* B1013 four miles north of Southend. Parkland course. 18 holes, 6132 yards. S.S.S. 69. *Green Fees:* information not provided. *Eating facilities:* full restaurant and snack facilities and bars. *Society Meetings:* catered for. Professional: Gary Shipley (0702 548968). Secretary: A.H. Bondfield.

ROMFORD. **Havering Municipal Golf Course,** Risebridge Chase, Lower Bedfords Road, Romford. *Location:* Gallows Corner, straight road, left turn at junction, Collier Row. 18 holes, 6342 yards. S.S.S. 70. *Green Fees:* information not provided. *Visitors:* welcome without reservation. Professional: Paul Jennings. Pro Shop: (0708 741429).

ROMFORD. **Maylands Golf and Country Club,** Harold Park, Romford RM3 0AZ (0708 342055). *Location:* directly on A12 between Romford and Brentwood. 18 holes, 6182 yards. S.S.S. 70. Buggy hire. *Green Fees:* £20.00 per round, £30.00 per day. *Eating facilities:* by arrangement. *Visitors:* welcome with reservation. *Society Meetings:* catered for. Professional: John Hopkin (0708 346466). Secretary/Proprietor: P. S. Taylor (0708 373080).

ROMFORD. **Risebridge Golf Club,** Risebridge Chase, Lower Bedfords Road, Romford (Romford (0708) 41429). *Location:* Gallows Corner, straight road, left turn at junction, Collier Row. 18 holes, 6342 yards. S.S.S. 70. *Green Fees:* information not available. *Eating facilities:* available. *Visitors:* welcome without reservation. *Society Meetings:* catered for. Professional: Paul Jennings. Secretary: Mrs Joan Simper (0708 765084).

SAFFRON WALDEN. **Saffron Walden Golf Club,** Windmill Hill, Saffron Walden CB10 1BX (Saffron Walden (0799) 22786). *Location:* end of town on A130 to Cambridge. 18 holes, 6617 yards. S.S.S. 72. *Green Fees:* £25.00 per day or round (weekdays only). *Eating facilities:* lunches and snacks available. *Visitors:* welcome with current Handicap Certificate. *Society Meetings:* catered for Mondays, Wednesdays and Thursdays. Professional: Philip Davis. General Manager: David Smith.

SOUTH BENFLEET. **Boyce Hill Golf Club Ltd,** Vicarage Hill, South Benfleet SS7 1PD (Benfleet (0268) 793625). *Location:* one-and-a-half-miles from A13 or A127. Hilly course, 18 holes. S.S.S. 68. *Green Fees:* weekdays £25.00 per round, £30.00 per day. *Eating facilities:* full dining facilities. *Visitors:* welcome, except Tuesday mornings. *Society Meetings:* catered for Thursdays only. Professional: G. Burroughs (0268 752565). Secretary: J.E. Atkins (0268 793625).

SOUTHEND-ON-SEA. **Southend-on-Sea Golf Club,** Belfairs Park, Eastwood Road North, Leigh-on-Sea SS9 4LR (0702 524836). *Location:* A127 London to Southend Road. Parkland/wooded course (Belfairs Municipal course). 18 holes, 5857 yards. S.S.S. 68. *Green Fees:* weekdays £11.20; weekends £16.80. *Eating facilities:* restaurant in the park. *Visitors:* welcome, unrestricted, but bookings required for weekends and Bank Holidays. Booking by phone to Starters Hut (0702 525345). Professional: Roger Foreman (0702 520202). Secretary: N.A. Dye (0702 340472).

SOUTHEND-ON-SEA. **Thorpe Hall Golf Club,** Thorpe Hall Avenue, Thorpe Bay, Southend-on-Sea. *Location:* one mile east of Southend-on-Sea. Parkland. 18 holes, 6286 yards. S.S.S. 71. *Green Fees:* on application. *Eating facilities:* restaurant open every day except Mondays. *Visitors:* welcome weekdays with Handicap Certificate, weekends with members only. *Society Meetings:* catered for. Professional: Gary Harvey (0702 588195). Secretary: G.R.G. Winkless (0702 582205).

STAPLEFORD ABBOTTS. **Stapleford Abbotts Golf Club,** Horsemans Side, Tysea Hill, Stapleford Abbotts RM4 1JU. *Location:* three miles from Junction 28 M25. Off main Romford – Ongar Road B175 at Stapleford

Abbotts, Essex. Parkland with many water hazards. Abbotts – 18 holes, 6684 yards. S.S.S. 71. Priors – 18 holes, 6005 yards. S.S.S. 70. Friars – 9 holes, 1140 yards. S.S.S. 27. Two practice areas. *Green Fees:* Abbotts – £20.00 per round; Priors £15.00 per round; Friars £5.00 per round. *Eating facilities:* stud bar and restaurant. *Visitors:* midweek no restrictions. *Society Meetings:* ring for booking brochure. Professional: Scott Cranfield (04023 81278). Secretary: Keith Fletcher (04023 81108). Tee Reservations: Abbotts (04023 70040), Priors (0277 373344).

STAPLEFORD TAWNEY. **Abridge Golf and Country Club,** Epping Lane, Stapleford Tawney RM4 1ST (Stapleford (Essex) (04028) 396 and 397). *Location:* A113 from London through Chigwell to Abridge, left at White Hart, right after 200 yards. Two miles on. 18 holes, 6609 yards. S.S.S. 72. *Green Fees:* information not provided. *Eating facilities:* lunch and teas served at club except Fridays. *Visitors:* welcome but must be a member of a recognised golf club and produce evidence of current handicap, weekdays only. Tennis courts and heated swimming pool. *Society Meetings:* catered for on Mondays and Wednesdays only. Professional: Bernard Cooke (04028 333). Secretary: P.G. Pelling.

WOODFORD GREEN. **Woodford Golf Club,** Sunset Avenue, Woodford Green (081-504 4254). Woodland with gorse. Centenary 1990. 18 holes, 5806 yards. S.S.S. 68. *Green Fees:* £15.00 per round. *Eating facilities:* available except Mondays. *Visitors:* no green fees Tuesday or Thursday mornings or after 3.00pm weekdays. Red (scarlet) clothing must be worn – trousers or top. *Society Meetings:* welcome. Professional: A. Johns (081-504 4254). Secretary: G.J. Cousins (081-504 3330).

# Gloucestershire

BROADWAY. **Broadway Golf Club,** Willersey Hill, Broadway WR12 7LG (0386 853683). *Location:* one-and-a-half-miles east Broadway (A44). 18 holes, 6211 yards. S.S.S. 70 *Green Fees:* on application. *Eating facilities:* available daily (except Monday). *Visitors:* welcome; reservation advised. Handicap Certificates required. Saturdays (April/September) with member only before 3pm. October/March no restrictions. *Society Meetings:* by arrangement. (Wednesday, Thursday and Friday). Professional: Martyn Freeman (0386 853275). Managing Secretary: B. Carnie (0386 853683).

CHELTENHAM. **Cleeve Cloud Golf Club,** Near Prestbury, Cheltenham (Bishops Cleeve (024-267) 2592. *Location:* three miles north of Cheltenham on A46. 18 holes, 6217 yards. S.S.S. 70. *Green Fees:* information not provided. *Eating facilities:* full restaurant and bar snack facilities available every day. *Society*

*Meetings:* catered for by arrangement. *Visitors:* welcome without reservation. Professional: D. Finch. Secretary: R. East.

CHELTENHAM. **Lilley Brook Golf Club,** Cirencester Road, Charlton Kings, Cheltenham GL53 8EG (Cheltenham (0242) 526785). *Location:* two miles south-east of Cheltenham on main Cirencester road (A435). Parkland, 18 holes, 6226 yards, 5979 metres. S.S.S. 70. Practice field. *Green Fees:* weekdays £20.00. *Eating facilities:* full catering available. *Visitors:* welcome weekdays, weekends as a guest of a member only. Handicap Certificates required. *Society Meetings:* by arrangement. Professional: Forbes E. Hadden (0242 525201). Secretary: K.A. Skeen (0242 526785).

CHELTENHAM near. **Cotswold Hills Golf Club Ltd,** Ullenwood, Near Cheltenham GL53 9QT

(Cheltenham (0242) 522421). *Location:* at Ullenwood, off the A436 south of Cheltenham (two miles from town). Undulating Cotswold country course, excellent drainage. 18 holes, 6750 yards. S.S.S. 72. Large practice ground. *Green Fees:* weekdays £21.00 per round; weekends £26.00 per round. *Eating facilities:* full restaurant and bars. *Visitors:* no restrictions as a rule, but it is wise to telephone. *Society Meetings:* catered for by arrangement with Secretary. Professional: Noel Boland (0242 515263). Secretary: Andrew O'Reilly (0242 515264).

CIRENCESTER. **Cirencester Golf Club,** Cheltenham Road, Cirencester (Cirencester (0285) 653939). *Location:* one mile north of Cirencester on A435 Cheltenham road. 18 holes, 6108 yards. S.S.S. 69. *Green Fees:* weekdays £20.00, weekends and Bank Holidays £25.00. *Eating facilities:* lunches and suppers by arrangement. Hot and cold snacks always available. *Visitors:* welcome, Handicap Certificate required. *Society Meetings:* catered for Tuesday, Wednesday and Friday only. Professional: Geoff Robbins (0285 656124). Secretary: N.D. Jones (0285 652465).

COLEFORD. **Forest Hills Golf Club Ltd.,** Mile End Road, Coleford (0594 810620; Fax: 0594 562899). *Location:* half a mile outside Coleford town centre on Gloucester Road. 18 holes, 6000 yards. *Green Fees:* weekdays £13.00; weekends £15.00. *Eating facilities:* temporary clubhouse with bar, lounge serving bar

meals. *Visitors:* welcome, no restrictions. Pro shop. Changing facilities and showers.

COLEFORD. **Royal Forest of Dean Golf Club,** Lords Hill, Coleford GL16 8BD (Dean (0594) 832583; Fax: 0594 832584). *Location:* 10 miles from Severn Bridge. M4, M5 and M50, on B4431 Coleford to Parkend Road, quarter of a mile from Coleford town centre. Parkland course in Forest of Dean. 18 holes, 5535 yards. S.S.S. 67. Practice area. *Green Fees:* weekdays £15.00, weekends £17.00. Bargain Daily Break – golf, snack lunch, dinner only £24.00 available Mondays to Thursdays. *Eating facilities:* restaurant, bar snacks, bar open all day. *Visitors:* always welcome, please book teeing-off times with Professional. Own 32 bedroom Hotel (all en-suite), outdoor swimming pool, tennis court, bowling green, golf cars available. *Society Meetings:* welcome; conference facilities available at special rates. Professional: John Nicol (0594 833689). Secretary: Mrs K. Cave (0594 832583).

DURSLEY. **Stinchcombe Hill Golf Club,** Stinchcombe Hill, Dursley GL11 6AQ (Dursley (0453) 542015). *Location:* M5 between Junctions 13 and 14, A38 to Dursley. At traffic lights in centre of Dursley enter May Lane, continue to top of Hill and turn right onto Golf Course. A gently undulating course situated on a hilltop at the southern edge of the Cotswolds, extensive views. 18 holes, 5723 yards. S.S.S. 68. Practice and teaching areas. *Green Fees:* £20.00 weekdays (£10.00 with member); £25.00 weekends and Bank Holidays

(£12.50 with member). *Eating facilities:* full catering and bar service available. *Visitors:* welcome with recognised handicaps, time restrictions at weekends and Bank Holidays. *Society Meetings:* catered for by arrangement. Professional: Brendan Wynne (0453 543878). Secretary: John R. Clarke (0453 542015).

GLOUCESTER. **Gloucester Hotel, Golf and Country Club,** Matson Lane, Gloucester GL4 9EA (Gloucester (0452) 525653 Ext. 316). *Location:* situated on Robinwood Hill, turn off Gloucester to Painswick Road and head for Ski slopes. Parkland-type. Back 9 holes on top of hill. 18 holes, 6137 yards, 5613 metres. S.S.S. 69. 9 holes Par 3 course, driving range. *Green Fees:* weekdays £19.00; weekends £25.00. *Eating facilities:* full catering available. *Visitors:* welcome any time but where recommended by telephoning Secretary. *Society Meetings:* welcome weekdays, weekends by special arrangement. Professional/Manager: P. Darnell (0452 411331).

LYDNEY. **Lydney Golf Club,** The Links, off Lakeside Avenue, Lydney GL15 5QA (Dean (0594) 842614). *Location:* on front left-hand side of town when entering on A48 Cardiff road from Gloucester. Meadowland. 9 holes, 5382 yards. S.S.S. 66. Small practice area. *Green Fees:* £15.00 per day. Reductions when playing with a member. *Eating facilities:* snack meals only. *Visitors:* welcome, but only with a member at weekends/Bank Holidays. *Society Meetings:* welcome by prior arrangement (maximum 30/36). Hon. Secretary: D.A. Barnard (0594 843940).

MINCHINHAMPTON. **Minchinhampton Golf Club,** New Course, Minchinhampton, Stroud (Nailsworth (045-383) 3858). *Location:* New Course between Minchinhampton and Avening. Old Course between Minchinhampton and Stroud. Both courses 18 holes. New Course 6675 yards, Old Course 6295 yards. S.S.S. New Course 72, Old Course 70. *Green Fees:* New Course: weekdays £22.50 day, weekends and Bank Holidays £28.00 day. Old Course: weekdays £10.00 day, weekends and Bank Holidays £12.00. *Eating facilities:* normal catering at both New Course and Old Course Clubhouses. *Visitors:* New Course: welcome, must have handicap. Old Course: welcome. *Society Meetings:* both courses cater for groups by arrangement. Professional: New and Old Courses C. Steele (045-383 3860). Secretary: D.R. Vickers (045-383 3866). Old Course Golf Shop (045-383 2642).

PAINSWICK. **Painswick Golf Club,** Painswick, Near Stroud (Painswick (0452) 812180). *Location:* three miles north-east of Stroud on A46. 18 holes, 4900 yards. S.S.S. 64. *Green Fees:* weekdays £8.00; Saturdays £12.00. *Eating facilities:* lunches at Club (prior notice requested). *Visitors:* welcome weekdays and Saturday mornings. Saturday afternoons and Sunday mornings only with member. Saturday morning without reservation. *Society Meetings:* catered for, welcome most days. Secretary: R.J. May.

TETBURY. **Westonbirt Golf Course,** c/o Bursar, Westonbirt School Ltd, Westonbirt, Near Tetbury GL8 8QP (0666 880 242). *Location:* three miles south from Tetbury on A433, A439 to Bath on Bath road. Parkland. 9 holes, 4504 yards. S.S.S. 61. Practice area. *Green Fees:* weekdays £6.50 per day; weekends and Bank Holidays £6.50 per round. *Eating facilities:* available. *Visitors:* welcome without reservation. *Society Meetings:* catered for, limited facilities. Professional: C. Steele (visiting from Minchinhampton Golf Club). Secretary: Mr Nolan.

TEWKESBURY. **Tewkesbury Park Hotel, Golf and Country Club,** Lincoln Green Lane, Tewkesbury GL20 7DN (Tewkesbury (0684) 295054). *Location:* leave Junction 9 of M5 continue into Tewkesbury onto Gloucester Road. Parkland. 18 holes, 6533 yards. S.S.S. 72. *Green Fees:* weekdays £25.00; weekends £30.00. *Eating facilities:* hotel restaurant, coffee shop. *Visitors:* welcome without reservation weekdays. Valid Handicap Certificate required. Leisure complex. 78 bedroomed hotel. *Society Meetings:* catered for, residential only at weekends. Professional: Mr Robert Taylor (0684 294892). Secretary: Mr Bob Nicholl (0684 295054 extension 409).

WOTTON-UNDER-EDGE. **Cotswold Edge Golf Club,** Upper Rushmire, Wotton-under-Edge GL12 7PT (Dursley (0453) 844167). *Location:* eight miles from Junction 14 M5, on B4058 Tetbury road. Fairly flat course with magnificent views. 18 holes, White Tees - 6170 yards. S.S.S. 70; Yellow Tees - 5816 yards. S.S.S. 68. *Green Fees:* weekdays £15.00. *Eating facilities:* good catering service, usual bar facilities. *Visitors:* welcome weekdays. Telephone call in advance advisable. *Society Meetings:* by arrangement with Secretary. Professional: David Gosling (0453 844398). Secretary: N.J. Newman (0453 844167).

# Hampshire

ALDERSHOT. **Army Golf Club**, Laffan's Road, Aldershot GU11 2HF (0252 540638; Fax: 0252 376562). Clubhouse (0252 541104). Pro's Shop (0252 547232). *Location:* access from Eelmoor Bridge off A323 Aldershot Fleet Road. 18 holes, 6533 yards. S.S.S. 71. *Green Fees:* no casual green fees for civilians, only with member. Special rates for servicemen. *Eating facilities:* a range of catering is available by arrangement with the Secretary. *Visitors:* must be members' guests or servicemen. *Society Meetings:* catered for. Professional: Mr Nigel Turner. Secretary/Manager: R.T. Crabb.

ALRESFORD. **Alresford Golf Club**, Cheriton Road, Tichborne Down, Alresford SO24 0PN (Alresford (0962) 733746). *Location:* one mile south of A31 (Winchester/Alton). Two miles north A272 (Winchester/Petersfield). Flat parkland – wooded. 18 holes, 5989 yards. S.S.S. 69. *Practice area. Green Fees:* weekdays £16.50 per round, £27.50 per day; weekends and Bank Holidays £32.00 per round (not before 12 noon). *Eating facilities:* full catering except Mondays. *Visitors:* welcome but not before 12 noon weekends/Bank Holidays. Handicap Certificate required. *Society Meetings:* catered for by prior arrangement. Professional: Malcolm Scott (0962 733998). Secretary: Peter Kingston (0962 733746).

ALTON. **Alton Golf Club**, Old Odiham Road, Alton GU34 4BU (Alton (0420) 82042). *Location:* off A32, two miles north of Alton. Odiham six miles. Undulating wooded course. 9 holes, Alternate tees. 5744 yards. S.S.S. 68. Practice area. *Green Fees:* weekdays £12.00 per round, £16.00 per day; weekends £20.00 per round, £30.00 per day. Half green fees if with a member. *Eating facilities:* bar. *Visitors:* weekdays welcome without reservation, except on competition days. Weekends and Bank Holidays with member or 18 Handicap maximum. *Society Meetings:* welcome weekdays only, catering provided. Professional: Mr A. Lamb (0420 86518). Secretary: Mrs M.J. Woodhead (0420 82042).

AMPFIELD. **Ampfield Par Three Golf and Country Club**, Winchester Road, Ampfield, Near Romsey SO51 9BQ (Braishfield (0794) 68480). *Location:* A31 Winchester to Romsey road, next door to White Horse Public House. Parkland course designed by Henry Cotton. All holes par 3. 18 holes, 2478 yards. S.S.S. 53. *Green Fees:* on application. *Eating facilities:* light meals

and snacks, bar facilities. *Visitors:* welcome, but best to phone first. Handicap Certificate required at weekends and Bank Holidays.Recognised golf shoes must be worn. *Society Meetings:* catered for by prior arrangement. Professional: Richard Benfield (0794 68750). Secretary: Mrs Stella Baker.

ANDOVER. **Andover Golf Club**, 51 Winchester Road, Andover SP10 2EF (Andover (0264) 323980). *Location:* half-mile south of town centre on the A3057 Winchester/Stockbridge road. Parkland. 9 holes, 5933 yards. S.S.S. 68. *Green Fees:* £12.00 weekdays, £22.00 weekends. *Eating facilities:* full catering available. *Visitors:* welcome but not before 12 noon weekends and Bank Holidays. *Society Meetings:* catered for with prior arrangement. Professional: A. Timms (0264 324151). Secretary: D.A. Fairweather (0264 358040). Clubhouse Manager: (0264 323980).

BARTON-ON-SEA. **Barton-on-Sea Golf Club**, Milford Road, New Milton BH25 5PP. *Location:* one mile east of New Milton on B3508 Milford-on-Sea Road. Seaside course. 18 holes, 5325 yards. S.S.S. 66. *Green Fees:* on request. *Eating facilities:* full catering available. *Visitors:* welcome but not before 11.15am at weekends and Bank Holidays. *Society Meetings:* catered for Wednesdays and Fridays only with three months' notice in writing. Professional: P. Coombs (0425 611210). Secretary: C.J. Wingfield (0425 615308).

BASINGSTOKE. **Basingstoke Golf Club**, Kempshott Park, Basingstoke RG23 7LL (Basingstoke (0256) 465990). *Location:* on A30, three miles west of town on road to Winchester; from Winchester leave M3 at Exit 7. Parkland course. 18 holes, 6259 yards. S.S.S. 70. *Green Fees:* information not provided. *Eating facilities:* lunches and teas in clubhouse. *Visitors:* welcome on weekdays if member of a golf club, visitors at weekends and Bank Holidays only if playing with a member. *Society Meetings:* Wednesdays and Thursdays. Professional: I. Hayes (0256 51332). Secretary: J.E. Osborough.

BASINGSTOKE. **Bishopswood Golf Club**, Bishopswood Lane, Tadley, Basingstoke RG26 6AT (Tadley (0734) 815213). *Location:* six miles north of Basingstoke off the A340. Parkland/wooded course. 9 holes, 6474 yards. S.S.S. 71. 12 bay floodlit driving range open seven days a week. *Green Fees:* weekdays £7.15

111

for 9 holes, £12.25 for 18 holes. *Eating facilities:* lounge and spike bars – snacks, bar meals and 50 seater restaurant facility. *Visitors:* welcome weekdays only by prior booking. *Society Meetings:* welcome by arrangement. Professional: S. Ward (0734 815213). Manager: M.W. Phillips (0734 812200).

BASINGSTOKE. **Sandford Springs Golf Club,** Wolverton, Basingstoke (0635 297881; Fax: 0635 298065). *Location:* A339 Basingstoke to Newbury at Kingsclere. Wooded parkland course with lakes. 27 holes. *Green Fees:* weekdays £20.00. *Eating facilities:* available all day. *Society Meetings:* always welcome weekdays. Professional: G. Edmunds. Secretary: G. Tipple. Professional/Managing Director: K. Brake.

BASINGSTOKE. **Tylney Park Golf Club,** Rotherwick, near Basingstoke (Hook (0256) 762079). *Location:* one mile Hook A30. Parkland. 18 holes, 6135 yards. S.S.S. 69, Par 70. *Green Fees:* weekdays £18.00; weekends £28.00. *Eating facilities:* catering available. *Visitors:* weekdays unrestricted, weekends with Handicap Certificate or member. Professional: C. DeBruin. Secretary: A.D. Bewley.

·BORDON. **Blackmoor Golf Club,** Whitehill, Bordon GU35 9EH (0420 472775). *Location:* lies midway between Petersfield and Farnham on A325. 18 holes, 6213 yards. S.S.S. 70. *Green Fees:* £34.00 per day, after 1pm £26.00. *Eating facilities:* dining room. *Visitors:* welcome with reservation, handicaps necessary. *Society Meetings:* catered for all day. Morning coffee, lunch, evening meal. Professional: A. Hall. Secretary: Major (Retd.) H.R.G. Spiller.

BORDON near. **Kingsley Golf Club,** Main Road, Kingsley, Near Bordon GU35 9NG (0420 476118). *Location:* B3004 off A325 (Farnham to Petersfield Road). Parkland public course, a challenging short course. 9 holes, 1797 yards. S.S.S. Men 53, Ladies 60. *Green Fees:* weekdays £4.00 9 holes, £6.50 18 holes, (Juniors £2.50); weekends £4.00 9 holes, £8.00 18 holes. *Eating facilities:* bar and cafeteria. *Visitors:* no visitors on Sundays without prior booking. Driving range, indoor computerised driving bay, equipment superstore, golf school for tuition. *Society Meetings:* by prior arrangement. Professional: Richard Adams (0420 488478). Secretary: Alex Cook (0420 476118).

BROCKENHURST. **Brokenhurst Manor Golf Club,** Sway Road, Brockenhurst SO4 7SG (Lymington (0590) 22383). *Location:* from M27 take A337 to Brockenhurst then B3055 (to Sway). Approximately one mile to golf club. Beautiful New Forest course – wet in winter. 18 holes, 6222 yards. S.S.S. 70. *Green Fees:* weekdays £25.00 per round, £30.00 per day; weekends and Bank Holidays £35.00. *Eating facilities:* available all day; to 5pm in winter. *Visitors:* welcome

any day but please book in advance as there are restrictions on some days. Club Handicap Certificate required. *Society Meetings:* Thursdays only; small groups catered for by arrangement Mondays, Wednesdays and Fridays. Professional: B. Plucknett (0590 23092). Secretary: R.E. Stallard (0590 23332).

CRONDALL. **Oak Park Golfing Complex,** Heath Lane, Crondall, Near Farnham, Surrey GU10 5PB (0252 850880). *Location:* one and a half miles off A287 Farnham-Odiham road, five miles from Junctions 4 and 5 of M3 motorway. Gently undulating parkland course. 18 holes, 6437 yards. S.S.S. 71. Putting green and 16 bay covered driving range. *Green Fees:* weekdays £16.00 per round (reductions for Juniors); weekends £22.00 per round. *Eating facilities:* à la carte restaurant: Mon to Fri lunchtime and Sunday lunch. Tues to Sat evenings. Bar snacks available. *Visitors:* welcome; must book through Professional; reserved tee system weekends and Public Holidays. Conference facilities. *Society Meetings:* by arrangement with Secretary, welcome every day subject to availability. Professional: Simon Coaker (0252 850066). Secretary: Mrs R. Smythe (0252 850851).

DIBDEN. **Dibden Golf Centre,** Main Road, Dibden, Southampton (Hythe (0703) 845060). *Location:* half-mile off A326 Totton to Fawley road at Dibden very close to New Forest. 18 holes, 6206 yards. S.S.S. 70. 9 hole course and 19 bay driving range. *Green Fees:* summer rate: weekdays £5.50, weekends £8.00. *Eating facilities:* available. *Visitors:* welcome without reservation. *Society Meetings:* catered for. Professional: Alan Bridge (0703 845596). Course administration by Professional.

EASTLEIGH. **Fleming Park Golf Club,** Fleming Park, Eastleigh (Eastleigh (0703) 2797). *Location:* two miles off M27 Eastleigh Airport turning. Parkland. 18 holes, 4494 yards. S.S.S. 65. *Green Fees:* information not provided. *Eating facilities:* available plus bar. *Visitors:* welcome, book at least one week in advance. *Society Meetings:* all welcome. Professional: D. Miller. Secretary: D. Ainsworth-Lay.

FAREHAM. **Southwick Park Golf Club,** Pinsley Drive, Southwick, Fareham PO17 6EL. *Location:* near Southwick village, within HMS Dryad. Parkland. 18 holes, 5972 yards. S.S.S. 68. Practice area, pitch and putt. *Green Fees:* weekdays £16.00 per round. *Eating facilities:* bar and snacks available. *Visitors:* weekdays only. *Society Meetings:* Tuesdays only, book through Manager. Professional: J. Green (0705 380442). Manager: N.W. Price (0705 380131).

FARNBOROUGH. **Southwood Golf Course,** Ively Road, Cove, Farnborough GU14 0LJ (0252 515139). *Location:* approximately half a mile west of A325. Flat parkland. 18 holes, 5553 yards. S.S.S. 67. Putting green. *Green Fees:* information not available. *Eating facilities:* bar and diningroom available. *Visitors:* welcome, bookable at all times. *Society Meetings:* catered for by arrangement. Professional: Bob Hammond (0252 548700).

FLEET. **Hartley Wintney Golf Club,** London Road, Hartley Wintney, Basingstoke RG27 8PT (0252 842214). *Location:* on A30 between Camberley and Basingstoke. Parkland, wooded. 9 holes, 6096 yards. S.S.S. 69. Practice area. *Green Fees:* under review. *Eating facilities:* full catering facilities available except Mondays. *Visitors:* restricted Wednesdays Ladies' Day; weekends and Bank Holidays with member only. *Society Meetings:* catered for Tuesdays and Thursdays on application. Professional: Martin Smith (0252 843379). Secretary: B.D. Powell (0252 844211).

FLEET. **North Hants Golf Club,** Minley Road, Fleet GU13 8RE (0252 616443; Fax: 0252 811627). *Location:* B3013 off A30, M3 Junction 44. 400 yards from railway station. Heathland. 18 holes, 6257 yards. S.S.S. 70. Practice ground. *Green Fees:* weekdays £21.00 per round, £26.00 per two rounds. *Eating facilities:* lunch daily, evening meals by prior arrangement. *Visitors:* welcome weekday only by prior arrangement, Handicap Certificates required, Thursdays ladies day. *Society Meetings:* Tuesdays and Wednesdays only, maximum 42. Professional: Steve Porter (0252 616655). Secretary: I.R. Goodliffe.

GOSPORT. **Fleetlands Golf Club,** RNAY Fleetlands, Fareham Road, Gosport PO13 0AW. *Location:* two miles south of Fareham on Fareham/Gosport Road. Flat/wooded Course. 9 holes, 4777 yards. S.S.S. 63. *Green Fees:* £3.00 weekdays, £5.00 weekends. *Eating facilities:* bar/clubhouse. *Visitors:* by appointment with member only. *Society Meetings:* by appointment with member only. Secretary: Mr A. Eade (0705 822351 extension 44384).

GOSPORT. **Gosport and Stokes Golf Club,** off Fort Road, Haslar, Gosport (Gosport (0705) 581625). *Location:* A32 to Gosport, course is one mile east of Stokes Bay, near Gilkicker Point. Water course, natural hazards. 9 holes, 5800 yards. S.S.S. 68. Nets and putting green. *Green Fees:* £12.00 per day weekdays, £16.00 per day Sundays. *Eating facilities:* bar snacks, meal by arrangement. *Visitors:* welcome all week, restricted Sundays and Thursdays. *Society Meetings:* by arrangement. Secretary: A.P. Chubb (0705 527941).

HAVANT. **Rowlands Castle Golf Club,** 31 Links Lane, Rowlands Castle PO9 6AE (Portsmouth (0705) 412216). *Location:* four miles north of Havant or Horndean/Rowlands Castle Junction from A3M. Flat

parkland, wooded course. 18 holes, 6627 yards White Tees, 6381 yards Yellow Tees. S.S.S. 72 (White), 70 (Yellow). *Green Fees:* weekdays £24.00 per round/ day; weekends £30.00. *Eating facilities:* full catering available except Mondays. *Visitors:* welcome, except Saturdays unless playing with a member, maximum 12 visitors on a Sunday and Bank Holidays. *Society Meetings:* catered for, bookings through Professional. Professional: Peter Klepacz (0705 412785). Secretary: Captain A.W. Aird (0705 412784).

HAYLING ISLAND. **Hayling Golf Club,** Links Lane, Hayling Island PO11 0BX (Hayling Island (0705) 463777). *Location:* A3023 five miles south of Havant. Seaside links. 18 holes, 6489 yards. S.S.S. 71. *Green Fees:* £25.00 per day, weekends £35.00. *Eating facilities:* lunches and afternoon teas available. *Visitors:* welcome with current Handicap Certificate and must be members of recognised clubs. *Society Meetings:* Tuesdays and Wednesdays only by arrangement with the Secretary. Professional: Ray Gadd (0705 464491). Secretary: R.C.W. Stokes (0705 464446).

LEE-ON-THE-SOLENT. **Lee-On-The-Solent Golf Club,** Brune Lane, Lee-on-the-Solent PO13 9PB (Lee-on-the-Solent (0705) 551170). *Location:* M27 Exit 9, three miles south of Fareham on the B3385 then signposted. Flat parkland course. 18 holes, 5959 yards. S.S.S. 69. Practice range. *Green Fees:* weekdays £20.00; weekends £24.00. *Eating facilities:* catering and bar. *Visitors:* welcome weekdays, Handicap Certificate required. *Society Meetings:* Thursdays by arrangement. Professional: Mr. John Richardson (0705 551181). Secretary: P.A. Challis (0705 551170).

LIPHOOK. **Liphook Golf Club,** Wheatsheaf Enclosure, Liphook GU30 7EH (Liphook (0428) 723271). *Location:* one mile south of Liphook off A3. Heathland. 18 holes, 6250 yards. S.S.S. 70. *Green Fees:* on application. *Eating facilities:* bar and restaurant. *Visitors:* welcome, Handicap Certificate required, check with Secretary. *Society Meetings:* catered for. Professional: Ian Large (0428 723271). Secretary: Major J.B. Morgan MBE (0428 723785).

LIPHOOK. **Old Thorns Golf Course and Hotel,** Longmoor Road, Liphook GU30 7PE (Liphook (0428) 724555). *Location:* A3 to Liphook, then one mile down Longmoor Road (B2131). Parkland, wooded, with natural streams and lakes. 18 holes, 6529 yards. S.S.S. 72. Practice ground and putting green. *Green Fees:* £24.00 per round, £42.00 per day, £40.00 per round weekends. Telephone to arrange a starting time. *Eating facilities:* full catering available. Choice of European or Japanese cuisine. *Visitors:* welcome at all times. *Society Meetings:* welcome all week. Society days £52.00. Company days £65.00. Facilities: 33 en suite bedrooms, indoor heated swimming pool, sauna,

KOSAIDO
**OLD THORNS**
GOLF COURSE·HOTEL·RESTAURANTS

**Longmoor Road, Liphook, Hampshire. Telephone: Liphook (0428) 724555.** *See Colour Advertisement on Page 10.*

solarium, massage, 2 tennis courts, conference and banqueting rooms. Professional: Philip Loxley. General Manager: G.M. Jones.

LYNDHURST. **Bramshaw Golf Club,** Brook, Lyndhurst (Soton (0703) 813433). *Location:* M27 (interchange 1) one mile from M27 (north) at Brook. Two courses: one parkland, one woodland. Both 18 holes, Forest Course 5774 yards. S.S.S. 68. Manor Course 6233 yards. S.S.S. 70. Practice facilities. *Green Fees:* £30.00 weekdays, weekends with member only or Bell Inn Hotel guest. *Eating facilities:* clubhouse and restaurant, also Bell Inn close by. *Visitors:* welcome Monday to Friday. No visitors at weekends unless playing with a member or Bell Inn resident, Handicap Certificates required. Accommodation in 22 bedroomed hotel. *Society Meetings:* catered for by arrangement. Professional: Clive Bonner (0703 813434). General Manager: Bob Tingey (0703 813433).

LYNDHURST. **New Forest Golf Club,** Southampton Road, Lyndhurst SO43 7BU (0703 282450). *Location:* on the A35 Southampton to Lyndhurst road. Forest heathland course. 18 holes, 5742 yards. S.S.S. 68. Practice area. *Green Fees:* weekdays £12.00; weekends and Bank Holidays £14.00. *Eating facilities:* 11.00am to 3.00pm snacks and light meals. Bar open from 11.00am. *Visitors:* welcome, bookings available one week in advance. *Society Meetings:* catered for Tuesdays, Wednesdays and Thursdays only; maximum number 24, advance booking only. Professional: Ken Gilhespy (0703 282450). Secretary: Mrs W. Swann (0703 282752/282450).

PETERSFIELD. **Petersfield Golf Club,** Heath Road, Petersfield GU31 4EJ (Petersfield (0730) 63725). *Location:* turn off A3 in town centre, clubhouse one mile east. Heathland and parkland. 18 holes, 5649 yards. S.S.S. 67. *Green Fees:* £15.00 weekdays, £21.00 weekends. *Eating facilities:* available Tuesday to Saturday. *Visitors:* welcome weekdays, also Saturday and Sunday afternoon. *Society Meetings:* welcome except at weekends. Professional: Stephen Clay (0730 67732). Secretary: Lt Cdr P. Heraud RN (0730 62386; Fax: 0730 62386).

PORTSMOUTH. **Great Salterns Municipal Golf Course,** Burrfields Road, Portsmouth. *Location:* Junction of A2030 (eastern road) and Burrfield Road, one mile from M27. Parkland with easy walking. 18 holes, 5894 yards. S.S.S. 68. 25 bay floodlit driving range. *Green Fees:* adults £8.90, Juniors £5.50. Daily rates £13.30. *Eating facilities:* local farmhouse pub. *Visitors:* welcome, time booking required. *Society Meetings:* only by prior arrangement. Professional: Terry Healy (0705 664549; Fax: 0705 650525).

PORTSMOUTH. **Portsmouth Golf Club (1926),** Crookhorn Lane, Widley, Waterlooville PO7 5QL (0705 201827). *Location:* two thirds of a mile from junction of B2177 and A3. 18 holes, 6081 yards. S.S.S. 70. Practice area and putting green. *Green Fees:* £8.90. *Eating facilities:* full restaurant and bar. *Visitors:* welcome, tee bookings required. *Society Meetings:* as arranged with Pro Shop. Professional: R. Brown (0705 372210). Secretary: D. Houlihan (0705 201827).

PORTSMOUTH. **Southsea Golf Club,** Eastern Road, Portsmouth. *Location:* half a mile from M27 exit A2030 Southsea. Plays over Great Salterns Golf Course. Flat parkland. 18 holes, 6050 yards. S.S.S. 68. Floodlit golf driving range. *Green Fees:* £10.00. *Eating facilities:* at adjacent farmhouse bar/restaurant. *Visitors:* welcome – public course. Professional: Terry Healy (0705 690816). Secretary: K. Parker (0705 812435).

PORTSMOUTH. **Waterlooville Golf Club,** Cherry Tree Avenue, Cowplain, Waterlooville PO8 8AP. *Location:* off A3 or A3 (m), 10 miles north of Portsmouth. Parkland course. 18 holes, 6647 yards. S.S.S. 72. *Green Fees:* £20.00 per round, £30.00 per day, weekdays only. *Eating facilities:* full catering service available, bar facilities. *Visitors:* welcome weekdays, weekends as members' guests only. *Society Meetings:* catered for by prior arrangement. Professional: John Hay (0705 256911). Secretary: Mr C. Chamberlain (0705 263388).

RINGWOOD. **Burley Golf Club,** Cott Lane, Burley, Ringwood BH24 4BB (Burley (04253) 3737). *Location:* A31 from Ringwood and turn right at Picket Post and on through Burley Street. Heathland course, 9 holes, 6149 yards. S.S.S. 69. *Green Fees:* weekdays £13.00, weekends £15.00. Under 18's half price. *Visitors:* welcome, but not before 4pm Saturdays and 1.45pm Wednesdays. *Society Meetings:* not catered for. Professional: Wm. P. Tye. Secretary: Major G.R. Kendall (04253 2431).

ROMSEY. **Dunwood Manor Country Club,** Shootash Hill, Near Romsey SO51 0GF (0794 40549). *Location:* four miles from Romsey off A27. Undulating parkland. 18 holes, 6004 yards. S.S.S. 69. Practice area. *Green Fees:* £20.00 round, £30.00 day weekdays; £30.00 per round weekends. Society rates £18.00 per round, £24.00 per day. *Eating facilities:* full catering facilities. *Visitors:* welcome, by arrangement. *Society Meetings:* welcome, by arrangement. Professional: Richard Pilbury (0794 40663). Manager: Patrick Dawson (0794 40549).

SHEDFIELD. **Meon Valley Hotel, Golf and Country Club,** Sandy Lane, Shedfield SO3 2HQ (0329 833455; Fax: 0329 834411). *Location:* leave M27 at exit 7, take A334 to Botley then towards Wickham. Sandy Lane is 2 miles on the left. Wooded course. 18 holes, 6519 yards. S.S.S. 71. 9 holes, 2714 yards. S.S.S. 34. *Green Fees:* weekdays £22.00; weekends £30.00. *Eating facilities:* Treetops Restaurant, poolside grillroom and three bars. *Visitors:* welcome, no restrictions. Handicap Certificates required to play. *Society Meetings:* catered for. Professional: Mr John Stirling (0329 832184). Secretary: Mr George McMenemy.

SOUTHAMPTON. **Botley Park Golf Club,** Winchester Road, Botley, Southampton SO3 2UA (0489 780888). *Location:* approximately two miles from Junction 7 on M27. Parkland. 18 holes, 5714 yards. S.S.S. 69. Driving range. *Green Fees:* £23.00. *Eating facilities:* two bars, main restaurant and club lounge. *Visitors:* welcome by prior booking by phone. Handicap Certificate required. 100 bedroomed hotel on site;

## NOTE

All the information in this book is given in good faith in the belief that it is correct. However, the
publishers cannot guarantee the facts given in these pages, neither are they responsible for changes in
policy, ownership or terms that may take place after the date of going to press. Readers should always
satisfy themselves that the facilities they require are available and that the terms, if quoted, still apply.

tennis, squash, swimming, sauna, solarium, steam room, fitness suite, snooker. *Society Meetings:* Wednesdays and Thursdays only. Professional: Tim Barter. Secretary: Keith Pearson.

SOUTHAMPTON. **Corhampton Golf Club,** Sheeps Pond Lane, Droxford, Southampton SO3 1QZ (Droxford (0489) 877279). *Location:* one mile from Corhampton on the Bishops Waltham – Corhampton road (B3135). 18 holes, 6088 yards. S.S.S. 69. *Green Fees:* weekdays £20.00 per round, £32.00 per day. *Eating facilities:* full catering, except Tuesdays. *Visitors:* welcome Monday to Friday; weekends and Bank Holidays with a member. *Society Meetings:* Mondays and Thursdays. Professional: Garry Stubbington (0489 877638). Secretary: P. Taylor (0489 877279). Steward: J. Smith (0489 878749).

SOUTHAMPTON. **Southampton Golf Club** (Play over the Municipal Golf Course), Course Road, Southampton. 18 holes, 6218 yards, S.S.S. 70. 9 holes separate course also, S.S.S. 33. *Green Fees:* 18 holes weekdays £7.40, weekends and Bank Holidays £10.80; 9 holes weekdays £3.70, weekends and Bank Holidays £5.40. *Eating facilities:* bar and full catering. *Visitors:* welcome but must book at weekends. *Society Meetings:* by arrangement with Sports Centre Manager's Office (0703 790732). Professional: John Cave (0703 768407). Hon. Secretary: K.G. Kennard (0703 760472).

SOUTHAMPTON. **Stoneham Golf Club,** Bassett Green Road, Bassett, Southampton SO2 3NE

(Southampton (0703) 768151; Fax: 0703 769272). *Location:* A33/M27 north of Southampton find Chilworth roundabout take road to Airport (A27), half mile on left. Hilly heathery course. 18 holes, 6310 yards. S.S.S. 70. *Green Fees:* £25.00 per round or day; weekends £27.50 telephone re availability. *Eating facilities:* full catering, bar open all day. *Visitors:* welcome, except competition days. *Society Meetings:* catered for. Professional: Ian Young (0703 768397). Secretary: Mrs. A. M. Wilkinson (0703 769272).

WINCHESTER. **Hockley Golf Club,** Twyford, Near Winchester SO21 1PL (Winchester (0962) 713461). *Location:* on A333 (Twyford road), two miles south east of Winchester off M3. Parkland course. 18 holes, 6279 yards. S.S.S. 70. Practice areas. *Green Fees:* £25.00 per day or round. *Eating facilities:* restaurant and bar available. *Visitors:* welcome weekdays, weekends with members only. Check first with Professional. *Society Meetings:* welcome, catered for Wednesdays only. Professional: Terry Lane (0962 713678). Secretary: J.R. Digby (0962 713165).

WINCHESTER. **Royal Winchester Golf Club,** Sarum Road, Winchester (Winchester (0962) 851694). *Location:* one mile west of Winchester, left off A272, right at A31. 18 holes, 6218 metres. S.S.S. 70. *Green Fees:* weekdays £25.00. Weekends with member only. *Eating facilities:* full catering available except Thursdays. *Visitors:* welcome with Handicap Certificate. *Society Meetings:* by prior booking. Professional: D.P. Williams (0962 862473). Manager: (0962 852462).

# Hereford & Worcester

BELMONT. **Belmont House Golf Course,** Belmont House, Belmont HR2 9SA (0432 352666). Riverside and parkland. 18 holes, 6448 yards. S.S.S. 71. *Green Fees:* on application. Discounts for groups over 10. *Eating facilities:* restaurant and bar. *Visitors:* welcome with advance booking. 30 en-suite bedrooms, tennis, fishing, meeting rooms. *Society Meetings:* catered for. Professional: Mike Welsh (0432 352717).

BEWDLEY. **Little Lakes Golf Club,** Lye Head, Bewdley, Worcester (Rock (0299) 266385). *Location:* two miles west of Bewdley off A456, turn left opposite Alton Glasshouses. 9 holes, 6247 yards. S.S.S. 72. *Green Fees:* weekdays £15.00 per round, £18.00 per day, weekends only by invitation of a member. *Eating*

*facilities:* full restaurant service. *Visitors:* no restrictions weekdays. *Societies:* welcome by prior arrangement. Professional: M. Laing. Secretary: R.A. Norris (0562 67495).

BLACKWELL. **Blackwell Golf Club,** Blackwell, Near Bromsgrove B60 1PY (021-445 1470). *Location:* approximately 10 miles south of Birmingham and three miles east of Bromsgrove. Parkland. 18 holes, 6202 yards. S.S.S. 71. *Green Fees:* £36.00 per day. *Eating facilities:* full catering by prior arrangement. *Visitors:* welcome Monday to Friday without reservation. *Society Meetings:* catered for by arrangement through Secretary. Professional: N. Blake (021-445 3113). Secretary: R.W.A. Burns (021-445 1994).

BLAKEDOWN. **Churchill and Blakedown Golf Club,** Churchill Lane, Blakedown, Near Kidderminster DY10 3NB (Kidderminster (0562) 700200). *Location:* off A456 Birmingham/Kidderminster road at Blakedown. Elevated, hilly parkland course. 9 holes, 6472 yards. S.S.S. 71. *Green Fees:* £15.00 weekdays. *Eating facilities:* snacks and full meals except Monday. *Visitors:* welcome with reservation. Weekends with member only. *Society Meetings:* weekdays only by arrangement through the Hon. Secretary. Professional: Mr Keith Wheeler (0562 700454). Secretary: Mr G. Hull (0562 700018).

BRANSFORD. **Bransford Golf Club,** Bank House Hotel, Bransford WR6 5JD. *Location:* on A4103 Hereford Road, four miles south west of Worcester, at Bank House Hotel. Flat, undulating course incorporating 14 lakes – "Florida" style course – island greens, etc. 18 holes, 6175 yards. S.S.S. 68. 20 bay floodlit driving range. *Green Fees:* weekdays £15.00 18 holes; weekends £15.00 or £25.00 per day. *Eating facilities:* available in Bank House Hotel. *Visitors:* welcome after 10am. Handicap Certificates required. Smart golf attire. Accommodation in hotel. *Society Meetings:* welcome after 9.30am – accommodation and meals available. Professional: Graham Hawkings (0886 833621). Secretary: Patrick A.D. Holmes (0886 833551; Fax: 0886 832461).

BROMYARD near. **Sapey Golf Club,** Upper Sapey, Worcester WR6 6XT (08867 288; Fax: 08867 485). *Location:* situated six miles north of Bromyard on B4203. Parkland course with trees, ditches and water; outstanding views over Malvern Hills. 18 holes, 5885 yards. S.S.S. 69. Driving range. *Green Fees:* weekdays £15.00; weekends £20.00. *Eating facilities:* bar and restaurant meals available Wednesday to Sunday. *Visitors:* welcome always. *Society Meetings:* catered for Wednesdays to Sundays. Professional: Chris Knowles. Secretary: Shirley Dykes.

DROITWICH. **Droitwich Golf and Country Club Ltd,** Westford House, Ford Lane, Droitwich WR9 0BQ (Droitwich (0905) 770129). *Location:* between Junction 5 of M5 and Droitwich just off A38. Parkland – undulating – wooded. 18 holes, 6040 yards. S.S.S. 69. Practice area. *Green Fees:* £22.00 weekdays, member only £5.00; £8.00 weekends playing with a member only. *Eating facilities:* full catering available. *Visitors:* welcome without reservation Mondays to Fridays, weekends with member only. *Society Meetings:* catered for Wednesdays or Fridays. Professional: C.S. Thompson (0905 770207). Secretary: M.J. Taylor (0905 774344).

DROITWICH near. **Ombersley Golf Club,** Bishops Wood Road, Lineholt, Ombersley, Near Droitwich WR9 0LE (0905 620747; Fax: 0905 621016). *Location:* A449. High undulating course above the Severn Valley. 18 holes, 6289 yards. S.S.S. 68. Practice range £1.40 per 40 balls. *Green Fees:* £9.00 weekdays (£6.50 veterans and juniors); £12.00 weekends. *Eating facilities:* bar facilities, snacks and meals available. *Visitors:* all visitors welcome. *Society Meetings:* welcome by arrangement. Professional: Mr Graham Glenister. Secretary: Mr Robert Dowty.

EVESHAM. **Evesham Golf Club,** Craycombe Links, Fladbury Cross, Pershore WR10 2QS (Evesham (0386) 860395). *Location:* M5 at Junction 6, A4538 and B4084 to Evesham approximately 10 miles. Evesham take B4084 towards Worcester about three miles. Meadowland, heavily bunkered, tree-lined fairways. 9 holes (18 tees), 6415 yards, 5866 metres. S.S.S. 71. Practice area. *Green Fees:* £15.00 or £7.00 per round if playing with member. *Eating facilities:* diningroom and bar, except Mondays. *Visitors:* must be members of recognised club and have a certified handicap. On Tuesdays, Ladies' Day, play is not possible in Summer until after 3.15pm approx. *Society Meetings:* catered for by prior arrangement. Professional: Charles Haynes (0386 861145). Hon. Secretary: Frank G. Vincent (home 0386 552373). Steward: J.A. Webber.

HAGLEY. **Hagley Country Club Golf Club,** Wassell Grove, Hagley (Hagley (0562) 883701). *Location:* Wassell Grove is off A456 Birmingham to Kidderminster Road. 18 holes, 6353 yards. S.S.S. 72. *Green Fees:* £20.00 per round, £25.00 per day weekdays. *Eating facilities:* a la Carte Restaurant and bar snacks, Tuesday to Saturday. *Visitors:* welcome. *Society Meetings:* welcome by prior arrangement. Professional: Iain Clark (0562 883852). Secretary: Graham F. Yardley.

HEREFORD. **Burghill Valley Golf Club,** Tillington Road, Burghill, Hereford HR4 7RW (Hereford [0432] 760456). *Location:* three miles west of Hereford on B road to Weobley. Pleasantly undulating parkland including a lake, and interesting holes through mature cider orchards. 9 holes (18 holes open summer 1993), 6146 yards. S.S.S. 69. *Green Fees:* £6 for 9 holes, £10 for 18 holes. *Eating facilities:* bar and light refreshments. *Visitors:* welcome at any time. *Society Meetings:* by prior arrangement with the Professional. Professional: Tim Morgan (0432 760456).

HEREFORD. **The Herefordshire Golf Club,** Ravens Causeway, Wormsley, Hereford HR4 8LY (0432 71219). *Location:* six miles north-west of Hereford on a B road to Weobley. Undulating parkland course. 18 holes, 6036 yards. S.S.S. 69. *Green Fees:* £14.00 per round, £20.00 per day weekdays; £18.00 per round, £26.00 per day weekends and Bank Holidays. As members' guests weekdays £9.00 per round, £15.00 per day; weekends £11.00 per round, £19.00 per day. *Eating facilities:* catering available, limited on Mondays. *Visitors:* welcome. *Society Meetings:* catered for. Early application advised, weekends restricted. Professional: David Hemming (0432 71465). Secretary: W.J. Bullock.

KIDDERMINSTER. **Habberley Golf Club,** Habberley, Kidderminster DY11 5LG (0562 822381). *Location:* north west side of Kidderminster. Hilly parkland course. 9 holes, 5481 yards. S.S.S. 68. *Green Fees:* £12.00 weekdays, £5.00 weekends with member. *Eating facilities:* food and bar available. *Visitors:* welcome weekdays, without reservation; weekends with member only. *Society Meetings:* by negotiation. Secretary: Mr D.B. Lloyd (0562 745756).

KIDDERMINSTER. **Kidderminster Golf Club,** Russell Road, Kidderminster DY16 3HT (Kidderminster (0562) 822303). *Location:* signposted off A449

Worcester-Wolverhampton Road. Wooded parkland course. 18 holes, 6405 yards. S.S.S. 71. Practice ground. *Green Fees:* £22.00 weekdays. *Eating facilities:* bar and restaurant available. *Visitors:* welcome weekdays only if bona fide member of another club, weekends if guest of member. Snooker room with bar. *Society Meetings:* catered for Thursdays only. Professional: N.P. Underwood (0562 740090). Secretary: Alan Biggs (0562 822303).

KINGTON. **Kington Golf Club,** Bradnor Hill, Kington (Kington (0544) 230340). *Location:* one mile out of Kington, on B4355 to Presteigne. Hill course, with views of seven counties. Highest 18 hole course in England and Wales. 18 holes, 5820 yards. S.S.S. 68. *Green Fees:* £13.00 per round, £16.00 per day weekdays; weekends and Bank Holidays £18.00 per round, £22.00 per day. *Eating facilities:* meals at club. *Visitors:* welcome. Please contact Professional to ensure course is available. *Society Meetings:* catered for by arrangement. Professional: Dean Oliver (0544 231320). Hon. Secretary: G.E. Long (0497 820542).

LEOMINSTER. **Leominster Golf Club,** Ford Bridge, Leominster HR6 0LE (Leominster (0568) 612863). *Location:* three miles south of Leominster on A49 bypass, clearly signed. Undulating parkland with holes alongside River Lugg. 18 holes, 6045 yards. S.S.S. 69. Small practice area and putting green. *Green Fees:* weekdays £17.00, weekends £21.00. *Eating facilities:* full bar and catering daily except Mondays. *Visitors:* welcome weekdays, weekends by prior bookings. *Society Meetings:* by prior booking weekdays and some weekends. Professional: Mr. Russell Price (0568 611402). Secretary: J.A. Ashcroft (0432 880493).

MALVERN WELLS. **The Worcestershire Golf Club,** Wood Farm, Malvern Wells WR14 4PP (Malvern (0684) 575992). *Location:* two miles south of Great Malvern, near Junction of A449 and B4209. Exceptionally scenic – Malvern Hills and Vale of Evesham. 18 holes, 6449 yards. S.S.S. 71. *Green Fees:* £22.00 weekdays, £27.00 weekends. With member £10. Seven Day ticket £80. *Eating facilities:* available. *Visitors:* visitors unaccompanied by a member must provide evidence of Golf Club membership. Weekends after 10am. *Society Meetings:* catered for Thursday and Fridays only on application. Professional: G.M. Harris (0684 564428). Secretary: G.R. Scott (0684 575992).

PERSHORE. **The Vale Golf and Country Club,** Hill Furze Road, Bishampton, Pershore WR10 2LZ (0386 82781; Fax: 0386 82597). *Location:* from Evesham on B4084 right at Vale Golf sign/from Worcester to Wyre Piddle, left at Vale Golf sign. Meadowland course. 27 holes, 6519 yards, 5867 metres. S.S.S. 73. *Green Fees:* weekdays £6.50 9 holes, £18.00 18 holes; weekends £8.50 9 holes, £24.00 18 holes. *Eating facilities:* spike bar, bar/bar snacks members and non members, Vale bar for members; full à la carte. *Visitors:* welcome at all times. *Society Meetings:* very welcome. Professional: Russell Gardner (0386 82520; Fax: 0386 82660). General Manager: Nigel Brunner (0386 82 781/2/3/4).

REDDITCH. **Abbey Park Golf and Country Club,** Abbey Park, Dagnell End Road, Redditch B98 7BD (Redditch (0527) 63918). *Location:* leave M42 at A435 Evesham – through Beoley towards Redditch or off A441 Birmingham to Redditch. Parkland. 18 holes, 6411 yards, 5827 metres. S.S.S. 71. Driving range. *Green Fees:* weekdays £5.00, weekends £10.00. *Eating facilities:* bars, restaurant and bar snacks. *Visitors:* welcome, no restrictions. Booking usually necessary at weekends and Bank Holidays. Accommodation available, special rates for Weekend Breaks. Snooker room available. *Society Meetings:* welcome. Professional: R.K. Cameron. Secretary: M.E. Bradley.

REDDITCH. **Redditch Golf Club,** Green Lane, Lower Grinsty, Callow Hill, Redditch B97 5PJ (Redditch (0527) 543309). *Location:* three miles west of Redditch town centre, off Redditch to Bromsgrove road (A448), or Astwood Bank to Redditch (A441), take Windmill Drive, look for Callow Hill signs. First 9 holes parkland, second 9 holes wooded. White – 18 holes, 6671 yards. S.S.S. 72; Yellow – 18 holes, 6285 yards. S.S.S. 70. Two practice areas. *Green Fees:* £25.00 weekdays; weekends £7.50 with member only. *Eating facilities:* restaurant and bar with bar snacks except Mondays. *Visitors:* welcome, weekends with member. *Society Meetings:* catered for by arrangement. Professional: Mr F. Powell (0527 546372). Secretary: Mr C. Holman.

REDDITCH. **Redditch Kingfisher Golf Club,** Plymouth Road, Redditch (0527 541043). *Location:* Junction 3 M42 Redditch signposts. Wooded course. Separate winter and summer courses. 9 holes, 2700 yards. S.S.S. 64 for 18 holes. *Green Fees:* weekdays £5.00 18 holes; weekends £6.00 18 holes. *Eating* *facilities:* full catering and bar facilities. *Visitors:* welcome at all times. Showers/changing rooms. *Society Meetings:* welcome at all times. Professional: Mr David Stewart (0527 541054). Secretary: Mr John Russell (0527 503166).

ROSS-ON-WYE. **Ross-on-Wye Golf Club,** Two Park, Gorsley, Ross-on-Wye HR9 7UT (098982 457). *Location:* adjacent Junction 3 M50, midway Ross-on-Wye and Newent. Parkland course. 18 holes, 6500 yards. S.S.S. 73. Practice area. *Green Fees:* weekdays £25.00; weekends £30.00. Member's guest £8.00. *Eating facilities:* full catering, diningroom. *Visitors:* welcome, Handicap Certificate advised. Must be members of recognised golf club. Book in advance with Professional. *Society Meetings:* two per week, booking well in advance with Secretary. Minimum number 20, maximum 60. Snooker tables also available. Professional: Nick Catchpole (098982 439). Secretary: G.H. Cason (098982 267).

WORCESTER. **Tolladine Golf Club,** The Fairway, Tolladine Road, Worcester WR4 9BA (Worcester (0905) 21074). *Location:* M5, exit 6. Warndon turn off, one mile. 9 holes, 18 holes, 5630 yards. S.S.S. 67, Par 68. *Green Fees:* £12.00 weekdays, £5.00 with member; £6.00 weekends with member only. *Visitors:* welcome weekends. Professional: (0905 726180). Secretary: A.J. Wardle.

WORCESTER. **Worcester Golf and Country Club,** Boughton Park, Worcester WR2 4EZ (Worcester (0905) 421132). *Location:* one-and-a-quarter miles west of city on A4103 (to Hereford). Parkland. 18 holes, 5946 yards. S.S.S. 68. Practice ground. *Green Fees:* £23.00 per weekday. Weekends only with a member. *Eating facilities:* full catering available. *Visitors:* welcome weekdays. Handicap Certificate required. *Society Meetings:* catered for. Professional: Colin Colenso (0905 422044). Secretary: J.M. Kennedy (0905 422555). Caterer: Mrs J. Swale.

WYTHALL. **Fulford Heath Golf Club Ltd,** Tanners Green Lane, Wythall (Wythall (0564) 822806). *Location:* one mile from Alcester Road, via Tanners Green Lane. 18 holes, 6216 yards. S.S.S. 70. *Green Fees:* weekdays £25.00 (Societies £20). *Eating facilities:* available. *Visitors:* welcome weekdays with reservation, not at weekends and Bank Holidays. *Society Meetings:* catered for on application. Professional: Mr. K. Hayward (0564 822930). Secretary: R. Bowen (0564 824758).

# Hertfordshire

BARNET. **Arkley Golf Club,** Rowley Green Road, Barnet EN5 3HL (081-449 0394). *Location:* A1000 from London, turn by Elstree Moat House, two miles from Barnet. Parkland. 9 holes, 6045 yards. S.S.S. 69. *Green Fees:* weekdays £20.00 per round or £25.00 day; weekends with a member only. *Eating facilities:* available, no catering Mondays. *Visitors:* welcome weekdays, please phone, weekends with member only. *Society Meetings:* catered for Wednesdays, Thursdays and Fridays. Professional: M. Squire (081-440 8473). Secretary: G.D. Taylor (081-499 0394).

BARNET. **Hadley Wood Golf Club,** Beech Hill, Near Barnet (081-449 4328). *Location:* off the exit from M25 at Junction 24 on to A111 Cockfosters. Down hill, third turning on the right. 18 holes, 6473 yards. S.S.S. 71. *Green Fees:* on application. *Eating facilities:* available Tuesday to Friday. *Visitors:* welcome weekdays, (not Tuesday a.m.), with club Handicap Certificate or letter of introduction. *Society Meetings:* catered for Wednesday to Friday. Professional: Alan McGinn (081-449 3285). Secretary/General Manager: P.S. Bryan.

BERKHAMSTED. **Ashridge Golf Club,** Little Gaddesden, Berkhamsted (044284 2244). *Location:* five miles north west of Berkhamsted. 18 holes, 6508 yards. S.S.S. 71. *Green Fees:* on application. *Eating facilities:* daily. *Visitors:* welcome with reservation. Professional/Golf Manager: Geoffrey Pook. Secretary: Mrs Maggie West.

BERKHAMSTED. **Berkhamsted Golf Club,** The Common, Berkhamsted HP4 2QB (Berkhamsted (0442) 863730). *Location:* A41 to Berkhamsted, up past the castle to the common. Heathland, wooded, grass bunkers. 18 holes, 6605 yards. S.S.S. 72. Two practice grounds. *Green Fees:* weekdays £24.00 18 holes, £34.00 36 holes, £12.50 after 4pm; weekends £30.50 18 holes, £41.00 36 holes, £20.00 after 4pm. *Eating facilities:* daily although limited on Mondays. *Visitors:* welcome most days by arrangement. Handicap Certificate required. *Society Meetings:* catered for Wednesdays and Fridays. Professional: B.J. Proudfoot (0442 865851). Secretary: Colin Nextall (0442 865832).

BISHOP'S STORTFORD. **Bishop's Stortford Golf Club,** Dunmow Road, Bishop's Stortford CM23 5HP (Bishop's Stortford (0279) 654027). *Location:* M11 Junction 8, follow signs for Bishop's Stortford, after third (mini) roundabout entrance about half a mile on left hand side of road. Parkland. 18 holes, 6440 yards. S.S.S. 71. *Green Fees:* weekdays £21.00, with a member £10.50; weekends £16.00 (with full member only). *Eating facilities:* restaurant and bar meals. *Visitors:* welcome weekdays; weekends and Public Holidays with member only. *Society Meetings:* catered for weekdays except Tuesdays (minimum 15, maximum 40). Professional: Vince Duncan (0279 651324). Secretary: Major C. Rolls (0279 654715).

BUNTINGFORD. **East Herts Golf Club Ltd,** Hamels Park, Buntingford SG9 9NA (Ware (0920) 821978). *Location:* one mile north of Puckeridge on A10. 18 holes, 6416 yards. S.S.S. 71. *Green Fees:* details on application. *Eating facilities:* no catering Tuesdays. *Visitors:* welcome, with members only at weekends. *Society Meetings:* catered for weekdays. Professional: J. Hamilton (0920 821922). Secretary: J.A. Harper.

BUSHEY. **Bushey Hall Golf Club,** Bushey Hall Drive, Bushey WD2 2EP (Watford (0923) 229759). *Location:* Bushey Hall Road, Aldenham Road roundabout, one mile from M1. Parkland. 18 holes, 6099 yards. S.S.S. 69. *Green Fees:* weekdays £21.00; weekends £13.50 with member only. *Eating facilities:* full catering available, two bars. *Visitors:* welcome weekdays with Handicap Certificate. *Society Meetings:* catered for Monday, Tuesday and Thurday. Professional: D. Fitzsimmons (0923 222253). Secretary: Colin M. Brown (0923 225802).

BUSHEY HEATH. **Hartsbourne Golf and Country Club,** Hartsbourne Avenue, Bushey Heath WD2 1JW. *Location:* five miles south east of Watford. Parkland. 18 holes, 6305 yards. S.S.S. 70. 9 holes, 5342 yards. S.S.S. 66. *Green Fees:* information not supplied. *Eating facilities:* restaurant and snack bar available. *Visitors:* guests of members only. *Society Meetings:* catered for Mondays and Fridays. Professionals: Geoff Hunt and Martin Hattam (081-950 2836). Secretary: David J. Woodman (081-950 1133 or 4346).

CHORLEYWOOD. **Chorleywood Golf Club Ltd.,** Common Road, Chorleywood WD3 5LN (Chorleywood (0923) 282009). *Location:* half a mile off A404, three miles from Rickmansworth. Flat common land with woods. 9 holes, 5676 yards. S.S.S. 67. *Green Fees:* £14.00 weekdays, £17.50 weekends. *Eating facilities:* meals served if ordered by phone. *Visitors:* welcome weekdays except Tuesday and Thursday mornings, restricted at weekends. Secretary: R.M. Lennard.

DAGNALL. **Whipsnade Park Golf Club,** Studham Lane, Dagnall HP4 1RH (Little Gaddesden (044 284) 2330/2331). *Location:* between Dagnall and Studham. Junction 11 M1 (from north), Junction 9 (from south). Parkland. 18 holes, 6800 yards. S.S.S. 72. Large practice area. *Green Fees:* £20.00 per round, £30.00 per day weekdays, weekends with member only. *Eating facilities:* restaurant open daily, 2 bars. *Visitors:* welcome weekdays with reservation. *Society Meetings:* welcome with reservation. Professional: Mike Lewendon (044284 2331). Secretary: Andrea King (044284 2330).

GRAVELEY. **The Chesfield Downs Family Golf Centre,** Jack's Hill, Graveley, Near Hitchin SG4 7EQ (0462 482929). *Location:* just off Junction 8 of the A1 (M), approximately two miles along the B197. Inland

# VISITORS WELCOME

## Open Daily from 7.00 a.m. - 11.00 p.m.

- Superb 18 hole Chesfield Downs Course.

- 9 hole Lannock Links Course.

- 25 Bay floodlit, covered Driving Range, equipped with top grade two-piece range balls and superior quality practice mats.

- Well stocked Family Golf Superstore. Huge Choice - Competitive Prices - Expert Advice.

- The Family Golf Academy, featuring individual and group tuition from our team of Professionals.

- Hire Clubs available.

- "19th Hole" Bar & Bistro.

- 18 Hole Putting Green.

- Purpose built and well designed modern Clubhouse, including changing facilities and a fully equipped Function Room.

- Golf Societies and Corporate Golf Days available.

- Specialist Repair Centre.

- Creche and Adventure Playground.

 **0462 482929**

## The Chesfield Downs F.G.C.
## Jack's Hill
## Graveley
## Herts
## SG4 7EQ

FAX:  0462 482930

links/downland. Two Courses: Chesfield – 18 holes, 6630 yards. S.S.S. 72. Par 71. Lannock Links – 9 holes, 975 yards. S.S.S. 27. 25 bay floodlit driving range, putting green. *Green Fees:* weekdays £12.25 (£3.50); weekends £17.50 (£4.50). *Eating facilities:* "19th Hole" bar and bistro. *Visitors:* welcome, advance booking system available to reserve tee-off times. Golf Superstore, Golf Academy, changing facilities, creche/ playground. *Society Meetings:* Catered for by arrangement. Professionals: Dale Brightman/Beverly Huke. Secretary: David C.M. Carter.

HARPENDEN. **Harpenden Common Golf Club,** East Common, Harpenden AL5 1BL (0582 712856). *Location:* on A1081 between Harpenden and St. Albans. Flat heathland. 18 holes, 5613 yards, 5133 metres. S.S.S. 67. *Green Fees:* weekdays £20.00 per round, £25.00 per day; weekends £25.00 per day. *Eating facilities:* bar and restaurant daily. *Visitors:* welcome weekdays only with reservation (not Tuesdays). Weekends with member only. *Society Meetings:* Thursday and Friday only. Professional: B. Puttick (0582 460655). Secretary: R.D. Parry (0582 715959).

HARPENDEN. **Harpenden Golf Club,** Hammonds End, Redbourn Lane, Harpenden (Harpenden (0582) 712580). *Location:* turn off A1081, four miles after St. Albans on B487. Parkland course. 18 holes, 6363 yards. S.S.S. 70. *Green Fees:* £30 per day. *Eating facilities:* lunches at club, order in advance. *Visitors:* welcome by arrangement. *Society Meetings:* by arrangement only. Professional: Doug Smith. Secretary: R.A. Mortimer.

HATFIELD. **Brookmans Park Golf Club,** Golf Club Road, Brookmans Park, Hatfield AL9 7AT (Potters Bar (0707) 52459). *Location:* between A1 and A1000, also just off M25, exit for Potters Bar. Parkland. 18 holes, 6454 yards, 5901 metres. S.S.S. 71. Practice ground and putting green. *Green Fees:* weekdays £25.00 per round, £30.00 per day. Handicap Certificate required. *Eating facilities:* bar snacks and lunches weekdays. *Visitors:* welcome weekdays; weekends with member only. *Society Meetings:* catered for Wednesdays and Thursdays. Professionals: M.M.R. Plumbridge and I. Jelley (0707 52468). Secretary: P.A. Gill (0707 52487).

HATFIELD. **Hatfield London Country Club,** Bedwell Park, Essendon, Hatfield AL9 6JA (Potters Bar (0707) 42624 or 42626). *Location:* B158, 5 miles north east of Potters Bar, one mile south of Essendon village. 18 holes and 9 holes Pitch and Putt. 6359 yards. S.S.S. 70. *Green Fees:* information not provided. *Eating facilities:* lunch except Mondays. *Visitors:* welcome, advance bookings only. *Society Meetings:* catered for. Professional: Norman Greer.

HEMEL HEMPSTEAD. **Boxmoor Golf Club,** 18 Box Lane, Boxmoor, Hemel Hempstead HP1 1DZ (Hemel Hempstead (0442) 242434). *Location:* two miles from Hemel Hempstead, three-quarters of a mile from Hemel Hempstead Station on A41. Hilly/moorland course, 9 holes, 4112 yards. S.S.S. 62. *Green Fees:* £10.00 weekdays; £15.00 weekends. Half fee if playing with member. *Eating facilities:* ring Steward. *Visitors:* welcome without reservation, except on Sundays.

*Society Meetings:* catered for on application. Hon. Secretary: Neville James.

HEMEL HEMPSTEAD. **Little Hay Golf Complex,** Box Lane, Bovingdon, Hemel Hempstead HP3 0DQ (0442 833783). *Location:* just off A41, along Chesham Road from Hemel Hempstead. 18 holes, 6678 yards. S.S.S. 72. 9 hole pitch & putt course, 18 hole putting green, floodlit driving range. *Green Fees:* information not provided. *Eating facilities:* open from 8am to 10pm seven days a week. *Visitors:* all members of the public welcome. *Society Meetings:* made most welcome, special rates. Professional: David Johnson and Stephen Proudfoot (0442 833798). Director of Golf: David Johnson (0442 833798).

HERTFORD. **Brickendon Grange Golf and Country Club,** Brickendon, Near Hertford SG13 8PD. *Location:* three miles south of Hertford, one mile from Bayford Railway Station. Undulating parkland with specimen trees. 18 holes, 6315 yards. S.S.S. 70. *Green Fees:* £30.00 day ticket, £24.00 per round. *Eating facilities:* bar and restaurant, snack meals available lunchtimes. *Visitors:* welcome weekdays only, Handicap certificate required. *Society Meetings:* catered for by arrangement. Professional: J. Hamilton (0992 511218). Secretary: N. Martin (0992 511258).

KNEBWORTH. **Knebworth Golf Club,** Deards End Lane, Knebworth SG3 6NL (Stevenage (0438) 814681). *Location:* one mile south of Stevenage. Parkland. 18 holes, 6492 yards. S.S.S. 71. *Green Fees:* details on application. *Eating facilities:* available. *Visitors:* welcome (with members only at weekends). *Society Meetings:* welcome weekdays. Professional: R.Y. Mitchell (0438 812757). Secretary: J.C. Wright (0438 812752).

LETCHWORTH. **Letchworth Golf Club,** Letchworth Lane, Letchworth SG6 3NQ. *Location:* two miles from A1 (M) near village of Willian, adjacent to Letchworth Hall Hotel. Parkland course. 18 holes, 6181 yards. S.S.S. 69. Practice ground. *Green Fees:* weekdays £23.50 per round, £32.50 per day; weekend accompanied only. *Eating facilities:* bars and restaurant except Mondays. *Visitors:* weekdays Handicap Certificate required, weekends accompanied only. *Society Meetings:* catered for Wednesdays, Thursdays and Fridays. Professional: John Mutimer (0462 682713). Secretary: A.R. Bailey (0462 683203).

POTTERS BAR. **Potters Bar Golf Club,** Darkes Lane, Potters Bar EN6 1DF (0707 52020). *Location:* M25 (exit 24), signposted Potters Bar. Through one set of traffic lights, turn right at second set into Darkes Lane, club on left end of shopping centre. Parkland course, well wooded and undulating. 18 holes, 6279 yards. S.S.S. 70. Small practice ground. *Green Fees:* £27.50 weekdays; weekends with member only. *Eating facilities:* luncheons and bar available from 11.30am. *Visitors:* weekdays only, must produce valid Handicap Certificate. *Society Meetings:* Mondays/Tuesdays/ Fridays only. Professional: Kevin Hughes (0707 52987). Secretary: Arthur Williams. Secretary/ Manager: A. St.J. Williams (0707 52020).

RADLETT. **Porters Park Golf Club,** Shenley Hill, Radlett WD7 7AZ (0923 856262). *Location:* approximately 3 miles south west of Junction 22 (M25), 3 miles north-east Junction 5 (M1), half a mile north of Radlett Station on Shenley Hill. Park-type course with fine trees and a brook. 18 holes, 6313 yards. S.S.S. 70. Two practice areas, putting. *Green Fees:* £27.50 per 18 holes, £39.00 per day. (£13.50 per round with a member). *Eating facilities:* full diningroom and bar snack menus. *Visitors:* welcome weekdays if pre-booked, with members only at weekends and Bank Holidays. Handicap Certificate required. *Society Meetings:* catered for Wednesday and Thursday March to October only. Professional: David Gleeson (0923 854366). Manager: J.H. Roberts (0923 854127).

RICKMANSWORTH. **Moor Park Golf Club,** Moor Park, Rickmansworth WD3 1QN (Rickmansworth (0923) *Location:* A404 to Northwood Hills, Batchworth Heath. Course no. 1: 18 holes, 6695 yards. S.S.S. 72. Course no. 2: 18 holes, 5823 yards. S.S.S. 68. *Green Fees:* information not provided. *Eating facilities:* full catering always available at club. *Visitors:* welcome on weekdays by prior arrangement, and on weekends with a member. Professional: E.R. Whitehead. Secretary: J.A. Davies.

RICKMANSWORTH. **Rickmansworth Golf Club,** Moor Lane, Rickmansworth WD3 1QL (Rickmansworth (0923) 773163). *Location:* from town centre along A404 to Waterworks, left along B4504, then first right. Testing, undulating parkland course. 18 holes, 4500 yards, 4115 metres. S.S.S. 62. *Green Fees:* weekdays £8.00 per round, £13.50 per day; weekends 13.00. *Eating facilities:* bars, restaurant. *Visitors:* no restrictions. *Society Meetings:* catered for, contact Professional. Professional: Iain Duncan (0923 775278). Secretary: W.F. Stokes (0923 772948).

ROYSTON. **Royston Golf Club,** Baldock Road, Royston SG8 5BG (Royston (0763) 242177). *Location:* alongside the A505 on right hand side when approaching from Baldock, clubhouse at top of hill before entering town. Undulating heathland. 18 holes, 6032 yards. S.S.S. 69. Practice fairway. *Green Fees:* £20.00 weekdays; weekends with a member only. *Eating facilities:* bar and restaurant meals – two bars. *Visitors:* welcome weekdays; weekends only with member. *Society Meetings:* catered for weekdays only with 12 or more members. Professional: M. Hatcher (0763 243476). Secretary: Mrs S. Morris (0763 242696).

SAWBRIDGEWORTH. **The Manor of Groves Golf and Country Club,** High Wych, Sawbridgeworth CM21 0LA (0279 722333; Fax: 0279 726972). *Location:* one mile north of Harlow off the A1184. Parkland and meadowland course. 18 holes, 6198 yards. S.S.S. 70. *Green Fees:* £15.00 weekdays; £20.00 Saturdays, £22.00 Sundays. *Eating facilities:* restaurant and bar. *Visitors:* welcome anytime weekdays, after noon weekends. Must have Handicap Certificate or proficiency certificate. Accommodation available in our 35 bedroomed Hotel. *Society Meetings:* welcome anytime. Professionals: S. James and L. Jones. Secretary: S. Sharer.

ST. ALBANS. **Batchwood Hall Golf Club,** Batchwood Drive, St. Albans (St. Albans (0727)

833349). *Location:* north west corner of town. 18 holes, 6463 yards. S.S.S. 71. *Green Fees:* on application from Pro's shop. *Eating facilities:* bar meals. *Visitors:* welcome with reservation (0727 44250) except 0630 to 1000 hours weekends. *Society Meetings:* not catered for. Professional: J. Thomson (0727 52101). Secretary: B.R. Mercer.

ST. ALBANS. **Mid-Herts Golf Club,** Gustard Wood, Wheathampstead, St. Albans (Wheathampstead (058 283) 3118). *Location:* B651, six miles north of St. Albans. Heathland, short and tight course. 18 holes, 6094 yards. S.S.S. 69. Course record 67. *Green Fees:* weekdays £21.00 per round; weekends and Bank Holidays with member only. *Eating facilities:* by arrangement. *Visitors:* welcome weekdays with reservation; Handicap Certificate required. *Society Meetings:* catered for by arrangement. Professional: N. Brown (058 283 2788). Secretary: R.J.H. Jourdan (058 283 2242).

ST. ALBANS. **Redbourn Golf Club,** Kingbourne, Green Lane, Redbourn, Near St. Albans AL3 7QA (0582 793363). *Location:* four miles north of St. Albans, 4 miles south of Luton, one mile south of M1 Junction 9. Parkland. 18 holes, 6407 yards. S.S.S. 71. 9 holes, 1361 yards. S.S.S. 27. Driving range. *Green Fees:* £14.00 weekdays, £17.00 weekends and Bank Holidays. *Eating facilities:* licensed bar, snacks and hot meals readily available. *Visitors:* welcome weekdays except between 4.15pm – 6pm, weekends and Bank Holidays after 3.00pm. *Society Meetings:* catered for by arrangement Mondays to Thursdays. Professional: Steve Baldwin (0582 793493). Secretary: W.M. Dunn (0582 792150).

ST. ALBANS. **Verulam Golf Club,** 226 London Road, St. Albans AL1 1JG (St. Albans (0727) 53327). *Location:* Junction 22 M25, then A1081 St. Albans. Parkland. 18 holes, 6457 yards. S.S.S. 71. Practice ground. *Green Fees:* weekdays £20.00 per round, £25.00 per day (Mondays £11.00 per round, £18.00 per day). *Eating facilities:* bar snacks, lunches. *Visitors:* welcome except weekends and Bank Holidays. *Society Meetings:* catered for by arrangement. Professional: Paul Anderson (0727 861401). Secretary: G.D. Eastwood (0727 53327; Fax: 0727 812201).

STEVENAGE. **Stevenage Golf Centre,** Aston Lane, Stevenage SG2 7EL (0438 880424). *Location:* turn off A1(M) at Stevenage South Junction onto A602 to Hertford. 18 holes, 6451 yards. S.S.S. 71. Par 72. 20-bay driving range. *Green Fees:* telephone the Professional for details. *Eating facilities:* restaurant and bar. *Visitors:* welcome, advance booking system available to reserve tee-off times. Shower facilities. *Society Meetings:* catered for by arrangement. Professional: K. Bond.

WALTHAM CROSS. **Cheshunt Golf Club,** The Clubhouse, Park Lane, Cheshunt (Waltham Cross (0992) 29777). *Location:* M25 Junction 25, then A10 towards Hertford, second set of traffic lights to Flanstead End. Flat parkland course. 18 holes, 6608 Yards. S.S.S. 71. Practice area. *Green Fees:* weekdays £7.00; weekends and Bank Holidays £9.00. Senior Citizens £4.00 weekdays only. *Eating facilities:* public cafe. *Visitors:* welcome any time. For tee-off times phone

Pro's shop (0992 24009). *Society Meetings:* catered for by arrangement. Professional: C. Newton (0992 24009). Secretary: J.G. Duncan (0992 29777).

WARE. **Chadwell Springs Golf Club,** Hertford Road, Ware SG12 9LE (0920 461447). *Location:* A10 Hertford or Ware. Heathland. 9 holes, 6418 yards. S.S.S. 71. *Green Fees:* £14.00 weekdays; weekends £10.00 with a member only. *Eating facilities:* bar meals. *Visitors:* welcome weekdays; weekends with member only. *Society Meetings:* by arrangement. Professional: Adrian Shearn (0920 462075). Secretary: D. Evans (0920 461447).

WARE. **Whitehill Golf Club,** Whitehill Golf Centre, Dane End, Ware SG12 0JS (0920 438495; Fax: 0920 438891). *Location:* turn off A10 at Happy Eater, High Cross. Undulating course. 18 holes, 6636 yards. S.S.S. 72. 25 bay floodlit driving range. *Green Fees:* weekdays £15.00 per round, £20.00 per day; weekends £18.00. *Eating facilities:* bar, restaurant, function room. *Visitors:* welcome, must have Handicap. Snooker room. *Society Meetings:* catered for, groups of 12 or more. Professional: Robert Green (0920 438326). Secretary: Andrew Smith.

WATFORD. **Aldenham Golf and Country Club,** Church Lane, Aldenham, Near Watford WD2 8AL (Radlett (0923) 853929). *Location:* Junction 5 on M1, take A41 to South Watford, turn left at 1st roundabout to Church Lane. Flat parkland. 18 holes, 6500 yards. S.S.S. 71. New 9 hole course, 2500 yards. Practice area. *Green Fees:* £18.00 per round weekdays, £25.00 per round weekends. *Eating facilities:* three bars, snack bar, restaurant. *Visitors:* welcome weekdays, weekends not before 12 noon. Teaching. Swing Analyser video. *Society Meetings:* by arrangement. Professional: Alistair McKay (0923 857889). Secretary: D.W. Phillips (0923 853929).

WATFORD. **West Herts Golf Club,** Cassiobury Park, Watford WD1 7SL (Watford (0923) 224264). *Location:* south Watford 3 minutes off A412 at Croxley Green. 18 holes, 6488 yards. S.S.S. 71. *Green fees:* information not provided. *Eating facilities:* no catering Mondays. *Visitors:* welcome weekdays only without reservation (restrictions Thursdays). *Society Meetings:* catered for Wednesdays and Fridays. Professional: C.S. Gough (0923 220352). General Manager: A.D. Bluck (0923 236484).

WELWYN GARDEN CITY. **Panshanger Golf Complex,** Old Herns Lane, Panshanger, Welwyn Garden City AL7 2ED (Welwyn Garden (0707) 333132). *Location:* Junction 6 A1(M), 10 minutes from M25. Parkland set in the Mimram Valley. 18 holes, 6347 yards. S.S.S. 70. Practice ground, 9 hole pitch and putt. *Green Fees:* weekdays £9.80; weekends £10.80. *Eating facilities:* Fairway Tavern pub and servery. *Visitors:* municipal course, pay as you play, all welcome, dress conditions. *Society Meetings:* welcome. Professionals: Bryan Lewis and Mick Corlass (0707 333350). Secretary: Sheila (0707 332837).

WELWYN GARDEN CITY. **Welwyn Garden City Golf Club Ltd.,** Mannicotts, High Oaks Road, Welwyn Garden City AL8 7BP (Welwyn Garden (0707) 322722). *Location:* from north Junction 5 on A1M take B197 to Valley Road. From south Junction 4 on A1M to Lemsford Lane and Valley Road. Undulating parkland. 18 holes, 6200 yards. S.S.S. 69. Practice ground. *Green Fees:* £25.00 weekdays. *Eating facilities:* by order for lunches; sandwiches available. *Visitors:* welcome weekdays with Handicap Certificate; weekends with member only. *Society Meetings:* Wednesdays and Thursdays only. Professional: Simon Bishop (0707 325525). Secretary/Manager: J.L. Carragher (0707 325243).

# Humberside

BEVERLEY. **Beverley and East Riding Golf Club,** Westwood, Beverley, North Humberside (0482 868757). *Location:* one mile from Beverley town centre. 18 holes, 5949 yards. S.S.S. 68. *Green Fees:* £10.00 weekdays, £12.50 weekends and Bank Holidays. *Eating facilities:* lunch and high teas, prior ordering. *Visitors:* welcome with reservation. *Society Meetings:* catered for, prior notice for approval of committee. Professional: Ian Mackie. Secretary: A. Walker.

BEVERLEY. **Hainsworth Park Golf Club,** Brandesburton, Near Driffield YO25 8RT (Hornsea (0964) 542362). *Location:* A165 between Beverley and Bridlington, 8 miles north of Beverley. Parkland with mature trees. 18 holes, 6000 yards. S.S.S. 69. Practice area. *Green Fees:* weekdays £10.00; weekends £15.00. *Eating facilities:* bar and full catering. *Visitors:* welcome anytime. Hotel accommodation. *Society Meetings:* welcome. Secretary: R. Hounsfield (0964 542362).

BRIDLINGTON. **Bridlington Golf Club,** Belvedere Road, Bridlington YO15 3NA (0262 672092). *Location:* one mile south from Bridlington town centre, adjacent A165. Flat parkland. 18 holes, 6491 yards. S.S.S. 71. Two small practice areas. *Green Fees:* weekdays £14.00; weekends and Bank Holidays £20.00. Reductions for parties over 25 in number. *Eating facilities:* full catering. *Visitors:* welcome most days but limited on Wednesdays/Sundays. Advisable to book in advance. *Society Meetings:* catered for. Professional: D.M. Rands (0262 674721). Hon. Secretary: Clive Wilson (0262 606367).

BRIDLINGTON. **Flamborough Head Golf Club,** Flamborough, Bridlington (Bridlington (0262) 850333). *Location:* five miles north-east of Bridlington on B1255. 18 holes, 5438 yards. S.S.S. 66. *Green Fees:* weekdays £12.00 per day; weekends and Bank Holidays £16.00 per day. *Visitors:* welcome, limited Sunday and Wednesday mornings. *Society Meetings:* catered for, apply to Secretary. Secretary: W.R. Scarle (0262 676494).

BRIGG. **Elsham Golf Club,** Barton Road, Elsham, South Humberside (0652 688382). *Location:* off Junction 5 M180. Parkland. 18 holes, 6411 yards. S.S.S. 71. *Green Fees:* £20.00 weekdays; weekends only with a member £15.00. *Eating facilities:* full catering. *Visitors:*

welcome mid week on application to Manager. *Society Meetings:* catered for on weekdays except Thursdays on application to Manager. Steward (0652 688382). Professional: Stuart Brewer (0652 680432). Secretary: B.P. Nazer (0652 680291).

BROUGH. **Brough Golf Club,** Cave Road, Brough HU15 1HB (0482-667374). *Location:* 10 miles west of Hull off A63. Parkland. 18 holes, 6153 yards. S.S.S. 69. Practice facilities. *Green Fees:* weekdays £22.50; weekends £30.00. *Eating facilities:* snacks etc. *Visitors:* welcome Monday to Friday subject to club events, not weekends or Bank Holidays. Wednesdays only after 2pm. *Society Meetings:* catered for. Professional: G. Townhill (0482 667483). Secretary/Manager: W.G. Burleigh (0482 667291).

BROUGH. **Cave Castle Hotel Golf Club,** South Cave, Brough HU15 2EU (0430 422245; Fax: 0430 421118). *Location:* end of M62 east, 10 miles from Hull. Parkland at the foot of the wolds with views of the River Humber. 18 holes, 6400 yards. S.S.S. 71. *Green Fees:* £12.50 per round, £18.00 per day weekdays; £18.00 per round, £25.00 per day. *Eating facilities:* golf bar plus hotel à la carte, banqueting and conference facilities for 300. *Visitors:* welcome, no restrictions. Hotel has 70 bedrooms. *Society Meetings:* welcome. Professional: Chris Gray (0430 421286). Secretary: Mr J.R. Bean (0430 421286).

CLEETHORPES. **Cleethorpes Golf Club Ltd.,** Golf House, Kings Road, Cleethorpes DN35 0PN (0472 812059). *Location:* approximately one mile south of Cleethorpes. Flat meadowland crossed by large dykes. 18 holes, 6018 yards, 5503 metres. S.S.S. 69. Restricted practice area. *Green Fees:* weekdays £17.00; weekends £22.00. £5.00 reduction weekdays if with member, £10.00 weekends. *Eating facilities:* lunch time hot and cold snacks, evening meals by arrangement. *Visitors:* welcome except Wednesdays, but must be member of another golf club. Ladies do not play Saturday afternoon and Sunday morning. Men do not play Wednesday afternoon. *Society Meetings:* weekdays only by arrangement with the Secretary. Professional: P. Davies (0472 814060). Secretary: G.B. Standaloft (0472 814060).

CONISTON.**Ganstead Park Golf Club,** Longdales Lane, Coniston, Near Hull HU11 4LB (Hull (0482) 811280). *Location:* east of Hull, on A165 to Bridlington. Flat parkland. 18 holes, 6801 yards. S.S.S. 73.

*Green Fees:* weekdays £14.00 per round, £18.00 per day; weekends £24.00 per day. *Eating facilities:* full catering facilities. *Visitors:* welcome without reservation except Wednesday 9.00 – 11.00am and Sunday 8.00am – 1.00pm. *Society Meetings:* catered for subject to availability. Professional: Mike Smee (0482 811121). Secretary: J. Kirby (0482 874754).

COTTINGHAM. **Hessle Golf Club,** Westfield Road, Raywell, Cottingham (Hull (0482) 659187) *Location:* three miles south west of Cottingham. Parkland. 18 holes, 6290 yards, S.S.S. 70. Two practice areas. *Green Fees:* £20.00 per round, £25.00 per day weekdays; weekends and Bank Holidays £25.00 per round. *Eating facilities:* snack lunches Tuesday to Sunday, set lunches by arrangement. *Visitors:* midweek unrestricted except Tuesdays 9am – 1pm. Weekends visitors may play after 11am at Professional's discretion. *Society Meetings:* catered for weekdays only by arrangement. Professional: G. Fieldsend (0482 650190). Secretary: R. L. Dorsey (0482 650171).

DRIFFIELD. **Driffield Golf Club,** Sunderlandwick, Driffield (Driffield (0377) 43116). *Location:* one mile south of Driffield off the A161. 18 holes, 6199 yards. S.S.S. 69. *Green Fees:* weekdays £15.00; weekends £20.00. *Eating facilities:* bar, dining facility. *Visitors:* welcome weekdays, restrictions weekends. *Society Meetings:* catered for by prior arrangement. Secretary: M. Winn (0377 44167).

GRIMSBY. **Grimsby Golf Club Ltd,** Littlecoats Road, Grimsby DN34 4LU (Grimsby (0472) 342823). *Location:* one mile west of Grimsby town centre off A18. 18 holes, 6058 yards. S.S.S. 69. Practice area. *Green Fees:* weekdays £17.00, £12 with member; weekends £22.00, £12.00 with member. *Eating facilities:*snack lunches most days, set lunches by arrangement, afternoon teas most days, evening meals by arrangement with Steward. *Visitors:* welcome weekdays, must be members of golf clubs. Ladies do not play Saturday between 1.00pm – 5.00pm and Sunday mornings. *Society Meetings:* catered for Mondays and Fridays by arrangement with Secretary (Club ladies' day Tuesday, club ladies have priority). Professional: Steve Houltby (0472 356981). Secretary: A.D. Houlihan (0472 342630).

HORNSEA. **Hornsea Golf Club,** Rolston Road, Hornsea HU18 1XG (Hornsea (0964) 535488). *Location:* follow signs for Hornsea Pottery – Golf Course 200 yards past Pottery. Parkland. 18 holes, 6475 yards. S.S.S. 71. Large practice area. *Green Fees:* weekdays £16.50; weekends £25.00. *Eating facilities:* available every day. *Visitors:* welcome, please ring Professional for a time. Ladies' Day Tuesdays. *Society Meetings:* catered for by arrangement with the Secretary. Professional: B. Thompson (0964 534989). Secretary: B.W. Kirton (0964 532020).

HOWDEN. **Boothferry Golf Club,** Spaldington Lane, Howden, Near Goole DN14 7NG (Howden (0430) 430364; Fax: 0430 430567). *Location:* M62 Junction 37 – Howden – B1228 towards Bubwith. Flat meadowland, with bunkers, ditches and ponds. 18 holes, 6651 yards. S.S.S. 72. Two large practice areas. *Green Fees:* weekdays £6.50 per round, weekends £10.50 per round. *Eating facilities:* bar and catering facilities. *Visitors:* welcome seven days a week, must book times; dress restrictions. *Society Meetings:* welcome all week, numbers over 12. Professional: (0430 430364). Secretary: (0405 765141). Caterer: (0430 430371).

HULL. **Hull Golf Club (1921) Ltd.,** The Hall, 27 Packman Lane, Kirk Ella, Hull HU10 7TJ (Hull (0482) 653026). *Location:* five miles west of Hull. Parkland and wooded. 18 holes, 6242 yards. S.S.S. 70. *Green Fees:* on application. *Eating facilities:* available. *Visitors:* welcome weekdays except Wednesday. *Society Meetings:* by prior arrangement. Professional: D. Jagger (0482 653074). General Manager: R. Toothill (0482 658919).

HULL. **Springhead Park Golf Club,** Willerby Road, Hull HU5 5JE (Hull (0482) 656309). *Location:* west boundary. Parkland. 18 holes, 6102 yards. S.S.S. 69. *Green Fees:* weekdays £4.50 per round, weekends £6.00 per round. *Visitors:* unrestricted. Professional: B. Herrington (0482 594969). Secretary: M.J. Kemp.

HULL. **Sutton Park Municipal Golf Club,** Saltshouse Road, Hull HU8 9HF (Hull (0482) 74242). *Location:* three miles east of city centre on A164. Parkland course. 18 holes, 6295 yards, 5719 metres. S.S.S. 70. *Green Fees:* weekdays £4.50, weekends £6.00. Reductions for Juniors and Senior Citizens.

*Eating facilities:* available, parties by pre-booking. *Visitors:* no restrictions except Sunday mornings. *Society Meetings:* by application to Hull Corporation Leisure Services Dept. Professional: Paul Rushworth (0482 711450). Secretary: Mr Platten (0482 706088).

IMMINGHAM. **Immingham Golf Club,** Church Lane, Immingham DN40 2EU (Immingham (0469) 575298). *Location:* two miles off A180, behind St. Andrew's Church, Immingham. Flat-ridge and furrow, wide and deep dykes. 18 holes, 6100 yards. S.S.S. 69. *Green Fees:* weekdays £11.00 per round; weekends £18.00. *Eating facilities:* full catering facilities, normal bar. *Visitors:* welcome anytime except Thursday pm, Saturday pm and Sunday am. *Society Meetings:* catered for if booked in advance. Professional: Mr N. Harding (0469 575493). Secretary: (0469 575298).

SCUNTHORPE. **Grange Park Golf Club,** Butterwick Road, Messingham, Scunthorpe DN17 3PP (0724 762945). *Location:* five miles south of Scunthorpe between Messingham and East Butterwick, four miles south of Junction 3 of M180. New parkland course. 9 holes, 2970 yards. S.S.S. 69. Par 35. Driving range. *Green Fees:* £4.00 weekdays; £6.00 weekends. Juniors half price. *Eating facilities:* coffee bar. *Visitors:* welcome at all times. Pro shop. Manager: Ian Cannon.

SCUNTHORPE. **Holme Hall Golf Club,** Holme Lane, Bottesford, Scunthorpe DN16 3RF (Scunthorpe (0724) 849185). *Location:* M180 Exit 4 (Scunthorpe East). Heathland with sandy subsoil. 18 holes, 6475 yards. S.S.S. 71. *Green Fees:* to be decided. *Eating facilities:* daily except Mondays. Bar meals or restaurant. *Visitors:* welcome if members of affiliated clubs, not weekends or Bank Holidays unless with a member. *Society Meetings:* catered for by arrangement with Secretary. Professional: Richard McKiernon (0724 851816). Secretary: Mr G.D. Smith (0724 862078).

SCUNTHORPE. **Normanby Hall Golf Club,** Normanby Park, Near Scunthorpe DN15 9HU (Scunthorpe (0724) 720252). *Location:* five miles north of Scunthorpe on B1130. Follow signs for Normanby Country Park. Parkland. 18 holes, 6500 yards. S.S.S. 71. Practice area. *Green Fees:* weekdays £9.50 per round, £14.00 per day; weekends £11.50 per round. *Eating facilities:* fully licensed Clubhouse with restaurant, Societies should notify Catering Manager in advance. *Visitors:* welcome on most occasions, check times in advance with golf Professional. *Society Meetings:* bookings taken for weekdays, Thursdays and Friday pm. Professional: Mr Chris Mann (0724 720226). Bookings Secretary: I.D. Reekie (0724 280444). Secretary: Mr Graham Kirk (0724 844303).

SCUNTHORPE. **Scunthorpe Golf Club,** Burringham Road, Scunthorpe DN17 2AB (Scunthorpe (0724) 842913). *Location:* M181 – Burringham Road opposite Asda Superstore. Flat wooded course. 18 holes, 6281 yards. S.S.S. 71. *Green Fees:* weekdays £16.00. *Eating facilities:* full catering and bar available. *Visitors:* welcome weekdays only. *Society Meetings:* catered for weekdays. Professional: A. Lawson (0724 868972). Secretary: E. Willsmore (0724 866561).

WITHERNSEA. **Withernsea Golf Club,** Chestnut Avenue, Withernsea HU19 2PG (0964 612258). *Location:* 25 miles north-east of Kingston-upon-Hull. Seaside links. 9 holes, 5112 yards. S.S.S. 64. *Green Fees:* weekdays £8.00 per day, £5.00 if with a member; weekends £8.00 with a member only. *Eating facilities:* bar and meals available. *Visitors:* welcome any day except weekends unless playing with a member. *Society Meetings:* by reservation. Special rates. Professional: G. Harrison. Secretary: F. Buckley (0964 612214).

# Isle of Wight

COWES. **Cowes Golf Club,** Crossfield Avenue, Cowes, Isle of Wight (Cowes (0983) 292303). Parkland with sea views. 9 holes, 5934 yards. S.S.S. 68. *Green Fees:* weekdays £15.00; weekends £18.00. *Eating facilities:* snack meals available in bar in summer. Bar open 11am to 2pm summer months. *Visitors:* welcome except Sunday before 1pm and Thursday, Ladies' Day (11.30am to 3pm). *Society Meetings:* by arrangement with Secretary. Society rates by arrangement. Secretary: D.C. Weaver.

EAST COWES. **Osborne Golf Club,** Osborne House, East Cowes PO32 6JX (Cowes (0983) 295421). *Location:* off A3027 north of East Cowes, in Osborne Estate. Parkland. 9 holes, 6286 yards. S.S.S. 70. Practice area. *Green Fees:* weekdays £15.00; weekends and Bank Holidays £18.00. *Eating facilities:* catering available each day. *Visitors:* welcome except on Saturdays and Sundays before 12.00 noon and Tuesdays before 1.00pm. *Society Meetings:* catered for (24 maximum). Professional: Andrew Scullion (0983 295649). Secretary: Roy Jones.

## NOTE

FRESHWATER. **Freshwater Bay Golf Club,** Afton Down, Freshwater (Freshwater (0983) 752955). *Location:* western end of Island, approximately half-a-mile east of Freshwater Bay on coast road to Ventnor. 18 holes, 5379 yards. S.S.S. 67. *Green Fees:* £16.00 per day, £20.00 weekends and Bank Holidays. *Eating facilities:* licensed bar, catering. *Visitors:* welcome. *Society Meetings:* by arrangement. Secretary: G. Smith.

NEWPORT. **Newport (Isle of Wight) Golf Club,** St. Georges Down, Near Shide, Newport, Isle of Wight (Newport (0983) 525076). *Location:* one mile south east of Newport. 9 holes, 5704 yards. S.S.S. 68. *Green Fees:* £15.00 per day weekdays; £17.50 weekends. *Eating facilities:* snacks available. *Visitors:* welcome, except Saturday after 3.30pm and Sunday afternoons. *Society Meetings:* welcome by arrangement. Secretary: Mr P.J. Mills (0983 525076).

RYDE. **Ryde Golf Club,** Binstead Road, Ryde, Isle of Wight PO33 3NF (Ryde (0983) 614809). *Location:* on A3054 very close to town. Parkland course. 9 holes, 5287 yards. S.S.S. 66. Practice area. *Green Fees:* weekdays £15.00 per day; weekends and Bank Holidays £20.00. *Eating facilities:* available during bar

hours. *Visitors:* welcome, restrictions Wednesdays and Sundays. *Society Meetings:* catered for. Professional: Mark Wright. Secretary: F. Cockayne (0983 614809).

SANDOWN. **Shanklin and Sandown Golf Club,** The Fairway, Lake, Sandown PO36 9PR (0983 403170). *Location:* one mile from Sandown. Heathland. 18 holes, 6068 yards. S.S.S. 69. *Green Fees:* £20/£25 weekdays; £25 weekends. Three day ticket weekdays £50. *Eating facilities:* available 10/11am to dusk. *Visitors:* welcome, restrictions weekends. Handicap Certificate preferred. Bona fide golfers only. *Society Meetings:* by arrangement. Professional: Peter Hammond (0983 404424). Secretary: G.A. Wormald (0983 403217).

UPPER VENTNOR. **Ventnor Golf Club,** Steephill Down Road, Upper Ventnor (Ventnor (0983) 853326). *Location:* north-west boundary of Ventnor. Downland undulating with side slopes windy. 9 holes, 5752 yards. S.S.S. 68. *Green Fees:* weekdays £12.00; weekends £14.00. Ladies £2.00 less; Juniors under 16 half price. *Eating facilities:* bar snacks only. *Visitors:* welcome, Sundays after 1pm, Ladies' Day Fridays 12 noon to 3pm. Secretary: R. Hose (0983 853198).

# PUBLISHER'S NOTE

While every effort is made to ensure accuracy, we regret that FHG Publications cannot accept responsibility for errors, omissions or misrepresentation in our entries or any consequences thereof. Prices in particular should be checked because we go to press early. We will follow up complaints, but cannot act as arbiters or agents for either party.

# Kent

ASHFORD. **Ashford (Kent) Golf Club,** Sandyhurst Lane, Ashford TN25 4NT (Ashford (0233) 620180). *Location:* just off A20, one and a half miles west of Ashford. Parkland – stream cutting through course. 18 holes, 6246 yards. S.S.S. 70. *Green Fees:* weekdays £24.00, weekends and Bank Holidays £40.00 (November to February reduced green fees). *Eating facilities:* every day. *Visitors:* welcome. Handicap Certificate required. *Society Meetings:* catered for Tuesdays and Thursdays by arrangement. Professional: Hugh Sherman (0233 629644). Secretary: A.H. Story (0233 622655).

BECKENHAM. **Beckenham Place Park Golf Club,** Beckenham Hill Road, Beckenham. *Location:* on A222 north of Bromley. Parkland. 18 holes, 5672 yards. S.S.S. 68. Practice ground, nets, putting green. *Green Fees:* information not available. *Eating facilities:* bar and cafeteria. *Visitors:* welcome without reservation on weekdays, but must book for weekends. *Society Meetings:* not catered for. Other facilities include tennis courts and putting green. Professional: B. Woodman (081-658 5374). Secretary: K. Tregunno (081-778 4116).

BECKENHAM. **Braeside Golf Club,** Beckenham Place Park, Beckenham Hill, Beckenham (081-650 2292). Parkland course. 18 holes, 5722 yards, 5230 metres. S.S.S. 68. Practice area and nets. *Green Fees:* £8.30 midweek, £13.30 weekends, plus £2.80 booking fee. 9 holes: £5.15 weekdays, £7.70 weekends and Bank Holidays. *Eating facilities:* cafe and bar. *Visitors:* welcome any time. Professional: Bill Woodman (081-658 5374). Secretary: R. Oliver (081-304 3818).

BECKENHAM. **Langley Park Golf Club,** Barnfield Wood Road, Beckenham BR3 2SZ (081-650 2090). *Location:* one mile from Bromley South station. Flat parkland. 18 holes, 6488 yards, 5931 metres, S.S.S. 71. Practice nets. *Green Fees:* on application. *Eating facilities:* bar snacks, restaurant/dining room. *Visitors:* welcome by arrangement with Professional. *Society Meetings:* by arrangement with Secretary. Professional: George Ritchie (081-650 1663). Secretary: J.L. Smart (081-658 6849).

BEXLEY HEATH. **Bexley Heath Golf Club,** Mount Row, Mount Road, Bexley Heath DA6 8JS (081-303 6951). *Location:* adjacent to A2. Hilly parkland. 9 holes, 5239 yards, 4788 metres. S.S.S. 66. *Green Fees:* £15.00 (approximately). Weekends with member only. *Eating facilities:* catering available. *Visitors:* weekdays only. Professional: To be appointed. Secretary: S.E. Squires.

BIGGIN HILL. **Cherry Lodge Golf Club,** Jail Lane, Biggin Hill, Near Westerham TN16 3AX (Biggin Hill (0959) 572250; Fax: 0959 540672). *Location:* from Bromley, A233 to Westerham, Jail Lane on left 400 yards past Biggin Hill Airfield. Parkland. 18 holes, 6652

yards. S.S.S. 72. Practice ground. *Green Fees:* weekdays £24.00; weekends with member only £22.00. *Eating facilities:* a la carte restaurant and lounge bar. *Visitors:* weekdays only. *Society Meetings:* welcome weekdays only. Professional: Nigel Child (0959 572987). General Manager/Secretary: Mr J.R. Macarthur (0959 576712).

BROADSTAIRS. **North Foreland Golf Club,** The Clubhouse, Convent Road, Broadstairs CT10 3PU (Thanet (0843) 862140). *Location:* outside Broadstairs, near North Foreland Lighthouse. Seaside downland. 18 holes, 6382 yards. S.S.S. 71. Short Course: 18 holes, 1752 yards. Par 3. *Green Fees:* £20.00 per round, £30.00 per day weekdays. Short Course: £5.50 weekdays, £6.50 weekends and Public Holidays. *Eating facilities:* bar and dining room. *Visitors:* weekdays and weekend afternoons with current Handicap Certificate. Tennis. *Society Meetings:* Wednesdays and Fridays by prior arrangement with Secretary. Professional: Mike Lee (0843 869628). Secretary: B.J. Preston (0843 862140).

BROMLEY. **Magpie Hall Lane Municipal Golf Club,** Magpie Hall Lane, Bromley (081-462 7014). *Location:* off Bromley Common on A21. 9 holes, 5538 yards. S.S.S. 67. *Green Fees:* information not provided. *Visitors:* welcome without reservation. Professional: A. Hodgson (081-462 7014). Clubhouse (081-462 8001).

BROMLEY. **Shortlands Golf Club,** Postal Meadow Road, Shortlands, Bromley BR2 0PB (081-460 2471). *Location:* car park and entrance in Ravensbourne Avenue, off the main Beckenham to Bromley Road, adjacent Shortlands B.R. Station. 9 holes, 5261 yards. S.S.S. 65. *Green Fees:* no green fees allowed except when introduced and playing with a member £10.00. *Eating facilities:* available. *Visitors:* restricted to playing with a member. *Society Meetings:* only when member involved. Professional: J. Bates (081-464 6182). Hon. Secretary: Mrs Leah Burrows (081-460 8828 or 2471).

BROMLEY. **Sundridge Park Golf Club,** Garden Road, off Plaistow Lane, Bromley BR1 3NE (081-460 1822). *Location:* five minutes walk from Sundridge Park station. Wooded parkland. 36 holes. East 6467 yards. West 6007 yards. S.S.S. 71 and 69. Two practice grounds. *Green Fees:* £36.00 per day weekdays. *Eating facilities:* restaurant, spike bar, lounge bar, members bar. *Visitors:* welcome weekdays only, with Handicap Certificate. *Society Meetings:* catered for by arrangement. Professional: Bob Cameron (081-460 5540). Secretary: Derek Lowton (081-460 0278).

CANTERBURY. **Broome Park Golf and Country Club,** Broome Park Estate, Barham, Near Canterbury CT4 6QX (Canterbury (0227) 831701). *Location:* off the A2 at the A260, half a mile on right hand side. Parkland, undulating, lake in front of 18th green. 18

holes, 6610 yards, S.S.S. 72. *Green Fees:* £23.00 weekdays; £25.00 weekends. *Eating facilities:* available all week. *Visitors:* weekdays. *Society Meetings:* weekdays. Professional: Tienie Britz (0227 831701 extension 264). Hon. Secretary: Don Lees (0227 831701 extension 298).

CANTERBURY. **Canterbury Golf Club,** Scotland Hills, Littlebourne Road, Canterbury CT1 1TW (0227 781871). *Location:* one mile from town centre on the A257 road to Sandwich. 18 holes, 6209 yards. S.S.S. 70. *Green Fees:* weekdays £24.00 per round, £32.00 per day; weekends £32.00 per round. Saturday/Sunday after 3pm only. *Eating facilities:* snacks, sandwiches, lunches, dinners each day. *Visitors:* welcome without reservation. *Society Meetings:* catered for Tuesday and Thursday. Professional: Paul Everard (0227 462865). Secretary: E.L. Ruckert. (0227 453532).

CHISLEHURST. **Chislehurst Golf Club,** Camden Park Road, Chislehurst BR7 5HJ (081-467 3055). *Location:* between Bromley and junction of A222 and Sidcup bypass. Parkland. 18 holes, 5128 yards. S.S.S. 65. *Green Fees:* £25.00 weekdays; £10.00 weekends with member only. *Eating facilities:* catering available. Large parties by prior arrangement. *Visitors:* welcome but restricted to weekdays (except Wednesday mornings) and only with a member at weekends. *Society Meetings:* catered for by arrangement, 36 hole Societies only on Thursdays. Professional: S. Corstorphine (081-467 6798). Secretary: N.E. Pearson (081-467 2782).

CRANBROOK. **Cranbrook Golf Club Ltd.,** Benenden Road, Cranbrook TN17 4AL (Cranbrook (0580) 712833). *Location:* situated between Sissinghurst and Benenden. Parkland – tree lined. 18 holes, 6351 yards. S.S.S. 70. Practice area. *Green Fees:* weekdays £19.00, £11.00 with a member; weekends £27.50, £17.00 with a member. *Eating facilities:* clubhouse facilities available all day. *Visitors:* welcome anytime except Tuesday and Thursdays before 10.30am and weekends before 11.30am. *Society Meetings:* company days available. Secretary: (0580 712833).

DARTFORD. **Corinthian Golf Club,** Fawkham Road, Fawkham, Dartford DA3 8LZ (0474 707559). *Location:* off the A2 east of Dartford. Wooded with artificial tees and greens. 9 holes. S.S.S. 70. Practice area. *Green Fees:* £10.00, with a member £6.00.

*Eating facilities:* bar with snacks, catering by arrangement. *Visitors:* welcome except weekends and Bank Holiday mornings. *Society Meetings:* welcome. Secretary: John Wood.

DARTFORD. **Dartford Golf Club Ltd.,** The Clubhouse, Dartford Heath, Dartford DA1 2TN (Dartford (0322) 223616). *Location:* backing on to A2, one mile from Dartford Tunnel and M25. Flat parkland. 18 holes, 5914 yards. S.S.S. 68. *Green Fees:* weekdays £28.00. *Eating facilities:* catering available. *Visitors:* welcome on weekdays with reservation, must be member of another golf club. *Society Meetings:* welcome on Mondays and Fridays by prior arrangement with Secretary. Professional: A. Blackburn (0322 226409). Secretary: Margaret Gronow (0322 226455).

DEAL. **Royal Cinque Ports Golf Club,** Golf Road, Deal (Deal (0304) 374007; Fax: 0304 379530). *Location:* A258 from Sandwich. In Upper Deal leave for Middle Deal Road, left turn into Albert Road, Western Road, on to Golf Road (or from Dover, A258 via Sea front and Godwin Road). Links course. 18 holes, Championship 6785 yards, Medal 6406 yards. S.S.S. 71. *Green Fees:* weekdays £40.00 per day, £30.00 per round after 1pm. No fees accepted at weekends. *Eating facilities:* hot snacks provided Monday to Friday, through bar. *Visitors:* welcome with reservation, introduction preferred. *Society Meetings:* catered for on application. Professional: A.W. Reynolds (0304 374170). Secretary: C.W. Greaves.

DEAL. **Walmer and Kingsdown Golf Club,** The Leas, Kingsdown, Deal CT14 8ER (Deal (0304) 373256). *Location:* on A258 from Dover (A2) to Deal, club signposted at village of Ringwood. Seaside links on clifftop near Dover. 18 holes, 6451 yards. S.S.S. 71. *Green Fees:* weekdays £20.00 per day, £22.00 weekends after 12 noon. *Eating facilities:* full catering and bar service. *Visitors:* welcome without reservation if members of another club. *Society Meetings:* catered for except Saturdays and Sundays. Professional: Ian Coleman (0304 363017). Secretary: B.W. Cockerill.

DEANGATE. **Deangate Ridge Golf Club,** Hoo, Rochester (Medway (0634) 250374). *Location:* three miles from Rochester off A228 towards Isle of Grain. Wooded. 18 holes, 6300 yards. S.S.S. 70. 18 hole Pitch and Putt. *Green Fees:* £8.60 weekdays, £11.30 weekends. *Eating facilities:* available. *Visitors:* welcome

without reservation, bookings required for weekends. *Society Meetings:* catered for. Professional: Barry Aram (0634 251180). Secretary: R. Worthington (0634 271749).

EDENBRIDGE. **Edenbridge Golf and Country Club,** Crouch House Road, Edenbridge TN8 5LQ (Edenbridge (0732) 865097). *Location:* from M25 take A25, at Limpsfield take B2026 to Edenbridge. Parkland. 18 holes, 6643 yards. S.S.S. 73. Second Course 18 holes, 5671 yards. S.S.S. 67. 16 bay floodlit driving range. *Green Fees:* weekdays £15.00 per round, weekends and Bank Holidays £18.00 per round; Skeynes Course £12.00 weekdays, £15.00 weekends. *Eating facilities:* bar and restaurant. *Visitors:* welcome, call for start time. *Society Meetings:* welcome by arrangement. Professional: B. Hemsley (0732 865202). Secretary: Judith Scully (0732 867381; Fax: 0732 867029).

EYNSFORD. **Austin Lodge Golf Club,** Upper Austin Lodge Road, Eynsford DA4 0HU (0322 868944; Fax: 0322 862406). *Location:* Eynsford – 10 minutes' drive from Junction 3 of M25, M20, A20. Secluded rolling countryside with lakes. 18 holes, 6575 yards Yellow Tees, 7118 yards White Tees. S.S.S. 73. Practice ground. *Green Fees:* weekdays £15.00; weekends £20.00. *Eating facilities:* bar, restaurant with light meals all day. *Visitors:* welcome weekdays, possibly after 2pm weekends, telephone booking only. *Society Meetings:* welcome, telephone booking only. Professional: Philip Clark. Secretary: A. McAdams.

FARNBOROUGH. **High Elms Golf Club,** High Elms Road, Downe (0689 58175). *Location:* two miles from Farnborough Hospital on A21, turn right at Shire Lane, second left. 18 holes, 5626 metres. S.S.S. 70. *Green Fees:* information not available. *Eating facilities:* food by arrangement with publican, ring (0689 50177). Professionals: Alan Hodgson, John Kane and Peter Remy. Secretary: Mrs P. O'Keeffe (081-300 2734).

FAVERSHAM. **Faversham Golf Club Ltd.,** Belmont Park, Faversham ME13 0HB (0795 890251). *Location:* M2 Faversham Exit (A251) to A2 junction, left to Brogdale Road, left to Belmont. 18 holes, 6021 yards. S.S.S. 69. *Green Fees:* weekdays £21.00 per round, £28.00 all day; weekends with members only £22.00 per round, £30.00 per day. *Eating facilities:* by arrangement with Steward. *Visitors:* welcome with member. *Society Meetings:* Wednesday and Friday catered for, Tuesdays limited numbers. Professional: G. Nixon (0795 890275). Secretary: D.B. Christie (0795 890561).

FOLKESTONE. **Sene Valley, Folkestone and Hythe Golf Club Ltd.,** Blackhouse Hill, Folkestone CT18 8BZ (0303 66726). *Location:* A20 then B2065 by Channel Tunnel initial works. Downland course overlooking sea. 18 holes, 6287 yards. S.S.S. 70. Practice ground. *Green Fees:* information not available. *Eating facilities:* bar and restaurant (no catering Mondays). *Visitors:* welcome with Handicap Certificate (preferably not weekends or Bank Holidays). *Society Meetings:* welcome. Professional: Trevor Dungate (0303 68514). Secretary: G. Hills (0303 268513).

GILLINGHAM. **Gillingham Golf Club Ltd.,** Woodlands Road, Gillingham ME7 2AP (Medway (0634) 850999). *Location:* M2 to Gillingham turn off, left to A2. Turn left towards Gillingham, course on right hand side. Parkland. 18 holes, 5863 yards, 5364 metres. S.S.S. 68. *Green Fees:* weekdays with a member £10.00 per round, £15.00 per day; without a member £20.00 per round or day. Weekends only with a member. *Eating facilities:* available Wednesday – Sunday. *Visitors:* not weekends; must hold Handicap Certificate and be member of a golf club. *Society Meetings:* welcome, maximum 30 players. Professional: Brian Impett (0634 855862). Secretary: L.P. O'Grady (0634 853017).

GRAVESEND. **Mid-Kent Golf Club,** Singlewell Road, Gravesend DA11 7RB (Gravesend (0474) 352387). *Location:* A227 off A2. Parkland. 18 holes, 6206 yards. S.S.S. 70. *Green Fees:* weekdays £28.00 per round, £35.00 per day; weekends with member only. *Eating facilities:* breakfast, dinner by arrangement, lunch every day, bar 11am to 11pm. *Visitors:* welcome weekdays except competition days with Handicap Certificate. *Society Meetings:* catered for Tuesdays only. Professional: R. Lee (0474 332810). Secretary: T. Potter (0474 568035).

HAWKHURST. **Hawkhurst Golf Club,** High Street, Hawkhurst TN18 4JS (Hawkhurst (0580) 752396). *Location:* on A268 from Hawkhurst to Flimwell. Parkland. 9 holes, 5769 yards. S.S.S. 68. *Green Fees:* £18.00 weekdays; weekends only with member. *Eating facilities:* snacks/meals available. Please check before arriving. *Visitors:* welcome. *Society Meetings:* weekdays, catered for with prior notice. Professional: Tony Collins (0580 753600). Secretary: Richard C. Fowles.

HERNE BAY. **Herne Bay Golf Club,** Canterbury Road, Herne Bay (Herne Bay (0227) 373964). 18 holes, 5466 yards. S.S.S. 67. *Green Fees:* weekdays £18.00 per round, £25.00 per day; weekends £25.00. *Eating facilities:* available except Monday. *Visitors:* welcome weekdays unrestricted. Weekends and Bank Holidays after 12 noon only. Handicap Certificate required. *Society Meetings:* catered for weekdays. Professional: D. Lambert. Secretary: B. Warren.

HEVER. **Hever Golf Club,** Hever TN8 7NG (0732 70778). *Location:* at Junction 6 take A22 turning to Godstone, then turn left onto the A25 to Sevenoaks, after three and a half miles take the Edenbridge road. Follow signs for Hever Castle. Go past the entrance to castle and the club is half a mile further on the right. 18 holes, 6951 yards (6319 metres). S.S.S. 72. *Green Fees:* on application. *Eating facilities:* available in the clubhouse. *Visitors:* members only.

HYTHE. **Hythe Imperial Golf Club,** Princes Parade, Hythe CT21 6AE. *Location:* come off M20 Junction 11 directions for Hythe A261. Flat seaside course. 9 holes, 5533 yards. S.S.S. 67. Practice ground. *Green Fees:* information not provided. Reductions if playing with a member. *Eating facilities:* available at the hotel. *Visitors:* welcome weekdays, no fees weekends up to 1pm. *Society Meetings:* welcome weekdays only. Professional: Gordon Ritchie (0303 267441). Secretary: Mr R. Barrett (0303 267554).

MAIDSTONE. **Bearsted Golf Club,** Ware Street, Bearsted, Maidstone ME14 4PQ (0622 38389). *Location:* Junction 7 off M20. Secluded parkland course with view of North Downs. 18 holes, 6253 yards, 5715 metres. S.S.S. 70. Practice area/net. *Green Fees:* £22.00 per round weekdays only. *Eating facilities:* bar/restaurant. *Visitors:* welcome on proof of membership of bona fide golf club. Current Handicap Certificate required. Weekends with member only. *Society Meetings:* catered for Tuesdays and Thursdays, limited numbers Wednesday/Fridays. Professional: T. Simpson (0622 38024). Secretary: Mrs L.M. Siems (0622 38198).

MAIDSTONE. **Cobtree Manor Park Golf Club,** Chatham Road, Sandling, Maidstone ME14 3AZ (0622 681560). *Location:* M20, A229 Chatham (not Maidstone). Undulating course with trees, and interesting 6th hole over lake. 18 holes, 5716 yards. S.S.S. 68. Tuition, practice, putting. *Green Fees:* information not available. *Eating facilities:* restaurant and bar. *Visitors:* welcome, book one week in advance through Professional. *Society Meetings:* weekdays by arrangement only. Professional: Martin Drew (0622 753276).

MAIDSTONE. **Leeds Castle Golf Course,** Leeds Castle, Leeds, Maidstone ME17 1PL (0622 880467). *Location:* M20-A20 near Maidstone. Situated in the grounds of Leeds Castle, parkland. 9 holes, 2880 yards S.S.S. 34. Practice putting green and nets. *Green Fees:* £8.50. Reductions Juniors and Senior Citizens weekdays. *Eating facilities:* Park Gate Inn (situated in golf course car park). *Visitors:* welcome anytime, bookings taken from six days in advance. Correct dress must be worn – no denim jeans allowed, golf shoes preferred. *Society Meetings:* welcome midweek. Professional: Chris Miller PGA. Secretary: Jill Skinner.

MAIDSTONE. **Tudor Park Golf and Country Club,** Ashford Road, Bearsted ME14 4NQ (Maidstone (0622) 735891). *Location:* east of Maidstone, on A20 at Bearsted. Off Junction 8 of M20. Parkland. 18 holes, 6041 yards. S.S.S. 69. Practice area. *Green Fees:* weekdays £30.00, weekends £36.00 (special rates if guest of member). *Eating facilities:* restaurants and bars. *Visitors:* current Handicap Certificate required. Hotel, leisure and conference facilities. *Society Meetings:* societies and company days catered for. Professional: Marc Boggia (0622 39412). Secretary: Christopher May (0622 34334).

MAIDSTONE. **West Malling Golf Club,** London Road, Addington, Maidstone (West Malling (0732) 844785). *Location:* A228 turn off M20. Parkland, 18 holes, 6142 yards. S.S.S. 70 (Spitfire Course). 18 holes, 6300 yards. S.S.S. 70 (Hurricane Course). *Green Fees:* weekdays £18.00 per round, £25.00 per day; weekends £25.00 after 12 noon. *Eating facilities:* restaurant available. *Visitors:* welcome except Bank Holidays or before 11.30am weekends. Conference/function facilities available. *Society Meetings:* catered for. Professional: Paul Foston (0732 844022). Secretary: Mike Ellis (0732 844785).

NEW ROMNEY. **Littlestone Golf Club,** St. Andrews Road, Littlestone, New Romney TN28 8RB (New Romney (0679) 62310). *Location:* A20 to Ashford, B2070 to New Romney, one mile from New Romney.

Seaside links course. 18 holes, 6417 yards. S.S.S. 71. Also 9 hole course, 1998 yards. S.S.S. 32. Driving range. *Green Fees:* £20.00 per round, £28.00 per day weekdays; £23.00 per round, £33.00 per day weekends. 9 hole course £7.00 weekdays; £8.50 weekends. *Eating facilities:* available. *Visitors:* Handicap Certificate required, visitors not allowed at weekends in Winter, in Summer only after 3pm. Weekdays by prior arrangement with the Secretary. Professional: Stephen Watkins (0679 62231). Secretary: J.D. Lewis (0679 63355).

NEW ROMNEY. **Romney Warren Golf Club,** St. Andrews Road, Littlestone, New Romney TN28 8RB. *Location:* M20 to Ashford B2070 to New Romney, one mile from town centre. Seaside links. 18 holes, 5000 yards. S.S.S. 65. Practice area, chipping and putting green. *Green Fees:* £8.50 per round weekdays; £10.00 per round weekends. *Eating facilities:* clubhouse open for breakfast, lunch and dinner. *Visitors:* no restrictions on visitors except that starting times should be booked in advance. *Society Meetings:* welcomed. Professional: Stephen Watkins (0679 62231). Secretary: J.D. Lewis (0679 63355).

ORPINGTON. **Cray Valley Golf Club,** Sandy Lane, St. Paul's Cray, Orpington BR5 3HY (Orpington (0689) 831927). *Location:* Ruxley roundabout A20; turn off into Sandy Lane, half-a-mile on left. Parkland. 18 holes, 5624 yards. S.S.S. 67. *Green Fees:* weekdays £10.00, weekends £16.00. Also 9 hole course: weekdays £4.00, weekends £5.50. *Eating facilities:* hot meals available lunchtimes, also bar. *Visitors:* welcome all week. *Society Meetings:* welcome weekdays. Professional: Mr John Gregory (0689 837909). Secretary: Ron Hill (0689 839677).

ORPINGTON. **Ruxley Park Golf Centre,** Sandy Lane, St. Paul's Cray, Orpington BR5 3HY (Orpington (0689) 871490). *Location:* off Ruxley roundabout on the old A20. Undulating parkland. 18 holes, 4466 yards. S.S.S. 65. Floodlit driving range. *Green Fees:* information not provided. *Eating facilities:* bar and catering facilities. *Visitors:* welcome, except weekends before 11.00am. *Society Meetings:* welcome. Professional: J. Gregory. Secretary: Les Dyke.

ORPINGTON. **West Kent Golf Club,** West Hill, Downe, Near Orpington BR6 7JJ (0689 853737). *Location:* from Downe village south along Luxted Lane, 600 yards turn right into West Hill. 18 holes, 6399 yards. S.S.S. 70. *Green Fees:* £25.00 per round, £40.00 per day. *Eating facilities:* meals by arrangement. *Visitors:* welcome with letter of introduction and recognised handicap. Casual golfers must phone in advance. *Society Meetings:* catered for. Professionals: R.S. Fidler and G. Ryan (0689 856863). Secretary: A.J. Messing (0689 851323).

RAMSGATE. **St. Augustine's Golf Club,** Cottington Road, Cliffsend, Ramsgate CT12 5JN (Thanet (0843) 590333). *Location:* two miles south-west of Ramsgate – approaching from A253 or A256 follow signs to St. Augustine's Cross. Entrance 75 yards beyond Cross by railway bridge. Mainly parkland, flat – tight and challenging course. 18 holes, 4999 yards, 4572 metres. S.S.S. 64. *Green Fees:* £21.00 weekdays, £23.00 weekends and Bank Holidays. Weekly £65.00

monthly £195. *Eating facilities:* full catering except Mondays when sandwiches and beverages only, usual bar facilities. *Visitors:* welcome, proof of Handicap required, advisable to ring Professional the day before to check periods booked for competitions, societies, etc. *Society Meetings:* catered for, book through Secretary. Professional: D. Scott (0843 590222). Secretary: R. James (0843 590333).

ROCHESTER. **Rochester and Cobham Park Golf Club,** Park Pale, by Rochester ME2 3UL (Shorne (047 482) 3411). *Location:* on A2, 2 miles east of Gravesend turn-off. 18 holes, 6467 yards. S.S.S. 71. *Green Fees:* on application. *Eating facilities:* lunch, tea, dinner and snacks available, lunches should be ordered in advance. *Visitors:* with Handicap Certificates – welcome without reservation on weekdays. *Society Meetings:* catered for on Tuesdays and Thursdays. Professional: Matt Henderson (047 482 3658). Manager: J.W. Irvine (047 482 3411).

SANDWICH BAY. **Prince's Golf Club,** Sandwich Bay (Sandwich (0304) 611118). *Location:* four miles from Sandwich through the Sandwich Bay Estate. 27 holes arranged as 3 loops of 9 holes named "Dunes", "Himalayas", "Shore". D & H 6262 – 6776 yds par 71, S.S.S. 70-73. H & S 6238 – 6813 yds, Par 71, S.S.S. 70-73, S & D 6466-6947 yds. Par 72, S.S.S. 71-73. *Green Fees:* weekdays £26.50 round, £29.00 day; Saturdays £31.00 round, £34.00 day; Sundays £36.00 round, £39.00 day. *Eating facilities:* breakfast, lunch, dinner available every day (pre-booking advisable); bar buffet/Ploughman's lunchtime & evenings; light snacks throughout the day. *Visitors & Societies:* welcome without restriction, Company days and private parties our speciality. Brochure available on request. *Starting Times:* Philip Sparks (Professional) (0304 613797). Information & Bookings: Geoff Ramm (0304 611118).

SANDWICH. **Royal St. Georges Golf Club,** Sandwich CT13 9PB (0304 617308; Fax: 0304 611245). *Location:* one mile from Sandwich on the road to Sandwich Bay. From Canterbury A257, from Dover A258. Links. 18 holes, Championship 6903 yards, Medal 6534 yards. S.S.S. Championship 74. Medal 72. Large practice ground. *Green Fees:* £45.00 per round, £65.00 per day weekdays. *Eating facilities:* snack bar and dining room. *Visitors:* welcome

weekdays only. Must have Handicap Certificate and be member of club with membership of E.G.U. *Society Meetings:* catered for by arrangement. All players must meet requirements for visitors. Professional: Niall Cameron (0304 615236). Secretary: Gerald E. Watts (0304 613090).

SEVENOAKS. **Darenth Valley Golf Course,** Station Road, Shoreham, Near Sevenoaks TN14 7SA (0959 522944). *Location:* A225 between Otford and Eynsford, approximately four miles north of Sevenoaks. Parkland course. 18 holes, 6356 yards. S.S.S. 72. Practice area, putting greens. *Green Fees:* weekdays £10.00 for 18 holes; weekends and Bank Holidays £13.00. *Eating facilities:* bar snacks, diningroom, functions up to 100 covers. *Visitors:* welcome with reservation through Pro's shop. *Society Meetings:* catered for by arrangement. Professional: Scott Fotheringham (0959 522922). Clubhouse Manager/Steward: Neil Morgan.

SEVENOAKS. **Knole Park Golf Club,** Seal Hollow Road, Sevenoaks TN15 0HJ (Sevenoaks (0732) 452709). *Location:* one mile south-east of Sevenoaks town. Parkland. 18 holes, 6249 yards, 5711 metres. S.S.S. 70. *Green Fees:* weekdays only, £25.50 per round, £36.00 for two rounds. *Eating facilities:* full catering and bar. *Visitors:* by appointment only, must have a club handicap. *Society Meetings:* catered for by arrangement only. Professional: P.E. Gill (0732 451740). Secretary: D.J.L. Hoppe (0732 452150).

SEVENOAKS. **Wildernesse Golf Club,** Park Lane, Seal, Sevenoaks TN15 0JE (Sevenoaks (0732) 761526). *Location:* A25 between Sevenoaks and Borough Green. Park and woodland. 18 holes, 6478 yards, 5924 metres. S.S.S. 72. Large practice ground. *Green Fees:* £25.00/£35.00 weekdays. *Eating facilities:* by arrangement. *Visitors:* welcome, weekdays only by prior arrangement; letter of introduction. *Society Meetings:* catered for Thursdays. Professional: Bill Dawson (0732 761527). Secretary: K.L. Monk (0732 761199).

SEVENOAKS. **Woodlands Manor Golf Club,** Tinkerpot Lane, Woodlands, Near Otford, Sevenoaks TN15 6AB (Otford (09592) 3805). *Location:* Junction 3, M25 take "Brands Hatch" sign on A20, seven miles. Parkland. 18 holes, 6000 yards. S.S.S. 68. Six acre practice ground. *Green Fees:* on application. *Eating facilities:* bar daily. *Visitors:* welcome weekdays, Handicap Certificate required at weekends after 1pm. *Society Meetings:* welcome by arrangement Monday to Friday. Professional: Nick Allen (09592 4161). Secretary: E.F. Newman (09592 3806).

SEVENOAKS. **Wrotham Heath Golf Club,** Seven Mile Lane, Comp, Sevenoaks TN15 8QZ (Borough Green (0732) 884800). *Location:* on B2016 half-a-mile

south of junction with A20. Woods and heather. 9 holes with alternate tees for 18. 5918 yards. S.S.S. 68. *Green Fees:* weekdays £20.00; weekends only with a member. *Eating facilities:* bar and snacks, meals by arrangement, except Mondays. *Visitors:* welcome on weekdays with Handicap Certificate, but not Bank Holidays. *Society Meetings:* catered for Fridays only, no more than 20 people. Professional: H. Dearden (0732 883854). Secretary: T.J. Fenson (0732 884800).

SHEERNESS. **Sheerness Golf Club,** Power Station Road, Sheerness ME12 3AE (Sheerness (0795) 662585). *Location:* follow A249 then A250 towards Sheerness. Flat marshland/meadowland – numerous water hazards. 18 holes, 6500 yards. S.S.S. 71. Practice area. *Green Fees:* weekdays £15.00 (£8.00) per round, £20.00 (£12.00) per day; weekends £12.00 only if playing with a member. *Eating facilities:* available. *Visitors:* weekdays only except with member. *Society Meetings:* catered for Tuesdays, Wednesdays and Thursdays by previous arrangement. (16-40). Professional: Alan Gillard (0795 666840). Secretary: J.W. Gavins.

SIDCUP. **Sidcup Golf Club (1926) Ltd,** 7 Hurst Road, Sidcup DA15 9AE (081-300 2150). *Location:* three minutes' walk from Sidcup Station. Parkland. 9 holes, 5722 yards. S.S.S. 68. Practice area. *Green Fees:* weekdays £16.00. *Eating facilities:* restaurant and bar. *Visitors:* welcome weekdays except Bank Holidays. *Society Meetings:* (up to 30 members) catered for by arrangement. Professional: Nick Terry (081-309 0679). Secretary: Sandy Watt (081-300 2150).

SITTINGBOURNE near. **Upchurch River Valley Golf Courses,** Oak Lane, Upchurch, near Sittingbourne ME9 7AY (0634 360626; Fax: 0634 387784). *Location:* M2, Junction 4 (A278) A2 Rainham 2.5 miles L, Upchurch (opposite Little Chef). Undulating parkland with ponds and panoramic views. 18 holes, 6160 yards. S.S.S. 69. 16 bay driving range. *Green Fees:* weekdays £9.20 18 holes, £5.50 9 holes; weekends £12.30 18 holes, £6.50 9 holes. *Eating facilities:* 120 seater à la carte restaurant, all day poolside food and drinks lounge. *Visitors:* unrestriceed. Swimming pool. *Society Meetings:* welcome weekdays. Professional: Martin Daniels (0634 379592). Secretary: (Members only) A.J. New ACIB. Course Controller: URVGC Ltd.

SITTINGBOURNE. **Sittingbourne and Milton Regis,** Wormdale, Newington, Sittingbourne ME9 7PX (Newington (0795 842261). *Location:* Junction 5 M2, A249 to Sheerness three-quarters of a mile. Undulating course with trees. 18 holes, 6121 yards. S.S.S. 69. *Green Fees:* £20.00 (18 holes), £32.00 (36 holes) weekdays. No green fees weekends. *Eating facilities:* available. *Visitors:* welcome weekdays. Handicap Certificate or letter of introduction required. *Society Meetings:* catered for Tuesdays and Thursdays

by arrangement. Professional: J. Hearn (0795 842775). Manager: H.D.G. Wylie.

TENTERDEN. **Tenterden Golf Club,** Woodchurch Road, Tenterden TN30 7DR (Tenterden (05806) 3987). *Location:* one mile south east of Tenterden on B2067. Parkland course. 18 holes, 6030 yards. S.S.S. 69. *Green Fees:* weekdays £18.00. *Eating facilities:* catering available. *Visitors:* welcome except weekends and Bank Holidays. *Society Meetings:* by prior arrangement. Professional: Garry Potter (05806 2409). Secretary: D.F. Hunt.

TONBRIDGE. **Nizels Golf Club,** Nizels Lane, Hildenborough, Nr. Tonbridge TN11 8NX (Tonbridge (0732) 833138). 18 holes, 6408 yards. S.S.S. 69. *Green Fees:* £25.00 per round, £35 per day. *Eating facilities:* bar with high class catering, open all day. *Society Meetings:* welcome. Professional: M. Jarvis. Secretary: T.J. Fensom.

TONBRIDGE. **Poult Wood Public Golf Course,** Higham Lane, Tonbridge (Tonbridge (0732) 364039 – Golf Shop). *Location:* A227, two miles north of town centre. Wooded, 18 holes, 5569 yards. S.S.S. 67. Practice ground. *Green Fees:* £7.70 per round (£4.40 Juniors/Senior Citizens) weekdays; £11.60 per round weekends. Day ticket (Society) £20.00, £10.50 for 18 holes. *Eating facilities:* full catering available. *Visitors:* all welcome. *Society Meetings:* by arrangement with Clubhouse Manager. Other facilities, squash courts, meeting room, showers, toilets, changing, lockers. Non- Resident Professional: Ken Adwick. Club House Manager: (0732 366180).

TUNBRIDGE WELLS. **Lamberhurst Golf Club,** Church Road, Lamberhurst TN3 8DT (Lamberhurst (0892) 890241). *Location:* A21 from Tunbridge Wells to Hastings, turn left prior to descending hill to Lamberhurst then first right. Attractive parkland course. 18 holes, 6232 yards. S.S.S. 70. Small practice ground. *Green Fees:* £30.00 per weekday, £36.00 weekends and Bank Holidays. *Eating facilities:* full catering by arrangement. *Visitors:* welcome after 8am weekdays, 12 noon weekends and Bank Holidays. Handicap Certificate required. *Society Meetings:* catered for Tuesdays, Wednesdays and Thursdays by arrangement. Professional: M. Travers (0892 890552). Secretary: Mr P. Gleeson (0892 890591).

TUNBRIDGE WELLS. **Nevill Golf Club,** Benhall Mill Road, Tunbridge Wells TN2 5JW (0892 527820). *Location:* off Forest Road, follow signs. 18 holes, 6336

yards. S.S.S. 70. *Green Fees:* £30.00 weekdays; £42.00 weekends and Bank Holidays. *Eating facilities:* lunches at club by prior arrangement. *Visitors:* welcome with reservation. Handicap Certificate required. *Society Meetings:* catered for. Professional: Paul Huggett (0892 532941). Secretary: Miss K.N.R. Pudner (0892 525818).

TUNBRIDGE WELLS. **Tunbridge Wells Golf Club,** Langton Road, Tunbridge Wells (Tunbridge Wells (0892) 523034). *Location:* behind Marchants Garages. 9 holes, 4525 yards. S.S.S. 62. *Green Fees:* £21.00, £28.00 per day. *Eating facilities:* snacks at bar or by arrangement. *Visitors:* welcome weekdays except Tuesdays. *Society Meetings:* only by previous arrangement. Professional: K. Smithson (0892 541386). Secretary: E.M. Goulden.

WESTGATE ON SEA. **Westgate and Birchington Golf Club,** 176 Canterbury Road, Westgate on Sea CT8 8LT (0843 833905). Seaside course between Westgate on Sea and Birchington (A28). Seaside links course. 18 holes, 4926 yards, 4547 metres. S.S.S. 64. *Green Fees:* weekdays £14.00 per day (after 10am), weekends and Bank Holidays £17.00 (after 11 am, Sun after 12 noon). *Eating facilities:* full service available except Mondays and Fridays. *Visitors:* welcome if members of a recognised golf club. *Society Meetings:* by arrangement with Secretary. Professional: R. Game (0843 831115). Secretary: J.M. Wood (0843 831115).

WHITSTABLE. **Chestfield (Whitstable) Golf Club,** 103 Chestfield Road, Chestfield, Whitstable CT5 3LU (0227 792243). *Location:* half a mile south of Thanet Way (A299). Seaside links with woods – slightly hilly. 18 holes, 6181 yards. S.S.S. 70. *Green Fees:* £22.00 weekdays. *Eating facilities:* full catering facilities. *Visitors:* welcome weekdays with Handicap Certificate, weekends with member only. *Society Meetings:* catered for weekdays. Professional: John Brotherton (0227 793563). Secretary: R.W. Leaver (0227 79441).

WHITSTABLE. **Whitstable and Seasalter Golf Club,** Collingwood Road, Whitstable CT5 1EB (0227 272020). *Location:* course adjoins town centre, take Nelson Road turning off main street. Flat seaside links. 9 holes, 5276 yards. S.S.S. 63. Practice net. *Green Fees:* £15.00, green fees are accepted at weekends only if accompanied by a member. *Eating facilities:* bar snacks. Hon. Secretary: Derek Spratt (0227 272020 or 273589).

# Lancashire

ACCRINGTON. **Accrington and District Golf Club,** New Barn Farm, West End, Oswaldtwistle, Accrington (Accrington (0254) 32734). *Location:* on A679, 2 miles from Blackburn. 18 holes, 5954 yards. S.S.S. 69. *Green Fees:* weekdays £15.00, weekends £18.00. *Eating facilities:* lunches and evening meals. *Visitors:* welcome without reservation. *Society Meetings:* prior bookings catered for. Professional: Bill Harling (0254 31091). Hon Secretary: J. Pilkington (0254 232734).

ACCRINGTON. **Green Haworth Golf Club,** Green Haworth, Accrington (Accrington (0254) 237580). *Location:* off A679, one mile Town Centre, via Willows Lane, turn left 300 yards beyond Red Lion Inn. 9 holes, 5513 yards. S.S.S. 67. *Green Fees:* weekdays £10.00; weekends and Bank Holidays £14.00. *Eating facilities:* meals may be ordered in advance. *Visitors:* welcome, restricted to weekdays and Saturday with reservation. *Society Meetings:* catered for weekdays only. Secretary: C. Gaskell.

BACUP. **Bacup Golf Club,** Bankside Lane, Bacup (Bacup (0706) 3170). *Location:* one mile from Bacup centre. 9 holes, 5656 yards. S.S.S. 67. *Green Fees:* information not provided. *Eating facilities:* by arrangement except Mondays. *Visitors:* welcome without reservation except Mondays. Secretary: J. Garvey (0706 874485).

BLACKBURN. **Blackburn Golf Club,** Beardwood Brow, Blackburn BB2 7AX. *Location:* off A677 within easy reach of M6 (Junction 31), M61 and M65; west end of Blackburn. Meadowland with superb views of Lancashire coast and Pennine hills. 18 holes, 6140 yards, 5614 metres. S.S.S. 70. Par 71. Outdoor practice ground and indoor net. *Green Fees:* weekdays £16.00 (£6.00 with a member); weekends and Bank Holidays £19.00 (£7.00 with a member). Special rates for parties of 12 or more. *Eating facilities:* full catering and bar facilities (restricted Mondays). *Visitors:* welcome without reservation except on competition days. *Society Meetings:* catered for by arrangement (not Tuesdays or weekends). Professional: Alan Rodwell (0254 55942). Secretary: P.D. Haydock (0254 51122).

BLACKBURN. **Great Harwood Golf Club,** Harwood Bar, Great Harwood, Blackburn BB6 7TE (Great Harwood (0254) 884391). Flat wooded course. 9 holes, 6411 yards, 5862 metres. S.S.S. 71. Practice area. *Green Fees:* weekdays £12.00; weekends £15.00. *Eating facilities:* all meals catered for, bar hours 12-2pm, 4-11pm. *Visitors:* welcome Tuesday – Friday. *Society Meetings:* catered for by advance bookings. Professional: (0254 884391). Secretary: A. Garraway.

BLACKBURN. **Pleasington Golf Club,** Pleasington, Near Blackburn (Blackburn (0254) 201028). *Location:* M6 north to Junction 31. Blackburn eight miles. Undulating woodland. 18 holes, 6445 yards. S.S.S. 71.

*Green Fees:* weekdays £23.00, weekends and Bank Holidays £28.00. *Eating facilities:* full catering available. *Visitors:* welcome by prior arrangement. *Society Meetings:* Mondays, Wednesdays, Fridays by arrangement. Professional: G.J. Furey (0254 201630). Secretary: J. Hacking (0254 202177).

BLACKBURN. **Rishton Golf Club,** Eachill Links, Rishton (Great Harwood (0254) 884442). *Location:* three miles east of Blackburn. 9 holes, 6094 yards. S.S.S. 69. *Green Fees:* weekdays £10.00; weekends £7.50 with a member. *Visitors:* welcome on weekdays and with a member at weekends and on Bank Holidays. *Society Meetings:* visiting parties welcome by prior arrangement. Secretary: G. Haworth.

BLACKBURN. **Whalley Golf Club,** Portfield Lane, Whalley, Blackburn BB6 9DR (Whalley (0254) 822236). *Location:* seven miles east of Blackburn on A59. Parkland. 9 holes, 5912 yards, 5406 metres. S.S.S. 69. *Green Fees:* weekdays £15.00 (with a member £8.00); weekends £20.00 (with a member £12.00). *Eating facilities:* full catering and bar facilities. *Visitors:* welcome except Thursday afternoons and Saturdays April to September. *Society Meetings:* welcome by appointment. Professional: H. Smith (0254 824766). Secretary: R. Bolsover (0254 824259).

BLACKBURN. **Wilpshire Golf Club Ltd,** Whalley Road, Wilpshire, Blackburn (Blackburn (0254) 248260 or 249691). *Location:* A666 three miles north of Blackburn on Blackburn to Whalley road. 18 holes, 5911 yards. S.S.S. 68. *Green Fees:* £20.00 weekdays, £25.00 weekends. *Eating facilities:* lunch, high tea, dinner except Mondays. *Visitors:* welcome without reservation except competition days. *Society Meetings:* catered for by prior booking through the Secretary. Professional: W. Slaven. Secretary: B. Grimshaw.

BLACKPOOL. **Blackpool North Shore Golf Club,** Devonshire Road, Blackpool FY2 0RD (0253 51017). *Location:* north Blackpool on A587 behind North Prom. Undulating parkland. 18 holes, 6431 yards. S.S.S. 71. *Green Fees:* £21.00 weekdays; £23.00 weekends. Special package rates Mondays, Tuesdays, Wednesdays and Fridays. *Eating facilities:* full catering and bar facilities. *Visitors:* welcome except Saturdays. *Society Meetings:* welcome except Thursdays and weekends. Professional: Brendan Ward (0253 54640) Secretary: Mr R. Yates (0253 52054).

BLACKPOOL. **Blackpool Park Golf Club,** North Park Drive, Stanley Park, Blackpool FY3 8LS (Blackpool (0253) 393960). *Location:* within the boundary of Stanley Park. Undulating parkland course 18 holes, 6060 yards. S.S.S. 69. *Green Fees:* £7.50 weekdays; £8.50 weekends. *Eating facilities:* full catering services except Tuesday, bar. *Visitors:* welcome. *Society Meetings:* welcome (booking to b made through Blackpool Parks Dept.). Professional: B. Purdie (0253 391004). Secretary: Terence Lee (0253 397916).

BLACKPOOL. **Knott End Golf Club Ltd,** Wyre Side, Knott-End-on-Sea, Blackpool FY6 0AA (Knott End (0253) 810254). *Location:* M55 Exit 3, A585 Fleetwood Road and A588 to Knott End, or by passenger ferry from Fleetwood. Scenic seaside undulating course. 18 holes, 5852 yards. S.S.S. 68. Practice ground. *Green Fees:* £20.00 weekdays, weekends £24.00. *Eating facilities:* full catering available. *Visitors:* welcome weekdays, restricted weekends. *Society Meetings:* by arrangement weekdays only. Professional: Kevin Short (02530 811365). Secretary: C. Desmond (0253 810576).

BLACKPOOL. **Poulton-le-Fylde Golf Club,** Myrtle Farm, Breck Road, Poulton-le-Fylde, Blackpool FY6 7HJ (Blackpool (0253) 893150). *Location:* three miles east of Blackpool. 9 holes, 2972 yards. *Green Fees:* £4.80 weekdays, £6.60 weekends per round. *Eating facilities:* meals at lunch time and light snacks available all day. *Visitors:* welcome without reservation. *Society Meetings:* catered for by prior booking. Professional: D. Spencer (0253 892444). Secretary: K. Audis.

BOLTON. **Bolton Municipal Golf Course,** Links Road, Chorley New Road, Bolton BL2 9XX (Bolton (0204) 44170). *Location:* midway between Horwich and Bolton, A673. Fairly flat parkland. 18 holes, 6336 yards, 5570 metres. S.S.S. 70. Practice ground. *Green Fees:* weekdays £4.30; weekends £6.50. *Eating facilities:* snack and meal facilities available and bar. *Visitors:* welcome at any time. *Society Meetings:* advance booking. Mid-week Society package available. Professional: A.K. Holland (0204 42336). Secretary: J. Leeming (0204 44170).

BURNLEY. **Burnley Golf Club,** Glen View, Burnley BB11 3RW (Burnley (0282) 21045). *Location:* 300 yards from junction of A56 and A646. Moorland. 18 holes, 5899 yards, 5391 metres. S.S.S. 69. *Green Fees:* weekdays £14.00, weekends and Bank Holidays £23.00. *Eating facilities:* available except Wednesdays from lunchtime and Mondays. *Visitors:* welcome except Saturdays. *Society Meetings:* catered for. Professional: W. Tighe (0282 55266). Hon. Secretary: G.J. Butterfield (0282 54434).

BURNLEY. **Towneley Golf Club,** Todmorden Road, Burnley (0282 3843 – Pro's shop). *Location:* east of town centre on Burnley centre. Parkland course, reasonably flat. 18 holes, 5862 yards, 5357 metres. S.S.S. 68. Small practice area. *Green Fees:* £4.50 weekdays, £5.50 weekends. *Eating facilities:* clubhouse with diningroom, lounge bar and games room. *Visitors:* welcome, reservations recommended and tee reservation advisable. New 9 hole course recently opened in addition. *Society Meetings:* contact Steward at clubhouse for catering requirements (0282 51636). Secretary: D. Rigby (0282 29339).

CHORLEY. **Chorley Golf Club,** Hall o' th' Hill, Heath Charnock, Chorley PR6 9HX (0257 480263). *Location:* south of Chorley, just off the A673 at the junction with the A6. Scenic course. 18 holes, 6317 yards.

S.S.S. 70. *Green Fees:* weekdays £20.00 per round, £22.50 per day. *Eating facilities:* restaurant and lounge bar. *Visitors:* welcome by prior arrangement not Mondays, Bank Holidays or weekends. *Society Meetings:* catered for by arrangement. Professional: Paul Wesselingh (0257 481245). Secretary: A.K. Tyrer. Catering: (0257 474664).

CHORLEY. **Duxbury Park Golf Club (Municipal),** Duxbury Hall Road, Duxbury Park, Chorley PR7 4AS (02572 41634). *Location:* one mile south of town centre off A6. Wooded parkland with water hazards on several holes. 18 holes, 5843 yards. S.S.S. 70. Small practice area. *Green Fees:* weekdays £5.40; weekends £6.50. *Eating facilities:* can be arranged. *Visitors:* welcome, book seven days in advance. *Society Meetings:* weekdays. Professional: David Clarke (02572 65380). Secretary: Reg Blease (02572 68665).

CHORLEY. **Shaw Hill Hotel Golf and Country Club,** Preston Road, Whittle-le-Woods, Chorley PR6 7PP (Chorley (02572) 69221). *Location:* one mile north of Junction 8 on M61 and two miles M6 Junction 28. Championship course in superb parkland with the clubhouse in a beautiful Georgian mansion. 18 holes, 6405 yards. S.S.S. 71. Practice area. *Green Fees:* weekdays £30.00 per round; weekends £40.00 per round. *Eating facilities:* spike bar and formal bar, à la carte restaurant. *Visitors:* welcome all week, must hold current Handicap Certificate. Accommodation available, sauna, solarium. Golf trolleys and buggies also available. *Society Meetings:* catered for midweek only. Professional: David Clarke (0257 279222). General Manager: Mrs A.M. Lawless. Secretary: Bernard Brodrick (0257 269221; Fax: 0257 261223).

CLITHEROE. **Clitheroe Golf Club,** Whalley Road, Pendleton, Clitheroe BB7 1PP (Clitheroe (0200) 22618). *Location:* off A59, two miles south of Clitheroe. Flat parkland course. 18 holes, 6326 yards, 5785 metres. S.S.S. 71. Practice ground and range. *Green Fees:* weekdays £19.00; weekends and Bank Holidays £24.00. *Eating facilities:* full service available. *Visitors:* welcome with reservation. Saturdays some restrictions. No jeans/trainers/tracksuits. Jackets and ties in diningroom after 7pm. *Society Meetings:* catered for by arrangement. Professional: John E. Twissell (0200 24242). Secretary: G. Roberts JP (0200 22292).

COLNE. **Colne Golf Club,** Law Farm, Old Skipton Road, Colne BB8 7EB (Colne (0282) 863391). *Location:* come off eastern end of M65. Carry on one mile to next roundabout and take first exit on left. Goup Hill. Flat scenic moorland course with trees beginning to come into play. 9 holes, 5961 yards, 5451 metres. S.S.S. 69. Full practice facilities. *Green Fees:* £10.00 weekdays, £12.00 weekends and Bank Holidays (subject to review). Parties of 2 or more £9.00 per person (not at weekends, Thursdays or competition days). *Eating facilities:* excellent. *Visitors:* welcome except on competition days; two-balls only on Thursdays. *Society Meetings:* welcome except weekends, Thursdays and competition days. Secretary: K. Hargreaves.

DARWEN. **Darwen Golf Club,** Winter Hill, Darwen BB3 0LB (0254 701287). *Location:* one and a half miles from Darwen centre. Moorland. 18 holes, 5752 yards. S.S.S. 68. Large practice area. *Green Fees:* weekdays £15.00; weekends and Bank Holidays £20.00. *Eating facilities:* full catering. *Visitors:* welcome, except Saturdays. *Society Meetings:* welcome, except Saturdays. Professional: Wayne Lennon (0254 776370). Secretary: J. Kenyon (0254 704367).

FLEETWOOD. **Fleetwood Golf Club Ltd.,** The Golf House, Princes Way, Fleetwood FY7 8AF (0253 873114). *Location:* on Fylde Coast, eight miles from Blackpool. Seaside links. White course 18 holes, 6723 yards, S.S.S. 72; Yellow course 18 holes, 6433 yards, S.S.S. 71. *Green Fees:* weekdays £20.00; weekends £25.00. *Eating facilities:* full catering facilities except Thursday. *Visitors:* welcome with Handicap Certificate. *Society Meetings:* catered for by arrangement. Professional: C.T. Burgess (0253 873661). Secretary: H. Fielding (0253 873661).

HEYSHAM. **Heysham Golf Club,** Trumacar Park, Middleton Road, Heysham LA3 3JH (Lancaster (0524) 851240). *Location:* five miles from M6 via Lancaster and Morecambe. Parkland, flat, part-wooded. 18 holes, 6338 yards. S.S.S. 70. Two practice grounds. *Green Fees:* weekdays £20.00; weekends and Bank Holidays £25.00. Special rates for parties on application. *Eating facilities:* full catering seven days. Bar open all day Sunday. *Visitors:* welcome without reservation. Tee reserved for members 1 to 1.45pm. *Society Meetings:* catered for by arrangement with Secretary. Professional: S. Fletcher (0524 852000). Secretary: F.A. Bland (0524 851011).

LANCASTER. **Lancaster Golf and Country Club Ltd,** Ashton Hall, Ashton-with-Stodday, Lancaster LA2 0AJ. *Location:* three miles south of Lancaster on A588. Parkland. 18 holes, 6282 yards. S.S.S. 71. *Green Fees:* weekdays £25.00. *Eating facilities:* available (Caterer: 0524 751105). *Visitors:* welcome weekdays only unless staying in the Dormy House. Club has a Dormy House (part of Ashton Hall) which accommodates 18 persons, 2 night minimum stay. *Society Meetings:* catered for weekdays only. Professional: David Sutcliffe (0524 751802). Secretary: Mr Duncan D.J. Palmer (0524 751247).

LANCASTER. **Lansil Golf Club,** Caton Road, Lancaster LA1 3PE (Lancaster (0524) 39269). *Location:* A683, towards Lancaster from Junction 34 M6. Parkland, quite hilly. 9 holes, 5608 yards. S.S.S. 67. *Green Fees:* £12.00 (£6.00 with a member). *Eating facilities:* light refreshments only by arrangement. *Visitors:* welcome, not before 1pm Saturday and Sunday. *Society Meetings:* catered for by arrangement weekdays only. Secretary: Derrick Crutchley (0524 418007).

LEYLAND. **Leyland Golf Club Ltd.,** Wigan Road, Leyland, Preston PR5 2UD (Leyland (0772) 421359). *Location:* leave M6 at Exit 28, turn right to traffic lights, (200 yards) turn right onto the A49, course located one mile on left. Flat parkland. 18 holes, 6123 yards. S.S.S. 69. *Green Fees:* £22.00 weekdays. *Eating facilities:* full catering except Mondays. *Visitors:* welcome weekdays only unless with a member. *Society Meetings:* welcome

but by arrangement with Secretary. Professional: C. Burgess (0772 423425). Secretary: G.D. Copeman (0772 436457).

LYTHAM ST. ANNES. **Fairhaven Golf Club Ltd.,** Lytham Hall Park, Ansdell, Lytham St. Annes FY8 4JU (Lytham (0253) 736741). *Location:* on B5261, two miles from Lytham, eight miles from Blackpool. 18 holes, 6880 yards. S.S.S. 73. Practice ground and net. *Green Fees:* weekdays £25.00 per round, £32.00 per day; weekends £30.00 per round. *Eating facilities:* full catering except Mondays. *Visitors:* welcome with reservation. *Society Meetings:* catered for by arrangement Mondays, Tuesdays, Wednesdays and Fridays. Professional: Mr I. Howieson (0253 736976). Secretary: Brian Hartley.

LYTHAM ST. ANNES. **Lytham Green Drive Golf Club,** Ballam Road, Lytham St. Annes FY8 4LE (Lytham (0253) 737390). *Location:* one mile from Lytham Square. 18 holes, 6159 yards. S.S.S. 69. *Green Fees:* £19.00 per round, £24.00 per day weekdays; £31.00 per round weekends. *Eating facilities:* catering available daily. *Visitors:* welcome without reservation. *Society Meetings:* catered for mid-week. Professional: F.W. Accleton (0253 737379). Secretary: R. Kershaw.

LYTHAM ST. ANNES. **Royal Lytham and St. Annes Golf Club,** Links Gate, Lytham St. Annes FY8 3LQ (0253 724206; Fax: 0253 780946). *Location:* within one mile of the centre of St. Annes on Sea. Seaside links course. 18 holes, 6673 yards. S.S.S. 73. Practice ground. *Green Fees:* weekdays £45.00 per round, £60.00 per day; Sundays (limited times) £50.00. *Eating facilities:* restaurant and bar. *Visitors:* welcome weekdays, limited Sundays, times by arrangement. Dormy House accommodation available. *Society Meetings:* by arrangement. Professional: Eddie Birchenough (0253 720094). Secretary: Major A.S. Craven.

LYTHAM ST. ANNES. **St. Annes Old Links Golf Club,** Highbury Road, Lytham St. Annes FY8 2LD (St. Annes (0253) 721826). *Location:* M55 via Blackpool South Shore, following airport signs. Past airport down to coast road, turn left and first left at next real traffic lights. The only true links course in Lancashire. 18 holes, 6616 yards. S.S.S. 72. Practice ground, putting and chipping greens. *Green Fees:* £25.00 weekdays; £30.00 weekends. *Eating facilities:* restaurant and snack facilities, bar. *Visitors:* welcome, not Saturdays, restricted Sundays. Tuesday is ladies day. *Society Meetings:* restricted to those with Handicaps and membership of other clubs. Professional: G.G. Hardiman (0253 722432). Secretary: P.W. Ray (0253 723597).

MORECAMBE. **Morecambe Golf Club Ltd.,** The Club House, Bare, Morecambe LA4 6AJ (Morecambe (0524) 418050). *Location:* on A589, coastal road leaving Morecambe towards Carnforth. Parkland course affected by sea breezes offering superb views. 18 holes, 5766 yards. S.S.S. 68. *Green Fees:* weekdays £19.00; weekends and Bank Holidays £24.00. *Eating facilities:* diningroom and bar snacks, except Mondays. *Visitors:* welcome at all times, tee reserved for members

8am to 9.30am and 12 noon to 1.30pm. *Society Meetings:* welcome at all times. Professional: P. De Valle (0524 415596). Secretary: T.H. Glover (0524 412841).

NELSON. **Marsden Park Golf Club,** Nelson Municipal Golf Course, Townhouse Road, Nelson BB9 8DG (0282 67525). *Location:* just off M65, heading towards Colne. Hilly parkland. 18 holes, 5806 yards. S.S.S. 68. *Green Fees:* information not available. *Eating facilities:* bar, meals to order. *Visitors:* welcome without restriction. *Society Meetings:* by arrangement. Professional: N. Brown (0282 67525). Secretary: J.L. Beck.

NELSON. **Nelson Golf Club,** King's Causeway, Brierfield, Nelson BB9 0EU (Nelson (0282) 614583). *Location:* on A682 two miles north of Burnley, one mile from Junction 12 M65. Moorland with trees. 18 holes, 5967 yards. S.S.S. 69. *Green Fees:* £16.00 weekdays, £18.00 weekends and Public Holidays. *Eating facilities:* lunches, dinners by arrangement except Mondays. *Visitors:* weekdays except Thursdays, no Saturdays, Sundays by arrangement. *Society Meetings:* weekdays except Thursdays. Professional: M.J. Herbert (0282 617000). Secretary: R.W. Baldwin (0282 611834).

ORMSKIRK. **Ormskirk Golf Club,** Cranes Lane, Lathom L40 5UJ (Ormskirk (0695) 572112). *Location:* two miles east of Ormskirk. 18 holes, 6358 yards. S.S.S. 70. *Green Fees:* weekdays (except Wednesday) £25.00 per round, £30.00 per day; weekends and Wednesdays £30.00 per round, £35.00 per day. *Eating facilities:* available except Monday. *Visitors:* welcome, Handicap Certificates required, notice advised with reservation. *Society Meetings:* catered for, book in advance. Professional: J. Hammond. Secretary: P.D. Dromgoole.

PRESTON. **Ashton and Lea Golf Club Ltd,** Tudor Avenue, off Blackpool Road, Lea, Preston PR4 0XA (Preston (0772) 726480). *Location:* on A583, three miles west of Preston, turn right opposite Pig and Whistle Hotel. Parkland with water features. 18 holes, 6289 yards. S.S.S. 70. Small practice ground. *Green Fees:* Mondays to Thursdays £18.00, Fridays £20.00; weekends and Bank Holidays £24.00. Reduced rates if playing with member. *Eating facilities:* full catering every day. *Visitors:* welcome but please telephone to reserve tee time. *Society Meetings:* catered for Mondays, Tuesdays and Wednesdays only. Small parties on Thursdays and Fridays, apply in writing to the Secretary. Professional: Mr P.G. Laugher (0772 720374). Secretary: Mr M.G. Gibbs (0772 735282).

PRESTON. **Fishwick Hall Golf Club,** Glenluce Drive, Farringdon Park, Preston PR1 5TD (Preston (0772) 798300). *Location:* two minutes from Exit 31 M6, off A49 Blackburn to Preston Road. Parkland, part wooded, bounded by river. 18 holes, 6028 yards. S.S.S. 69. Practice ground and net. *Green Fees:* weekdays £20.00; weekends and Public Holidays £25.00. Reductions if playing with members. *Eating facilities:* bar, full catering available. *Visitors:* welcome by arrangement. *Society Meetings:* catered for by arrangement. Professional: S. Bence (0772 795870). Secretary: R.R. Gearing (0772 798300).

PRESTON. **Ingol Golf and Squash Club,** Tanterton Hall Road, Ingol, Preston PR7 1BY (Preston (0772) 734556). *Location:* two miles from Junction 32 M6 (joins M55). Parkland. 18 holes, 5868 yards. S.S.S. 68. *Green Fees:* weekdays £20.00 (reduction with member), weekends and Bank Holidays £25.00 (reduction with member). Reductions for parties. *Eating facilities:* restaurant, lounge and spike bar. *Visitors:* welcome by appointment. Snooker room. *Society Meetings:* welcome by arrangement. Professional: Mark Cartwright. Manager: Harold Parker.

PRESTON. **Longridge Golf Club,** Fell Barn, Jeffrey Hill, Longridge, Preston PR3 2TU (Longridge (0772) 783291). *Location:* eight miles north-east of Preston off B6243. Moorland with extensive spectacular views. 18 holes, 5726 yards. S.S.S. 68. *Green Fees:* £15.00 Mondays to Thursdays, £18.00 Fridays, Saturdays, Sundays and Bank Holidays. *Eating facilities:* full catering except Mondays. *Visitors:* welcome at all times. *Society Meetings:* welcome by arrangement. Professional: Neil James. Secretary: J. Greenwood (0772 782765 evenings).

PRESTON. **Penwortham Golf Club Ltd.,** Blundell Lane, Penwortham, Preston PR1 0AX (Preston (0772) 743207). *Location:* one mile west of Preston on main Southport to Liverpool road. Parkland. 18 holes, 5667 yards. S.S.S. 68. *Green Fees:* £20.00 weekdays, £25.00 weekends. *Eating facilities:* lunches and dinners served at Club. *Visitors:* weekdays only. *Society Meetings:* catered for by arrangement. Professional: J. Wright (0772 742345; Fax: 0772 741677). Secretary: J. Parkinson (0772 744630).

PRESTON. **Preston Golf Club,** Fulwood Hall Lane, Fulwood, Preston PR2 4DD (0772 794234). *Location:* exit 32 on M6 marked Preston & Garstang, partway to Preston turning at Watling Street Road. Parkland course. 18 holes, 6267 yards. S.S.S. 70. *Green Fees:* weekdays £20.00 per round, £25.00 per day. *Eating facilities:* first class diningroom, bars. *Visitors:* welcome Mondays, Wednesdays and Fridays, maximum 48, Thursdays maximum 32, Tuesdays maximum 16. *Society Meetings:* catered for, Handicap Certificate required. Professional: P. Wells (0772 700022). Secretary: J.B. Dickinson (0772 700011).

ROSSENDALE. **Rossendale Golf Club Ltd.,** Ewood Lane Head, Haslingden, Rossendale BB4 6LH (Rossendale (0706) 213056). *Location:* 14 miles north of Manchester, easy access from M66 and A56. 18 holes, 6260 yards. S.S.S. 70. *Green Fees:* weekdays £20.00; weekends and Bank Holidays £25.00. *Eating facilities:* full catering except Mondays; bar. *Visitors:* welcome except Saturdays during season. *Society Meetings:* special terms including full catering available. Professional: S.J. Nicholls (0706 213616). Secretary: J.R. Swain (0706 831339).

SKELMERSDALE. **Beacon Park Golf Centre,** Beacon Lane, Dalton, Upholland WN8 7RU (Upholland (0695) 622700). *Location:* M6 Junction 26, follow signs for Upholland. Parkland, tree lined – undulating. 18 holes, 5995 yards. S.S.S. 72. Large practice ground, 24 bay floodlit driving range. *Green Fees:* weekdays £4.50 adults, £2.80 Senior Citizens; weekends £6.00

adults, £3.50 Senior Citizens. *Eating facilities:* bar/restaurant. *Visitors:* welcome anytime. Public course, open seven days. *Society Meetings:* Society and Group bookings available on request. Professional: Ray Peters (0695 622700; Fax: 0695 633066).

UPHOLLAND. **Dean Wood Golf Club,** Lafford Lane, Upholland, Skelmersdale WN8 0QZ (0695 622980). *Location:* on A577 one and a half miles west of Junction 26 M6 motorway. Parkland course set in

pleasant countryside with fine views of Pennine Hills. 18 holes, 6137 yards. S.S.S. 70. Practice area. *Green Fees:* weekdays £22.00; weekends and Bank Holidays restricted. *Eating facilities:* three bars, full catering service available. *Visitors:* welcome except Tuesdays (ladies day), visitors may only play with a member at weekends or on Bank Holidays. *Society Meetings:* catered for by prior arrangement. Professional: Tony Coop. Secretary: Geoff Rimmer (0695 622219).

# Leicestershire

ASHBY DE LA ZOUCH. **Willesley Park Golf Club,** Tamworth Road, Ashby de la Zouch (0530 411532). *Location:* on B5006 towards Tamworth, one mile from centre of Ashby. Wooded park, semi-heathland. 18 holes, 6304 yards. S.S.S. 70. *Green Fees:* weekdays £25.00 per round/day, weekends and Bank Holidays £30.00. *Eating facilities:* dining room and bar, no catering Mondays. *Visitors:* welcome with reservation. *Society Meetings:* catered for Wednesday, Thursday and Friday. Professional: C.J. Hancock (0530 414820). Secretary: N.H. Jones (0530 414596).

BIRSTALL. **Birstall Golf Club,** Station Road, Birstall LE4 3BB (Leicester (0533) 674450). *Location:* 3 miles north of Town just off the A6 Leicester to Derby. Parkland. 18 holes, 5988 yards. S.S.S. 69. Practice ground and net. *Green Fees:* weekdays £25.00 per day. *Eating facilities:* bar, diningroom. No catering Mondays. *Visitors:* welcome Mondays, Wednesdays and Fridays. *Society Meetings:* minimum 20, catered for by prior arrangement £20.00 per person. Professional: D. Clark (0533 675245). Secretary: Mrs S.E. Chilton (0533 674322).

COSBY. **Cosby Golf Club,** Chapel Lane, off Broughton Road, Cosby, Leicester (Leicester (0533) 864759). *Location:* eight miles south of Leicester, four miles from Junction 21 M1. Undulating parkland. 18 holes, 6277 yards. S.S.S. 70. *Green Fees:* weekdays £18.00 per round, £20.00 per day; weekends £6.00 only with a member. Special rates for societies over 20 in number. *Eating facilities:* bar and food available by arrangement with the Steward. *Visitors:* no visitors after 4pm weekdays or weekends. Handicap Certificates may be required for all visitors. *Society Meetings:* welcome, prior booking essential. Professional: David Bowring (0533 848275). Secretary: M.D. Riddle.

ENDERBY. **Enderby Golf Club,** Enderby Golf Course, Enderby Leisure Centre, Mill Lane, Enderby (0533 849388). *Location:* two miles from M1/M69 Junction 21 roundabout. Flat parkland course. 9 holes, 2178 yards. S.S.S. 61. *Green Fees:* weekdays 9 holes £2.90, 18 holes £4.00; weekends 9 holes £4.00, 18 holes £5.25. *Eating facilities:* bar open normal bar hours, light snacks available at lunchtime. *Visitors:* welcome at all times. Full range of recreational facilities available – swimming, squash, indoor bowls, sauna, solarium, badminton, snooker, etc. Professional: Chris d'Araujo.

HINCKLEY. **Hinckley Golf Club,** Leicester Road, Hinckley LE10 3DR (Hinckley (0455) 615124). *Location:* situated one mile from Hinckley on A47 Leicester-Hinckley road. Parkland with lakeside features. 18 holes, 6517 yards, 5959 metres. S.S.S. 71. Practice area for members. *Green Fees:* weekdays £20.00 per round, £25.00 per day. *Eating facilities:* bar and meals daily except Sunday evenings. *Visitors:* welcome except Tuesdays and weekends. *Society Meetings:* Mondays and Wednesdays by appointment. Professional: R. Jones (0455 615014). Secretary: J. Toon (0455 615124).

KIRBY MUXLOE. **Kirby Muxloe Golf Club,** Station Road, Kirby Muxloe LE9 9EP (Leicester (0533) 393107). *Location:* four miles west of Leicester on A47. M1 Exit 21. Undulating parkland with lake. 18 holes, 6303 yards, 5766 metres. S.S.S. 70. Practice area and tuition from Professional. *Green Fees:* weekdays £20.00 per round, £25.00 per day; weekends with member or by Captain's permission only. *Eating facilities:* bars, dining room. *Visitors:* welcome weekdays. Advisable to phone in advance. *Society Meetings:* Wednesdays, Thursdays, Friday afternoons only. Professional: R.T. Stephenson (0533 392813). Secretary: S.F. Aldwinckle (0533 393457).

LEICESTER. **Humberstone Heights Golf Club,** Gipsy Lane, Leicester (Leicester (0533) 761905). *Location:* opposite Towers Hospital, Uppingham side of Leicester. Parkland. 18 holes, 6444 yards. S.S.S. 71. Practice area, pitch and putt course. *Green Fees:* weekdays £5.30 per round, weekends £6.50 (reduced rates for Juniors). *Eating facilities:* bar, snacks. *Visitors:* welcome (Municipal Golf Course). Green Fee ticket gains entry to Clubhouse. *Society Meetings:* welcome. Professional: Philip Highfield (0533 764674). Secretary: Stephen Day (0533 674835).

LEICESTER. **Kibworth Golf Club Ltd.,** Weir Road, Kibworth Beauchamp, Leicester LE8 0LP (0533 792301). *Location:* A6, four miles Market Harborough, 12 miles Leicester. Flat wooded course. 18 holes, 6298 yards. S.S.S. 70. *Green Fees:* £16.00. *Eating facilities:* restaurant – book through Steward in advance avoiding Monday. *Visitors:* welcome, Handicap Certificate required or introduction from club member. *Society Meetings:* catered for if booked. Professional: Alan Strange (0533 792283). Secretary: W. Potter (0533 792301).

LEICESTER. **Leicestershire Golf Club,** Evington Lane, Leicester LE5 6DJ (Leicester (0533) 736035). *Location:* two miles from city centre off A6 road. Parkland. 18 holes, 6312 yards. S.S.S. 70. *Green Fees:* weekdays £25.00, weekends £30.00. *Eating facilities:* bar snacks, full catering available by order. *Visitors:* welcome, Handicap Certificate required. *Society Meetings:* by arrangement. Professional: John R. Turnbull (0533 736730). Secretary: J.L. Adams (0533 738825).

LEICESTER. **Scraptoft Golf Club,** Beeby Road, Scraptoft, Leicester LE7 9SJ (Leicester (0533) 419000). *Location:* off A47 Peterborough. Undulating. 18 holes, 6166 yards. S.S.S. 69. *Green Fees:* £20.50 weekdays, £25.50 weekends. Sunday mornings with club member only. *Eating facilities:* full restaurant service except Mondays. *Visitors:* welcome, proof of Handicap required. *Society Meetings:* catered for on application weekdays only. Professional: Simon Sherratt (0533 419138). Secretary: A.M. Robertson (0533 418863).

LEICESTER. **Western Park Golf Club,** Scudamore Road, Braunstone Frith, Leicester (0533 876158). *Location:* four miles west of Junction 21 on M1 motorway. Flat, wooded course. 18 holes, 6532 yards. S.S.S. 71. Practice area. *Green Fees:* information not available. *Eating facilities:* full catering facilities. *Visitors:* contact Professional. *Society Meetings:* contact Professional. Professional: Bruce Whipham (0533 872339). Secretary: Brian Wells (0533 773543).

LEICESTER. **Whetstone Golf Club and Driving Range,** Cambridge Road, Cosby (Leicester (0533) 861424). *Location:* south of Leicester between Corby and Whetstone. Parkland. 18 holes, 5795 yards. S.S.S. 68. Driving range, putting green. *Green Fees:* weekdays £10.00; weekends £12.50. *Eating facilities:* bar serving snacks. *Visitors:* welcome midweek and after 1pm Saturday and Sunday. *Society Meetings:* welcome by prior arrangement. Professionals: N. Leatherland and D. Raitt. Secretary: Mr D.H. Dalby.

LOUGHBOROUGH. **Charnwood Forest Golf Club,** Breakback Road, Woodhouse Eaves, Near Loughborough LE12 8TA (Woodhouse Eaves (0509) 890259). *Location:* Beacon Hill, Charnwood Forest. A6 to B591 two miles. M1 Junction 22 two miles east. Rocks, bracken, heather, woods – in the heart of Charnwood Forest. 9 holes, 5960 yards. S.S.S. 69. *Green Fees:* weekdays £17.50 (£8.50 with member); weekends £21.50 (£10.00 with member). *Eating facilities:* full catering except Mondays; snacks available. *Visitors:* welcome, but not Tuesdays (Ladies' Day). *Society Meetings:* not more than 40 catered for by prior arrangement. Professional: Mark Lawrence (0509 890509). Secretary: A.G. Stanley (0509 890259).

LOUGHBOROUGH. **Longcliffe Golf Club,** Snell's Nook Lane, Nanpantan, Loughborough (0509 216321). *Location:* two miles west of Loughborough Town Centre, 13 miles north of Leicester. Approximately one mile from Exit 23, M1. 18 holes, 6551 yards. S.S.S. 71. *Green Fees:* £22.00 per round, £27.00 per day. *Eating facilities:* full catering facilities, except Tuesdays. *Visitors:* restricted, must be introduced and playing with member at weekends and Bank

Holidays. *Society Meetings:* by arrangement only accepted on Mondays, Wednesdays, Thursdays and Fridays. Professional: I. Bailey (0509 231450). Secretary: G. Harle (0509 239129).

LUTTERWORTH. **Lutterworth Golf Club,** Rugby Road, Lutterworth, Leicester LE17 5HN (Lutterworth (0455) 557141). *Location:* on A4114. Hilly parkland-type course – open fairways. 18 holes, 5570 yards. S.S.S. 67. *Green Fees:* £15.00 per round, £20.00 per day. *Eating facilities:* lunches and evening meals available every day. *Visitors:* welcome on weekdays and with a member at weekends. Professional: N. Melvin (0455 567199). Secretary: Mrs Tranter (0455 552532). Steward: C.D. Sholl (0455 557141).

LUTTERWORTH near. **Ullesthorpe Court Golf Club,** Frolesworth Road, Ullesthorpe, Near Lutterworth LE17 5BZ (0455 209023). *Location:* 10/15 minutes M1, M69, M6, between Leicester and Coventry. 18 holes, 6650 yards. S.S.S. 72. *Green Fees:* £17.50 weekdays. Golf Day Specials from £20.00. *Eating facilities:* restaurant, bar snacks and functions. *Visitors:* welcome weekdays except Bank Holidays. 40 bedroomed hotel and leisure centre. *Society Meetings:* catered for weekdays except Bank Holidays. Professional: I. Sadler (0455 209150). Secretary: Mrs P. Woolley (0455 202361).

MARKET HARBOROUGH. **Market Harborough Golf Club,** Harborough (0858) 63684). *Location:* two miles south of town on A508. Parkland. 9 holes, 6090 yards. S.S.S. 69. Extending to 18 holes opening in 1993. Practice ground. *Green Fees:* £10.00 per day. *Eating facilities:* full catering available. *Visitors:* welcome weekdays; weekends only with a member, with permission. *Society Meetings:* welcome, minimum 10, maximum 30; reduced rates. Professional: F. Baxter. Secretary: J. Lord (0536 771771).

MELTON MOWBRAY. **Melton Mowbray Golf Club,** Thorpe Arnold, Melton Mowbray LE14 4SD (Melton Mowbray (0664) 62118). *Location:* A607 road two miles north-east of Melton Mowbray. 18 holes, 6241 yards, S.S.S. 70. Practice ground. *Green Fees:* weekdays £12.00; weekends £18.00. *Eating facilities:* full catering and bar facilities. *Visitors:* welcome before 3pm. *Society Meetings:* by prior arrangement weekdays only. Professional: James Wilson (0664 69629). Secretary: E.A. Sallis.

OADBY. **Glen Gorse Golf Club,** Glen Road, Oadby LE2 4RF (Leicester (0533) 712226). *Location:* on A6, four and a half miles south of Leicester. Flat but wooded course. 18 holes, 6615 yards, 6048 metres. S.S.S. 72. Par 72. *Green Fees:* weekdays £20.00 (£7.00 with member); weekends £7.00 with member only. *Eating facilities:* bar and meals/snacks (not Mondays). *Visitors:* welcome weekdays without reservation, weekends with members only. *Society Meetings:* welcome Tuesday to Friday. Professional: Bob Larratt (0533 713748). Secretary: M. Goodson (0533 714159).

OADBY. **Oadby Golf Club,** Leicester Road, Oadby, Leicester LE2 4AB (Leicester (0533) 700215). *Location:* on A6 south of Leicester, one mile from City boundary, at Leicester Racecourse. Parkland. 18 holes,

6228 yards, 5692 metres. S.S.S. 69. Practice ground, coaching. *Green Fees:* information not provided. *Eating facilities:* snacks always available, bar with meals on prior notice. *Visitors:* welcome on application to the Professional or booked through Oadby and Wigston Borough Council. *Society Meetings:* booking as for Visitors (weekdays only). Professional: Simon Ward (0533 709052). Hon. Secretary: C. Chamberlain (0533 889862 home).

ROTHLEY. **Rothley Park Golf Club,** Westfield Lane, Rothley, Leicester LE7 7LH (Leicester (0533) 302019). *Location:* off A6, north of Leicester. Parkland. 18 holes, 6481 yards. S.S.S. 71. *Green Fees:* £25.00 per round, £30.00 per day (mid-week). *Eating facilities:* available except Mondays. *Visitors:* welcome except Tuesdays, weekends and Bank Holidays, must be members of recognised golf club with handicap. *Society Meetings:*

catered for Wednesdays and Thursdays. Professional: P.J. Dolan (0533 303023). Secretary: Bernard Durham (0533 302809).

WOODHOUSE EAVES. **Lingdale Golf Club,** Joe Moore's Lane, Woodhouse Eaves, Near Loughborough LE12 8TF (Woodhouse Eaves (0509) 890035). *Location:* on B5300, Ansty-Shepshed road, three miles from Exit 23 on M1. Woodland and parkland – set in Charnwood Forest. 18 holes, 6545 yards. S.S.S. 71. Practice ground. *Green Fees:* weekdays £18.00 per day; weekends £20.00. Societies £15.00. *Eating facilities:* full catering available. *Visitors:* welcome, but please telephone first. *Society Meetings:* catered for Mondays, Wednesdays, Thursdays and Fridays (one month's notice required). Professional: P. Sellears (0509 890684). Secretary: M. Green (0509 890703).

# Lincolnshire

BOSTON. **Boston Golf Club Ltd,** Cowbridge, Horncastle Road, Boston PE22 7EL (Boston (0205) 352533). *Location:* two miles north of Boston on B1183. Look for sign to right if travelling north. Parkland with featured water. 18 holes, 5825 yards, 5326 metres. S.S.S. 68. *Green Fees:* weekdays £14.00 per round, £20.00 per day; weekends and Bank Holidays £20.00 per round, £30.00 per day. *Eating facilities:* daily by arrangement with resident Steward. *Visitors:* welcome without reservation. *Society Meetings:* small groups catered for midweek. Professional: T.R. Squires (0205 362306). Secretary: D.E. Smith (0205 350589).

GAINSBOROUGH. **Gainsborough Golf Club,** Gainsborough DN21 1PZ (Gainsborough (0427) 613088). *Location:* one mile north east of Gainsborough, between A159 and A631. Flat parkland. 18 holes, 6620 yards. S.S.S. 72. Putting green and driving range. *Green Fees:* weekdays £19.00 per round, £25.00 per day. *Eating facilities:* restaurant and coffee shop. *Visitors:* welcome weekdays without reservation; weekends with member only. *Society Meetings:* welcome if booked in advance. Professional: S. Cooper (0427 612278). Manager: D.J. Garrison (0427 613088).

GRANTHAM. **Belton Park Golf Club,** Belton Lane, Londonthorpe Road, Grantham NG31 9SH (0476 63355). *Location:* two miles from Grantham. 250 acre Deer Park adjacent to the historical Belton House. Three courses as follows: Brownlow Course 6420 yards (Championship). S.S.S. 71. Ancaster Course 6252 yards. S.S.S. 70. Belmont Course 6016 yards. S.S.S. 69. Two large practice areas. *Green Fees:* weekdays £16.00 per round, half price if playing with member; weekends and Bank Holidays £26.00 per

round, half price with member. All including VAT. *Eating facilities:* full restaurant facilities every day; three bars. *Visitors:* welcome without reservation. *Society Meetings:* catered for by arrangement weekdays only (except Tuesday). Special day package. Professional: B. McKee (0476 63911). Secretary and General Manager: T. Measures (0476 67399 – all enquiries; Fax: 0476 592078).

GRANTHAM near. **Belton Woods Hotel and Country Club,** Belton, Near Grantham NG32 2LN (0476 593200). *Location:* two miles north of Grantham on A607 to Lincoln. Five minutes off A1 at Gonerby Moor. Parkland with mature and young trees. Three courses – Lancaster course: 18 holes, 7021 yards. S.S.S. 74; Wellington Course: 18 holes, 6875 yards. S.S.S. 73; Spitfire Course: 9 holes, 1184 yards. S.S.S. not yet available. Putting green, 24-bay driving range. *Green Fees:* £16.00 weekdays; £25.00 weekends. Special rates for societies and groups. *Eating facilities:* three bars, two restaurants. *Visitors:* welcome Monday to Friday, no advance booking. Accommodation in Hotel, 96 bedrooms and suites, families welcome. Golfing Breaks a speciality. *Society Meetings:* weekday bookings, weekends subject to availability. Professional: T. Roberts (0476 593200).

GRANTHAM. **Stoke Rochford Golf Club,** Stoke Rochford, Near Grantham NG33 5EW (Great Ponton (047-683 275). *Location:* five miles south of Grantham on A1. Entrance at "A.J.S." service area. Parkland. 18 holes, 6209 yards. S.S.S. 70. Small practice ground. *Green Fees:* £17.00 per round, £24.00 per day weekdays (estimated); weekends and Bank Holidays £26.00 per round, £35.00 per day (estimated). If playing with a member £8.00 weekdays, £10.00 weekends. *Eating facilities:* meals available daily, to be booked before playing. *Visitors:* cannot commence play before 10.30am at weekends or on Public Holidays. No visitors at weekends November, December and January. *Society Meetings:* by prior arrangement. Professional: A.E. Dow (047-683 218). Secretary: J.M. Butler (0476) 67030).

HORNCASTLE near. **Horncastle Golf Club,** West Ashby, Near Horncastle LN9 5PP (0507 526800). *Location:* just off A158 between Horncastle and Baumber. Parkland course – water on 14 holes. 18 holes, 5800 yards. S.S.S. 70. Floodlit golf range. *Green Fees:* £10.00 per round, £15.00 per day. *Eating facilities:* bar, restaurant. *Visitors:* welcome anytime. Ballroom and conference facilities. Accommodation available in 24 bedrooms. *Society Meetings:* please phone in advance. Professional: E.C. Wright. Secretary: T. Bullimore.

LINCOLN. **Blankney Golf Club,** Blankney, near Metheringham, Lincoln LN4 3AZ (0526 20263). *Location:* on B1188, 10 miles south of Lincoln. Parkland, slightly undulating. 18 holes, 6378 yards. S.S.S. 71. Practice area. *Green Fees:* weekdays £15.00 per round, £20.00 per day; weekends £20.00 per round, £25.00 per day. *Eating facilities:* bar snacks/meals, catering in dining room by prior arrangement. *Visitors:* welcome weekdays except Bank Holidays – telephone beforehand. *Society Meetings:* by advance booking only. Professional: Graham Bradley (0526 20202). Secretary: D.A. Priest (0526 20263).

LINCOLN. **Canwick Park Golf Club,** Canwick Park, Washingborough Road, Lincoln LN4 1EF (Lincoln (0522) 522166). *Location:* one and a half miles approximately east of Lincoln, first left (turning) off Canwick Road from Lincoln is Washingborough Road. Wooded parkland course. 18 holes, 6257 yards, 5726 metres, S.S.S. 70. Practice ground. *Green Fees:* £10.00 per round, £17.00 per day Mondays; £12.00 per round, £18.00 per day Tuesdays to Fridays (£14.00 per day with a member). Weekends £13.00 per round, £20.00 per day (£15.00 per day with a member). *Eating facilities:* bar snacks and meals to order. *Visitors:* welcome weekdays; weekends after 3.00pm. Professional: Steve Williamson (0522 536870). Secretary: Mr A.C. Hodgkinson (0522 791757).

LINCOLN. **Carholme Golf Club,** Carholme Road, Lincoln LN1 1SE (Lincoln (0522) 523725). *Location:* one mile from city centre on A57 to Worksop. Flat parkland. 18 holes, 6150 yards. S.S.S. 69. *Green Fees:* on application; no green fees weekends. *Eating facilities:* full service except Mondays. *Visitors:* welcome (not Sundays). *Society Meetings:* by prior arrangement only. Professional: G. Leslie (0522 536811). Secretary: F.J. Branson (0522 523725).

LINCOLN. **Lincoln Golf Club,** Torksey, Lincoln (Torksey (042 771) 210. *Location:* East Lincolnshire, between Lincoln, Gainsborough and Newark. Flat testing inland course with quick drying sandy subsoil. 18 holes, 6438 yards. S.S.S. 71. *Green Fees:* weekdays £18.00 per round, £21.00 per day. *Eating facilities:* full facilities except Tuesday (ladies day). *Visitors:* welcome by arrangement, weekends with members only. *Society Meetings:* catered for. Professional: Ashley Carter (042 771 273). Secretary: D. Boag (042 771 721).

LOUTH. **Louth Golf Club,** 59 Crowtree Lane, Louth LN11 9LJ (Louth (0507) 602554). *Location:* one mile west of town centre. Undulating parkland. 18 holes, 6477 yards. S.S.S. 71. Practice ground. *Green Fees:* £15.00 per round, £18.00 per day weekdays; £18.00 per round, £20.00 per day weekends and Bank Holidays. *Eating facilities:* full catering 10am to 10pm. *Visitors:* welcome without reservation. *Society Meetings:* catered for. Professional: A.J. Blundell (0507 604648). Secretary: P.C. Bell (0507 603681). Manager: A. Covey (0507 604864).

MABLETHORPE. **Sandilands Golf Club,** Roman Bank, Sandilands, Sutton-on-Sea LN12 2RJ (0521 41432). *Location:* A52 one mile south of Sutton-on-Sea. Seaside links adjacent to sea and sand. 18 holes, 5995 yards, 5483 metres. S.S.S. 69. *Green Fees:* weekdays £12.00 round, £18.00 day; weekends and Bank Holidays £18.00 per round. *Eating facilities:* meals and drinks in clubhouse. *Visitors:* welcome. *Society Meetings:* catered for weekdays. Professional: D. Vernon (0521 41600). Secretary: D. Mumby (0521 41617).

MARKET RASEN. **Market Rasen and District Golf Club,** Legsby Road, Market Rasen LN8 3DZ (Market Rasen (0673) 842319). *Location:* A46 to Market Rasen – one mile east of town. Wooded course. 18 holes, 6043 yards, 5527 metres. S.S.S. 69. Practice ground. *Green Fees:* weekdays £20.00 per day, £15.00 per round; weekends only with member. *Eating facilities:* by arrangement with the Steward, but not Mondays. *Visitors:* welcome with reservation, must be member of bona fide golf club. Not Wednesdays after 10.30am. Weekends with members only. *Society Meetings:* catered for Tuesdays and Fridays. Professional: A.M. Chester (0673 842416). Hon. Secretary: E. Hill (0673 842319).

SKEGNESS. **North Shore Hotel and Golf Club,** North Shore Road, Skegness PE25 1DN (Skegness (0754) 763298). *Location:* north of town one mile. Half seaside links, half parkland overlooking the sea. 18 holes, 6134 yards. Par 71, S.S.S. 69. *Green Fees:* weekdays £14.00 per round, £20.00 per day; weekends and Bank Holidays £20.00 per round, £26.00 per day. *Eating facilities:* hotel on the course. *Visitors:* welcome, prior notice essential. *Society Meetings:* welcome. Professional: Golf instruction given by John Cornelius (0754 764822).

SKEGNESS. **Seacroft Golf Club,** Seacroft, Skegness PE25 3AU (Skegness (0754) 763020). *Location:* towards Gibraltar Nature Reserve. Seaside links course. 18 holes, 6490 yards. S.S.S. 71. *Green Fees:* £20.00 per round, £25.00 per day; weekends and Bank Holidays £25.00 round, £35.00 per day. *Eating facilities:* available on prior booking. *Visitors:* welcome after 9.30am if members of recognised club, Handicap Certificate required; not between 12noon and 2pm. *Society Meetings:* catered for, limited to 24 at weekends. Professional: R. Lawie (0754 769624). Secretary: H.K. Brader (0754 763020).

SLEAFORD. **Sleaford Golf Club,** Willoughby Road, South Rauceby, Sleaford NG34 8PL (South Rauceby (05298) 273). *Location:* off A153, two miles west of Sleaford. Inland links-type course, fairly flat and lightly wooded. 18 holes, 6443 yards, 5947 metres. S.S.S. 71. Practice field, 6 hole pitch and putt. *Green Fees:* weekdays £17.00, weekends £25.00. *Eating facilities:* full catering except Mondays. Bar open seven days. *Visitors:* welcome without reservation, except winter Sundays. Handicap Certificate required and must be members of a recognised club. *Society Meetings:* catered for weekdays only by prior arrangement. Professional: S.D. Harrison (05298 644). Secretary: D.B.R. Harris (05298 326).

SOUTH KYME. **South Kyme Golf Club,** Skinners Lane, South Kyme LN4 4AE (0526 861113). *Location:* approximately four miles off A153 road from Sleaford to Horncastle, turn right before North Kyme. Six miles off A17 from Sleaford to Boston, turn left before East Heckington. A long and testing fenland course. 18 holes, 6597 yards. S.S.S. Men 71, Ladies 70. 6 hole pitch and putt. *Green Fees:* weekdays £10.00; weekends £12.00. £2.00 reduction when playing with a member. *Eating facilities:* bar and restaurant. Snacks available all day. Lunch menu available from 1pm to 2.30pm. *Visitors:* no restrictions at present but advisable to check at weekends in case of competitions. *Society Meetings:* welcome with prior booking. Secretary: Anne Mablethorpe.

SPALDING near. **Gedney Hill Golf Course,** West Drove, Gedney Hill, Near Spalding PE12 0NT (0406 330183). *Location:* six miles from Radnor Tower in Crowland, follow signs to Gedney Hill, golf course signposted. Flat, testing conditions, playing characteristics of a links course with fen winds. 18 holes, 5429 yards. S.S.S. 66. 10 bay driving range. *Green Fees:* weekdays £5.75; weekends £9.75. *Eating facilities:* two bars (one casual spike bar), restaurant (80 seater). *Visitors:* welcome always. Full snooker room. *Society Meetings:* by arrangement. Professional: David Creek (0406 330922). Secretary: Steve McGregor (0406 330922).

SPALDING. **Sutton Bridge Golf Club,** New Road, Sutton Bridge, Spalding (Holbeach (0406) 350323). *Location:* off A17, 18 miles east of Spalding. 9 holes, 5804 yards. S.S.S. 68. *Green Fees:* information not available. *Eating facilities:* available. *Visitors:* welcome, except weekends and not on match or competition days. *Society Meetings:* not catered for. Professional: R. Wood (0406 351080). Secretary: K.C. Buckle (0945 870455).

SPALDING. **The Spalding Golf Club,** Surfleet, Spalding PE11 4EA (0775 85234). *Location:* four miles from Spalding on A16 to Boston. 18 holes, 5807 yards. S.S.S. 67. *Green Fees:* £20.00 weekdays; £22.00 weekends. *Visitors:* welcome, Handicap Certificate required. *Society Meetings:* catered for on Thursdays only. Professional: John W. Spencer (0775 85474). Secretary: T.I. Chambers (0775 85386).

STAMFORD. **Burghley Park (Stamford) Golf Club,** St. Martins Without, Stamford PE9 3JX (0780 53789). *Location:* leave A1 at roundabout for Stamford, club one mile on right. Flat parkland. 18 holes, 6133 yards. S.S.S. 69. *Green Fees:* weekdays £20.00, weekends as members' guests only. *Eating facilities:* restaurant and bar. *Visitors:* welcome weekdays. Handicap Certificates required. *Society Meetings:* Wednesdays and Thursdays only. Professional: Glenn Davies (0780 62100). Secretary: Howard Mulligan (0780 53789).

STAMFORD. **Luffenham Heath Golf Club,** Ketton, Stamford PE9 3UU (Stamford (0780) 720218). *Location:* one-and-a-half miles south-west of Ketton on A6121. Undulating heathland, in conservation area for flora and fauna. 18 holes, 6254 yards. S.S.S. 70. *Green Fees:* on application. *Eating facilities:* catering available by arrangement. *Visitors:* welcome, advisable to contact Professional first. Handicap Certificate preferred. Changing room/showers. *Society Meetings:* by arrangement through the Secretary. Professional: J.A. Lawrence (0780 720298). Secretary: Ian F. Davenport (0780 720205).

WOODHALL SPA. **Woodhall Spa Golf Club,** Woodhall Spa LN10 6PU (Woodhall Spa (0526) 52511). *Location:* 19 miles from Lincoln, Boston, Sleaford; 33 miles from Skegness; 50 miles from Nottingham. Flat, wooded heathland. 18 holes, 6907 yards. S.S.S. 73. Practice ground and driving net. *Green Fees:* weekdays £22.00 per round, £32.00 per day; weekends and Bank Holidays £25.00 per round, £35.00 per day (all fees are estimates). *Eating facilities:* full catering available. *Visitors:* welcome with reservation. Handicap Certificates required (maximum handicap permitted Gents 20, Ladies 30). *Society Meetings:* catered for if booked in advance. Professional: P. Fixter (0526 53229). Secretary: B.H. Fawcett.

# Greater Manchester

ALTRINCHAM. **Altrincham Golf Course**, Stockport Road, Timperley, Altrinchram, Cheshire (061-928 0761). *Location:* one mile east of Altrincham on A560. Parkland. 18 holes, 6190 yards, 5659 metres. S.S.S. 69. *Green Fees:* £4.80 weekdays; £5.60 weekends. *Eating facilities:* Old Hall Hotel attached to course. *Visitors:* welcome any time, book one week in advance. Public course. Secretary: P. Yates.

ALTRINCHAM. **Dunham Forest Golf and Country Club**, Oldfield Lane, Altrincham WA14 4TY (061-928 2605; Fax: 061-929 8975). *Location:* approximately 9 miles south of Manchester off A56. Wooded parkland. 18 holes, 6772 yards. S.S.S. 72. *Green Fees:* weekdays £25.00, weekends and Bank Holidays £30.00. *Eating facilities:* clubhouse restaurant and bar open daily. *Visitors:* welcome, but should telephone to check availability. *Society Meetings:* welcome by prior arrangement. Professional: I. Wrigley (061-928 2727). Secretary: Mrs S. Klaus (061-928 2605).

ALTRINCHAM. **The Ringway Golf Club Ltd**, Hale Mount, Hale Barns, Altrincham WA15 8SW (061-904 9609). *Location:* Junction 6, M56 then A538 towards Altrincham for one mile. Parkland. 18 holes, 6494 yards. S.S.S. 71. *Green Fees:* weekdays £24.00, weekends and Bank Holidays £30.00. *Eating facilities:* full diningroom facilities available. *Visitors:* generally not on Tuesdays or Saturdays which are Ladies' and Gentlemen's Competition Days, or Fridays (members only). *Society Meetings:* catered for by arrangement. Professional: Nick Ryan (061-980 8432). Secretary: D. Wright (061-980 2630).

ASHTON-IN-MAKERFIELD. **Ashton-in-Makerfield Golf Club Ltd**, Garswood Park, Liverpool Road, Ashton-in-Makerfield (Wigan (0942) 727269). *Location:* M6, Junction 23 from south, M6 Junction 24 from north. Wooded course. 18 holes, 6140 yards. S.S.S. 69. *Green fees:* £20.00. *Eating facilities:* available, except Mondays. *Visitors:* welcome mid-week (except Wednesday) with reservation but not before 9.45am. *Society Meetings:* catered for Tuesdays and Thursdays by prior appointment. Professional: P. Allan (0942 724229). Secretary: J.R. Hay (0942 719330).

ASHTON-UNDER-LYNE. **Ashton-under-Lyne Golf Club**, Gorsey Way, Ashton-under-Lyne OL6 9HT (061-330 1537). *Location:* three miles from town centre, Mossley Road, left at Queens Road, right at Nook Lane, Clubhouse top of St. Christopher's Road. Wooded course. 18 holes, 6209 yards. S.S.S. 70. *Green Fees:* weekdays £20.00 per day, weekends with member only. *Eating facilities:* full catering except Mondays. *Visitors:* welcome weekdays except Wednesdays; members of recognised golf clubs welcome without reservation. *Society Meetings:* catered for on application: special daily rates. Professional: C. Boyle (061-308 2095). Secretary: G.J. Musgrave (061-339 8655).

BOLTON. **Bolton Golf Club Ltd**, Lostock Park, Chorley New Road, Bolton BL6 4AJ (Bolton (0204) 43067). *Location:* off main road half-way between Bolton and Horwich. 18 holes, 6215 yards. S.S.S. 70. *Green Fees:* information not provided. *Eating facilities:* luncheons (evening meals except Monday and Sunday). *Visitors:* welcome with reservation. *Society Meetings:* catered for on Thursdays and Fridays. Professional: R. Longworth. Secretary: H. Cook.

BOLTON. **Breightmet Golf Club**, Red Bridge, Ainsworth, Bolton (Bolton (0204) 27381). *Location:* leave Bolton on main road to Bury, turn left two miles on Milnthorpe road for the bridge. 9 holes, 6418 yards. S.S.S. 71. *Green Fees:* weekdays £15.00, weekends and Bank Holidays £18.00 (half-price with a member). *Eating facilities:* lunches and light refreshments. *Visitors:* welcome, preliminary phone call advisable. *Society Meetings:* catered for on application. Secretary: R. Weir.

BOLTON. **Deane Golf Club**, Broadford Road, Deane, Bolton (Bolton (0204) 61944). *Location:* one mile east of Junction 5 of M61 towards Bolton Centre. Rolling parkland with number of small ravines to cross. 18 holes, 5583 yards, 5105 metres. S.S.S. 67. *Green Fees:* weekdays £16.50; weekends £22.50. *Eating facilities:* lunches and evening meals by arrangement. *Visitors:* welcome. *Society Meetings:* Tuesdays, Thursdays and Fridays only. Secretary: P. Flaxman (0204 651808).

BOLTON. **Dunscar Golf Club Ltd**, Longworth Lane, Bromley Cross, Bolton BL7 9QY (Bolton (0204) 303321). *Location:* one and a half miles north of Bolton on A666. Parkland, moorland course. 18 holes, 6045 yards. S.S.S. 69. Practice facilities available. *Green Fees:* weekdays £20.00; weekends and Bank Holidays £30.00. With a member £10.00. *Eating facilities:* available. *Visitors:* welcome except weekends. *Society Meetings:* catered for by arrangement. Professional: Gary Treadgold (0204 592992). Secretary: Thomas Michael Yates (0204 301090).

BOLTON. **Great Lever and Farnworth Golf Club Ltd**, Lever Edge Lane, Bolton BL3 3EN (Bolton (0204) 62582). *Location:* A666 or M61, one and a half miles from Bolton town centre. Parkland. 18 holes, 5859 yards. S.S.S. 69. Practice ground. *Green Fees:* weekdays £11.00, weekends £17.00. *Eating facilities:* restaurant and bar every day except Mondays. *Visitors:* welcome weekdays, preferably by appointment. *Society Meetings:* catered for by arrangement weekdays. Professional: Mr L. Griffiths (0204 656650). Secretary: Mrs J. Ivill (0204 656137).

BOLTON. **Harwood Golf Club**, Roading Brook Road, Harwood, Bolton BL2 4JD (Bolton (0204) 22878). *Location:* three miles east of Bolton – A58 to Bury, turn left through Ainsworth village. Flat meadowland. 9 holes, 5958 yards. S.S.S. 69. Small practice area. *Green Fees:* weekdays £15.00, £5.00 with a member; weekends only with a member. *Eating facilities:* bar not open during weekdays, except Wednesdays; catering on request. *Visitors:* welcome any weekday, weekends only with a member. Should be members of recognised golf club or society. *Society Meetings:* catered for on written application to Secretary. Professional: Max Evans (0204 398472). Secretary: J.S. Fairhurst (0204 28028).

BOLTON. **Old Links (Bolton) Ltd,** Chorley Old Road, Montserrat, Bolton BL1 5SU (0204 40050). *Location:* on B6226, 400 yards north of roundabout on ring road. Championship course, moorland. 18 holes, 6410 yards. S.S.S. 72. Practice facilities. *Green Fees:* weekdays £26.00, weekends £30.00. Special rates for groups over 20. *Eating facilities:* available except Mondays. *Visitors:* welcome, not Saturdays until 4pm. *Society Meetings:* catered for weekdays. Professional: P. Horridge (0204 43089). Secretary: E. Monaghan (0204 42307).

BOLTON. **Regent Park Golf Club Ltd,** Links Road, Chorley New Road, Bolton BL6 4AF (0204 44170). *Location:* midway between Bolton and Horwich. Parkland. 18 holes, 6069 yards. S.S.S. 69. Practice area. *Green Fees:* weekdays £4.50; weekends £6.50. *Eating facilities:* meals/bar available. *Visitors:* welcome seven days – municipal course. *Society Meeetings:* welcome midweek, book in advance. Professional: A.K. Holland (0204 42336). Secretary: J. Leeming.

BOLTON. **Turton Golf Club,** Wood End Farm, Chapeltown Road, Bromley Cross, Bolton (0204 852235). *Location:* three miles north of Bolton on the A666. Moorland course with extensive views. 9 holes, 5805 yards. S.S.S. 68. Practice area. *Green Fees:* £12.00. *Eating facilities:* to order except Mondays. *Visitors:* welcome. *Society Meetings:* welcome on Thursdays by arrangement. Secretary: B.E. Stanley (0204 306881).

BRAMHALL. **Bramhall Golf Club,** The Clubhouse, Ladythorn Road, Bramhall, Stockport SK7 2EY (061-439 4057). *Location:* three quarters of a mile from Bramhall Railway Station, half a mile from Bramhall Moat House Hotel. Parkland. 18 holes, 6361 yards, 5816 metres. S.S.S. 70. *Green Fees:* information not provided. *Eating facilities:* Steward will provide meals on request, subject to club and visiting party occasions. *Visitors:* welcome except Thursdays and Competition Days. *Society Meetings:* catered for Wednesday, minimum 24. Professional: Brian Nield (061-439 1171). Secretary: J.G. Lee (061-439 6092).

BURY. **Bury Golf Club,** Unsworth Hall, Blackford Bridge, Bury (061-766 4897). *Location:* A56 eight miles north of Manchester. 18 holes, 5953 yards. S.S.S. 69. *Green Fees:* information not provided. *Eating facilities:* grill room service except Mondays. *Visitors:* welcome without reservation. *Society Meetings:* catered for. Professional: M. Peel (061-766 2213). Secretary: J. Meikle.

BURY. **Greenmount Golf Club,** Greenhaigh Fold Farm, Greenmount, Bury (Tottington (020-488 3712).

*Location:* three miles north of Bury. 9 holes, 4915 yards. S.S.S. 64. *Green Fees:* weekdays £10.00 per day. *Eating facilities:* lunches at club except on Thursdays. *Visitors:* welcome, Tuesday – ladies' day. *Society Meetings:* catered for. Secretary: G.J. Lowe (0204 883712).

BURY. **Lowes Park Golf Club Ltd.,** Hill Top, Walmersley, Bury BL9 6SU (061-764 1231). *Location:* take A56 north from Bury, turn right at Bury General Hospital into Lowes Road. Hilly course, usually windy. 9 holes, 6009 yards, 5500 metres. S.S.S. 69. *Green Fees:* information not provided. *Eating facilities:* full catering except Mondays. *Visitors:* welcome weekdays except Wednesdays (Ladies' Day). *Society Meetings:* catered for weekdays (not Saturday), Sundays by appointment. Secretary: E. Brierley (0706 67331).

BURY. **Walmersley Golf Club,** Garretts Close, Walmersley, Bury (061-764 1429). *Location:* leave A56 approximately two miles north of Bury at Walmersley Post Office into Old Road, right at Masons Arms Inn. Moorland course. 9 holes, 6114 yards, 5588 metres. S.S.S. 70. *Green Fees:* £12.00 per day, £6.00 with member. *Eating facilities:* lunches and evening meals served except Mondays. *Visitors:* welcome weekdays without reservation. *Society Meetings:* catered for weekdays. Secretary: C. Stock (061-764 5057).

CHEADLE. **Cheadle Golf Club,** Shiers Drive, Cheadle SK8 1HW (061-428 2160). *Location:* one-and-a-half miles Junction 11 M63. 9 holes, 5006 yards. S.S.S. 65. *Green Fees:* information not provided. *Eating facilities:* by arrangement. *Visitors:* welcome with reservation and playing with member. *Society Meetings:* catered for by arrangement. Professional: M. Redrup (061-428 9878). Secretary: P.P. Webster (061-491 4452).

DAVYHULME. **Davyhulme Park Golf Club,** Gleneagles Road, Davyhulme, Urmston M31 2SA (061-748 2856). *Location:* one mile from M63/M62. Wooded parkland course. 18 holes, 6237 yards. S.S.S. 70. *Green Fees:* weekdays £19.00; weekends £23.00. *Eating facilities:* lunches and dinners. *Visitors:* welcome except Competition days. *Society Meetings:* catered for by prior arrangement. Professional: Hugh Lewis (061-748 3931). Secretary: H.A. Langworthy (061-748 2260).

DENTON. **Denton Golf Club,** Manchester Road, Denton M34 2NU (061-336 3218). *Location:* A57, five miles from Piccadilly, Manchester. 18 holes, 6290 yards. S.S.S. 70. *Green Fees:* information not provided. *Eating facilities:* meals catered for except all day Monday and Thursday afternoon. *Visitors:* welcome with club members and handicap, without reservation weekdays only. *Society Meetings:* catered for on weekdays except Tuesday by application. Professional: Roger Vere. Secretary: R. Wickham.

DUKINFIELD. **Dukinfield Golf Club,** Lyne Edge, Dukinfield (061-338 2340). *Location:* six miles east of Manchester via Ashton-under-Lyne. Hillside with wooded areas. 18 holes, 5556 yards. S.S.S. 67. *Green Fees:* weekdays £14.50. *Visitors:* welcome except Wednesdays and weekends. *Society Meetings:* catered for by prior arrangement. Secretary: L. Holmes (061-338 2669).

ECCLES. **Worsley Golf Club,** Stableford Avenue, Monton, Eccles M30 8AP (061-789 4202). *Location:* one mile from Junction 13 M62. Parkland. 18 holes, 6200 yards. S.S.S. 70. *Green Fees:* weekdays £18.00; weekends and Bank Holidays £25.00 (£11.00 with member). *Eating facilities:* snacks, lunches and evening meals. *Visitors:* welcome, if past or present members of recognised golf clubs. *Society Meetings:* catered for Mondays, Wednesdays and Thursdays. Professional: Ceri Cousins. Secretary: B. Dean.

FLIXTON. **Acre Gate Golf Club,** Pennybridge Lane, Flixton, Manchester (061-748 1226). *Location:* Flixton Road. Flat course. 18 holes, 4395 yards. S.S.S. 64. *Green Fees:* weekdays £4.60; weekends £6.50. *Eating facilities:* catering and bar facilities weekend and Monday/Wednesday/Friday. *Visitors:* course is municipal therefore no restrictions. *Society Meetings:* welcome (on application to the club Secretary) to use club facilities. Secretary: Julie Wilde (061-748 1226 or 061-747 7230 home).

HYDE. **Werneth Low Golf Club,** Werneth Low, Hyde, Cheshire SK14 3AF (061-368 2503). *Location:* one mile from centre of Hyde via Gee Cross. Scenic, hilly course with excellent greens. 9 holes, 6114 yards. S.S.S. 66. *Green Fees:* weekdays £15.00; weekends £23.00. *Eating facilities:* light refreshments normally available except Wednesdays. *Visitors:* welcome any time except Sunday mornings and Tuesday evenings; Sundays with member only. *Society Meetings:* catered for by prior arrangement. Professional: T. Bacchus (061-336 6908). Secretary: R. Watson (061-368 7388).

LEIGH. **Pennington Golf Club (Municipal),** Pennington Golf Course, Pennington Country Park, off St. Helens Road, Leigh. *Location:* Junction 17 on M6 to Leigh. Flat parkland with water coursing through. 9 holes, 2919 yards. S.S.S. 34. *Green Fees:* on request. *Eating facilities:* snack bar facilities. *Visitors:* welcome without reservation. Professional: Mr T. Kershaw (0942 607278). Secretary: Mr P.A. Cartwright (061-794 5316).

LITTLEBOROUGH. **Whittaker Golf Club,** Whittaker Lane, Littleborough OL15 0LH (Littleborough (0706) 378310). *Location:* one mile from town centre along Blackstone Edge Old Road. Moorland course. 9 holes, 5632 yards. S.S.S. 67. *Green Fees:* weekdays £8.00; weekends £10.00. *Eating facilities:* bar only. *Visitors:* welcome without reservation, except Tuesday afternoons and Sundays. *Society Meetings:* weekdays and Saturdays only by prior arrangement with Secretary. Secretary: Mr G.A. Smith (0484 428546).

MANCHESTER. **Blackley Golf Club,** Victoria Avenue East, Blackley, Manchester M9 2HW (061-643 2980). *Location:* five miles north from City Centre. Parkland. 18 holes, 6237 yards, 5708 metres. S.S.S. 70. *Green Fees:* £15.00 weekdays. *Eating facilities:* diningroom/bar. *Visitors:* welcome, Thursdays and weekends with member only. *Society Meetings:* catered for. Professional: Martin Barton (061-643 3912). Secretary: C.B. Leggott (061-654 7770).

MANCHESTER. **Brookdale Golf Club Ltd,** Ashbridge, Woodhouse, Failsworth, Manchester (061-681 4534). *Location:* five miles north of Manchester. 18 holes, 6040 yards. S.S.S. 68. *Green Fees:* weekdays £18.00; weekends and Bank Holidays £21.00. *Eating facilities:* available with ample notice. *Visitors:* welcome without reservation except Sundays. *Society Meetings:* catered for with one month's notice. Professional: B. Connor (061-681 2655). Hon. Secretary: G. Glass.

MANCHESTER. **Chorlton-cum-Hardy Golf Club,** Barlow Hall Road, Chorlton-cum-Hardy M21 2JJ (061-881 3139). *Location:* near junction of A5145 and A5103 (M63 Junction 9). Meadowland. 18 holes, 6003 yards. S.S.S. 69. *Green Fees:* weekdays £20.00; weekends and Bank Holidays £25.00. *Eating facilities:* catering provided – seasonal limited hours, sandwiches only Mondays. *Visitors:* welcome without reservation, except on Competition days, must provide proof of recognised handicap. *Society Meetings:* catered for Thursdays only by arrangement with Secretary. Professional: David Screeton (061-881 9911). Secretary: Mrs H.M. Stuart (061-881-5830).

MANCHESTER. **Didsbury Golf Club Ltd,** Ford Lane, Northenden, Manchester M22 4NQ (061-998 2743). *Location:* Junction 3 on M56 to Palatine Road to Church Road, to Ford Lane. Parkland. 18 holes, 6276 yards. S.S.S. 70. Good practice facilities. *Green Fees:* weekdays £20.00; weekends £24.00. *Eating facilities:* fully-equipped bar and restaurant. *Visitors:* Thursday/Friday – Tuesday small societies. *Society Meetings:* catered for. Professional: P. Barber (061-998 2811). Secretary/Manager: C.B. Turnbull (061-998 9278).

MANCHESTER. **Ellesmere Golf Club,** Old Clough Lane, Worsley, Near Manchester M28 5HZ (061-790 2122). *Location:* off A580 East Lancs Road, adjacent to M62 northbound, (eastbound) access. Wooded parkland. 18 holes, 5954 yards. S.S.S. 69. *Green Fees:* weekdays: visitors £16.00, guests £5.00; weekends: visitors £20.00, guests £6.00. *Eating facilities:* bar; catering available, with or without reservation. *Visitors:* members of recognised golf clubs welcome, but not during club competitions or Bank Holidays, contact Professional for restrictions. *Society Meetings:* catered for by appointment. Professional: Terry Morley (061-790 8591). Hon. Secretary: A.C. Kay (061-799 0554).

MANCHESTER. **Fairfield Golf and Sailing Club,** "Boothdale", Booth Road, Audenshaw, Manchester M34 5WW (061-370 1641). *Location:* off A635, five miles east of Manchester. Parkland bounded in part by reservoir. 18 holes, 4956 yards. S.S.S. 68. *Green Fees:* weekdays £16.00; weekends £20.00. *Eating facilities:* available. *Visitors:* welcome, restrictions Wednesdays, Thursdays and weekends. *Society Meetings:* catered for by arrangement mid-week. Professional: D. Butler (061-370 2292). Secretary: J. Humphries (061-336 3950).

MANCHESTER. **Flixton Golf Club,** Church Road, Flixton, Urmston (061-748 2116). *Location:* five miles from Manchester. Parkland. 9 holes, 6410 yards. S.S.S. 71. *Green Fees:* £15.00 weekdays. £7.00 weekends, Bank Holidays and Christmas and New Year holiday period (playing with a member only). *Eating facilities:*

daily except Tuesdays. *Visitors:* welcome with reservation. *Society Meetings:* catered for by arrangement. Professional: B. Ling (061-746 7160). Hon. Secretary: J.G. Frankland (061-747 0296). Catering: (061-748 7545).

MANCHESTER. **Heaton Park Golf Club,** Heaton Park, Prestwich, Manchester (061-798 0295). *Location:* north Manchester, M62 to exit 19 M66 to A576, right to park entrance (200 yards). Undulating parkland. 18 holes, 5840 yards. S.S.S. 68. *Green Fees:* weekdays £5.50, weekends and Bank Holidays £6.60 per round. *Visitors:* welcome, book week in advance. Secretary: F. Lewis (061-773 1113).

MANCHESTER. **Houldsworth Golf Club Ltd,** Wingate House, Higher Levenshulme, Manchester M19 3JW (061-224 5055). *Location:* off A6 between Manchester and Stockport, adjacent to M63 and M6. Flat parkland with water hazards. 18 holes, 6078 yards, 5558 metres. S.S.S. 69. Practice area. *Green Fees:* weekdays £13.00; weekends £16.00. Reduced rates for parties. *Eating facilities:* bar snacks, or full restaurant service. *Visitors:* must be pre-arranged with Professional or Hon. Secretary. *Society Meetings:* catered for on application. Professional: David Naylor (061-224 4571). Secretary: S.W. Zielinski (061-224 5055).

MANCHESTER. **Manchester Golf Club,** Hopwood Cottage, Middleton, Manchester M24 2QP (061-643 2718). *Location:* Exit 20 from M62, three minutes from motorway. Moorland/parkland. 18 holes, 6454 yards, 5895 metres. S.S.S. 72. Large practice ground. Driving range. *Green Fees:* weekdays, £25.00 per day, weekends £30.00 per day. *Eating facilities:* two bars and first class restaurant. *Visitors:* welcome weekdays. *Society Meetings:* parties up to 120 catered for by arrangement. Professional: B. Connor (061-643 2638). Secretary: K.G. Flett (061-643 3202).

MANCHESTER. **New North Manchester Golf Club Ltd,** Rhodes House, Manchester Old Road, Middleton, Manchester (061-643 2941). *Location:* A576, less than one mile from Junction 18 on M62/M66. Undulating and sometimes hilly terrain. 18 holes, 6527 yards, 5987 metres. S.S.S. 72. Large practice ground. *Green Fees:* £18.00 per round £22.00 per day weekdays. *Eating facilities:* catering every day except Tuesday. *Visitors:* welcome except weekends. *Society Meetings:* welcome. Professional: P.J. Lunt (061-643 7094). Secretary: B.L. Woodhead (061-643 9033).

MANCHESTER. **Northenden Golf Club,** Palatine Road, Northenden, Manchester M22 4FR (061-998 4079). *Location:* five miles south of Manchester city centre, one mile north east of M56/M63 motorways. Parkland. 18 holes, 6469 yards, 5915 metres. S.S.S. 71. Practice net. *Green Fees:* £20.00 weekdays, £25.00 weekends. Reduced rates if playing with member. *Eating facilities:* available, diningroom and bar snacks. *Visitors:* welcome most days, preferably with reservation. *Society Meetings:* catered for Tuesdays and Fridays only. Professional: W. McColl (061-945 3386). Secretary: V.A. Holcroft (061-998 4738). Stewards: Mr and Mrs J. Penny.

MANCHESTER. **Pikefold Golf Club,** Cooper Lane, Manchester M9 2QQ (061-740 1136). *Location:* four miles north of city centre off Rochdale Road A664, then A6104 Victoria Avenue. Undulating wooded course. 9 holes, 5789 yards. S.S.S. 68. *Green Fees:* weekdays £12.00 per round/day (£5.00 with member); Saturdays and Bank Holidays £7.00, must play with member. No visitors Sundays. *Eating facilities:* full catering and bar facilities. *Visitors:* welcome weekdays without reservation. *Society Meetings:* catered for by prior arrangement. Secretary: F.J. Ashworth.

MANCHESTER. **Prestwich Golf Club,** Hilton Lane, Prestwich, Manchester (061-773 2544). *Location:* on A6044, one mile from junction with A56. 18 holes, 4757 yards. S.S.S. 63. *Green Fees:* information not provided. *Eating facilities:* by arrangement. *Visitors:* welcome weekdays. *Society Meetings:* catered for weekdays. Professional: Gary Coope.

MANCHESTER. **Stand Golf Club,** The Dales, Ashbourne Grove, Whitefield, Bury, Manchester M25 7NL (061-766 2388). *Location:* M62 Exit 17, A56/A665 one mile. Undulating parkland with sandy subsoil, playable all year round. 18 holes, 6426 yards. S.S.S. 71. *Green Fees:* weekdays £18.00; weekends £25.00. Reduced rates for parties over 16. *Eating facilities:* meals served daily and bar except Mondays, order in advance. *Visitors:* welcome Monday to Friday; weekends by prior arrangement. *Society Meetings:* welcome Wednesday/Friday by prior arrangement. Professional: Mark Dance (061-766 2214). Hon. Secretary: Eric B. Taylor (061-766 3197).

MANCHESTER. **Swinton Park Golf Club,** East Lancashire Road, Swinton, Manchester M27 1LX (061-794 1785). *Location:* on the A580 Manchester to Liverpool road, five miles from Manchester centre. Parkland course. Three courses. Practice area. *Green Fees:* on application. *Eating facilities:* available. *Visitors:* welcome Tuesdays, Wednesdays and Fridays, Tee reservations 10am-noon, 2pm-4pm. *Society Meetings:* catered for by prior arrangement. Professional: J. Wilson (061-793 8077). General Secretary: F. Slater (061-794 0861).

MANCHESTER. **Withington Golf Club,** 243 Palatine Road, West Didsbury, Manchester M20 8UD (061-445 3912). *Location:* three miles from Manchester city centre, adjacent M56 and M63. Flat parkland. 18 holes, 6410 yards. S.S.S. 71. *Green Fees:* (1992) weekdays only (except Thursdays) £20.00 per round. *Eating facilities:* lunches and evening meals to order. Snacks available at all times except Mondays. *Visitors:* ring Professional for times. *Society Meetings:* catered for by arrangement with the Secretary. Professional: R.J. Ling (061-445 4861). Secretary/Manager: A. Larsen (061-445 9544).

MARPLE. **Marple Golf Club,** Hawk Green, Marple SK6 7EL (061-427 2311). *Location:* off A6 at High Lane, then left at Hawk Green. 18 holes. *Green Fees:* information not available. *Eating facilities:* full catering. *Society Meetings:* Special Golf and Catering packages available. Professional: Nick Wood. Secretary: M. Gilbert.

OLDHAM. **Crompton and Royton Golf Club Ltd,** High Barn, Royton, Oldham OL2 6RW (061-624 2154). *Location:* A671 Oldham to Rochdale, turn off in Royton. Heathland. 18 holes, 6215 yards. S.S.S. 70. Practice ground and nets. *Green Fees:* weekdays £17.00; weekends £21.00. *Eating facilities:* lunches and meals served, except Mondays. *Visitors:* welcome without reservation, not at weekends. *Society Meetings:* catered for by arrangement with Secretary. Professional: D.A. Melling (061-624 2154). Secretary: Ron Butler (061-624 0986).

OLDHAM. **Oldham Golf Club,** Lees New Road, Oldham (061-624 4986). *Location:* B6194 between Ashton-under-Lyne and Oldham. Moorland course, no bunkers. 18 holes, 5045 yards. S.S.S. 65. *Green Fees:* information not available. *Eating facilities:* full catering. *Visitors:* welcome, telephone to check for competitions, especially weekends. *Society Meetings:* catered for by prior arrangement with Secretary. Professional's shop (061-626 8346). Secretary: J. Brooks (061-624 1955).

OLDHAM. **Saddleworth Golf Club,** Mountain Ash, Ladcastle Road, Uppermill, Near Oldham OL3 6LT (0457 872059). *Location:* five miles from Oldham – M62. A moorland course with superb views of the Pennines. 18 holes, 5976 yards. S.S.S. 69; Par 71. Practice area. *Green Fees:* weekdays £22 (£7 per day with member), weekends and Bank Holidays £25 (£10 per day with member). Visiting parties £30 per day. *Eating facilities:* snacks and meals provided. *Visitors:* welcome. *Society Meetings:* catered for, groups of 12 or more, except weekends. Professional: T. Shard (0457 873653). Secretary: H.A. Morgan (0457 873653).

OLDHAM. **Werneth Golf Club,** 124 Green Lane, Garden Suburb, Oldham (061-624 1190). 18 holes, 5275 yards. S.S.S. 66. Practice ground. *Green Fees:* £14.00 weekdays only. *Eating facilities:* full catering service available. *Visitors:* welcome, ring for details. *Society Meetings:* catered for, ring for details. Professional: Terence Morley. Secretary: J. Richardson.

ROCHDALE. **Lobden Golf Club,** Whitworth, Near Rochdale (Rochdale (0706) 343228). *Location:* take A671 from Rochdale, turn right at Dog and Partridge Pub in Whitworth. Moorland. 9 holes, 2885 yards. S.S.S. 68. *Green Fees:* weekdays £6.00; weekends £10.00. *Eating facilities:* by prior arrangement. *Visitors:* welcome all week except Saturday. *Society Meetings:* catered for by arrangement. Secretary: C. Buchanan (0706 343197).

ROCHDALE. **Rochdale Golf Club,** The Clubhouse, Edenfield Road, Bagslate, Rochdale OL11 5YR (Rochdale (0706) 46024). *Location:* M62 at Exit 20, three miles on A680. Parkland. 18 holes, 6002 yards. S.S.S. 69. *Green Fees:* £18.00 weekdays (£8.00 with member); £22.00 weekends and Bank Holidays (£9.00 with member). *Eating facilities:* meals available, order in advance, sandwiches only Mondays. *Visitors:* welcome, except Tuesdays between 12 noon and 7pm, Thursday between 12.30pm and 6pm and Saturday between 8.30am and 4pm (summer period only).

*Society Meetings:* catered for by arrangement Wednesdays and Fridays. Professional: A. Laverty (0706 522104). Secretary: S. Cockroft (0706 43818).

ROCHDALE. **Springfield Park Golf Club,** Springfield Park, Marland, Rochdale (0706 56401). *Location:* A58 out of Rochdale, along Bolton Road on right. Parkland. 18 holes, 5237 yards. S.S.S. 66. *Green Fees:* on request. *Eating facilities:* none available. *Visitors:* welcome, no restrictions. Professional: D. Wills (0706 49801). Secretary: B. Wynn (0706 526064).

SALE. **Ashton on Mersey Golf Club,** Church Lane, Ashton on Mersey, Sale M33 5QQ (061-937 3220). *Location:* M63, two miles from Sale Station. Parkland course. 9 holes, 6242 yards. S.S.S. 69. *Green Fees:* £16.00 weekdays, £8.00 with a member. *Eating facilities:* available weekdays except Mondays. *Visitors:* welcome on weekdays. Saturdays, Sundays and Bank Holidays only with member. *Society Meetings:* Thursdays. Professional: P. Preston (061-962 3727). Secretary: J.H. Edwards (061-976 4390).

SALE. **Sale Golf Club,** Sale Lodge, Golf Road, Sale M33 2LU (061-973 3404). *Location:* Junction 8 M63, A6144. Parkland. 18 holes, 6346 yards. S.S.S. 71. *Green Fees:* £20.00 weekdays, £30.00 weekends. *Eating facilities:* dining room daily except Mondays. *Visitors:* welcome weekdays, weekends and Bank Holidays with a member. *Society Meetings:* by arrangement. Professional: M. Stewart (061-973 1730). Secretary: J. Blair (061-973 1638).

SALFORD. **Brackley Municipal Golf Course,** Bullows Road (off Captain Fold Road), Little Hulton, Salford (061-790 6076). *Location:* M61 to Junction 4 onto A6, left at roundabout onto A6 (Walkden), half a mile turn left at White Lion pub. Flat course with interesting doglegs. 9 holes, 3003 yards, 2747 metres. S.S.S. 69. *Green Fees:* £3.00 for 9 holes weekdays, £5.00 for 18 holes. Senior Citizens £2.00, Juniors £2.50 weekdays. *Eating facilities:* none. *Visitors:* welcome anytime. Secretary: S. Lomax.

STOCKPORT. **Bramall Park Golf Club,** 20 Manor Road, Bramhall, Stockport (061-485 3119). *Location:* 10 miles south of Manchester, 3 miles south of Stockport, half a mile from Cheadle Hulme. Parkland. 18 holes, 6214 yards. S.S.S. 70. *Green Fees:* weekdays £25.00; weekends and Bank Holidays £35.00. *Eating facilities:* full eating facilities except Fridays. *Visitors:* welcome, apply to Professional. *Society Meetings:* catered for. Professional: M. Proffitt (061-485 2205). Secretary: J.C. O'Shea (061-485 3119).

STOCKPORT. **Disley Golf Club Ltd,** Stanley Hall Lane, Disley, Stockport SK12 2JX (Disley (0663) 62071). *Location:* six miles south-east of Stockport on A6. Moorland course with marvellous scenic views. 18 holes, 6015 yards. S.S.S. 69. *Green Fees:* information not available. *Eating facilities:* full service except Mondays. *Visitors:* welcome most days except Thursdays and Fridays. *Society Meetings:* catered for Tuesdays only. Professional: A.G. Esplin (0663 64001). Secretary: R.A. Clayton (0663 64001).

STOCKPORT. **Hazel Grove Golf Club,** Buxton Road, Hazel Grove, Stockport SK7 6LU (061-483 3217). *Location:* A6 to Buxton, three miles south of Stockport. Flat parkland with tree-lined fairways. 18 holes, 6300 yards. S.S.S. 70. *Green Fees:* weekdays £22.50; Friday, Saturday, Sunday and Bank Holidays £27.50. *Eating facilities:* available daily except Mondays. *Visitors:* welcome, ring Professional first to check availability. *Society Meetings:* catered for on Thursdays and Fridays. Professional: M.E. Hill (061-483 7272). Secretary: H.A.G. Carlisle (061-483 3978).

STOCKPORT. **Heaton Moor Golf Club,** Mauldeth Road, Heaton Mersey, Stockport SK4 3NX (061-432 2134). *Location:* A34 off M56. Flat parkland course. 18 holes, 5909 yards. S.S.S. 68. *Green Fees:* weekdays £18.00; weekends £30.00. *Eating facilities:* lunches and evening meals by arrangement. *Visitors:* welcome weekdays. *Society Meetings:* catered for. Professional: Clive Loydall (061-432 0846). Secretary: A.D. Townsend.

STOCKPORT. **Mellor and Townscliffe Golf Club,** Gibb Lane, Tarden, Mellor, Stockport SK6 5NA (061-427 2208). *Location:* seven miles south east of Stockport off A626. Parkland with trees/moorland. 18 holes, 5925 yards. S.S.S. 69. *Green Fees:* weekdays £16.00 per day, £6.00 with a member; weekends and Bank Holidays £25.00, with a member £8.00. *Eating facilities:* available daily except Tuesdays. *Visitors:* welcome weekdays, no casual visitors weekends. *Society Meetings:* catered for by prior arrangement. Professional: Michael J. Williams (061-427 5759). Secretary: D.A. Ogden.

STOCKPORT. **Reddish Vale Golf Club,** Southcliffe Road, Reddish, Stockport SK5 7EE (061-480 2359). *Location:* one mile north east of Stockport. Varied undulating heathland course, designed by Dr A. MacKenzie. 18 holes, 6086 yards. S.S.S. 69. *Green Fees:* weekdays £20.00. *Eating facilities:* bar and catering. *Visitors:* welcome on weekdays (not 12.30 – 1.30pm). *Society Meetings:* catered for by arrangement. Professional: Richard Brown (061-480 3824). Secretary: J.L. Blakey.

STOCKPORT. **Romiley Golf Club Ltd,** Goosehouse Green, Romiley, Stockport SK6 4LJ (061-430 2392). *Location:* B6104 off A560, signposted from Romiley village. Parkland. 18 holes, 6421 yards. S.S.S. 71. *Green Fees:* weekdays £20.00 per round, £25.00 per day; weekends and Bank Holidays £30.00 per round, £40.00 per day. Reduced rates for visitors by arrangement, over 30 in number £15.00 per round, £16.00 per day. *Eating facilities:* full catering by arrangement except Mondays. *Visitors:* welcome any day. *Society Meetings:* catered for by prior arrangement with Secretary. Professional: Gary Butler (061-430 7122). Secretary: Frank Beard (061-430 7257).

STOCKPORT. **Stockport Golf Club Ltd,** Offerton Road, Offerton, Stockport, Cheshire SK2 5HL (061-427 2001). *Location:* one mile from lights at Hazel Grove, along Torkington Road. Parkland. 18 holes, 6326 yards. S.S.S. 71. *Green Fees:* weekdays £25.00 per round, £35.00 per day; weekends £35.00 per round. *Eating facilities:* available, excellent. *Visitors:* welcome without reservation. *Society Meetings:* catered for. Professional: R.G. Tattersall (061-427 2421). Secretary: P. Moorhead (061-427 8369).

TRAFFORD. **William Wroe Municipal Golf Course,** Pennybridge Lane, off Flixton Road, Flixton, Trafford (061-748 8680). Course and shop managed by Trafford Borough Council, Acre Gate Golf Club play over the course. *Location:* M63 Exit 4, B5124 to Davyhulme Circle then one mile on B5158, left at Bird-in-Hand Hotel, Flixton. 18 holes, 3935 yards. *Green Fees:* information not provided. *Visitors:* welcome anytime, but advisable to book the day before. Teaching Professional: Roland West. Secretary: Mrs P. Rowan. Golf Course Manager: Mr B. Davies.

WESTHOUGHTON. **Westhoughton Golf Club,** Long Island, School Street, Westhoughton (Westhoughton (0942) 811055). *Location:* four miles south west of Bolton on A58. Parkland. 9 holes, 5702 yards. S.S.S. 68. *Green Fees:* weekdays £12.00 per day; weekends with a member only £5.00. *Eating facilities:* bar meals and function room. *Visitors:* welcome, Tuesdays Ladies' Day. Snooker room. *Society Meetings:* catered for by arrangement, maximum 30/32. Thursdays Society Day. Professional: P. Wesselingh/S. Bryan. Secretary: D.J. Kinsella.

WHITEFIELD. **Whitefield Golf Club,** Higher Lane, Whitefield, Manchester (061-766 2728). *Location:* Exit 17, off M62 then take road to Radcliffe for half a mile. 18 holes, 6041 yards. S.S.S. 69. *Green Fees:* on application. *Eating facilities:* restaurant facilities every day. *Visitors:* welcome. *Society Meetings:* catered for. Professional: P. Reeves. Secretary: Mrs R. L. Vidler (061-766 2904).

WIGAN. **Gathurst Golf Club,** 62 Miles Lane, Shevington, Wigan WN6 8EW (Appley Bridge (02575) 2861). *Location:* one mile south of Junction 27 M6. Parkland. 9 holes, 6308 yards. S.S.S. 70. *Green Fees:* weekdays £15.00. *Eating facilities:* available bar hours, daily except Monday. *Visitors:* welcome Monday, Tuesday, Thursday and Friday with reservation. *Society Meetings:* catered for by appointment. Professional: D. Clarke (02575 4909). Secretary: H. Marrow (02575 3056).

WIGAN. **Haigh Hall Golf Club,** Haigh Country Park, Aspull, Near Wigan WN2 1PE (Wigan (0942) 833337). *Location:* Junction 27 M6, at Standish. Parkland. 18 holes, 6400 yards, 5800 metres. S.S.S. 71. Practice area. *Green Fees:* weekdays £5.50, weekends £8.00. *Eating facilities:* Cafeteria. *Visitors:* welcome, book by telephone. Professional: Mr I. Lee (0942 831107) Secretary: Mr J.M. Parker.

WIGAN. **Hindley Hall Golf Club,** Hall Lane, Hindley, Wigan (Wigan (0942) 55131). *Location:* two miles east of Wigan, Junction 6 M61, or A58 to Ladies Lane/Hall Lane. 18 holes, 5841 yards. S.S.S. 68. *Green Fees:* £18.00 weekdays; £25.00 weekends and Bank Holidays. *Eating facilities:* not Mondays, book

before playing. *Visitors:* welcome without reservation if members of a recognised golf club. *Society Meetings:* catered for by arrangement with the Secretary. Special rates for parties of 25 or more. Professional: N. Brazell (0942 523116). Secretary: R. Bell.

WIGAN. **Wigan Golf Club,** Arley Hall, Haigh, Near Wigan WN1 2UH (Standish (0257) 421360). *Location:* M6 Exit 27, two miles on B5329, east of Standish. Parkland. 9 holes, 6058 yards. S.S.S. 69. *Green Fees:* £17.00 weekdays; £22.00 weekends. *Eating facilities:* meals and bar available. *Visitors:* welcome anytime except Tuesdays and Saturdays. *Society Meetings:* catered for on Thursdays and Fridays. Secretary: E. Walmsley (0942 43455).

# Merseyside

BIRKENHEAD. **Arrowe Park Golf Course,** Arrowe Park, Birkenhead. *Location:* Mersey Tunnel into Brough Road, then Woodchurch Road, head for Arrowe Park roundabout, bear left approximately 400 yards, turn right into Arrowe Park. Parkland. 18 holes, 6435 yards, 5885 metres. S.S.S. 71. 9 hole pitch and putt, putting green. *Green Fees:* £4.70 per round. *Eating facilities:* cafe – bar. *Visitors:* EVERYBODY WELCOME! *Society Meetings:* by arrangement through Professional. Professional: Clive Scanlon (051-677 1527). Secretary: K. Finlay.

BIRKENHEAD. **Prenton Golf Club,** Golf Links Road, Prenton, Birkenhead L42 8LW (051-608 1053). *Location:* M53 Junction 3, off A552 towards Birkenhead. Parkland course. 18 holes, 6411 yards. S.S.S. 71. *Green Fees:* £23.00 weekdays; £25.00 weekends. *Eating facilities:* full catering facilities available. *Visitors:* welcome, reservation advisable. *Society Meetings:* catered for Wednesdays and Fridays. Professional: Robin Thompson (051-608 1636). Secretary: W.F.W. Disley.

BIRKENHEAD. **The Wirral Ladies' Golf Club Ltd,** 93 Bidston Road, Oxton, Birkenhead (051-652 5797). *Location:* on boundary of town, Bidston Hill area. 18 holes, 4966 yards (Ladies), 5170 yards (Men). S.S.S. 70 (Ladies), S.S.S. 66 (Men). *Green Fees:* information not provided. *Eating facilities:* meals during day to order. *Visitors:* welcome with reservation. Introduction from Club Secretary. Professional: Philip Chandler (051-652 2468). Secretary: D.P. Cranston-Miller (051-652 1255).

BLUNDELLSANDS. **West Lancashire Golf Club,** Hall Road West, Blundellsands, Liverpool L23 8SZ (051-924 4115). *Location:* A565 Liverpool – Southport to Crosby, follow signposts for club – Waterloo Rugby Club. Links course. 6756 yards. S.S.S. 73. *Green Fees:* £33.00 per day, £22.00 per round; £38.50 per round weekends. *Eating facilities:* lunch, tea

and dinner every day. *Visitors:* welcome on weekdays. Electric trolleys by prior agreement only. *Society Meetings:* catered for by advance application. Professional: D.G. Lloyd (051-924 5662). Secretary: D.E. Bell (051-924 1076; Fax: 051-931 4448).

BOOTLE. **Bootle Golf Club,** Dunnings Bridge Road, Bootle L30 2PP (051-928 6196). *Location:* five miles north of Liverpool, one mile from M57 and M58. Links course. 18 holes, 6362 yards. S.S.S. 70. *Green Fees:* £3.40 weekdays; £4.85 weekends. *Eating facilities:* full catering as required by arrangement. *Visitors:* welcome weekdays and afternoons at weekends. *Society Meetings:* by appointment. Professional: Gary Brown (051-928 1371). Secretary: John F. Morgan (051-922 4792).

BROMBOROUGH. **Bromborough Golf Club,** Raby Hall Road, Bromborough, Wirral, Merseyside L63 0NN (051-334 2155). *Location:* Exit 4 Wirral Motorway M53. Parkland. 18 holes, 6650 yards, 6080 metres. S.S.S. 73. *Green Fees:* weekdays £22.00, weekends £29.00, reduced rates for Societies over 24. *Eating facilities:* bar and full catering facilities. *Visitors:* welcome without reservation weekdays, but essential to ring in advance for weekends and Bank Holidays. *Society Meetings:* catered for by prior arrangement. Professional: G. Berry (051-334 4499). Secretary: L.B. Silvester (051-334 2978).

EASTHAM. **Eastham Lodge Golf Club,** 117 Ferry Road, Eastham, Wirral, Merseyside L62 0AP (051-327 1483). *Location:* exit Junction 5 M53 into Eastham village from A41, follow signs for Eastham Country Park. Flat pleasant parkland course with many trees. 15 holes, 5864 yards (for 18). S.S.S. 68. *Green Fees:* weekdays £20.00; weekends with a member only £8.50. *Eating facilities:* bar snacks, full restaurant (book in advance). *Visitors:* welcome weekdays, with member weekends. *Society Meetings:* Tuesdays only; £15.00 per day, £12.00 per round. Professional: Bob Boobyer (051-327 3008). Secretary: C.S. Camden (051-327 3003).

FORMBY. **Formby Golf Club,** Golf Road, Formby, Liverpool L37 1LQ (Formby (07048) 72164). *Location:* one mile west of A565 by Freshfield Station. Seaside links, wooded. 18 holes, 6781 yards. S.S.S. 73. *Green Fees:* £40.00 weekdays only. *Eating facilities:* available. *Visitors:* welcome, except Wednesdays, weekends and Bank Holidays. Accommodation available. *Society Meetings:* catered for. Professional: C.F. Harrison (07048 73090). Secretary: A. Thirlwell (07048 72164).

FORMBY. **Formby Ladies' Golf Club,** Golf Road, Formby, Liverpool L37 1YH (Formby (07048) 74127). Seaside links. 18 holes, 5374 yards, 4914 metres. S.S.S. 71. Practice area. *Green Fees:* weekdays £25.00; weekends £31.00. *Eating facilities:* light lunches, afternoon teas. *Visitors:* welcome with prior reservation, contact the Secretary. *Society Meetings:* catered for with prior reservation. Professional: C. Harrison (07048 73090). Secretary: Mrs V. Bailey (07048 73493).

HESWALL. **Heswall Golf Club,** Cottage Lane, Gayton, Wirral L60 8PB (051-342 2193). *Location:* off A540, eight miles north-west of Chester. Parkland on the banks of River Dee estuary overlooking Welsh coast and hills. 18 holes, 6472 yards, 5909 metres. S.S.S. 72. Large practice area. *Green Fees:* weekdays £30.00,

weekends and Bank Holidays £35.00. *Eating facilities:* bar snacks, full meals by arrangement. *Visitors:* welcome anytime subject to availability. Must have accredited Handicaps. *Society Meetings:* catered for fully on Wednesdays and Fridays only, minimum 24 players. Professional: Alan Thompson (051-342 7431). Secretary: C.P.R. Calvert (051-342 1237). Catering (051-342 2193).

HOYLAKE. **Royal Liverpool Golf Club,** Meols Drive, Hoylake, Wirral, Merseyside L47 4AL (051-632 3102). *Location:* 10 miles west of Liverpool on Wirral Peninsula. Approach from M6, M56 and M53. Championship links. 18 holes, 6804 yards. S.S.S. 74. Large practice area. *Green Fees:* weekdays £35-£50(d); weekends £50-£75(d). *Eating facilities:* hot and cold snacks and lunches daily, bars. *Visitors:* welcome weekdays except Thursday mornings (Ladies Day) and limited at weekends. Snooker available. *Society Meetings:* catered for by agreement with the Secretary. Professional: John Heggarty (051-632 5868). Secretary: Robin White (051-632 3101; Fax: 051-632 6737).

HUYTON. **Bowring Golf Club,** Bowring Park, Roby Road, Huyton (051-489 1901). 9 holes, 5580 yards. S.S.S. 66. *Green Fees:* on application. *Visitors:* unrestricted. Secretary: E. Hatton. Professional: Michael Sarsfield.

**Restaurant and Motel**

💃💃💃💃 AA** RAC**
Ashley Courtenay Recommended

Where better to relax than Tree Tops in its country setting with heated pool and patio area (available May to September), yet close to Southport with its famous Lord Street for shopping, theatres, cinemas and all sporting activities including five championship golf courses.

All accommodation is to a high standard with every comfort for our guests. The restaurant, which is exquisitely furnished is renowned in the area for its cuisine offering both à la carte and table d'hôte menu. SPECIAL BREAKS – 2 nights Dinner, Bed and Breakfast only £99 per person.

**SOUTHPORT OLD ROAD, FORMBY, MERSEYSIDE. TEL: 07048 79651.**

# KING'S GAP COURT HOTEL 💃💃💃
## Valentia Road, Hoylake, Wirral L47 2AN
## Telephone: 051 632 2073

Set in pleasant gardens within easy reach of eight golf courses, beach, marina and railway station. Most rooms en-suite; colour TV, tea and coffee making facilities. Full central heating. Large car park. Reduced terms for golfers or sailing enthusiasts Monday to Friday (4 nights). LICENSED BAR & RESTAURANT.

HUYTON. **Huyton and Prescot Golf Club Ltd,** Hurst Park, Huyton Lane, Huyton, Liverpool L36 1UA (051-489 3948 office), (051-489 1138 members). *Location:* M57 and M62. 18 holes, 5732 yards. S.S.S. 68. *Green Fees:* weekdays £20.00, weekends by special permission only (one visitor only per member). Golf Societies Package arrangement. *Eating facilities:* dining facilities from 11.00am to 5.00pm. *Visitors:* welcome, Handicap Certificate required. Dress restrictions on and off course. Tee reserved for members between 12 and 2pm. *Society Meetings:* catered for mid-week only. Professional: R. Pottage (051-489 2022). Secretary: Mrs E. Holmes (051-489 3948).

LIVERPOOL. **Allerton Park Golf Club,** Allerton Road, Liverpool 18 (051-427 8510). *Location:* Menlove Avenue. 18 holes, 5081 yards. S.S.S. 67. *Green Fees:* information not available. *Eating facilities:* lunches at club. *Visitors:* welcome. Professional: Barry Large.

LIVERPOOL. **Dudley Golf Club,** Allerton Municipal Golf Course, Menlove Avenue, Allerton, Liverpool 18 (051-428 8510). *Location:* end of M62, then two miles on Allerton road. Wooded parkland. 18 holes, 5459 metres. S.S.S. 67. 9 holes, 1685 metres. S.S.S. 34. *Green Fees:* information not provided. *Eating facilities:* hot meals available in clubhouse. *Visitors:* welcome at any time. *Society Meetings:* welcome. Professional: Barry Large (051-428 1046). Secretary: Terry Tollitt (051-427 6189).

LIVERPOOL. **Lee Park Golf Club,** Childwall Valley Road, Liverpool L27 3YA (051-487 9861). *Location:* Queens Drive, Childwall Valley Road. Parkland. 18 holes, 6074 yards. Medal tees: 5569 yards. Front tees: S.S.S. 68. Ladies' tee: 5650 yards. S.S.S. 72. *Green Fees:* £17.00 weekdays; £25.00 weekends. *Eating facilities:* restaurant and bar snacks daily. *Visitors:* welcome anytime except between 12.15pm and 2.15pm daily (reserved for members). *Society Meetings:* catered for. Secretary: Mrs Doris Barr (051-487 3882).

LIVERPOOL. **The Childwall Golf Club Ltd.,** Naylors Road, Gateacre, Liverpool L27 2YB (051-487 9982). *Location:* Exit 6 M62 to Liverpool follow Huyton A5080 to second set of traffic lights, turn left into Wheathill Road. Parkland, flat, designed by James Braid. 18 holes, 6425 yards. S.S.S. 72. Practice area. *Green Fees:* £19.50 weekdays; £28.00 weekends. *Eating facilities:* bar, snacks and restaurant. *Visitors:* no visitors weekends and Tuesdays. *Society Meetings:* catered for on weekdays, contact the Secretary. Groups over 20, £17.50. Professional: Mr N.M. Parr (051-487 9871). Secretary: Mr L. Upton (051-487 0654).

LIVERPOOL. **West Derby Golf Club,** Yew Tree Lane, West Derby, Liverpool L12 9HQ. 18 holes, 6346 yards. S.S.S. 70. *Green Fees:* weekdays £20.00 per day; weekends £28.00. *Eating facilities:* soup and sandwiches, light meals available at lunch. Evening meals by prior arrangement. *Visitors:* welcome if members of a recognised golf club. *Society Meetings:* catered for only by arrangement with Secretary. Professional: Nick Brace (051-220 5478). Secretary/Manager: S. Young (051-254 1034).

LIVERPOOL. **Woolton Golf Club,** Doe Park, Speke Road, Woolton, Liverpool L25 7TZ (051-486 1601). *Location:* south Liverpool, one mile from Woolton Village. Parkland. 18 holes, 5706 yards. S.S.S. 68. *Green Fees:* weekdays £18.00; weekends £25.00. *Eating facilities:* bar snacks daily. *Visitors:* welcome without reservation, except Tuesdays. *Society Meetings:* catered for by arrangement. Professional Shop: (051-486 1298). Secretary: K.G. Jennions (051-486 2298).

MORETON. **Bidston Golf Club,** Scoresby Road, Leasowe, Moreton L46 1QQ (051-638 3412). *Location:* leave M53 Junction 1 (from Chester), Wallasey, Leasowe, one mile left Catholic Church, approximately one mile. Flat course. 18 holes, 6204 yards. S.S.S. 70. Practice ground. *Green Fees:* weekdays £15.00. Reduced rates for Societies. *Eating facilities:* available. *Visitors:* welcome weekdays with prior notification. *Society Meetings:* catered for, early application by letter required. Professional: J. Law (051-630 6650). Secretary/Manager: L.A. Kendrick (051-638 8685).

MORETON. **Leasowe Golf Club,** Leasowe Road, Moreton, Wirral, Merseyside L46 3RD (051-677 5852). *Location:* one mile west of Wallasey Village and one mile from M53. Links course. 18 holes, 6204 yards. S.S.S. 70. *Green Fees:* £16.00 weekdays, £20.00 weekends and Bank Holidays. *Eating facilities:* catering and bar. *Visitors:* welcome on weekdays, by arrangement weekends and Bank Holidays. *Society Meetings:* catered for by arrangement. Professional: C. Gill (061-678 5460). Secretary: T. Lee.

NEWTON-LE-WILLOWS. **Haydock Park Golf Club,** Rob Lane, Newton-le-Willows WA12 0HX (Newton-le-Willows (0925) 224389). *Location:* off East Lancs Road (A580) and M6, three quarters of a mile from Newton-le-Willows High Street. Flat, wooded parkland course in beautiful setting. 18 holes, 6043 yards. S.S.S. 69. Large practice ground. *Green Fees:* weekdays £25.00. *Eating facilities:* restaurant and two bars. *Visitors:* welcome weekdays except Tuesdays, identification (club membership card) or letter of introduction required. *Society Meetings:* catered for by arrangement. Professional: P. Kenwright (0925 226944). Secretary: G. Tait (0925 228525).

SOUTHPORT. **Hesketh Golf Club,** Cockle Dicks Lane, Cambridge Road, Southport PR9 9QQ (Southport (0704) 530226). *Location:* one mile north of town centre. Seaside links Championship course. 18 holes, 6478 yards. S.S.S. 72. Practice ground. *Green Fees:* weekdays £25.00 per round, £35.00 per day; weekends and Bank Holidays £40.00 per day. *Eating facilities:* bar snacks and dining room; three bars. *Visitors:* welcome by prior arrangement with Secretary. *Society Meetings:* catered for by arrangement with Secretary. Professional: John Donoghue (0704 530050). Secretary: Peter B. Seal (0704 536897; Fax: 0704 539250).

SOUTHPORT. **Hillside Golf Club,** Hastings Road, Hillside, Southport PR8 2LU (0704 69902). *Location:* south of town, Hillside station one mile. Links. 18 holes, 6850 yards. S.S.S. 74. Practice ground. *Green Fees:* weekdays £45.00 per day, £35.00 per round;

weekends £45.00 if available. *Eating facilities:* dining-room, bars. *Visitors:* welcome weekdays, some Sundays and Tuesdays afternoons only. *Society Meetings:* welcome with prior reservations. Professional: Brian Seddon (0704 68360). Secretary: P.W. Ray (0704 67169; Fax: 0704 63192).

SOUTHPORT. **Park Golf Club,** Park Road West, Southport (Southport (0704) 530133). Play over Southport Municipal Links. S.S.S. 69. Secretary: J.A.V. Turner. Professional: (0704) 535286).

SOUTHPORT. **Royal Birkdale Golf Club,** Waterloo Road, Birkdale, Southport PR8 2LX (0704 67920). *Location:* one mile south of Southport town centre. Classic Links on the Open Championship rota. 18 holes, 6703 yards. S.S.S. 73. *Green Fees:* contact the Secretary. *Visitors:* welcome by arrangement with Secretary, offical golf Handicap required. *Society Meetings:* catered for, package prices for 20 plus, diningroom facilities. Professional: Richard Bradbeer (0704 68857). Secretary: Norman Crewe (0704 67920).

SOUTHPORT. **Southport and Ainsdale Golf Club,** Bradshaw's Lane, Off Liverpool Road, Ainsdale, Southport PR8 3LG (Southport (0704) 78092). *Location:* south of Southport on A565. Links course. 18 holes, 6615 yards. S.S.S. 73. *Green Fees:* weekdays £30.00 per round, £40.00 per day; weekends £45.00 per day. *Eating facilities:* full catering available. *Visitors:* advance booking recommended. *Society Meetings:* catered for by arrangement. Professional: M. Houghton (0704 77316). Secretary: I.F. Sproule (0704 78000; Fax: 0704 70896).

SOUTHPORT. **Southport Municipal Golf Club,** Park Road West, Southport (Southport (0704) 55130). *Location:* Park Road West, north end of Promenade, near Marine Lake, Southport. Flat seaside links. 18 holes, 6139 yards. S.S.S. 70. *Green Fees:* information not available. *Eating facilities:* licensed cafe. *Visitors:* booking system operates up to seven days in advance (visitors unrestricted). *Society Meetings:* welcome, book in advance. Professional: William Fletcher (0704 35286).

SOUTHPORT. **Southport Old Links Golf Club,** Moss Lane, Churchtown, Southport PR9 7QS (0704 28207). *Location:* end of Roe Lane, Churchtown. Tree lined links course. 9 holes, 6378 yards (x2). S.S.S. 71. *Green Fees:* weekdays £15.00; weekends and Bank Holidays £20.00. Seven Day Ticket (restricted) £40.00 (any seven consecutive days). *Eating facilities:* available. *Visitors:* welcome except Wednesdays, Sundays and Bank Holidays. *Society Meetings:* catered for by arrangement, not more than 24. Secretary: G.M. Rimington (0704 24294).

ST. HELENS. **Grange Park Golf Club,** Prescot Road, St. Helens WA10 3AD (St. Helens (0744) 22980). *Location:* one and a half miles south west of St. Helens on A58. Wooded parkland. 18 holes, 6429 yards. S.S.S. 71. Practice area. *Green Fees:* weekdays £21.00; weekends £26.00. *Eating facilities:* full catering and bar facilities. *Visitors:* welcome anytime but times are often not available at weekends/Bank Holidays;

reservation through Professional recommended. *Society Meetings:* catered for Mondays, Wednesdays or Thursdays by advance reservation through Secretary. Professional: Paul Evans (0744 28785). Secretary: David A. Wood (0744 26318).

ST HELENS. **Sherdley Park Golf Club,** St. Helens (0744 813149). Clubhouse (0744 815518). *Location:* two miles east of town on A570. 18 holes, 5941 yards. S.S.S. 69. *Green Fees:* information not provided. *Visitors:* unrestricted. Professional: P.R. Parkinson. Secretary: B.M. Healiss.

WALLASEY. **Wallasey Golf Club,** Bayswater Road, Wallasey L45 8LA (051-639 3630). *Location:* via M53 through Wirral or 15 minutes from Liverpool centre via Wallasey Tunnel. Seaside links. 18 holes, 6607 yards, 6038 metres. S.S.S. 73. *Green Fees:* weekdays £23.00 per round, £28.00 per day; weekends and Bank Holidays £27.00 per round, £34.00 per day. *Eating facilities:* snacks and full catering facilities. *Visitors:* welcome with reservation. *Society Meetings:* catered for by arrangement. Professional: Mike Adams (051-638 3888). Secretary: Mrs L.M. Dolman (051-691 1024).

WALLASEY. **Warren Golf Club,** The Grange, Grove Road, Wallasey (051-639 8323). Links course. 9 holes, 5914 yards. S.S.S. 68. *Green Fees:* information not provided. Professional: Kenneth Lamb. Secretary: Paul Warrington.

WIRRAL. **Brackenwood Golf Club,** Bracken Lane, Bebington, Wirral (051-608 5394). *Location:* M53 Clatterbridge turnoff Birkenhead and Bebbington near Clatterbridge Hospital. Flat parkland. 18 holes, 6285 yards, 5747 metres. S.S.S. 70. *Green Fees:* £4.70. *Eating facilities:* snacks available. *Visitors:* welcome, book through Pro's shop. Professional: Colin Disbury (051-608 3093). Secretary: N.D. Taylor (051-327 2387).

WIRRAL. **Hoylake Golf Club,** Carr Lane, Hoylake (051-632 2956). *Location:* 10 miles from Liverpool. 18 holes, 6330 yards, S.S.S. 70. *Green Fees:* £4.70; Juniors and Senior Citizens £2.35. *Eating facilities:* available all week. Phone Steward (M. Down) in advance (051-632 4883). *Visitors:* midweek unrestricted. Weekends phone to book tee. *Society Meetings:* weekdays only. Professional: S.N. Hooton. Secretary: M.E. Down (051-632 4883).

WIRRAL. **The Caldy Golf Club Ltd,** Links Hey Road, Caldy, Wirral L48 1NB (051-625 5515). *Location:* one mile south of West Kirby on the River Dee. 10 miles from Chester. Undulating parkland, links, open aspect with views across the Dee to the North Wales hills. 18 holes, 6675 yards, 6105 metres. S.S.S. 73. Practice ground and putting green. *Green Fees:* weekdays £25.00 per round, £30.00 per day; weekends with member only. *Eating facilities:* bars and restaurant throughout the day. *Visitors:* welcome weekdays with advance booking and Handicap Certificate. Restrictions Tuesdays and Wednesdays. Jeans not allowed on course or in Clubhouse. *Society Meetings:* Thursdays by prior arrangement. Professional: Kevin Jones (051-625 1818). Secretary: T.D.M. Bacon (051-625 5660).

# Norfolk

BAWBURGH. **Bawburgh Golf Club,** Long Lane, Bawburgh, Norwich NR9 3LX (0603 746390; Fax: 0603 811110). *Location:* three miles west of Norwich off A47, at rear of Norfolk Showground. Undulating open parkland. 9 holes, 6066 yards. S.S.S. 70. Driving range – covered and floodlit, group tuition. *Green Fees:* information not provided. *Eating facilities:* bar and snacks only, meals by arrangement. *Visitors:* restricted at weekends and Bank Holidays, advisable to ring in advance. Ladies have preference Monday mornings. *Society Meetings:* Tuesdays and Thursdays on application to Secretary before beginning of year. Professional: C. Potter (0603 742323). Secretary: R.J. Mapes (0953 606776).

CROMER. **Links Country Park Hotel and Golf Club,** Sandy Lane, West Runton, Cromer NR27 9QH (0263 838383). *Location:* midway between Cromer and Sheringham on the A149, turn left opposite the village inn. Undulating parkland with narrow fairways and tricky greens. 9 holes, 4814 yards, S.S.S. 64. *Green Fees:* £19.00 per day weekdays, £23.00 weekends. *Eating facilities:* grill room, snacks, hotel restaurant table d'hôte and à la carte. *Visitors:* welcome weekdays, restrictions weekends. Adjoining Hotel offers free golf to residents; Sauna, Solarium, Swimming Pool etc. *Society Meetings:* welcome weekdays and some weekends. Professional: Mike Jubb (0263 838215). Hon. Secretary: S. Mansfield (0263 838383).

CROMER. **Royal Cromer Golf Club,** 145 Overstrand Road, Cromer NR27 0JH (Cromer (0263) 512219). *Location:* one mile east of town centre on coast road. Undulating seaside course. 18 holes, 6508 yards. S.S.S. 71. Large practice ground. *Green Fees:* £25.00 weekdays, £30.00 weekends. *Eating facilities:* full catering and bar snacks. *Visitors:* welcome, booking essential from 1st April to 31st October, Handicap Certificates required. *Society Meetings:* welcome except weekends. Professional: Robin J. Page (0263 512267). Secretary: B.A. Howson (0263 512884).

DEREHAM. **Dereham Golf Club,** Quebec Road, Dereham NR19 2DS (Dereham (0362) 695900). *Location:* three-quarters-of-a mile from town centre on B1110. Wooded parkland. 9 holes (double tees), 6225 yards. S.S.S. 70. *Green Fees:* weekdays £16.00; weekends with member only. *Eating facilities:* full restaurant except Mondays (Summer). *Visitors:* welcome weekdays with prior notice, not weekends; players must produce proof of Handicap and club membership. *Society Meetings:* catered for with advance booking. Professional: Steven Fox (0362 698471). Secretary: George Dalrymple (0362 695900).

DISS. **Diss Golf Club,** Stuston Common, Diss, Norfolk (0379 642847). The course is in Suffolk but Postal Address is Diss, Norfolk. *Location:* B1077 off A140, half-a-mile from Diss railway station, one mile from town centre. Flat common land. 18 holes, 6238 yards. S.S.S. 70. *Green Fees:* £20.00, £10.00 if playing with a member. *Eating facilities:* excellent facilities – newly refurbished. *Visitors:* welcome without reservation. *Society Meetings:* all welcome and catered for. Professional: N. Taylor (0379 644399). Secretary: J.A. Bell (0379 641025).

DOWNHAM MARKET. **Ryston Park Golf Club,** Ely Road, Denver, Downham Market PE38 0HH (Downham (0366) 382133).*Location:* one mile south Downham Market on A10. 36 miles north Cambridge. Parkland. 9 holes, 6292 yards. S.S.S. 70. Practice ground. *Green Fees:* weekdays £20.00, £8.00 with a member. *Eating facilities:* meals served to order. *Visitors:* welcome weekdays, one guest per member weekends. *Society Meetings:* restricted, catered for by arrangement. Secretary: A.J. Wilson (0366 383834).

FAKENHAM. **Fakenham Golf Club,** Gallow Sports Centre, Hempton Road, Fakenham (Fakenham (0328) 862867). *Location:* half-a-mile town centre on Swaffham Road. Parkland. 9 holes, 5992 yards. S.S.S. 69. Large practice area. *Green Fees:* weekdays £12.00, weekends and Bank Holidays £16.00 after 3pm. 10 per cent reduction for Societies. *Eating facilities:* available in Sports Centre. *Visitors:* welcome by appointment. *Society Meetings:* welcome, reduced rates. Professional: J. Westwood (0328 863534). Secretary: G.G. Cocker (0328 855665).

GREAT YARMOUTH. **Gorleston Golf Club,** Warren Road, Gorleston, Great Yarmouth NR31 6JT (Great Yarmouth (0493) 661082). *Location:* off A12 at Gorleston to Links Road. Seaside links. 18 holes, 6400 yards, 5850 metres. S.S.S. 71. *Green Fees:* weekdays £18.00; weekends and Public Holidays £25.00. Reductions if playing with member. *Eating facilities:* available all week. *Visitors:* welcome, check before for closed days, etc. *Society Meetings:* catered for by prior arrangement (membership of recognised club required). Professional: R.L. Moffitt (0493 662103). Secretary: C.B. Court (0493 661911).

GREAT YARMOUTH. **Great Yarmouth and Caister Golf Club,** Beach House, Caister-on-Sea, Great Yarmouth NR30 5TD (Great Yarmouth (0493) 720214). *Location:* A149 coast road, two miles north of Great Yarmouth. Links. 18 holes, 6235 yards. S.S.S. 70. Practice ground. *Green Fees:* £23.50, £15.00 after 3.30pm weekdays; £28.00, £18.00 after 3.30pm weekends. Members' guests 50 per cent. *Eating facilities:* full range of catering; bar. *Visitors:* welcome, not before 10.30am Saturdays and not before 11.30am Sundays. *Society Meetings:* catered for. Professional:

R. Foster (0493 720421). Secretary: Mrs H.M. Marsh (0493 728699).

HELLESDON. **Royal Norwich Golf Club,** Drayton High Road, Hellesdon, Norwich NR6 5AH (Norwich (0603) 429928). *Location:* centre of city and thence by A1067 Fakenham or via Ring Road, then 500 yards along A1067. 18 holes, 6603 yards. S.S.S. 72. *Green Fees:* £26.00 per round or day. *Eating facilities:* lunches and teas served at club. *Visitors:* welcome during week only, but must have membership card of a recognised golf club and a bona fide handicap. Professional: Alan Hemsley. Secretary: D.F. Cottier.

HUNSTANTON. **Hunstanton Golf Club,** Golf Links Road, Old Hunstanton PE36 6JQ (Hunstanton (0485) 532811). *Location:* adjoins Old Hunstanton village, approximately half a mile north east of Hunstanton. Links. 18 holes, 6670 yards. S.S.S. 72. Practice ground. *Green Fees:* weekdays £28.00 per day, weekends £34.00. *Eating facilities:* available except Mondays (soup and sandwiches only). *Visitors:* welcome weekdays, restricted weekends. Must be members of recognised golf club and have current Handicap Certificate. Please contact Secretary. *Society Meetings:* catered for, contact Secretary. Professional: J. Carter (0485 532751). Secretary: R.H. Cotton (0485 532811).

KINGS LYNN. **Eagles Golf Club,** 39 School Road, Tilney All Saints, Kings Lynn PE34 4RS (0553 827147). *Location:* off A47 road between Kings Lynn and Wisbech. Parkland. 9 holes, 4284 yards. S.S.S. 61. Par 3 course, driving range. *Green Fees:* weekdays £5.50 9 holes; weekends £6.50 9 holes. *Eating facilities:* bar/restaurant. *Visitors:* welcome, no restrictions. *Society Meetings:* apply to Secretary. Secretary: David W. Horn.

KING'S LYNN. **King's Lynn Golf Club,** Castle Rising, King's Lynn PE31 6BD (Castle Rising (0553) 631656). *Location:* four miles north-east of King's Lynn. Undulating wooded course. 18 holes, 6646 yards. S.S.S. 72. Practice areas. *Green Fees:* weekdays £25.00, weekends £33.00. *Eating facilities:* snacks, lunches, teas available; other meals by prior arrangement, two bars. *Visitors:* welcome on production of Handicap Certificate. *Society Meetings:* catered for by prior arrangement Thursdays and Fridays. Professional: C. Hanlon (0553 631655). Secretary: G.J. Higgins (0553 631654).

KING'S LYNN. **Royal West Norfolk Golf** Brancaster, Near King's Lynn PE31 8AX (Brancaster (0485) 210223). *Location:* one mile off A149, Beach Road junction, seven miles east of Hunstanton. Seaside links. 18 holes, 6428 yards. S.S.S. 71. *Green Fees:* weekdays £30.00 per day; weekends £40.00 per day. *Eating* *facilities:* available. *Visitors:* all visitors to be members of a recognised Golf Club, hold an official Handicap and must make prior arrangements with the Secretary to play. No visitors prior to 10.00am Sundays and no visitors during last week in July and until first week in September. *Professional:* R.E. Kimber (0485 210616). *Secretary:* Major N.A. Carrington Smith (0485 210087).

NORWICH. **Barnham Broom Hotel, Golf and Country Club,** Honingham Road, Norwich NR9 4DD (Barnham Broom (060-545) 393). *Location:* eight miles south-west of Norwich between A11 and A47. River valley parkland and hill course. 36 holes. Full practice facilities. *Green Fees:* weekdays £25.00 per round, £30.00 per day; weekends on application. *Eating facilities:* snack bar and full restaurant. *Visitors:* casual and residential with prior notice. 50 bedroomed hotel. *Society Meetings:* welcome on application. Professional: Steve Beckham (060545 393 ext. 132). Director of Golf: Peter Ballingall (060545 393 ext. 138).

NORWICH. **Costessey Park Golf Course,** Old Costessey, Norwich NR8 5AL (Norwich (0603) 746333). *Location:* off the A47 Norwich to King's Lynn road, in the village of Old Costessey (adjacent to Norwich). Set in river valley with some parkland. 18 holes, 5964 yards. S.S.S. 69. Par 72. Practice area. *Green Fees:* weekdays £14.00; weekends £17.00. *Eating facilities:* bar and bar snacks; carvery and set meals available. *Visitors:* welcome anytime except weekends when visitors allowed only after 11.30am. Golf cart available for hire by physically handicapped golfers. *Society Meetings:* catered for by arrangement. Professional: Simon Cook (0603 747085). Secretary: Colin House.

NORWICH. **Eaton (Norwich) Golf Club,** Newmarket Road, Norwich NR4 6SF (Norwich (0603) 52881). *Location:* half a mile from A11, approximately one and a half miles from Norwich city centre. Parkland course. 18 holes, 6135 yards. S.S.S. 69. Practice areas available. *Green Fees:* £25.00 weekdays, £30.00 weekends and Bank Holidays. *Eating facilities:* snacks, lunches, dinners by arrangement. *Visitors:* welcome;

only after 11.30am weekends. Handicap Certificate required. *Society Meetings:* on application. Professional: Frank Hill (0603 52478). Secretary: D.L.P. Sochon (0603 51686).

NORWICH. **Mundesley Golf Club,** Links Road, Mundesley, Norwich NR11 8ES (Mundesley (0263) 720297). *Location:* one mile from village centre. Undulating fairly exposed parkland course. 9 holes, 5410 yards, 4949 metres. S.S.S. 66. Small practice area. *Green Fees:* on application. *Eating facilities:* full catering except Tuesdays. *Visitors:* welcome, but not before 11.30am at weekends. *Society Meetings:* catered for (not Wednesday 12 noon – 3.30pm). Professional: T.G. Symmons (0831 455461). Secretary: Peter Hampel (0263 720095).

NORWICH. **Sprowston Park Golf Club,** Wroxham Road, Norwich NR7 8RP (0603 409188). *Location:* A1151 to Wroxham off Norwich ring road. Parkland, flat with quite a few trees. 18 holes, 5676 yards, 5187 metres. S.S.S. 67. 29 bay covered floodlit driving range. *Green Fees:* weekdays £12.00 per round; weekends £14.00 per round. *Eating facilities:* spacious clubhouse with bar and diningroom. *Visitors:* always welcome. *Society Meetings:* catered for anytime with notice. Professional: P.G. Crice PGA (0603 417264). Secretary: J.A. Butterfield (Mrs) (0603 410657; Fax: 0603 788884).

NORWICH. **Wensum Valley Golf Club,** Beech Avenue, Taverham, Norwich NR8 6HP (0603 261012 extension 3). *Location:* out of Norwich on the A1067 to Taverham. Two courses. Parkland and very picturesque set in the valley. Wensum Course – 4862 yards, 4447 metres. S.S.S. 66. Valley Course – 18 holes, 6000 yards, 5486 metres. S.S.S. 69. Driving range. *Green Fees:* weekdays £12.00; weekends £15.00. *Eating facilities:* full catering and bar facilities. *Visitors:* welcome, restrictions at weekends and Bank Holidays. Accommodation for 11 people available. *Society Meetings:* all welcome. Professional: Peter Briggs (0603 261012 extension 2). Secretary: Bridgette Todd (0603 261012 extension 4).

SHERINGHAM. **Sheringham Golf Club,** Weybourne Road, Sheringham NR26 8HG (Sheringham (0263) 822038). *Location:* one mile west of town on Weybourne Road (A149). Clifftop course. 18 holes, 6464 yards. S.S.S. 71. Large practice area. *Green Fees:* weekdays £28.00; weekends and Bank Holidays £33.00. *Eating facilities:* full catering to order. *Visitors:* welcome, telephone first, with reservation for members of other clubs, Handicap Certificate required. Accommodation in Dormy House, details from Secretary. *Society Meetings:* catered for by prior arrangement with Secretary except weekends from 1st April to 31st October. Professional: R.H. Emery (0263 822980). Secretary: M.J. Garrett (0263 823488).

SWAFFHAM. **Swaffham Golf Club,** Cley Road, Swaffham PE37 8AE (Swaffham (0760) 721611). *Location:* two miles south-west of Swaffham Market Place (signposted) on Cley Road. Heathland course. 9 holes, 6252 yards. S.S.S. 70. Practice ground. *Green Fees:* £18.00 weekdays. *Eating facilities:* full catering except Mondays and Tuesdays, bar snacks all week. *Visitors:* welcome without reservation weekdays, weekends only if playing with member. *Society Meetings:* catered for subject to prior notice being given. Professional: Peter Field. Secretary: R. Joslin.

THETFORD. **Thetford Golf Club,** Brandon Road, Thetford IP24 3NE (Thetford (0842) 752258). *Location:* half a mile from A11. Wooded heathland course. 18 holes, 6879 yards. S.S.S. 73. *Green Fees:* £28.00 weekdays. *Eating facilities:* bar snacks, teas, meals available. *Visitors:* welcome weekdays. *Society Meetings:* catered for weekdays if members of golf clubs. Professional: N. Arthur (0842 752662). Secretary: R.J. Ferguson (0842 752169).

# Northamptonshire

CORBY. **Corby Public Golf Course,** Priors Hall Complex, Corby (Corby (0536) 400497). *Location:* off A43 Kettering to Stamford Road one mile east of village of Weldon. 18 holes, 6677 yards. S.S.S. 72. *Green Fees:* weekdays £4.50; weekends and Bank Holidays £6.00. *Eating facilities* available, and licensed bar. *Society Meetings:* by arrangement with Professional. Professional: M. Summers (0536 60756). Secretary: Jack Marr.

CORBY near. **Priors Hall Golf Club,** Stamford Road, Weldon, Near Corby NN17 3JH (0536 400497). *Location:* on the A43, four miles from Corby on the Stamford Road. 18 holes, 6700 yards. S.S.S. 72. Practice nets and ground. *Green Fees:* weekdays £4.80; weekends £6.90. *Eating facilities:* bar meals. *Visitors:* no restrictions mid week, booking system.

*Society Meetings:* no restrictions mid week. Professional: Malcolm Summers (0536 60756). Secretary: J. Marr.

DAVENTRY. **Daventry and District Golf Club,** Norton Road, Daventry (Daventry (0327) 702829). 9 holes, 5812 yards. S.S.S. 67. *Green Fees:* weekdays £9.00; weekends £12.00. *Visitors:* welcome weekdays and weekends. Summer all welcome except Sunday before 11.00am. Professional: Mike Higgins. Secretary: F. Higham.

DAVENTRY. **Staverton Park Hotel and Golf Club,** Daventry Road, Staverton, Near Daventry NN11 6JT (Daventry (0327) 705911). *Location:* one mile from Daventry on A425 to Leamington Spa. Easy access from M1 Junctions 16 or 18. Undulating parkland. 18

holes, 6634 yards. S.S.S. 72. Practice range. *Green Fees:* weekdays £18.50 per round; weekends and Bank Holidays £21.50 per round. After 4pm summer £16.00 (not bookable in advance). *Eating facilities:* full catering available at all times. *Visitors:* welcome by booking only (two weeks prior). 52 bedroomed hotel with leisure facilities. Residential golf packages available. *Society Meetings:* book through main office. Professional: Brian and Richard Mudge (0327 705506). General Golf Manager: Rex Burdett. Fax (0327 300821).

HELLIDON. **Hellidon Lakes Golf Club,** Hellidon NN11 6LN (0327 62550; Fax: 0327 62559). *Location:* six miles from Daventry off A361. Parkland. 18 holes, 6700 yards. S.S.S. 72. Driving range, putting green. *Green Fees:* weekdays £19.00; weekends £26.00. Special rates on application. *Eating facilities:* bar with food available all day, à la carte restaurant. *Visitors:* always welcome, Handicap Certificates required at weekends. Accommodation available. *Society Meetings:* all welcome. Professional: Neil Dainton. Secretary: Mrs J.A. Nicoll.

KETTERING. **Kettering Golf Club,** Headlands, Kettering NN15 6XA (0536 512074). *Location:* course is at south end of Headlands which is continuation from High Street. Meadowland. 18 holes, 6035 yards, 5515 metres. S.S.S. 69. *Green Fees:* £20.00 day/round. *Eating facilities:* by prior arrangement. *Visitors:* welcome weekdays only, without reservation. *Society Meetings:* catered for Wednesdays and Fridays only by arrangement. Professional: K. Theobald (0536 81014). Secretary: B.C.L. Rumary (0536 511104).

NORTHAMPTON. **Cold Ashby Golf Club,** Cold Ashby, Northampton NN6 7EP (Northampton (0604) 740548). *Location:* midway between Rugby, Leicester and Northampton, with easy access M1 Junction 18. Undulating parkland. 18 holes, 6004 yards. S.S.S. 69. *Green Fees:* midweek £12.00 per round, £18.00 per day; weekends £15.00 per round. *Eating facilities:* meals and bar snacks available daily. *Visitors:* welcome midweek anytime, weekends after 2pm. *Society Meetings:* catered for weekdays. Professional: Tony Skingle (0604 740099). Secretary: David Croxton.

NORTHAMPTON. **Collingtree Park Golf Club,** Windingbrooke Lane, Northampton NN4 0XN (0604-700000). *Location:* take Junction 15 off M1-A508 Northampton. 18 holes, 6692 yards. S.S.S. 72. 18th hole is an island green, set in parkland. *Green Fees:* weekdays: £25.00 18 holes, £40.00 per day; weekends: £40.00 18 holes, £70.00 per day. *Eating facilities:* Conservatory Restaurant, à la carte and table d'hôte, and bar snacks at all times. *Visitors:* welcome – advised to book in advance. *Society Meetings:* corporate golf packages available. Golf Academy which includes two par 4 and one par 3 practice holes, as well

as 16 driving range bays. Hi-tech indoor teaching rooms also. The finest teaching facility for golf, 5 special programmes available. Professional: John Cook. Secretary: Gill Peters.

NORTHAMPTON. **Delapre Park Golf Club,** Eagle Drive, Nene Valley Way, Northampton NN4 0DU (Northampton (0604) 764036; Fax: 0604 763957). *Location:* two and a half miles from Junction 15 (M1), A45 to Wellingborough (exit at Swallow Hotel). Parkland. 18 holes, 6943 yards. Additional 9 holes 2146 yards. S.S.S. 32. Floodlit covered driving range, 39 bays; Par 3 courses, pitch and putt course. *Green Fees:* weekdays £6.20; weekends and Bank Holidays £7.70. 9 hole courses £4.45 weekdays; £5.30 weekends and Bank Holidays. Pitch and putt £1.10 weekdays; £1.25 weekends. Par 3 Courses £2.75 weekdays; £3.00 weekends. *Eating facilities:* meals available all day 9am to 9.30pm, bar – regular hours. *Visitors:* welcome without reservation, except 18 hole and 9 hole course. Start times bookable and must be paid and booked in advance unless vacancies occur on the day. *Society Meetings:* catered for by appointment and advance payment. Professional/Secretary: John Corby (0604 763957).

NORTHAMPTON. **Kingsthorpe Golf Club,** Kingsley Road, Northampton NN2 7BU (Northampton (0604) 711173). *Location:* off M1 and A43. Undulating parkland. 18 holes, 6006 yards. S.S.S. 69. *Green Fees:* (provisional) weekdays £16.00 per round/day, weekends £8.00 per round/day (must play with member). *Eating facilities:* full catering. *Visitors:* welcome weekdays, but must have a Certificate of Handicap. Weekends must be guest of member. *Society Meetings:* catered for by arrangement Mondays and Thursdays only. Professional: Paul Smith (0604 719602). Secretary: P.L. Voke (0604 710610).

NORTHAMPTON. **Northampton Golf Club,** Harlestone, Northampton NN7 4EF (Northampton (0604) 845102). *Location:* on A428 north-west of the village of Harlestone. Parkland with a lake coming into play 16th and 18th holes. 18 holes, 6534 yards. S.S.S. 71. Practice ground. *Green Fees:* £25.00 weekdays, weekends must play with a member. *Eating facilities:* restaurant and bar snacks. *Visitors:* welcome weekdays but must have a Certificate of Handicap. *Society Meetings:* weekdays except Wednesdays. Inclusive packages available. Professional: Mark Chamberlain (0604 845167). Secretary: I.M. Kirkwood (0604 845155).

NORTHAMPTON. **Northamptonshire County Golf Club,** Sandy Lane, Church Brampton, Northampton NN6 8AZ (Northampton (0604) 842170). *Location:* four miles north of Northampton between A50 and

A428. Heathland with woods, gorse and stream. 18 holes, 6503 yards, 5946 metres. S.S.S. 71. Practice ground, indoor net. *Green Fees:* £30.00 (£10.00 with a member). *Eating facilities:* restaurant and bar. *Visitors:* by prior arrangement, must have Club Handicap. *Society Meetings:* catered for Wednesdays, some Thursdays and Mondays. Professional: T. Rouse (0604 842226). Secretary: M.E. Wadley (0604 843025).

OUNDLE. **Oundle Golf Club,** Benefield Road, Oundle (Oundle (0832) 273267). *Location:* on A427 Oundle to Corby road. 18 holes, 5410 yards. S.S.S. 67. *Green Fees:* weekdays £18.00; weekends £25.00. *Eating facilities:* by prior arrangement. *Visitors:* welcome without reservation, not Saturday and Sunday mornings or Bank Holidays. *Society Meetings:* catered for. Secretary: R.K. Davis.

TOWCESTER near. **West Park Golf and Country Club,** Whittlebury, Near Towcester NN12 8XW (0327 858092; Fax: 0327 858009). *Location:* off the A43 – onto the A413 through Whittlebury. Three 9 hole courses and 9 hole academy. Mature oak parkland with 14 lakes and large copses. Golf-o-Drome range. *Green Fees:* weekdays £20.00 per round; weekends £25.00. *Eating facilities:* bar/bistro within clubhouse. *Visitors:* welcome weekdays, slight restrictions weekends, tee times must be booked in advance. Accommodation

planned. *Society Meetings:* catered for. Director of Golf: Peter Cane.

WELLINGBOROUGH. **Rushden Golf Club,** Kimbolton Road, Chelveston, Wellingborough NN9 6AN (Rushden (0933) 312581). *Location:* on A45 two miles east of Higham Ferrers. Undulating parkland. 10 holes, 6335 yards. S.S.S. 70. Small practice area. *Green Fees:* weekdays £12.00 per round, £8.00 with member; no visitors weekends. *Eating facilities:* bar and dining area – no catering Mondays. *Visitors:* welcome except Wednesday afternoons, weekends must play with member. *Society Meetings:* small societies catered for weekdays. Secretary: E.W. Richardson (0933 314910).

WELLINGBOROUGH. **Wellingborough Golf Club,** Great Harrowden Hall, Wellingborough NN9 5AD (Wellingborough (0933) 673022). *Location:* one mile out of Wellingborough on A509, turn right at crossroads by Great Harrowden Church. Undulating parkland. 18 holes, 6604 yards, 6039 metres. S.S.S. 72. Practice ground. *Green Fees:* £22.00 per round, £27.00 per day weekdays; weekends as member's guest only. *Eating facilities:* bar with casual lunch or dinner menu, restaurant. *Visitors:* weekdays only by appointment and with Handicap Certificate. *Society Meetings:* welcome by appointment. Conference facilities available. Professional: David Clifford (0933 678752). Secretary: (0933 677234).

# Northumberland

ALNMOUTH. **Alnmouth Golf Club Ltd,** Foxton Hall, Foxton Drive, Lesbury, Alnwick NE66 3BE (Alnmouth (0665) 830231). Stewardess (0665 830687). *Location:* four miles east of Alnwick. 18 holes, 6414 yards, 5855 metres. S.S.S. 71. *Green Fees:* weekdays £22.00. *Eating facilities:* diningroom and bars. *Visitors:* welcome Mondays, Tuesdays, Thursdays by prior arrangement, Handicap Certificate required. Dormy House accommodation available. *Society Meetings:* catered for by arrangement. Secretary: P.K. McIlroy (0665 830231).

ALNMOUTH. **Alnmouth Village Golf Club,** Marine Road, Alnmouth (Alnmouth (0665) 830370). *Location:* five miles from Alnwick, leave A1 and join A1068. Seaside links course. 9 holes, 6090 yards, 5572 metres. S.S.S. 70. Small practice area. *Green Fees:* weekdays

£10.00 per 18 holes; weekends £15.00 per 18 holes. *Eating facilities:* bar, meals to order. *Visitors:* welcome, restrictions on club competition days. *Society Meetings:* book in advance and only with official Golf Club Handicaps. Secretary: W. Maclean (0665 602096).

ALNWICK. **Alnwick Golf Club,** Swansfield Park, Alnwick (Alnwick (0665) 602632). *Location:* south-west of town, top of Swansfield Park Road, off A1. Mature wooded parkland. 9 holes, 5387 yards. S.S.S. 66. *Green Fees:* weekdays £10.00 per round, £15.00 per day; weekends and Bank Holidays £15.00 per round, £20.00 per day. Half price with member at any time. *Eating facilities:* available on request; bar. *Visitors:* welcome without reservation, some restrictions on competition days. *Society Meetings:* welcome by prior arrangement. Secretary: L.E. Stewart (0665 602499).

ALNWICK. **Dunstanburgh Castle Golf Club,** Embleton, Alnwick NE66 3XQ (Embleton (0665) 576562). *Location:* eight miles off A1, to the north-east of Alnwick. Seaside links course in area of outstanding natural beauty. 18 holes, 6298 yards. S.S.S. 70. *Green Fees:* weekdays £10.50 per day; weekends £12.50 per round, £16.50 per day. *Eating facilities:* snacks, lunches, high teas; bar. *Visitors:* welcome without reservation. Clubs for hire. *Society Meetings:* catered for. Secretary: P.F.C. Gilbert.

BAMBURGH. **Bamburgh Castle Golf Club,** Bamburgh NE69 7DE (Bamburgh (06684) 378). *Location:* north of Alnwick on A1, take B1341 or B1342 to Bamburgh. Links course with outstanding coastal views. 18 holes, 5465 yards, 4991 metres. S.S.S. 67. Practice area. *Green Fees:* weekdays £20.00 per day or round; weekends £25.00 per round, £30.00 per day. Five-day ticket £50.00. *Eating facilities:* full catering and bar. *Visitors:* welcome, except Bank Holidays and Competition weekends. Handicap Certificate required. Buggy hire available. *Society Meetings:* by written application. Hon. Secretary: T.C. Osborne (06684 321).

BEDLINGTON. **Bedlingtonshire Golf Club,** Acorn Bank, Bedlington NE22 6AA (Bedlington (0670) 822457). *Location:* one mile south west of Bedlington on A1068. Parkland. 18 holes, 6546 metres. S.S.S. 73. Practice ground and putting green. *Green Fees:* weekdays £12.00 per round, £15.00 per day; weekends £14.50 per round, £19.00 per day (estimated). *Visitors:* welcome, but not before 10.30am, time restrictions at weekends. *Society Meetings:* catered for. Applications to Chief Leisure and Publicity

Officer, Town Hall, Ashington. Professional: Marcus Webb (0670 822087). Secretary: B.W. Munro (0670 822457).

BERWICK-UPON-TWEED. **Berwick-upon-Tweed (Goswick) Golf Club,** Beal, Berwick-upon-Tweed TD15 2RW (0289 87256). *Location:* signposted off A1, eight miles south of Berwick-upon-Tweed. Seaside links. 18 holes, 6425 yards, 5871 metres. S.S.S. 71. Practice ground. *Green Fees:* weekdays £18.00 per day, £14.00 per round; weekends £24.00 per day, £18.00 per round. *Eating facilities:* catering except Mondays, bar meals. *Visitors:* welcome anytime, parties by arrangement, after 9.30am weekdays, after 10am weekends. *Society Meetings:* catered for by arrangement. Professional: P. Terras (0289 87380). Secretary: R.C. Oliver (0289 87256).

BERWICK-UPON-TWEED. **Magdalene Fields Golf Club,** Magdalene Fields, Berwick-upon-Tweed TD15 1NE (0289 306384). *Location:* to coast from town centre, A1 Scotland/England border. Seaside, parkland course in clifftop setting. 18 holes, 6300 yards. S.S.S. 71. Practice area. *Green Fees:* weekdays £12.00; weekends £14.00. Discount for party bookings. *Eating facilities:* bar and eating facilities. *Visitors:* welcome Monday to Saturday, restrictions on Sundays. *Society Meetings:* all welcome. Secretary: R. Patterson (0289 305758). Green Ranger: (0289 330700).

BLYTH. **Blyth Golf Club Ltd,** New Delaval, Blyth NE24 9DB (Blyth (0670) 367728). *Location:* 12 miles north of Newcastle near the coast. Flat parkland, water hazards. 18 holes, 6533 yards, 6300 metres. S.S.S. 71.

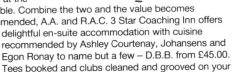
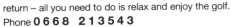

162

Large practice area. *Green Fees:* £12.00 per round, £14.00 per day (with a member £6.00) weekdays; weekends only with a member £6.00. *Eating facilities:* bar and full catering. *Visitors:* welcome weekdays before 3pm, weekends with member only. *Society Meetings:* welcome weekdays only by prior arrangement. Professional: B. Rumney (0670 356514). Secretary: Miss J. Tate (0670 540110).

CARLISLE. **Haltwhistle Golf Course,** Banktop, Greenhead, Via Carlisle (06977 47367). *Location:* off the A69 at the village of Greenhead, two and a half miles west of Haltwhistle. Undulating parkland course with wooded areas. 12 holes, 6154 yards over 18 holes. S.S.S. 69. Practice area. *Green Fees:* £10.00 per day. £30.00 weekly ticket for bona fide holidaymakers. *Eating facilities:* clubhouse bar, catering by prior arrangement. *Visitors:* welcome, no restrictions except on club competition days when course is closed until 4.00pm. *Society Meetings:* welcome by arrangement. Professional: Joe Metcalfe. Secretary: Bill Barnes (0434 320337).

GATESHEAD. **Ravensworth Golf Club Ltd,** Moss Heaps, Wrekenton, Gateshead NE9 7VU (091-4876014). *Location:* two miles south of Gateshead town centre. 18 holes, 5872 yards, 5374 metres. S.S.S. 68. *Green Fees:* £13.00 per round weekdays; £21.00 weekends and Bank Holidays. *Eating facilities:* meals served with reasonable notice (not Mondays). *Visitors:* welcome without reservation. *Society Meetings:* catered for. Professional: Grant Noble. Secretary: L. Winter.

HEXHAM. **Allendale Golf Club,** High Studdon, Allendale, Hexham. *Location:* one and a half miles south of Allendale on B6295. Parkland course, hilly. 9 holes, (new course in full use 1993). *Green Fees:* weekdays £4.00; weekends and Bank Holidays £5.00. Special rates for visiting parties. *Eating facilities:* no catering apart from tea-making facilities, but several good hotels and pubs in Allendale. *Visitors:* welcome anytime except August Bank Holiday Monday; Sundays from May to September by prior booking. *Society Meetings:* catered for by arrangement. Secretary: Jim Hall (091-267 5875).

HEXHAM. **Bellingham Golf Club,** Bogglehole, Bellingham, Hexham (0434 220530). *Location:* four miles west of A68. 9 holes (18 tees), 5245 yards. S.S.S. 66. Practice area. *Green Fees:* weekdays £7.00; weekends and Bank Holidays £10.00. *Eating facilities:* meals available. *Visitors:* welcome, no restrictions except during club competitions. *Society Meetings:* catered for not Sundays. Secretary: T.H. Thompson (0434 220281).

HEXHAM. **Hexham Golf Club,** Spital Park, Hexham NE46 3RZ(Hexham (0434) 602057). *Location:* 20 miles west of Newcastle upon Tyne, one mile west of Hexham town centre. 18 holes, 6272 yards. S.S.S. 70. *Green Fees:* weekdays £18.00 per round, weekends and Bank Holidays £24.00 per round. *Eating facilities:* lunch, high tea and dinner. *Visitors:* welcome without reservation. Preliminary booking advisable. *Society Meetings:* catered for Monday to Friday by arrangement. Professional: Ian Waugh (0434 604904).

Secretary: J.C. Oates (0434 603072; Fax: 0434 601865).

HEXHAM. **Tynedale Golf Club,** Tyne Green Road, Hexham (0434 608154). *Location:* off A69 towards Hexham over Tyne Bridge; immediate right along riverside. 9 holes, 5640 yards. S.S.S. 67. *Green Fees:* weekdays £8.00 adults, £4.00 Juniors and Senior Citizens; weekends £9.00 adults. *Visitors:* welcome except Sunday mornings (club competitions). *Society Meetings:* welcome, please contact Secretary. Secretary: Mr S. Plemper. Private Club, but course maintained by Tynedale District Council.

MORPETH. **Morpeth Golf Club,** The Common, Morpeth NE61 2BT (Morpeth (0670) 519980). *Location:* turn off A1 for Morpeth; south side of town. Parkland. 18 holes, 6206 yards. S.S.S. 70. Practice area. *Green Fees:* weekdays £15.00 per round, £20.00 per day; weekends £20.00 per round, £28.00 per day. *Eating facilities:* restaurant/bar meals/snacks etc., *Visitors:* welcome, mid week after 9.30am, Handicap Certificates may be asked for. *Society Meetings:* catered for weekdays by prior arrangement. Professional: M.R. Jackson (0670 512065). Secretary: G. Hogg (0670 519980).

MORPETH. **Newbiggin-by-the-Sea Golf Club,** Newbiggin-by-the-Sea NE64 6DW (Ashington (0670) 817344). *Location:* take signpost for Newbiggin off A189 (spine road from Tyne Tunnel). Clubhouse at most easterly point of village, adjacent to Church Point Caravan Park. Seaside links. 18 holes, 6452 yards. S.S.S. 71. Practice area. *Green Fees:* weekdays £12.00, £8.00 with a member; weekends £17.00, £12.00 with a member. *Eating facilities:* bar, lounge bar, dining room. *Visitors:* welcome, not before 10am, check by telephone with Professional. *Society Meetings:* catered for by prior arrangement with Secretary. Professional: D. Fletcher (0670 817833). Secretary: Derek Lyall (Office: 0670 520236; 0670 815062 after 6pm).

MORPETH. **Warkworth Golf Club,** The Links, Warkworth, Morpeth NE65 0SW (Alnwick (0665) 711596). *Location:* off A1 to B6345 at Felton, on to A1068 to Warkworth. Links course. 9 holes, 5817 yards. S.S.S. 68. Practice area. *Green Fees:* weekdays £10.00 per day; weekends £15.00 per day. Half price with member. *Eating facilities:* by arrangement only, bar open at nights. *Visitors:* welcome, avoid Tuesdays and Saturdays. *Society Meetings:* welcome by arrangement with Secretary. Secretary: J.W. Anderson (0665 575608).

NEWCASTLE. **Arcot Hall Golf Club Ltd,** Arcot Hall, Dudley, Cramlington NE23 7QP (091-236 2794). *Location:* seven miles north of Newcastle. Turn off A1 for Ashington and then signposted. 18 holes, 6389 yards, 5840 metres. S.S.S. 70. *Green Fees:* weekdays £20.00; weekends £25.00 by invitation only. *Eating facilities:* lunch and high tea. *Visitors:* welcome without reservation midweek only. Clubs for hire. *Society Meetings:* catered for on application to Secretary. Professional: Graham Cant (091-236 2147). Secretary: A.G. Bell (091-236 2794).

NEWCASTLE-UPON-TYNE. **Ponteland Golf Club,** Bell Villas, Ponteland, Newcastle-upon-Tyne NE20 9BD (0661 22689). *Location:* A696, one and a half miles north of Newcastle Airport. Parkland. 18 holes, 6524 yards. S.S.S. 71. Large practice area. *Green Fees:* £21.00 per day or round (inclusive VAT). *Eating facilities:* full menu in restaurant and bar. *Visitors:* welcome Monday to Thursday, must be members' guest Friday, weekends and Bank Holidays. *Society Meetings:* Tuesdays or Thursdays, catered for with pre-booking agreed by Secretary/Manager. Professional: Alan Crosby (0661 22689). Secretary: Mr John Hillyer (0661 22689).

PRUDHOE. **Prudhoe Golf Club,** Eastwood Park, Prudhoe NE42 5DX (Prudhoe (0661) 832466). *Location:* 10 miles west of Newcastle-upon-Tyne, A695 to Hexham. Undulating parkland, highly rated course. 18 holes, 5856 yards, 5319 metres. S.S.S. 68. Large practice area. *Green Fees:* £18.00 weekdays; £25.00 weekends after 4.30pm only. Special rates for parties over 20. *Eating facilities:* bar snacks, dining room and evening meals. *Visitors:* welcome midweek with reservation (contact Professional); weekends after 4.30pm. *Society Meetings:* catered for weekdays with prior booking. Professional: John Crawford (0661 836188). Secretary: G.B. Garratt. Bookings Secretary: W. Wray.

ROTHBURY. **Rothbury Golf Club,** Old Race Course, Thorpton Road, Rothbury, Morpeth (0669 21271). *Location:* 15 miles north of Morpeth, take A697 turn off at Weldon Bridge for Rothbury. Flat on Haugh course alongside river. 9 holes, 5560 yards. S.S.S. 67. *Green Fees:* £9.00 weekdays, £14.00 weekends. *Eating facilities:* none available, but there are plenty of good hotels in Rothbury and there is a bar open Wednesday nights and weekends. *Visitors:* welcome during weekdays, but limited at weekends due to club competitions. *Society Meetings:* catered for weekdays by arrangement only. Hon. Secretary: W.T. Bathgate (0669 20718 or 20313).

SEAHOUSES. **Seahouses Golf Club,** Beadnell Road, Seahouses NE68 7XT (Alnwick (0665) 720794).

*Location:* 15 miles north of Alnwick, turn off A1 for B1340. Flat seaside links with water hazard. 18 holes, 5462 yards. S.S.S. 67. Practice net. *Green Fees:* weekdays £13.00 per day; weekends £16.50 per day. Juniors under 16 half rates. *Eating facilities:* full catering and bar. *Visitors:* welcome with no restrictions, please telephone clubhouse. *Society Meetings:* by arrangement. Secretary: J.A. Stevens (0665 720809).

STOCKSFIELD. **Stocksfield Golf Club,** New Ridley, Stocksfield NE43 7RE (Stocksfield (0661) 843041). *Location:* 15 miles west of Newcastle on A69, and three miles east of A68. Wooded parkland. 18 holes, 5594 yards. S.S.S. 68. Practice area. *Green Fees:*weekdays £20.00, weekends and Bank Holidays £25.00. *Eating facilities:* available, also bar. *Visitors:* welcome weekdays and after 4.30pm at weekends. *Society Meetings:* catered for. Professional: Ken Driver. Secretary: D.B. Moon.

TYNEMOUTH. **Tynemouth Golf Club Ltd,** Spital Dene, Tynemouth (North Shields (091) 2574578). *Location:* on A695. 18 holes, 6403 yards (forward tees). S.S.S. 71. *Green Fees:* weekdays £20.00; weekends and Bank Holidays must be signed in and play with a member. *Eating facilities:* lunches and high teas served at club. *Visitors:* welcome with reservation. *Society Meetings:* catered for. Professional: John McKenna. Secretary: W. Storey.

WOOLER. **Wooler Golf Club,** Dod Law, Doddington, Wooler. *Location:* situated on the high ground named Dod Law to the east of the B6525 Wooler – Berwick road. The route is signposted from Doddington village. 9 holes, 6358 yards. S.S.S. 70. Large practice area. *Green Fees:* weekdays £8.00 per day; weekends and Bank Holidays £10.00 per day. Juniors £2.00 per round, as adults after 6pm. *Eating facilities:* bar open evenings (operated voluntarily). *Visitors:* always welcome except during all day competitions. *Society Meetings:* welcome by arrangement with Secretary. Secretary: James Henry Curry (0668 81956).

# Nottinghamshire

BULWELL. **Bulwell Forest Golf Club,** Hucknall Road, Bulwell (0602 770576) *Location:* A610 north of Nottingham, M1 Junction 26, three miles from course. Parkland, very tight course. 18 holes, 5572 yards. S.S.S. 67. *Green Fees:* weekdays £6.50; weekends £8.10. *Eating facilities:* meals served at all times. *Visitors:* welcome except Tuesdays and weekends, time sheets in operation every day. *Society Meetings:* catered for, but book well in advance. Professional: C. D. Hall (0602 763172). Secretary: D. Stubbs.

EAST LEAKE. **Rushcliffe Golf Club,** Stocking Lane, East Leake, Near Loughborough LE12 5RL (0509 852209). *Location:* on A60 signposted eight miles south of Nottingham. Wooded hills on edge of the Wolds. 18 holes, 6057 yards, 5539 metres. S.S.S. 69. Practice ground. *Green Fees:* weekdays £22.00; weekends £25.00. *Eating facilities:* full catering except Mondays when bar snacks only. *Visitors:* welcome with reservation, weekends without a member between 9.30am to 11am and 3pm to 4.30pm. *Society Meetings:* catered for Mondays, Wednesdays, Thursdays and Fridays strictly by prior booking. Professional: Tim Smart (0509 852701). Secretary: D.J. Barnes (0509 852959).

EDWALTON. **Edwalton Municipal Golf and Social Club,** Wellin Lane, Edwalton (0602 234713). *Location:* follow Nottingham ring road, course signposted from island on ring road. Gently sloping parkland. 9 holes, 3342 yards. S.S.S. 72. Also 9 hole par 3 course. Large practice ground. *Green Fees:* £4.00 for 9 holes. Students, Senior Citizens, disabled and UB40's £2.00 before 5pm, weekdays only. Par 3 course £2.20, special rate £1.00. *Eating facilities:* first class catering, bar open all day. *Visitors:* welcome anytime except club competitions (contact Professional for dates). Professional: J.A. Staples (0602 234775). Secretary: E. Watts (0602 231576).

KIRKBY-IN-ASHFIELD. **Notts. Golf Club Ltd,** Hollinwell, Kirkby-in-Ashfield, Nottingham NG17 7QR (Mansfield (0623) 753225). *Location:* three miles from Exit 27 on M1, turn off M1 then left on A611. 18 holes, 7020 yards. S.S.S. 74. *Green Fees:* on application. *Visitors:* welcome on production of Handicap Certificate (weekends and Bank Holidays with member only). Advisable to book beforehand. *Society Meetings:* catered for Mondays and Tuesdays. Professional: Brian Waites. Secretary: J.R. Walker.

MANSFIELD. **Coxmoor Golf Club,** Coxmoor Road, Sutton in Ashfield, Mansfield NG17 5LF (Mansfield (0623) 559878). *Location:* exit Junction 27 M1 and A611 for three miles. Heathland. 18 holes, 6251 yards, 5944 metres. S.S.S. 72. Practice area and nets. *Green Fees:* weekdays £25.00. *Eating facilities:* restaurant. *Visitors:* welcome except weekends, pre-book through Professional. (Tuesday Ladies' Day). *Society Meetings:* catered for by prior application. Professional: D. Ridley (0623 559906). Secretary: Mr J.W. Tyler (0623 557359).

MANSFIELD. **Mansfield Woodhouse Golf Club,** Leeming Lane North, Mansfield Woodhouse NG19 9EU (0623 23521). *Location:* Junction 27 of M1, A60 Mansfield-Warsop. Flat parkland. 9 holes, 2446 yards. S.S.S. 64. *Green Fees:* £2.95 9 holes, £4.30 18 holes. *Eating facilities:* bar snacks. *Visitors:* welcome, unrestricted - pay and play. Professional: L. Highfield Jnr. (0623 23521). Secretary: T. Mason.

MANSFIELD. **Sherwood Forest Golf Club,** Eakring Road, Mansfield NG18 3EW (Mansfield (0623) 23327). *Location:* leave M1 at Exit 27, take signs for Mansfield, proceed via Southwell Road and Oak Tree Lane. Traditional heathland course designed by James Braid (Championship standard). 18 holes, 6710 yards. S.S.S. 73. Two practice grounds. *Green Fees:* weekdays £28.00 per round, £33.00 per day; weekends and Bank Holidays £33.00 per round. *Eating facilities:* two dining rooms, gents' bar and mixed lounge. *Visitors:* welcome Mondays, Thursdays and Fridays, must be member of a golf club with a handicap. *Society Meetings:* catered for Mondays, Thursdays and Fridays. Professional: K. Hall (0623 27403). Secretary: K. Hall (0623 26689).

MAPPERLEY. **Mapperley Golf Club,** Central Avenue, Plains Road, Mapperley NG3 5RH (Nottingham (0602) 265611). *Location:* B684, four miles north east of centre of Nottingham. Hilly picturesque course. 18 holes, 6283 yards. S.S.S. 70. Practice ground. *Green Fees:* weekdays £14.00; weekends £16.00. *Eating facilities:* 11.30am to 2.30pm daily, except Wednesdays. *Visitors:* welcome except on match and competition days, Ladies Day Tuesdays. *Society Meetings:* catered for. Professional: R. Daibell (0602 202227). Secretary: A. Newton.

NEWARK. **Newark Golf Club,** Coddington, Newark NG24 2QX (0636 626241). *Location:* off the A17 Sleaford road four miles east of Newark. Parkland, wooded course. 18 holes, 6486 yards. S.S.S. 71. Practice ground. *Green Fees:* £18.00 per round, £24.00 per day weekdays; weekends £24.00. *Eating facilities:* full catering, bar all day. *Visitors:* welcome with reservation. Handicap Certificates will be required. Restriction at peak times Saturday and Sunday, Ladies' Day Tuesday. Snooker. Professional tuition and computer/video analysis. *Society Meetings:* welcome except Tuesdays, weekends. Booking fee payable. Professional: H.A. Bennett (0636 626492). Secretary: A.W. Morgans (0636 626282).

NOTTINGHAM. **Beeston Fields Golf Club,** Old Drive, Wollaton Road, Beeston NG9 3DD (Nottingham (0602) 257062). *Location:* Wollaton road off A52 Derby road, M1, Exit 25. Parkland. 18 holes, 6414 yards. S.S.S. 71. Practice ground and net available. *Green Fees:* weekdays £20.00; weekends £30.00. *Eating facilities:* available daily. *Visitors:* welcome with reservation, Tuesday not until 2.30pm. *Society Meetings:* catered for Mondays and Wednesdays. Professional: Alun Wardle (0602 220872). Secretary: J.E.L. Grove (0602 257062).

NOTTINGHAM. **Chilwell Manor Golf Club,** Meadow Lane, Chilwell, Nottingham NG9 5AE (Nottingham (0602) 258958). *Location:* four miles from Nottingham on main Nottingham to Birmingham road. 18 holes, 6379 yards. S.S.S. 69. *Green Fees:* £24.00 at all times. *Eating facilities:* available. *Visitors:* welcome weekdays with reservation, restricted at certain busy times. *Society Meetings:* societies of 30 or more is minimum number catered for. Professional: E. McCausland. Hon. Secretary: G.A. Spindley.

NOTTINGHAM. **Nottingham City Golf Club,** Lawton Drive, Bulwell, Nottingham NG6 8BL (Nottingham (0602) 278021). *Location:* three miles north west of city centre, Exit 26 M1. Parkland. 18 holes, 6218 yards. S.S.S. 70. Practice area. *Green Fees:* weekdays £7.00 per round; weekends £8.50. *Eating facilities:* available. *Visitors:* welcome without reservation except weekends. *Society Meetings:* catered for. Professional: C.R. Jepson (0602 272727). Secretary: D.A. Griffiths (0602 276916).

NOTTINGHAM. **Ruddington Grange Golf Club,** Wilford Road, Ruddington, Nottingham NG11 6NB (0602 214139). *Location:* M1 Junction 24 Nottingham road, A52 to Nottingham Knight island, right to Ruddington, half a mile outside Ruddington. Parkland. 18 holes, 6490 yards, 5935 metres. S.S.S. 71. *Green Fees:* weekdays £20.00/£22.00; weekends £24.00/£26.00. *Eating facilities:* full restaurant. *Visitors:* welcome all the time but at weekends members have priority. Swimming pool. *Society Meetings:* welcome. Professional: Robert Ellis (0602 211951). Secretary: R.L. Westgate (0602 846141).

NOTTINGHAM. **Wollaton Park Golf Club,** Wollaton Park, Nottingham (0602 787574). *Location:* turning off Ring Road Middleton Boulevard. 18 holes, 6545 yards.

S.S.S. 71. *Green Fees:* weekdays £19.00 per round, weekends £22.00 per round. *Eating facilities:* available except Monday lunch. Bar snacks. *Visitors:* welcome without reservation. *Society Meetings:* catered for Tuesdays and Fridays. Professional: J. Lower (0602 784834). Secretary: O.B. Kirk.

RADCLIFFE-ON-TRENT. **Radcliffe-on-Trent Golf Club,** Dewberry Lane, Cropwell Road, Radcliffe-on-Trent NG12 2JH (0602 333125). *Location:* A52 from Nottingham turn right at traffic lights on Cropwell Road. Flat, wooded parkland. 18 holes, 6423 yards. S.S.S. 71. Two large practice areas. *Green Fees:* weekdays £21.00 per day, weekends £26.00 per day (reductions for members' guests). *Eating facilities:* snacks, meals and bar. *Visitors:* welcome, confirm course availability with Professional or Secretary. *Society Meetings:* catered for on Wednesdays. Professional: Nigel Birkitt (0602 332396). Secretary: Major B.C. Hodgson (0602 333000).

RETFORD. **Retford Golf Club Ltd,** Brecks Road, Ordsall, Retford DN22 7UA (0777 703733). *Location:* south off A620. 18 holes, 6301 yards. S.S.S. 71. *Green Fees:* weekdays £15.00 per round (£8.00 with a member), £20.00 per day; weekends and Bank Holidays £8.00 (must be accompanied by a member). *Eating facilities:* meals at club. *Visitors:* welcome. Professional: S. Betteridge (0777 703733). Secretary: A. Harrison (0777 860682).

SOUTHWELL. **Oakmere Park,** Oaks Lane, Oxton, Near Southwell NG25 0RH (Nottingham (0602) 655628). *Location:* eight miles north east of Nottingham on A614 and A6097. Parkland course. North Course – 18 holes, 6617 yards, 6046 metres. S.S.S. 72. South Course – 9 holes, 3495 yards, 3193 metres. 30 bay floodlit driving range. *Green Fees:* North – weekdays £16.00 per round, £24.00 per day; weekends £20.00 per round, £30.00 per day. South – weekdays £6.00; weekends £8.00. *Eating facilities:* clubhouse bar, spike bar, restaurant, resident chef. *Visitors:* welcome but should make reservations. Weekends require maximum notice possible. *Society Meetings:* welcome. Professional: G.C. Norton.

SOUTHWELL. **Oxton Golf Course Ltd,** Oaks Lane, Oxton, Southwell (Nottingham (0602) 653545). *Location:* adjoining A614 north of Nottingham. Attractive wooded estate courses. 18 holes. S.S.S. 72; also 9 hole course. 30-bay floodlit driving range. *Green Fees:* information not provided. *Eating facilities:* bar and restaurant open to all golfers. *Visitors:* pay-as-you-play courses. Professional/Secretary: G.C. Norton.

STANTON-ON-THE-WOLDS. **Stanton-on-the-Wolds Golf Club,** Stanton-on-the-Wolds NG12 5BH (0602 372044). *Location:* seven miles south of Nottingham, one mile west of main Nottingham – Melton road. Agricultural land. 18 holes, 6437 yards, 5886 metres. S.S.S. 71. Practice ground. *Green Fees:* weekdays £24.00; weekends with member only. *Eating facilities:* restaurant and bar. *Visitors:* welcome with prior arrangement with Secretary, weekends with member only. *Society Meetings:* catered for by arrangement with Secretary. Professional: Nick Hernon (0602 372390). Secretary: H.G. Gray, F.C.A. (0602 372006).

WORKSOP. **Kilton Forest Golf Club,** Worksop (0909 486563). *Location:* one mile north of Worksop on B6045. 18 holes, 6569 yards. S.S.S. 72. *Visitors:* unrestricted. Secretary: E.L. James. Professional: Peter Foster.

WORKSOP. **Lindrick Golf Club,** Lindrick, Worksop S81 8BH (Worksop (0909) 485802). *Location:* on A57 four miles west of Worksop. M1 junction 31 on to A57 Worksop. 18 holes, 6615 yards, 6048 metres. S.S.S. 72. *Green Fees:* on application. *Eating facilities:* by arrangement. *Visitors:* welcome weekdays, except Tuesday mornings. Prior booking required. *Society Meetings:* catered for weekdays. Professional: P. Cowen (0909 475820). Secretary: (0909 475282).

WORKSOP. **Worksop Golf Club,** Windmill Lane, Worksop S80 2SQ (Worksop (0909) 472696). *Location:* south east of town centre, best approach from A57 bypass at Junction with B. Heathland with gorse, broom, birch and oak; easy walking. 18 holes, 6666 yards. S.S.S. 73. Practice ground. *Green Fees:* £18.00 per round, £25.00 per day weekdays; £25.00 per round weekends and Bank Holidays. *Eating facilities:* diningroom and bar. *Visitors:* welcome, except weekends and Bank Holidays. Advise preliminary phone call. Snooker table. *Society Meetings:* by arrangement with Professional. Professional: J.R. King (0909 477732). Secretary: P.G. Jordan (0909 477731).

# Oxfordshire

ABINGDON. **Frilford Heath Golf Club,** Abingdon OX13 5NW (Frilford Heath (0865) 390864). *Location:* on A338 Oxford/Wantage Road seven miles south-west of Oxford, four miles west of Abingdon. Flat, wooded heathland. Red course: 18 holes, 6768 yards. S.S.S. 73; Green course: 18 holes, 5763 yards. S.S.S. 69. Two practice areas. *Green Fees:* weekdays £40.00, after 5pm £30.00; weekends and Bank Holidays £50.00, after 5pm £35.00. *Eating facilities:* first class restaurant and bars. *Visitors:* welcome weekdays with Handicap Certificate, phone ahead for weekends and Bank Holidays. *Society Meetings:* welcomed Mondays, Wednesdays and Fridays. Professional: D.C. Craik (0865 390887). Secretary: J. Kleynhans (0865 390864).

BANBURY. **Cherwell Edge Golf Club,** C/o Cherwell Edge Public Course, Chacombe, Banbury OX17 2EN (0295 712067). *Location:* M40, Junction 11, two miles; four miles east of Banbury. 18 holes, 5600 metres. S.S.S. 68 (men), 69 (ladies). *Green Fees:* weekdays local residents £6.80, non residents £7.80; weekends £8.90 local residents, £10.20 non residents. All-day rates £12.10 and £14.00. *Eating facilities:* bar and lounge. *Visitors:* welcome, open to the public. *Society Meetings:* contact the Golf Professional. Professional Manager: Mr R. Davies (0295 711591).

BANBURY. **Tadmarton Heath Golf Club,** Wigginton, Banbury OX15 5HL (0608 737278). *Location:* off M40, off A41, off B4035, five miles west of Banbury.

Heathland. 18 holes, 5917 yards. S.S.S. 69. Practice area. *Green Fees:* by application. *Eating facilities:* full catering. *Visitors:* welcome weekdays (restrictions Thursdays); weekends with member only. Must be member of another golf club with Handicap Certificate. *Society Meetings:* welcome weekdays except Thursdays. Professional: Les Bond (0608 730047). Secretary: R.E. Wackrill (0608 737278).

BICESTER. **Chesterton Golf Club,** Chesterton, Near Bicester OX6 8TE (Bicester (0869) 241204). *Location:* one mile off A421, Bicester/Oxford. Two miles south-west of Bicester. 18 holes, 6224 yards. S.S.S. 70. Practice ground and putting green. *Green Fees:* weekdays £12.00 per day, weekends and Bank Holidays £18.00 per day. *Eating facilities:* bars and lunchtime bar food, diningroom by arrangement. *Visitors:* welcome weekdays without reservation, weekends may book through Pro shop. Snooker room. *Society Meetings:* catered for except weekends. Professional: Jack Wilkshire (0869 242023). Secretary: Brian Carter (0869 241204).

BURFORD. **Burford Golf Club,** Burford OX18 4JG (Burford (0993) 822149). *Location:* A40 – Burford roundabout. Flat parkland. 18 holes, 6405 yards, 6083 metres. S.S.S. 71. *Green Fees:* £25.00 per day weekdays. *Eating facilities:* full catering. *Visitors:* welcome weekdays only by arrangement on application. *Society Meetings:* catered for on application to Secretary. Professional: Norman Allen (0993 822344). Secretary: Richard Cane (0993 822583).

*If you are writing, a stamped, addressed envelope is always appreciated.*

CHIPPING NORTON. **Chipping Norton Golf Club,** Southcombe, Chipping Norton OX7 5QH (0608 641150). *Location:* Junction of A34 and A44, 18 miles from Oxford. 20 miles from Stratford-on-Avon. Downland, with many planted trees and lake. 18 holes, 6280 yards, 5743 metres. S.S.S. 70. Practice ground and putting green. *Green Fees:* weekdays £22.00; weekends only with a member £10.00. £38.00 per day for societies, including catering. *Eating facilities:* dining-room and bar. *Visitors:* welcome Monday to Friday but not Bank Holidays. *Society Meetings:* Mondays, Tuesdays, Wednesdays and some Fridays. Professional: Robert Gould (0608 643356). Secretary: John Norman (0608 642383).

HENLEY-ON-THAMES. **Badgemore Park Golf Club,** Badgemore, Henley-on-Thames RG9 4NR (0491 573667). *Location:* just west of Henley-on-Thames, on B290 Henley-Peppard road. Flat but wooded course. 18 holes, 6112 yards. S.S.S. 69. *Green Fees:* weekdays £26.00 per day; weekends £29.00. *Eating facilities:* full catering and bar facilities. *Visitors:* welcome though must play with a member weekends and Bank Holiday mornings. Handicap Certificate required. *Society Meetings:* complete Company and Society Golf Days available. Professional: Mark Wright (0491 574175). Manager: R. Park (0491 572206; Fax: 0491 567899).

HENLEY-ON-THAMES. **Henley Golf Club,** Harpsden, Henley-on-Thames RG9 4HG (Henley (0491) 573304). *Location:* from centre of Henley-Reading, one mile from Harpsden Way to clubhouse. Parkland with many trees. 18 holes, 6329 yards. S.S.S. 70. *Green Fees:* £30.00; weekends with member only £10. *Eating facilities:* bar snacks at all times, meals by arrangement. *Visitors:* welcome with reservation weekdays, not at weekends or Bank Holidays (Handicap Certificate holders only). *Society Meetings:* catered for Wednesdays and Thursdays only. Professional: Mark Howell (0491 575710). Secretary: John Hex (0491 575742).

HENLEY-ON-THAMES. **Huntercombe Golf Club,** Nuffield, Henley-on-Thames RG9 5SL (0491 641207). *Location:* A432, six miles west of Henley-on-Thames. Downland wooded course. 18 holes, 6301 yards. S.S.S. 70. Practice ground. *Green Fees:* £30.00 weekdays, no weekend green fees. *Eating facilities:* catering and bar facilities. *Visitors:* welcome weekdays, after 10.00am by prior arrangement. *Society Meetings:* Tuesdays and Thursdays by arrangement. Professional: J.B. Draycott (0491 641241). Secretary: Lt Col T.J. Hutchison.

MAPLEDURHAM. **Mapledurham Golf Club,** Chazey Heath, Mapledurham (0734 724751). *Location:* leave Reading towards Mapledurham, Woodcote and Wallingford, club is on the right immediately after leaving built up area. Parkland. 18 holes. Practice ground. *Green Fees:* weekdays £13.00; weekends £18.00. *Eating facilities:* restaurant and bar. *Visitors:* welcome. *Society Meetings:* welcome.

OXFORD. **North Oxford Golf Club,** Banbury Road, Oxford OX2 8ED (Oxford (0865) 54415). *Location:* just north of Oxford on the Banbury Road to Kidlington. 18 holes, 5805 yards, S.S.S. 67. *Green Fees:* £28.00 weekdays; weekends and Bank Holidays with members only. *Eating facilities:* limited on Mondays. *Visitors and Societies:* welcome. Professional: Bob Harris (0865 53977). Secretary: W. Forster (0865 54924).

OXFORD. **Southfield Golf Club,** Hill Top Road, Oxford OX4 1PF. *Location:* one mile from Rover Works, along Cowley Road, turn right into Southfield Road, then right at end of road. Hilly parkland. 18 holes, 6328 yards. S.S.S. 70. *Green Fees:* £24.00 per day weekdays. *Eating facilities:* full catering except Mondays, bar open seven days. *Visitors:* welcome except weekends and Public Holidays. Handicap Certificates required. *Society Meetings:* welcome by arrangement (not weekends or Bank Holidays). Professional: Tony Rees (0865 244258). Secretary: A.G. Hopcraft (0865 242158).

WALLINGFORD near. **RAF Benson,** Near Wallingford OX10 6AA. *Location:* three and a half miles north-east of Wallingford, follow signposts to RAF Benson. Airfield course, through airfield installations. 9 holes, 4395 yards. S.S.S. 61. *Green Fees:* £5.00. *Visitors:* casual visitors not permitted must be accompanied by members. Secretary: Flt Lt J.W. (Taff) Williams (0491 35376).

# Shropshire

BRIDGNORTH. **Bridgnorth Golf Club,** Stanley Lane, Bridgnorth WV16 4SF (Bridgnorth (0746) 763315). *Location:* one mile from town centre on Broseley road. Parkland, alongside River Severn. 18 holes, 6627 yards. S.S.S. 72. Practice ground. *Green Fees:* £18.00 – £22.00 weekdays; £25.00 – £30.00 weekends and Bank Holidays. *Eating facilities:* full catering available except Mondays. *Visitors:* welcome weekdays except Wednesday with Handicap Certificate or if bona fide club member. *Society Meetings:* catered for Tuesday, Thursday, Friday only. Professional: Paul Hinton (0746 762045). Secretary: K.D. Cole (0746 764179).

CHURCH STRETTON. **Church Stretton Golf Club,** "Hunters Moon", Trevor Hill, Church Stretton SY6 6JH (Church Stretton (0694) 722281). *Location:* one mile west of A49, adjacent to Carding Mill Valley. Hillside, heathland course. 18 holes, 5008 yards. S.S.S. 65. *Green Fees:* £12.00 weekdays, £18.00 weekends and Bank Holidays. *Eating facilities:* snacks and meals by arrangement; bar. *Visitors:* welcome, Saturday not 9am to 10.30am and 1pm to 3pm, Sundays not before 10.30am or between 12.30pm and 3pm.*Society Meetings:* catered for by arrangement with Secretary. Hon. Secretary: R. Broughton (0694 722633).

LUDLOW. **Ludlow Golf Club,** Bromfield, Ludlow SY8 2BT (0584 77285). *Location:* A49 one mile north of Ludlow bypass, turn right onto the Bridgnorth road. Well signposted. Parkland with hills to north east; two quarry holes. 18 holes, 6239 yards. S.S.S. 70. Practice ground. *Green Fees:* weekdays £18.00; weekends £24.00 (£7.00 with member). *Eating facilities:* full catering and bar service. *Visitors:* welcome weekdays with prior booking, weekends with member only. *Society Meetings:* catered for Wednesday and Thursdays April to October. Professional: G. Farr. Administrator: M. Cropper.

MARKET DRAYTON. **Market Drayton Golf Club,** Sutton, Market Drayton (Market Drayton (0630) 652266). *Location:* south of town leaving by Walkmill Road one mile past the swimming baths. Parkland with exceptional views. 18 holes, 6214 yards, 5702 metres. S.S.S. 70. *Green Fees:* weekdays £20.00; weekends only with a member. Reduced fees if playing with member. *Eating facilities:* bar with high class catering open all day. *Visitors:* welcome weekdays only. Tuesday Ladies' Day, first tee closed 9am to 11am.

Bungalow (sleeps 6) available for letting. *Society Meetings:* catered for weekdays by prior arrangement. Professional: R. Clewes. Secretary: J.J. Moseley (0630 653661).

NEWPORT. **Lilleshall Hall Golf Club,** Lilleshall, Near Newport TF10 9AS (Telford (0952) 603840). *Location:* at Lillyhurst turn north off Abbey Road, which joins Wellington Road near Lilleshall and the B4379 near Sheriffhales. Wooded parkland. 18 holes, 5906 yards. S.S.S. 68. Practice ground. *Green Fees:* weekdays £18.00 (half price with member), weekends £15.00 only with member. Bank Holidays and following day plus Christmas holiday week £30.00 (half price with a member). *Eating facilities:* meals served 9am to 5pm, order in advance. *Visitors:* welcome on weekdays, check with Professional for tee restrictions. *Society Meetings:* catered for by prior arrangement with Secretary. Professional: N.W. Bramall (0952 604104). Secretary: H. Fothergill (0952 604776).

OSWESTRY. **Llanymynech Golf Club,** Pant, Near Oswestry SY10 8LB (Llanymynech (0691) 830542). *Location:* one mile west of A483 Welshpool to Oswestry, six miles south of Oswestry. Turn by Cross Guns Inn, Pant signposted to club. Upland course with extensive views. 18 holes, 6114 yards, 5899 metres. S.S.S. 69. Practice area. *Green Fees:* weekdays £18.00 per day, £13.00 per round; weekends £23.00 per day, £19.00 per round. Half price with member. Reductions for Juniors. *Eating facilities:* restaurant and bar (not Mondays). *Visitors:* welcome weekdays; some weekends by prior arrangement. *Society Meetings:* by arrangement with the Secretary. Professional: A.P. Griffiths (0691 830879). Secretary: N. Clews (0691 830983).

OSWESTRY. **Oswestry Golf Club,** Aston Park, Oswestry SY11 4JJ (Queens Head (069188) 221). *Location:* four miles south-east of Oswestry on A5. Parkland course. 18 holes, 6038 yards. S.S.S. 69. *Green Fees:* weekdays £17.00; weekends £25.00. *Eating facilities:* diningroom and bar. *Visitors:* welcome; must be members of another club or playing with a member. *Society Meetings:* catered for Wednesday and Friday, by arrangement, application necessary. Professional: D. Skelton (069188 448). Secretary: Mrs. P.M. Lindner (069188 535).

SHIFNAL. **Shifnal Golf Club,** Decker Hill, Shifnal TF11 8QL (Telford (0952) 460330). *Location:* one mile north east of Shifnal, one mile from A5, Junction 4 M54. Parkland course. 18 holes, 6504 yards. S.S.S. 71. *Green Fees:* £18.50 per round, £25.00 per day; weekends with member only. *Eating facilities:* full catering service. *Visitors:* welcome, phone first, not weekends or Bank Holidays. *Society Meetings:* catered for by arrangement with Secretary. *Professional:* J. Flanagan (0952 460457). *Secretary:* P.W. Holden (0952 460330).

SHREWSBURY. **Hawkstone Park Leisure Ltd,** Weston-under-Redcastle, Shrewsbury SY4 5UY. Where Sandy Lyle, '85 Open Champion, learned his game. (Lee Brockhurst (0939 200611). *Location:* 14 miles north of Shrewsbury on A49 Whitchurch road. Parkland course with hills. 18 holes, Par 72, S.S.S. 71. *Green Fees:* from £27.50 per round. *Eating facilities:* hotel restaurant and bar. *Visitors:* welcome but advisable to book tee times in advance. Residential bargain breaks available all year round with starting times reserved. *Society Meetings:* comprehensive super value packages available. *Golf Professional:* Keith Williams (0939 200209). Buggies available for hire through the Professional's Shop.

SHREWSBURY. **Shrewsbury Golf Club,** Condover, Shrewsbury SY5 7BL. *Location:* A49 two miles south west of Shrewsbury. Parkland. 18 holes, 6212 yards. S.S.S. 70. Large practice ground. *Green Fees:* £15.00 per round, £20.00 per day weekdays; £25.00 per day or round weekends and Bank Holidays. *Eating facilities:* full restaurant facilities available seven days.

*Visitors:* welcome at all times. *Society Meetings:* by arrangement if over 16 players, not Wednesdays, preferably Monday and Fridays, some Sundays. *Professional:* Peter Seal (0743 723751). *Secretary:* Mrs S.M. Kenney (0743 722977).

TELFORD. **Telford Hotel, Golf and Country Club,** Great Hay, Sutton Hill, Telford TF7 4DT (0952 585642). *Location:* turn off A442 between Bridgnorth and Telford, two miles to M54 Junction 4. Rolling wooded parkland with lake features. 18 holes, 6766 yards, 6187 metres. S.S.S. 72. 9 hole par 3 course. All-weather driving range. *Green Fees:* £25.00 weekdays; £35.00 weekends. *Eating facilities:* clubroom, coffee bar and restaurant, also private rooms for Societies. *Visitors:* welcome anytime but advance booking essential. Handicap Certificates or membership of bona fide golf club essential. Leisure Centre with swimming pool, gym, etc. *Society Meetings:* by arrangement with Golf Co-ordinator extension 307. *Professional:* Steve Marr (0952 586052). *Secretary:* Cdr John Brigham (0952 585642 ext. 274).

TELFORD. **Wrekin Golf Club,** Ercall Woods, Wellington, Telford (Telford (0952) 244032). *Location:* end of M54, turn back along Holyhead road to golf club sign. Undulating parkland. 18 holes, 5699 yards. S.S.S. 67. Small practice ground. *Green Fees:* weekdays £18.00; weekends £25.00 numbers limited. *Eating facilities:* by arrangement with Stewardess. *Visitors:* welcome except weekends and Bank Holidays. *Society Meetings:* by arrangement. *Professional:* K. Houseden (0952 223101). *Secretary:* S. Leys (0952 255586 after 7pm).

**TELFORD**
**HOTEL**
**Golf & Country**
**CLUB**

## GREAT HAY, SUTTON HILL, TELFORD TF7 4DT.
## TEL: 0952 585642 · FAX: 0952 582836 · TELEX: 35481

Spend some time at one of Shropshire's premier Hotel and Golf complexes and enjoy a range of Golfing Packages, each one designed to make your visit one to remember.

The challenging 18 hole championship golf course stands along with our 9 hole par 3 course, high above the splendour of the Ironbridge Gorge. Telford offers amenities such as buggy hire, pro shop, 8 bay floodlit driving range and expert video tuition to name but a few.

Lying to the south of Telford the Hotel complex is close to Junctions 4 and 5 of the M54, giving easy access to both the M1 and M6 motorways.

We have 86 comfortable double/twin bedded rooms, each having en-suite bathroom and shower, colour television, direct dial telephone and tea and coffee making facilities. The Hotel prides itself on its golf course, but why not make use of our excellent indoor heated pool, squash courts, snooker and sauna, steam room, gymnasium, spa pool and solariums, before choosing from our à la carte or table d'hôte menus.

For more information on our Special Golf Weekend Classic, Summer Saver Packages, Company Golf Days, and Society Golf Days please contact the Golf Co-ordinator on (0952) 585642 or Fax (0952) 582836. Conference and meeting facilities available.

**Please note we now have full course irrigation.**

Please rush details to me on the following:

Special Golf Weekend Classic ☐

Summer Saver Packages ☐

Company Golf Days ☐

Society Golf Days ☐

Name ...........................................................................................................

Address .......................................................................................................

...................................................................................................................

**Great Hay, Sutton Hill, Telford TF7 4DT**
**Telephone: (0952) 585642      Fax: (0952) 582836      Telex: 35481**

# Hill Valley Golf & Country Club

## PLAY AND STAY
## FOR HOLIDAY, LEISURE
## AND BUSINESS GOLF

Hill Valley provides an enjoyable test of golf, ideally suited to the club and scratch golfer alike. The courses, designed by golf stars Peter Alliss and Dave Thomas, thread their challenging way through Hill Valley's trees, lakes and picturesque streams to American-style 'holding' greens trapped by sand and water. **Championship Course was designed in 1973 and opened in 1975.** The modern clubhouse overlooking the 18th green has bars, restaurant and games room and offers modern dormy-style accommodation with all facilities.

| TWO-DAY GOLF BREAKS | |
|---|---|
| Nov-Feb: | £75 per person |
| March: | £85 |
| July/Aug: | £99 |
| (4 days) | £190 |

**WINTER 'SPECIAL'**
3rd Jan – 21st Feb 1993
Any 2 nights (Sun-Thurs)
£49 per person
Friday & Sat. £59

| BED & BREAKFAST RATES | |
|---|---|
| SINGLE: | from £37.50 pp |
| TWIN: | from £27.50 pp |

'Single' supplement: £10 per person per night

**'SPECIAL' FOR GOLF SOCIETIES & COMPANY DAYS**
Programme includes: morning coffee · 9 holes play · soup and sandwich lunch · 18 hole championship course golf · roast evening meal.
£29 per person; £34 at weekends.

**WITH GOLF**
Sun-Thurs: TWIN from £55
Friday/Sat: from £60 per person per night

Hill Valley is a parkland course, 18-hole Championship, measuring 6600 yards par 72 with 9-hole par 34 and further 9-hole opening April 1993. Modern accommodation in dormy-style rooms, all en-suite with colour TV, direct-dial phone and tea/coffee making facilities. The club has snooker, squash and a large function room.

Our Sportsman's Bar and Restaurant offer table d'hôte and à la carte menus as well as bar snacks and refreshments. Health and beauty treatments available include Body Massage and Conditioning and Apidermie Facials.

*For further details and brochure please contact:*
**Hill Valley Golf & Country Club, Terrick Road, Whitchurch, Shropshire
Telephone: 0948 3584    Fax: 0948 5927**

WHITCHURCH. **Hill Valley Golf and Country Club,** Terrick Road, Whitchurch SY13 4JZ (0948 3584). *Location:* fully signposted off A41/A49 trunk road in Whitchurch. Undulating course. No 1 Course – 18 holes, 6050 yards. S.S.S. 69. No 2 Course – 18 holes, 4406 yards. S.S.S. 62. Also Par 3 9 hole course. *Green Fees:* No 1 Course – weekdays £18.00, weekends and Bank Holidays £24.00; No 2 Course – weekdays £9.00, weekends and Bank Holidays £14.00. *Eating facilities:* full restaurant and bar facilities 8am – 11pm. *Visitors:* welcome without reservation. Motel accommodation, squash, tennis, snooker room. *Society Meetings:* fully catered for every day. Professional: Tony Minshall (0948 3032). Secretary: R.B. Walker (0948 3584; Fax: 0948 5927).

WOLVERHAMPTON. **Patshull Park Hotel, Golf and Country Club,** Patshull Park, Pattingham, Near Wolverhampton WV6 7HR (Tel/Fax: 0902 700100/ 700874). *Location:* take Junction 3 off M54 turn, left on A41 back towards Wolverhampton and fork right into Albrighton. From the main crossroads turn right along Cross Road, taking T-junction with the A464 Wolverhampton/Shifnal Road and turning right towards Shifnal. Signposted Patshull Park Golf Course. Set in glorious parkland landscaped by Capability Brown; John Jacobs designed course. 18 holes, 6412 yards. S.S.S. 72. Excellent practice area. *Green Fees:* weekdays £22.50 per round; weekends £27.50 per round. *Eating facilities:* available, one restaurant and three bars, coffee shop. *Visitors:* welcome on application. 48 bedroomed hotel, leisure club and swimming pool, fishing lakes (80 acres). Residential Breaks. *Society Meetings:* corporate and society meetings welcome; special group rates and facilities. Professional: Duncan J. McDowall (0902 700342).

WORFIELD. **Worfield Golf Club,** Bridgnorth Road, Worfield, Near Bridgnorth WV15 5HE (07464 541). *Location:* A454 Wolverhampton to Bridgnorth Road, three miles from Bridgnorth. Parkland and seaside links mixture. 18 holes, 6801 yards. S.S.S. 73. Large practice area. *Green Fees:* weekdays £15.00 per round, £20.00 per day; weekends £20.00 per round, £25 per day. *Eating facilities:* dining room, bar and patio. *Visitors:* no restrictions other than weekends only from 10am. *Society Meetings:* all welcome. Professional: David Thorp (07464 372). Secretary: William Weaver (07464 541 or 546 evenings).

# Somerset

BRIDGWATER. **Enmore Park Golf Club,** Enmore, Bridgwater TA5 2AN (0278 671244). *Location:* M5 Exit 23, left at lights in town for one mile, course signposted two miles on left. Wooded parkland course on Quantock foothills. 18 holes, 6406 yards. S.S.S. 71. Practice area. *Green Fees:* £18.00/£25.00 weekdays; £25.00/ £30.00 weekends. *Eating facilities:* lunch and evening meal available. *Visitors:* welcome weekdays, weekends if no competitions. *Society Meetings:* welcome by arrangement. Professional: Nigel Wixon (0278 671519). Secretary: David Weston (0278 671481).

BURNHAM-ON-SEA. **Brean Golf Club,** Coast Road, Brean, Burnham-on-Sea TA8 2RF (0278 751570). *Location:* leave M5 at Junction 22, follow Brean signs for five miles; three miles north of Burnham-on-Sea. Flat moorland. 18 holes, 5714 yards. S.S.S. 68 (Par 69). *Green Fees:* weekdays £12.00 per round; weekends £15.00 per round. *Eating facilities:* bar snacks at Clubhouse; meals at adjoining Leisure Centre on request. *Visitors:* welcome without reservation; Saturdays and Sundays after 1pm. Large caravan park. *Society Meetings:* welcome with prior notice. Over 12 players £8.00 per round, £15.00 per day. Professional: Sue Spencer. Secretary: Bill Martin (0278 751409). Manager: Albert Clarke.

BURNHAM-ON-SEA. **Burnham and Berrow Golf Club,** St. Christopher's Way, Burnham-on-Sea TA8 2PE (Burnham-on-Sea (0278) 783137). *Location:* one mile north of Burnham-on-Sea. Leave M5 at Exit 22. Seaside links. 18 holes, 6327 yards. S.S.S. 72. *Green Fees:* £28.00 weekdays, £40.00 weekends and Bank Holidays. *Eating facilities:* catering available daily 11.00am to 6.00pm (other meals by arrangement). *Visitors:* welcome with reservation if members of a recognised golf club and with Handicap Certificate. *Society Meetings:* catered for. Professional: M. Crowther-Smith (0278 784545). Secretary: Mrs E.L. Sloman (0278 785760).

CHARD. **Windwhistle Golf, Squash and Country Club Ltd,** Cricket St. Thomas, Near Chard TA20 4DG (0460 30321; Fax: 0460 30055). *Location:* on A30 between Chard and Crewkerne, opposite Cricket St. Thomas Wildlife Park, follow signs. Unique elevated course with unsurpassed panoramic scenery, flora and fauna. 18 holes, 6500 yards. S.S.S. 71, Par 73; 9 holes, 3000 yards. S.S.S. 69, Par 70. Practice areas. *Green Fees:* on application. *Eating facilities:* comprehensive and extensive clubhouse facilities. *Visitors:* welcome weekdays, weekends and holidays, booking preferred. Senior PGA tuition available. Trolley hire. *Society Meetings:* catered for – comprehensive arrangements available. Professional: visiting. Secretary/Manager: Ian Neville Dodd.

MINEHEAD. **Minehead and West Somerset Golf Club,** The Warren, Minehead TA24 5SJ (Minehead (0643) 705095). *Location:* beside the beach at eastern end of the town, three-quarters of a mile from town centre. Flat seaside links. 18 holes, 6137 yards. S.S.S. 70. *Green Fees:* weekdays £19.50; weekends and Bank Holidays £23.00. *Eating facilities:* available at clubhouse, bar open every day. *Visitors:* welcome with tee reservation at Pro's shop. *Society Meetings:* catered for, subject to prior arrangement with the Secretary. Society groups numbering 15 or more qualify for 10% discount. Wide wheel trolleys only. Professional: Ian Read (0643 704378). Secretary: Laurie Harper (0643 702057).

SHEPTON MALLET. **Mendip Golf Club Ltd,** Gurney Slade, Shepton Mallet, Near Bath BA3 4UT (Oakhill (0749) 840570). *Location:* three miles north of Shepton Mallet (A37). Downland, undulating course. 18 holes, 6330 yards. S.S.S. 70. Practice ground. *Green Fees:* weekdays £20.00 per round, £25.00 per day (with a member £8.00); weekends and Bank Holidays £30.00 per day (with a member £10.00). *Eating facilities:* bar and restaurant open seven days a week. *Visitors:* welcome every day, telephone Professional to check availability. *Society Meetings:* catered for Mondays to Fridays by arrangement. Professional: R.F. Lee (0749 840793). Secretary: Mrs J.P. Howe (0749 840570).

STREET. **Kingweston Golf Club,** (Millfield School), Street (0458 43921). *Location:* one mile south of Butleigh Village, near Street, Somerset. Flat course – trees. 9 holes, 2378 yards. S.S.S. 62. Practice area. *Green Fees:* £2.00. *Eating facilities:* pub half a mile.

*Visitors:* welcome only with a member. Secretary: J.G. Willetts (0458 43921).

TAUNTON. **Taunton and Pickeridge Golf Club,** Corfe, Taunton TA3 7BY (0823 42240). *Location:* B3170 four miles south of Taunton, first left. Undulating parkland course. 18 holes, 5921 yards. S.S.S. 68. Practice ground. *Green Fees:* £19.00 weekdays, £25.00 weekends. *Eating facilities:* bar and dining-room. *Visitors:* by arrangement with Secretary, must produce Handicap Certificates. *Society Meetings:* catered for by arrangement. Professional: Graham Glew (0823 42790). Secretary: G.W. Sayers (0823 42537).

TAUNTON. **Taunton Golf Club,** Vivary Park, Taunton (Taunton (0823) 81946). 18 holes, 4280 yards. S.S.S. 62. *Green Fees:* information not provided.

TAUNTON. **Vivary Park Public Golf Course,** Vivary Park, Fons George, Taunton TA1 3JW. *Location:* one mile from town centre off main Wellington road. Access to course is through Vivary Park in central Taunton. Pleasant parkland course with spectacular water hazards. 18 holes, 4620 yards. S.S.S. 63. Practice ground. *Green Fees:* information not available. *Eating facilities:* restaurant and bar available. *Visitors:* always welcome but will need to book on the day of play. *Society Meetings:* catered for by prior arrangement. Professional: Jeremy Wright (0823 33875).

WELLS. **Wells (Somerset) Golf Club Ltd,** East Horrington Road, Wells BA5 3DS (Wells (0749) 672868). *Location:* one mile east of city centre opposite Mendip Hospital. Parkland, wooded. 18 holes, 5354 yards, 4950 metres. S.S.S. 66. Practice area. *Green Fees:* weekdays £16.00 per round, £19.00 per day; weekends and Bank Holidays £20.00 per round, £22.00 per day. *Eating facilities:* restaurant and bar. *Visitors:* welcome, Handicaps required weekends and no play before 9.30am weekends and Public Holidays. Caravan park adjacent. *Society Meetings:* catered for weekdays. Professional: Andrew England (0749 679059). Secretary: George Ellis (0749 675005).

YEOVIL. **Yeovil Golf Club,** Sherborne Road, Yeovil BA21 5BW (Yeovil (0935) 75949). *Location:* on A30, one mile from town centre towards Sherborne on right before Babylon Hill. Parkland. 18 holes, 6144 yards. S.S.S. 70. 9 holes, 5016 yards. S.S.S. 66. Practice ground and putting green. *Green Fees:* (18 holes course) weekdays £20.00; weekends and Bank Holidays £25.00. 9 hole course fees on application. *Eating facilities:* bars and dining room. Tuesdays 11.45am to 4.45pm only. *Visitors:* midweek unrestricted subject to Society bookings; weekends players with current handicaps only. Telephone Pro Shop to check. *Society Meetings:* welcome weekdays. Professional: G. Kite (0935 73763; Fax: 0935 78605). Secretary/Manager: J. Riley (0935 22965).

# Staffordshire

BARLASTON. **Barlaston Golf Club,** Meaford Road, Stone ST15 8UX (Barlaston (078 139) 2795). *Location:* one mile south of Barlaston off A34. 18 holes, 5800 yards. S.S.S. 68. *Green Fees:* weekdays £18.00; £22.50 weekends. *Eating facilities:* available on request in advance. *Visitors:* welcome anytime except before 10am at weekends and Bank Holidays. Professional: Ian Rogers (078-139 2795). Secretary: M.J. Degg (078-139 2867).

BURTON UPON TRENT. **Craythorne Golf Centre,** Craythorne Road, Stretton, Burton upon Trent DE13 0AZ (Burton upon Trent (0283) 64329). *Location:* A38 (Burton North) A5121 signposted Stretton. Parkland. 18 holes, 5243 yards. S.S.S. 66. Floodlit driving range. *Green Fees:* £12.00 weekdays, £14.00 Saturdays, £16.00 Sundays and Bank Holidays. *Eating facilities:* bars and restaurant open daily. *Visitors:* welcome every day, booking necessary at weekends. 9 hole pitch and putt, golf hotel. *Society Meetings:* welcome. Professional: Steve Hadfield (0283 33745). Secretary/General Manager: John Bissell (0283 37992; Fax: 0283 511908).

BURTON-ON-TRENT. **Branston Golf Club,** Burton Road, Branston, Burton-on-Trent DE14 3DP (Burton-on-Trent (0283) 43207). *Location:* A38 Junction A5121. Flat/parkland. 18 holes, 6541 yards, 5978 metres. S.S.S. 71. Practice area. *Green Fees:* weekdays £18.00, weekends £22.00. *Eating facilities:* dining room and bar. *Visitors:* welcome, weekend restrictions only. *Society Meetings:* welcome, special rates. Professional: S.D. Warner (0283 43207). Secretary: K.L. George (0283 66984).

BURTON-ON-TRENT. **Burton-on-Trent Golf Club,** 43 Ashby Road East, Burton-on-Trent DE15 0PS (Burton-on-Trent (0283) 68708). *Location:* three miles east of Burton-on-Trent on the left hand side of the A50. Undulating and mature parkland course. 18 holes, 6555 yards. S.S.S. 71. Practice ground. *Green Fees:* weekdays £20.00 per round, £25.00 per day, weekends and Bank Holidays £25.00 per round, £30.00 per day. *Eating facilities:* bar open daily, diningroom/bar snacks except Mondays. *Visitors:* welcome during the week, not weekends. Ladies' day Tuesday, therefore some restrictions. *Society Meetings:* catered for, write to enquire. Professional: Gary Stafford (0283 62240). Secretary: D. Hartley (0283 44551).

CANNOCK. **Beau Desert Golf Club,** Hazel Slade, Hednesford, Cannock WS12 5PJ (0543 422773). *Location:* A460 Hednesford, signposted. Parkland/heathland course. 18 holes, 6279 yards. S.S.S. 71. Practice ground. *Green Fees:* £30.00 weekdays. *Eating facilities:* full catering and bar. *Visitors:* welcome Monday to Thursday. *Society Meetings:* catered for. Professional: Barrie Stevens (0543 422492). Secretary: A.J.R. Fairfield (0543 422626).

CANNOCK. **Cannock Park Golf Club,** Stafford Road, Cannock WS11 2AL. *Location:* on the A34 Stafford Road. Quarter of a mile from Cannock town centre. Parkland course, playing alongside Cannock Chase. 18 holes, 5151 yards. S.S.S. 65. *Green Fees:* £4.40 weekdays, £6.60 weekends. Senior Citizen reductions and half price 16-year-olds and under.

*Eating facilities:* available. *Visitors:* welcome every day. Golf shop, inside leisure centre. *Society Meetings:* welcome weekdays. Professional/Secretary: David Dunk (0543 578850).

LEEK. **Leek Golf Club,** Birchall, Cheddleton Road, Leek (Leek (0538) 385889). *Location:* one mile south of Leek on A520. Undulating semi-moorland. 18 holes, 6240 yards. S.S.S. 70. *Green Fees:* weekdays £25.00; weekends £35.00. *Eating facilities:* full bar facilities 11.30am-2pm and 4-11.30pm. Light refreshments from 9am. *Visitors:* welcome most times by prior arrangement. *Society Meetings:* catered for by arrangement Wednesdays only. Professional: P.A. Stubbs (0538 384767). Secretary: Frank Cutts B.E.M. (0538 384779).

LEEK. **Westwood Golf Club,** Newcastle Road, Leek ST13 7AA (Leek (0538) 383060). *Location:* A53 south of Leek. Moorland/parkland. 18 holes, 6156 yards. S.S.S. 69. *Green Fees:* weekdays £15.00. *Eating facilities:* full facilities. *Visitors:* welcome weekdays, Saturdays with member, no visitors Sundays. *Society Meetings:* Mondays and Thursdays by arrangement with Secretary. Secretary: Colin Plant (0538 399119).

LICHFIELD near. **The Seedy Mill Golf Club,** Elmhurst, Near Lichfield WS13 8HE (0543 417333). *Location:* a mile north of Lichfield off the A515. Parkland with lakes, ponds and streams. 18 holes, 6247 yards. S.S.S. 70. 26 bay floodlit driving range. New Par 3 9-hole course opens Spring 1993. *Green Fees:* weekdays £16.00; weekends £20.00. *Eating facilities:* full clubhouse facilities open 7.30am to 11pm. *Visitors:* welcome at all times. *Society Meetings:* welcome weekdays and weekends. Professional: Adrian Jones. Director of Golf: Tony McGuire.

LICHFIELD. **Whittington Barracks Golf Club,** Tamworth Road, Lichfield WS14 9PW (0543 432212). *Location:* on A51 Tamworth-Lichfield Road. Wooded heathland. 18 holes, 6457 yards. S.S.S. 71. *Green Fees:* weekdays £28.00. *Eating facilities:* lunches served at club. *Visitors:* welcome with prior notification and Handicap Certificate or letter of introduction. *Society Meetings:* catered for Wednesdays and Thursdays by arrangement. Professional: Adrian Sadler (0543 432261). Secretary: D.W.J. Macalester (0543 432317).

NEWCASTLE-UNDER-LYME. **Newcastle-under-Lyme Golf Club,** Whitmore Road, Newcastle-under-Lyme ST5 2QB (0782 616583). *Location:* one mile from Newcastle on A53, Shrewsbury Road. Parkland. 18 holes, 6450 yards. S.S.S. 71. *Green Fees:* weekdays £25.00; Societies £25.00. *Eating facilities:* dining room. *Visitors:* welcome weekdays. *Society Meetings:* catered for Wednesdays and Thursdays. Professional: Paul Symonds (0782 618526). Secretary: D.B. Saunders (0782 617006).

NEWCASTLE-UNDER-LYME. **Newcastle-under-Lyme Municipal Golf Club,** Keele Road, Newcastle-under-Lyme (0782 627596). *Location:* A525 Newcastle to Whitchurch, opposite University of Keele. Undulating parkland. 18 holes, 6300 yards, 5822 metres. S.S.S. 70. Driving range. *Green Fees:* weekdays £6.50, Juniors £3.00; weekends £8.00,

Juniors £6.50. *Eating facilities:* available. *Visitors:* welcome, no restrictions but start times must be pre-booked. Professional: Mr C. Smith. Secretary: Mr G.A. Bytheway (0782 619317).

RUGELEY. **Lakeside Golf Club,** Rugeley Power Station, Armitage Road, Rugeley WS15 1PR (0889 583181 extension 2739). *Location:* nearest town Rugeley (between Lichfield and Stafford), course over power station grounds. Flat parkland adjacent River Trent. 18 holes, 5508 yards, 5037 metres. S.S.S. 67. Limited practice area. *Green Fees:* £6.00 with member. *Eating facilities:* evening snacks and bar facilities. *Visitors:* must be accompanied by member. *Society Meetings:* by arrangement. Secretary: Mr E.G. Jones (0889 584472).

STAFFORD. **Brocton Hall Golf Club,** Brocton, Stafford ST17 0TH (Stafford (0785) 662627). *Location:* off A34 Stafford to Cannock four miles south east of Stafford. Undulating parkland. 18 holes, 6095 yards. S.S.S. 69. *Green Fees:* weekdays £25.00; weekends and Bank Holidays £30.00. *Visitors:* by arrangement. *Society Meetings:* by arrangement Tuesdays and Thursdays. Professional: Bob Johnson (0785 661485). Secretary: W.R. Lanyon (0785 661901).

STAFFORD. **Ingestre Park Golf Club,** Ingestre, Near Stafford (Weston (0889) 270061). *Location:* six miles east of Stafford. Parkland. 18 holes, 6334 yards. S.S.S. 70. *Green Fees:* weekdays £20.00 before 3.30pm, £8.00 with a member; weekends £10.00 with member only. *Eating facilities:* lunch and dinner menu. *Visitors:* welcome weekdays. *Society Meetings:* welcome with reservation except Wednesday; £15.00 18 holes, £20.00 27 holes, £25.00 36 holes. Professional: Danny Scullion (0889 270304). Manager: D.D. Humphries (0889 270845).

STAFFORD. **Stafford Castle Golf Club,** Newport Road, Stafford ST16 1BP (Stafford (0785) 223821). *Location:* M6 junction 13 or 14, 2 miles from club. Parkland course. 9 holes, 6073 yards. S.S.S. 69, Par 71. *Green Fees:* £14.00 weekdays; £18.00 weekends. *Eating facilities:* snacks and full catering available except Mondays. *Visitors:* welcome except Sunday mornings. *Society Meetings:* catered for by arrangement. Secretary: M.H. Fisher.

STOKE ON TRENT. **Parkhall Golf Course,** Hulme Road, Weston Coyney, Stoke on Trent ST3 5BH (0782 599584). *Location:* one mile outside Longton. Parkland. 18 holes, 2335 yards, 2136 metres. S.S.S. 54. *Green Fees:* weekdays £4.00 adults, £2.40 juniors; weekends £4.50 adults, £3.50 juniors. *Visitors:* welcome. Seven days advance booking required for weekends and Bank Holidays. *Society Meetings:* welcome. Professional: T. Clingan.

STOKE-ON-TRENT. **Burslem Golf Club Ltd,** Wood Farm, High Lane, Tunstall, Stoke-on-Trent ST6 7ST (Stoke-on-Trent (0782) 837006). *Location:* leave Burslem centre by Hamil Road, turn left at High Lane junction, 2 miles on right. 9 holes, 5800 yards. S.S.S. 68. *Green Fees:* information not provided. *Eating facilities:* meals and refreshments by arrangement except Wednesday and Sunday. *Visitors:* welcome weekdays with reservation. Bona fide golf club members only. *Society Meetings:* catered for. Secretary: F. Askey.

STOKE-ON-TRENT. **Greenway Hall Golf Club,** Greenway Hall, Stockton Brook, Stoke-on-Trent (Stoke-on-Trent (0782) 50318). 18 holes, 5803 yards. *Green Fees:* information not provided. *Visitors:* only with member during week, not weekends.

STOKE-ON-TRENT. **Trentham Golf Club,** 14 Barlaston Old Road, Trentham, Stoke-on-Trent ST3 8HB (Stoke-on-Trent (0782) 642347). *Location:* off A34 travelling south of Newcastle (Staffs.). Turn left at Trentham Gardens on Longton Road. Turn right at National Westminster Bank. Parkland with a sprinkling of trees. 18 holes, 6644 yards. S.S.S. 72. Practice ground. *Green Fees:* £25.00 weekdays; Sundays 12 noon onwards £30.00. Playing with member £8.00. *Eating facilities:* lunches and dinners available. *Visitors:* welcome except weekends, can only play from 12 noon onwards. Handicap Certificate required. *Society Meetings:* limited numbers catered for. Professional: Mark Budz (0782 657309). Secretary: I.B. Irving (0782 658109).

STOKE-ON-TRENT. **Trentham Park Golf Club,** Trentham Park, Trentham, Stoke-on-Trent ST4 8AE. *Location:* off A34 adjoining Trentham Gardens near Junction 15 on M6. 18 holes, 6403 yards. S.S.S. 71. *Green Fees:* £20.00 weekdays, £25.00 weekends. *Eating facilities:* available at clubhouse except Mondays. *Visitors:* welcome weekdays with reservation. *Society Meetings:* catered for Wednesdays and Fridays only. Professional: R. Clarke. Secretary: C.H. Lindop (0782 658800).

STONE. **Stone Golf Club,** Filleybrooks, Stone ST15 0NB (Stone (0785) 813103). *Location:* one mile north of Stone on the A34 adjacent to the Wayfarer Hotel. Parkland. 9 holes, 6272 yards. S.S.S. 70. *Green Fees:* weekdays £15.00 per round £20.00 per day. *Eating facilities:* full meals to order, snacks always available, bar. *Visitors:* welcome weekdays only except Bank Holidays. *Society Meetings:* catered for by arrangement. Secretary: M.G. Pharaoh (08897 224).

STOURBRIDGE. **Enville Golf Club Ltd,** Highgate Common, Enville, Stourbridge DY7 5BN (Kinver (0384) 872551). *Location:* leave A449 at Stewpony Hotel taking Bridgnorth Road A458, fork right after Fox Inn following signs for Halfpenny Green Airport. Two flat wooded heathland courses. Highgate Course - 18 holes, 6556 yards. S.S.S 72; Lodge Course - 18 holes, 6217 yards. S.S.S. 70. *Green Fees:* weekdays £22.00 18 holes, £26.50 27 holes, £32.00 36 holes. *Eating facilities:* meals available except Mondays. *Visitors:* welcome weekdays with Handicap Certificate, advisable to phone prior to visit. Ladies' day, Thursday, weekends with members only. *Society Meetings:* welcome except Thursdays and weekends. Professional:

S. Power (0384 872585). Secretary/Manager: R.J. Bannister (0384 872074).

STREETLY. **Little Aston Golf Club,** Streetly (021-353 2066). *Location:* off A454. Parkland course. 18 holes, 6724 yards. S.S.S. 73. *Green Fees:* information not provided. *Eating facilities:* lunches served at club except Mondays. *Visitors:* welcome on weekdays by prior arrangement, weekends with a member. *Society Meetings:* catered for on weekdays only. Professional: John Anderson.

TAMWORTH. **Drayton Park Golf Club,** Drayton Park, Tamworth B78 3TN (Tamworth (0827) 251139). *Location:* two miles south of Tamworth on A4091, next to Drayton Manor Leisure Park. Parkland with wooded areas. 18 holes, 6214 yards. S.S.S. 70. Practice area. *Green Fees:* weekdays £25.00 per round/day. Special rates for Societies over 12. *Eating facilities:* full catering facilities. *Visitors:* welcome weekdays, weekends with member only. *Society Meetings:* catered for Tuesdays and Thursdays, booked through Secretary. Professional: M.W. Passmore (0827 251478). Secretary: A.O. Rammell (0827 251139).

TAMWORTH. **Tamworth Municipal Golf Club,** Eagle Drive, Amington, Tamworth B77 4EG (Tamworth (0827) 53858). *Location:* Junction 10 M42 direction - Amington, Tamworth, signposted. Parkland course. 18 holes, 6083 metres. S.S.S. 72. Practice area. *Green Fees:* £7.40. *Eating facilities:* bar and catering all week. *Visitors:* welcome every day, no restrictions. *Society Meetings:* welcome. Professional/Manager: Barry Jones (0827 53850).

UTTOXETER. **Uttoxeter Golf Club,** Woodgate Farm, Wood Lane, Uttoxeter ST14 8JR (Uttoxeter (0889) 565108). *Location:* approximately half a mile from Uttoxeter Racecourse. Undulating course with scenic views. 18 holes, 5700 yards, 5215 metres. S.S.S. 67. Practice net and putting area. *Green Fees:* £13.00 per day weekdays, £17.00 per day weekends and Bank Holidays. *Eating facilities:* by arrangement (not Mondays). *Visitors:* welcome, restrictions on major competition days. *Society Meetings:* welcome. Professional: Mr John Pearsall (0889 564884). Secretary: Mrs G. Davies (0889 566552).

WOLSTANTON. **Wolstanton Golf Club,** Dimsdale Old Hall, Hassam Parade, Wolstanton, Newcastle (Newcastle (0782) 616995). *Location:* one mile north of Newcastle, turn right off A34 (Dimsdale Parade), first right (Hassam Parade) then right again 75 yards. Flat parkland. 18 holes, 5807 yards. S.S.S. 68. *Green Fees:* weekdays £18.00, £7.00 as member's guest; weekends as member's guest only £18.00. *Eating facilities:* full catering service and bar. *Visitors:* welcome weekdays; weekends only as member's guest. *Society Meetings:* catered for by arrangement. Professional: (0782 622718). Secretary: D. Shelley (0782 622413).

# Suffolk

ALDEBURGH. **Aldeburgh Golf Club,** Aldeburgh (Aldeburgh (0728) 452890). *Location:* one mile from town centre on A1094. Heathland course. 18 holes, 6366 yards. S.S.S. 71; also 9 holes. *Eating facilities:* lunches served daily at club. *Visitors:* welcome all year round with introduction from own club secretary. *Society Meetings:* by special arrangement. Professional: K.R. Preston. Secretary: R.C. Van de Velde.

BECCLES. **Wood Valley (Beccles) Golf Club,** The Common, Beccles NR34 9BX (Beccles (0502) 712244). *Location:* A146 Norwich, Lowestoft, River Waveney, Church Tower, Safeway. Flat course. 9 holes, 5562 yards, 5086 metres. S.S.S. 67. *Green Fees:* weekdays £9.00 (with member £7.00); weekends and Bank Holidays £10.00 (with member £8.00). *Eating facilities:* two bars, snacks available. Meals to order. *Visitors:* welcome, must play with member on Sundays and Bank Holidays, course closed Sunday 1.30pm-5.30pm April to September. *Society Meetings:* catered for (not Sundays or Bank Holidays). Secretary: Mrs L.W. Allen (0502 712479).

BUNGAY. **Bungay and Waveney Valley Golf Club,** Outney Common, Bungay NR35 1DS (Bungay (0986) 892337). *Location:* a quarter mile from town centre and alongside A143. Flat, links-type course. 18 holes, 5950 yards. S.S.S. 68. *Green Fees:* £18.00 per day. *Eating facilities:* available. *Visitors:* welcome weekdays, weekends with member only. *Society Meetings:* by arrangement with Secretary. Professional: N. Whyte (0986 892337). Secretary: W.J. Stevens (0986 892337).

BURY ST. EDMUNDS. **Bury St. Edmunds Golf Club,** Tuthill, Fornham All Saints, Bury St. Edmunds IP28 6LG (0284 755977). *Location:* two miles from Bury St. Edmunds on A45 towards Newmarket, leave A45 at roundabout following A1106, 400 yards. Parkland. 9 holes, 2332 yards. S.S.S. 63 (18 tees). *Green Fees:* £10.00 weekdays, weekends only with member. *Eating facilities:* lunches and snacks (dinner by arrangement). *Visitors:* welcome, except weekends. *Society Meetings:* catered for. Professional: Mark Jillings (0284 755978). Secretary: C. Preece (0284 755979).

BURY ST. EDMUNDS. **Flempton Golf Club,** Flempton, Bury St. Edmunds IP28 6EQ (0284 728291). *Location:* follow A1101 from Bury St. Edmunds towards Mildenhall for about four miles, course on right. 9 holes, 6240 yards. S.S.S. 70. *Green Fees:* weekdays £17.00 per round of 18 holes, £22.00 per day, weekends only with member. *Eating facilities:* by arrangement. *Visitors:* not weekends or Bank Holidays. Must produce Handicap Certificate. Professional: G. Kitley (0284 728817). Secretary: P.H. Nunn.

BURY ST. EDMUNDS. **Fornham Park Golf Club,** The Street, Fornham All Saints, Bury St. Edmunds IP28 6JQ (0284 706777). *Location:* two miles from Bury St. Edmunds (A45), A1101 to Mildenhall through village of Fornham St. Genevieve. Flat parkland, interesting

water hazards. 18 holes, 6229 yards. S.S.S. 70. Practice ground and putting green. *Green Fees:* weekdays £15.00 per round, £20.00 per day; weekends and Bank Holidays after 1pm £25.00 per round. Reduction if playing with a member. *Eating facilities:* Lark River Restaurant and two bars. *Visitors:* welcome weekdays except Tuesdays pm after 1pm weekends. *Society Meetings:* welcome by prior arrangement. Professional/Director of Golf/Secretary: Sean Clark (0284 706777; Fax: 0284 706721).

BURY ST. EDMUNDS. **Royal Worlington and Newmarket Golf Club,** Worlington, Bury St. Edmunds IP28 8SD (Mildenhall (0638) 712216). *Location:* six miles north east of Newmarket, signposted off A11 just south of Barton Mills roundabout. 9 holes, 3105 yards. S.S.S. 70 (18 holes). Practice ground. *Green Fees:* weekdays £29.00. *Eating facilities:* lunch and tea available with prior notice; no evening meals. *Visitors:* welcome weekdays, Handicap Certificate or letter of introduction from home club required. *Society Meetings:* catered for Tuesdays or Thursdays – booking well in advance essential. Professional: M. Hawkins (0638 715224). Secretary: Colin P. Simpson (0638 712216).

COLCHESTER. **Stoke by Nayland Golf Club,** Keepers Lane, Leavenheath, Colchester CO6 4PZ (Nayland (0206) 262836). *Location:* just off A134 on B1068 towards Stoke by Nayland. Undulating parkland with water hazards. Two courses (1) Gainsborough – 18 holes, 6516 yards. S.S.S. 71. (2) Constable – 18 holes, 6544 yards. S.S.S. 71. *Green Fees:* weekdays £25.00; weekends £27.50 (handicap golfers only). *Eating facilities:* full catering and bar. *Visitors:* welcome weekdays, phone call advisable; weekends after 10.30am, must produce Handicap Certificate. Squash courts also available. *Society Meetings:* welcome weekdays, book well in advance. Professional: Kevin Lovelock (0206 262769). Secretary: Jonathan Loshak (0206 262836).

FELIXSTOWE. **Felixstowe Ferry Golf Club,** Ferry Road, Felixstowe IP11 9RY (0394 283060). *Location:* near Felixstowe Ferry, one mile north of Felixstowe. Links course. 18 holes, 6308 yards. S.S.S. 70. Practice area. *Green Fees:* £18.00 per day, weekends and Bank Holidays £21.00. *Eating facilities:* diningroom and bar. *Visitors:* welcome, but advisable to check first. Two self catering flats available, free golf included in charges. *Society Meetings:* catered for Tuesdays, Wednesdays and Fridays. Professional: Ian MacPherson (0394 283975). Secretary: Ian H. Kimber (0394 286834).

FRAMLINGHAM. **Cretingham Golf Club,** Grove Farm, Cretingham, Woodbridge IP13 7BA (Earl Soham (072882) 275). *Location:* turn off A1120 at Earl Soham, nearest town Framlingham. Parkland. 9 holes, 1955 yards. S.S.S. 30. *Green Fees:* weekdays £7.00; weekends £10.00 (for 18 holes). *Eating facilities:* hot drinks and snacks available. *Visitors:* welcome, no restrictions. Other sports facilities available. *Society Meetings:* welcome. Secretary: J. Austin.

179

HAVERHILL. **Haverhill Golf Club Ltd,** Coupals Road, Haverhill CB9 7UW (Haverhill (0440) 61951). *Location:* A604 Sturmer road turn into Chalkestone Way, near railway viaduct, right into Coupals Road. Club is one mile on right. Undulating parkland with river features. 9 holes, 5707 yards. S.S.S. 68. Practice ground. *Green Fees:* weekdays £15.00; weekends and Bank Holidays £21.00. *Eating facilities:* bar. *Visitors:* welcome at all times except when first tee booked for matches and societies. *Society Meetings:* by arrangement with Secretary. Professional: Mr S.P. Mayfield (0440 712628). Secretary: Mrs J. Webster (0440 61951).

IPSWICH. **Fynn Valley Golf Club,** Witnesham, Ipswich IP6 9JA (0473 785202). *Location:* B1077 two miles due north of Ipswich. Rolling countryside overlooking Fynn Valley. 18 holes, 5850 yards, 5400 metres. S.S.S. 68. Golf range and Par 3 course. *Green Fees:* £7.50 per 9 holes, £12.00 per 18 holes; £15.00 per day. *Eating facilities:* bar, light meals, bar snacks. *Visitors:* welcome, members only Sunday mornings, Ladies Thursdays mornings. *Society Meetings:* welcome weekdays. Professional: Robin Mann (0473 785463). Secretary: Merryn Tyrrell (0473 785267; Fax: 0473 785632).

IPSWICH. **Hintlesham Hall Golf Club,** Hintlesham, Ipswich IP8 3NS (0473 87761). *Location:* four miles west of Ipswich on the A1071 to Sudbury. Parkland, championship standard – Architect: Martin Hawtree. 18 holes, 6630 yards. S.S.S. 72. Full practice facilities. *Green Fees:* weekdays £26.00. *Eating facilities:* full

catering facilities. *Visitors:* please telephone for tee off times. Accommodation available at Hintlesham Hall Hotel. *Society Meetings:* telephone enquiries welcome. We have a growing national reputation for the organisation of golf days. Professional: Alastair Spink.

IPSWICH. **Ipswich Golf Club,** Purdis Heath, Bucklesham Road, Ipswich IP3 8UQ (Ipswich (0473) 727474). *Location:* three miles east of Ipswich on Bucklesham Road, A12 and A45. Heathland. 18 holes, 6405 yards. S.S.S. 71. 9 holes 1930 yards. S.S.S. 59. *Green Fees:* 18 hole course £28.00 weekdays, £35.00 weekends per day. 9 hole course £7.50 per day, £10.00 weekends and Bank Holidays. *Eating facilities:* full catering facilities available for visitors to 18 hole course only. *Visitors:* by prior arrangement for 18 hole course, and must produce Handicap Certificate or letter of introduction. No restriction for 9 hole course. *Society Meetings:* by special reservation only and on Society terms. Professional: S.J. Whymark (0473 724017). Secretary: Brig A.P. Wright MBE (0473 728941).

IPSWICH. **Rushmere Golf Club,** Rushmere Heath, Woodbridge Road, Ipswich IP4 5QQ (Ipswich (0473) 727109). *Location:* off A12 north from Ipswich, 300 yards signposted. Heathland course. 18 holes, 6287 yards. S.S.S. 70. Practice facilities. *Green Fees:* £18.00. *Eating facilities:* full catering available. *Visitors:* welcome except 4.30 – 5.30pm, weekends after 2.30pm. Handicap Certificate required. *Society Meetings:* welcome. Professional: N.T.J. McNeill (0473 728076). Secretary: R.W. Whiting (0473 725648).

LOWESTOFT. **Rookery Park Golf Club,** Beccles Road, Carlton Colville, Lowestoft (Lowestoft (0502) 574009). *Location:* west of Lowestoft on A146. Flat parkland. 18 holes, 6898 yards, S.S.S. 72. 9 holes par 3 course. Practice ground. *Green Fees:* weekdays £20.00; weekends £25.00. Half price when playing with a member. *Eating facilities:* full catering and two bars. *Visitors:* welcome if members of recognised golf club, please telephone before coming. *Society Meetings:* welcome. Professional: M. Elsworthy (0502 515103). Secretary: S.R. Cooper (0502 560380).

NEWMARKET. **Links Golf Club,** Cambridge Road, Newmarket CB8 0TG (Newmarket (0638) 662708). *Location:* one and a half miles south of Newmarket High Street, opposite racecourse. Relatively flat parkland. 18 holes, 6378 yards. S.S.S. 71. Two practice grounds. *Green Fees:* £22.00 weekdays; £27.00 weekends and Bank Holidays. *Eating facilities:* full service available daily. *Visitors:* current Handicap Certificate required weekdays/weekends except for members of organised golf societies. Not before 11.30am Sunday unless member's guest. *Society Meetings:* mid-week only by prior arrangement. Professional: Mr John Sharkey (0638 662395). Secretary: Mrs T. MacGregor (0638 663000)

SOUTHWOLD. **Southwold Golf Club,** The Common, Southwold (Southwold (0502) 723234). *Location:* from A12 Blythburgh turn off on A1095 to Southwold. Flat common land with sea views. 9 holes, 6050 yards. S.S.S. 69. *Green Fees:* £14.00 per round weekdays; £18.00 weekends. *Visitors:* welcome, phone for availability. *Society Meetings:* welcome, subject to availability. Professional: B.G. Allen (0502 723790). Secretary: Mr D.F. Randall (0502 723248).

STOWMARKET. **Stowmarket Golf Club Ltd,** Lower Road, Onehouse, Stowmarket IP14 3DA (0449 736473). *Location:* on B1508 from Stowmarket to Onehouse. Parkland. 18 holes, 6101 yards. S.S.S. 69. Driving range. *Green Fees:* weekdays £18.50 per day; weekends £29.00 per day. *Eating facilities:* lunches except Monday and Tuesday, snacks all week. *Visitors:* welcome, avoid Wednesdays. Handicap Certificate required at weekends. *Society Meetings:* catered for Thursdays and Fridays only. Professional: C. S. Aldred (0449 736392). Secretary: P.W. Rumball (0449 736473).

SUDBURY. **Newton Green Golf Club,** Newton Green, Sudbury (Sudbury (0787) 77501). *Location:* on A134 east of Sudbury. Flat course. 9 holes, 5488 yards, 5022 metres. S.S.S. 67. *Green Fees:* £15.00,

weekends only with member. *Eating facilities:* available. *Visitors:* welcome Monday to Friday (except Tuesday). *Society Meetings:* not more than 20 persons. Professional: K. Lovelock (0787 210910). Secretary: G. Bright (0787 77217).

THORPENESS. **Thorpeness Golf Club Hotel,** Thorpeness (Aldeburgh (0728-45) 2176). *Location:* leave A12 at Saxmundham, on to B119 then B1353. 18 holes, 6208 yards. S.S.S. 70. *Green Fees:* on application. *Visitors:* welcome without reservation. Accommodation available – 22 twin bedded rooms. *Society Meetings:* catered for. Professional: T. Pennock. Secretary: N. Griffin.

WOODBRIDGE. **Ufford Park Hotel, Golf and Leisure Centre,** Yarmouth Road, Ufford, Woodbridge IP12 1QW (0394 383555). *Location:* A12 northwards to A1152 to Melton. In Melton turn left at traffic lights one mile on the right hand side. Parkland course with 10 water hazards. 18 holes, 6078 yards (6335 Medal). S.S.S. 71. *Green Fees:* weekdays £12.00; weekends £15.00. *Eating facilities:* spikes bar, restaurant, bar and patio. *Visitors:* welcome anytime. Hotel, conference and banqueting. Large leisure centre and indoor swimming pool. *Society Meetings:* welcome. Golf Director: Jon Marks (0394 382836). Golf Co-ordinator: David Cotton.

WOODBRIDGE. **Waldringfield Heath Golf Club,** Newbourne Road, Waldringfield, Woodbridge IP12 4PT (0473 36 426). *Location:* three miles north of Ipswich off old A12. Flat easy walking heathland course. 18 holes, 6153 yards. S.S.S. 69. Limited practice area. *Green Fees:* weekdays £10.00 per round, £15.00 per day; weekends £12.00 per round. Special rates available by arrangement. *Eating facilities:* full service. *Visitors:* welcome weekdays, weekends after 12 noon. *Society Meetings:* welcome weekdays by arrangement. Professional: A. Dobson (0473 36 417). Secretary: L.J. McWade (0473 36 768).

WOODBRIDGE. **Woodbridge Golf Club,** Bromeswell Heath, Woodbridge IP12 2PF (0394 383212). *Location:* leave A12 at Melton Roundabout. After traffic lights, follow A1152 over level crossing, fork left at roundabout. Club is 400 yards on right. Heathland. 18 or 9 holes. Large practice ground. *Green Fees:* £24.00 weekdays. Societies £28.00 per round or day. *Eating facilities:* main bar, casual bar and restaurant. *Visitors:* not before 9.30am, not at weekends. Handicap Certificates mandatory. Telephone call advisable. *Society Meetings:* by prior arrangement, maximum number 36. Professional: L.A. Jones (0394 383213). Secretary: Capt L.A. Harpum RN (0394 382038).

# Surrey

BAGSHOT. **Pennyhill Park Country Club,** London Road, Bagshot GU19 5ET (0276 771774). *Location:* south west. Exit 3 of M3, about 27 miles from London, 13 miles from Heathrow. Parkland course. 9 holes, 2000 yards. *Green Fees:* available with members and residents only. *Eating facilities:* available on hotel premises. *Visitors:* welcome with members/hotel guests and at the discretion of the management. A 120 acre estate with parkland and lake. 76 bedroom hotel, clay shooting, fishing, sauna and solarium. Green fees included in accommodation rates. *Society Meetings:* on application to the Sales Office. Secretary: John Henriques.

BANSTEAD. **Cuddington (Banstead) Golf Club Ltd,** Banstead Road, Banstead SM7 1RD (081-393 0952; Fax: 081-786 7025). *Location:* 200 yards from Banstead Railway Station. 18 holes, 6352 yards, 5995 metres. S.S.S. 70. *Green Fees:* information not provided. *Visitors:* welcome with reservation. *Society Meetings:* catered for on Thursdays. Professional: J. Morgan. Secretary: D. M. Scott.

BROOKWOOD. **West Hill Golf Club,** Badshot Road, Brookwood GU24 0BH (0483 474365). *Location:* M3, Junction 3, A322 entrance adjacent railway bridge Brookwood. Heathland. 18 holes, 6368 yards. S.S.S. 70. Practice range and net. *Green Fees:* weekdays £32.00 per round, £42.00 per day. *Eating facilities:* bar snacks available, meals including dinner by prior arrangement. *Visitors:* by arrangement through the Professional. *Society Meetings:* catered for by arrangement through the Secretary. Professional: John Clements (0483 473172). Secretary: W.D. Leighton (0483 474365).

CAMBERLEY. **Camberley Heath Golf Club,** Golf Drive, Portsmouth Road, Camberley GU15 1JG (0276 23258; Fax: 0276 692505). *Location:* adjacent to Ravenswood roundabout on the A325. Heathland and pine, designed by Harry Colt – his best. 18 holes, 6402 yards, 5888 metres. S.S.S. 71. Practice ground. *Green Fees:* weekdays £30.00 per round, Saturdays accompanied by a member, £40.00 per round. *Eating facilities:* restaurants and Teppan Yaki (Japanese cuisine). *Visitors:* welcome weekdays only. *Society Meetings:* welcome by prior arrangement weekdays only. Professional: Gary Smith (0276 27905). Secretary/General Manager: J. Greenwood (0276 23258).

CARSHALTON. **Oaks Sports Centre Ltd,** Woodmansterne Lane, Carshalton SM5 4AN (081-643 8363; Fax: 081-770 7303). *Location:* on the B2032 past Carshalton Beeches Station, Oaks Sports Centre signposted north of A2022, half way between A217 and A237. Meadowland course. 18 holes, 5975 yards. S.S.S 69. 9 holes, 1590 yards. S.S.S 28. 18 bay golf range. *Green Fees:* £8.00 18 hole, £4.00 9 hole weekdays; £10.00 18 hole, £4.90 9 hole weekends. *Eating facilities:* bar lounge, restaurant (no smoking).

*Visitors:* public course, everyone welcome. Squash courts, sauna, solarium. *Society Meetings:* by arrangement. Professional: Mr G.D. Horley. Secretary: Mr J. Bremer.

CHERTSEY. **Barrow Hill Golf Club,** Longcross, Chertsey KT16 0DS. *Location:* four miles west of Chertsey. 18 holes, 3090 yards. S.S.S. 53. *Green Fees:* information not provided. *Visitors:* only with a member. *Society Meetings:* not accommodated. Secretary: R.W. Routley (0932 848117).

CHERTSEY. **Laleham Golf Club,** Laleham Reach, Mixnams Lane, Chertsey KT16 8RP (Chertsey (0932) 564211). *Location:* M25 take directions to Thorpe Park, entrance opposite through Penton Park. Parkland course. 18 holes, 6203 yards. S.S.S. 70. *Green Fees:* weekdays £23.50 per round or day (£16.00 1st November – 31st March); weekends with member only. *Eating facilities:* lunches and snacks available. *Visitors:* welcome weekdays only. *Society Meetings:* catered for Mondays to Wednesdays April to October; Monday, Wednesday and Friday November to March. Professional: T. Whitton (0932 562877). Secretary: D.G. Lee (0932 564211).

CHESSINGTON. **Chessington Golf Club,** Garrison Lane, Chessington KT9 2LW (081-391 0948). *Location:* off A243, 500 yards from Chessington World of Adventure. Opposite Chessington South Station, Junction 9 M25. Flat course. 9 holes, 1530 yards, 1401 metres. S.S.S. 28. Covered floodlit driving range. *Green Fees:* weekdays £3.10; weekends and Bank Holidays £3.75 (for 9 holes). Reductions for Juniors and Senior Citizens. *Eating facilities:* public bar and food available. *Visitors:* welcome, must book for weekend mornings. Facilities open to public 8am until 10pm seven days a week. *Society Meetings:* welcome. Professional: (081-391 0948). Secretary: Tony Maxted (081-974 1705).

CHESSINGTON. **Surbiton Golf Club,** Woodstock Lane, Chessington KT9 1UG (081-398 2056). *Location:* two miles east of Esher, off A3 at Ace of Spades roundabout. Undulating parkland. 18 holes, 6211 yards. S.S.S. 70. Limited practice area. *Green Fees:* £27.00 per round, £40.50 per day. *Eating facilities:* snacks and lunches to order by reservation weekdays. *Society Meetings:* catered for Monday and Friday only. Professional: Paul Milton (081-398 6619). Secretary: G.A. Keith MBE (081-398 3101).

CHIDDINGFOLD. **Shillinglee Park Golf Club,** Chiddingfold, Godalming GU8 4TA (Haslemere (0428) 653237; Fax: 0428 644391). *Location:* off A283 near Chiddingfold. Parkland. 9 holes, 4950 yards. S.S.S. 63. 6 hole pitch and putt course, ideal for learners. Well equipped Pro Shop. *Green Fees:* weekdays £8.50 for 9 holes, £15.00 for 18; weekends £9.00 for 9 holes,

£16.50 for 18 holes. Daily rate, plus Senior Citizens' and Junior rates. Season tickets and club membership available. _Eating facilities:_ excellent menu from snacks to à la carte. _Visitors:_ welcome at all times, advisable to book. Instruction available. _Society Meetings:_ always welcome. Professional/Secretary: Roger Mace.

CHIPSTEAD. **Chipstead Golf Club Ltd,** How Lane, Chipstead (Downland (0737) 555781). _Location:_ by Chipstead Station (Tattenham Corner Line). 18 holes, 5454 yards, 4351 metres. S.S.S. 67. _Green Fees:_ £25.00 before 2.00pm, £20.00 after 2.00pm. _Eating facilities:_ by arrangement. _Visitors:_ welcome with reservation, weekends with member. _Society Meetings:_ catered for Thursdays. Professional: Gary Torbett. Secretary: S. Spencer-Skeen.

COBHAM. **Silvermere Golf and Leisure Complex,** Redhill Road, Cobham (Cobham (0932) 866007). Individual bookings (0932) 867275). Open for the public seven days a week. Administration enquiries for Society bookings and Company days (Cobham (0932) 866007). _Location:_ from Junction 10, M25 take B366 to Byfleet, half a mile on right. From London take Cobham turn-off then A245 to Byfleet, half a mile on left into Redhill Road. London 25 minutes, Heathrow 15 minutes, Gatwick 25 minutes. Seven holes tight heathland, 10 holes open parkland, one hole (17th) completely over water. 18 holes, 6333 yards. S.S.S. 71. 34 bay floodlit (till 10.00pm) driving range. _Green Fees:_ weekdays £16.00; weekends £20.00 bookable by telephone. Members only Saturday/Sunday mornings. Professional's Golf Superstore open seven days till 10.00pm. All top named brands stocked. Clubs may be tried on range prior to purchase. _Eating facilities:_ full service from 7.00am – breakfast, lunch, snacks and dinner; bar facilities seven days a week. _Society Meetings:_ welcome, £47.50 for full day including dinner. All enquiries to Secretary. Professional: Doug McClelland PGA (0932 867275). Secretary: Mrs Pauline Devereux (0932 866007).

COULSDON. **Coulsdon Court,** Coulsdon Road, Coulsdon CR5 2LL (081-668 0414). _Location:_ off M23/M25 A23 London to Brighton road. Parkland. 18 holes, 6030 yards. S.S.S. 68. _Green Fees:_ information not available. _Eating facilities:_ elegant restaurant offering table d'hôte and à la carte menus. Two relaxing bars with top quality bar food. _Visitors:_ welcome. _Society Meetings:_ welcome. Extensive banquet and conference facilities, 35 luxurious bedrooms, all en-suite. Professional: Colin Staff (081-660 6083). General Manager: Mr MacArthur.

COULSDON. **Woodcote Park Golf Club Ltd,** Bridle Way, Meadow Hill (off Smithambottom Lane), Coulsdon (081-660 2577). _Location:_ south of Croydon, on B2030. 18 holes, 6669 yards. S.S.S. 72 _Green Fees:_

information not available. _Eating facilities:_ meals by arrangement, bar snacks. _Visitors:_ welcome with reservation. _Society Meetings:_ up to 60 catered for, by arrangement. Professional: Ian Martin (081-668 1843). Secretary: Brian Dunn (081-668 2788).

CRANLEIGH. **Fernfell Golf and Country Club,** Barhatch Lane, Cranleigh GU6 7NG (0483 268855). _Location:_ Guildford A281 Horsham take Cranleigh turn-off. Interesting parkland course. 18 holes, 5599 yards. S.S.S. 67. Par 68. _Green Fees:_ £20.00 per round, £30.00 per two rounds weekdays. _Eating facilities:_ bar, bar snacks, banqueting facilities available. _Visitors:_ welcome weekdays only. Tennis. _Society Meetings:_ welcome weekdays (£45.00). Professional: Trevor Longmuir (0483 277188). Secretary: Catherine Kimberley (0483 268855; Fax: 0483 267251).

CROYDON. **Addington Court Golf Courses,** Featherbed Lane, Addington, Croydon CR0 9AA (081-657 0281-3). _Location:_ two miles east of Croydon. Leave B281 at Addington Village. Undulating. Four courses – Old Championship 5577 yards, S.S.S. 67. New Falconwood 5513 yards, S.S.S. 66. Lower 9 hole course 1812 yards, S.S.S 62. 18 hole, Par 3 course. _Green Fees:_ £2.40 – £11.00. _Eating facilities:_ full range available. _Visitors:_ golfers and non-golfers welcome. _Society Meetings:_ catered for weekdays only. Professional/Managing Director: G.A. Cotton.

CROYDON. **Addington Palace Golf Club,** Gravel Hill, Addington, Croydon CR0 5BB (081-654 3061). _Location:_ two miles East Croydon Station. 18 holes, 6262 yards. S.S.S. 71. _Green Fees:_ information not available. _Visitors:_ welcome weekdays, weekends and Bank Holidays must be accompanied by a member. Secretary: Mr J. Robinson. Professional: J. M. Pilkington.

CROYDON. **Croham Hurst Golf Club,** Croham Road, South Croydon CR2 7HJ (081-657 2075). _Location:_ one mile from South Croydon Station, on road to Selsdon. 18 holes, 6274 yards. S.S.S. 70. _Green Fees:_ weekdays £32.00 per round/day (subject to increase). Weekends and Bank Holidays as members' guests only. _Eating facilities:_ lunches, teas, snacks. _Visitors:_ welcome with reservation on weekdays. _Society Meetings:_ catered for booked one year ahead. Professional: E. Stillwell (081-657 7705).

CROYDON. **Selsdon Park Hotel Golf Course,** Sanderstead, South Croydon, Surrey CR2 8YA (081-657 8811; Fax: 081-651 6171). _Location:_ three miles south of Croydon on A2022 Purley-West Wickham road. Parkland course, designed by J.H. Taylor. 18 holes, 6402 yards, 5854 metres. S.S.S. 71. Practice ground. _Green Fees:_ weekdays £20.00 (18), £30.00 (36); Saturdays £25.00, Sundays and Bank Holidays

£30.00. Reduced rates if starting after 4.00pm weekends, 2.00pm winter. Reduced fees for resident guests. *Eating facilities:* hotel bars, restaurant and grill. *Visitors:* welcome all week with pre-bookable tee-off times, some times reserved for hotel guests. *Society Meetings:* welcome by prior arrangement. P.G.A. Professionals: Iain Naylor, Tom O'Keefe (081-657 4129). Golf Reservations: (081-657 8811).

CROYDON. **Shirley Park Golf Club Ltd,** 194 Addiscombe Road, Croydon CR6 7LB (081-654 1143). *Location:* on A232 one mile from East Croydon Station. Parkland. 18 holes, 6210 yards. S.S.S. 70. Practice area. *Green Fees:* £26.00 weekdays. *Eating facilities:* breakfast/snack lunch/dinner, two bars. *Visitors:* welcome weekdays 9.30am/12 noon and 1pm/4pm; weekends only with a member. *Society Meetings:* catered for Tuesdays and half day Mondays, Thursdays and Fridays (afternoon). Professional: Hogan Stott (081-654 8767). Secretary: Andrew Baird (081-654 1143).

DORKING. **Betchworth Park Golf Club (Dorking) Ltd,** Reigate Road, Dorking (Dorking (0306) 885929). *Location:* on A25 one mile east of Dorking on Reigate Road. Parkland course. 18 holes, 6266 yards. S.S.S. 70. *Green Fees:* weekdays £28.00; Sunday afternoons only, £39.00. *Eating facilities:* lunches to order. *Visitors:* welcome with reservation, Handicap Certificate required. *Society Meetings:* Thursdays, catered for lunch or dinner. Professional: Rick Blackie (0306 884334). Secretary: D.A.S. Bradney (0306 882052).

DORKING. **Dorking Golf Club,** Chart Park, Dorking RH5 4BX (Dorking (0306) 886917). *Location:* on A24 half-a-mile south of junction with A25. Parkland/downland. 9 holes, alternative tees second 9, 5106 yards. S.S.S. 65. *Green Fees:* £16.00 per round. *Eating facilities:* full catering except Mondays. *Visitors:* weekdays only without reservation. *Society Meetings:* catered for up to 24, over this number by arrangement. Professional: P. Napier. Secretary: R. Payne.

DORKING. **Gatton Manor Hotel and Golf Club,** Ockley, Near Dorking RH5 5PQ (030-679 555). *Location:* one-and-a-half miles off A29 at Ockley, nine miles south of Dorking, midway between London and the coast. Undulating, wooded course with scenic water holes. 18 holes, 6903 yards. S.S.S. 72. Practice range. *Green Fees:* weekdays £26.00 per day, £15.00 per round (after 4.00pm £9.00); weekends £40.00 per day, £20.00 per round (after 4.00pm £12.00). *Eating facilities:* bar snacks and restaurant. *Visitors:* welcome every day except Sunday mornings. Conference suites, bowls, fishing, tennis. *Society Meetings:* catered for Monday to Friday only. Professional: R. Sargent (030-679 557). Managing Director: D.G. Heath (030-679 555; Fax: 030-679 713).

EAST HORSLEY. **Drift Golf Club,** The Drift, Off Forest Road, East Horsley (East Horsley (04865) 4641). *Location:* the club is located just off the Drift Road which runs between Ockham Road and Forest Road, East Horsley. 18 holes, 6414 yards. S.S.S. 71. *Green Fees:* information not provided. *Eating facilities:* restaurant/buffet service. *Visitors:* welcome Monday to Friday. *Society Meetings:* catered for. Professional: Joe Hagan. Secretary: Charles Rose.

EFFINGHAM. **Effingham Golf Club,** Guildford Road, Effingham KT24 5PZ (0372 52203). *Location:* A246 between Guildford and Leatherhead. Downland course with magnificent views towards London. 18 holes, 6488 yards. S.S.S. 71. Large practice ground. *Green Fees:* on application. *Eating facilities:* full bar and restaurant service all week. *Visitors:* welcome with reservation Monday-Friday. *Society Meetings:* Wednesdays, Thursdays, Fridays catered for. Professional: S. Hoatson (0372 52606). Secretary: Lt Col (Rtd) S.C. Manning OBE (0372 52204).

EPSOM. **Epsom Golf Club,** Longdown Lane South, Epsom KT17 4JR (Epsom (0372) 723363). *Location:* off A240 into B288, 200 yards south of Epsom Downs Station. Downland, links-type course. 18 holes, 5700 yards. S.S.S. 67. Practice nets and putting green. *Green Fees:* £14.00 weekdays, £16.50 weekends. *Eating facilities:* lounge bar, spike bar, two diningrooms with full catering facilities. *Visitors:* welcome all day Monday, Wednesday, Thursday and Fridays; after mid-day Tuesdays, weekends and Bank Holidays. Advisable to phone in advance at all times. *Society Meetings:* Wednesdays, Thursdays and Fridays, by prior arrangement through Secretary/Manager. Professional: R. Wynn (0372 721666). Secretary: Mr R.R. Fry (0372 741867).

EPSOM. **Horton Park Country Club,** Hook Road, Epsom KT19 8QG (081-393 8400). *Location:* off A3 London to Guildford Road, Epsom. Parkland. 18 holes, 5197 yards. S.S.S. 66. *Green Fees:* weekdays £10.25; weekends £13.00. *Eating facilities:* bars, restaurant and function suite. *Visitors:* welcome. *Society Meetings:* welcome except weekends. Professionals: Mr M. Hirst and Mr G. Clements (081-394 2626). Secretary: Paul Hart.

EPSOM. **R.A.C. Country Club,** Wilmerhatch Lane, Woodcote Park, Epsom KT18 7EW (0372 276311; Fax: 0372 276117). *Location:* one mile from Epsom Station. 2 courses by 18 holes. S.S.S.: Old Course 72, Coronation Course 67. *Green Fees:* information not provided. *Eating facilities:* full catering. *Visitors:* welcome with members only. *Society Meetings:* catered for by arrangement if sponsored by a member. Professional: Peter Butler (0372 276311 extension 248). Estate and Sports Manager: Keith Symons (0372 273091).

ESHER. **Moore Place Golf Club,** Portsmouth Road, Esher KT10 9LN (0372 463533). *Location:* half a mile from Esher town centre on Portsmouth Road. Parkland course with featured trees. 9 holes, 2047 yards. S.S.S. 32. Practice ground. *Green Fees:* weekdays £4.50; weekends £6.00. *Eating facilities:* two restaurants and two bars. *Visitors:* unrestricted. *Society Meetings:* welcome anytime. Professional: David Allen (0372 463533). Hon. Secretary: K.J. Sargeant (081-941 1168).

ESHER. **Sandown Golf Centre,** More Lane, Esher KT10 8AN (Esher (0372) 463340). *Location:* centre of Sandown Park racecourse. Parkland. 9 holes, 2829 yards. S.S.S. 67 (18 holes). 9-hole par 3; 9-hole Pitch and Putt. Floodlit 33-bay driving range, open until 10.30pm. *Green Fees:* £4.80 weekdays; £6.00 weekends. Subject to review. *Eating facilities:* bar and coffee shop. *Visitors:* welcome. *Society Meetings:* welcome. Professional: Neal Bedward. General Manager: Peter Barriball.

ESHER. **Thames Ditton and Esher Golf Club,** Marquis of Granby, Portsmouth Road, Esher (081-398 1551). 9 holes played twice from different tees. 5190 yards. S.S.S. 65. *Green Fees:* £10.00 weekdays, £12.00 weekends. *Eating facilities:* breakfast-lunches, evening meals served on advance bookings by arrangement. *Society Meetings:* welcome except mornings or Sundays. Professional: R. Hutton. Secretary: B.A.J. Chandler.

FARNHAM. **Farnham Golf Club Ltd,** Sands, Farnham GU10 1PX (Runfold (02518) 3163). *Location:* off A31 Crooksbury Road, Near "Jolly Farmer", signposted. Mixture of wooded parkland and heathland. 18 holes, 6313 yards. S.S.S. 70. Putting green and practice ground. *Green Fees:* £25.00 round, £30.00 day. Playing with member £10.00 per day. *Eating facilities:* three bars and diningroom, full high standard catering. *Visitors:* welcome if member of another club with Handicap Certificate. *Society Meetings:* groups up to 60 catered for, Wednesdays and Thursdays preferred. Must have Handicap Certificate. Professional: Grahame Cowlishaw (02518 2198). Secretary: James Pevalin (02518 2109).

FARNHAM. **Hankley Common Golf Club,** Tilford Road, Tilford, Farnham GU10 2DD (Frensham (025 125) 3145). *Location:* off A3, right at lights at Hindhead. Off A31 (Farnham by-pass) left at lights, three miles beyond level crossing on A287. Heathland, dry and sandy links-type course. 18 holes, 6418 yards. S.S.S. 71. Practice ground. *Green Fees:* weekdays £25.00 per round, £32.00 per day; weekends £32.00 after 2pm. *Eating facilities:* full range available, restaurant and two bars. *Visitors:* welcome weekdays, weekends after 2pm only. Handicap Certificate required. *Society Meetings:* catered for on Tuesdays and Wednesdays. Professional: Peter Stow (025125 3761). Secretary: J.K.A. O'Brien (025125 2493).

GODALMING near. **Hurtmore Golf Club,** Hurtmore Road, Hurtmore, Near Godalming GU7 2RN (0483 426492; Fax: 0483 426121). *Location:* A3 London – Portsmouth Road, Norney Hurtmore, Shackleford turnoff. Undulating parkland with large lakes. 18 holes, 5500 yards. S.S.S. 70. *Green Fees:* weekdays £15.00;

weekends £20.00. *Eating facilities:* bar, restaurant. *Visitors:* welcome, pay as you play course with 200 members. *Society Meetings:* welcome.

GODALMING. **West Surrey Golf Club,** Enton Green, Godalming GU8 5AF (Godalming (0483) 421275). *Location:* off the A3 south of Guildford, half mile past Milford Station/crossing. Wooded parkland. 18 holes, 6259 yards, 5722 metres. S.S.S. 70. Practice ground. *Green Fees:* weekdays £22.50 and £32.00; weekends £39.50. *Eating facilities:* bar, diningroom. *Visitors:* welcome, must be member of recognised golf club and have current Handicap Certificate. *Society Meetings:* catered for by prior arrangement. Professional: J. Hoskison (0483 417278). Secretary: R.S. Fanshawe (0483 421275).

GUILDFORD. **Bramley Golf Club,** Bramley, Near Guildford GU5 0AL (0483 893042). *Location:* three miles south of Guildford on the Horsham road, A281. Parkland. 18 holes, 5990 yards. S.S.S. 67. Practice area, driving range. *Green Fees:* weekdays £20.50 per round, £25.50 per day; weekends with member only. *Eating facilities:* bar, breakfast from 8am, lunches, snacks, evening meals. *Visitors:* welcome Monday to Friday. *Society Meetings:* by prior arrangement with Secretary. Professional: Gary Peddie (0483 893685). Secretary: Ms M. Lambert (0483 892696).

GUILDFORD. **Guildford Golf Club,** High Path Road, Merrow, Guildford (Guildford (0483) 63941). Steward: (0483 31842). *Location:* from Guildford take Epsom Road (A246) turn right at the third set of traffic lights. Downland course. 18 holes, 6080 yards. S.S.S. 70. Practice area. *Green Fees:* £25.00 per round, £33.00 per day weekdays; weekends with a member only. *Eating facilities:* snacks and restaurant service. *Visitors:* welcome weekdays, with member weekends. *Society Meetings:* catered for Monday to Friday. Professional: P. G. Hollington (0483 66765). Secretary: R.E. Thomas (0483 63941).

GUILDFORD. **Puttenham Golf Club,** Guildford GU3 1AL (Guildford (0483) 810498). *Location:* Farnham and Guildford, 600 yards south of Hog's Back (A31). Wooded/heathland course. 18 holes, 6220 yards. S.S.S. 70. *Green Fees:* on application. *Visitors:* welcome weekdays only by prior arrangement. (Weekends playing with a member). Handicap Certificate required. *Society Meetings:* catered for Wednesdays and Thursdays. Secretary and Professional: Gary Simmons.

HINDHEAD. **Hindhead Golf Club,** Churt Road, Hindhead GU26 6HX (Hindhead (0428) 604614). *Location:* one and a half miles north of Hindhead on A287 to Farnham. The Course is played over heathland and wooded valleys. 18 holes, 6349 yards, 5806 metres. S.S.S. 70. *Green Fees:* £41.00 weekends and Bank Holidays; £34.00 weekdays. *Eating facilities:* restaurant, snack bar, summer bar and members' bar. *Visitors:* welcome with Handicap Certificate, weekends by appointment. *Society Meetings:* Wednesdays and Thursdays only. Professional: Neil Ogilvy (0428 604458). General Manager: D. Browse.

KINGSTON-UPON-THAMES. **Coombe Hill Golf Club,** Golf Club Drive, off Coombe Lane West, Kingston KT2 7DG (081-942 2284). *Location:* from A3 take A238 to Kingston. Hilly and tree lined. 18 holes, 6040 yards. S.S.S. 71. *Green Fees:* weekdays £45.00. *Eating facilities:* diningroom 11.30am to 5pm, bar (varying hours). *Visitors:* weekdays only. *Society Meetings:* please contact Secretary. Professional: Craig De Foy (081-949 3713). Secretary: C.A. Fereday.

KINGSTON-UPON-THAMES. **Coombe Wood Golf Club,** George Road, Kingston Hill KT2 7NS (081-942 3828). *Location:* on A307. Wooded course. 18 holes, 5296 yards, 4842 metres. S.S.S. 66. *Green Fees:* weekdays £25.00, weekends with member only. *Eating facilities:* catering all week. *Visitors:* welcome weekdays. *Society Meetings:* by arrangement Wednesday to Friday. Professional: D. Butler (081-942 6764). Secretary: T. Duncan (081-942 0388).

KINGSWOOD. **Kingswood Golf and Country Club Ltd,** Sandy Lane, Kingswood, Tadworth KT20 6NE (0737 833316: Fax: 0737 833920). *Location:* five miles south of Sutton just off A217/Junction 8 M25. 18 holes, 6855 yards. S.S.S. 73. Large practice area. *Green Fees:* weekdays £28.00 per round, weekends £40.00 per round. *Eating facilities:* full range available. *Visitors:* welcome anytime, restricted times at weekends. Squash courts, snooker tables. *Society Meetings:* catered for. Professional: Mr Martin Platts (0737 832334). Administrator: Miss Lynn Thompson (0737 832188).

LEATHERHEAD. **Leatherhead Golf Club,** Kingston Road, Leatherhead KT22 ODP (0372 843966; Fax: 0372 842241). *Location:* off Junction 9 of M25, onto A243 to Kingston. Parkland, many mature trees. 18 holes, 6107 yards. S.S.S. 71. Practice ground, putting green. *Green Fees:* weekdays £30.00 one round, £35.00 two rounds; weekends £42.50 one round afternoons only. *Eating facilities:* à la carte restaurant, cafe/brasserie and lounge bar. *Visitors:* welcome, no visitors Thursday, Saturday or Sunday mornings. *Society Meetings:* welcome, from 16 to 100 by reservation. Professional: Richard Hurst (0372 843956). Secretary: W.G. Betts (0372 843966).

LEATHERHEAD. **Tyrrells Wood Golf Club Ltd,** Leatherhead KT22 8QP (Leatherhead (0372) 376025). *Location:* south-east on A24 Leatherhead by-pass after A.A. caravan, one mile left to Headley, then 200 yards right into M25. Hillside, wooded course with glorious views. 18 holes, 6234 yards. S.S.S. 70. Small practice ground. *Green Fees:* weekdays £30.00 per round, £45.00 per day; Sunday afternoons only, £40.00. *Eating facilities:* full catering and bar. *Visitors:* Handicap Certificates or proof of membership of a club required. No visitors Saturdays or Sunday mornings. *Society Meetings:* catered for by arrangement with Manager. Professional: Philip Taylor (0372 375200). Secretary: Mrs P. Humphries (0372 376025).

LINGFIELD. **Lingfield Park Golf Club,** Racecourse Road, Lingfield Park, Lingfield RH7 6PQ (0342 834602). *Location:* A22 turn off at Blindley Heath, six miles from M25 Junction 6. Parkland. 18 holes, 6500 yards. S.S.S. 72. Driving range and practice ground. *Green Fees:* weekdays £20.00 per round, £30.00 per day; weekends £30.00 per round. *Eating facilities:* snacks available all day, other catering by arrangement. *Visitors:* welcome weekdays only. Horse racing. *Society Meetings:* catered for weekdays only. Professional: Trevor Collingwood (0342 832659). Manager: Greer Milne.

MITCHAM. **Mitcham Golf Club,** Carshalton Road, Mitcham Junction, Mitcham (081-648 1508). *Location:* off A217, off A23. Flat course. 18 holes, 5935 yards. S.S.S. 68. *Green Fees:* £9.00. *Eating facilities:* meals and snacks daily. *Visitors:* welcome with restriction at weekends, book via Professional. *Society Meetings:* catered for, book through Secretary. Professional: J.A. Godfrey (081-640 4280). Secretary: C.A. McGahan (081-648 4197).

NEW MALDEN. **Malden Golf Club,** Traps Lane, New Malden KT3 4RS (081-942 0654). *Location:* half a mile from Maldon Station – near A3, between Wimbledon and Kingston. Parkland. 18 holes, 6201 yards. S.S.S. 70. *Green Fees:* weekdays £30.00, with a member £12.00; weekends £45.00, with a member £15.00. *Eating facilities:* restaurant and bar. *Visitors:* welcome weekdays, weekends restricted. Advisable to telephone Professional. *Society Meetings:* catered for Wednesday, Thursday and Friday. Professional: Robert Hunter (081-942 6009). Secretary: Peter G. Fletcher (081-942 6433).

OTTERSHAW. **Foxhills Country Club,** Stonehill Road, Ottershaw KT16 OEL (Ottershaw (0932) 872050). *Location:* 20 miles London, 10 miles London Heathrow off A320 Chertsey/Woking road behind St. Peter's Hospital. 45 holes, two 18 hole courses. Chertsey 6880 yards, S.S.S. 73. Longcross 6747 yards, S.S.S. 72. Par 3 course. *Green Fees:* weekdays £40.00. *Eating facilities:* three restaurants, service 7 days a week. *Visitors:* welcome on weekdays only. Bedroom suites, tennis, squash, two pools and health club available. *Society Meetings:* catered for by arrangement – contact Karen John. Professional: Bernard Hunt. Golf Executive: Arthur Dupuy.

OXTED. **Limpsfield Chart Golf Club,** Westerham Road, Limpsfield, Oxted RH8 OSL (0883 723405). *Location:* on A25 between Westerham and Oxted. Heathland, fairly flat course. 9 holes – alternate tees for 18 holes, 5718 yards. S.S.S. 68 men, 70 ladies. *Green Fees:* weekdays £17.00, weekends £20.00 with a member only. *Eating facilities:* by prior arrangement. *Visitors:* welcome weekdays except Thursday (Ladies'

★ **18 hole parkland course**   ★ **Restaurant**
★ **Practice ground**           ★ **Café/Brasserie**
★ **Professional's shop**        ★ **Visitors welcome**
**Kingston Road, Leatherhead KT22 ODP**
**Telephone: (0372) 843966 Fax: (0372) 842241**

Day) when only after 3.30pm. *Society Meetings:* catered for by prior arrangement. Secretary: W.G. Bannochie (0883 723405).

OXTED. **Tandridge Golf Club,** Oxted (Oxted (0883) 712274). *Location:* A25 between Godstone and Sevenoaks. 18 holes, 6260 yards. S.S.S. 70. *Green Fees:* information not provided. *Eating facilities:* full catering facilities. *Visitors:* welcome Monday, Wednesday and Thursday only. *Society Meetings:* catered for Mondays, Wednesdays and Thursdays. Professional: A. Farquhar (0883 713701). Secretary: A.S. Surnival.

PIRBRIGHT. **Goal Farm Golf Course,** Golf Road, Pirbright, Woking GU24 0PZ (0483 433183). *Location:* between Woking and Guildford, off A322. Challenging, picturesque course. 9 holes, 1273 yards. S.S.S. 48. Practice net, putting green, bunker. *Green Fees:* weekdays £2.75; weekends £3.00. *Eating facilities:* bar, light refreshments. *Visitors:* welcome, restrictions Saturday and Thursday mornings (Club Competitions). Professional: Kevin Warn. Secretary: Bruce Tapsfield.

PURLEY. **Purley Downs Golf Club,** 106 Purley Downs Road, Purley, South Croydon CR2 0RB (081-657 1231). *Location:* three miles south of Croydon, one mile east of A235. Downland (hilly). 18 holes, 6212 yards. S.S.S. 70. Practice area, nets. *Green Fees:* weekdays £25.00. Visitors are not allowed to play at weekends unless with a Full Member of the club. *Eating facilities:* diningroom, bar snacks, two bars. *Visitors:* welcome weekdays, Handicap Certificate required. *Society Meetings:* catered for Mondays and Thursdays. Professional: G. Wilson (081-651 0819). Secretary: C.H.D. Cross (081-657 8347).

REDHILL. **Redhill and Reigate Golf Club,** Clarence Lodge, Pendleton Road, Redhill (Reigate (0737) 244626). *Location:* one mile south of Reigate between A23 and A25. Well wooded course. 18 holes, 5261 yards. S.S.S. 66. Small practice area. *Green Fees:* weekdays £12.00 per round; weekends £18.00 per round. No green fees before 11.00am at weekends. No play after 2.00pm Sundays June to September. *Eating facilities:* available but very limited on Mondays. *Visitors:* welcome without reservation most days. Telephone enquiry advised weekends. *Society Meetings:* catered for by arrangement with Secretary. Professional: Barry Davies (0737 244433). Secretary: Frank R. Cole (0737 240777).

REIGATE. **Reigate Heath Golf Club,** The Clubhouse, Reigate Heath, Reigate RH2 8QR (Reigate (0737) 242610). *Location:* south of A25 on western boundary of Reigate. Heathland. 9 holes, 5554 yards. S.S.S. 67. *Green Fees:* on application. *Eating facilities:* meals by arrangement with Steward. Light lunches and snacks available except Mondays. *Visitors:* welcome

weekdays, advisable to telephone before coming. *Society Meetings:* catered for Wednesdays or Thursdays. Professional: G. Gow. Secretary: Mrs D.M. Howard (0737 245530).

RICHMOND. **Richmond Golf Club,** Sudbrook Park, Petersham, Richmond TW10 7AS (081-940 1463). *Location:* off A307 two miles south of Richmond, end of Sudbrook Lane. Parkland. 18 holes, 6602 metres, 6040 yards. S.S.S. 69. *Green Fees:* weekdays £32.00. *Eating facilities:* lunches available Monday to Friday; teas daily. *Visitors:* welcome weekdays without reservation. *Society Meetings:* welcome Tuesdays, Thursdays and Fridays by arrangement with Secretary. Professional: Nicholas Job (081-940 7792). Secretary: John F. Stocker (081-940 4351).

RICHMOND. **Royal Mid-Surrey Golf Club,** Old Deer Park, Richmond TW9 2SB (081-940 1894). *Location:* in Old Deer Park off A316 at Richmond. Parkland course. Two 18 hole courses, Inner – 5544 yards, S.S.S. 67 men, 5446 yards, S.S.S. 71 ladies; Outer – 6337 yards, S.S.S. 70 men, 5755 yards, S.S.S. 73 ladies. *Green Fees:* weekdays £43.00 Summer, £30.50 Winter. *Eating facilities:* The Buttery daily, the diningroom daily except Mondays, the bar daily. *Visitors:* welcome weekdays only, accompanied by introduction from own club. *Society Meetings:* welcome by prior arrangement. Professional: D. Talbot (081-940 0459). Secretary: M.S.R. Lunt.

SUNNINGDALE. **Sunningdale Golf Club,** Ridgemount Road, Sunningdale, Ascot SL5 9RR (0344 21681; Fax: 0344 24154). *Location:* 350 yards west of station, off A30, 25 miles from London. Heathland, 36 holes, 2 courses. *Green Fees:* weekdays £80.00 day ticket. *Eating facilities:* diningroom and three bars. *Visitors:* require introduction from Secretary of own club on weekdays. At weekends with member only. *Society Meetings:* accepted Tuesday, Wednesday, Thursday only, by arrangement. Professional: Keith Maxwell (0344 20128). Secretary: Stewart Zuill. Caddiemaster for bookings (0344 26064).

SUTTON. **Banstead Downs Golf Club,** Burdon Lane, Belmont, Sutton SM2 7DD (081-642 2284). *Location:* A217 (10 minutes from Belmont Station). 18 holes, 6190 yards. S.S.S. 69. *Green Fees:* weekdays £30.00 mornings, £20.00 afternoons. *Eating facilities:* lunches served at Club except on Mondays. *Visitors:* welcome on weekdays with letter of introduction, at weekends with member. *Society Meetings:* catered for all day Thursday and Wednesday, Friday afternoons. Professional: Ian Marr (081-642 6884). Secretary/Manager: A.W. Schooling.

TADWORTH. **Walton Heath Golf Club,** Deans Lane, Tadworth KT20 7TP (Tadworth (0737) 812060). *Location:* Junction 8 M25, A217 towards London,

B2032 towards Dorking, turning right hand side Deans Lane. Two 18 hole courses. Old – 6883 yards, S.S.S. 73. New – 6659 yards. S.S.S. 72. Practice ground and shed. *Green Fees:* £55.00 weekdays, after 11.30am £45.00. *Eating facilities:* restaurant and two bars. *Visitors:* welcome by previous arrangement, Handicap Certificate or letter of introduction required. *Society Meetings:* catered for. Professional: Ken MacPherson (0737 812152). Secretary: (0737 812380).

VIRGINIA WATER. **Wentworth Club Ltd,** Wentworth Drive, Virginia Water GU25 4LS (0344 842201/2/3; Fax: 0344 842804). *Location:* 21 miles south-west of London, just off the A30 at junction with A329 to Ascot. M25 and M3 three miles. Wooded heathland. West course – 18 holes, 6945 yards, S.S.S. 72; East course – 18 holes, 6500 yards, S.S.S. 70; Edinburgh course – 18 holes, 6979 yards, S.S.S. 73; Executive course – 9 holes. Driving range. *Green Fees:* weekdays from £55 to £80 including VAT. *Eating facilities:* diningroom, private rooms, bar. *Visitors:* welcome weekdays only by appointment. *Society Meetings:* welcome by prior arrangement. Professional: Bernard Gallacher (0344 843353). Secretary: Robbie James (0344 842201).

WALTON-ON-THAMES. **Burhill Golf Club,** Walton-on- Thames KT12 4BL (Walton (0932) 227345). *Location:* off A3 to A245, right into Seven Hills Road and again into Burwood Road or from Walton Railway Bridge through Burwood Park. 18 holes, 6224 yards. S.S.S. 70. *Green Fees:* information not provided. Professional: Lee Johnson. Secretary: M.B. Richards.

WEST BYFLEET. **West Byfleet Golf Club,** Sheerwater Road, West Byfleet KT14 6AA (Byfleet (0932) 345230). *Location:* Junction 10 M25 onto A245 – half a mile west of West Byfleet. Flat, wooded course. 18 holes, 6211 yards. S.S.S. 70. *Green Fees:* weekdays £27.00 per round, £33.00 per day. *Eating facilities:* lunches, bar snacks, teas and evening meals available. Catering: 0932 353525. Bar 0932 352501. *Visitors:* welcome weekdays with reservation, weekends with member only. *Society Meetings:* catered for, advance bookings, minimum group size 25. Professional: David Regan (0932 346584). Secretary: D.G. Smith (0932 343433).

WEYBRIDGE. **New Zealand Golf Club,** Woodham Lane, Woodham, Addlestone KT15 3QD (Byfleet (0932) 345049). *Location:* junction Woodham Lane and Sheerwater Road on A245. 18 holes, 6012 yards. S.S.S. 69. *Green Fees:* information on request. *Eating facilities:* lunch available Tuesdays to Fridays. *Visitors:* welcome Monday to Friday with reservation. *Society Meetings:* catered for Tuesday, Wednesday, Thursday and Friday. Professional: V.R. Elvidge. Secretary: Cdr J. Manley OBE RN.

WEYBRIDGE. **St. George's Hill Golf Club,** St. George's Hill, Weybridge KT13 0NL (0932 842406). *Location:* A3 off Junction 10 A3 off toward London, turn left is Byfleet, Outer estate at S.P's St. George's Hill. Hilly, Surrey heathland – well wooded with plentiful heather and rhododendron. 27 holes, 6569 yards. S.S.S. 71. *Green Fees:* £45.00 weekdays, £35.00 after 1.45pm. *Eating facilities:* diningroom, two bars. *Visitors:* by prior arrangement. *Society Meetings:* catered for on Wednesdays, Thursdays and Fridays by prior arrangement. Professional: A.C. Rattue (0932 843523). Secretary: M.R. Tapsell (0932 847758).

WOKING. **Hoebridge Golf Centre,** Old Woking Road, Old Woking GU22 8JH (0483 722611). Parkland with some trees. 18 holes, 6587 yards. S.S.S. 71. Par 3 course. (9 hole intermediate course). Covered driving range. *Green Fees:* Main Course £12.00; Intermediate £6.75; 9-hole Par 3 £6.50. *Eating facilities:* large dining room and bar. *Visitors:* welcome. *Society Meetings:* welcome weekdays. Professional/Secretary: Tim Powell.

WOKING. **Windlemere Golf Club,** Windlesham Road, West End, Near Woking (0276 858727). *Location:* off A322. Well designed parkland course. 9 holes, 2673 yards. S.S.S. 33. Floodlit 12-bay driving range. *Green Fees:* weekdays £7.00; weekends £8.50. Reduced rates for Senior Citizens and Juniors. *Eating facilities:* bar with light menu, normal clubhouse facilities. *Visitors:* always welcome, may book up to one week in advance. Snooker, pool facilities. *Society Meetings:* welcome to book. Professionals: Dave Thomas and Alistair Kelso. Secretary: Simon Hodsdon (0276 857405).

WOKING. **Woking Golf Club,** Pond Road, Hook Heath, Woking GU22 0JZ (Woking (0483) 760053). *Location:* via Hollybank Road, just south of first road

# Wentworth

*Wentworth Club, set in glorious countryside, offers one 9 and three 18-hole golf courses, tennis, and a heated outdoor swimming pool. Complementing its prestigious sporting reputation with comfortable and friendly ambience the Club is charmingly informal.*

Wentworth Club, Wentworth Drive, Virginia Water, Surrey GU25 4LS  Telephone 0344 842201

bridge over Woking/Brookwood railway. 18 holes, 6365 yards. S.S.S. 70. *Green Fees:* on application. *Eating facilities:* lunches and snacks available. *Visitors:* welcome with reservation, please telephone. *Society Meetings:* catered for. Professional: J. Thorne (0483 769582). Secretary: A.W. Riley.

WOKING. **Worplesdon Golf Club,** Woking. *Location:* off A322 Guildford, Bagshot Road, Heath House Lane, first left south of West Hill G.C. Heather parkland course. 18 holes, 6440 yards. S.S.S. 71. *Green Fees:* £50.00 per day. *Eating facilities:* lunches served at club. *Visitors:* weekdays only. *Society Meetings:* by

arrangement. Professional: Jim Christine (0483 473287). Secretary: Major R.E.E. Jones (0483 472277; Fax: 0483 473303).

WOLDINGHAM. **North Downs Golf Club,** Northdown Road, Woldingham CR3 7AA (Woldingham (0883) 653397). *Location:* Eastbourne Road roundabout at Caterham. 2 miles Woldingham road. 18 holes, 5787 yards, S.S.S. 68. *Green Fees:* enquire from Professional. *Eating facilities:* full restaurant facilities. *Visitors:* welcome with Handicap Certificate. *Society Meetings:* catered for. Professional: P. Ellis (0883 653004). Secretary: J.A.L. Smith (0883 652057).

# East Sussex

BEXHILL-ON-SEA. **Cooden Beach Golf Club,** Cooden Sea Road, Bexhill-on-Sea TN39 4TR (Cooden (04243) 2040). *Location:* A259 Eastbourne to Hastings road, follow 'Cooden Beach' sign at Little Common roundabout (one mile). Seaside course, slightly undulating. 18 holes, 6450 yards. S.S.S. 71. Practice facilities. *Green Fees:* £22.50 weekdays, weekends and Bank Holidays £27.50. *Eating facilities:* catering and bar every day. *Visitors:* welcome, preferably by prior arrangement. Accommodation for five in Club's own guest house alongside 18th green. *Society Meetings:* prior booking necessary. Professional: Keith Robson (04243 3938). Secretary: R.L. Wilkins (04243 2040). Caterers: (04243 3936).

BEXHILL-ON-SEA. **Highwoods Golf Club,** Ellerslie Lane, Bexhill-on-Sea TN39 4LJ (0424 212625). *Location:* off A259 north west of town. Parkland, wooded course. 18 holes, 6218 yards. S.S.S. 70. *Green Fees:* weekdays £22.00; weekends £25.00. *Eating facilities:* snacks always available, lunch by prior arrangement. *Visitors:* Handicap Certificate required. Sunday mornings with member only. *Society Meetings:* welcome Thursdays by arrangement. £24.00 per play green fee plus coffee/ploughmans/evening meal £13.50 approximately per head. Professional: M. Andrews (0424 212770). Secretary: J.K. McIver (0424 212625).

BRIGHTON. **Brighton and Hove Golf Club,** Dyke Road, Brighton BN1 8YJ (Brighton (0273) 507861). *Location:* south from A23, at Patcham traffic lights turn right and right again at mini roundabout to Devil's Dyke. Downland course. 9 holes, 5722 yards. S.S.S. 68. *Green Fees:* (18 holes) weekdays £15.00; weekends and Bank Holidays £20.00. *Visitors:* every day except Mondays and Tuesdays. *Visitors:* welcome without reservation. *Society Meetings:* catered for. Secretary: C. S. Cawkwell (0273 556482).

BRIGHTON. **Dyke Golf Club,** Dyke Road, Brighton BN1 8YJ (0273 857230). *Location:* off A23 on to A2038 on entering Brighton; follow signs to Devil's Dyke. Downland course. 18 holes, 6588 yards. S.S.S. 71. Practice fairway. *Green Fees:* weekdays £21.00 per round, £31.00 per day; weekends and Bank Holidays £31.00 per round. *Eating facilities:* full restaurant and bar available. *Visitors:* welcome with reservation, not Sunday mornings. *Society Meetings:* catered for by appointment, £45.00 for full day inclusive of lunch and dinner. Professional: P. Longmore (0273 857260). Secretary: (0273 857296).

BRIGHTON. **East Brighton Golf Club,** Roedean Road, Brighton BN2 5RA (Brighton (0273) 603989). *Location:* east end of Brighton just off A259, behind the

Marina. Undulating downland course. 18 holes, 6346 yards, 5802 metres. S.S.S. 70. *Green Fees:* weekdays £21.00, weekends and Bank Holidays £30.00. *Eating facilities:* diningroom and bars, lunches and teas served except Mondays. *Visitors:* welcome from 9am weekdays, after 11am weekends. *Society Meetings:* catered for weekdays (not Wednesdays) on application. Professional: W. Street (0273 603989). Secretary: K.R. Head (0273 604838).

BRIGHTON. **Hollingbury Park Golf Club,** Ditchling Road, Brighton (0273 552010). *Location:* between A23 and A27. 18 holes, 6502 yards. S.S.S. 71. *Green Fees:* weekdays £13.00 per round, £18.00 per day; weekends £15.00 per round. *Eating facilities:* full catering service seven days. *Visitors:* welcome without reservation. *Society Meetings:* catered for weekdays only. Professional: Peter Brown (0273 500086). Secretary: J. Walling.

BRIGHTON. **Pyecombe Golf Club,** Clayton Hill, Pyecombe, Brighton BN4 7FF (Hassocks (07918) 4176). *Location:* four miles north on A273 Burgess Hill Road. Downland. 18 holes, 6234 yards. S.S.S. 70. Two practice areas. *Green Fees:* weekdays £17.00, weekends and Bank Holidays £20.00. *Eating facilities:* club diningroom and bar. *Visitors:* welcome, some time restrictions. *Society Meetings:* catered for on application. Professional: C.R. White (07918 5398). Secretary: W.M. Wise (07918 5372).

BRIGHTON. **Waterhall Golf Club,** Seddlescombe Road, off Devil's Dyke Road, Brighton BN1 8YN (Brighton (0273) 508658). *Location:* three miles north

of Brighton. Downland course. 18 holes, 5773 yards, 5328 metres. S.S.S. 68. Practice area. *Green Fees:* weekdays £11.30 per round, £16.70 per day; weekends £14.00 per round. *Eating facilities:* catering available every day except Tuesdays. *Visitors:* welcome except Saturday and Sunday mornings. *Society Meetings:* catered for, except Tuesdays, weekends or Bank Holidays, by prior arrangement with Secretary. Professional: Paul Charman-Mitchell. Secretary: David Birch.

CROWBOROUGH. **Crowborough Beacon Golf Club,** Beacon Road, Crowborough (Crowborough (0892) 661511). *Location:* nine miles south of Tunbridge Wells on the A26. Heathland. 18 holes, 6279 yards. S.S.S. 70. Practice ground. *Green Fees:* £22.50 per round, £34.00 per day weekdays. *Eating facilities:* available. *Visitors:* welcome after 9.30am weekdays, not allowed at weekends. *Society Meetings:* catered for. Professional: D. Newnham (0892 653877). Secretary: M.C. Swatton (0892 661511).

EAST GRINSTEAD. **Royal Ashdown Forest Golf Club (Old Course),** Forest Row, Near East Grinstead RH18 5LR (0342 822018/823014). *Location:* four miles south of East Grinstead; take B2110 (off A22) in Forest Row and then turn right into Chapel Lane, bear left at top of Chapel Lane. Undulating heathland. 18 holes, 6477 yards. S.S.S. 71. *Green Fees:* weekdays £33.00; weekends £38.00. *Eating facilities:* lunch and tea (prior arrangement), bar snacks. *Visitors:* welcome but always phone beforehand. *Society Meetings:* catered for – prior reservation essential. Professional:

M. Landsborough (0342 822247). Secretary: D.J. Scrivens.

EASTBOURNE. **Eastbourne Downs Golf Club,** East Dean Road, Eastbourne BN20 8ES (Eastbourne (0323) 21844). *Location:* five minutes from town centre via Old Town on A259. Downland. 18 holes, 6635 yards. S.S.S. 72. *Green Fees:* weekdays £20.00; weekends £15.00. *Eating facilities:* food available except Monday and Tuesday, two bars. *Visitors:* welcome weekdays, after 1pm weekends. *Society Meetings:* catered for by arrangement. Professional: Terry Marshall (0323 32264). Secretary: D.J. Eldrett (0323 20827).

EASTBOURNE. **Eastbourne Golfing Park,** Lottbridge Drove, Eastbourne, East Sussex BN23 6QJ (Eastbourne (0323) 520400). *Location:* half a mile south of Hampden Park and one mile north of the sea. Parkland, with water on 7 of the 9 holes. 9 holes, 5046 yards. S.S.S. 65 and a 24-bay floodlit driving range. *Green Fees:* £12 weekdays, £15 weekends, plus cheaper 9-hole rounds, look out for specials. *Eating facilities:* all day snack bar and order by intercom from the course. *Visitors:* very welcome on a "pay as you play" basis, please book tee times. Professionals: Kyle Kelsall and David Ashton. Golf Director: David Ashton.

EASTBOURNE. **Royal Eastbourne Golf Club,** Paradise Drive, Eastbourne BN20 8BP (0323 30412) (Steward and Members). *Location:* one mile from town centre via Meads Road and Compton Place Road. (a) 18 holes, 6109 yards. S.S.S. 69. (b) 9 holes, 2147 yards 2. S.S.S. 61. *Green Fees:* weekdays £21.50; weekends and Bank Holidays £27.50. *Eating facilities:* full catering. *Visitors:* welcome. Handicap Certificate required Long Course only. Cottage accommodation for four people. *Society Meetings:* catered for. Professional: Richard Wooller (0323 36986). Secretary: (0323 29738).

EASTBOURNE. **Willingdon Golf Club,** Southdown Road, Eastbourne BN20 9AA (Eastbourne (0323) 410983). *Location:* north of Eastbourne, one mile from station, just off A22 at traffic lights (signposted). Downland course of particular beauty. 18 holes, 6049 yards, 5530 metres. S.S.S. 69. Practice ground and nets. *Green Fees:* weekdays £24.00; Saturdays and Bank Holidays £27.00. *Eating facilities:* diningroom, lounge and casual bar. *Visitors:* welcome after 9.00am weekdays, Saturdays check for tee bookings, not Sunday mornings, check for tee bookings. *Society Meetings:* welcome – book well in advance. Professional: J. Debenham (0323 410984). Secretary: Brian Kirby (0323 410981).

FOREST ROW. **Ashdown Forest Hotel and Royal Ashdown Forest New Course,** Chapel Lane, Forest Row RH18 5BB (0342-82 4866; Fax: 0342-82 4869). *Location:* three miles south of East Grinstead on A22 in village of Forest Row. Take Tunbridge Wells road. Chapel Lane is fourth turning on right. Undulating forest and heathland course – no sand bunkers! Adjoins Royal Ashdown Forest Old Course. 18 holes, 5549 yards. S.S.S. 67. *Green Fees:* information on request. *Eating facilities:* bar snacks, restaurant, banqueting up to 100. *Visitors:* welcome seven days of the week, best to phone in advance, specific tee time can be reserved 24 hours in advance by Access/Visa. 15 rooms available. *Society Meetings:* welcome. Professional: Martyn Landsborough (0342-82 2247). Proprietors: Mr R.L. Pratt and Mr A.J. Riddick.

HASTINGS. **Beauport Park Golf Club** (Associated to Hastings Golf Course), Battle Road, St. Leonards on Sea TN38 0TA (Hastings (0424) 851165). *Location:* A2100 Battle to Hastings Road. Parkland, wooded, hilly course. 18 holes, 6248 yards, 5767 metres. S.S.S. 70. Driving range. *Green Fees:* weekdays £10.00; weekends £12.50. *Eating facilities:* dining room. *Visitors:* welcome at all times. *Society Meetings:* catered for weekdays. Professional: M. Barton (0424 852981). Secretary: R. Thompson (0424 852977).

HEATHFIELD. **Horam Park Golf Course,** Chiddingly Road, Horam, Near Heathfield TN21 0JJ (04353 3477). Wooded course, with several lakes and ponds. 9 holes, 2911 yards. S.S.S. 68. Floodlit driving range. *Green Fees:* weekdays £8.50 for 9 holes, £14.50 for 18 holes; weekends £9.00 for 9 holes, £15.00 for 18 holes. *Eating facilities:* restaurant and bar; Golf Society catering a speciality. *Visitors:* welcome all week, advisable to book in advance. *Society Meetings:* catered for weekdays, we specialise in Company Days. Professional: Richard Foster (04353 3477). Secretary: Howard Fisher (04353 3477). Club Manager: M. Consens.

HOVE. **West Hove Golf Club,** Church Farm, Hangleton Valley, Hove BN3 8AN (Brighton (0273) 413411). *Location:* north of new bypass off A27 Link Road. Downland course, new, Hawtree designed. 18 holes, 6252 yards. S.S.S. 70. Practice range. *Green Fees:* £20.00 weekdays; £25.00 weekends. Weekdays £10.00 after 4pm. *Eating facilities:* catering and bar. *Visitors:* welcome, phone Professional. *Society Meetings:* welcome by booking. Professional: D. Mills (0273 413494). Secretary: R.W. Charman (0273 419738).

LEWES. **Lewes Golf Club,** Chapel Hill, Lewes BN7 2BB (Lewes (0273) 473245). *Location:* A27 – A22. Undulating downland with panoramic views. 18 holes, 6204 yards. S.S.S. 70. Practice area. *Green Fees:* £15.50 weekdays; £26.00 weekends. *Eating facilities:* full catering. *Visitors:* welcome without reservation. *Society Meetings:* catered for by prior arrangement. Professional: Paul Dobson (0273 483823). Secretary: R.B.M. Moore (0273 483474).

NEWHAVEN. **Peacehaven Golf Club,** The Clubhouse, Brighton Road, Newhaven BN9 9UH (0273 514049). *Location:* one mile from Newhaven on the right hand side of the main South Coast road towards Brighton and on the left hand side just out of Peacehaven. 9 holes, 5235 yards. S.S.S. 66. *Green Fees:* information not provided. *Eating facilities:* light meals unless previously ordered. *Visitors:* welcome without reservation. *Society Meetings:* catered for up to 20. Professional: G. Williams. Secretary: D. Wright.

RYE. **Rye Golf Course,** Camber, Rye (Rye (0797) 225241). *Location:* A259 from Rye, take Camber road to coast. Seaside links. 18 holes, 6310 yards. S.S.S. 71. 9 holes, 6141 yards. S.S.S. 71. *Green Fees:* information not provided. *Eating facilities:* lunch and tea only, but not Tuesdays. Bars. *Visitors:* welcome, only playing with a member or on introduction by a member. *Society Meetings:* very limited. Professional: Peter Marsh (0797 225218). Secretary: Commander J.M. Bradley (0797 225241).

SEAFORD. **Seaford Head Golf Club,** Southdown Road, Seaford (Seaford (0323) 890139). *Location:* midway between Eastbourne and Brighton on A259. 18 holes, 5812 yards. S.S.S. 68. *Green Fees:* information not provided. *Eating facilities:* at Club by appointment. *Visitors:* welcome without reservation. *Society*

*Meetings:* catered for by written appointment. Professional: A.J. Lowles. Secretary: A.T. Goodman.

SEAFORD. **Seaford Golf Club,** East Blatchington, Seaford BN25 2JD (Seaford (0323) 892597). *Location:* turn inland at War Memorial in Seaford, follow the road for one and a quarter miles. Downland course. 18 holes, 6233 yards, 5700 metres. S.S.S. 70. Practice ground. *Green Fees:* weekdays £30.00 (£24.00 after 12 noon, £14.00 after 3pm). *Eating facilities:* diningroom for all meals and bar snacks available in the bar. *Visitors:* welcome weekdays other than Tuesdays. Telephone first. *Society Meetings:* catered for Wednesdays, Thursdays and Fridays if club members with Handicap Certificates. Residential accommodation for 18 guests. Professional: P. Stevens (0323 894160). Secretary: M.B. Hichisson (0323 892442).

SEDLESCOMBE. **Aldershaw Golf Club,** Sedlescombe TN33 0SD (0424 870898; Fax: 0424 870855). *Location:* A21 near Sedlescombe. Gently undulating parkland. 9 holes, 3109 yards. S.S.S. 70. Driving range. *Green Fees:* weekdays £12.00 18 holes; weekends £15.00 18 holes. 9 hole rates available. *Eating facilities:* bar and snacks always available. *Visitors:* welcome, telephone for booking details. *Society Meetings:* contact Professional for availability. Professional: Mike Palmer.

UCKFIELD. **East Sussex National Golf Club,** Little Horsted, Uckfield TN22 5TS. *Location:* off the A22 Eastbourne road following the Uckfield by-pass, 30 minutes from Gatwick. American style, wooded, bent grasses. Two courses; 1: 18 holes, 7081 yards. S.S.S. 74 Championship; 2: 18 holes, 7154 yards. S.S.S. 74 Championship. 3 hole teaching academy, driving range. *Green Fees:* £60.00 per round, £80.00 per day. Twilight rate of £30.00 from 4.30pm (May 31st to September 30th). *Eating facilities:* full restaurant facilities. *Visitors:* welcome anytime booking seven days in advance. Luxury country house hotel accommodation. *Society Meetings:* minimum 12 people, booking allowed six months in advance. Professional: Mr Greg Dukart (0825 841217). C E O: Rt Hon. John Sinclair (0825 750577).

UCKFIELD. **Piltdown Golf Club,** Piltdown, Uckfield TN22 3XB (0825 722033). *Location:* one mile west of Marefield off A272, signposted Isfield. Undulating

---

Enjoy the ultimate golfing break by choosing the luxury of Horsted Place country house hotel combined with the supreme excellence of the East Sussex National Golf Club. Half price green fees are available to resident guests and there is also a range of attractive mid-week packages. Other leisure facilities include a heated indoor swimming pool, all-weather tennis court and croquet lawn.

## EAST SUSSEX
### NATIONAL GOLF CLUB
See also our colour display on page 8.

gorse and heather. 18 holes, 6070 yards. S.S.S. 69. Practice ground, putting green. *Green Fees:* any day round or day £30.00. *Eating facilities:* bar, full catering – please telephone to book. *Visitors:* welcome but must bring Handicap Certificate or letter of introduction from own club Secretary. Some time restrictions. Jacket and tie obligatory in lounge and diningroom. Smart dress on course. *Society Meetings:* catered for by arrangement Mondays, Wednesdays and Fridays only. Professional: John Amos (0825 722389). Secretary: J.C. Duncan (0825 722033).

WADHURST. **Dale Hill Golf Club,** Ticehurst, Wadhurst TN5 7DQ (0580 200113). *Location:* on B2087, one mile off A21, 50 miles south of London, 16 miles north of Hastings. Wooded/parkland course. 18 holes, men 6063 (5221 ladies) yards, S.S.S. 69 (ladies 70.) Practice area and green, indoor practice area. *Green Fees:* weekdays £20.00; weekends £25.00. Reductions for SCGU members. *Eating facilities:* breakfast and dinner to order, lunches and snacks always available. *Visitors:* welcome with reservation, handicap players only at weekends. 27-room luxury hotel with leisure centre. *Society Meetings:* catered for by prior arrangement. Professional: Ian Connelly (Director of Golf) (0580 201090). Secretary: L.E. Irvine (0580 200112).

# West Sussex

ANGMERING. **Ham Manor Golf Club Ltd,** Angmering BN16 4JE (0903 783288). *Location:* on A259 between Worthing and Littlehampton. 18 holes, 6216 yards. S.S.S. 70. *Green Fees:* on application. *Eating facilities:* lunches served at club except on Mondays. *Visitors:* welcome with reservation. Handicap Certificate required. *Society Meetings:* catered for weekdays only. Professional: Simon Buckley. Secretary: P.H. Saubergue.

BOGNOR REGIS. **Bognor Regis Golf Club,** Downview Road, Felpham, Bognor Regis (Bognor Regis (0243) 865867). *Location:* turn north at traffic lights on A259 at Felpham village. Flat parkland. 18 holes, 6238 yards. S.S.S. 70. Practice area. *Green Fees:* £24.00 weekdays, £30.00 weekends and Bank Holidays. *Eating facilities:* bar snacks available most days. *Visitors:* welcome weekdays, weekends only with a member. Handicap Certificate required. *Society Meetings:* catered for, minimum 20. Professional: R. Day (0243 865209). Secretary: B.D. Poston (0243 821929).

CHICHESTER. **Goodwood Golf Club,** Goodwood, Chichester PO18 0PN (Chichester (0243) 774105). *Location:* three and a half miles north east Chichester on Racecourse Road. Downland course, hilly with fine views to Isle of Wight. 18 holes, 6383 yards. S.S.S. 70. Limited practice only. *Green Fees:* weekdays £25.00, weekends and Bank Holidays £35.00. *Eating facilities:* bar meals at all times, others by prior arrangement. *Visitors:* welcome most days except during competitions, advisable to phone prior to play. Handicap Certificates required at all times. *Society Meetings:* limited to Wednesdays and Thursdays only. Professional: Keith MacDonald (0243 774994). Secretary: Colin Pickup (0243 774968).

CHICHESTER. **Selsey Golf Club,** Golf Links Lane, Selsey, Chichester (0243 602203/602165). *Location:* B2145, seven miles south of Chichester. Flat course. 9 holes playing 18, 5932 yards. S.S.S. 68. *Green Fees:* information not available. *Eating facilities:* lunches served at club. *Visitors:* welcome weekends and Bank Holidays only if holding a bona fide Handicap Certificate or playing with a member. *Society Meetings:* catered for weekdays only. Professional: P. Grindley. Secretary: E.C. Rackstraw (0243 602029).

CRAWLEY. **Copthorne Golf Club,** Borers Arms Road, Copthorne, Crawley RH10 3LL (Copthorne (0342) 712033). *Location:* off Exit 10 M23, one mile on A264 towards East Grinstead. Flat wooded course. 18 holes, 6505 yards. S.S.S. 71. Practice area. *Green Fees:* weekdays £25.00 per round, £33.00 per day; weekends £45.00 after 1pm. Half fees if playing with member. *Eating facilities:* catering all day, bar. *Visitors:* welcome weekdays without reservation, after 1pm weekends. *Society Meetings:* catered for Thursdays and Fridays. Professional: Joe Burrell (0342 712405). Secretary: J. Appleton (0342 712508; Fax: 0342 717682).

CRAWLEY. **Cottesmore Golf and Country Club,** Buchan Hill, Pease Pottage, Crawley RH11 9AT (Crawley (0293) 528256). *Location:* Junction 11 of M23, signposted Pease Pottage. Wooded course. 36 holes, Old Course – 6100 yards. S.S.S. 70. New Course – 5700 yards. S.S.S. 68. Practice ground. *Green Fees:* £27.00 Old Course, £16.00 New Course weekdays, £34.00 Old Course, £20.00 New Course weekends. *Eating facilities:* three bars, two dining-rooms, licensed spikes bar with snacks. *Visitors:* welcome anytime except weekends and Bank Holidays when they can play after 11am. Full health club with all facilities. En-suite accommodation available. *Society Meetings:* catered for. Professional: Steve Laycock (0293 535399). Secretary: Vaughan Williams (0293 529196).

CRAWLEY. **Ifield Golf and Country Club,** Rusper Road, Ifield, Crawley RH11 0LW (Crawley (0293) 513627). *Location:* outskirts of Crawley near A23 to Glossops Green. Parkland. 18 holes, 6314 yards. S.S.S. 70. Practice area. *Green Fees:* £27.00 per round or day, £20.00 after 1pm. *Eating facilities:* all day bar and catering. *Visitors:* welcome Monday, Tuesday and Wednesday afternoons, Thursday, Friday till 3.30pm. *Society Meetings:* catered for. Professional: Jon Earl (0293 523088). Secretary: Brian Gazzard (0293 612973).

CRAWLEY. **Tilgate Forest Golf Centre,** Titmus Drive, Tilgate, Crawley RH10 5EU (0293 530103). *Location:* one mile off the M23 Junction 10 Pease Pottage. Take signs for Crawley and follow signs for Tilgate Park. Wooded. 18 holes, 6127 yards. S.S.S. 69. Also 9 hole course. Driving range. *Green Fees:* weekdays £11.00; weekends £15.00. Twilight half price. *Eating facilities:* restaurant and bar. *Visitors:* welcome anytime. Pay as you play. Pro shop. *Society Meetings:* welcome, contact Sheila Bevan. Professional: H. Spencer.

EAST GRINSTEAD. **Chartham Park,** Lingfield Road, Felcourt, East Grinstead RH19 2JT (0342 870340; Fax: 0342 870719). *Location:* Lingfield Road off A22 on north side of East Grinstead. Parkland. 18 holes, 6680 yards. S.S.S. 72. Practice area, putting green. *Green Fees:* £23.00 per round weekdays; £29.00 per round weekends. £35.00 day ticket. *Eating facilities:* light snacks and refreshments available all day. *Visitors:*

pre-booking required. Golf carts and trolleys can be hired. *Society Meetings:* by prior arrangement. Secretary: Lindsey Irvine.

EAST GRINSTEAD. **Holtye Golf Club,** Holtye Common, Cowden, Near Edenbridge TN8 7ED (0342 850635). *Location:* four miles east of East Grinstead on A264, seven miles west of Tunbridge Wells. Undulating forest course; alternate tees. 9 holes, 5265 yards. S.S.S. 66. Large practice ground. *Green Fees:* information not available. *Eating facilities:* available by arrangement. *Visitors:* welcome, restrictions Thursday and weekend mornings. *Society Meetings:* catered for. Professional: Kevin Hinton (0342 850635). Secretary: J.P. Holmes (0342 850576).

EFFINGHAM. **Effingham Park Golf Club,** Copthorne Effingham Park Hotel, Copthorne (0342 716528). *Location:* Junction 10 M23, two miles east on A264. Wooded parkland around lake. 9 holes, 1750 yards. S.S.S. 57. *Green Fees:* information not provided. *Eating facilities:* Wellingtonia Restaurant, McLaren Restaurant and Charlie's Bar. *Visitors:* not before 1pm at weekends or on a Tuesday evening. Four star Hotel on site and leisure club. *Society Meetings:* catered for on request. Professional: I. Dryden. Secretary: Mr J.O'Donovan.

HAYWARDS HEATH. **Haywards Heath Golf Club,** High Beech Lane, Haywards Heath RH16 1SL (Haywards Heath (0444) 414310). *Location:* two miles north of Haywards Heath. Parkland. 18 holes, 6204 yards. S.S.S. 70. Practice area. *Green Fees:* weekdays £20.00 per round £25.00 for more than 18 holes; weekends and Bank Holidays £25.00 per round, £30.00 for more than 18 holes. *Eating facilities:* bar and catering both available. *Visitors:* by arrangement, phone Professional. *Society Meetings:* catered for Wednesdays and Thursdays only, numbers over 20. Professional: M. Henning (0444 414866). Secretary: John Duncan (0444 414457).

HORSHAM. **Mannings Heath Golf Club,** Goldings Lane, Mannings Heath, Near Horsham RH13 6JU (Horsham (0403) 210228; Fax: 0403 270974). *Location:* three miles south-east of Horsham off A281, seven miles west of M23. Undulating wooded course with featured streams. 18 holes, 6402 yards. S.S.S. 71. Restricted practice area and net. *Green Fees:* weekdays £25.00; weekends £33.00. *Eating facilities:* bar and diningroom (not Mondays); bar hours 11am-11pm. Caterers: (0403 210168). *Visitors:* welcome weekdays and weekends, can book tee reservation one week in advance. Handicap Certificate essential. *Society Meetings:* welcome during week, full or half day. Professional: (0403 210332). Director of Golf: J.D. Owen. Golf Administrator: J.D. Windwood.

HORSHAM near. **Slinfold Park Golf Club,** Stane Street, Slinfold, Near Horsham RG13 7RE (0403 791154). *Location:* A29 Slinfold, near Horsham. Wooded parkland with lakes and streams. 18 holes. S.S.S. 72. 9 hole course, driving range, practice course. *Green Fees:* weekdays £18.00 18 hole course, £6.00 9 hole course; weekends £25.00 18 hole course, £8.00 9 hole course. *Eating facilities:* full restaurant and bar facilities. *Visitors:* welcome at all times. Pro shop

194

Society Meetings: bookings taken. Professionals: George McKay and Donald Slicer. Secretaries: David Drew and Colin Duncton.

LITTLEHAMPTON. **Littlehampton Golf Club,** 170 Rope Walk, Riverside West, Littlehampton BN17 5DL (Littlehampton (0903) 717170). *Location:* leave A259 one mile west of Littlehampton at sign. Seaside links. 18 holes, 6244 yards. S.S.S. 70. *Green Fees:* £22.00 weekdays, £30.00 weekends. *Eating facilities:* restaurant and two bars. *Visitors:* welcome weekdays, weekends after midday, but phone prior to arrival. *Society Meetings:* recognised societies only. Professional: Neill Thirkell (0903 716369). Secretary: Keith Palmer.

MIDHURST. **Cowdray Park Golf Club,** Midhurst GU29 0BB (0730) 812088). *Location:* one mile east of Midhurst on A272. Undulating parkland. 18 holes, 6212 yards. S.S.S. 70. Two practice grounds. *Green*

*Fees:* £20.00 weekdays, £25.00 weekends. Reduction when playing with member. *Eating facilities:* available. *Visitors:* welcome weekends only after 11.00am. *Society Meetings:* catered for except Tuesdays, Fridays, weekends and Bank Holidays. Professional: Stephen Hall (0730) 812091). Secretary: Mrs J.D. Huggett (0730) 813599).

PULBOROUGH. **West Sussex Golf Club,** Hurston Warren, Pulborough RH20 2EN (Pulborough (07982) 2563). between Storrington and Pulborough on the A283. Heathland. 18 holes, 6221 yards. S.S.S. 70. Large practice ground. *Green Fees:* on application. *Eating facilities:* lunch and tea daily, bars. *Visitors:* welcome by prior arrangement (not Tuesdays). No three or four balls. *Society Meetings:* catered for Wednesdays and Thursdays. Professional: T. Packham (07982 2426). Secretary: G.R. Martindale (07982 2563).

# NOTE

All the information in this book is given in good faith in the belief that it is correct. However, the publishers cannot guarantee the facts given in these pages, neither are they responsible for changes in policy, ownership or terms that may take place after the date of going to press. Readers should always satisfy themselves that the facilities they require are available and that the terms, if quoted, still apply.

## West Chiltington Golf Club

Tel: (0798) 813574
Fax: (0798) 812631

**Broadford Bridge Road, West Chiltington, West Sussex RH20 2YA**

All facilities are open to the public. 27 hole course . . . 18 hole course 5939 yards par 72 and 9 hole course par 3 1360 yards. Bar and restaurant open all day every day. 18 bay driving range (8 covered). Golf societies and company days welcome. Set in a unique position with spectacular views over the South Downs. Resident golf professional is Ryder Cup star Brian Barnes.

WEST CHILTINGTON. **West Chiltington Golf Club,** Broadford Bridge Road, West Chiltington RH10 2YA (0798 813574; Fax: 0798 812631). *Location:* A29 Bognor from London Road, left at Adversane village B2132 then signposted. Gently undulating parkland with spectacular views of South Downs. 18 holes, 6389 yards. S.S.S. 69. 9 holes, 1360 yard short pitch and putt course ideal for beginners. 13 bay driving range. *Green Fees:* weekdays £14.00; weekends £19.00. *Eating facilities:* bar and restaurant open all day every day. *Visitors:* always welcome, smart dress. *Society Meetings:* welcome, apply to Secretary. Professionals: Brian Barnes/Roland Tisdall (0798 812089). Secretary: S.G. Coulson.

WORTHING. **Hill Barn Golf Course,** Hill Barn Lane, Worthing BN14 9QE (Worthing (0903) 233918). *Location:* signposted on the roundabout at the top of Broadwater, Worthing on the A27. Downland course with a few trees but generally fairly open. 18 holes, 6224 yards. S.S.S. 70. Small practice area (balls not provided) and putting green. *Green Fees:* weekdays £10.00, weekends £11.70. Juniors £4.50 weekdays only. *Eating facilities:* clubhouse and bar. *Visitors:* welcome at all times. *Society Meetings:* catered for by pre-booking, 25 people minimum. Professional: A.P. Higgins (0903 237301). Secretary: M. Pettit (0903 207179).

WORTHING. **Worthing Golf Club,** Links Road, Worthing BN14 9QZ (Worthing (0903) 260801; Fax: 0903 694664). *Location:* on A27 near junction with A24 (Offington Roundabout). Two downland courses. Lower course: 18 holes, 6519 yards. S.S.S. 72. Upper course: 5243 yards. S.S.S. 66. *Green Fees:* weekdays £28.00 per day, weekends and Bank Holidays £35.00 per day. *Eating facilities:* first class restaurant facilities. *Visitors:* welcome, check in advance with Secretary. No visitors during December, January and February. *Society Meetings:* catered for by arrangement. Professional: Stephen Rolley (0903 260718). Secretary: D. Morgan (0903 260801).

# Tyne & Wear

BIRTLEY. **Birtley (Portobello) Golf Club,** Birtley Lane, Birtley (Tyneside (091-4102207). *Location:* off A1 (M) Chester-le-Street, A647 to Birtley. 9 holes, 5660 yards. S.S.S. 67. *Green Fees:* information not available. *Visitors:* not allowed after 2pm on Fridays or at weekends unless accompanied by a member. *Society Meetings:* only by special arrangement. Secretary: B. Richardson.

CHOPWELL. **Garesfield Golf Club,** Chopwell NE17 7AP (Ebchester (0207) 561278). *Location:* leave A694 at Rowlands Gill, follow signposts for Chopwell, approximately three miles. Parkland, wooded. 18 holes, 6203 yards. S.S.S. 70. *Green Fees:* weekdays £11.00 per round, £14.00 per day; weekends and Bank Holidays after 4.30pm, £14.00. Reduced for parties over 20 with prior booking. *Eating facilities:* full catering and bar service. *Visitors:* welcome weekdays, weekends after 4.30pm. *Society Meetings:* by arrangement. Secretary: J.R. Peart (0207 561309).

EAST BOLDON. **Boldon Golf Club Ltd,** Dipe Lane, East Boldon (Wearside (091-536) 4182). *Location:* near Sunderland approximately one mile from rounda-

bout at junction of A19 and A1 highways. Fairly flat parkland. 18 holes, 6348 yards. S.S.S. 70. *Green Fees:* £12.00 weekdays, £15.00 weekends. Reduced rates for parties of over 20. *Eating facilities:* bar snacks and restaurant. *Visitors:* welcome, not between 9am and 10am, 12.30pm and 1.30pm and 4.30pm and 6.00pm. Not before 3.30pm at weekends. *Society Meetings:* catered for. Professional: Phipps Golf (091-536 5835). Hon. Secretary: R.E. Jobes (091-536 5360).

GATESHEAD. **Heworth Golf Club,** Gingling Gate, Heworth, Gateshead (091-4692137). *Location:* A1 (M) south east boundary of Gateshead. Flat wooded course. 18 holes, 6437 yards. S.S.S. 71. *Green Fees:* £15.00 weekdays; £18.00 weekends. *Eating facilities:* diningroom except Wednesdays. *Visitors:* weekdays up to 4pm, no visitors Saturdays; but after 10am or Sundays. *Society Meetings:* mid-week only. Secretary G. Holbrow (091-4699832).

HEDDON-ON-THE-WALL. **Close House Golf Club,** Heddon-on-the-Wall, Newcastle-upon-Tyne NE15 0HT (0661 852953). *Location:* nine miles west of city on A69. Parkland/part wooded. 18 holes, 558 yards. S.S.S. 67. Private golf club. *Eating facilities:* b arrangement with Steward (Mr R. Nairn). *Visitors:* with member only. *Society Meetings:* weekdays only by arrangement with Secretary. Secretary: to be appointed.

HOUGHTON-LE-SPRING. **Houghton-le-Spring Golf Club,** Copt Hill, Houghton-le-Spring (Tyneside (091) 5841198). *Location:* off A690 Durham Road, take Houghton to Seaham road, course is situated at the top of Copt Hill bank. Testing hillside course. 18 holes, 6416 yards, 5867 metres. S.S.S. 71. *Green Fees:* weekdays £12.00, weekends £18.00. *Eating facilities:* available most days, bar open every day. *Visitors:* welcome most days but not on competition days (Sundays). *Society Meetings:* catered for by arrangement. Professional: S.J. Bradbury (091-584 7421). Secretary: N. Wales (091-528 5481).

NEWCASTLE UPON TYNE. **City of Newcastle Golf Club,** Three Mile Bridge, Gosforth, Newcastle upon Tyne NE3 2DR (091-285 1775). *Location:* B1318 three miles north of city. Flat parkland. 18 holes, 6510 yards. S.S.S. 71. *Green Fees:* weekdays £18.50; weekends and Bank Holidays £20.50. *Eating facilities:* bar, meals (not Mondays). *Visitors:* welcome without reservation, restricted times Fridays and no visitors on men's competition days. *Society Meetings:* very welcome. Professional/Secretary: A.J. Matthew (091-285 5481).

NEWCASTLE UPON TYNE. **Gosforth Golf Club,** Broadway East, Gosforth, Newcastle upon Tyne NE3 5ER (091-285 6710). *Location:* three miles north of Newcastle city centre, on A6127. Parkland with stream. 18 holes, 6030 yards. S.S.S. 69. *Green Fees:* weekdays £18.00; weekends and Bank Holidays £18.00 only after 4pm. £6.00 at all times as member's guest. *Eating facilities:* full catering except Mondays, order in advance. *Visitors:* welcome weekdays. *Society Meetings:* catered for by arrangement with the Secretary. Not weekends or Bank Holidays. Professional: D. Race (091-285 0553). Secretary: A. Sutherland (091-285 3495).

NEWCASTLE UPON TYNE. **Newcastle United Golf Club,** 60 Ponteland Road, Cowgate, Newcastle upon Tyne NE5 3JW (Tyneside (091-2864693). *Location:* two miles west of city centre in direction of airport. Moorland. 18 holes, 6573 yards, 6010 metres. S.S.S. 71. Practice area. *Green Fees:* weekdays £11.50 (£6.50 with member); weekends £14.50. *Eating facilities:* bar meals available. *Visitors:* no restrictions midweek, welcome weekends if no competitions. *Society Meetings:* welcome, book through Secretary. Professional: Brian Hall. Golf Shop: (091-2869998). Secretary: J. Simpson.

NEWCASTLE UPON TYNE. **Parklands Golf Club,** High Gosforth Park, Newcastle upon Tyne NE3 5HQ (091-236 4867). *Location:* just off A1 north of Newcastle, follow signs for Gosforth Park. Parkland. 18 holes, 6060 yards, 5530 metres. S.S.S. 71. 9 holes pitch and putt, 45 bay floodlit driving range. *Green Fees:* weekdays £9.00, weekends £11.00. *Eating facilities:* restaurant and bar. *Visitors:* welcome, no restrictions. *Society Meetings:* catered for. Professional: Malcolm Leighton (091-236 4480). Secretary: Brian Woof (091-236 4480).

NEWCASTLE UPON TYNE. **The Northumberland Golf Club Ltd,** High Gosforth Park, Newcastle upon Tyne NE3 5HT (Tyneside (091-236 2498). *Location:* off A1. 18 holes, 6629 yards. S.S.S. 72. *Green Fees:* £27.50 per round, £33.00 two rounds. *Visitors:* welcome with prior reservation or introduction. *Society Meetings:* catered for except on Mondays, Wednesdays and weekends. Secretary: M.E. Anderson (091-236 2498).

NEWCASTLE UPON TYNE. **Tyneside Golf Club Ltd,** Westfield Lane, Ryton NE40 3QE (091-413 2177). *Location:* seven miles west of Newcastle upon Tyne, off A695 in Ryton Village. Parkland, hilly with water hazards. 18 holes, 6042 yards, 5522 metres. S.S.S. 69. Practice field. *Green Fees:* weekdays £16.00, weekends £25.00. *Eating facilities:* full catering. *Visitors:* bona fide golfers welcome. *Society Meetings:* by arrangement with Secretary, weekdays only. Professional: M. Gunn (091-413 2177). Secretary: J.R. Watkin (091-413 2742).

NEWCASTLE UPON TYNE. **Westerhope Golf Club,** Whorlton Grange, Westerhope, Newcastle-upon-Tyne NE5 1PP (Tyneside (091-2869125). *Location:* A69, Jingling Gate Public House. Parkland/wooded. 18 holes, 6468 yards, 5912 metres. S.S.S. 71. Two practice areas. *Green Fees:* weekdays £14.00, £8.00 with a member; weekends £10.00 with a member only. All day £18.00, with a member £12.00. *Eating facilities:* lunches and high teas. *Visitors:* welcome weekdays, weekends and Bank Holidays with a member only. *Society Meetings:* by appointment. Professional: N. Brown (091-2860594). Secretary: J.W. Hedley (091-2867636).

NEWCASTLE-UPON-TYNE. **Hobson Municipal Golf Club,** Hobson, Burnopfield, Newcastle-upon-Tyne (0207 70941). *Location:* on main Newcastle to Consett road. Fairly flat, well designed course. 18 holes, 6582 yards, 6018 metres. S.S.S. 71. Practice area. *Green Fees:* weekdays £8.00 per round; weekends £10.00 per round. *Eating facilities:* bar, lounge and restaurant. *Visitors:* no restrictions; booking system at weekends. *Society Meetings:* by prior arrangement with Professional (all bookings). Professional: J.W. Ord (0207 71605). Secretary: R.J. Handrick (0207 570189).

NEWCASTLE-UPON-TYNE. **Whickham Golf Club,** Hollinside Park, Whickham, Newcastle-upon-Tyne NE16 5BA (091-488 7309). *Location:* five miles south west of Newcastle. Parkland. 18 holes, 6179 yards. S.S.S. 69. *Green Fees:* information not available. *Eating facilities:* lunches, teas, evening meals available by prior order. *Visitors:* welcome without reservation. *Society Meetings:* catered for by arrangement. Professional: Brian Ridley (091-488 8591). Secretary: N. Weightman (091-488 1576).

RYTON. **Ryton Golf Club,** Dr. Stanners, Clara Vale, Ryton NE40 3TD (091-413 3737). *Location:* off A695 at Crawcrook to Clara Vale. 18 holes, 6034 yards. S.S.S. 69. *Green Fees:* weekdays £13.00 per day; weekends £13.00 per round. *Eating facilities:* available by arrangement with Steward. *Visitors:* welcome weekdays, weekends with member. Visiting parties weekends one round only. *Society Meetings:* catered for by arrangement with Secretary. Secretary: Mr F.R. Creed.

SHIREMOOR. **Backworth Golf Club,** The Hall, Backworth, Shiremoor (Tyneside (091) 2681048). *Location:* from Newcastle to Shiremoor Crossroads then left for one mile. 9 holes, 5930 yards. S.S.S. 69. *Green Fees:* information not provided. *Visitors:* welcome by arrangement.

SOUTH SHIELDS. **South Shields Golf Club Ltd,** Cleadon Hills, South Shields NE34 8EG (Tyneside (091-456) 0475). *Location:* near A19 and A1 M, Cleadon Chimney prominent landmark. 18 holes, 6264 yards, 5729 metres. S.S.S. 70. *Green Fees:* weekdays £20.00; weekends and Bank Holidays £25.00. *Eating facilities:* meals available at all times, bar. *Visitors:* welcome at all times without reservation. *Society Meetings:* catered for. Professional: Gary Parsons (091-456 0110). Secretary: W.H. Loades (091-456 8942).

SOUTH SHIELDS. **Whitburn Golf Club,** Lizard Lane, South Shields NE34 7AF (Wearside (091-529) 2144). *Location:* between Sunderland and South Shields adjoining Coast Road. 18 holes, 6046 yards. S.S.S. 69. *Green Fees:* weekdays £15.00, introduced by and playing with member £8.00. Saturdays, Sundays and Bank Holidays £20.00, introduced by and playing with a member £10.00. *Eating facilities:* available. *Visitors:* welcome except on Saturday or Sunday when competitions being held and restricted Tuesdays (Ladies' Day). *Society Meetings:* catered for on weekdays by prior reservations. Professional: D. Stephenson (091-529 4210). Secretary: Mrs V. Atkinson.

SUNDERLAND. **Wearside Golf Club,** Cox Green, Sunderland SR4 9JT (091-534 2518). *Location:* on south bank of River Wear, one mile west of A19. From A19 exit for A183, direction Chester-le-Street, at 200 yards turn right, signposted Offerton/Cox Green, then left at T junction, down hill over humped bridge.

Parkland, bordered on north by River Wear, deep wooded gully traverses course. 18 holes, 6323 yards. S.S.S. 70. 4 holes par 3 field and separate practice tees. *Green Fees:* weekdays £20.00; weekends and Bank Holidays £25.00. *Eating facilities:* full catering and bar service. *Visitors:* welcome most times, telephone Professional for information. *Society Meetings:* by advance application. Professional: Mr Steven Wynn (091-534 4269). Secretary: N. Hildrew (091-534 1193).

WALLSEND. **Wallsend Golf Club,** Bigges Main, Wallsend. *Location:* western boundary. Parkland. 18 holes, 6608 yards, 6324 metres. S.S.S. 72. *Green Fees:* weekdays £10.00; weekends £12.00. *Eating facilities:* meals available on request. *Visitors:* restricted weekends – not before 12.30pm April to October. *Society Meetings:* weekdays only. Professional: K. Phillips (091-262 4231). Secretary: L. Rowe (091-262 1973).

WASHINGTON. **Washington Moat House Golf Club,** Stonecellar Road, Washington NE33 1PH (091-4172626). *Location:* half a mile from A1 M junction A184. Parkland. 18 holes, 6604 yards, 6038 metres. S.S.S. 72. *Green Fees:* weekdays £13.00; weekends £19.00. *Eating facilities:* fully licensed hotel on site. *Visitors:* by arrangement. Special rates for visiting parties of over 15 mid-week. Hotel with 150 plus bedrooms. *Society Meetings:* by arrangement. Professional: David Howdon (091-4178346). Secretary: D.V. Duffy (091-4162609).

WHITLEY BAY. **Whitley Bay Golf Club,** Claremont Road, Whitley Bay NE26 3UF (Tyneside (091-252 0180). *Location:* north side of town. Undulating parkland. 18 holes, 6617 yards. S.S.S. 72. *Green Fees:* information not provided. *Eating facilities:* available except on Mondays. *Visitors:* welcome with reservation weekdays, weekends only with member. *Society Meetings:* catered for by arrangement with Secretary. Professional: W.J. Light (091-252 5688). Secretary: B. Dockar (091-252 0180).

# Warwickshire

ATHERSTONE. **Atherstone Golf Club,** The Outwoods, Coleshill Road, Atherstone CV9 2RL (Atherstone (0827) 713110). *Location:* five miles north of Nuneaton and seven miles south of Tamworth. Undulating parkland. 11 holes (18 played), 6239 yards. S.S.S. 70. Practice ground. *Green Fees:* £17.00 weekdays, £7.00 with a member; Saturdays with member only. *Eating facilities:* bar and dining room. *Visitors:* welcome weekdays without reservation, Saturdays with member only, not Sundays. Ladies' Day Wednesday. *Society Meetings:* on application to Secretary. Professional: (0827 713110). Secretary: V.A. Walton (0827 892568).

KENILWORTH. **Kenilworth Golf Club Ltd,** Crew Lane, Kenilworth (0926 54038). *Location:* A429 Coventry to Kenilworth adjacent to A46 Coventry to Warwick Road. Parkland and wooded course. 18 holes, 6410 yards. S.S.S. 71. Practice ground and 9 hole Par 3 course. *Green Fees:* £25.00 weekdays, £37.15 weekends and Bank Holidays. *Eating facilities:* diningroom, bar snacks, two bars. *Visitors:* must be members of another club with official Handicap Certificate. *Society Meetings:* groups (under 20 in number) weekdays, Societies (over 20) Wednesday only. Professional: S. Yates (0926 512732). Secretary: J.S. Morrison (0926 58517).

LEAMINGTON SPA. **Leamington and County Golf Club,** Golf Lane, Whitnash, Leamington Spa (Leamington Spa (0926) 420298). *Location:* two miles south of town centre of Royal Leamington Spa. 18 holes, 6430 yards, 5878 metres. S.S.S. 71. *Green Fees:* information not provided. *Eating facilities:* luncheons, teas, evening meals and snacks. *Visitors:* welcome without reservation. *Society Meetings:* catered for. Professional: I. Grant (0926 428014). Secretary: S.M. Cooknell (0926 425961).

LEAMINGTON SPA. **Newbold Comyn Golf Club,** Newbold Terrace East, Leamington Spa (0926 421157). *Location:* central, off Willes Road B4099. Parkland, front 9 hilly, back 9 flat. 18 holes, 6259 yards, 5719 metres. S.S.S. 70. Pitch and putt course 9 holes. *Green Fees:* 18 holes – weekdays £6.30, weekends £8.00; 9 holes – weekdays £4.00, weekend and Bank Holidays £5.80. *Eating facilities:* restaurant and bar. *Visitors:* welcome, unrestricted. *Society Meetings:* catered for, book through Professional. Professional: D.R. Knight (0926 421157). Secretary: A.A. Pierce (0926 422660).

NORTH WARWICKSHIRE. **Purley Chase Golf and Country Club "1990",** Ridge Lane, Near Nuneaton CV10 0RB (Chapel End (0203) 397468). *Location:* three miles off A5 between Atherstone and Nuneaton. Slightly undulating. 18 holes, 6650 yards, 6040 metres. S.S.S. 71. Driving range. *Green Fees:* weekdays £18.00; weekends £25.00. Reductions if member's guest. *Eating facilities:* restaurant. *Visitors:* welcome all the time. *Society Meetings:* all welcome, special rates. Professional/Secretary: David Llewellyn (0203 395348 or 393118).

NUNEATON. **Nuneaton Golf Club,** Golf Drive, Whitestone, Nuneaton CV11 6QF (Nuneaton (0203 383281). *Location:* Junction 3 off M6. Wooded course. 18 holes, 6429 yards. S.S.S. 71. Practice ground. *Green Fees:* weekdays £22.00, with a member £6.00; weekends £22.00 playing with a member only. *Eating facilities:* catering available except Mondays; bar open usual hours. *Visitors:* welcome weekdays. *Society Meetings:* Wednesdays and Fridays only, must clear tee by 2pm on Fridays. Professional: (0203 340201). Secretary/Manager: G. Pinder (0203 347810).

RUGBY. **Rugby Golf Club,** Clifton Road, Rugby CV21 3RD (0788 542306). *Location:* one mile from Rugby town centre on the Clifton road. Parkland course. 18 holes, 5457 yards. S.S.S. 67. Practice ground. *Green Fees:* £18.00 per round (£6.00 with a member), £25.00 per day. *Eating facilities:* bar and diningroom, meals served daily except Tuesdays. *Visitors:* welcome weekdays, weekends and Bank Holidays only with a member. Ladies' Day Wednesday. Snooker room. *Society Meetings:* welcome if pre-booked. Professional: D. Sutherland (0788 575134). Secretary: J.B. Poxon.

STRATFORD-UPON-AVON. **Stratford Oaks Golf Club,** Bearly road, Snitterfield, Stratford-upon-Avon CV37 0JH (0789 731571; Fax: 0789 731700). *Location:* from Junction 15 off M40 head south to Stratford-upon-Avon, take signpost to Snitterfield and club is between Snitterfield and Bearly. Flat parkland with lakes. 18 holes, 6500 yards. S.S.S. 72. 26 bay floodlit driving range. *Green Fees:* weekdays £12.00; weekends £15.00. Juniors half price. *Eating facilities:* available. *Visitors:* welcome, no restrictions. *Society Meetings:* catered for, no restrictions. Professional: Derwynne Honnan. Secretary: Paul Davidson.

*If you are writing, a stamped, addressed envelope is always appreciated.*

**The Crown & Cushion Hotel & Leisure Centre**

**Nr. Oxford, Chipping Norton OX7 5AD.**

500 year old Coaching Inn, tastefully modernised to provide 40 excellent en-suite bedrooms. Some 4 Poster suites. "Old World Bar", log fires, real ale, good food. Indoor pool, Squash court, Multi gym, Solarium, (full sized snooker table subject to availability). A fully equipped modern conference centre. Hotel located in a picturesque Cotswold town midway between Oxford and Stratford-upon-Avon. Convenient for London, Heathrow Airport and M40 Motorway. Blenheim Palace, Warwick Castle, Broadway, Bourton-on-the-Water, Bibury, Stow-on-the-Wold, Shakespeare Country are all nearby. Price Busters start at just £19.50 or B&B plus full Restaurant Dinner at just £32. Lyneham Golf Club (18 hole, Tel: 0993 831841) is just 4 miles away and costs £12 midweek, £15 weekends per round. Chipping Norton Golf Club (18 hole, Tel: 0608 642383) costs £22 mid-week.

**For colour brochure, freephone 0800 585251 or fax: 0608 642926**      ETB ♨♨♨♨ Approved

---

STRATFORD-UPON-AVON. **Stratford-on-Avon Golf Club,** Tiddington Road, Stratford-upon-Avon CV37 7BA (0789 297296). *Location:* half a mile from town on B4086. Flat parkland. 18 holes, 6309 yards. S.S.S. 70. Practice ground. *Green Fees:* weekdays £25.00; weekends £33.00. *Eating facilities:* full catering/bar service. *Visitors:* welcome any time subject to domestic commitments. *Society Meetings:* catered for Tuesdays and Thursdays. Professional: N.D. Powell (0789 205677). Secretary: J.H. Standbridge (0789 205749).

STRATFORD-UPON-AVON. **Welcombe Hotel Golf Course,** Warwick Road, Stratford-upon-Avon CV37 0NR (0789 299012). *Location:* exit M40 at Junction 15, follow signs to Stratford. Club is on A439 after five miles. Or take A439 out of town and club is on left after one mile. Parkland (once owned by Shakespeare). 18

holes, 6202 yards. S.S.S. 70. Practice area and putting green. *Green Fees:* weekdays £25.00; weekends and Bank Holidays £35.00. *Eating facilities:* bar serving pub style food. *Visitors:* welcome subject to availability. Hotel on site, four star facilities. *Society Meetings:* weekdays by prior arrangement, rates on request. Golf Manager: P.J. Day (0789 299012).

WARWICK. **Warwick Golf Club,** Warwick Golf Centre, Racecourse, Warwick (Warwick (0926) 494316). *Location:* off M40, from A41/A46 junction, travel half a mile towards Warwick, turn right into racecourse. Flat parkland. 9 holes, 2682 yards. S.S.S. 66. Driving range (floodlit). *Green Fees:* weekdays £3.80 per 9 holes, weekends £5.50 per 9 holes. *Eating facilities:* bar, no catering. *Visitors:* welcome any time except Sunday mornings. Professional: S. Hutchinson. Secretary: R. Dunkley.

# West Midlands

BIRMINGHAM. **Brandhall Golf Club,** Heron Road, Oldbury, Warley B68 8AQ (021-552 7475). *Location:* Junction 2 M5, A4123, right at traffic lights, signposted from there. Wooded course. 18 holes, 5734 yards, 5243 metres. S.S.S. 68. Practice area. *Green Fees:* weekdays £5.75; weekends £6.50. *Eating facilities:* cafe and bar. *Visitors:* welcome, no restriction except weekends. Tee reserved for club members only Saturdays 8-10am and Sundays 8-10.30am. *Society Meetings:* phone Pro Shop (021-552 2195) to book times. Professional: Garry Mercer. Secretary: D. Wood (0676 42482).

BIRMINGHAM. **Cocks Moors Woods Golf Club,** Alcester Road, Kings Heath, Birmingham B14 4ER (021-444 3584). *Location:* A435 Kings Heath, nearest motorway M42. Parkland/wooded course. 18 holes, 5820 yards. S.S.S. 69. *Green Fees:* £6.20 weekdays and weekends. *Eating facilities:* full catering and bar. *Visitors:* welcome at all times. Full range of leisure facilities within complex. *Society Meetings:* not catered for. Professional: Steve Ellis. Secretary: Glyn Spencer.

BIRMINGHAM. **Edgbaston Golf Club,** Church Road, Edgbaston, Birmingham B15 3TB (021-454 1736). *Location:* from centre of city take A38 (Bristol Road). After one mile and at second traffic lights turn right into Priory Road, at end turn left into Church Road, club entrance 200 yards on left. Parkland course. 18 holes, 6172 yards. S.S.S. 69. *Green Fees:* weekdays £30.00; weekends £35.00. Playing with a member £8.00. *Eating facilities:* lunches and teas daily except Sundays, other meals by arrangement. *Visitors:* welcome. Must have Handicap Certificate. *Society Meetings:* catered for by arrangement with Secretary. Professional: A.H. Downes (021-454 3226; Fax: 021 454 8295). Secretary: Lt Col G. Donald MBE.

BIRMINGHAM. **Gay Hill Golf Club,** Hollywood Lane, Hollywood, Birmingham B47 5PP (021-43 6523). *Location:* M42 Junction 3, three miles. Parkland/wooded course. 18 holes, 6532 yards. S.S.S. 71. Practice area. *Green Fees:* £28.50 weekdays. *Eating facilities:* available. *Visitors:* welcome all week; weekends by invitation only. *Society Meetings:* catered for by arrangeme

Thursdays. Professional: Andrew Hill (021-474 6001). Secretary: Mrs E.K. Devitt (021-430 8544).

BIRMINGHAM. **Great Barr Golf Club,** Chapel Lane, Great Barr, Birmingham B43 7BA (021-357 1232). *Location:* six miles north-west of Birmingham M6 Junction 7. 18 holes, 6545 yards. S.S.S. 72. *Green Fees:* £25.00 weekdays and weekends. *Eating facilities:* meals served, order in advance. *Visitors:* welcome weekdays, restricted at weekends. Weekends maximum handicap 18. Handicap Certificate required. *Society Meetings:* small groups catered for. Professional: S.M. Doe (021-357 5270). Secretary: Mrs J.S.Pembridge (021-358 4376).

BIRMINGHAM. **Handsworth Golf Club,** 11 Sunningdale Close, Handsworth Wood, Birmingham B20 1NP (021-554 0599). *Location:* M5 Junction 1. A41 left at first lights, left at next set of lights, second left, second left/M6 Junction 7. A34 Birmingham Road, Old Walsall Road, Vernon Avenue, Westover Road, Craythorne Avenue. Parkland course. 18 holes, 6272 yards, 5733 metres. S.S.S. 70. Large practice area and putting green. *Green Fees:* £25.00 per day, £7.00 with a member; weekends with member only, £10.00. *Eating facilities:* bar snacks to à la carte menu in restaurant. *Visitors:* welcome weekdays with Handicap Certificate. *Society Meetings:* catered for by arrangement with Secretary. Special packages available. Professional: Mr L. Bashford (021-523 3594). Secretary: P.S. Hodnett (021-554 3387).

BIRMINGHAM. **Harborne (Church Farm) Golf Club,** Vicarage Road, Harborne, Birmingham B17 0SN (021-427 1204). *Location:* signposted from Harborne Centre. Parkland. 9 holes, 4062 yards. S.S.S. 63. *Green Fees:* on application. *Eating facilities:* lunches and sandwiches available anytime. *Visitors:* welcome anytime. *Society Meetings:* by arrangement with the Professional. Professional: Mark Hampton. Secretary: Keith Williams (021-427 7889).

BIRMINGHAM. **Harborne Golf Club,** 40 Tennal Road, Harborne, Birmingham B32 2JE (021-427 1728). *Location:* A4123, A456, B4124 three miles west Birmingham city centre. Undulating parkland/moorland. 18 holes, 6240 yards, 5703 metres. S.S.S. 70. *Green Fees:* weekdays £27.00; weekends and Bank Holidays £10.00 (must play with a member). *Eating facilities:* bar and dining area, daily except Mondays. *Visitors:* must be members of golf club with Handicap Certificate. *Society Meetings:* Wednesday to Friday. Special rates for parties over 20 players. Professional: A. Quarterman (021-427 3512). Secretary: E.J. Humphreys (021-427 3058).

BIRMINGHAM. **Harborne Municipal Golf Club,** Vicarage Road, Harborne, Birmingham B17 0SN (021-427 1204). *Location:* A456 to Harborne Village then course is signposted. Parkland course, beware of rooks! 9 holes, 2366 yards. S.S.S. 63. *Green Fees:* information not available. *Eating facilities:* restaurant. *Visitors:* welcome anytime. Free car parking. *Society Meetings:* welcome weekdays only. Professional: M.J. Hampton (021-427 1204). Secretary: K. Williams (021-427 1204).

BIRMINGHAM. **Hatchford Brook Golf Club,** Coventry Road, Sheldon, Birmingham B26 3PY (021-743 9821). *Location:* A45 next to Birmingham Airport, M6 Exit 4. North of M42 Junction 6. Parkland. 18 holes, 6157 yards. S.S.S. 69. Practice ground. *Green Fees:* £5.60 per round weekdays; £6.00 per round weekends. *Eating facilities:* cafe/restaurant. *Visitors:* welcome without reservation. Professional: P. Smith. Secretary: D. Williams (0676 23383).

BIRMINGHAM. **Hilltop Public Golf Course,** Park Lane, Handsworth, Birmingham B21 8LJ (021-554 4463). *Location:* M5 exit West Bromwich, take Birmingham road first left past W.B.A. football ground. Parkland, gently sloping fairways, large greens. 18 holes, 6114 yards. S.S.S. 69. *Green Fees:* weekdays £5.40 per round, weekends £6.20 per round. *Eating facilities:* cafe serving drinks and hot meals. *Visitors:* welcome anytime, Municipal course. *Society Meetings:* bookings available through Professional. Professional: Kevin Highfield. Secretary: M. Adams.

BIRMINGHAM. **Kings Norton Golf Club Ltd,** Brockhill Lane, Weatheroak, Alvechurch, Birmingham B48 7ED (Wythall (0564) 822821). *Location:* M42 Junction 3, towards Birmingham. Sign on left to Weatheroak, follow for two miles, over first crossroads. Club on left hand side. Parkland. 27 holes, 7000 yards. S.S.S. 72. *Green Fees:* £27.00 per round; £29.50 per day. *Eating facilities:* available. *Visitors:* welcome weekdays only, weekends with member. *Society Meetings:* catered for weekdays only. Professional: C. Haycock (0564 822822). Secretary: L.N.W. Prince (0564 826789).

BIRMINGHAM. **Maxstoke Park Golf Club,** Castle Lane, Coleshill, Birmingham B46 2RD (Coleshill (0675) 462158). *Location:* three miles north east of Coleshill on B4114, turn right for Maxstoke. Parkland with trees and lake. 18 holes, 6478 yards, 5925 metres. S.S.S. 71. Two practice areas. *Green Fees:* £22.00 per round, £32.00 per day. *Eating facilities:* restaurant and bar. *Visitors:* welcome weekdays only, weekends with member. *Society Meetings:* catered for. Professional: R.A. Young (0675 464915). Secretary: J.C. Evans.

BIRMINGHAM. **Moseley Golf Club,** Springfield Road, Kings Heath, Birmingham B14 7DX (021-444 2115). *Location:* south Birmingham. 18 holes, 6227 yards. S.S.S. 70. *Green Fees:* £30.00. *Eating facilities:* in clubhouse. *Visitors:* welcome only by prior arrangement with Secretary. *Society Meetings:* catered for. Professional: G. Edge (021-444 2063). Secretary: P. Muddiman (021-444 4957 10am-1pm).

BIRMINGHAM. **North Worcestershire Golf Club,** Frankley Beeches Road, Northfield, Birmingham B31 5LP (021-475 1026). *Location:* from city centre main Bristol road (A38) to Northfield, turning right into Frankley Beeches Road by Black Horse Public House. Parkland, established inland course. 18 holes, 5954 yards. S.S.S. 69. *Green Fees:* £20.50 weekdays. *Eating facilities:* full restaurant and bar. *Visitors:* welcome weekdays without reservation. *Society Meetings:* catered for Mondays and Thursdays. Professional: K.E. Jones (021-475 5721). Secretary: B.C. Lediard (021-475 1026).

COVENTRY. **Ansty Golf Club,** Brinklow Road, Ansty, Coventry CV7 9HZ (0203 621347). *Location:* Junction 2 M6, head toward Ansty/Shilton, turn right onto Brinklow Road. Parkland. 18 holes, 5628 yards, 5146 metres. S.S.S. 67. Driving range. *Green Fees:* weekdays £9.00; weekends £11.00. Reductions for Juniors and Senior Citizens. *Eating facilities:* full restaurant/bar. *Visitors:* always welcome. Network Golf Shop. *Society Meetings:* welcome. Professional and Secretary/Manager: John Kennedy (0203 621341).

COVENTRY. **Brandon Wood Golf Course,** Brandon Lane, Wolston, Near Coventry CV8 3GQ (0203 543133). *Location:* six miles south of Coventry off southbound carriageway A45. Parkland on banks of River Avon. 18 holes. 6610 yards, 6043 metres. S.S.S. 72. 11 bay floodlit driving range. *Green Fees:* telephone Professional for details. *Eating facilities:* bar and restaurant. *Visitors:* unrestricted.*Society Meetings:* phone for details. Professional/Secretary: Chris Gledhill (0203 543141).

COVENTRY. **City of Coventry Golf Club,** Brandon Lane, Wolston, Near Coventry CV8 3GQ (Coventry (0203) 543133). *Location:* six miles south-east from City centre off A45. Parkland on banks of River Avon. 18 holes, 6610 yards. S.S.S. 72. Floodlit driving range. *Green Fees:* please telephone Secretary for details. *Eating facilities:* licensed bar and restaurant. *Visitors:* anytime – advance bookings available anyday up to seven days in advance on payment of one green fee – telephone bookings available 24 hours in advance. *Society Meetings:* telephone Professional for details. Professional/Secretary: C. Gledhill (0203 543141).

COVENTRY. **Coventry Golf Club,** Finham Park, Coventry CV3 6PJ (Coventry (0203) 411123). *Location:* on A444 south of A45, one mile on left. Parkland, wooded. 18 holes, 6613 yards. S.S.S. 72. Practice ground. *Green Fees:* on application. *Eating facilities:* available. *Visitors:* welcome weekdays only, without reservation. *Society Meetings:* catered for on Wednesdays and Thursdays by arrangement. Rates dependent on numbers. Professional: P. Weaver (0203 411298). Secretary: J.E. Jarman (0203 414152).

COVENTRY. **Coventry Hearsall Golf Club,** Beechwood Avenue, Coventry CV5 6DF (Coventry (0203) 675809). *Location:* off A46 south of Coventry, one mile south of city centre. 18 holes, 5958 yards. S.S.S. 69. *Green Fees:* Mondays to Fridays £23.00, weekends only as guest of a member. *Eating facilities:* full restaurant facilities. *Visitors:* welcome weekdays. *Society Meetings:* limited. Professional: (0203 713156). Secretary: W.G. Doughty (0203 713470).

COVENTRY. **Forest of Arden Hotel, Golf and Country Club,** Maxstoke Lane, Meriden, Coventry CV7 7HR (0676 22335). *Location:* three miles from Junction 6 off M42, three miles from Junction 4 off M6; very close to N.E.C. Two 18 hole parkland courses. The Arden – 6915 yards. S.S.S. 73; The Aylesford – 6525 yards. S.S.S. 71. *Green Fees:* on application. *Eating facilities:* bars and restaurant available. *Visitors:* residential visitors only at weekends before 1pm. 152 bedroom four star hotel with extensive conference and luxurious leisure facilities. *Society Meetings:* enquiries

welcome. Professional: M. Tarn (0676 22118). Golf Operations Manager: Richard Woolston (0676 22335 extension 421; Fax: 0676 23711).

COVENTRY. **Grange Golf Club,** Copeswood, Coventry (Coventry (0203) 451465). *Location:* three miles from centre of Coventry on A427/A428 road to Rugby, Lutterworth. 9 holes, 6002 yards. S.S.S. 69. *Green Fees:* weekdays £10.00 per round, Sundays £15.00 per round. *Visitors:* welcome except Saturdays, weekday evenings or Sunday mornings. Secretary: E. Soutar.

COVENTRY. **North Warwickshire Golf Club Ltd,** Hampton Lane, Meriden, Coventry CV7 7LL (Meriden (0676) 22259). *Location:* on B4102, one mile from Stonebridge on A45, approximately midway between Birmingham and Coventry. 9 holes, 6352 yards. S.S.S. 70. *Green Fees:* £20.00 weekdays, weekends £18.00 with member only. *Eating facilities:* full catering and bar. *Visitors:* welcome without reservation except Thursdays. *Society Meetings:* catered for by prior arrangement, limited numbers. Professional: Simon Edwin (0676 22259). Secretary: E.G. Barnes (0676 22915).

COVENTRY. **Windmill Village Hotel and Golf Club,** Birmingham Road, Allesley, Coventry CV5 9AL (0203 407241). *Location:* six miles from NEC Birmingham Airport on the A45 westbound. Parkland. 18 holes, 4661 yards. S.S.S. 64. Par 67. *Green Fees:* weekdays £9.40; weekends £10.50. *Eating facilities:* 180 seater restaurant, cellar bar, varied menus. *Visitors:* welcome, no restrictions. Leisure Club, 100 rooms all en-suite available at hotel, sauna, jaccuzi, etc. *Society Meetings:* welcome. Professional: Mr Rob Hunter. Secretary: Paul Tranter.

DUDLEY. **Dudley Golf Club Ltd,** Turners Hill, Rowley Regis, Warley (Dudley (0384) 253719). *Location:* one mile south of Dudley town centre on Blackheath Road. 18 holes, 6000 yards. S.S.S. 68. *Green Fees:* £18.00 weekdays. *Eating facilities:* full catering facilities available. *Visitors:* welcome but only with a member at weekends. *Society Meetings:* by prior arrangement. Professional: Paul Taylor (0384 254020) Secretary: R.P. Fortune (0385 233877).

DUDLEY. **Himley Hall Golf Centre,** Log Cabin Himley Hall Park, Himley Road, Dudley DY3 4D (0902 895207). *Location:* just off A449 at Himley near Dudley. Parkland. 9 holes, 3185 yards. S.S.S. 35 for holes. Practice ground, pitch and putt. *Green Fee* weekdays £3.50 for 9 holes, £5.00 for 18 hole weekends £4.00 for 9 holes, £5.50 for 18 holes. Junio and Senior Citizens £2.20 for 9 holes, £3.50 for 1 holes weekdays; £3.50 for 9 holes, £4.50 for 18 hol weekends. *Eating facilities:* cafe. *Visitors:* welcom weekdays, weekends with booking. Secretary: Mr I Harris (0384 239929).

DUDLEY near. **Swindon Golf Club,** Bridgno Road, Swindon, Near Dudley DY3 4PU (09 897031). *Location:* B4176 Dudley/Bridgnorth Roa three miles from A449 at Himley. Woodland a parkland course with exceptional views. 27 holes, 1135 yards, 18 – 6042 yards. S.S.S. 18 – 69, 9 – Pa *Green Fees:* £15.00 per round, £25.00 per weekdays; £25.00 per round, £40.00 per day weekends and Bank Holidays. *Eating facilities:* fully licensed bar and restaurant. *Visitors:* always welcome, booking not required. Buggies available. Fishing. *Society Meetings:* by arrangement weekdays only. Secretary: Rosemary Pope (0902 897031).

DUDLEY. **Sedgley Golf Club,** Sandyfields Road, Sedgley, Dudley DY3 3DL (0902 880503). *Location:* half a mile from Sedgley town centre near Cotwall End Valley Nature Reserve, just off the A463. Undulating contours and mature trees with extensive views over surrounding countryside. 9 holes, 3147 yards. S.S.S. 71 (18 holes). Covered and floodlit golf range. *Green Fees:* £3.00 9 holes, £5.00 18 holes weekdays; £3.50 9 holes, £5.50 18 holes weekends. Reductions weekdays for Juniors and Senior Citizens. *Eating facilities:* only hot drinks available. *Visitors:* pay and play course throughout the week, booking advisable at weekends. *Society Meetings:* weekdays preferred by prior arrangement. Professional: David Fereday (0384 287996). Secretary: J.A. Cox (0902 672452).

DUDLEY. **Swindon Ridge Driving Range and Golf Club,** Bridgnorth Road, Swindon, Dudley DY3 4PU (0902 896765). *Location:* B4176 Bridgnorth/Dudley Road, three miles from Himley A449. Wooded. 18 holes, 6026 yards. S.S.S. 69. *Green Fees:* £18.00 per round weekdays; £25.00 per round weekends. *Eating facilities:* restaurant/bar. *Visitors:* welcome at all times. *Society Meetings:* welcome. Professionals: Phil Lester and Simon Price (0902 896191). Secretary: Rosemary Pope (0902 897031).

HALESOWEN. **Halesowen Golf Club,** The Leasowes, Leasowes Lane, Halesowen B62 8QF (021-550 1041). *Location:* exit Junction 3 M5, A456 (Kidderminster) two miles, Halesowen town centre one mile. Parkland course. 18 holes, 5754 yards. S.S.S. 68. *Green Fees:* weekdays £16.00 per round, £21.00 per day; weekends must play with a member. *Eating facilities:* no catering Mondays. *Visitors:* welcome weekdays. *Society Meetings:* by arrangement with Secretary. Professional: David Down (021-503 0593). Secretary: Mrs M. Bateman (021-501 3606).

REDNAL. **Lickey Hills (Municipal) Golf Club,** Old Birmingham Road, Rednal, Near Birmingham (021-453 3159). *Location:* M5 Exit 4 on city boundary. 18 holes, 5721 yards. S.S.S. 67. *Green Fees:* information not provided. *Eating facilities:* restaurant at club. *Visitors:* welcome.

REDNAL. **Rose Hill Golf Club,** Rednal, near Birmingham (021-453 7600). *Location:* M5 Junction 4 to Birmingham South, at 156 turn right, one mile. Parkland, wooded. 18 holes, 6010 yards. S.S.S. 69. *Green Fees:* £5.80 weekdays, £6.20 weekends. *Eating facilities:* cafe. *Visitors:* welcome without reservation. *Society Meetings:* catered for. Professional: M. March (021-453 3159). Secretary: M.R. Billingham.

SOLIHULL. **Copt Heath Golf Club,** 1220 Warwick Road, Knowle, Solihull B93 9LN (Knowle (0564) 772650). *Location:* on A4141 half a mile south of Junction 5 with M42. Flat parkland. 18 holes, 6500 yards. S.S.S. 71. Full practice facilities available. *Green*

*Fees:* weekdays £35.00. Weekends and Public Holidays must be introduced by a member. *Eating facilities:* lunch and evening meal available except Mondays. *Visitors:* no restrictions weekdays. *Society Meetings:* by arrangement with Secretary. Professional: Brian Barton. Secretary: W. Lenton.

SOLIHULL. **Ladbrook Park Golf Club Ltd,** Poolhead Lane, Tanworth-in-Arden, Solihull B94 5ED (Tanworth-in-Arden (05644) 2220). *Location:* south from Junction 3 M42. Parkland gently undulating. 18 holes, 6418 yards. S.S.S. 71. *Green Fees:* £27.00 per day; weekends with a member only. *Eating facilities:* excellent dining. *Visitors:* welcome weekdays, prior telephone call suggested. Weekends with member only. *Society Meetings:* catered for by prior arrangement with Secretary. Professional: Steve Harrison (05644 2581). Secretary: Ted Gadd (05644 2264).

SOLIHULL. **Olton Golf Club Ltd,** Mirfield Road, Solihull B91 1JH (021-705 1083). *Location:* approximately two miles off Junction 5 (M42), A41 – Solihull. Parkland. 18 holes, 6229 yards, 5694 metres. S.S.S. 71. *Green Fees:* £30.00 weekdays. *Eating facilities:* by arrangement. *Visitors:* welcome weekdays only except Wednesdays. *Society Meetings:* catered for by arrangement. Professional: David Playdon (021-705 7296). Secretary: M.A. Perry (021-704 1936 am).

SOLIHULL. **Robin Hood Golf Club,** St. Bernards Road, Solihull B92 7DJ (021-706 0159). *Location:* eight miles south of Birmingham, off A40 Birmingham to Warwick road. Flat parkland. 18 holes, 6635 yards, 6067 metres. S.S.S. 72. *Green Fees:* £26.00 per round, £31.00 per day weekdays. *Eating facilities:* by prior arrangement with Steward (021-706 0159). *Visitors:* welcome weekdays only subject to limitations. Arrange with Professional. *Society Meetings:* catered for. Professional: R.S. Thompson (021-706 0806). Secretary: A.J. Hanson (021-706 0061).

SOLIHULL. **Shirley Golf Club,** Stratford Road, Monkspath, Shirley, Solihull (021-744 7024). *Location:* 8 miles from Birmingham on A34 to Stratford. 18 holes, 6411 yards. S.S.S. 71. *Green Fees:* £25.00 per round, £35.00 per day. *Eating facilities:* meals at club except Mondays. *Visitors:* welcome weekdays without reservation. *Society Meetings:* catered for weekdays. Professional: Chris Wicketts (021-745 4979). Secretary: A.J. Phillips (021-744 6001).

SOLIHULL. **Whitelakes Golf Club,** Tilehouse Lane, Tidbury Green, Solihull B90 1PT (0564 824414). *Location:* two miles from Shirley and three miles off the M42. To play over numerous ponds, lakes and the River Coal. 9 holes, 987 yards. S.S.S. 27. 15-bay golf range. *Green Fees:* information not available. *Eating facilities:* excellent bar and restaurant facilities. *Visitors:* welcome, no restrictions. Facilities for fishing, clay pigeon shooting, archery, swimming pool available. *Society Meetings:* catered for.

STOURBRIDGE. **Stourbridge Golf Club,** Worcester Lane, Pedmore, Stourbridge DY8 2RB (Stourbridge (0384) 393062). *Location:* one mile from town centre on Worcester road. Parkland. 18 holes, 6231 yards.

S.S.S. 70. Practice ground. *Green Fees:* £22.00 weekdays only. *Eating facilities:* available except Mondays. *Visitors:* welcome weekdays, weekends with member. *Society Meetings:* catered for Tuesdays. Professional: W.H. Firkins (0384 393129). Secretary: F.R. McLachlan (0384 395566).

SUTTON COLDFIELD. **Boldmere Municipal Golf Club,** Monmouth Drive, Sutton Coldfield (021-354 3379). *Location:* A34, seven miles from centre of Birmingham. 18 holes, 4463 yards. S.S.S. 61. *Green Fees:* weekdays £5.60; weekends £6.10. *Eating facilities:* meals daily. *Visitors:* welcome without reservation. *Society Meetings:* not catered for. Professional: T.J. Short. Secretary: D. Duffy.

SUTTON COLDFIELD. **Moor Hall Golf Club Ltd,** Moor Hall Drive, Sutton Coldfield B75 6LN (021-308 0103). *Location:* one mile east of Sutton Coldfield, A446. Parkland. 18 holes, 6249 yards. S.S.S. 70. Practice area. *Green Fees:* £25.00 per round, £32.00 day ticket. *Eating facilities:* available weekdays except for Mondays. *Visitors:* welcome weekdays only (not Thursday mornings). *Society Meetings:* catered for Tuesdays and Wednesdays only. Professional: Alan Partridge (021-308 5106). Secretary: R.V. Wood (021-308 6130).

SUTTON COLDFIELD. **Pype Hayes Golf Club,** Eachelhurst Road, Walmley, Sutton Coldfield B76 8EP (021-351 1014). *Location:* off the A38 Kingsbury Road by M6 Junction 5, one and a half miles from Junction 9 M42. Wooded course. Smallish demanding greens as well as four demanding Par 3 holes. 18 holes, 5373 yards. S.S.S. 69. *Green Fees:* weekdays £5.60; weekends £6.20. *Eating facilities:* full facilities available. *Visitors:* welcome, subject to availability. Professional: J. Bayliss. Secretary: K. Haden (021-779 2357).

SUTTON COLDFIELD. **Sutton Coldfield Golf Club,** Thornhill Road, Streetly, Sutton Coldfield B74 3ER (021-353 9633). *Location:* situated in Sutton Park, one mile off A452, seven miles from centre of Birmingham. 18 holes, 6491 yards. S.S.S. 71. *Green Fees:* weekdays £30.00. *Eating facilities:* by arrangement with Steward. *Visitors:* welcome without reservation. Handicap Certificate required. *Society Meetings:* catered for by arrangement with Secretary. Professional: J.K. Hayes. Administrator: Mrs T. Thomas.

SUTTON COLDFIELD. **Walmley Golf Club (Wylde Green) Ltd,** Brooks Road, Sutton Coldfield B72 1HR (021-373 0029). *Location:* Birmingham/Sutton Coldfield main road, turn right at Greenhill Road. Flat parkland. 18 holes, 6537 yards. S.S.S. 72. Practice area. *Green Fees:* weekdays £22.00 18 holes, £27.00 18+ holes; weekends playing with member only. *Eating facilities:* lunch and evening meals available except Mondays. *Visitors:* welcome with member. *Society Meetings:* catered for weekdays except Mondays. Secretary: J.P.G. Windsor. Professional: Mike Skerritt (021-373 7103).

WALSALL. **Bloxwich Golf Club (1988) Ltd,** Stafford Road, Bloxwich, Walsall WS3 3PQ (Bloxwich (0922) 405724). *Location:* off main Walsall-Cannock road

(A34). Semi parkland. 18 holes, 6286 yards. S.S.S. 70. *Green Fees:* weekdays £20.00 per round, £25.00 per day. *Eating facilities:* available. *Visitors:* welcome with or without reservation except weekends and Bank Holidays. *Society Meetings:* catered for preferably midweek, reduced rates for 20 or more. Professional: Mr G. Broadbent (0922 476889). Secretary: Mrs J.N. Loveridge (0922 476593).

WALSALL. **Calderfields Golf Club Ltd,** Aldridge Road, Walsall WS4 2JS (0922 640540). *Location:* A454 Dilke Public Arms. Parkland, lake. 18 holes, 6700 yards, 6100 metres. S.S.S. 73. Practice hole and putting green. *Green Fees:* weekdays £10.00; weekends £16.00. *Eating facilities:* restaurant and bar. *Visitors:* welcome always. *Society Meetings:* very welcome, package deals available. Professional: Roger Griffin (0922 32243). Secretary: Mr Colin Andrew (0922 640540; Fax: 0922 38787).

WALSALL. **Druids Heath Golf Club,** Stonnall Road, Aldridge, Walsall WS9 8JZ (Aldridge (0922) 55595). *Location:* between Sutton Coldfield and Walsall, near A454. 18 holes, 6914 yards. S.S.S. 73. *Green Fees:* £22.00 weekdays; £29.00 weekends. *Eating facilities:* diningroom and bar snacks. *Visitors:* welcome without reservation weekdays, with member at weekends. Ladies' Day Thursdays. *Society Meetings:* catered for on weekdays. Professional: M.P. Daubney (0922 59523). Secretary: P.M. Halldron.

WALSALL. **Walsall Golf Club,** The Broadway, Walsall WS1 3EY (0922 20014 or 22710). *Location:* one and a half miles from M6/M5 junction. Wooded course. 18 holes, 6243 yards. S.S.S. 70. *Green Fees:* £33.00 per round, £40.00 per day. Reduced rates for organised societies, minimum 16. *Eating facilities:* all facilities available. *Visitors:* welcome weekdays only. *Society Meetings:* catered for. Professional: R. Lambert (0922 26766). Secretary: E. Murray (0922 613512).

WARLEY. **Warley Golf Club,** Lightwood Hill, Warley (021-429 2440). *Location:* five miles west of Birmingham centre, just off main Hagley Road West. 9 holes 2606 yards. S.S.S. 64. *Green Fees:* £4.40 weekdays £5.20 weekends. *Eating facilities:* cafe. *Visitors:* welcome without reservation. *Society Meetings:* catered for, but not advised (Municipal Golf Course). Professional: David Owen. Secretary: C. Lowndes.

WEST BROMWICH. **Dartmouth Golf Club,** Vale Street, West Bromwich (021-588 2131). *Location:* one mile from West Bromwich town centre, rear of Churchfields High School, All Saints Way. Part flat, part undulating course. 9 holes, 6060 yards. S.S.S. 70. *Green Fees:* weekdays £17.50; weekends only with member £14.00. *Eating facilities:* bar open mid-day and evenings except Tuesday and Sunday evening Meals by arrangement. *Visitors:* welcome weekday and on some Sundays with member. *Society Meeting* welcome by prior arrangement. Professional: Carl Yates (021-588 2131). Secretary: M. Morton (021-58 2131).

WEST BROMWICH. **Sandwell Park Golf Clu** Birmingham Road, West Bromwich (021-553 463 *Location:* on A41 to Birmingham close to Junctior

M5. 18 holes, 6470 yards. S.S.S. 72. *Green Fees:* weekdays £30.00. *Eating facilities:* lunches except Mondays. *Visitors:* welcome except weekends and Bank Holidays. *Society Meetings:* by prior arrangement. Professional: N. Wylie (021-553 4384).

WISHAW. **The Belfry,** Lichfield Road, Wishaw, Near Sutton Coldfield B76 9PR (Curdworth (0675) 470301; Fax: 0675 470178). *Location:* M42 junction 9 just off the Lichfield Road (A446). Two parkland courses. Brabazon: 18 holes, 6975 yards. S.S.S. 73. Derby: 18 holes, 6077 yards. S.S.S. 69. Driving range and putting green. *Green Fees:* Brabazon: weekdays £46.00; weekends £51.00. Derby: weekdays £20.50; weekends £26.00. *Eating facilities:* bar food, buffet. *Visitors:* welcome weekday and weekends. Can only book 14 days in advance. The Belfry is a 4 Star Hotel with extensive leisure facilities. *Society Meetings:* welcome at all times. Professional: Peter McGovern (0675 470301 extension 267). Assistant Professional: Glenn Williams.

WOLVERHAMPTON. **Oxley Park Golf Club Ltd,** Stafford Road, Bushbury, Wolverhampton WV10 6DE (0902 20506). *Location:* one and a half miles M54/A449 junction. One and a half miles Wolverhampton town centre. Undulating parkland. 18 holes, 6168 yards, 5639 metres. S.S.S. 69. *Green Fees:* weekdays £18.00 per round, £22.00 per day; weekends £20.00 per round, £24.00 per day. *Eating facilities:* each day except Monday. *Visitors:* welcome weekdays, weekends by arrangement with Professional. *Society Meetings:* catered for Wednesdays only. Professional: Leslie Burlison (0902 25445). Secretary: Mrs Kathryn Mann (0902 25892).

WOLVERHAMPTON. **Penn Golf Club,** Penn Common, Penn, Wolverhampton (Wolverhampton (0902) 341142). *Location:* two miles south west of Wolverhampton, off A449. Heathland. 18 holes, 6465 yards. S.S.S. 71. *Green Fees:* £20.00. *Eating facilities:* available, excluding Sunday and Monday. *Visitors:* welcome weekdays, without advance booking. *Society Meetings:* catered for. Professional: A. Briscoe (0902 330472). Secretary: P.W. Thorrington (0384 256220).

WOLVERHAMPTON. **Perton Park Golf Club,** Wrottesley Park Road, Perton, Wolverhampton WV6 7HL (0902 380103). *Location:* just off the A454 Bridgnorth Road or A41 Wolverhampton to Newport road. Flat meadowland. 18 holes, 7007 yards. S.S.S. 71. Driving range, putting green. *Green Fees:* weekdays £5.00; Saturdays £6.00; Sundays and Bank Holidays £7. *Eating facilities:* available also bar. *Visitors:* pay as you play course. *Society Meetings:* catered for. Secretary: E.G.J. Greenway (0902 380073).

WOLVERHAMPTON. **South Staffordshire Golf Club,** Danescourt Road, Tettenhall, Wolverhampton WV6 9BQ (Wolverhampton (0902) 756401). *Location:* A41 north from Wolverhampton. Parkland. 18 holes, 6653 yards. S.S.S. 72. Two practice grounds. *Green Fees:* weekdays £25.00; weekends £30.00. *Eating facilities:* full catering and bar, except Mondays. *Visitors:* welcome by arrangement with Secretary. *Society Meetings:* catered for weekdays. Professional: J. Rhodes (0902 754816). Secretary: Ralph J. Crofts (0902 751065).

WOLVERHAMPTON. **Wergs Golf Club,** Keepers Lane, Tettenhall, Wolverhampton WV6 8UA (0902 742225; Fax: 0902 744748). *Location:* from centre of Wolverhampton, take A41 (to Newport), after two and a half miles turn right, half a mile on right. Open parkland. 18 holes, 6949 yards. S.S.S. 73. *Green Fees:* weekdays £15.00; weekends £20.00. *Eating facilities:* full catering and bar facilities. *Visitors:* always welcome. *Society Meetings:* welcome anytime during week, after 10am at weekends. Secretary: Mrs G. Parsons.

# Wiltshire

CALNE. **Bowood Golf and Country Club,** Derby Hill, Calne SN11 9PQ (0249 822228; Fax: 0249 822218). *Location:* A4 between Marlborough and Chippenham, signposted off M4. Grade I listed. Capability Brown landscaped, parkland. 18 holes, 7317, 6890, 6566, 6229 yards. S.S.S. 74, 73, 71, 77. 3 academy holes, driving range. *Green Fees:* weekdays £25.00 per round, £40.00 per day; weekends £40.00 per round, £65.00 per day. *Eating facilities:* private diningrooms, public restaurant. *Visitors:* welcome at all times except from 9am – 12 noon on weekend mornings. Four double bedroomed house in centre of course. *Society Meetings:* welcome. Professional: Ian Brake. Chief Executive: Sally-Jane Coode. Director of Golf: Nigel Blenkarae.

CASTLE COMBE. **Castle Combe Golf Club,** Castle Combe SN14 7PL (0249 782982). *Location:* M4 between Junctions 17 and 18. Parkland divided by river valley in area of outstanding natural beauty. 18 holes, 6340 yards. S.S.S. 71. Practice ground. *Green Fees:* £25.00. *Eating facilities:* bar and catering available all day. *Visitors:* welcome with members only. Snooker, sauna available. Professional: Miss Christine Langford. Secretary: Michael Spring-Rice (0249 782982; Fax: 0249 782992).

CHIPPENHAM. **Chippenham Golf Club,** Malmesbury Road, Chippenham SN15 5LT (Chippenham (0249) 652040). *Location:* A429 one mile from Chippenham, two miles from M4 (Junction 17). Parkland. 18 holes, 5540 yards. S.S.S. 67. *Green Fees:* weekdays £20.00, weekends £25.00. *Eating facilities:* snacks and evening à la carte (not Mondays). *Visitors:* welcome; current Handicap Certificate required. Prior arrangement necessary. *Society Meetings:* catered for weekdays only. Professional: Bill Creamer (0249 655519). Secretary: D. Maddison (0249 652040).

CORSHAM. **Kingsdown Golf Club,** Corsham SN14 9BS (Box (0225) 742530). *Location:* five miles east of Bath. Heathland. 18 holes, 6445 yards, 5891 metres.

S.S.S. 71. *Green Fees:* weekdays £22.00. *Eating facilities:* lounge bar and diningroom. *Visitors:* welcome except at weekends and Bank Holidays and must have current Handicap Certificate. *Society Meetings:* catered for by arrangement. Professional: Peter Evans (0225 742634). Secretary: S.H. Phipps (0225 743472).

DEVIZES. **Erlestoke Sands Golf Club,** Erlestoke, Devizes SN10 5UA (0380 830507). *Location:* six miles east of Westbury on B3098. Downland, spectacular 7th hole, 170 yards Par 3, one of the finest short holes in the west country. 18 holes, 6500 yards. S.S.S. 72. Par 71. Large practice ground. *Green Fees:* weekdays £10.00; weekends £14.00 per round. *Eating facilities:* full catering service, lounge, bar and diningroom. *Visitors:* welcome, booking advisable. *Society Meetings:* catered for by prior arrangement. Steward: Pauline and Trevor Head (0380 830507). Professional: Tony Valentine (0380 831027). Manager: Adrian Stiff.

DEVIZES. **North Wilts Golf Club,** Bishop's Cannings, Devizes SN10 2LP (Cannings (0380 860257). *Location:* one and a half miles from A4 east of Calne. Four miles from Devizes. Downland, undulating course. 18 holes, 6451 yards, 5898 metres. S.S.S. 71. *Green Fees:* weekdays £18.00 per round, £25.00 per day; weekends £30.00 when accepted. *Eating facilities:* full catering service. *Visitors:* welcome all weekdays, some weekends but not December to March. *Society Meetings:* catered for by prior arrangement. Professionals: Graham Laing and Richard Blake (0380 860330). Secretary: Stuart Musgrove (0380 860627).

HIGHWORTH. **Highworth Community Golf Centre,** Swindon Road, Highworth SN6 7SJ. *Location:* on A361 just south of the town. Undulating parkland. 9 holes, 3120 yards, 2851 metres. Par 35. 9 hole pitch and putt, practice ground. *Green Fees:* weekdays £4.60; weekends £5.50. Concession rates for under 16s, Senior Citizens and unemployed. *Eating facilities:* vending machines. *Visitors:* municipal course,

no restrictions. *Society Meetings:* welcome any day. Professional: Kevin Pickett (0793 766014).

HIGHWORTH. **Wrag Barn Golf Club,** Shrivenham Road, Highworth SN6 7QQ (0793 861325). *Location:* Junction 15 M4, take A419 Cirencester Road to Highworth roundabout fourth exit B14000. Undulating, set in beautiful Wiltshire countryside, three lakes and moat around 17th green. 18 holes, 6548 yards. S.S.S. 71. Excellent practice facilities. *Green Fees:* weekdays £15.00; weekends £22.00 after 11.30am. *Eating facilities:* good bar snacks available all day and bar – à la carte Friday, Saturday, Sunday and Sunday lunch. *Visitors:* welcome but members have priority, no green fee players at weekends before 11.30am. *Society Meetings:* welcome any weekday. Two rounds, coffee, lunch, dinner £35.00 per head minimum of 20 players. Professional: Barry Loughrey (0793 766027). Secretary: Mrs Suzanne Manners (0793 861327).

MARLBOROUGH. **Marlborough Golf Club,** The Common, Marlborough SN8 1DU (Marlborough (0672) 512147). *Location:* about one mile from town centre on A345 travelling towards Swindon. Downland. 18 holes, 6241 yards. S.S.S. 70. Practice ground and putting green. *Green Fees:* weekdays only £19.50 per round, £29.00 per day; weekends £40.00 per round. *Eating facilities:* restaurant serving snacks and full meals open most of day. *Visitors:* welcome generally, but it is best to telephone in advance as course may be too busy to allow green fees; some weekends course is closed to green fees. *Society Meetings:* catered for with advance notice. Professional: Billy McAdams (0672 512493). General Manager: Laurence Ross (0672 512147).

PEWSEY. **RAF Upavon Golf Club,** York Road, Upavon, Pewsey SN9 6BQ (0980 630787). *Location:* one mile south east of Upavon village on A342. On Salisbury Plain. Parkland/downland course. 9 holes, 5600 yards, 5116 metres. S.S.S. 67. Practice ground available. *Green Fees:* weekdays £14.00; weekends £17.00 payable at guardroom. *Eating facilities:* available by prior arrangement. *Visitors:* welcome but must be accompanied by a member at weekends. *Society Meetings:* welcome, contact Manager Mr D.L. Simpson (0980 630787). Secretary: Sqn Ldr R.G. Pegrum (0980 630351 ext. 4169).

SALISBURY. **High Post Golf Club Ltd,** Great Durnford, Salisbury SP4 6AT (0722 73231). *Location:* midway between Salisbury and Amesbury on A345. Downland and blackthorn. 18 holes, 6267 yards, 5730 metres. S.S.S. 70. Large practice ground. *Green Fees:* weekdays £20.00 per round, £25.00 per day; weekends £25.00 per round, £30.00 per day. *Eating facilities:* full catering and bars available. *Visitors:* welcome with valid Handicap Certificate. *Society*

*Meetings:* catered for mid-week by arrangement. Professional: Tony Harman (072 273 219). Secretary: W. Goodwin (072 273 356).

SALISBURY. **Salisbury and South Wilts Golf Club,** Netherhampton, Salisbury SP2 8PR (Salisbury (0722) 742131). *Location:* on A3094, two miles Salisbury, two miles Wilton, opposite Netherhampton village. Parkland. 27 holes, 6528 yards. S.S.S. 71. Practice ground. *Green Fees:* weekdays £23.00 per day, weekends and Bank Holidays £35.00 per day. *Eating facilities:* full catering service and bar. *Visitors:* welcome without reservation at all times, but preliminary phone call advised. *Society Meetings:* catered for by prior arrangement. Professional: G. Emerson (0722 742929). Secretary: John Newcomb (0722 742645).

SHRIVENHAM. **Shrivenham Park Golf Course,** Penny Hooks, Near Swindon SN6 8EX (0793 783853). *Location:* M4 exit 15. Follow signs to Shrivenham, go through village, golf club on right. A delightful parkland course in excellent condition and extensive, open to all. 18 holes, 5412 yards. S.S.S 68 (men's), 70 (ladies'). Practice area. *Green Fees:* £10.00 per round weekdays; £13.00 per round weekends. Discounts for Senior Citizens and Juniors. *Eating facilities:* bar open all day every day, restaurant open to all with a good all round menu. *Visitors:* welcome at all times, starting times must be booked to avoid disappointment. *Society Meetings:* we specialise in company days, societies, etc. Professional: Paul Young. Secretary: Vic Sedgwick.

SWINDON. **Broome Manor Golf Complex,** Pipers Way, Swindon SN3 1RG (Swindon (0793) 495761). *Location:* two miles from Junction 15, M4 (follow signs for "Golf Complex"). Wooded parkland. 18 holes, 6359 yards, 5815 metres. S.S.S. 71. 9 holes, 5610 yards, 5130 metres. S.S.S. 67. Floodlit covered driving range. *Green Fees:* weekdays £4.50 for 9 holes, £7.50 for 18 holes; weekends £5.50 for 9 holes, £9.00 for 18 holes. *Eating facilities:* full facilities. *Visitors:* welcome, no restrictions, booking essential for 18 hole course. Simulated clay pigeon shooting. *Society Meetings:* catered for Monday to Thursday. Professional: Barry Sandry (0793 532403). Manager: Tom Watt (0793 495761). Catering: (0793 490939):

SWINDON. **Swindon Golf Club,** Ogbourne St. George, Marlborough SN8 1TB (Ogbourne St. George (067-284) 217). *Location:* A345, four miles south of Junction 15 (M4), two miles north of Marlborough. Downland course. 18 holes, 6226 yards. S.S.S. 70. Practice area. *Green Fees:* on application weekdays; with a member only at weekends. *Eating facilities:* full daily catering available, full bar service. *Visitors:* welcome with reservation weekdays. Weekends and Bank Holidays with member only. Handicap Certificates

required. *Society Meetings:* catered for Mondays, Wednesdays and Fridays only by prior arrangement with Secretary. Professional: Colin Harraway (067-284 287). Secretary: P.V. Dixon (067-284 327).

TIDWORTH. **Tidworth Garrison Golf Club,** Bulford Road, Tidworth SP9 7AF (0980 42321). *Location:* A338 Salisbury to Marlborough Road, golf course off Bulford Road. Undulating downland course. 18 holes, 6075 yards. S.S.S. 69. Practice driving area, chipping and putting greens. *Green Fees:* weekdays £19.00; weekends £24.00 (£15.00 after 2pm). *Eating facilities:* full bar and catering facilities except for Mondays (sandwiches only). *Visitors:* welcome at all times, but normally after 2pm at weekends. *Society Meetings:*

catered for Tuesdays, Thursdays and Fridays. Professional: T. Gosden (0980 42393). Secretary: Lt. Col. D.F.T. Tucker RE (0980 42301).

WARMINSTER. **West Wilts Golf Club,** Elm Hill, Warminster BA12 0AU (Warminster (0985) 212702). *Location:* on A350 half-a-mile out of Warminster on Westbury Road. Downland. 18 holes, 5709 yards. S.S.S. 68. *Green Fees:* weekdays £20.00, weekends £30.00. *Eating facilities:* full meals and snacks available at all times. *Visitors:* welcome, but must produce a Handicap Certificate. Afternoons only at weekends. *Society Meetings:* catered for Wednesday to Friday. Professional: John Jacobs (0985 212110). Secretary: L.R. Weaver (0985 213133).

# North Yorkshire

ALDWARK. **Aldwark Manor Golf Club,** Aldwark Alne, York YO6 2NF (Tollerton (03473) 353. Fax: 03473 8867). *Location:* in village of Aldwark, five miles from A1 and five miles from A19. Flat parkland. 18 holes, 6171 yards. S.S.S. 66. *Green Fees:* weekdays £16.00 per round, £20.00 per day; weekends and Bank Holidays £20.00 per round, £24.00 per day. *Eating facilities:* two restaurants and two bars. *Visitors:* always welcome weekdays, restricted weekends. 20 bedroomed hotel. *Society Meetings:* always welcome, restricted weekends. Golf Director: G. Platt (03473 353).

BEDALE. **Bedale Golf Club,** Leyburn Road, Bedale (Bedale (0677) 422568). *Location:* close to northern boundary of town. Parkland. 18 holes, 6565 yards. S.S.S. 71. *Green Fees:* £18.00 weekdays; £24.00 weekends. *Eating facilities:* caterer employed. *Visitors:* welcome without reservation. *Society Meetings:* catered for on application. Professional: A.D. Johnson (0677 422443). Secretary: G.A. Shepherdson (0677 422451).

BENTHAM. **Bentham Golf Club,** Robin Lane, Bentham, Near Lancaster LA2 7AG (Bentham (05242) 61018). *Location:* B6480 north-west of Lancaster towards Settle. Parkland with magnificent views. 9 holes, 5760 yards. S.S.S. 69. *Green Fees:* weekdays £14.00, Juniors £7.00; weekends and Bank Holidays £18.00, Juniors £9.00. Weekly tickets £40.00, Juniors

£20.00. *Eating facilities:* hot and cold snacks and meals available. *Visitors:* welcome all week without reservation. *Society Meetings:* welcome – contact Secretary. Secretary: J.M. Philipson (05242 62455).

CATTERICK. **Catterick Garrison Golf Club,** Leyburn Road, Catterick Garrison, Catterick DL9 3QE (Richmond (0748) 833401). *Location:* six miles south-west Scotch Corner, A1 turn off to Catterick Garrison. Undulating parkland/moorland with spectacular views. 18 holes, 6331 yards, 5789 metres. S.S.S. 70. Practice ground. *Green Fees:* weekdays £15.00, weekends and Bank Holidays £22.00. *Eating facilities:* bar and restaurant. *Visitors:* welcome without reservation. *Society Meetings:* catered for by appointment only. Professional: Andy Marshall (0748 833671). Secretary: J.K. Mayberry (0748 833268).

EASINGWOLD. **Easingwold Golf Club,** Stillington Road, Easingwold, York YO6 3ET (Easingwold (0347) 21486). *Location:* 12 miles north of York, course one mile along Stillington Road. Flat, wooded parkland. 18 holes, 5679 metres. S.S.S. 70. *Green Fees:* weekdays £20.00 per day; weekends and Bank Holidays £25.00. £10.00 playing with a member at any time. *Eating facilities:* catering except Mondays, order in advance. *Visitors:* welcome without reservation. *Society Meetings:* maximum 48, weekdays only, prior booking essential. Contact G.C. Young. Professional: John

Hughes (0347 21964). Secretary: K.C. Hudson (0347 22474).

FILEY. **Filey Golf Club,** The Clubhouse, West Avenue, Filey YO14 9BQ (Scarborough (0723) 513116). *Location:* one mile from town centre. Seaside links. 18 holes, 6030 yards. S.S.S. 69. Practice area. *Green Fees:* weekdays £18.00, weekends £23.00. *Eating facilities:* full dining and bar facilities. *Visitors:* welcome most days if members of a golf club and hold current Handicap Certificate. *Society Meetings:* welcome, must be pre-arranged. Professional: D. England (0723 513134). Secretary: T.M. Thompson (0723 513293).

HARROGATE. **Crimple Valley Golf Club,** Hookstone Wood Road, Harrogate HG2 8PN (0423 883485; Fax: 0423 881018). *Location:* one mile south from town centre. Turn off A61 at Appleyards Garage on to Hookstone Road, signposted to right. Gently sloping fairways in rural setting. 9 holes, 2500 yards. S.S.S. 33. *Green Fees:* information not provided. *Eating facilities:* licensed bar, lunches available weekdays, breakfasts weekends. *Visitors:* welcome at all times. Professional: R.A. Lumb. Secretary: A.M. Grange.

HARROGATE. **Harrogate Golf Club Ltd,** Forest Lane Head, Harrogate HG2 7TF (Harrogate (0423) 863158). *Location:* two miles from Harrogate on the A59 Harrogate/Knaresborough road. Parkland. 18 holes, 6241 yards. S.S.S. 70. Practice ground. *Green Fees:* weekdays £25.00 per round or day; weekends £35.00. *Eating facilities:* 19th Hole bar, lounge bar, diningroom, full catering. *Visitors:* welcome but enquiry advised. *Society Meetings:* catered for. Professional: P. Johnson (0423 862547). Secretary: J. McDougall (0423 862999).

HARROGATE. **Oakdale Golf Club,** Oakdale, off Kent Road, Harrogate HG1 2LN (Harrogate (0423) 502806). *Location:* three-quarters of a mile from town centre, leave Ripon road (A61 from Leeds) at Kent Road. Parkland, with featured stream. 18 holes, 6456 yards. S.S.S. 71. Practice ground. *Green Fees:* weekdays £21.00 per round, £28.00 per day; weekends £26.00 per round. *Eating facilities:* full dining facilities. *Visitors:* welcome, groups by prior arrangement. *Society Meetings:* welcome by arrangement. Professional: Richard Jessop (0423 560510). Secretary: Frank Hindmarsh (0423 567162).

HARROGATE. **Pannal Golf Club,** Follifoot Road, Pannal, Harrogate HG3 1ES (Harrogate (0423) 871641). *Location:* two miles south of Harrogate A61 (Leeds Road). 18 holes, 6659 yards. S.S.S. 72. Large practice ground. *Green Fees:* weekdays £28.00 per round, £35.00 per day; weekends £35.00 per round. *Eating facilities:* lunch available daily, dinner by arrangement. *Visitors:* welcome Monday to Friday without reservation, enquiry advised. *Society Meetings:* catered for Monday, Tuesday (pm only), Wednesday and Thursday, Friday (limited to 16 only). Professional: Murray Burgess (0423 872620). Secretary: T.B. Davey MBE (0423 872628).

KIRKBYMOORSIDE. **Kirkbymoorside Golf Club,** Manor Vale, Kirkbymoorside, York YO6 6EG (0751 31525). *Location:* nearest road A170. Undulating parkland. 18 holes, 6017 yards. S.S.S. 69. *Green Fees:* £15.00 weekdays, £20.00 weekends and Public Holidays. Reduced fees in winter when temporary greens and shortened course in use. *Eating facilities:* available except Mondays. *Visitors:* welcome except on Competition Days by arrangement with Steward. *Society Meetings:* catered for by arrangement with Steward except weekends. Secretary: D.G. Saunders (0439 71625).

KNARESBOROUGH. **Knaresborough Golf Club,** Boroughbridge Road, Knaresborough HG5 0QQ (Harrogate (0423) 863219). *Location:* one-and-a-half miles from town centre, direction A1 Boroughbridge. Wooded parkland. 18 holes, 6232 yards. S.S.S.70. Large practice area. *Green Fees:* weekdays £16.00 per round, £20.00 per day; weekends £26.00. *Eating facilities:* resident Steward provides full catering. *Visitors:* welcome without reservation. *Society Meetings:* catered for. Professional: Keith Johnstone (0423 864865). Secretary/Manager: J.I. Barrow (0423 862690).

MALTON. **Malton and Norton Golf Club,** Welham Park, Malton YO17 9QE (Malton (0653) 692959). *Location:* off A64 to Malton between York and Scarborough. One mile south on Welham road turn right at Norton level crossing. 18 holes, 6411 yards. S.S.S. 71. Medal course: 6141 yards. S.S.S. 69 (club). Practice ground. *Green Fees:* weekdays £18.00; weekends and Public Holidays £23.00. *Eating facilities:* full bar and catering available. *Visitors:* welcome without reservation except club match days, and weekends from 1st November to 31st March unless with member. *Society Meetings:* catered for by arrangement with Secretary. Professional: S. Robinson (0653 693882). Secretary: W.G. Wade (0653 697912).

RICHMOND. **Richmond (Yorkshire) Golf Club,** Bend Hagg, Richmond DL10 5EX (0748 825319). *Location:* Scotch Corner, Richmond, traffic lights, turn right, Barrack Hill. Wooded, parkland, some hills. 18 holes, 5704 yards. S.S.S. 68. *Green Fees:* weekdays £11.00 per round, £13.00 per day; weekends £17.00 per round, £22.00 per day. *Eating facilities:* bar and

catering. *Visitors:* welcome except before 11.30am on Sunday. *Society Meetings:* catered for, book with Professional. Professional: Paul Jackson (0748 822457). Secretary: B.D. Aston (0748 825319).

RIPON. **Masham Golf Club,** Masham, Ripon (Ripon (0765) 689379). *Location:* nine miles north of Ripon. 9 holes, two courses of 2654 yards and 5308 yards. S.S.S. 66. *Green Fees:* £15.00 U/A. *Visitors:* welcome weekdays but must be accompanied by a member weekends and Bank Holidays. Party visits by arrangement. Secretary: Mrs M.A. Willis (0765 689491).

RIPON. **Ripon City Golf Club,** Palace Road, Ripon HG4 1UW (Ripon (0765) 603640). *Location:* one mile from town centre on A6108. Parkland. 9 holes, 5861 yards. S.S.S. 68. *Green Fees:* Saturday, Sunday and Bank Holidays £20.00 per day, £12.00 other days. *Eating facilities:* bar open 11am to 5pm Tuesday to Sunday, snacks and meals available. *Visitors:* welcome, no restrictions – starting sheet in operation weekends. *Society Meetings:* catered for, apply in writing. Professional: T. Davies (0765 600411). Secretay: J.L. Wright (0765 603640).

SCARBOROUGH. **Ganton Golf Club Ltd,** Ganton, Near Scarborough YO12 4PA. *Location:* on A64, nine miles west of Scarborough. 18 holes, 6693 yards. *Green Fees:* on request. *Eating facilities:* available. *Visitors:* welcome by prior arrangement. *Society Meetings:* catered for with reservation. Professional: Gary Brown. Secretary: Air Vice-Marshal R.G. Price, CB.

SCARBOROUGH. **Raven Hall Country House Hotel Golf Course,** Ravenscar, Near Scarborough YO13 0ET. *Location:* twelve miles north of Scarborough, off coastal road to Whitby. Cliff top. 9 holes, 1938 yards. *Green Fees:* £12.00 per day, every day. *Eating facilities:* full catering available in Hotel Restaurant. Bar snacks. *Visitors:* welcome. Golf clinics available. *Society Meetings:* arranged through Mr Davies, General Manager. Prior booking not necessary. For further details (0723 870353).

SCARBOROUGH. **Scarborough North Cliff Golf Club,** North Cliff Avenue, Scarborough YO12 6PP (Scarborough (0723) 360786). *Location:* two miles north of Scarborough on coastal road to Whitby.

Parkland. 18 holes, 6425 yards. S.S.S. 71. Practice area. *Green Fees:* weekdays £20.00 per day, weekends and Bank Holidays £25.00. *Eating facilities:* available. *Visitors:* welcome (restrictions on competition days, not allowed Sundays before 10am.). *Society Meetings:* catered for, from 12 to 40. Prior booking through Secretary. Professional: S.N. Deller (0723) 365920). Secretary: J.R. Freeman (0723) 360786).

SCARBOROUGH. **Scarborough South Cliff Golf Club Ltd,** Deepdale Avenue, Scarborough YO11 2UE (Scarborough (0723) 360522). *Location:* one mile south of town centre on Filey road. Parkland and clifftop with panoramic sea views. 18 holes, 6039 yards. S.S.S. 69. *Green Fees:* £19.00 weekdays; £25.50 weekends and Bank Holidays. *Eating facilities:* full restaurant service. *Visitors:* welcome when course available. *Society Meetings:* catered for by arrangement. Professional: D.M. Edwards (0723 365150). Secretary: R. Bramley B.E.M. (0723 374737).

SELBY. **Selby Golf Club,** Mill Lane, Brayton Barff, Brayton, Selby YO8 9LD (0757 228622). *Location:* three miles south of Selby off A19 Selby-Doncaster road. Inland links type course, very well drained.18 holes, 6246 yards. S.S.S. 70. Practice ground. *Green Fees:* weekdays £20.00 per round, £22.00 per day; weekends casual visitors not accepted. *Eating facilities:* pleasant restaurant and bar. *Visitors:* Wednesdays, Thursdays and Fridays, suitable dress both on course and in diningroom. All visitors must have Handicap Certificates. Tuition available, snooker tables. *Society*

*Meetings:* same as visitors. Professional: Mr C.A.C. Smith (0757 228785). Secretary/Manager: Mr Barrie Moore.

SETTLE. **Settle Golf Club,** Buck Haw Brow, Giggleswick, Settle (Settle (0729) 825288). *Location:* one mile north of Settle on main A65. Moorland. 9 holes, 4600 yards. S.S.S. 62. *Green Fees:* £7.50. *Eating facilities:* bar facilities open Sundays only. *Visitors:* welcome, restrictions Sundays. *Society Meetings:* welcome, must book in advance through Secretary. Secretary: R.G. Bannier (0729 823596).

SKIPTON. **Skipton Golf Club,** off North West Bypass, Skipton BD23 1LL (Skipton (0756) 793922). *Location:* one and a half miles from Skipton centre on the northern bypass A65. Undulating, with panoramic views, some water hazards. 18 holes, 6010 yards. S.S.S. 70. Practice ground. *Green Fees:* weekdays £17.00; weekends and Bank Holidays £22.00. Half-price if playing with member or juniors (under 18 years). *Eating facilities:* available every day except Mondays. *Visitors:* welcome at all times, some restrictions weekends and Thursdays. *Society Meetings:* welcome, accepted with prior booking. Professional: (0756 793257). Secretary: D. Farnsworth (0756 795657).

THIRSK. **Thirsk and Northallerton Golf Club,** Thornton-le-Street, Thirsk YO7 4AB (Thirsk (0845) 522170). *Location:* off the A168 Northallerton Road, two miles north of Thirsk. Flat parkland with excellent

views. 9 holes, 6257 yards. S.S.S. 70. Small practice area. *Green Fees:* weekdays £15.00 per round, £20.00 per day; Saturdays and Public Holidays £25.00; Sundays only with a member. *Eating facilities:* bars open normal times, food available except Tuesdays. *Visitors:* must be members of a recognised golf club and have a handicap. Not at weekends. Dress regulations must be strictly followed. *Society Meetings:* application must be made in writing to, and confirmed by, the Secretary well in advance of a society visit. Not at weekends. Professional: Andrew Wright. Secretary: Henry D. Swarbrick (0845 587350).

THORNTON-IN-CRAVEN. **Ghyll Golf Club,** Ghyll Brow, Barnoldswick, Colne, Lancs BB8 6JQ (Earby (0282) 842466). *Location:* M65 to Colne. Parkland, hilly course. 9 holes, 5706 yards, 5213 metres. S.S.S. 68. *Green Fees:* weekdays £12.50 (£5.00 with member), weekends and Bank Holidays £16.50 restricted (£12.00 with member). *Eating facilities:* bar, evening only. *Visitors:* welcome except Sundays and some Saturdays. *Society Meetings:* catered for by arrangement. Secretary: John L. Gill (0282 813205).

WHITBY. **Whitby Golf Club,** Low Straggleton, Whitby YO21 3SR (Whitby (0947) 602768). *Location:* Sandsend Road out of Whitby. Coastal course. 18 holes, 5560 yards. S.S.S. 67. *Green Fees:* weekdays £17.50, weekends and Bank Holidays £25.00. *Eating facilities:* meals available daily except Mondays, bar facilities. *Visitors:* welcome, parties over 12 by prior reservation, all must be bona fide golfers. *Society Meetings:* catered for by prior arrangement. Professional: A.S. Brook (0947 602719). Secretary: Alan Dyson (0947 600660).

YORK. **Forest Park Golf Club,** Stockton on Forest, York YO3 9UX (0904 400425). *Location:* one and a half miles from East End of York bypass, follow signs for Stockton on Forest. Flat parkland type course with stream running through. 18 holes, 6200 yards. S.S.S. 70. Driving range and practice area. *Green Fees:* weekdays £13.00 per round, £18.00 per day; weekends £18.00 per round, £23.00 per day. *Eating facilities:* full bar and all golf club type meals. *Visitors:* welcome mid week, limited availability weekends. *Society Meetings:* welcome by prior arrangement. Secretary: David Crossley (0904 400688).

YORK. **Fulford (York) Golf Club Ltd,** Heslington Lane, York YO1 5DY (York (0904) 413212). *Location:* A19 (Selby) from city, turn left to Heslington. Heathland. 18 holes, 6775 yards. S.S.S. 72. Practice ground. *Green Fees:* weekdays £30.00; weekends £35.00. *Eating facilities:* both lounge/diningroom and bar. *Visitors:* welcome during week, prior reservation recommended. *Society Meetings:* by prior reservation – enquiries to Secretary. Professional: B. Hessay (0904 412882). Secretary: Judith Hayhurst (0904 413579; Fax: 0904 416918).

YORK. **Heworth Golf Club,** Muncaster House, Muncastergate, York YO3 9JX (York (0904) 424618). *Location:* within city boundaries, adjacent A1036 (A64) for Malton/Scarborough. Parkland. 11 holes, 6141 yards. S.S.S. 69. *Green Fees:* weekdays £13.00; weekends and Bank Holidays £16.00. *Eating facilities:* available every day except Monday. *Visitors:* generally welcome except Sunday mornings and competition days, but advisable to telephone. *Society Meetings:* only by written application. Professional: Neil Cheetham (0904 422389). Secretary: J.R. Richards (0904 426156).

YORK. **Pike Hills Golf Club,** Tadcaster Road, Askham Bryan, York YO2 3UW (York (0904) 706566). *Location:* four miles from York on Tadcaster Road, right hand side going west. 18 holes, 6048 yards. S.S.S. 69. *Green Fees:* £18.00 per day. *Eating facilities:* full catering except Mondays. *Visitors:* welcome but not weekends or summer evenings. *Society Meetings:* catered for. Professional: Ian Gradwell (0904 708756). Secretary: G. Rawlings (0904 706566).

YORK. **York Golf Club,** Lordsmoor Lane, Strensall, York YO3 5XF (York (0904) 490304). *Location:* six miles north-east of York. Wooded heathland. 18 holes, 6285 yards. S.S.S. 70. Practice ground; Professional shop. *Green Fees:* £24.00 weekdays, £28.00 weekends and Bank Holidays. *Eating facilities:* full catering except Fridays. *Visitors:* welcome, but advisable to ring before visiting. *Society Meetings:* catered for Mondays, Wednesdays, Thursdays and Sundays. Professional: A.B. Mason (0904 490304). Secretary: Gp Captain F. Appleyard (0904 491840).

# South Yorkshire

BARNSLEY. **Barnsley Golf Club,** Wakefield Road, Staincross, Barnsley S75 6JZ (Barnsley (0226) 382856). *Location:* A61 three miles north of Barnsley, five miles south of Wakefield. Parkland course. 18 holes, 6048 yards, 5529 metres. S.S.S. 69. *Green Fees:* weekdays £6.00 per day, weekends £7.00. *Eating facilities:* meals available. *Visitors:* welcome, no restrictions. *Society Meetings:* course extremely busy and not suitable for Societies. Professional: M. Melling (0226 382954). Secretary: L.E. Lammas (0226 382856).

BARNSLEY. **Silkstone Golf Club,** Field Head, Elmhirst Lane, Silkstone, Barnsley S75 4OD (Barnsley (0226) 790328). *Location:* one mile beyond Dodworth village on the A628 and one mile from M1. Parkland. 18 holes, 6045 yards. S.S.S. 70. *Green Fees:* information not available. *Eating facilities:* available. *Visitors:* welcome weekdays only. *Society Meetings:* by arrangement. Professional: Kevin Guy (0226 790128). Secretary: L. Depledge (0226 287053).

DONCASTER. **Austerfield Park Golf Club,** Cross Lane, Austerfield, Doncaster DN10 6RF (Doncaster (0302) 710841). *Location:* two miles from Bawtry on the A614. Parkland. 18 holes, 6828 yards. S.S.S. 73. 10 bay floodlit golf range, flat bowling green. *Green Fees:* midweek £14.00 per day; weekends £18.00 per day. *Eating facilities:* bar snacks and full restaurant. *Visitors:* welcome without reservation. *Society Meetings:* welcome, special package rates. Professional: Chris Gray (0302 710841). Secretary: Alan Bradley (0709 540928).

DONCASTER. **Crookhill Park (Municipal) Golf Club,** Crookhill Park, Conisborough, Doncaster (Rotherham (0709) 862974). *Location:* leave A1(M) Doncaster by-pass, on to A630 Sheffield, after two miles turn left in Conisborough on to B60694. 18 holes, 5846 yards. S.S.S. 68. Practice area. *Green Fees:* £7.00. *Eating facilities:* buffet lunches at club. *Visitors:* welcome. Professional: Richard Swaine (0709 862979). Hon. Secretary: M. Belk.

DONCASTER. **Doncaster Town Moor Golf Club,** c/o Belle Vue Club, Belle Vue, Doncaster DN4 5HT (Doncaster (0302) 535286). *Location:* clubhouse approximately 300 yards from racecourse roundabout travelling south towards Bawtry, same entrance as Doncaster Rovers Football Club. Flat wooded parkland. 18 holes, 6094 yards. S.S.S. 69. *Green Fees:* weekdays £12.00, £8.00 with a member per round, £14.00, £10.00 with a member per day; weekends and Public Holidays £14.00, £10.00 with a member per round, £16.00, £12.00 with a member per day. *Eating facilities:* available except Sundays. *Visitors:* welcome without reservation, not before 11.30am Sundays. *Society Meetings:* catered for by arrangement with Secretary. Professional: Steve Poole (0302 535286). Secretary: Gerry Sampson (0302 538423).

DONCASTER. **Hickleton Golf Club,** Hickleton, Near Doncaster (Rotherham (0709) 892496). *Location:* six miles from Doncaster on A635 to Barnsley. In Hickleton village turn right to Thurnscoe, 500 yards on right. Undulating parkland. 18 holes, 6403 yards. S.S.S. 71. Practice facilities. *Green Fees:* weekdays £17.00; weekends and Bank Holidays £25.00. *Eating facilities:* available by arrangement with Steward/ess. *Visitors:* welcome by arrangement, restricted times at weekends. *Society Meetings:* welcome by arrangement. Professional: Paul Shepherd (0709 895170). Secretary: R. Jowett (0709 896081 office).

DONCASTER. **Serlby Park Golf Club,** Serlby, Doncaster DN10 6BA (Retford (0777) 818268). *Location:* 12 miles south of Doncaster, between A614 and A638. 9 holes, 5370 yards. S.S.S. 66. *Green Fees:* information not provided. *Visitors:* welcome only if playing with member. *Society Meetings:* not catered for. Hon. Secretary: R. Wilkinson (0302 536336).

DONCASTER. **Thorne Golf Club,** Kirkton Lane, Thorne, Near Doncaster (Thorne (0405) 815173). *Location:* A18, Parkland. 18 holes, 5366 yards. S.S.S. 66. Practice ground. *Green Fees:* weekdays £8.00 per round, weekends and Bank Holidays £6.50 per round. *Eating facilities:* snacks or full meals booked in advance. *Visitors:* welcome, no restrictions. *Society Meetings:* welcome, please book in advance. Professional: R.D. Highfield (0405 812084). Secretary: P. Kettridge (0405 812084).

DONCASTER. **Wheatley Golf Club,** Armthorpe Road, Doncaster DN2 5QB (Doncaster (0302) 831655). *Location:* follow East Coast route alongside Racecourse boundary to water tower at first crossroads. Flat parkland, water hazards between 10th and 18th holes. 18 holes, 6209 yards. S.S.S. 70 (yellow markers); 6405 yards. S.S.S. 71 (white markers). Practice area and putting green. *Green Fees:* weekdays £17.50 per round, £21.00 per day; weekends and Bank Holidays £21.00 per round, £25.00 per day. Reductions if playing with member. *Eating facilities:* restaurant and bars. *Visitors:* welcome if member of another club. Non-members may play in the company of a member. *Society Meetings:* catered for weekdays only on written application. Professional: S. Fox. Secretary: T.A.D. Crumpton.

ROTHERHAM. **Grange Park Golf Club,** Upper Wortley Road, Kimberworth Park, Rotherham (Rotherham (0709) 558884). Municipal golf course, private clubhouse. *Location:* A629 from Rotherham, easy access from M1. Parkland. 18 holes, 6353 yards. S.S.S. 71. Practice ground. *Green Fees:* £5.00 weekdays, £6.00 weekends. *Eating facilities:* licensed bar and full catering. *Visitors:* welcome without restriction. *Society*

213

*Meetings:* contact Professional in first instance. Professional: Eric Clark (0709 559497). Secretary: R. Charity (0709 583400).

ROTHERHAM. **Phoenix Golf Club,** Pavilion Lane, Brinsworth, Rotherham (Rotherham (0709) 363864). *Location:* M1 Tinsley roundabout, Bawtry Road, Pavilion Lane one mile on left. 18 holes, 6145 yards. S.S.S. 69. *Green Fees:* weekdays £12.00, £6.00 with a member; weekends £16.00, £8.00 with a member. *Eating facilities:* snacks or full meals. *Visitors:* welcome weekdays. *Society Meetings:* welcome, reduced rates for parties. Professional: A. Limb (0709 382624). Secretary: J. Burrows (0709 370759).

ROTHERHAM. **Rotherham Golf Club Ltd,** Thrybergh Park, Doncaster Road, Thrybergh, Rotherham S65 4NU (Rotherham (0709) 850466). *Location:* three and a half miles east of Rotherham on A630. Wooded parkland. 18 holes, 6234 yards, 5701 metres. S.S.S. 70. Practice ground. *Green Fees:* weekdays £22.00, weekends £27.00. Reductions for parties over 16. *Eating facilities:* full catering, bar and restaurant. *Visitors:* welcome all days with limitations. *Society Meetings:* catered for weekdays only except Wednesdays. Professional: Simon Thornhill (0709 850480). Secretary: F. Green (0709 850812).

ROTHERHAM. **Sitwell Park Golf Club,** Shrogswood Road, Rotherham S60 4BY (Wickersley (0709) 700799). *Location:* A631 off M18, Bramley turn off to Rotherham thence to Sheffield, exit 33 off M1, follow A631 to Bawtry. Undulating parkland. 18 holes, 6203 yards. S.S.S. 70. Practice ground. *Green Fees:* weekdays £19.00 per round, £22.00 per day; weekends and Bank Holidays £22.00 per round, £26.00 per day. *Eating facilities:* restaurant and bar. *Visitors:* welcome with reservation, Saturdays only with member, Sundays after 11.30am. *Society Meetings:* catered for if pre-arranged with Secretary. Not Saturdays; Sundays after 11.30am only. Professional: N. Taylor (0709 540961). Secretary: G. Simmonite (0709 541046).

ROTHERHAM. **Wath Golf Club,** Abdy, Rawmarsh, Rotherham S62 7SJ (Rotherham (0709) 872149). *Location:* A633 from Rotherham, through Rawmarsh, taking B6090 towards Wentworth, right along B6089 taking signed road to Clubhouse 300 yards on right. Flat parkland course with small green, dykes and two ponds. 18 holes, 5857 yards. S.S.S. 68. Limited practice area. *Green Fees:* weekdays £16.00; weekends with a member £16.00. *Eating facilities:* lounge bar and dining area with seating for up to 150 people. *Visitors:* weekdays only. No jeans or collarless shirts allowed. *Society Meetings:* welcome weekdays only by prior arrangement. Golf/meal Package £25.00. Professional: Chris Bassett (0709 878677). Secretary: John Pepper (0709 873153 day, 873730 evening; Fax: 0709 760179).

SHEFFIELD. **Abbeydale Golf Club,** Twentywell Lane, Dore, Sheffield S17 4QA (Sheffield (0742) 360763). *Location:* A621 five miles south of Sheffield. Parkland. 18 holes, 6419 yards. S.S.S. 71. Practice ground. *Green Fees:* weekdays £25.00, weekends and Bank Holidays £30.00. *Eating facilities:* restaurant and

bar meals. *Visitors:* welcome by arrangement. Starting time restrictions April-October. *Society Meetings:* catered for Tuesdays and Fridays by arrangement. Professional: N. Perry (0742 365633). Secretary: Mrs K.M. Johnston (0742 360763).

SHEFFIELD. **Beauchief Municipal Golf Club,** Abbey Lane, Beauchief, Sheffield S8 0DB (0742 620040). *Location:* the entrance to course is on the Sheffield Outer Ring Road, between the A621 Bakewell Road and the A61 Chesterfield Road. Mainly flat parkland course. 18 holes, 5452 yards, 4984 metres. S.S.S. 66. Practice area, net. *Green Fees:* £6.95 per round. Juniors half price. *Eating facilities:* cafe/bar, open till dusk every day except Tuesday. *Visitors:* welcome anytime, but starting times get booked up early and cannot be booked by telephone. *Society Meetings:* weekdays only, can be booked through Sheffield City Council Recreation Department, Meersbrook Park, Sheffield S8 9FL. Professional: B.T. English (0742 620648). Bookings: (0742 338 7274). Secretary: J.G. Pearson (0742 306720).

SHEFFIELD. **Birley Wood Golf Course,** Birley Lane, Sheffield S12 3BP (0742 647262). *Location:* four and a half miles south east of city centre, off A616 from Mosborough. Undulating meadowland course with well varied features, open plan and good views. 18 holes, 5452 yards. S.S.S. 67. Practice field near course. *Green Fees:* £6.90 per round. *Eating facilities:* bar and snacks at nearby Fairway Inn. *Visitors:* welcome with prior notice. *Society Meetings:* by prior arrangement. Professional: P. Ball (0742 647262). Secretary: D. Cronshaw (0742 471258).

SHEFFIELD. **Concord Park Golf Club,** Shiregreen Lane, Sheffield S5 6AE. *Location:* one-and-a-half miles from M1 Junction 34. Hilly wooded parkland. 18 holes, 4321 yards, 3929 metres. S.S.S. 62. *Green Fees:* information not provided. *Eating facilities:* available at adjacent Sports Centre. *Visitors:* welcome any time. Secretary: B. Shepherd (0742 456806).

SHEFFIELD. **Dore and Totley Golf Club,** The Clubhouse, Bradway Road, Bradway, Sheffield S17 4QR (Sheffield (0742) 360492). *Location:* leave M1 at Junction 33. Parkland. 18 holes, 6265 yards. S.S.S. 70. *Green Fees:* weekdays £20.00 per round or day; weekends with a member only. *Eating facilities:* bar available, catering facilities available except Mondays. *Visitors:* unintroduced visitors restricted to the hours of 9.30am to 12 noon and after 2pm. Restrictions also exist on Wednesday (Ladies' Day). *Society Meetings:* catered for Tuesday, Thursday, Friday by prior arrangement. Professional: M. Pearson (0742 366844). Secretary: Mrs C. Ward (0742 369872).

SHEFFIELD. **Hallamshire Golf Club Ltd,** Sandygate, Sheffield S10 4LA (Sheffield (0742) 301007). *Location:* A57 out of Sheffield four miles then fork left for Lodge Moor. Moorland course. 18 holes, 6396 yards. S.S.S. 71. *Green Fees:* £27.00 weekdays; £32.00 weekends. *Eating facilities:* full catering except Tuesdays – prior notice required. *Visitors:* welcome weekdays by arrangement, some weekends. Snooker table. *Society Meetings:* catered for by arrangement with Secretary. Professional: Geoffrey Tickell (0742 305222). Secretary: R. Burns (0742 302153).

SHEFFIELD. **Hallowes Golf Club,** Hallowes Lane, Dronfield, Sheffield S18 6UA (Dronfield (0246) 413734). *Location:* six miles south of Sheffield on old A61 (not by-pass to Chesterfield). Moorland/parkland. 18 holes, 6342 yards. S.S.S. 70. Large practice area. *Green Fees:* weekdays £18.00 per round, £25.00 per day. *Eating facilities:* bars, dining room (no catering Mondays). *Visitors:* weekdays only, no visitors except with members at weekends and Bank Holidays. *Society Meetings:* E.G.U. registered societies only. Company days welcome. Professional: Martin Heggie (0246 411196). Secretary: Keith Dowswell (0246 413734).

SHEFFIELD. **Hillsborough Golf Club Ltd,** Worral Road, Sheffield S6 4BE (Sheffield (0742) 343608). *Location:* three miles from city centre. Worrall Road via Middlewood Road, Dykes Hall Road. Undulating wooded parkland and heath. 18 holes, 6204 yards. S.S.S. 70. *Green Fees:* weekdays £24.00; weekends £35.00. *Eating facilities:* snacks available; lunches, teas, evening meals by arrangement (not Fridays). *Visitors:* welcome by arrangement. *Society Meetings:* catered for by arrangement. Professional: G. Walker (0742 332666). Secretary: A. Platts (0742 349151).

SHEFFIELD. **Lees Hall Golf Club Ltd,** Hemsworth Road, Norton, Sheffield S8 8LL (0742 554402). *Location:* three miles south of Sheffield, between A61 and A6102 ring road. Undulating parkland with extensive views over Sheffield. 18 holes, 6137 yards. S.S.S. 69. *Green Fees:* weekdays £18.00 per round, £25.00 per day; weekends and Bank Holidays £30.00 per round. *Eating facilities:* available daily except Tuesdays. *Visitors:* welcome, except Saturday and Sunday before 10.30am. *Society Meetings:* by arrangement only. Professional: J.R. Wilkinson (0742 554402). Secretary: N.E. Westworth (0742 552900).

SHEFFIELD. **Stocksbridge and District Golf Club Ltd,** 30 Royd Lane, Deepcar S30 5RZ (Sheffield (0742) 882003). *Location:* 10 miles from Sheffield on A616 heading towards Manchester. Parkland course. 18 holes, 5200 yards. S.S.S. 65. Practice ground. *Green Fees:* weekdays £15.00; weekends £24.00. *Eating facilities:* available. *Visitors:* welcome weekdays, restrictions weekends. *Society Meetings:* catered for by arrangement. Secretary: Stuart Lee (0742 882408).

SHEFFIELD. **Tankersley Park Golf Club,** High Green, Sheffield S30 4LG (Sheffield (0742) 468247). *Location:* take M1 north to Junction 35a, come off at 35a to island, straight on from island approximately quarter of a mile and turn right into golf club. Parkland. 18 holes, 6212 yards. S.S.S. 70. Practice area. *Green Fees:* £17.50 per round, £20.00 per day weekdays; £20.00 weekends. *Eating facilities:* sandwiches, bar meals, full evening meals. *Visitors:* welcome on weekdays without reservation but not before 3pm weekends. *Society Meetings:* catered for by prior arrangement. Professional: I. Kirk (0742 455583). Secretary: Mr P.A. Bagshaw (0742 468247).

SHEFFIELD. **Tinsley Park Golf Club (Municipal),** High Hazels Park, Darnall, Sheffield (0742 560237). *Location:* three miles from Junction 33 M1 – A6102. Wooded course. 18 holes, 6086 yards. S.S.S. 69. Practice facilities. *Green Fees:* £6.95. *Eating facilities:* cafe (closed Tuesday); meals if ordered from Stewardess. Time must be booked on arrival. *Visitors:* welcome without restriction, no booking facilities. *Society Meetings:* book through Sheffield City Council. Professional: Mr A.P. Highfield (0742 560237). Secretary: Mr C.E. Benson (0742 873110).

SHEFFIELD. **Wortley Golf Club,** Hermit Hill Lane, Wortley, Near Sheffield S30 4DF (Sheffield (0742) 882139). *Location:* leave M1 Junction 36 or 35A, off A629 west of Wortley Village. Parkland. 18 holes, 5983 yards, 5469 metres. S.S.S. 69. *Green Fees:* £19.00 weekdays; £25.00 weekends and Bank Holidays. *Eating facilities:* order in advance, not Mondays. *Visitors:* welcome by arrangement. *Society Meetings:* parties catered for by arrangement Wednesdays and Fridays. Professional: Jeremy Tilson (0742 886490). Secretary: J. Lewis Dalby (0742 885294).

# West Yorkshire

BINGLEY. **Bingley (St. Ives) Golf Club,** The Mansion, St. Ives, Harden, Bingley (Bradford (0274) 562436). Parkland/moorland. 18 holes, 6480 yards. S.S.S. 71. Practice ground. *Green Fees:* weekdays £15.00 per round, £20.00 per day; weekends and Bank Holidays £20.00 per round. *Eating facilities:* daily except Mondays. *Visitors:* welcome weekdays, limited availability weekends. *Society Meetings:* welcome, book through Professional. Professional: R.K. Firth (0274 562506). Secretary: Mary Welch (0274 562436).

BRADFORD. **Clayton Golf Club,** Thornton View Road, Clayton, Bradford BD14 6JX (Bradford (0274) 880047). *Location:* two miles south west of Bradford, via Thornton Road, then Listerhills Road. Moorland course, testing par 3 at third hole. 9 holes, 5515 yards. S.S.S. 67. *Green Fees:* information not provided. *Eating facilities:* bar snacks, meals if notice given. No bar Mondays. *Visitors:* welcome at all times except before 4.00pm on Sundays. *Society Meetings:* catered for by arrangement. Secretary: F. V. Wood (0274 574203).

BRADFORD. **East Bierley Golf Club,** South View Road, East Bierley, Bradford (Bradford (0274) 681023). *Location:* situated about three miles east of Bradford on the Wakefield/Heckmondwike Road. Turn off at Bierley Bar and down South View Road.

Undulating semi-moorland course. 9 holes, 4308 metres. S.S.S. 63. *Green Fees:* £10.00 per round weekdays; Saturdays £12.50. *Eating facilities:* lunchtime and evening catering. *Visitors:* welcome, not Sunday or Mondays after 4pm. Secretary: M. Welch (0274 683666). Steward: (0274 680450).

BRADFORD. **Headley Golf Club,** Headley Lane, Thornton, Bradford BD13 3LX (Bradford (0274 833481). *Location:* five miles west of Bradford. Hilly parkland. 9 holes, 4914 yards. S.S.S. 64. *Green Fees:* weekdays £10.00, £5.00 if playing with a member. *Eating facilities:* dining and bar. *Visitors:* weekdays only. *Society Meetings:* restricted facilities. Hon. Secretary: J.P. Clark (0274 832571).

BRADFORD. **Northcliffe Golf Club,** High Bank Lane, Shipley BD18 4LJ (Bradford (0274) 584025). *Location:* three miles west of Bradford on A650 Bradford-Keighley. Undulating wooded parkland. 18 holes, 6065 yards, 5546 metres. S.S.S. 69. *Green Fees:* weekdays £15.50; weekends and Bank Holidays £22.50. *Eating facilities:* bars, dining room (no catering Mondays) *Visitors:* unlimited apart from weekends (Competition Days). *Society Meetings:* welcome Wednesday, Thursday and Fridays. Professional: Simon Poot (0274 587193). Secretary: Ralph Anderson (0274 596731).

BRADFORD. **Queensbury Golf Club,** Brighouse Road, Queensbury, Bradford BD13 1QF (Bradford (0274) 882155). *Location:* M62 Junction 25, A644 to Brighouse, Hipperholme and Queensbury. Wooded course. 9 holes, 5024 yards. S.S.S. 65. *Green Fees:* weekdays £13.00; weekends £20.00. *Eating facilities:* lunches, teas except Monday. Bar available. *Visitors:* welcome any day, must have Handicap. No parties at weekends. *Society Meetings:* by arrangement. Professional: Mr Geoff Howard (0274 882956). Secretary: Mr H. Andrew (0422 201565).

BRADFORD. **Shipley Golf Club,** Beckfoot Lane, Cottingley Bridge, Bingley BD16 1LX (Bradford (0274) 563212). *Location:* off A650 at Cottingley Bridge, Bradford six miles, Bingley one mile (from Bradford left before Cottingley Bridge). Slightly undulating parkland. 18 holes. S.S.S. 70. Practice area and net putting green. *Green Fees:* weekdays £22.50; weekends and Bank Holidays £29.00. *Eating facilities:* available by arrangement with Steward, except Mondays. *Visitors:* welcome (Tuesdays after 2.00pm, Saturdays after 4.00pm). *Society Meetings:* catered for by arrangement. Professional: J.R. Parry (0274 563674). Hon. Secretary: Stuart Holman (0274 568652).

BRADFORD. **South Bradford Golf Club,** Pearson Road, Odsal, Bradford BD6 1BH (Bradford (0274) 679195). *Location:* follow signs for Odsal Stadium, then turn right down towards club entrance. Scenic, testing course, wooded. 9 holes, 6028 yards. S.S.S. 69. Practice ground. *Green Fees:* weekdays £10.00 per day (£6.00 with member); weekends £15.00 per day (£8.00 with member). *Eating facilities:* available daily except Mondays. *Visitors:* welcome. Must conform with club rules on dress. Parties accommodated when possible on application. *Society Meetings:* catered for on application to Secretary. Professional: M. Hillas (0274 673346). Secretary: R. Tiffany (0274 601505).

BRADFORD. **West Bowling Golf Club Ltd,** Newall Hall, Rooley Lane, Bradford BD5 8LB (Bradford (0274) 724449). *Location:* take M606 off the M62, course at top of M606. Parkland. 18 holes, 5657 yards. S.S.S. 67. *Green Fees:* weekdays £23.00 (£19.00 with Handicap Certificate); weekends and Bank Holidays £30.00 (restricted). *Eating facilities:* available excluding Mondays. *Visitors:* individuals welcome without reservation. *Society Meetings:* by arrangement. Professional: A. Swaine (0274 728036). Secretary: M.E. Lynn (0274 393207).

BRADFORD. **West Bradford Golf Club Ltd,** Chellow Grange Road, Haworth Road, Bradford BD9 6NP (Bradford (0274) 542767). *Location:* three miles west of city centre off Haworth Road. Undulating course. 18 holes, 5788 yards. S.S.S. 68. *Green Fees:* £14.50 weekdays; £20.50 weekends, including VAT. *Eating facilities:* available every day except Mondays. *Visitors:* welcome, except Saturdays. *Society Meetings:* welcome Wednesday to Friday. Golf package deals Wednesday to Friday £16.00. Professional: Nigel M. Barber (0274 542102). Secretary: D. Ingham (0274 542767).

BRIGHOUSE. **Castlefields Golf Club,** Rastrick Common, Rastrick, Brighouse HD6 3HL. *Location:* one mile out of Brighouse on A643. Parkland. 7 holes, 2406 yards. S.S.S. 51. *Green Fees:* information not provided. *Eating facilities:* Globe Inn 200 yards away. *Visitors:* welcome at all times but must be accompanied by a member. Secretary: P. Bentley (0484 712108).

CLECKHEATON. **Cleckheaton and District Golf Club Ltd,** Bradford Road, Cleckheaton BD19 6BU (0274 874118). *Location:* four miles south of Bradford on A638, Junction 26 M62. Parkland course. 18 holes, 5769 yards. S.S.S. 68. Practice area. *Green Fees:* £22.00 weekdays; £27.00 weekends and Bank Holidays. *Eating facilities:* available (except Mondays). *Visitors:* welcome all year, suggest prior enquiry. *Society Meetings:* catered for by prior arrangement except Mondays, Saturdays or Sundays. Professional: Mike Ingham (0274 851267). Secretary: Herbert Thornton (0274 851266).

DEWSBURY. **Hanging Heaton Golf Club,** White Cross Road, Dewsbury WF12 7DT (Dewsbury (0924) 461606). *Location:* one mile from town centre on main A653 Dewsbury to Leeds road. 9 holes, 5870 yards (for 18 holes). S.S.S. 67. *Green Fees:* weekdays £12.00 (£8.00 with member); weekends with member £10.00. Green fees not taken weekends or Bank Holidays without member's introduction. *Eating facilities:* available. *Visitors:* welcome without reservation, except weekends. *Society Meetings:* catered for by arrangement with Steward. Secretary: S.M. Simpson.

ELLAND. **Elland Golf Club,** Hammerstones, Leach Lane, Elland HX5 0QP (0422 372505). *Location:* M62 Junction 24 exit off roundabout for Blackley. Parkland. 9 holes, 5630 yards. S.S.S. 66. *Green Fees:* weekdays £8.00, weekends £12.00. *Eating facilities:* meals/bar snacks except Mondays. *Visitors:* welcome mid-week. *Society Meetings:* by arrangement. Professional: M. Allison (0422 374886). Secretary: D.B.J. Ward (0422 377294).

GUISELEY. **Bradford Golf Club,** Hawksworth Lane, Guiseley, Leeds LS20 8NP (Guiseley (0943) 877239). _Location:_ Shipley to Ilkley road, left at top of Hollins Hill, one mile up Hawksworth Lane. Moorland/parkland. 18 holes, 6259 yards. S.S.S. 71. _Green Fees:_ weekdays £25.00; weekends £32.00 (half price with member). _Eating facilities:_ every day, preferably by prior arrangement. _Visitors:_ welcome without reservation weekdays, not on weekends without prior arrangement. _Society Meetings:_ catered for on weekdays (except Tuesdays) by prior arrangement. Professional: Sydney Weldon (0943 873719). Secretary: A. Pinder (0943 875570).

HALIFAX. **Bradley Hall Golf Club,** Holywell Green, Halifax (0422 374108). _Location:_ three miles south of Halifax on B6112. Moorland, undulating. 18 holes, 6213 yards. S.S.S. 70. _Green Fees:_ weekdays £17.00; weekends £25.00. _Eating facilities:_ full catering by arrangement except Tuesdays. _Visitors:_ welcome. Snooker. _Societies:_ welcome with prior reservation weekdays. Professional: P. Wood (0422 372103). Secretary: P.M. Pitchforth (0422 376626 evenings).

HALIFAX. **Halifax Golf Club Ltd,** Union Lane, Ogden, Halifax (Halifax (0422) 244171). _Location:_ three miles out of Halifax, A629 towards Keighley. Moorland. 18 holes, 6037 yards. S.S.S. 70. _Green Fees:_ weekdays £20.00, with Handicap Certificate £15.00; weekends £30.00, with Handicap Certificate £25.00. _Eating facilities:_ luncheons and dinners served. Good restaurant facilities. _Visitors:_ welcome most days by arrangement. All-in Day £22.00. _Society Meetings:_ catered for by arrangement – mid-week £32.00; weekends £40.00. Professional: Mr Steve Foster (0422 240047). Secretary: Mr J.P. Clark (0422 244171).

HALIFAX. **Lightcliffe Golf Club,** Knowle Top Road, Lightcliffe, Halifax (Halifax (0422) 202459). _Location:_ three miles east of Halifax on A58 (Leeds) road. Parkland. 9 holes, 5368 metres. S.S.S. 68. _Green Fees:_ weekdays £10.00; weekends £16.00. _Eating facilities:_ bar snacks and meals (except Mondays). _Visitors:_ welcome without reservation but must confirm with Professional. Not Wednesdays. _Society Meetings:_ catered for. Professional: D.W. Lockett (0422 202459). Secretary: T.H. Gooder (0422 201051).

HALIFAX. **Ryburn Golf Club,** The Shaw, Norland, Near Halifax (Halifax (0422) 831355). _Location:_ Station Road Halifax to Sowerby Bridge, turn right up hill, right towards Hobbit Inn (signposted), left after cottages. Demanding, hilly, windy course. 9 holes, 4907 yards. S.S.S. 64. _Green Fees:_ information not available. _Eating facilities:_ good catering facilities and bar. _Visitors:_ welcome weekdays, weekends by prior arrangement. _Society Meetings:_ welcome by prior arrangement. Secretary: Jack Hoyle (0422 843070 home).

HALIFAX. **West End Golf Club (Halifax) Ltd,** Paddock Lane, Highroad Well, Halifax HX2 0NT (Halifax (0422) 353608). _Location:_ two miles from town centre. Parkland. 18 holes, 6003 yards. S.S.S. 69. _Green Fees:_ weekdays £15.00 per round, £18.00 per day; weekends and Bank Holidays £18.00 per round,

£23.00 per day. _Eating facilities:_ full bar and catering except Mondays. _Visitors:_ welcome – please check with Professional. _Society Meetings:_ catered for by arrangement with Secretary. Professional: D. Rishworth (0422 363293). Secretary: B.R. Thomas (0422 341878).

HEBDEN BRIDGE. **Hebden Bridge Golf Club,** Wadsworth, Hebden Bridge HX7 8PH (Hebden Bridge (0422) 842896). _Location:_ one mile upwards past Birchcliffe Centre. Moorland with superb Pennine views. 9 holes, 5202 yards. S.S.S. 66. _Green Fees:_ weekdays £7.50 (with a member £4.00); weekends £10.00 (with a member £5.00). _Eating facilities:_ bar and diningroom facilities. _Visitors:_ welcome, please check first at weekends. _Society Meetings:_ welcome by prior arrangement. Secretary: Dr R.G. Pogson.

HUDDERSFIELD. **Bradley Park Municipal Golf Course,** Off Bradley Road, Huddersfield HD2 1PZ (Huddersfield (0484) 539988). _Location:_ M62 Junction 25, one mile up A6107. Parkland, rolling hills with panoramic views. 18 holes, 6220 yards. S.S.S. 70. Floodlit driving range, 9 hole Par 3 course. _Green Fees:_ weekdays £8.50; weekends £9.75. _Eating facilities:_ full catering. _Visitors:_ no restrictions except booking at weekends. _Society Meetings:_ all welcome. Professional: P.E. Reilly. Secretary: J.A. Murphy.

HUDDERSFIELD. **Crosland Heath Golf Club Ltd,** Felk Stile Road, Crosland Hill, Huddersfield HD4 7AF (0484 653216). _Location:_ three miles from town centre off A62 Oldham road. Flat heathland with extensive views. 18 holes, 5963 yards. S.S.S. 70. Practice facilities. _Green Fees:_ on application. _Eating facilities:_ full catering except Mondays. _Visitors:_ welcome, suggest prior enquiry. _Society Meetings:_ catered for by arrangement. Professional: John Andrew (0484 653877). Secretary: D. Walker (0484 653262).

HUDDERSFIELD. **Huddersfield Golf Club,** Fixby Hall, Lightridge Road, Fixby, Huddersfield HD2 2EP (Huddersfield (0484) 420110). _Location:_ M62 Junction 24; A643 from Hilton Hotel; turn right first traffic lights by Sun Inn. Parkland course. 18 holes, 6402 yards. S.S.S. 71. Practice ground. _Green Fees:_ weekdays £25.00 for 18 holes, £35.00 for 27/36 holes; weekends and Public holidays £35.00 for 18 holes, £45.00 for 27/36 holes; £8.50 playing with a member. _Eating facilities:_ available. _Visitors:_ always welcome, reservation advised but not essential. Tuesday is Ladies' day and no visitors Saturdays. Snooker. _Society and Company Days:_ catered for except weekends, well appointed private rooms. Catering to suit all occasions. Professional: P. Carman (0484 426463). Secretary: Miss D. Rose (0484 426203). General Manager: D.L. Bennett (0484 426203).

HUDDERSFIELD. **Longley Park Golf Club,** Maple Street, Off Somerset Road, Huddersfield (Huddersfield (0484) 426932). _Location:_ one mile town centre, Wakefield side. 9 holes, 5324 yards. S.S.S. 66. _Green Fees:_ weekdays £12.00; weekends and Bank Holidays £15.00. _Eating facilities:_ available. _Visitors:_ welcome Mondays, Tuesdays and Fridays. Professional: Neil Suckling (0484 422304). Secretary: D. Palliser.

HUDDERSFIELD. **Marsden Golf Club,** Hemplow, Marsden, Huddersfield HD7 6JL (Huddersfield (0484) 844253). *Location:* eight miles south of Huddersfield on A62 to Manchester. Moorland. 9 holes, 5702 yards. S.S.S. 68. *Green Fees:* weekdays £10.00. *Eating facilities:* lunches and snacks available except Tuesdays. *Visitors:* welcome weekdays, with a member only weekends. *Society Meetings:* catered for by arrangement. Secretary: S. Shaw (0484 845869).

HUDDERSFIELD. **Woodsome Hall Golf Club,** Woodsome Hall, Fenay Bridge, Huddersfield HD8 0LQ (Huddersfield (0484) 602971). *Location:* off A629 Pemstone/Sheffield Road, three miles Huddersfield centre. Parkland. 18 holes, 6080 yards. S.S.S. 69. Practice ground. *Green Fees:* weekdays £25.00; weekends and Public Holidays £30.00. *Eating facilities:* on application to Stewardess. *Visitors:* applications in writing to Secretary, bookings commence September for following year. All visitors must hold EGU Handicaps. *Society Meetings:* welcome. Professional: M. Grantham (0484 602034). Secretary: Mrs P. Bates (0484 602739). Hon. Secretary: W.D.N. Woodhouse.

ILKLEY. **Ben Rhydding Golf Club,** High Wood, Ben Rhydding, Ilkley (0943 608759). 9 holes, 4711 yards (18 holes). S.S.S. 64. *Green Fees:* weekdays £8.00; Bank Holiday Mondays £10.00. *Visitors:* welcome without reservation, no visitors Wednesday afternoons, Saturdays and Sundays. Secretary: P. Atkinson (0943 876442).

ILKLEY. **Ilkley Golf Club,** Nesfield Road, Ilkley (Ilkley (0943) 607277). *Location:* 15 miles north of Bradford. Flat course. 18 holes, 6262 yards. S.S.S. 70. *Green Fees:* weekdays £28.00; weekends £35.00. Subject to review. *Eating facilities:* by arrangement. *Visitors:* welcome by arrangement. *Society Meetings:* catered for by arrangement. Professional: J. L. Hammond (0943 607463). Secretary: G. Hirst (0943 600214).

KEIGHLEY. **Branshaw Golf Club,** Branshaw Moor, Oakworth, Keighley BD22 7ES (Haworth (0535) 643235). *Location:* B6143 south west of Keighley. Moorland with extensive views. 18 holes, 5858 yards. S.S.S. 69. *Green Fees:* weekdays £12.00; weekends £17.00. Juniors half price. *Eating facilities:* meals and bar snacks served (except Monday). *Visitors:* welcome weekdays, limited Saturdays. *Society Meetings:* catered for if application tendered four weeks in advance. Professional: S.A. Dixon (0535 665370). Secretary: Mr D.A. Town (0535 605003).

KEIGHLEY. **Keighley Golf Club,** Howden Park, Utley, Keighley BD20 6DH (Keighley (0535) 604778). *Location:* one mile west of Keighley on A650. Parkland. 18 holes, 6139 yards, 5615 metres. S.S.S. 70. *Green Fees:* weekdays £20.00 per round, £24.00 per day; weekends £22.00 per round, £26.00 per day. *Eating facilities:* full catering available. *Visitors:* welcome by prior arrangement. Ladies' day, Tuesday. *Society Meetings:* catered for by arrangement. Professional: S.A. Dixon (0535 665370). Secretary: D.F. Coyle (0535 604778).

KEIGHLEY. **Riddlesden Golf Club,** Howden Rough, Riddlesden, Keighley BD20 5QN (Keighley (0535) 602148). *Location:* A650 Keighley-Bradford road, left into Bar Lane, left on Scott Lane, which leads on to Scott Lane West and Elam Wood Road approximately two miles. Moorland, with spectacular par 3s. 18 holes, 4247 yards. S.S.S. 61. *Green Fees:* weekdays £8.00 (£5.00 with member); weekends £12.00 (£8.00 with a member). *Eating facilities:* catering available during bar hours – weekdays 12 noon to 3pm then 7pm to 11pm; weekends noon onwards. *Visitors:* welcome except Saturdays 10am to 2pm and Sundays until after 2pm. *Society Meetings:* catered for by prior arrangement. Secretary: Mrs K.M. Brooksbank (0535 607646).

KEIGHLEY. **Silsden Golf Club,** High Brunthwaite, Silsden, Near Keighley BD20 0NH (Sleeton (0535) 652998). *Location:* five miles north of Keighley. Undulating downland. 14 holes, 4870 yards. S.S.S. 64. Practice area and putting green. *Green Fees:* £10.00 weekdays; £16.00 weekends. *Eating facilities:* licensed bar, food available. *Visitors:* restrictions at weekends – details from Secretary. *Society Meetings:* by arrangement with Secretary. Secretary: G. Davey.

KNOTTINGLEY. **Ferrybridge "C" P.S. Golf Club,** PO Box 39, Stranglands Lane, Knottingley WF11 8SQ. *Location:* off the A1 at Ferrybridge and quarter of a mile towards Castleford on the B6136. Undulating land within the boundaries of and surrounding the power station. 9 holes, 5138 yards. S.S.S. 65. Practice ground. *Green Fees:* £3.00 weekdays, £4.00 weekends. *Visitors:* welcome when accompanied by a member only because of security restrictions. *Society Meetings:* by special arrangement in parties of not more than 12. Secretary: Mr N.E. Pugh (0977 793884).

LEEDS. **Alwoodley Golf Club,** Wigton Lane, Alwoodley, Leeds LS17 8SA (Leeds (0532) 681680). *Location:* five miles north of Leeds on A61 (Leeds to Harrogate). 18 holes, 6686 yards. S.S.S. 72. *Green Fees:* £35.00 weekdays; £45.00 weekends. *Eating facilities:* available. *Visitors:* welcome by arrangement. *Society Meetings:* catered for by arrangement. Professional: J. Green (0532 689603). Secretary: R.C.W. Banks.

LEEDS. **Calverley Golf Club,** Woodhall Lane, Pudsey, Leeds LS28 5QY (0532 564362). *Location:* Leeds seven miles, Bradford four miles. Parkland. 27 holes: 18 holes – 5527 yards, 9 holes – 2581 yards. S.S.S. 67. *Green Fees:* weekdays £9.50, 9 holes £5.00; weekends £12.50, 9 holes £5.00. *Eating facilities:* available. *Visitors:* welcome, must book 18 hole course. *Society Meetings:* welcome. Professional: Derek Johnson (0532 569244). Secretary: W. Gardner.

LEEDS. **Garforth Golf Club Ltd,** Long Lane, Garforth, Leeds LS25 2DS (Leeds (0532) 862021). *Location:* six miles east of Leeds on A63, then turn left on to A642. Flat parkland. 18 holes, 6306 yards. S.S.S. 70. Practice area. *Green Fees:* £20.00 per round, £25.00 per day weekdays. *Eating facilities:* available. *Visitors:* welcome, but not before 9.30am or between 12 noon and 2.30pm or after 4.30pm. Weekend as members' guest only. *Society Meetings:* catered for. Professional: K. Findlater (0532 862063). Secretary/Manager: F.A. Readman (0532 863308).

LEEDS. **Gotts Park Municipal Golf Club,** Gotts House, Gotts Park, Armley Ridge Road, Leeds LS12 2QX (Leeds (0532) 310492). *Location:* three miles east of city centre off A647 Stanningley Road. Parkland, hilly, hard walking. 18 holes, 4960 yards. S.S.S. 64. Practice ground, lessons available. *Green Fees:* under review. *Eating facilities:* snack bar cafe, bar evenings only. *Visitors:* unrestricted except at weekends when booking system applies – no phone bookings. Professional: J.F. Simpson (0532 636600). Secretary: M. Gill (0532 562994).

LEEDS. **Headingley Golf Club,** Back Church Lane, Adel, Leeds LS16 8DW (Leeds (0532) 673052). *Location:* leave Leeds/Otley road (A660) at Church Lane, Adel about five miles from city centre. 18 holes, 6298 yards. S.S.S. 70. *Green Fees:* £22.00 per round, £27.50 per day weekdays; £36.00 per round or day weekends and Bank Holidays. *Eating facilities:* full catering except Fridays. *Visitors:* members of other golf clubs welcome, preferably with prior reservation. *Society Meetings:* catered for by arrangement. Professional: Andrew Dyson (0532 675100). Secretary: R.W. Hellawell (0532 679573).

LEEDS. **Horsforth Golf Club Ltd,** Layton Rise, Layton Road, Horsforth, Near Leeds LS18 5EX (0532 581703). *Location:* north-west of Leeds on A65 to Ilkley. 18 holes, 6293 yards. S.S.S. 70. *Green Fees:* £22.00 weekdays, £28.00 weekends and Bank Holidays. *Eating facilities:* full catering (except Monday), order in advance for dinner. *Visitors:* welcome, must be bona fide member of another club. *Society Meetings:* catered for by arrangement with Secretary. Professional: L.Turner (0532 585200). Secretary: C.B. Carrington (0532 586819).

LEEDS. **Howley Hall Golf Club,** Scotchman Lane, Morley, Leeds (Batley (0924) 472432). *Location:* turn off the A650 Bradford/Wakefield road at the Halfway House Public House, take the B6123 towards Batley – the course is on the left. Parkland. 18 holes, 6029 yards. S.S.S. 69. Practice ground. *Green Fees:* weekdays £18.00 per round, £22.00 per day; weekends £25.00. *Eating facilities:* diningroom, meals available up to 7pm. *Visitors:* welcome. *Society Meetings:* catered for by reservation. Professional: S.A. Spinks. Secretary: Mrs A. Pepper.

LEEDS. **Leeds Golf Club,** Cobble Hall, Elmete Lane, Leeds LS8 2LJ (Leeds (0532) 658775). *Location:* Leeds ring road to A58, turn left if from east, right if from west, fork right at next roundabout, turn right after 250 yards. 18 holes, 6097 yards. S.S.S. 69. *Green Fees:* £25.00 per day, £19.00 per round weekdays, weekends with member only. *Eating facilities:* full

catering, apply in advance. *Visitors:* welcome. *Society Meetings:* catered for. Professional: J. Longster. Secretary: G.W. Backhouse.

LEEDS. **Middleton Park (Municipal) Golf Club,** Ring Road, Beeston, Middleton, Leeds LS10 4NX (0532 700449). *Location:* ring road to Middleton off A653 (Water Tower). Parkland, wooded course. 18 holes, 5036 yards. S.S.S. 66. Practice ground. *Green Fees:* on request – fixed by Leeds County Council. *Visitors:* weekdays, contact the Professional. *Society Meetings:* contact the Professional. Professional: David Bulmer (0532 709506). Secretary: Fred Ramsey (0532 533993).

LEEDS. **Moor Allerton Golf Club,** Coal Road, Wike, Leeds LS17 9NH (Leeds (0532) 661154). *Location:* accessible from A61 at Alwoodley or from Harvester Scarcroft on A58. Undulating parkland, designed by Robert Trent Jones. 18 holes, 6552 yards. S.S.S. 72. 9 holes, 3541 yards. S.S.S. 37. Large practice area and driving range. *Green Fees:* £35.00 per day weekdays. Reduced rate November to March. *Eating facilities:* bars, full restaurant and snack facilities. *Visitors:* welcome weekdays with reservation. Tennis courts. *Society Meetings:* catered for weekdays by arrangement, brochure available. Professional: Richard Lane (0532 665209). Secretary: (0532 661154). Executive Vice-President: J.J. Harris.

LEEDS. **Moortown Golf Club,** Harrogate Road, Alwoodley, Leeds LS17 7DB (Leeds (0532) 681682). *Location:* five miles north of Leeds centre, A61 Leeds to Harrogate road. 18 holes, 6515 yards. S.S.S. 72. Large practice field. *Green Fees:* weekdays £33.00 per round, £39.00 per day, weekends £39.00 per round, £44.00 per day. *Eating facilities:* lunches except Mondays, evening meals Tuesday to Saturday. *Visitors:* welcome weekdays, some tee-off time restrictions. *Society Meetings:* catered for. Professional: B. Hutchinson (0532 683636). Secretary: R.H. Brown (0532 686521).

LEEDS. **Rawdon Golf and Lawn Tennis Club,** Buckstone Drive, Micklefield Lane, Rawdon, Leeds LS19 6BD (Leeds (0532) 506040). *Location:* eight miles north of Leeds on A65, left at Rawdon traffic lights on to Micklefield Lane. Undulating parkland, with trees a special feature. 9 holes (18 tees), 5964 yards. S.S.S. 69. *Green Fees:* weekdays £16.00; weekends £10.00 with a member. *Eating facilities:* meals and bar snacks except Mondays. *Visitors:* welcome, weekends must play with a member. Facilities for tennis, visitors welcome with members. *Society Meetings:* catered for on application to Secretary. Professional: Syd Wheldon (of Bradford Golf Club) (0532 505017). Secretary: Ray Adams (0532 506064).

LEEDS. **Roundhay Municipal Golf Club,** Park Lane, Leeds LS8 3QW (Leeds (0532) 662695). *Location:* four miles north of Leeds city centre, leave A58 to Wetherby at Oakwood. Wooded parkland. 9 holes, 5322 yards. S.S.S. 65. Practice ground. *Green Fees:* weekdays £5.80; weekends and Bank Holidays £6.15. *Eating facilities:* bar for members and guests, restaurant in evenings. *Visitors:* welcome without reservation. *Society Meetings:* arrangements to be made with Leeds City Council. Professional: J. Pape (0532 661686). Hon Secretary: R.H. McLauchlan (0532 492523).

LEEDS. **Sand Moor Golf Club,** Alwoodley Lane, Leeds LS17 7DJ (Leeds (0532) 681685). *Location:* five miles north of Leeds off A61. Moorland, overlooking picturesque Wharfedale. 18 holes, 6429 yards, 5876 metres. S.S.S. 71. *Green Fees:* weekdays £26.00 per round, £32.00 per day; weekends £38.00. *Eating facilities:* lunches daily, evening meals Tuesday to Friday. *Visitors:* welcome most weekdays by arrangement. *Society Meetings:* catered for. Professional: J.R. Foss (0532 683925). Secretary: B.F. Precious (0532 685180).

LEEDS. **Scarcroft Golf Club,** Syke Lane, Leeds LS14 3BQ (Leeds (0532) 892263). *Location:* A58 Wetherby road; turn left at New Inn, Scarcroft village seven miles north of Leeds. Undulating parkland. 18 holes, 6426 yards. S.S.S. 71. Practice ground and indoor net. *Green Fees:* £25.00 per round, £30.00 per day weekdays; £35.00 per round weekends. *Eating facilities:* bar and restaurant except Mondays. *Visitors:* casuals after 9.30am. *Society Meetings:* catered for Tuesdays, Wednesdays and Thursdays only April to October, must have official Handicaps. Professional: Martin R. Ross (0532 892780). Secretary: R.D. Barwell (0532 892311).

LEEDS. **South Leeds Golf Club,** Parkside Links, Gipsy Lane, Off Middleton Ring Road, Leeds LS11 5TU (Leeds (0532) 700479). *Location:* M62 and M1 within five minutes' drive, Leeds City Centre 5 minutes' drive. Links course with undulating fairways. 18 holes, 5769 yards. S.S.S. 68. Practice fairway. *Green Fees:* £17.00 weekdays; £25.00 weekends and Bank Holidays (rates may change). Special rates for visiting parties over 30. *Eating facilities:* full catering except Mondays and bar. *Visitors:* welcome most days and after 2pm on Sundays. *Society Meetings:* catered for by prior arrangement. Professional: Mike Lewis (0532 702598). Secretary: J. McBride (0532 771676).

LEEDS. **Temple Newsam Golf Club,** Temple Newsam, Leeds 15 (Leeds (0532) 645624). *Location:* easily reached by public transport from City (to Temple Newsam or Halton). Two 18 hole courses. No. 1 Course 6448 yards. S.S.S. 71. No. 2 Course 5731 yards. S.S.S. 70. *Green Fees:* as decided by City Council. *Eating facilities:* cafe open Saturdays and Sundays 7.30am till 4.00pm. *Visitors:* welcome without reservation, except that parties must book in advance. *Society Meetings:* catered for. Professional: David Bulmer (0532 641464). Secretary: G. Gower.

MELTHAM. **Meltham Golf Club,** Thick Hollins Hall, Meltham, Huddersfield HD7 3DQ (Huddersfield (0484) 850227). *Location:* half mile east of Meltham, six miles

south west of Huddersfield (B6107). Gently sloping course in wooded valley from Meltham. 18 holes, 6202 yards, 5673 metres. S.S.S. 70. Restricted practice area. *Green Fees:* weekdays £18.00, weekends £22.00. *Eating facilities:* lunches, dinners (with reservation). *Visitors:* welcome weekdays and Sundays without reservation, not Saturdays and with member Sundays. *Society Meetings:* catered for by arrangement. Professional: P. Davies (0484 851521). Secretary: J. Holdsworth.

MIRFIELD. **Dewsbury District Golf Club,** The Pinnacle, Sands Lane, Mirfield WF14 8HJ (0924 492399). *Location:* turn off A644 opposite Swan Inn, two miles west of Dewsbury. Undulating moorland/parkland with panoramic views over surrounding countryside. 18 holes, 6256 yards. S.S.S. 71. *Green Fees:* £18.00 weekdays. *Eating facilities:* full catering except Monday – order in advance. *Visitors:* welcome without reservation except weekends unless with member. Two full size snooker tables. *Society Meetings:* welcome. Professional: N.P. Hirst (0924 496030). Secretary: D.M. Scott.

NORMANTON. **Normanton Golf Club,** Snydale Road, Normanton WF6 1PA (Wakefield (0924) 892943). *Location:* Junction 31 M62, A655 towards Wakefield, left at lights, half a mile on left. Flat course with internal out of bounds. 9 holes, 5323 yards. S.S.S. 66. Large practice area. *Green Fees:* £8.00 weekdays; Saturday £14.00. £1.00 off if playing with a member. No green fees Sundays. *Eating facilities:* full catering and bar facilities. *Visitors:* welcome, no visitors on Sundays. *Society Meetings:* catered for weekdays only. Professional: Martin Evans (0924 220134). Secretary: Jack McElhinney (0977 702273).

OTLEY. **Otley Golf Club,** West Busk Lane, Otley LS21 3NG (0943 461015). *Location:* off main Bradford to Otley road. Parkland with magnificent views across Wharfedale. 18 holes, 6229 yards. S.S.S. 70. Good practice ground. *Green Fees:* weekdays £23.00; weekends £28.00. *Eating facilities:* large dining rooms. *Visitors:* welcome without reservation except Tuesday mornings and Saturdays. *Society Meetings:* catered for by arrangement. Professional: Stephen McNally (0943 463403). Secretary: A.F. Flowers (0943 465329).

OUTLANE. **Outlane Golf Club,** Slack Lane, off New Hey Road, Outlane, Near Huddersfield (Halifax (0422) 374762). *Location:* from Huddersfield (A640) through Outlane Village, entrance on left just after bus terminus. 18 holes, 6003 yards. S.S.S. 69. *Green Fees:* £16.00 mid week; £24.00 weekends and Bank Holidays. Reduced rates playing with member and after 3pm Sunday. *Eating facilities:* full catering available except Mondays. *Visitors:* welcome without reservation (but advisable to phone). Professional: D. Chapman. Secretary: G. Boyle.

POLLARD LANE. **Bradford Moor Golf Club,** Scarr Hill, Pollard Lane, Bradford 2 (Bradford (0274) 638313). *Location:* A658 two miles from M62. 9 holes, 5854 yards. *Green Fees:* information not available. *Eating facilities:* available, order in advance. *Visitors:* welcome except on competition days. Professional: M. R.J. Hughes. Secretary: D. Armitage.

PONTEFRACT. **Pontefract and District Golf Club,** Park Lane, Pontefract WF8 4QS (Pontefract (0977) 792241). *Location:* M62 Exit 32, one mile from Pontefract on B6134. Parkland. 18 holes, 6227 yards. S.S.S. 70. Practice ground. *Green Fees:* weekdays £22.00; weekends £27.00. *Eating facilities:* available except Mondays. *Visitors:* welcome, must be members of a golf club. *Society Meetings:* catered for Tuesdays, Thursdays and Fridays by arrangement. Professional: J. Coleman (0977 706806). Secretary: W. T. Smith (0977 792115).

PUDSEY. **Fulneck Golf Club Ltd,** Fulneck, Pudsey LS28 8NT (Pudsey (0532) 565191). *Location:* between Leeds and Bradford. Undulating wooded parkland course. 9 holes, 5564 yards. S.S.S. 67. *Green Fees:* £10.00 (£5.00 with member) weekdays, weekends with a member only. *Society Meetings:* catered for by arrangement. Secretary: J.A. Brogden (0532 574049).

PUDSEY. **Woodhall Hills Golf Club Ltd,** Woodhall Road, Calverley, Pudsey (Leeds (0532) 564771). *Location:* one mile from Pudsey roundabout on A647 Leeds to Bradford road, signposted Calverley. 18 holes, 6102 yards. S.S.S. 69. *Green Fees:* weekdays £20.50 per round/day, weekends and Bank Holidays £25.50. Juniors £10.50 any day. *Eating facilities:* available daily except Mondays. *Visitors:* welcome without reservation. *Society Meetings:* catered for by previous arrangement. Professional: D. Tear (0532 562857). Secretary: D. Harkness (0532 554594).

SHIPLEY. **Baildon Golf Club,** Moorgate, Baildon BD17 5PP (0274 584266). *Location:* five miles northwest of Bradford via Shipley. Hilly, moorland course. 18 holes, 6085 yards, 5692 metres. S.S.S. 70. *Green Fees:* weekdays £14.00, weekends and Bank Holidays £22.00. Reduced rates for groups of 12 and over. *Eating facilities:* catering except Mondays. Bar and separate restaurant. *Visitors:* welcome, restricted at weekends and Tuesdays. *Society Meetings:* welcome weekdays only, by written application. Professional: R. Masters (0274 595162). Secretary: A. Beuridge (0274 592320).

TODMORDEN. **Todmorden Golf Club,** Rive Rocks, Cross Stone Road, Todmorden (Todmorden (0706) 812986). *Location:* A646 Halifax Road, one mile left Cross Stone Road, one mile, bear left at top. Moorland. 9 holes, 5818 yards. S.S.S. 68. *Green Fees:* weekdays £10.00, weekends and Bank Holidays £15.00. *Eating facilities:* available except Monday, order in advance. *Visitors:* welcome without reservation. *Society Meetings:* catered for Tuesday to Friday. Secretary: R.A. Ward.

WAKEFIELD. **City of Wakefield Golf Club,** Lupset Park, Horbury Road, Wakefield WF2 8QS (Wakefield (0924) 374316). *Location:* one mile from city centre, two miles from M1 Junctions 39/40. Undulating partially wooded parkland. 18 holes, 6299 yards, 5760 metres. S.S.S. 70/71. *Green Fees:* weekdays £6.00; weekends and Bank Holidays £8.00; Juniors weekdays £2.40; weekends and Bank Holidays £3.60. *Eating facilities:* full or snack catering, bar available, except Thursdays. *Visitors:* weekdays only – ball chute operates, weekends – booked times only. *Society Meetings:* only by arrangement with Professional. Not weekends. Professional: Roger Holland (0924 360282). Secretary: Mrs P. Ambler (0924 367442 club or 0924 375008 home).

WAKEFIELD. **Low Laithes Golf Club Ltd,** Parkmill Lane, Flushdyke, Ossett, Wakefield WF5 9AP (Wakefield (0924) 273275). *Location:* one mile from Junction 40 M1, or along A638 Dewsbury to Wakefield road. Parkland, undulating. 18 holes, 6456 yards. S.S.S. 71. Practice area. *Green Fees:* £18.00 weekdays; £24.00 weekends and Bank Holidays. *Eating facilities:* bar and catering. *Visitors:* welcome weekdays after 10am, weekends after 2pm. *Society Meetings:* by arrangement, not weekends or Bank Holidays. Professional: Paul Browning (0924 274667). Secretary: Donald Walker (0924 376553).

WAKEFIELD. **Painthorpe House Golf and Country Club,** Painthorpe Lane, Crigglestone, Wakefield WF4 3HE (Wakefield (0924) 255083). *Location:* half a mile from Junction 39 M1. Undulating parkland. 9 holes, 4520 yards. S.S.S. 62. *Green Fees:* weekdays £5.00; weekends £7.00. *Eating facilities:* extensive catering for private functions. Two ballrooms (one holding 450, the other 60), Saturday dinner dances. *Visitors:* welcome, restrictions weekends. Bowling green. Secretary: H. Kershaw (0924 274527).

WAKEFIELD. **Wakefield Golf Club,** Woodthorpe Lane, Sandal, Wakefield WF2 6JH (Wakefield (0924) 255104). *Location:* three miles south of Wakefield. Parkland. 18 holes, 6611 yards. S.S.S. 72. *Green Fees:* weekdays £22.00; weekends and Bank Holidays £25.00 per round/day. *Eating facilities:* full catering available. *Visitors:* visiting parties by arrangement Mondays, Wednesdays, Thursdays and Fridays, no catering Mondays. *Society Meetings:* catered for by arrangement. Professional: I.M. Wright (0924 255380). Secretary: D.T. Hall (0924 258778).

WETHERBY. **Wetherby Golf Club,** Linton Lane, Wetherby LS22 4JF (0937 582527). *Location:* off the A1 at Wetherby. Parkland course. 18 holes, 6235 yards. S.S.S. 70. Two practice grounds. *Green Fees:* weekdays £22.50 per round, £27.50 per day; weekends £33.00 per round/day. *Eating facilities:* available except Mondays. *Visitors:* welcome, advisable to phone first. *Society Meetings:* catered for Wednesdays, Thursdays and Fridays. Professional: D. Padgett (0937 583375). Secretary: W.F. Gibb (0937 580089).

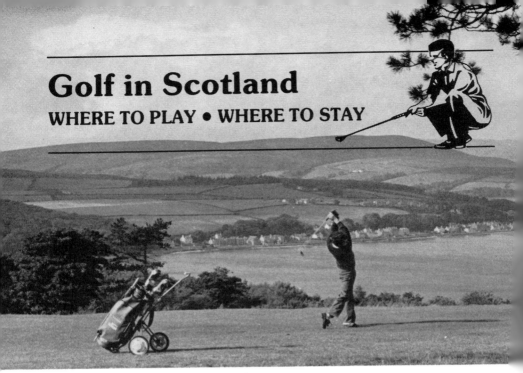

# Golf in Scotland
## WHERE TO PLAY • WHERE TO STAY

SCOTLAND is the traditional home of golf. The first written record is as early as 1457 but there is undoubtedly an earlier pedigree. The Royal and Ancient Golf Club of St. Andrews, with more recent assistance from the US Golf Association, is the law-maker and governing body of the game. The Honourable Company of Edinburgh Golfers has inherited, from the 'Gentlemen Golfers of Edinburgh', the oldest club in the world, playing over Muirfield Links at Gullane since at least 1744.

That a country so small and sparsely populated as Scotland has over 400 golf courses, therefore, is less surprising than might at first appear. Indeed, apart from more desolate, if scenic, stretches of the north west, one could almost play continuous golf around the borders and coasts of Scotland! And as one played, one would find many a good meal and comfortable bed in the hotels throughout Scotland which are so closely linked with the game of golf.

# Aberdeenshire

ABERDEEN. **Auchmill Golf Course,** Aberdeen District Council, Aberdeen Leisure, Howes Road, Bucksburn, Aberdeen. *Location:* approximately four miles from city centre, turn off A96 into Aberdeen at Howes Road. Open, fairly flat. 18 holes, 5952 yards, 5439 metres. S.S.S. 69. *Green Fees:* information not provided. *Visitors:* welcome. Contact: Outdoor Activities Officer, Aberdeen Leisure, Howes Road, Justice Mill Lane, Aberdeen AB1 2EQ (0224 587920).

ABERDEEN. **Balnagask Golf Course,** Aberdeen District Council, Aberdeen Leisure, Grey Hope Road, Aberdeen. *Location:* on coast beside Girdleness Lighthouse between Aberdeen Harbour and Nigg Bay, south east side of city. Seaside links. 18 holes, 5986 yards, 5472 metres. S.S.S. 69. *Green Fees:* information not provided. *Visitors:* welcome. Contact: Outdoor Activities Officer, Aberdeen Leisure, Bon Accord Baths, Justice Mill Lane, Aberdeen AB1 2EQ (0224 587920).

ABERDEEN. **Bon Accord Municipal Golf Club,** 19 Golf Road, Aberdeen (0224 633464). *Location:* next to Pittodrie Stadium at Aberdeen beach. Seaside links. 18 holes, 6433 yards, 5880 metres. S.S.S. 71. *Green Fees:* information not provided. *Eating facilities:* meals on request. *Society Meetings:* bookings in advance. Professional: Bruce Davidson (0224 641577). Secretary: G.S. Hunter (0224 782274).

ABERDEEN. **Caledonian Golf Club,** Kings Links, Aberdeen (Aberdeen (0224) 632443). 18 holes, 6396 yards. S.S.S. 71. *Green Fees:* information not provided. *Visitors:* welcome.

ABERDEEN. **Deeside Golf Club,** Golf Road, Bieldside, Aberdeen (Aberdeen (0224) 867697). *Location:* three miles west of Aberdeen on A93 to Braemar. Parkland. 18 holes, 5972 yards, 5460 metres. S.S.S. 69. New 9 hole course. Practice area. *Green Fees:* £15.00 weekdays, £17.00 weekends and Public Holidays. Weekly tickets £60.00. *Eating facilities:* diningroom and bar. *Visitors:* not permitted to play after 4pm weekdays nor before 4pm weekends or before 9am weekdays. *Society Meetings:* by arrangement, Thursdays only. Professional: F.G. Coutts (0224 861041). Secretary: Dr N.M. Scott (0224 869457).

ABERDEEN. **Hazlehead Golf Club,** Aberdeen District Council, Aberdeen Leisure, Groats Road, Aberdeen. *Location:* situated on west edge of city, four miles from city centre. From A944 into Aberdeen turn off into Groats Road. No. 1 course 18 holes, 6204 yards, 5673 metres. S.S.S. 70. No 2 course 18 holes, 5801 yards, 5303 metres. S.S.S. 68. 9 hole course, 2770 yards, 2531 metres. S.S.S. 34. *Green Fees:* information not provided. *Eating facilities:* restaurant adjoining park. *Visitors:* welcome. Professional: Iain Smith. Contact: Outdoor Activities Officer, Aberdeen Leisure, Bon Accord Baths, Justice Mill Lane, Aberdeen AB1 2EQ 0224 587920).

ABERDEEN. **King's Links Golf Course,** Golf Road, Aberdeen (0224 632269). *Location:* beach front course near Bridge of Don. Open plan, near Pittodrie Stadium. 18 holes, 6384 yards. S.S.S. 71. Driving range next door. *Green Fees:* £5.75 adult, £2.90 Junior. *Eating facilities:* four pubs all doing bar lunches etc nearby. *Visitors:* some bookings for after 4pm, must be done day before in person except Wednesday, Saturday and Sunday. *Society Meetings:* all welcome by writing to Aberdeen District Council (14 days notice). Professional: Bruce Davidson.

ABERDEEN. **Murcar Golf Club,** Murcar, Bridge of Don, Aberdeen (0224 704345). *Location:* five miles from Aberdeen on Peterhead – Fraserburgh road. 18 holes, 6240 yards. S.S.S. 70. *Green Fees:* weekdays £20.00 per day, £12.50 per round before 11.30am; weekends £22.50 per day. *Eating facilities:* meals served at club except Tuesday. *Visitors:* welcome without reservation. *Society Meetings:* catered for. Professional: A. White (0224 704370). Secretary: R. Matthews (0224 704354).

ABERDEEN. **Northern Aberdeen (Municipal) Golf Club,** 22 Golf Road, Aberdeen AB2 1QB (0224 636440). *Location:* off Beach Esplanade near Pittodrie Stadium. Seaside course – flat. 18 holes, 7204 yards. S.S.S. 70. *Green Fees:* information not available. *Eating facilities:* snacks available at the bar. *Visitors:* welcome. *Society Meetings:* catered for, contact Leisure and Recreation Department. Secretary: F. Sutherland. Steward: (0224 632134).

ABERDEEN. **Royal Aberdeen Golf Club,** Balgownie Links, Links Road, Balgownie AB23 8AT (Aberdeen (0224) 702571). *Location:* on A92, north side of Aberdeen, cross Bridge of Don, second right. Seaside links. Two Courses – Championship (Balgownie): 18 holes, 6372 yards, 5828 metres. S.S.S. 71; Silverburn: 18 holes, 4033 yards, 3717 metres. S.S.S. 60. Practice area. *Green Fees:* weekdays £25.00 per round, £30.00 per day; weekends and Public Holidays £30.00 per round. (Silverburn course green fees are half those quoted for Balgownie). *Eating facilities:* two bars and full catering. *Visitors:* welcome with reservation, Saturday after 3.30pm only. *Society Meetings:* catered for by arrangement with Secretary. Professional: R.A. MacAskill (0224 702221). Secretary: G.F. Webster (0224 702571; Fax: 0224 826591).

ABERDEEN. **Tarland Golf Club,** Aberdeen Road, Tarland, Aboyne (03398 81413). *Location:* from Aberdeen – A944 then A974. Parkland/wooded, easy walking, difficult upland course. 9 holes, 5816 yards for 18 holes, S.S.S. 68. Small practice area. *Green Fees:* weekdays £8.00, weekends £10.00. Weekly and fortnightly tickets available. (all rates to be reviewed). *Eating facilities:* catering available, bar 11am to midnight. *Visitors:* welcome without reservation, phone call advisable due to club competitions. *Society Meetings:* catered for except weekends. Secretary: Mr J.H. Honeyman.

ABOYNE. **Aboyne Golf Club**, Formaston Park, Aboyne (03398 86328). *Location:* A93, 30 miles west of Aberdeen. Part parkland, part hilly with lovely views. 18 holes, 5910 yards. S.S.S. 68. Practice ground. *Green Fees:* weekdays £17.00 per day, weekends £20.00 per day. *Eating facilities:* full restaurant and bar facilities. *Visitors:* welcome without reservation. *Society Meetings:* by arrangement with Secretary. Professional: Innes Wright (03398 86328). Secretary: Mrs M. MacLean (03398 87078).

ALFORD. **Alford Golf Club**, Montgarrie Road, Alford AB33 8AE (09755 62178). *Location:* A944, 26 miles west of Aberdeen. Flat course. 18 holes, 5290 yards. S.S.S. 67. Practice area. *Green Fees:* £8.00 per round, £9.50 per round, £12.50 per day weekends. Parties of 12 or over 10% discount. *Eating facilities:* snacks available, meals to order, bar. *Visitors:* always welcome, enquiries advised weekends during playing season. *Society Meetings:* catered for by arrangement. Secretary: Mrs M.J. Ball (09755 62843).

BALLATER. **Ballater Golf Club**, Victoria Road, Ballater AB3 5QX (Ballater (0338) 55200). *Location:* 40 miles west of Aberdeen on A93 in Upper Deeside. Wooded parkland course. 18 holes, 5704 yards. S.S.S. 67. *Green Fees:* £14.00 per round, £21.00 per day weekdays; £17.00 per round, £25.00 per day weekends. Weekly £63.00, season ticket £150. Reductions for players aged under 18. *Eating facilities:* restaurant, dining room – April to October, bar. *Visitors:* welcome, but advise phone call first, can be very busy especially weekends. *Society Meetings:* catered for. Professional: Joe Blair (03397 55658). Secretary: Bert Ingram (0338 55567).

BRAEMAR. **Braemar Golf Club**, Cluniebank Road, Braemar AB35 5XX (03397 41618). *Location:* about one mile from centre of the village, signposted. Flat parkland, 18 holes, 5011 yards. S.S.S. 64. Practice ground. Highest 18 hole course on mainland of Great Britain. Small practice area. *Green Fees:* weekdays £9.00 per round, £12.00 per day; weekends £12.00 per round, £15.00 per day. Weekly ticket £40.00. *Eating facilities:* restaurant and bar. *Visitors:* welcome (prior booking for weekends). *Society Meetings:* welcome by writing or phoning Secretary only. Secretary: John Pennet (0224 704471).

CRUDEN BAY. **Cruden Bay Golf Club**, Aulton Road, Cruden Bay, Peterhead AB42 7NN (Cruden Bay (0779) 812285). *Location:* seven miles south of Peterhead, 23 miles north east of Aberdeen. Traditional seaside links with magnificent views near Bay of Cruden. 18 holes, 6370 yards, 5859 metres. S.S.S. 71; 9 holes, 4710 yards. S.S.S. 62. Ample practice facilities. *Green Fees:* weekdays £18.50; weekends £25.50. *Eating facilities:* full bar and catering facilities. *Visitors:* welcome but restricted at weekends, telephone for details. *Society Meetings:* welcome weekdays only. Professional: Robbie Stewart (0779 812414). Manager: Ian A.D. McPherson (0779 812285; Fax: 0779 812945).

ELLON. **McDonald Golf Club**, Hospital Road, Ellon AB41 9AW (Ellon (0358) 20576). *Location:* A92 from Aberdeen to Ellon. One mile down A948, on left. Flat parkland with trees and stream. 18 holes, 5986 yards. S.S.S. 69. Putting green and practice nets. *Green Fees:* on application. *Eating facilities:* full catering except Mondays, bar all week. *Visitors:* welcome at all times weekdays, after 10am and booking advisable at weekends. *Society Meetings:* must book in advance. Professional: Ronnie Urquhart (0358 22891). Secretary: Fred Chadwick (0358 21397).

ELLON. **Newburgh-on-Ythan Golf Club**, c/o Andrew C. Stevenson, Newburgh, Ellon, Aberdeen AB4 0FB (03586 89438). *Location:* 12 miles north of Aberdeen. Seaside links course. 9 holes, 6300 yards, 5758 metres. S.S.S. 70. *Green Fees:* weekdays £10.00; weekends £12.00. Reduction of £2 for Senior Citizens. *Eating facilities:* at local hotels. *Visitors:* welcome, but tee reserved Tuesday evenings (Club competitions), Monday evenings (Juniors have priority) and Wednesday evenings (Ladies have priority). *Society Meetings:* by arrangement. Secretary: Andrew C. Stevenson.

FRASERBURGH. **Fraserburgh Golf Club**, Corbie Hill, Fraserburgh (0346 28287). *Location:* 38 miles north of Aberdeen. Seaside links. 18 holes, 6217 yards, 5688 metres. S.S.S. 70. Practice area. *Green Fees:* information not provided. *Eating facilities:* full catering provided, bar. *Visitors:* welcome, reservations at weekends. *Society Meetings:* catered for. Secretary: J. Grant (03465 2978).

HUNTLY. **Huntly Golf Club**, Cooper Park, Huntly AB54 4SH (0466 792643). *Location:* north side of Huntly, 38 miles from Aberdeen on A96. Open parkland course between Rivers Deveron and Bogie. 18 holes, 5399 yards. S.S.S. 66. Practice area. *Green Fees:* weekdays £10.00 day ticket; weekends £12.00. Weekly ticket £50.00. *Eating facilities:* full catering by arrangement, lounge bar. *Visitors:* welcome, no restriction except Wednesday and Thursday evenings. *Society Meetings:* by arrangement with Secretary, maximum of 40. Secretary: Gordon Alexander (0466 792877).

INSCH. **Insch Golf Club**, Golf Terrace, Insch (0464 20363). *Location:* A96 from Aberdeen. Parkland trees, water hazards. 9 holes, 2816 yards. S.S.S. 67. *Green Fees:* £6.00 per day weekdays; £8.00 weekends. *Eating facilities:* catering and bar by prior arrangement with caterer. *Visitors:* welcome except Monday and Tuesday. Secretary: James G. McCombie (0464 20291).

INVERALLOCHY. **Inverallochy Golf Club**, Inverallochy (03465 2324). *Location:* A92 from Aberdeen then B9107 for three and a half miles. Seaside links course. 18 holes, 5107 yards. S.S.S. 65. *Green Fees:* weekdays £5.00; weekends £7.00. *Eating facilities:* limited, unlicensed, advance booking required. *Visitors:* welcome. *Society Meetings:* catered for or limited basis. Secretary: R.A. Mutch (0346 28220).

INVERURIE. **Inverurie Golf Club**, Davah Wood Blackhall Road, Inverurie (Inverurie (0467) 20207) *Location:* main Aberdeen/Inverness trunk road, 1€ miles west of Aberdeen. Parkland, partly woode₁ course. 18 holes, 6000 yards. S.S.S. 66. Practice area

*Green Fees:* weekdays £8.00; weekends £12.00. *Eating facilities:* bar lounge, catering. *Visitors:* welcome anytime – reserve through Golf Shop (0467 20193). *Society Meetings:* catered for. Secretary: John Ramage (0467 21291).

INVERURIE. **Kintore Golf Club,** Balbithan Road, Kintore, Inverurie AB5 0UR (0467 32631). *Location:* off A96 12 miles north of Aberdeen. Undulating moorland course. 18 holes, 5985 yards. S.S.S. 69. *Green Fees:* weekdays £10.00 per day; weekends £15.00 per day. Evenings after 6pm £6.00. Weekly tickets available. *Eating facilities:* bar available, catering if booked in advance. *Visitors:* welcome daily except Mondays, Wednesdays and Fridays after 4pm. *Society Meetings:* welcome weekdays. Secretary: James D. Black.

KEMNAY. **Kemnay Golf Club,** Monymusk Road, Kemnay (0467) 42225). *Location:* from A96 main Aberdeen/Inverness road. Take B994 signposted Kemnay and pass through village of Kemnay to find golf course on left hand side on leaving village. Parkland. 9 holes, 5502 yards. S.S.S. 67. *Green Fees:* weekdays £6.00, weekends £7.00. *Eating facilities:* light snacks available at the bar. *Visitors:* welcome all week, Sundays if starting times available. *Society Meetings:* weekdays and weekends by arrangement, maximum number 25. Secretary: D. Imrie (0467 43047).

NEWMACHAR. **Newmachar Golf Club,** Swailend, Newmachar AB2 0UU (0651 8632002). *Location:* two and a half miles north of Dyce on A947. Championship standard wooded parkland course with ponds being main feature. 18 holes, 6605 yards. S.S.S. 73. *Green Fees:* weekdays £14.00 per round; weekends £20.00 per round. *Eating facilities:* fully licensed clubhouse, catering available. *Visitors:* welcome by prior arrangement. Handicap Certificate required. *Society Meetings:* welcome by prior arrangement. Professional: Glenn Taylor (0651 862127). Manager: George McIntosh.

OLDMELDRUM. **Oldmeldrum Golf Club,** Kirk Brae, Oldmeldrum, Inverurie AB51 0DJ (06512 2648). *Location:* 17 miles north-west of Aberdeen on A947 to Banff. First on right entering from Aberdeen direction. Undulating parkland with tree-lined fairways and water features. 18 holes, 5988 yards, 5479 metres. S.S.S. 69. Practice area. *Green Fees:* weekdays £10.00 per day,

weekends £15.00. *Eating facilities:* catering by arrangement, bar. *Visitors:* welcome, advisable to phone first. *Society Meetings:* catered for by arrangement. Secretary: Douglas Petrie (06512 2383).

PETERHEAD. **Peterhead Golf Club,** Craigewan Links, Peterhead AB42 6LT (Peterhead (0779) 72149). *Location:* off Golf Road at north end of town at mouth of River Ugie. Seaside links. 18 holes, 6189 yards. S.S.S. 70. Practice area. *Green Fees:* £10.00 weekdays, £14.00 weekends. *Eating facilities:* meals available, lounge bar. *Visitors:* welcome, no restrictions for individual visitors. *Society Meetings:* catered for anytime except Saturdays, prior booking necessary. Secretary: A. Brandie.

TORPHINS. **Torphins Golf Club,** Bog Road, Torphins, Banchory AB3 4JT (03398 82115). *Location:* Torphins is five miles north-west of Banchory, well signposted. 9 holes, 4376 yards. S.S.S. 63. *Green Fees:* £8.00 weekdays; £10.00 weekends. *Eating facilities:* light refreshments, unlicensed. *Visitors:* no play on medal days (alternate Saturdays or Sundays); members only Tuesday evenings. *Society Meetings:* no restrictions. Secretary: Mrs Sue Mortimer (03398 82563).

TURRIFF. **Turriff Golf Club,** Rosehall, Turriff AB53 7BB (0888 62745). *Location:* A947 signposted on south side of Turriff. Flat, parkland course. 18 holes, 6145 yards. S.S.S. 69. *Green Fees:* weekdays £9.00 per round, £13.00 per day; weekends £13.00 per round, £16.00 per day. *Eating facilities:* catering by arrangement. *Visitors:* no visitors before 10am weekends. Phone Professional for tee bookings. *Society Meetings:* welcome. Professional: Robin Smith (0888 63025). Secretary: James D. Stott (0888 62982).

WESTHILL. **Westhill Golf Club,** Westhill Heights, Westhill, Skene (0224 743361). *Location:* six miles from Aberdeen on A944. Undulating parkland course (hilly in places). 18 holes, 5921 yards. S.S.S. 69. Practice ground. *Green Fees:* weekdays £8.00 per round, £11.00 per day; weekends and public holidays £10.00 per round, £13.00 per day. Special package Monday-Friday for parties of 20 or more. *Eating facilities:* lounge bar with dining area. *Visitors:* welcome weekdays except between 4pm and 7pm, no visitors on Saturdays. *Society Meetings:* welcome per visitors times by arrangement. Professional: Ronnie McDonald (0224 740159). Secretary: John L. Webster (0224 740957).

# Angus

ARBROATH. **Arbroath Golf Course,** Elliot, By Arbroath (Arbroath (0241) 72069). *Location:* one mile south on Dundee to Arbroath Road A92. Seaside links. 18 holes, 6095 yards. S.S.S 69. Practice area, putting green and new sprinkler system. *Green Fees:* weekdays £10.00 per round, £15.00 per day; weekends £15.00 per round, £20.00 per day. *Eating facilities:* full catering and bar facility. *Visitors:* welcome, no visitors before 10am weekends. *Society Meetings:* all welcome (good rates midweek). Professional: L. Ewart (0241 75837). Secretary: Tom Pullar (0241 75837).

ARBROATH by. **Letham Grange Golf Club,** Colliston, By Arbroath DD11 4RL. *Location:* from Arbroath A933 – Brechin/Forfar road. Approximately four miles turn right at Colliston (signposted). OLD COURSE – 18 holes, 6939 yards. S.S.S. 73. NEW COURSE – 18 holes, 5528 yards. S.S.S. 68. Practice green, putting green and practice area. *Green Fees:* on application. *Eating facilities:* available at Hotel – catering and bars. *Visitors:* welcome, with valid handicap. Except: OLD COURSE – Tuesdays 9-10am, weekends prior to 10.30am and 1-2pm. Accommodation available. *Society Meetings/Company Outings:* welcome by arrangement. Bookings: 0241 89 373. Golf Professional: 0241 89 377.

BARRY. **Panmure Golf Club,** Burnside Road, Barry, By Carnoustie DD7 7RT (0241 53120). *Location:* two miles west of Carnoustie, south in centre at Barry village, then 200 yards turn right. Seaside links. 18 holes, 6317 yards, 5776 metres. S.S.S. 70. *Green Fees:* on application. *Eating facilities:* bar and diningroom. Soup and sandwiches only available on Mondays. *Visitors:* welcome daily – no visiting parties on Saturdays. *Society Meetings:* catered for. Professional: T. Shiel. Secretary: Captain J.C. Ray.

BRECHIN. **Brechin Golf and Squash Club,** Trinity, By Brechin DD9 6BJ (Brechin (0356) 622383). *Location:* Trinity Village, one mile north of Brechin on A94. Rolling parkland. 18 holes, 5287 yards. S.S.S. 66. *Green Fees:* weekdays £11.00 per round, £16.00 per day; weekends £14.00 per round, £22.00 per day. *Eating facilities:* excellent catering available at all times; large bar. *Visitors:* welcome without reservation. Squash courts, pool table available. *Society Meetings:* catered for, but prior booking necessary. Midweek packages for parties of 12 or more. Professional: Brian Young (0356 625270). Secretary: A.B. May (0356 622326).

CARNOUSTIE. **Carnoustie Golf Links,** Links Parade, Carnoustie DD7 7JE (0241 53789; Fax: 0241 52720). *Location:* 12 miles east of Dundee. Three 18-hole courses. Championship Course 6936 yards. S.S.S. 74; Burnside Course 6020 yards. S.S.S. 69; Buddon Links 5196 yards. S.S.S. 66. Golf trolleys permitted from May to October only. *Green Fees:* (1992 only) Weekly tickets for play over three courses £124.00. Three-day tickets for play over three courses £93.00. Championship Course: Single round £31.00. Burnside Course: Single round £12.00. Buddon Links Course: Single round £7.00. *Eating facilities:* catering facilities can be arranged with the local golf clubs. *Visitors:* welcome, times must be booked and ballot system in operation. Handicap Certificates required for play on Championship Course. *Society Meetings:* catered for by arrangement. Secretary: Earle J.C. Smith.

DUNDEE. **Caird Park Golf Club,** Mains Loan, Dundee (0382 453606). *Location:* northern edge of city, off Kingsway. Wooded parkland. 18 holes, 6273 yards, 5740 metres. S.S.S. 70. Practice range on course. *Green Fees:* information not available. *Eating facilities:* at clubhouse. *Visitors:* welcome, must book in

advance to ensure game. *Society Meetings:* see Dundee District Council, Parks Department. Professional: Jackie Black (0382 459438). *Secretary:* Douglas Farquhar Jnr.

DUNDEE. **Camperdown Golf Club,** Camperdown House, Camperdown Park, Dundee (Dundee (0382) 623398). *Location:* two miles north-west of city, enter at Kingsway/Coupar Angus road junction. Wooded parkland. 18 holes, 6561 yards. S.S.S. 72 par 71. *Green Fees:* £8.50. *Eating facilities:* (must be ordered beforehand) all year round. *Visitors:* welcome, bookable all week, contact Art and Recreation Division, Leisure Centre, Dundee. *Society Meetings:* by arrangement, catered for once booked by Parks Dept.

for date and times. Professional: R. Brown (0382 623398). Secretary: K. McCreery (0382 642925).

DUNDEE. **Downfield Golf Club,** Turnberry Avenue, Dundee DD2 3QP (0382 825595). *Location:* north end Dundee off A923 (Timex Circle). Map available on request. By rail Dundee Tay Bridge Station. Undulating wooded heathland course. 18 holes, 6804 yards. S.S.S. 73. Extensive practice ground. *Green Fees:* £33.00 per day, £22.00 per round. *Eating facilities:* full catering available. *Visitors:* welcome, weekend play arrange through Professional on day of play only. *Society Meetings:* catered for (reservation). Professional: C. Waddell (0382 89246). Managing Secretary: Brian F. Mole (0382 825595; Fax: 0382 813111).

EDZELL. **Edzell Golf Club,** High Street, Edzell DD9 7TF (03564 235). *Location:* turn left onto B966 from A94 north of Brechin by-pass on Forfar to Aberdeen road. Undulating heathland course. 18 holes, 6300 yards. S.S.S. 70. Practice area and putting green. *Green Fees:* weekdays £15.00 per round, £22.50 per day; weekends £20.00 per round, £30.00 per day. *Eating facilities:* dining room, lounge and bar. *Visitors:* welcome with some restrictions. *Society Meetings:* welcome with some restrictions, apply to Secretary. Professional: Jim Webster (03564 460). Secretary: J.M. Hutchison (03564 7283). Steward and Caterer: Mr and Mrs G. Milne.

FORFAR. **Forfar Golf Club,** Cunninghill, Forfar (Forfar (0307) 62120). *Location:* one mile from Forfar on A932 to Arbroath. Undulating wooded heathland course. 18 holes, 5497 metres. S.S.S. 69. *Green Fees:* weekdays £14.00 per round, £20.00 per day; Sundays £25.00 per day. *Visitors:* welcome. *Society Meetings:* catered for. Professional: Peter McNiven. Secretary: W. Baird (0307 63773).

KIRRIEMUIR. **Kirriemuir Golf Club Ltd,** Northmuir, Kirriemuir DD8 4LN (0575 72144). *Location:* on A926 and A928. Parkland and heathland course, relatively flat. 18 holes, 5591 yards, 5336 metres. S.S.S. 67. Practice area for members only. *Green Fees:* £17.50 weekdays; weekends with member only. *Eating facilities:* fully licensed, all catering facilities. *Visitors:* welcome weekdays only. *Society Meetings:* weekdays only. Professional: A. Caira (0575 73317). Secretary: Mrs Joan Knight (0575 73317; Fax: 0575 74608).

MONIFIETH. **Broughty Golf Club,** 6 Princes Street, Monifieth, Dundee DD5 4AW (0382 532147). Starter (0382 532767). *Location:* eight miles east of Dundee, in village of Monifieth. Seaside links, some fairways fringed with trees. Medal Course: 18 holes, 6657 yards, 6087 metres. S.S.S. 72. Ashludie Course: 18 holes, 5123 yards. S.S.S. 66. Practice area. *Green Fees:* Medal Course £16.00 per round, £24.00 per day; Sundays £18.00 per round, £27.00 per day. Ashludie Course £10.00 per round, £15.00 per day; Sundays £11.00 per round, £16.50 per day. *Eating facilities:* full catering; no catering Tuesdays or Thursdays. *Visitors:* no visitors before 2pm on Saturdays or before 10am Sundays. *Society Meetings:* by arrangement. Secretary: Samuel J. Gailey (0382 730014).

MONIFIETH. **Monifieth Golf Links,** Prince Street, Monifieth, Dundee DD5 4AW (0382 535553). *Location:* seven miles east of Dundee, Monifieth High Street. Seaside links. Medal Course 18 holes, 6657 yards. S.S.S. 72; Ashludie Course 18 holes, 5123 yards. S.S.S. 64. *Green Fees:* Medal Course £17.00 per round, £25.00 per day; Ashludie Course £11 per round, £16.00 per day Mondays to Saturdays; Medal Course £19.00 per round, £25.00 per day Sundays. Ashludie Course £12.00 per round, £16.00 per day Sundays. *Eating facilities:* clubs and Hotel. *Visitors:* welcome Monday to Friday at any time except before 9.30am; Saturdays after 2pm; Sundays after 10am. *Society Meetings:* parties over 12 must provide club Handicap Certificates. Professional: Ian McLeod (0382 532945). Secretary: H.R. Nicoll.

MONTROSE. **Montrose Links Trust,** Traill Drive, Montrose DD10 8SW (Montrose (0674) 72932). *Location:* A92 runs from Dundee to Aberdeen, through Montrose. Links Medal Course 6443 yards. Par 71. S.S.S. 71. Broomfield Course 4815 yards. Par 66. S.S.S. 63. *Green Fees:* April 1992/March 1993. Medal: weekdays £18.00 per day, £11.00 per round, Juniors £5.50 per round; weekends £25.00 per day, £16.00 per round, Juniors £8.00 per round; weekly tickets £60.00 adult, £30.00 Juniors. Broomfield: weekdays £10.00 per day, £6.50 per round, Juniors £2.00 per round; weekends £15.00 per day, £10.00 per round, Juniors £4.00 per round; weekly ticket £40.00 adult, £20.00 Junior. 'Special Deal' to parties for two rounds plus catering from £17.50. Details on request. *Eating facilities:* catering facilities available by arrangement in golf clubs. *Visitors:* welcome, except on Medal Course Saturdays and before 10am Sundays. *Society Meetings:* welcome by arrangement. Temporary membership available at the following clubs: Caledonia Golf Club (0674 72313); Mercantile Golf Club (0674 72408); Royal Montrose (0674 72376). Professional: Kevin Stables. Secretary: Mrs Margaret Stewart (0674 72932; Fax: 0674 72634).

MONTROSE. **Royal Montrose Golf Club,** Montrose (Montrose (0674) 72376). Private club playing over the Montrose courses. 18 holes, 6442 yards. S.S.S. 71. *Green Fees:* information not provided. *Eating facilities:* meals at club for temporary members. Hon. Secretary: J D. Sykes.

# Argyll

CAMPBELTOWN. **Machrihanish Golf Club,** Machrihanish, by Campbeltown (Machrihanish (058 681) 213). *Location:* five miles west of Campbeltown on B843 road. Championship standard, seaside links course. 18 holes, 6228 yards. S.S.S. 70. Also 9 holes, 2395 yards. Practice area. *Green Fees:* weekdays £13.50 per round, £18.00 per day; weekends day ticket only, £18.00. Discounts for parties of 12 and over. Advance booking necessary. *Eating facilities:* full catering and bar facilities. *Visitors:* welcome without reservation. (Some restrictions on competition days. Open competitions in summer). Special Flight/Golf packages available through Loganair, Glasgow Airport, Paisley. *Society Meetings:* as visitors. Professional: Ken Campbell (058 681 277). Secretary: Mrs Anna Anderson.

CARRADALE. **Carradale Golf Club,** Carradale PA28 6QT. *Location:* 15 miles north of Campbeltown on B842. Seaside, short but very demanding, unbelievable views. 9 holes, 2700 yards. S.S.S. 63 (18 holes). *Green Fees:* £5.00 per day. *Eating facilities:* hotel at first tee. *Visitors:* all welcome, no restrictions. Secretary: J.A. Duncan (05833 387).

DUNOON. **Blairmore and Strone Golf Club,** Strone, by Dunoon (Kilmun (036-984) 676). *Location:* on high road above Strone village, nine miles north of Dunoon on A880. Scenic hilly course, heavily wooded. 9 holes, 2112 yards, 1933 metres. S.S.S. 62. *Green Fees:* £5.00 per day or round. *Eating facilities:* bar only. *Visitors:* welcome except Saturday afternoons. Secretary: A.B. Horton (036-984 217).

DUNOON. **Cowal Golf Club,** Ardenslate Road, Kirn, Dunoon PA23 8LT (Dunoon (0369) 5673). *Location:* quarter mile off A815 at Kirn (north-east boundary of Dunoon). Wooded parkland. 18 holes, 6251 yards. S.S.S. 70. *Green Fees:* weekdays £12.00 per round, £18.00 per day; weekends £15.00 per round, £23.00 per day (prices may be subject to increase). *Eating facilities:* bar snacks all day, lunches and dinners to order. *Visitors:* welcome weekdays, some restrictions weekends. *Society Meetings:* welcome at special rates in groups of 12 (minimum) to 24 (maximum). Professional: R.D. Weir (0369 2395). Secretary: Brian Chatham (0369 5673).

DUNOON. **Innellan Golf Club,** c/o J.G. Arden, Hon. Secretary, Craigard, Royal Crescent, Dunoon (Clubhouse 0369 5276). *Location:* four miles from Dunoon by road, situated on hill behind village. Hilly wooded area. 9 holes, 4642 yards. S.S.S. 63. *Green Fees:* weekdays £6.00, Saturdays £6.00, Sundays £6.00. *Eating facilities:* by arrangement. *Visitors:* welcome, course closed Monday evenings from 5.00pm. *Society Meetings:* catered for subject to prior arrangement. Secretary: J.G. Arden (0369 3546).

OBAN. **Glencruitten Golf Club,** Glencruitten Road, Oban (Oban (0631) 62868). *Location:* one mile from town centre. Hilly parkland. 18 holes, 4452 yards. S.S.S. 63. Practice area. *Green Fees:* weekdays £9.00 per round, £11.00 per day; weekends £11.00 per round, £13.00 per day. *Eating facilities:* full catering and bar facilities. *Visitors:* welcome, restrictions on Saturdays and Thursdays during competition times. Starter: (0631 64115). Secretary: C.M. Jarvie (0631 62308).

SOUTHEND. **Dunaverty Golf Club,** Southend, By Campbeltown (0586 83 677). *Location:* about 10 miles south of Campbeltown on B842. Scenic seaside course. 18 holes, 4799 yards. S.S.S. 64. *Green Fees:* £7.00 per round, £10.00 per day. *Eating facilities:* snacks, tea and coffee. *Visitors:* welcome at all times except during competition ballot times (mainly Saturdays), telephone above number. *Society Meetings:* catered for on limited basis on prior application. Secretary: J. Galbraith (0586 83698).

TARBERT. **Tarbert Golf Club,** Kilberry Road, Tarbert PA29 6XX (0800 820565). *Location:* approximately one mile south of Tarbert on B8024. Hilly wooded parkland. 9 holes, 4460 yards. S.S.S. 64. *Green Fees:* £4.00 9 holes, £6.00 18 holes, £8.00 per day. *Eating facilities:* licensed clubhouse open evenings and weekends. *Visitors:* welcome at all times, Summer Saturday restrictions. *Society Meetings:* by arrangement. Secretary: Peter Cupples (0880 820536).

TIGHNABRUAICH. **Kyles Of Bute Golf Club,** Tighnabruaich. *Location:* access from Dunoon and Strachur. Clubhouse by Kames Farm, turn south off B8000 Kames to Millhouse road. Hillside course with magnificent views. 9 holes, 4778 yards. S.S.S. 64. *Green Fees:* £5.00 per day. *Eating facilities:* no bar, but snacks and soft drinks available. *Visitors:* welcome, except Sunday mornings. *Society Meetings:* by special arrangement only. Secretary: J.A. Carruthers (0700 811601).

# Ayrshire

AYR. **Belleisle Golf Course**, Doonfoot Road, Ayr KA7 4DU (Alloway (0292) 41258). *Location:* south of Ayr at Belleisle Park. Gently sloping parkland course with fine mature trees. 18 holes, 6477 yards. S.S.S. 71. Practice area. *Green Fees:* £12.00. One round Belleisle, one round Seafield £18.00. *Eating facilities:* hotel on site for catering. *Visitors:* no restrictions but booking in advance advisable. Juniors under 17 must have handicap of 12 or under. *Society Meetings:* catered for, groups up to 40. Professional: David Gummell (0292 41314). Starter: (0292 41258).

AYR. **Dalmilling (Municipal) Golf Club**, Westwood Avenue, Ayr KA8 0QY. *Location:* A77, on north-east boundary, one mile from town centre. Meadowland. 18 holes, 5752 yards. S.S.S. 68. Practice area. *Green Fees:* £9.00 per round, £16.00 per day. *Eating facilities:* snacks/lunches/high teas, table licence. *Visitors:* welcome without reservation (telephone for times available). *Society Meetings:* catered for by prior arrangement. Professional: Philip Cheyney (0292 263893). Secretary: Stewart Graham.

AYR. **Seafield Golf Course**, Doonfoot Road, Ayr KA7 4DU (0292 41258). *Location:* south Ayr at Belleisle Park. Reasonably flat links course. 18 holes, 5369 yards. S.S.S. 66. *Green Fees:* £9.00. One round Seafield, one round Belleisle £18.00. *Eating facilities:* hotel on site for catering. *Visitors:* welcome, no restrictions but booking in advance advisable. Juniors under 17 must have handicap of 12 or under. *Society Meetings:* catered for, groups up to 40. *Professional:* David Gummell (0292 41314). Starter: (0292 41258).

BEITH. **Beith Golf Club**, Threepwood Road, Beith (05055 3166). *Location:* off Beith by-pass road. Wooded and hilly course. 9 holes, 3400 yards, 3115 metres. S.S.S. 67. Practice area available. *Green Fees:*

weekdays £10.00 per round, £15.00 per day; weekends £15.00. *Eating facilities:* meals are available and bar open between 11am and 11pm. *Visitors:* welcome except no visitors on Saturdays and last visitors before 1pm on Sundays. *Society Meetings:* all welcome. Secretary: Mr A. McFarlane (0505 685562).

GALSTON. **Loudoun Gowf Club**, Galston KA4 8PA (Galston (0563) 820551). *Location:* five miles east of Kilmarnock on A71. Flat parkland. 18 holes, 5844 yards. S.S.S. 68. *Green Fees:* £13.00 per round, £20.00 per day weekdays. *Eating facilities:* full catering. *Visitors:* welcome weekdays only. *Society Meetings:* welcome by arrangement. Secretary: T.R. Richmond (0563 821993).

GIRVAN. **Girvan Golf Club,** Girvan (Girvan (0465) 4272). *Location:* A77 from Glasgow, through Ayr, on coast road to Stranraer. Links, parkland. 18 holes, 5078 yards. S.S.S. 65. Practice area. *Green Fees:* information not available. *Eating facilities:* available. *Visitors:* welcome, book through Starter. *Society Meetings:* welcome. Secretary: W.B. Tait (0465 2011).

IRVINE. **Glasgow Golf Club,** Gailes, Irvine KA11 5AE (0294 311347). *Location:* six miles from Kilmarnock, three miles south of Irvine, four miles north of Troon. Links. 18 holes, 6493 yards. S.S.S. 71. *Green Fees:* weekdays £27.00 per round, £33.00 per day; Saturdays and Sunday afternoons £33.00 per round. *Eating facilities:* full catering and bar facilities. *Visitors:* welcome weekdays, (not 4th Wednesday) and Saturday and Sunday afternoons if no club competitions. *Society Meetings:* by application to Club Secretary. Professional: Jack Steven (041-942 8507). Secretary: D.W. Deas (041-942 2011).

IRVINE. **Irvine Ravenspark Golf Club,** Municipal Clubhouse, Kidsneuk Lane, Irvine KA12 0SR (Irvine (0294) 71293 or 79550). *Location:* on A78 between Irvine and Kilwinning at Ravenspark Academy. Parkland course. 18 holes, 6453 yards. S.S.S. 71. *Green Fees:* weekdays £8.50, weekends £13.00 (day tickets). *Eating facilities:* entry to Club by arrangement with Secretary. *Visitors:* welcome, no jeans or training shoes allowed in the clubhouse. *Society Meetings:* groups of up to 20 welcome weekdays and Sundays. Professional: P.J. Bond (0294 76467). Secretary: G. Robertson (0294 54617).

IRVINE. **The Irvine Golf Club,** Bogside, Irvine KA12 8SN (Irvine (0294) 78139). *Location:* through Irvine going towards Kilwinning, turn left at Ravenspark Academy. Fairly flat and deemed a links course. 18

holes, 6408 yards. S.S.S. 71. Practice ground. *Green Fees:* £23.00 per round, £28.00 per day. *Eating facilities:* full catering every day except Mondays. *Visitors:* welcome with reservation. *Society Meetings:* catered for. Professional: Keith Erskine. Secretary: Andrew Morton (0294 75979).

IRVINE. **Western Gailes Golf Club,** Gailes, By Irvine KA11 5AE (0294 311649). *Location:* three miles north of Troon. Seaside links. 18 holes, 6664 yards, 6094 metres. S.S.S. 72. *Green Fees:* weekdays £33.00 per round, £40.00 per day. *Eating facilities:* full bar and catering facilities. *Visitors:* welcome Monday, Tuesday, Wednesday and Friday, must contact club in advance. Handicap Certificate required. *Society Meetings:* welcome by arrangement with Secretary. Secretary: Andrew M. McBean C.A.

KILBIRNIE. **Kilbirnie Place Golf Club,** Largs Road, Kilbirnie (Kilbirnie (0505) 683398). *Location:* on main Kilbirnie to Largs Road, left hand side just outside town boundary. Parkland. 18 holes, 5116 yards. S.S.S. 69. *Green Fees:* weekdays £10.00; weekends £17.50. Party bookings on application. *Eating facilities:* catering and bar. *Visitors:* welcome weekdays. No visitors Saturdays, no visiting parties Sundays. Secretary: J.C. Walker (0505 683283).

KILMARNOCK. **Annanhill Golf Club,** Irvine Road, Kilmarnock (0563 21644). *Location:* between Kilmarnock and Crosshouse on road to Irvine. Parkland course with excellent views. 18 holes, 6285 yards. S.S.S. 70. *Green Fees:* weekdays £8.00; weekends £12.00. *Eating facilities:* full catering available. *Visitors:* no parties on Saturdays, but welcome Sundays and weekdays by reservation. *Society Meetings:* catered for. Secretary: Mr D. McKie.

KILMARNOCK. **Caprington Golf Club,** Ayr Road, Kilmarnock (0563 23702). Parkland/wooded course. *Green Fees:* information not available. *Eating facilities:* available. *Visitors:* welcome except Saturdays. *Society Meetings:* all welcome. Secretary: F. McCulloch (0563 25848).

LARGS. **Inverclyde National Golf Training Centre,** Scottish Sports Council, Burnside Road, Largs KA30 8RW (Largs (0475) 674666). *Location:* Largs-Greenock-Glasgow (M8). Parkland, links, training bunkers. 6 holes, driving range. *Green Fees:* on application. *Eating facilities:* cafeteria, dining room, accommodation and bar. *Visitors:* groups only – pre-booked on a weekly residential basis. Professionals: Bob Torrance, Jack Steven, David Scott. Secretary: John Kent (Deputy Director).

LARGS. **Largs Golf Club,** Irvine Road, Largs KA30 8EU (Largs (0475) 673594). *Location:* on A78 28 miles from Glasgow. Parkland with scenic views. 18 holes, 6220 yards. S.S.S. 70. *Green Fees:* weekdays £24.00 per day, £18.00 per round; weekends £24.00 per round or day. *Eating facilities:* full catering and bar. *Visitors:* welcome, no restrictions except on competition days. *Society Meetings:* catered for Tuesdays and Thursdays only by prior arrangement. Professional: R. Collinson (0475 686192). Secretary: F. Gilmour (0475 672497).

LARGS. **Routenburn Golf Club,** Routenburn, Largs (Largs (0475) 673230). Hilly moorland course. 18 holes, 5765 yards. S.S.S. 67. *Green Fees:* information not provided. *Eating facilities:* lunches at club except Thursdays, order in advance. *Visitors:* welcome with reservation. *Society Meetings:* catered for on application to club. Professional: Greig McQueen (0475 687240). Secretary: J.E. Smeaton.

MAUCHLINE. **Ballochmyle Golf Club,** Mauchline KA5 6LE (Mauchline (0295) 50469). *Location:* turn left from A76 coming out of Mauchline from Kilmarnock, club adjacent to Ballochmyle Hospital. Wooded parkland course. 18 holes, 5952 yards. S.S.S. 69. *Green Fees:* £22.00 per day weekdays; £27.00 per day weekends. *Eating facilities:* all day bar opening from 1st April until 30th Sept, snacks and meals available during bar hours. *Visitors:* welcome every day except Saturdays. Dress both on and off the course must be adhered to. Two full size snooker tables and squash court. *Society Meetings:* all welcome to a total of 30 per party. Secretary: Douglas Munro (0295 50469).

MAYBOLE. **Maybole Golf Club,** Memorial Park, Kirkoswald Road, Maybole (0292 281511). *Location:* A77 from Glasgow. By-pass Ayr to Girvan road, on main Girvan road at Maybole. Hilly parkland. 9 holes, 5270 yards. S.S.S. 65. *Green Fees:* municipal rates. *Visitors:* welcome. *Society Meetings:* welcome.

NEW CUMNOCK. **New Cumnock Golf Club,** Lochhill, Cumnock Road, New Cumnock. *Location:* half a mile north of New Cummock on A76. Parkland. 9 holes, 4772 yards (18). S.S.S. 63. *Green Fees:* weekdays £6.00 adults; weekends £6.00 adults; £4.00 Juveniles. Senior Citizens within Cumnock and Doon Valley £1.00. *Eating facilities:* local hotel next to course.

*Visitors:* welcome at all times except Sunday competition days before 4pm. *Society Meetings:* welcome, contact Secretary. Secretary: Jim Bryce (0290 32037).

PRESTWICK. **Prestwick Golf Club,** Links Road, Prestwick (Prestwick (0292) 77404). *Location:* one mile from Prestwick airport, 40 minutes by car from Turnberry Hotel, 10 minutes from Troon, 15 minutes from Ayr. 18 holes, 6544 yards. (No LGU tees). S.S.S. 72. *Green Fees:* information not provided. *Eating facilities:* dining room (male only: prior booking required) open from 12.30pm to 2.30pm Cardinal Room (light lunches) open to ladies and gentlemen from 10.00am until 4.00pm. *Visitors:* welcome with reservation. *Society Meetings:* catered for. Professional: F.C. Rennie. Secretary: D.E. Donaldson.

PRESTWICK. **Prestwick St. Cuthbert Golf Club,** East Road, Prestwick KA9 2SX (0292 77101). *Location:* south-east area of Prestwick near A77 and Prestwick Airport. Flat, some trees; semi-parkland. 18 holes, 6470 yards, 6063 metres. S.S.S. 71. Limited practice area. *Green Fees:* £24.00 per day weekdays only. *Eating facilities:* full catering and bar service. *Visitors:* welcome except weekends unless introduced by and playing with member. *Society Meetings:* catered for. Secretary: R. Morton (0292 77101).

PRESTWICK. **Prestwick St. Nicholas Golf Club,** Grangemuir Road, Prestwick KA9 1SN (0292 77608). *Location:* proceed down Grangemuir Road from main street Prestwick. 18 holes, 5926 yards, 5418 metres. S.S.S. 68. *Green Fees:* weekdays £28.00 per day, £18.00 per round. *Eating facilities:* full service. *Visitors:* welcome most weekdays with club introduction, reserved for members at weekends. *Society Meetings:* catered for by arrangement. Professional: S. Smith (0292 79755). Secretary: J.R. Leishman (0292 77608).

SKELMORLIE. **Skelmorlie Golf Club,** Beithglass Road, Skelmorlie PA17 5ES (Wemyss Bay (0475) 520159). *Location:* two/three miles from Wemyss Bay Pier. Hillside course. 13 holes, 5056 yards. S.S.S. 65. *Green Fees:* weekdays £8.00 per round, £11.00 per day; Sundays only £10.00 per round, £15.00 per day. No visitors Saturdays. Discounts to local hotel residents. *Eating facilities:* bar with snacks available. *Visitors:* welcome except Saturdays before 4pm. *Society Meetings:* welcome by arrangement. Parties at discounted "all-in" rate. Secretary: Mr J. Blair (0475 35642).

STEVENSTON. **Ardeer Golf Club,** Greenhead, Stevenston KA20 4JX (0294 64542). *Location:* north of Ayr. Rural parkland, undulating fairways. 18 holes, 6630 yards. S.S.S. 72. *Green Fees:* weekdays £10.00 (£18.00 daily); weekends £12.00 (£24.00 daily). *Eating facilities:* lounge, restaurant, bars. *Visitors:* welcome except Saturdays and medal Sundays. *Society Meetings:* catered for. Professional: Bob Rodgers (0294 601327). Secretary: William F. Hand (0294 63538).

TROON. **Kilmarnock (Barassie) Golf Club,** 29 Hillhouse Road, Barassie, Troon KA10 6SY (Troon (0292) 311077). *Location:* 100 yards from Barassie Railway Station, nearest town Troon. Links course. 18

holes, 6473 yards. S.S.S. 71. Practice ground. *Green Fees:* £35.00 per day or round weekdays. *Eating facilities:* coffee, lunches, snacks, high teas. *Visitors:* welcome Mondays, Tuesdays, Thursdays and Friday afternoons. *Society Meetings:* catered for. Professional: W.R. Lockie (0292 311322). Secretary: Robert L. Bryce (0292 313920).

TROON. **Royal Troon Golf Club,** Craigend Road, Troon KA10 6EP (0292 311555). *Location:* three miles from A77 (Glasgow/Ayr trunk road). Old Course 18 holes, 7097 yards, 6488 metres. S.S.S. 74. Portland Course 18 holes, 6274 yards, 5738 metres. S.S.S. 71. *Green Fees:* £65.00 (Old); £40.00 (Portland). Lunch and morning coffee, etc included. *Eating facilities:* full restaurant service available, including bar snacks. *Visitors:* Mondays, Tuesdays and Thursdays between 9.30 and 11.00am and 14.30 and 15.00pm. Letter of introduction from own club and Handicap Certificate

(maximum of 20). (No ladies or those under 18 years on Old Course). *Society Meetings:* parties in excess of 24 not accepted. Professional: R. Brian Anderson (0292 313281). Secretary/Manager: J.D. Montgomerie (0292 311555 Fax: 0292 318204).

TROON. **Troon Municipal Golf Course,** Hayling Drive, Troon (0292 312464). *Location:* adjacent to railway station, one mile off the Ayr-Glasgow road. Three 18 hole courses. Lochgreen 6687 yards. S.S.S. 72. Darley 6327 yards. S.S.S. 70. Fullerton 4784 yards. S.S.S. 63. *Green Fees:* information not provided. *Eating facilities:* hot snacks, 8am – 6pm. Bar snacks and lunches, evening meals bookings only. *Visitors:* catered for. Broad wheeled trolleys only. *Society Meetings:* catered for. Caterer: John Darge. Professional: Gordon McKinley. Advance booking should be made in writing to Starter's Office, Troon Municipal Golf Courses, Harling Drive, Troon Ayrshire.

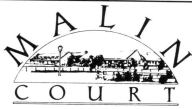

TURNBERRY. **Turnberry Hotel Golf Courses,** Turnberry KA26 9LT (0655 31000 extension 424; Fax: 0655 31706). *Location:* A77 between Girvan and Maybole. Seaside links, flat with magnificent views over Turnberry Bay to Arran and Ailsa Craig. 2 Championship Courses, Ailsa and Arran, each of 18 holes. Ailsa 6408 yards. S.S.S. 72, Arran 6249 yards. S.S.S. 70. Large practice area. *Green Fees:* on application. *Eating facilities:* hotel plus clubhouse, restaurant and bar. *Visitors:* written requests only. *Society Meetings:* same as visitors. Professional: Bob Jamieson (0655 31000 extension 440). Club Manager: R.L. Hamblett.

WEST KILBRIDE. **West Kilbride Golf Club,** 33-35 Fullerton Drive, Seamill, West Kilbride KA23 9HT (0294 823128). *Location:* on A78 Greenock to Ayr Road, leave at Seamill. Seaside links course. 18 holes, 6452 yards. S.S.S. 71. Practice area. *Green Fees:* on application. *Eating facilities:* diningroom and bar. *Visitors:* welcome weekdays only. Dormie House available sleeps four. *Society Meetings:* catered for Tuesdays and Thursdays. Certificates required. Professional: Gregor Howie (0294 823042). Secretary: E.D. Jefferies (0294 823911).

# Banffshire

BANFF. **Duff House Royal Golf Club,** The Barnyards, Banff AB45 3SX (0261 812062). *Location:* two minutes from town centre, A97, A98. Level parkland. 18 holes, 6161 yards. S.S.S. 69. *Green Fees:* weekdays £10.00 per round, £14.00 per day; weekends £15.00 per round, £20.00 per day. *Eating facilities:* lounge bar and full catering service. *Visitors:* welcome without reservation except restricted weekends. *Society Meetings:* catered for by prior arrangement. Professional: R.S. Strachan (0261 812075). Secretary: K.T. Morrison (0261 812062).

BUCKIE. **Buckpool Golf Club (Buckie),** Barhill Road, Buckie AB56 1DU (0542 32236). *Location:* turn off A98 signposted Buckpool. Links course with superlative view over Moray Firth. 18 holes, 6257 yards. S.S.S. 70. *Green Fees:* weekdays £9.00 per day, £5.00 (single rounds only) after 3.30pm; weekends £12.00 per day, £7.00 (single rounds only) after 3.30pm. *Eating facilities:* full catering daily. Normal bar hours. *Visitors:* no restrictions except when there are scheduled competitions. Squash, snooker and indoor

bowling. *Society Meetings:* welcome by prior arrangement. Secretary: Isabel E. Jagger.

CULLEN. **Cullen Golf Club,** The Links, Cullen, Buckie AB56 2SN (0542 40685). *Location:* off A98 midway between Aberdeen and Inverness, on Moray Firth coast. Seaside links with elevated section, natural rock landscaping and sandy beach coming into play at several holes. 18 holes, 4610 yards. S.S.S. 62. Putting green and net area. *Green Fees:* day tickets: weekdays £7.00, weekends £10.00. Weekly and fortnightly tickets available. Member of District Council's Rover Golf Ticket scheme. *Eating facilities:* catering and bar facilities. *Visitors:* welcome, may be restrictions Wednesdays and Saturdays (club competitions). *Society Meetings:* catered for. Secretary: I. Findlay (0542 40174).

DUFFTOWN. **Dufftown Golf Club,** Mether Cluny, Tomintoul Road, Dufftown (Dufftown (0340) 20325 or 20158). *Location:* one mile from Dufftown on Tomintoul Road. Hilly course, spectacular views. 18 holes, 5308 yards. S.S.S. 67. *Green Fees:* weekdays £7.00; weekends £8.00. Weekly (five day) ticket £25.00.

Juniors half price. *Eating facilities:* bar and snacks daily. *Visitors:* welcome at all times (minor restrictions on Wednesdays evenings). *Society Meetings:* welcome by arrangement, catering available. Treasurer: D.F. Duncombe (0340 20432).

KEITH. **Keith Golf Club,** Fife Park, Keith (Keith (05422) 2469). *Location:* off the Keith-Dufftown Road. Parkland. 18 holes, 5767 yards. S.S.S. 68. *Green Fees:* Day ticket: weekdays £7.00, weekends £10.00. *Eating facilities:* available all summer. *Visitors:* welcome without reservation at all times. *Society Meetings:* catered for by arrangement with Secretary. Secretary: G. Morrison (05422 2696).

MACDUFF. **Royal Tarlair Golf Club,** Buchan Street, Macduff (Macduff (0261) 32897). *Location:* A98 Fraserburgh to Inverness trunk road – A947 road. Seaside links. 18 holes, 5866 yards, 5373 metres. S.S.S. 68. *Green Fees:* weekdays £8.00 per day, weekends £10.00 per day. *Eating facilities:* full catering and bar available. *Visitors:* welcome. *Society Meetings:* catered for (bookings through Secretary). Secretary: Mrs E. Black (0261 851221).

*Please mention this guide when you write or phone to enquire about accommodation.*

# Berwickshire

COLDSTREAM. **Hirsel Golf Club,** Kelso Road, Coldstream (0890 2678). *Location:* A697 west of Coldstream. Parkland. 9 holes, 5830 yards. S.S.S. 72 (ladies), 68 (men). *Green Fees:* weekdays £10.00; weekends £15.00. Weekly tickets £45.00. *Eating facilities:* available. *Visitors:* welcome without reservation. *Society Meetings:* catered for on application. Secretary: W. Murray (0890 2661).

DUNS. **Duns Golf Club,** Hardens Road, Duns. *Location:* about one mile west of Duns just off A6105. 9 holes, 5826 yards (2913 x 2). S.S.S. 68. Practice ground. *Green Fees:* £8.00 weekdays; £10.00 weekends (half-price 1st November to 15th March). *Eating facilities:* lounge/bar open weekday evenings and weekends during season, snacks available. *Visitors:* welcome without reservation. *Society Meetings:* catered for. Secretary: A. Campbell (0361 82717).

EYEMOUTH. **Eyemouth Golf Club,** Gunsgreeen House, Eyemouth (Eyemouth (08907) 50551). *Location:* six miles north of Berwick-on-Tweed, off the A1 towards the coast. Seaside course on cliff tops with panoramic views, spectacular hole over North Sea inlet. 9 holes, 5000 metres. S.S.S. 65. *Green Fees:* £8.00 daily. *Eating facilities:* no eating facilities, normal bar hours in the evenings. *Visitors:* welcome most weekdays; after 10.30am on Saturdays and after 12 noon Sundays. *Society Meetings:* by prior arrangement with Secretary. Secretary: I. Fairbairn (08907 50074).

LAUDER. **Lauder Golf Club,** Galashiels Road, Lauder. *Location:* off A68, 28 miles south of Edinburgh. Undulating course, originally designed by W. Park of Musselburgh, on Lauder Hill. 9 holes, 6002 yards. S.S.S. 70. Practice ground. *Green Fees:* £5.00 weekdays; £6.00 weekends. *Eating facilities:* none – good Hotels in Lauder. *Visitors:* welcome without reservation. Secretary: D. Dickson (05782 526).

# Caithness

LYBSTER. **Lybster Golf Club,** Main Street, Lybster. *Location:* 14 miles south from Wick on A9, half-way down village street. One of smallest courses in Scotland, heathland/parkland. 9 holes, 1896 yards. S.S.S. 62. *Green Fees:* £3.00. *Eating facilities:* at nearby hotels in village. *Visitors:* welcome anytime. *Society Meetings:* welcome anytime. Secretary: N. Fraser (084 784 215).

THURSO. **Reay Golf Club,** Clubhouse, Reay, Thurso (Reay (084781) 288). *Location:* on A836 11 miles west of Thurso, two miles west of Dounreay. Seaside links. 18 holes, 5865 yards. S.S.S. 68. Practice area. *Green Fees:* £10.00. Weekly ticket £30.00. *Eating facilities:* bar lunches May to September weekdays, bar only weekends. *Visitors:* welcome anytime, restricted during competitions (Saturday mornings April to September). *Society Meetings:* welcome. Captain: Evan Sutherland (0847-81 439). Secretary: Miss P. Peebles (084781 37).

THURSO. **Thurso Golf Club,** Newlands of Geise, By Thurso (Thurso (0847) 3807). *Location:* two miles south west of Railway Station. Flat parkland, wonderful views of Pentland Firth and Orkneys. 18 holes, 5610 yards. S.S.S. 69. *Green Fees:* £10.00, with member £5.00 (clubs provided). *Eating facilities:* Tuesdays and Thursday evenings and weekends. *Visitors:* welcome without reservation. *Society Meetings:* catered for. Shop Manager: J. Conaghan. Secretary: J.R. Owens (0847 62144).

WICK. **Wick Golf Club,** Reiss, By Wick KW1 4RW (0955 2726). *Location:* three miles north of Wick on A9. Seaside links course. 18 holes, 5976 yards. S.S.S. 69, Ladies 72. Practice area. *Green Fees:* £10.00 per day. *Eating facilities:* licensed; snacks available. *Visitors:* welcome. *Society Meetings:* catered for. Secretary: Mrs M.S.W. Abernethy (0955 2702).

# Clackmannanshire

ALLOA. **Alloa Golf Club,** Shawpark, Sauchie (Alloa (0259) 722745). *Location:* on A908 between Alloa and Tillicoultry. Parkland. 18 holes, 6240 yards. S.S.S. 70. Two practice grounds. *Green Fees:* weekdays £12.00 per round, £20.00 per day. *Eating facilities:* dining room, bar meals. *Visitors:* welcome. *Society Meetings:* catered for. Professional: Bill Bennett (0259 724476). Secretary: A.M. Frame (0259 50100).

ALLOA. **Braehead Golf Club,** Cambus, By Alloa FK10 2NT (0259 722078). *Location:* one mile west of Alloa on A907. Parkland. 18 holes, 6013 yards. S.S.S. 69. Practice area. *Green Fees:* weekdays £12.00 per round, £17.00 per day; weekends £17.00 per round, £22.00 per day. *Eating facilities:* bar/catering available all day during Summer months; slightly restricted opening during Spring/Autumn. *Visitors:* no restrictions but advisable to telephone in advance. *Society Meetings:* catered for with prior booking. Professional: Paul Brookes. Secretary: Paul MacMichael.

ALVA. **Alva Golf Club,** Beauclerc Street, Alva FK12 5LD (0259 760431). *Location:* seven miles from Stirling on A91 Stirling to St Andrews Road – course lies at foot of Ochil Hills. Inland wooded hillside course with fast greens. 9 holes, 2423 yards, 2213 metres. S.S.S. 64. *Green Fees:* on application. *Eating facilities:* bar snacks only. *Visitors:* welcome at all times. Lounge and changing rooms available. Secretary: (0259 760431).

DOLLAR. **Dollar Golf Club,** Brewlands House, Dollar (Dollar (0259) 42400). *Location:* on A91. 18 holes, 5144 yards. S.S.S. 66. *Green Fees:* weekdays £6.00 round, £10.00 day; weekends £13.00. *Eating facilities:* full catering except Tuesdays. *Visitors:* welcome. *Society Meetings:* catered for. Secretary: M.B. Shea.

DOLLAR. **Muckhart Golf Club,** Muckhart, By Dollar (Muckhart (0259) 781423). *Location:* on A91, 14 miles east of Stirling. 18 holes, 6034 yards. S.S.S. 70. *Green Fees:* weekdays £12.50 per round, £18.00 per day; weekends £18.00 per round, £24.00 per day. Morning coffee, lunch and high tea plus 36 holes golf: £26.00 weekdays, £32.00 weekends. *Eating facilities:* meals available in clubhouse all day, every day. *Visitors:* welcome without reservation except before 9.45am and 12.00 noon to 2.30pm weekends. *Society Meetings:* catered for. Professional: Keith Salmoni. Secretary: A.B. Robertson.

# Dumfriesshire

ANNAN. **Powfoot Golf Club,** 27 Bank Street, Annan DG12 6AU (04617 227). *Location:* off Annan/Dumfries Road B724, signpost to course approximately three miles from Annan. Semi-links course on Solway shore with outstanding views. 18 holes, 6283 yards, 5745 metres. S.S.S. 70. Practice ground. *Green Fees:* weekdays £23.00 per day, after 2.45pm £14.00 per round. Sundays after 2.45pm £15.00. *Eating facilities:* morning coffee, lunches and teas in clubhouse – ordering in advance essential for large parties. *Visitors:* welcome weekdays but restrictions at weekends, no formal introduction required. *Society Meetings:* catered for weekdays by prior arrangement (up to 40 in number). Professional: Gareth Dick (04617 327). Secretary: R.G. Anderson (0461 202866/7).

DUMFRIES. **Dumfries and County Golf Club,** Nunfield, Edinburgh Road, Dumfries DG1 1JX (Dumfries (0387) 53585). *Location:* one mile north-east town centre on A701. 18 holes, 5928 yards. S.S.S. 68. Limited practice facilities. *Green Fees:* £18.00 weekdays; £20.00 weekends. *Eating facilities:* restaurant and bar snacks. *Visitors:* welcome except on Saturdays. *Society Meetings:* catered for by arrangement. Professional: G. Gray (0387 68918). Secretary: E.C. Pringle (0387 53585).

DUMFRIES. **Dumfries and Galloway Golf Club,** Laurieston Avenue, Dumfries (Dumfries (0387) 53582). *Location:* on Castle Douglas/Stranraer road, A75. Parkland course, 18 holes, 5803 yards. S.S.S. 68. Practice area. *Green Fees:* weekdays £16, weekends £20. *Eating facilities:* full catering during bar hours except Mondays. *Visitors:* welcome, except on competition days. *Society Meetings:* catered for weekdays except Tuesdays. Secretary: Jack Donnachie (0387 63848). Professional: Joe Fergusson (0387 56902).

DUMFRIES. **Southerness Golf Club,** Southerness, Kirkbean, Dumfries DG2 8AZ (Kirkbean (038 788) 677). *Location:* 16 miles south west of Dumfries on A710 (Solway Coast Road). Natural challenging Championship links, designed by MacKenzie Ross with panoramic views of Solway Firth and Galloway hills. Hosted British Ladies' Amateur 1989 and British Youths' 1990. 18 holes, 6554 yards. S.S.S. 72. Large practice area. *Green Fees:* weekdays £20.00 per day; weekends £26.00 per day. Weekly (Monday to Friday) ticket £80.00. *Eating facilities:* full bar and catering facilities. *Visitors:* reserved for members up to 10am (10.30am weekends) and from noon to 2pm (2.30pm weekends). Booking advisable. *Society Meetings:* on application to Secretary. Secretary: W.D. Ramage.

LANGHOLM. **Langholm Golf Club,** Whitaside, Langholm DG13 0JS (Langholm (03873) 80559). *Location:*on A7 Carlisle-Edinburgh road. Turn off at market place in centre of town. Hillside. 9 holes, 5744 yards. S.S.S. 68. Practice area available. *Green Fees:* £8.00; £4.00 if playing with member. *Eating facilities:* on request. *Visitors:* welcome without reservation; Saturday 9am to 9.45am, 1pm to 1.45pm, Sunday 9am

to 10am and 1pm Competition times. *Society Meetings:* in writing to Secretary. Secretary: Mr A. Edgar (03873 80878).

LOCKERBIE. **Lochmaben Golf Club,** Back Road, Lochmaben, Lockerbie DG11 1NT (Lochmaben (0387) 810552). *Location:* A709 Dumfries – Lockerbie Road. Parkland with panoramic views adjacent to Loch. 9 holes, 5304 yards, 4616 metres. S.S.S. 66. *Green Fees:* information not provided. *Eating facilities:* on request, lunch/evening. *Visitors:* welcome except on competition days and not after 5pm. Fishing. *Society Meetings:* welcome. Secretary: B.J. Graham (0387 810552).

LOCKERBIE. **Lockerbie Golf CLub,** 89 High Street, Lockerbie DG11 2ND (Lockerbie (05762) 3363). *Location:* on A74 at Lockerbie, take Corrie Road, 500 yards. Parkland featuring pond which is in play at three holes. 18 holes, 5418 yards. S.S.S. 66. *Green Fees:* weekdays £12.00; weekends £15.00. *Eating facilities:* catering in season 9am – 8pm, bar 11am – 11pm. *Visitors:* welcome. *Society Meetings:* welcome by arrangement. Secretary: Mr J. Thomson (05762 2462).

# FOR THE MUTUAL GUIDANCE OF GUEST AND HOST

Every year literally thousands of holidays, short-breaks and overnight stops are arranged through our guides, the vast majority without any problems at all. In a handful of cases, however, difficulties do arise about bookings, which often could have been prevented from the outset.

It is important to remember that when accommodation has been booked, both parties — guests and hosts — have entered into a form of contract. We hope that the following points will provide helpful guidance.

**GUESTS:** When enquiring about accommodation, be as precise as possible. Give exact dates, numbers in your party and the ages of any children. State the number and type of rooms wanted and also what catering you require — bed and breakfast, full board, etc. Make sure that the position about evening meals is clear — and about pets, reductions for children or any other special points.

Read our reviews carefully to ensure that the proprietors you are going to contact can supply what you want. Ask for a letter confirming all arrangements, if possible.

If you have to cancel, do so as soon as possible. Proprietors do have the right to retain deposits and under certain circumstances to charge for cancelled holidays if adequate notice is not given and they cannot re-let the accommodation.

**HOSTS:** Give details about your facilities and about any special conditions. Explain your deposit system clearly and arrangements for cancellations, charges, etc, and whether or not your terms include VAT.

If for any reason you are unable to fulfil an agreed booking without adequate notice, you may be under an obligation to arrange alternative suitable accommodation or to make some form of compensation.

MOFFAT. **The Moffat Golf Club,** Coatshill, Moffat DG10 9SB (Moffat (0683) 20020). *Location:* leave A74 at Beattock on A701, club notice one mile on left. Scenic moorland course. 18 holes, 5218 yards. S.S.S. 66. Putting green; small practice area. *Green Fees:* weekdays £12.00 per day; weekends £22.00 per day; 5-day ticket £35.00. *Eating facilities:* bar meals served all day. *Visitors:* welcome without reservation, except Wednesday after 12 noon. *Society Meetings:* catering provided. Secretary: T.A. Rankin (0683 20020). Clubmaster: Mr Ian Preston.

SANQUHAR. **Sanquhar Golf Club,** Euchan Course, Sanquhar (Sanquhar (0659) 50577). *Location:* situated quarter-of-a-mile from A76 Dumfries-Kilmarnock trunk road. 9 holes, 5144 metres. S.S.S. 68. *Green Fees:* weekdays £8.00 per round, weekends £10.00 per

round. *Eating facilities:* bar available if requested in advance. *Visitors:* welcome without reservation. *Society Meetings:* catered for with advance notice. Licensed clubhouse with full-size snooker table. Secretary: Mrs J. Murray (0659 58181).

THORNHILL. **Thornhill Golf Club,** Blacknest, Thornhill DG3 5DW (Thornhill (0848) 30546) *Location:* 14 miles north of Dumfries on A76. Parkland/ open moorland. 18 holes, 6011 yards. S.S.S. 69. Practice ground (two areas). *Green Fees:* weekdays £12.00; weekends £18.00. Weekly ticket £75.00. *Eating facilities:* catering available, except Mondays, bar facility. *Visitors:* welcome without reservation, but please contact club steward re competitions, etc. *Society Meetings:* welcome, contact club Steward. Secretary: Stuart Moscrop (0848 30151).

# Dunbartonshire

ALEXANDRIA. **Vale of Leven Golf Club,** Northfield Road, Bonhill, Alexandria (Alexandria (0389) 52351). *Location:* off A82 at Bonhill, follow signs to clubhouse, approximately one mile. Moorland overlooking Loch Lomond with splendid views. 18 holes, 5165 yards. S.S.S. 66. *Green Fees:* weekdays £8.50 per round, £12.00 per day; weekends £11.00 per round, £16.00 per day. *Eating facilities:* catering and bar available. *Visitors:* welcome except Saturdays between April 1st and September 30th. Full changing and locker facilities. *Society Meetings:* catered for, special rates available on application to Secretary. Secretary: W. McKinlay (0389 52508).

CARDROSS. **Cardross Golf Club,** Main Road, Cardross G82 5LB (Cardross (0389) 841213). *Location:* on A814 west of Dumbarton. Parkland course. 18 holes, 6469 yards. S.S.S. 71. Practice ground. *Green Fees:* weekdays £15.00 per round, £25.00 day ticket. *Eating facilities:* lunches/bar snacks available during bar hours. *Visitors:* weekdays only (by phoning Professional to book time). *Society Meetings:* catered for weekdays by application to Secretary. Professional: Robert Craig (0389 841350). Secretary: R. Evans, C.A. (0389 841754).

CLYDEBANK. **Clydebank and District Golf Club,** Glasgow Road, Hardgate, Clydebank G81 5QY (0389 73289). *Location:* Hardgate village. Off A8 10 miles west of Glasgow (off Great Western Road). 18 holes, 5832 yards, 5325 metres. S.S.S. 68. *Green Fees:* £12.00 per round. *Eating facilities:* catering as required. *Visitors:* welcome weekdays only. Professional: David Pirie (0389 78686). Secretary: W. Manson (0389 72832).

CLYDEBANK. **Clydebank Municipal Golf Course,** Overtoun Road, Clydebank G81 3RE (041-952 8698). *Location:* one mile west of Clydebank centre off Duntocher Road. Parkland course – one of the best Par 3's in Scotland. 18 holes, 5349 yards. S.S.S. 66. *Green Fees:* £4.00 per round weekdays; £4.40 per round weekends. Season Ticket £100, Juvenile Season Ticket £30.00, Senior Citizen Season Ticket £25.00. *Eating facilities:* tearoom. *Visitors:* municipal course, tee closed Saturdays in Summer 11am to 2pm. *Society Meetings:* contact District Council. Professional: Richard Bowman (041-952 6372). Secretary: District Council (041-941 1331).

CUMBERNAULD. **Palacerigg Golf Club,** Palacerigg Country Park, Cumbernauld, Near Glasgow G67 3HU (0236 734969). *Location:* Palacerigg Road, three miles south of Cumbernauld. Wooded parkland. 18 holes, 6440 yards. S.S.S. 71. Practice area. *Green Fees:* £6.50 per day weekdays, £7.50 per day weekends. *Eating facilities:* bar seven days, all day opening from March to October; meals available Wednesdays to Sundays or by arrangement. *Visitors:* welcome weekdays only. *Society Meetings:* by letter to Secretary. Secretary: Gordon McConkey (0236 734969).

CUMBERNAULD. **Westerwood Golf Club,** Westerwood, Cumbernauld (0236 51171; Fax: 0236 738478). *Location:* off M80 towards Dullatur. Undulating wooded course designed by Seve Ballesteros and Dave Thomas. 18 holes, 6721 yards. S.S.S. 73. *Green Fees:* £22.50 per round, £35.00 per day weekdays; £27.50 per round, £40.00 per day weekends. *Eating facilities:* clubhouse, restaurant and bar at all times, no restrictions. Advance booking of tee-off times recommended. Hotel golf packages available. *Society Meetings:* welcome by arrangement. Golf Professional: Tony Smith (0236 725281; Fax: 0236 738478).

DUMBARTON. **Dumbarton Golf Club,** Broadmeadow, Dumbarton G82 2BQ (Dumbarton (0389) 32830). *Location:* three-quarters of a mile from A82 on edge of town. Flat course. 18 holes, 5992 yards. S.S.S. 69. *Green Fees:* £15.00 weekdays. *Eating facilities:* bar available, meals by appointment. *Visitors:* welcome, Monday to Friday only. No jeans or shellsuits on course or in clubhouse. *Society Meetings:* catered for weekdays (£2.00 advance booking fee). Secretary: R. Turnbull.

HELENSBURGH. **Helensburgh Golf Club,** 25 East Abercromby Street, Helensburgh G84 9JD (Helensburgh (0436) 74173). *Location:* A82 Dumbarton. Moorland course with panoramic views. 18 holes, 6058 yards. S.S.S. 69. *Green Fees:* £15.00 per round, £23.00 per day weekdays. *Eating facilities:* full catering and bar. *Visitors:* welcome weekdays only, dress in recognised golfing attire. Professional: Robert Farrell (0436 75505). Secretary: Mrs A. McEwan (0436 74173).

KIRKINTILLOCH. **Kirkintilloch Golf Club,** Campsie Road, Kirkintilloch G66 1RN (041-776 1256). *Location:* from Glasgow to Bishopbriggs, then straight on to Kirkintilloch. Undulating, parkland course. 18 holes, 5269 yards. S.S.S. 66. Par 70. Putting green and practice areas. *Green Fees:* on application. *Eating facilities:* dining room and bar. *Visitors:* weekdays only, must be introduced by member. *Society Meetings:* catered for Mondays and Tuesdays, information from Secretary including catering. Secretary: I.M. Gray (041-775 2387).

LENZIE. **Lenzie Golf Club,** 19 Crosshill Road, Lenzie, Glasgow (041-776 1535). *Location:* six miles north-east of Glasgow. 18 holes, 5977 yards. S.S.S. 69. *Green Fees:* weekdays only, £12.50 per round, £20.00 per day. *Eating facilities:* dining room available. *Visitors:* welcome with introduction or prior reservation. *Society Meetings:* welcome. Professional: Jim McCallum (041-777 7748) Secretary: J.A. Chisholm (041-776 6020).

# Edinburgh and the Lothians

ABERLADY. **Kilspindle Golf Club,** The Clubhouse, Aberlady (087-57 216). *Location:* off A198 North Berwick Road at Aberlady. 18 holes, 5417 yards, 4957 metres. S.S.S. 66. Large practice area. *Green Fees:* weekdays £16.00 per round, £22.00 per day; Saturday and Sunday £20.00 per round, £26.00 per day. *Eating facilities:* diningroom and bar. *Visitors:* welcome after 9.15am and before 4pm on non-competition days. *Society Meetings:* welcome subject to above restrictions (no catering Fridays). Professional: Graham Sked (087-57 695). Secretary: Hugh F. Brown (087-57 358).

ABERLADY. **Luffness New Golf Club,** Aberlady EH32 0QA (Gullane (0620) 843114). Clubmaster (0620 843376). *Location:* A198 – 17 miles east of Edinburgh. One mile from Gullane. Links course, 18 holes, 6122 yards. S.S.S. 69. *Green Fees:* provided on application. *Eating facilities:* dining room except Mondays. *Visitors:* weekdays only (require introduction). *Society Meetings:* by prior arrangement. Secretary: Lt. Cd. J.G. Tedford (0620 843336).

BATHGATE **Bathgate Golf Club,** Edinburgh Road, Bathgate EH48 1BA (0506 52232). *Location:* three miles from M8, 400 yards east of George Square, in town centre. Flat course. 18 holes, 6328 yards. S.S.S. 70. Practice area. *Green Fees:* weekdays £11.00 per round, £14.00 per day; weekends £22.00 per day. *Eating facilities:* diningroom open all week. *Visitors:* welcome without reservation except on Competition days at weekends. Professional: Sandy Strachan (0506 630553). Secretary: Hugh G. Smith (0506 630505).

BROXBURN. **Uphall Golf Club,** Uphall, Broxburn (Broxburn (0506) 856404). *Location:* on outskirts of Uphall adjacent to A8 Edinburgh to Glasgow road. 18 holes, 5567 yards. S.S.S. 67. *Green Fees:* information not available. *Eating facilities:* available at The Houstoun House Hotel situated within the grounds of the golf course. *Visitors:* welcome without reservation. *Society Meetings:* catered for. Secretary: Aidin Dobie.

DALKEITH. **Newbattle Golf Club Ltd,** Abbey Road, Dalkeith (031-663 2123). *Location:* approximately seven miles south-east of Edinburgh A7 to Eskbank Toll (Newbattle exit). Parkland course. 18 holes, 6012 yards, 5498 metres. S.S.S. 69. Small practice area. *Green Fees:* £12.00 per round, £20.00 per day. *Eating facilities:* full catering available on request. *Visitors:* weekdays only. No jeans/trainers on course or in clubhouse. *Society Meetings:* restricted. Professional: (031-660 1631). Secretary: H.G. Stanners (031-663 1819).

DUNBAR. **Dunbar Golf Club,** East Links, Dunbar EH42 1LP (Dunbar (0368) 62317). *Location:* on sea side on eastern end of Dunbar. Seaside links. 18 holes, 6441 yards, 5890 metres. S.S.S. 71. *Green Fees:* weekdays £20.00; weekends £35.00. *Eating facilities:* full catering facilities. *Visitors:* no visitors on Thursday or before 9.30am and between 1.30pm and 2pm weekdays. No visitors before 9.30 and between 12 noon and 2pm weekends. *Society Meetings:* welcome. Professional: Derek Small (0368 62086). Secretary: Don Thompson.

DUNBAR. **Winterfield Golf Club,** North Road, Dunbar (0368 62280). Seaside course. 18 holes, 4686 metres. S.S.S. 65. *Green Fees:* information not available. *Eating facilities:* available, except Thursdays. *Visitors:* welcome without reservation. The Pro Shop: (0368 63562). Professional: Keven Phillips. Secretary: Michael O'Donnell.

EDINBURGH. **Baberton Golf Club,** Baberton Avenue, Juniper Green, Edinburgh EH14 5DU (031-453 3361). *Location:* five miles west of Edinburgh on the A70. 18 holes, 6098 yards. S.S.S. 69. *Green Fees:* weekdays £17.00 per round, £25.00 per day. *Eating facilities:* by arrangement (phone Mrs Goodsir 031-453 3361). *Visitors:* welcome by arrangement with Secretary. *Society Meetings:* catered for. Professional: K. Kelly (031-453 3555). Secretary: I.W. Horberry (031-453 4911).

EDINBURGH. **Braids United Golf Club,** 22 Braid Hills Approach, Morningside, Edinburgh EH10 6JY (031-452 9408). *Location:* Braid Hills on south side of Edinburgh. Two 18 hole courses. No. 1 – 5880 yards. S.S.S. 68. No. 2 – 4495 yards. S.S.S. 64. *Green Fees:* £5.00 weekdays; £6.00 weekends. *Visitors:* welcome without reservation. (Accommodation in Braid Hills Hotel – 400 yards). Public courses, clubs on hire. Sunday golf on No. 2 course only. Professional: John Boath. Hon. Secretary: Gerald Hind (031-445 2044).

EDINBURGH. **Broomieknowe Golf Club Ltd,** 36 Golf Course Road, Bonnyrigg (031-663 9317). *Location:* south of Edinburgh, A6094 from Dalkeith. 18 holes, 5754 yards. S.S.S. 68. *Green Fees:* weekdays £14.00 per round, £20.00 per day; £20.00 per round at weekends. *Eating facilities:* lunches, high teas except Mondays. *Visitors:* welcome Monday to Friday. *Society Meetings:* catered for by arrangement but not Fridays or weekends. Professional: Mark Patchett (031-660 2035). Secretary: I.J. Nimmo.

EDINBURGH. **Bruntsfield Links Golfing Society,** The Clubhouse, 32 Barnton Avenue, Edinburgh EH4 6JH (031-336 2006). *Location:* off A90 to Davidson's Mains. Parkland course. 18 holes, 6402 yards. S.S.S. 71. *Green Fees:* information not provided. *Eating facilities:* lunches served at club. *Visitors:* welcome on weekdays if playing with a member, or if suitably introduced. *Society Meetings:* catered for. Professional: Brian MacKenzie (031-336 4050). Secretary: Lieut. Col. M.B. Hext (031-336 1479).

EDINBURGH. **Craigmillar Park Golf Club,** 1 Observatory Road Edinburgh EH9 3HG (031-667 2837). *Location:* A702 from City centre on Mayfield Road, right at King's Buildings. Parkland. 18 holes, 5846 yards. S.S.S. 68. *Green Fees:* £12.00 per round, £18.00 per day. *Eating facilities:* lunches, snacks, high teas and dinners. *Visitors:* welcome with reservation on production of Handicap Certificate. Weekdays only before 3.30pm. *Society Meetings:* catered for by previous arrangement. Professional: B. McGee (031-667 0047). Secretary: Mrs J.H. Smith (031-667 0047).

EDINBURGH. **Duddingston Golf Club Ltd,** Duddingston Road West, Edinburgh EH15 3QD (031-661 1005). *Location:* adjacent to A1 Willowbrae Road, turn right at Duddingston crossroads then one mile on Duddingston Road West. Undulating parkland with stream. 18 holes, 6647 yards. S.S.S. 72. *Green Fees:* weekdays only £18.00 per round, £24.00 per day. *Eating facilities:* full catering and bar facilities. *Visitors:* welcome weekdays only. *Society Meetings:* catered for Tuesdays and Thursdays (rates on request). Professional: Alistair McLean (031-661 4301). Secretary: John C. Small (031-661 7688).

EDINBURGH. **Kingsknowe Golf Club,** 326 Lanark Road, Edinburgh EH14 2JD (031-441 1144). *Location:* on Edinburgh Corporation Bus No. 44 route. Parkland course. 18 holes, 5979 yards, 5466 metres. S.S.S. 69. Practice area. *Green Fees:* weekdays £14.00 per round, £18.00 per day; weekends £20.00 per round. *Eating facilities:* lounge bar, snacks and meals available. *Visitors:* welcome Monday to Friday, also weekends subject to availability. *Society Meetings:* catered for. Professional: W. Bauld (031-441 4030). Secretary: R. Wallace (031-441 1145).

EDINBURGH. **Liberton Golf Club,** Kingston Grange, 297 Gilmerton Road, Edinburgh EH16 5UJ (031-664 8580). *Location:* Corporation transport to Lodge Gate, buses 3 and 8 from Edinburgh. By car on A7 (Visitors' car park). Parkland, rolling. 18 holes, 5299 yards, 4845 metres. S.S.S. 66. *Green Fees:* weekdays £12.50 per round, £18.00 per day; weekends £21.50. *Eating facilities:* full catering and bar service. *Visitors:* not before 1.30pm weekends. *Society Meetings:* catered for by arrangememt except Fridays or weekends. Professional: I. Seath (031-664 1056). Secretary: A. Poole (031-664 3009).

EDINBURGH. **Lothianburn Golf Club,** 106a Biggar Road, Edinburgh EH10 6HG (031-445 2206). *Location:* south on the A702 approximately four miles from city centre or easily reached from Edinburgh bypass road coming off at Lothianburn junction. Hill course close to Pentland Hills. 18 holes, 5750 yards. S.S.S. 69. Two practice grounds. *Green Fees:* weekdays £9.50 per round, £14.00 per day; weekends £13.00 per round, £17.00 per day. *Eating facilities:* normal bar hours, no hot food on Wednesdays. *Visitors:* welcome mid-week, weekends restricted. *Society Meetings:* catered for by prior arrangement with the Secretary. Professional: Paul Morton (031-445 2288). Secretary: W.F.A. Jardine (031-445 5067).

EDINBURGH. **Merchants Of Edinburgh Golf Club,** Craighill Gardens, Edinburgh EH10 5PY (031-447 1219). *Location:* car park Glenlockhart Road, Edin-

burgh EH10. Hilly parkland. 18 holes, 4889 yards. S.S.S. 64. *Green Fees:* weekdays £12.00 per round, £14.00 per day. *Eating facilities:* by arrangement with Clubmaster, J. Wilson. *Visitors:* welcome weekdays until 4pm, not weekends. *Society Meetings:* catered for except weekends. Professional: C.A. Imlah (031-447 8709). Secretary: A.M. Montgomery.

EDINBURGH. **Mortonhall Golf Club,** 231 Braid Road, Edinburgh EH10 6PB (031-447 2411). *Location:* take A702 south from City to Morningside traffic lights, up Braid Road one mile, course on left. 18 holes, 6548 yards, 5987 metres. S.S.S. 71. *Green Fees:* information not provided. *Eating facilities:* lunch, tea and snacks every day (no lunches Mondays). *Visitors:* welcome with introduction. *Society Metings:* catered for (not at weekends). Professional: D. Horn. Secretary: Mr P. T. Ricketts (031-447 6974).

EDINBURGH. **Murrayfield Golf Club,** 43 Murrayfield Road, Edinburgh EH12 6EU (031-337 1009). *Location:* two miles west of city centre. Parkland on east side of Corstorphine Hill. 18 holes, 5725 yards. S.S.S. 68. Practice area, net and putting green. *Green Fees:* weekdays £18.00 per round, £24.00 per day. *Eating facilities:* lunch each day, snacks in casual bar, also full bar facilities. *Visitors:* welcome playing with member or by prior arrangement only. No visitors weekends. *Society Meetings:* catered for by prior arrangement. Professional: J.J. Fisher (031-337 3479). Secretary: J.P. Bullen (031-337 3478).

EDINBURGH. **Portobello Golf Club,** Stanley Street, Portobello, Edinburgh EH15 1JJ (031-669 4361). *Location:* on A1 at Milton Road East. Parkland course. 9 holes, 2400 yards, 2167 metres. S.S.S. 32. *Green Fees:* £3.00 per round (9 holes). Reductions for Juniors and Senior Citizens. *Visitors:* welcome, restrictions on competition days. *Society Meetings:* not catered for. Professional: J. Boath. Secretary: A. Cook (031-669 5271).

EDINBURGH. **Prestonfield Golf Club,** 6 Priestfield Road North, Edinburgh EH16 5HS (031-667 1273). *Location:* off Dalkeith Road, near Royal Commonwealth Pool on A68. Parkland. 18 holes, 6216 yards. S.S.S. 70. Practice area. *Green Fees:* weekdays £15.00 per round, £22.00 per day; weekends and Bank Holidays £22.00 per round, £30.00 per day. *Eating facilities:* full catering. *Visitors:* welcome weekdays anytime, weekends and Bank Holidays (Saturday not between 12 noon and 1.30pm, Sunday not before 10.30am). *Society Meetings:* welcome weekdays. Professional: Brian Commins (031-667 9665).

EDINBURGH. **Ravelston Golf Club Ltd,** 24 Ravelston Dykes Road, Blackhall, Edinburgh EH4 6RB (031-315 2486). *Location:* A90 Queensferry Road (leading to Forth Road Bridge). Left pedestrian crossing, Blackhall, into Craigcrook Road, then second left. Parkland course. 9 holes, 2600 yards, 2377 metres. S.S.S. 66. *Green Fees:* £12.50 weekdays. *Eating facilities:* tea, coffee, soft drinks and light snacks. *Visitors:* welcome during quiet period. *Society Meetings:* permitted by special application only. Secretary: Frank Philip (031-312 6850).

EDINBURGH. **Royal Burgess Golfing Society of Edinburgh,** 181 Whitehouse Road, Barnton, Edinburgh EH4 6BY. *Location:* A90 to Queensferry, behind Barnton Hotel. Parkland. 18 holes, 6494 yards. S.S.S. 71. *Green Fees:* on request. *Eating facilities:* snacks and lunches available. *Visitors:* welcome weekdays, male only. *Society Meetings:* male only, catered for Tuesdays, Thursdays and Fridays. Professional: George Yuille (031-334 6474). Secretary: John Audis (031-339 2075).

EDINBURGH: **Silverknowes Golf Club,** Silverknowes, Parkway, Edinburgh EH4 5ET (031-336 5359). *Location:* nearest main road Queensferry Road; signs Davidson Mains, Silverknowes. 18 holes, 6216 yards. S.S.S. 71. *Green Fees:* £6.00 per round (1992). *Eating facilities:* clubhouse – by invitation/Lauriston Farm restaurant. *Visitors:* only by invitation of club member. *Society Meetings:* by arrangement weekdays only. Secretary: D.W. Scobie.

EDINBURGH. **Swanston Golf Club,** 111 Swanston Road, Edinburgh EH10 7DS (031-445 2239). *Location:* five miles from centre of Edinburgh on the lower slopes of the Pentland Hills. Parkland course. 18 holes, 5024 yards. S.S.S. 66. *Green Fees:* weekdays £8.00 per round, £12.00 day ticket; weekends £10.00 per round, £15.00 per day. *Eating facilities:* full catering facilities. *Visitors:* welcome without reservation weekdays, weekends restricted. *Society Meetings:* catered for. Professional: (031-445 4002) (Post vacant). Secretary: John Allan (031-445 2239).

EDINBURGH. **Torphin Hill Golf Club,** Torphin Road, Edinburgh EH13 0PG (031-441 1100). *Location:* south west of Colinton Village at terminus of No. 9 and No. 10 bus. Holes 5 to 15 on plateau with outstanding views of Edinburgh. 18 holes, 5020 yards, 4597 metres. S.S.S. 66. *Practice area. Green Fees:* weekdays £10.00 per day; weekends £16.00. *Eating facilities:* dining room and bar snacks. *Visitors:* welcome without reservation except on Competition Days. *Society Meetings:* catered for weekdays only. Reduced rates for parties over 20. Secretary: E.H. Marchant (031-441 4061).

EDINBURGH. **Turnhouse Golf Club,** Turnhouse, Edinburgh (031-339 1014). *Location:* on road from Edinburgh to Turnhouse Airport. 18 holes, 6171 yards. S.S.S. 69. *Green Fees:* information not provided. *Eating facilities:* full service. *Visitors:* welcome with reservation with member or by letter of introduction from Secretary. Professional: John Murray. Secretary: A.B. Hay.

FAULDHOUSE. **Greenburn Golf Club,** 6 Greenburn Road, Fauldhouse EH47 9AY (Fauldhouse (0501) 70292). *Location:* four miles south of Junctions 4 and 5 of M8 motorway. Moorland. 18 holes, 6210 yards. S.S.S. 70. *Green Fees:* £11.00 per round, £16.50 per day weekdays; £13.00 per round, £19.50 per day weekends. *Eating facilities:* catering available except Tuesdays (catering on Tuesdays for visiting parties by prior arrangement only). *Visitors:* welcome, no restrictions though check with Professional regarding tee off times. *Society Meetings:* no visiting parties on Saturdays except on non competition days – check with Secretary for availability. Professional: Mr H. Ferguson (0501 71187). Secretary: Mr D. Watson (0501 71154).

GULLANE. **Gullane Golf Club,** Gullane EH31 2BB (0620 843115). *Location:* 18 miles east of Edinburgh on A198 Edinburgh to North Berwick Road. Links. Three 18 hole courses. No. 1 – 6466 yards, 5913 metres. S.S.S. 71. No. 2 – 6233 yards, 5666 metres. S.S.S. 70. No. 3 – 5166 yards, 4696 metres. S.S.S. 65. *Green Fees:* No. 1 course £31.00, No. 2 course £14.00, No. 3 course £10.00 weekdays; No. 1 course £41.00, No. 2 course £17.00, No. 3 course £12.00 weekends. *Eating facilities:* lunches and snacks daily except Mondays. *Visitors:* welcome with reservation. No. 1 Course visitors only in Clubhouse. *Society Meetings:* catered for. Professional: Jimmy Hume (0620 843111). Secretary: A.J.B. Taylor (0620 842255).

GULLANE. **The Honourable Company Of Edinburgh Golfers,** Muirfield, Gullane EH31 2EG (Gullane (0620) 842123). *Location:* 20 miles from Edinburgh along the coast road to North Berwick. 18 holes, 6601 yards. *Green Fees:* (1992) £45 per round, £60 per day. *Eating facilities:* morning coffee, lunches, afternoon teas, if ordered in advance. *Visitors:* on Tuesdays, Thursdays or the mornings of Fridays, except during July and August, by introduction of a member or by previous arrangement with the Secretary: Group Captain J.A. Prideaux.

HADDINGTON. **Haddington Golf Club,** Amisfield Park, Haddington, East Lothian EH41 4PT (062-082 3627). *Location:* on A1 Edinburgh. Wooded parkland, slightly undulating. 18 holes, 6280 yards, 5764 metres. S.S.S. 70. *Green Fees:* weekdays £9.25 per round, £12.75 per day; weekends £12.00 per round, £16.00 day. Fees subject to increase. *Eating facilities:* two bars and diningroom. *Visitors:* welcome, midweek no restrictions, weekends permitted 10am-12 noon, 2-4pm. *Society Meetings:* catered for. Pro-

fessional: J. Sandilands (062-082 2727). Secretary: T. Shaw.

KIRKNEWTON. **Dalmahoy Hotel, Golf and Country Club,** Kirknewton, Midlothian EH28 8EB (031-333 1845). *Location:* on A71, 7 miles west of Edinburgh, 3 miles from ring road. Two courses: East Course, 18 holes, 6664 yards. S.S.S. 72. West Course, 18 holes, 5317 yards. S.S.S. 66. Extensive practice area. *Green Fees:* East Course: weekdays £30.00 per round; West Course: weekdays £20.00 per round. *Eating facilities:* excellent choice of dining facilities. *Visitors:* weekend play restricted to members and Hotel residents only. Tee off times bookable in advance (031-333 4105). Professional: Scott Maxwell (031-333 4105). Secretary: Jennifer Wilson.

LINLITHGOW. **Linlithgow Golf Club,** Braehead, Linlithgow EH49 6QF (Linlithgow (0506) 842585). *Location:* M8, M9, 20 miles west of Edinburgh, west end of Linlithgow – fork left. Parkland and wooded course with panoramic views. 18 holes, 5858 yards, 5359 metres. S.S.S. 68. Small practice area and net. *Green Fees:* weekdays £10.00 per round, £14.00 per day; weekends £14.00 per round, £17.00 per day. *Eating facilities:* full facilities available. *Visitors:* welcome except Saturdays. *Society Meetings:* welcome. Professional: Derek Smith (0506 844356). Secretary: Mrs A. Bird (0506 842585).

LINLITHGOW. **West Lothian Golf Club,** Airngath Hill, Bo'ness EH49 7RH (Bo'ness (0506) 826030). *Location:* situated midway between Linlithgow and Bo'ness. Undulating parkland course. 18 holes, 6629 yards. S.S.S. 71. Practice area. *Green Fees:* weekdays £10.00 per round, £15.00 per day; weekends £14.00 per round, £20.00 per day. *Eating facilities:* available by arrangement. *Visitors:* welcome, no restrictions before 3.30pm midweek. After 3.30pm and at weekends by arrangement only. *Society Meetings:* by arrangement. Secretary: T.B. Fraser (0506 825476).

LIVINGSTON. **Deer Park Golf & Country Club,** Golf Course Road, Knightsridge, Livingston EH54 8PG (0506 31037). *Location:* near Edinburgh on M8. Parkland course. 18 holes, 6600 yards. S.S.S. 72. *Green Fees:* £14.00 per round weekdays; £22.00 per round weekends. *Eating facilities:* catering available every day; bar open all day. *Visitors:* welcome without reservation. Snooker, squash, swimming pool, jacuzzi, steam room, gym, ten pin bowling etc available at club as part of members' facilities. May be used if booked as a corporate outing with charges accordingly. *Society Meetings:* catered for. Professional/Secretary: W.J. Yule.

LIVINGSTON. **Pumpherston Golf Club,** Drumshoreland Road, Pumpherston, Livingston EH53 0LF (0506 32869). *Location:* one mile east of Livingston, one and a half miles south of M8. Undulating parkland course, well bunkered. 9 holes, 5154 yards, 4712 metres. S.S.S. 65. Small practice area. *Green Fees:* information not supplied. *Eating facilities:* snack meals, lounge bar. *Visitors:* only when introduced by member. *Society Meetings:* Mondays to Thursdays, maximum number 24. Secretary: A.H. Docharty (0506 854652).

LONGNIDDRY. **Longniddry Golf Club Ltd,** The Clubhouse, Links Road, Longniddry EH32 0NL (Longniddry (0875) 52228). *Location:* from Edinburgh by A1, left for Longniddry, A198 at Wallyford roundabout or left off A1 one mile after MacMerry. 18 holes, 6219 yards, 5678 metres. S.S.S. 70. Practice ground and putting green. *Green Fees:* weekdays £20.00 per round, £30.00 per day. *Eating facilities:* every day, bar snacks only on Fridays. *Visitors:* Monday to Thursday parties booked, otherwise Monday to Friday casual bookings within the previous seven days except on Public Holidays and competition days. *Society Meetings:* catered for (except Friday – Sunday). Professional: John Gray (0875 52228). Secretary: G.C. Dempster, C.A. (0875 52141).

MUSSELBURGH. **Musselburgh Golf Club,** Monktonhall, Musselburgh EH21 6SA (031-665 2005).

*Location:* from the A1 end of the Edinburgh City bypass, on the B6415 to Musselburgh. Wooded parkland, rivers. 18 holes, 6614 yards. S.S.S. 72. *Green Fees:* on application. *Eating facilities:* catering available except Tuesdays. *Visitors:* welcome with reservation. *Society Meetings:* catered for. Professional: T. Stangoe (031-665 7055). Secretary: G. McGill (031-665 2005). Administrator (for bookings): G. Finlay.

MUSSELBURGH. **Musselburgh Old Course Golf Club,** Silver Ring Clubhouse, 3B Millhill, Musselburgh EH21 7RG (031-665 3711). *Location:* Musselburgh racecourse one-and-a-half miles east of town centre. Seaside links course. 9 holes, 2690 yards. S.S.S. 67. Extensive practice area. *Green Fees:* information not available. *Eating facilities:* available. *Visitors:* welcome except during club competitions. *Society Meetings:* book through Mr Smith, Brunton Hall, Musselburgh (031-665 3711). Secretary: W. Finnigan (031-665 6014).

NEWBRIDGE. **Ratho Park Golf Club Ltd,** Ratho, Newbridge EH28 8NX (031-333 1252). *Location:* eight miles west of Edinburgh G.P.O., access from A71 or A8. Flat parkland. 18 holes, 5900 yards, 5398 metres. S.S.S. 68. *Green Fees:* weekdays £16.50 per round, £25.00 per day; weekends £30.00 per day. *Eating facilities:* full catering available. *Visitors:* welcome without reservation. *Society Meetings:* catered for Tuesdays, Wednesdays and Thursdays. Professional: Alan Pate (031-333 1406). Secretary: J.C. McLafferty (031-333 1752).

NORTH BERWICK. **Glen Golf Club,** East Links, Tantallon Terrace, North Berwick EH39 4LE (0620 2221; Fax: 0620 5288). *Location:* Firth of Forth – opposite Bass Rock, A198 one mile east of Railway Station. Seaside links with superb views. 18 holes, 6086 yards. S.S.S. 69. Practice area on course. Practice putting green at Clubhouse. *Green Fees:* weekdays £10.50 per round, £14.50 per day; weekends £13.50 per round, £18.50 per day. (Composite tickets available from hotels in East Lothian). Half price for Senior Citizens and Juniors weekdays. *Eating facilities:* full

catering available plus bar service. *Visitors:* welcome anytime. *Society Meetings:* catered for with advance booking. Professional: (shop only). Secretary: D.R. Montgomery (0620 2221). Starter: (0620 2726).

NORTH BERWICK. **North Berwick Golf Club,** New Clubhouse, Beach Road, North Berwick EH39 4BB (0620 4766; Fax: 0620 3274). *Location:* golf course stretches along the coast. First tee five minutes from town centre. Accessible from A198. Seaside links. 18 holes, 6315 yards. S.S.S. 70. *Green Fees:* weekdays £20.00 per round, £30.00 per day; weekends and Public Holidays £30.00 per round, £40.00 per day. *Eating facilities:* diningrooms and bar available. *Visitors:* welcome without restrictions. *Society Meetings:* catered for. Professional: D. Huish (0620 3233). Secretary: William Gray (0620 5040). Advance Bookings: (0620 3233).

PENICUIK. **Glencorse Golf Club,** Milton Bridge, Penicuik EH26 0RD (0968 77177). *Location:* A701 nine miles south of Edinburgh on Peebles Road. Parkland course with stream affecting 10 holes. 18 holes, 5205 yards. S.S.S. 66. *Green Fees:* weekdays £15.00 per round, £20.00 per day, weekends £20.00 per round. *Eating facilities:* full catering and bar. *Visitors:* welcome most days and times subject to Club Competitions. *Society Meetings:* catered for Tuesdays, most Wednesdays, Thursdays, most Fridays. Professional: C. Jones (0968 76481). Secretary: D.A. McNiven (0968 77189).

PRESTONPANS. **Royal Musselburgh Golf Club,** Prestongrange House, Prestonpans EH32 9PU (Prestonpans (0875) 810276). *Location:* A198 North Berwick road near Prestonpans. Parkland, 18 holes, 6237 yards. S.S.S. 70. *Green Fees:* weekdays £15.00 per round, £25.00 per day; weekends £25.00 per round, no day tickets. *Eating facilities:* full catering and licence. *Visitors:* welcome weekdays not before 9.30am, not after 3pm, not Friday afternoons. *Society Meetings:* catered for weekdays only – book in advance. Professional: John Henderson (0875 810139). Secretary: T.H. Hardie.

SOUTH QUEENSFERRY. **Dundas Parks Golf Club,** Dundas Estate, South Queensferry, West Lothian. *Location:* five miles west of Edinburgh, on South Queensferry to Kirkliston road on right of A8000. Parkland course in open countryside. 9 holes (x 2). Small practice area. *Green Fees:* £8.00. *Eating facilities:* not available. *Visitors:* welcome with member, or by prior arrangement with Secretary. *Society Meetings:* by prior arrangement with Secretary. Secretary: Keith D. Love (031-331 1416).

WEST CALDER. **Harburn Golf Club,** Harburn, West Calder EH55 8RS (West Calder (0506) 871256). *Location:* two miles south of West Calder on B7008. Parkland course. 18 holes, 5853 yards, 5436 metres. S.S.S. 68. Practice ground. *Green Fees:* £11.00 per round, £16.00 per day weekdays; £16.00 per round, £22.00 per day weekends. *Eating facilities:* full catering

and bar service except Tuesdays. *Visitors:* welcome any time – no restrictions. *Society Meetings:* catered for by advance arrangement. Professional: Stuart Crookston (0506 871582). Secretary: Frank Vinter (0506 871131).

WHITBURN. **Polkemmet Golf Course,** Polkemmet Country Park, Whitburn, West Lothian (Whitburn (0501) 43905). *Location:* off B7066, one mile west of Whitburn. Inland course set within old private estate, mature varied woodland with belts of Rhododendrons. 9 holes, 2969 metres. Par 37. Driving range. *Green Fees:* Monday to Saturday £2.10 adults, Juvenile/Senior Citizens/Concessions £1.15; Sunday £2.70 adult, Juvanile/Senior Citizens/Concessions £1.55. *Eating facilities:* restaurant and bar complex. *Visitors:*

welcome. Facilities include bowling green, picnic areas, etc. Caddy Cart hire 60p. Secretary: West Lothian District Council, Department of Leisure and Recreation, County Buildings, Linlithgow.

WINCHBURGH. **Niddry Castle Golf Club,** Castle Road, Winchburgh EH52 6RQ (0506 891097). *Location:* 10 miles west of Edinburgh on A803 between Kirkliston and Linlithgow. Wooded, natural parkland. 9 holes, 5450 yards. S.S.S. 67. *Green Fees:* £6.00 weekdays; £8.50 weekends. *Eating facilities:* none – but bar lunches available in village. *Visitors:* welcome anytime but not until 2pm on Saturdays of club competitions. *Society Meetings:* by arrangement. Secretary: A. Brockbank.

# Fife

ABERDOUR. **Aberdour Golf Club,** Seaside Place, Aberdour KY3 0TX (0383 860688). *Location:* take Shore Road from centre of village. Parkland course situated along the shoreline of the River Forth. 18 holes, 5469 yards. S.S.S. 67. *Green Fees:* £13.00 per round, £18.00 per day. *Eating facilities:* full catering. *Visitors:* welcome on weekdays. *Society Meetings:* catered for on weekdays and Sundays. On Sundays, maximum size of group 24. Professional: Gordon McCallum (0383 860256). Secretary: John Train (0383 860080).

ANSTRUTHER. **Anstruther Golf Club,** Marsfield, Shore Road, Anstruther KY10 3DZ (0333 310956). *Location:* nine miles south of St. Andrews, west side of Anstruther. Seaside links course. 9 holes, 4144 metres. S.S.S. 63. *Green Fees:* weekdays £10.00; weekends £14.00. *Eating facilities:* lounge bar and dining room. *Visitors:* welcome except during club competitions. *Society Meetings:* outwith May/September and com-

petition days. Secretary: A.B. Cleary (0333 310956/ 312283).

BURNTISLAND. **Burntisland Golf House Club,** Dodhead, Burntisland KY3 9EY (Burntisland (0592) 873247). *Location:* on B923, one mile north-east of town centre. Parkland. 18 holes, 5897 yards. S.S.S. 69. Practice net. *Green Fees:* weekdays £12.50 per round, £18.00 per day, weekends £18.00 per round, £20.00 per day. *Eating facilities:* meals and snacks in clubhouse. *Visitors:* welcome with advance bookings. Changing room. *Society Meetings:* advance booking. Professional: J. Montgomery (0592 873247). Secretary: Ian McLean (0592 874093).

CARDENDEN. **Auchterderran Golf Club,** Woodend Road, Cardenden (0592 721579). *Location:* seven miles on A910 from Kirkcaldy. 9 holes, 5250 yards. S.S.S. 66. *Green Fees:* information not provided. *Visitors:* welcome without reservation. Secretary: S.G. Miller.

CRAIL. **Crail Golfing Society,** Balcomie Clubhouse, Fifeness, Crail KY10 3XN (Crail (0333) 50278). Instituted 1786. *Location:* eleven miles south-east of St. Andrews on A917. Parkland/seaside links. 18 holes, 5720 yards. S.S.S. 68. Practice ground. *Green Fees:* weekdays £16.00 per round, £24.00 per day; weekends £20.00 per round, £30.00 per day. 3/4/5 day £16.00 per day, Fortnightly £128. (except Sundays). Subject to increase. *Eating facilities:* quality catering and bar. *Visitors:* welcome. *Society Meetings:* advance booking available for parties except latter half of July and first half August. Professional: Graeme Lennie (0333 50960). Secretary: Mrs C.W. Penhale (0333 50686).

CUPAR. **Cupar Golf Club,** Hilltarvit, Cupar (Cupar (0334) 53549). *Location:* near cemetery on Ceres Road. Hillside/parkland course. 9 holes, 5074 yards. S.S.S. 65. Practice putting green. *Green Fees:* weekdays £10.00; Sundays £12.00. *Eating facilities:* full catering/bar. *Visitors:* welcome, except Saturdays. *Society Meetings:* made very welcome. Secretary: J.P. McAndrew (0334 54312).

DUNFERMLINE. **Canmore Golf Club,** Venture Fair, Dunfermline (Dunfermline (0383) 724969). *Location:* one mile north of town centre on A823. Parkland. 18 holes, 5347 yards. S.S.S. 66. *Green Fees:* weekdays £10.00 per round, £15.00 per day. *Eating facilities:* full catering and bar. *Visitors:* welcome except on weekends. *Society Meetings:* visiting societies with prior reservation (not at weekends). Professional: John Hamlin (0383 728416). Secretary: J.C. Duncan (0383 726098).

DUNFERMLINE. **Dunfermline Golf Club,** Pitfirrane, Crossford, By Dunfermline KY12 8QV (0383 723534). *Location:* two miles west of Dunfermline on A994 to Kincardine Bridge. Undulating parkland. 18 holes, 6237 yards, 5739 metres. S.S.S. 70. Short 9 hole course and practice area. *Green Fees:* £15.00 per round, £25.00 per day weekdays. *Eating facilities:* full catering except Sunday evenings and Mondays; bar snacks available. *Visitors:* welcome weekdays 10am to 12 noon and 2pm to 4pm. Must have official club handicap. *Society Meetings:* accepted weekdays by prior arrangement. Professional: Steve Craig (0383 723534). Secretary: Hamish Mathston (0383 723534).

DUNFERMLINE. **Pitreavie (Dunfermline) Golf Club,** Queensferry Road, Dunfermline KY11 5PR (0383 722591). *Location:* M90 Edinburgh/Perth, leave at Junction 2 for Dunfermline. Undulating parkland with views across Firth of Forth. 18 holes, 6086 yards. S.S.S. 69. Practice range. *Green Fees:* weekdays £12.00 per round, £17.00 per day; weekends £22.00 per day. *Eating facilities:* full catering and bar facilities

available. *Visitors:* welcome except Competition Days. Please phone in advance, must have recognised Golf Union Handicap. *Society Meetings:* catered for, must be booked through Secretary. Professional: Jim Forrester (0383 723151). Secretary: Mr D. Carter (0383 722591).

DUNFERMLINE. **Saline Golf Club,** Kinneddar Hill, Saline (New Oakley (0383) 852591). *Location:* Dollar, turn left at Junction 4 M90. Hillside course. 9 holes, 5302 yards. S.S.S. 66. *Green Fees:* weekdays £10.00. *Eating facilities:* bar snacks; meals by prior arrangement. *Visitors:* welcome, no restrictions except Saturdays. *Society Meetings:* catered for mid-week or Sundays; maximum 24. Secretary: R. Hutchison (0383 852344).

ELIE. **Earlsferry Thistle Golf Club,** Melon Park, Rotton Row, Elie (0333 310053). 18 holes, 6241 yards. S.S.S. 70. *Green Fees:* set by Elie Golf House Club, on application. *Visitors:* welcome mid-week. Secretary: (0334 76770). The course belongs to Elie Golf House Club, Earlsferry Thistle play the same course.

ELIE. **Elie Sports Club,** Elie. *Location:* ten miles south of St. Andrews on A917. 9 holes, 2277 yards. S.S.S. 32. *Green Fees:* information not provided. *Eating facilities:* light snacks available. *Visitors:* welcome without reservation. Professional: R. Wilson. Secretary: J. Fyall (0333 330955).

ELIE. **Golf House Club,** Elie (Elie (0333) 330327). *Location:* 10 miles south of St Andrews on A917. Links course. 18 holes, 6253 yards. S.S.S. 70. *Green Fees:* weekdays £20.00 per round, £27.50 per day; weekends £30.00 per round, £37.50 per day (rates apply up to 31st May 1993 only). *Eating facilities:* lunches, teas, etc. *Visitors:* welcome with reservation. Elie Sports Centre nearby with leisure facilities and cafeteria. *Society Meetings:* catered for except at weekends. Professional: Robin Wilson (0333 330955). Secretary: A. Sneddon (0333 330301).

FALKLAND. **Falkland Golf Club,** The Myre, Falkland KY7 7AA (0337 57404). *Location:* entrance on A912, 12 miles from Kirkcaldy – approximately 20 minutes from St. Andrews. Lies at the foot of East Lomond Hills. Flat meadowland, beautiful views. 9 holes, 2608 yards, 2384 metres. S.S.S. 66 for 18 holes. *Green Fees:* £7.00 weekdays, £9.00 weekends. Weekly ticket £21.00. Contact 0337 57404 after 6pm. *Eating facilities:* meals by arrangement (evenings and weekends only), bar available for golfers. *Visitors:* welcome, no problem during weekdays, phone for availability weekends. *Society Meetings:* must book in advance. Secretary: Mrs H.H. Horsburgh (0337 756075).

GLENROTHES. **Glenrothes Golf Club,** Golf Course Road, Glenrothes (Glenrothes (0592) 758686). *Location:* west Glenrothes. Hilly wooded parkland. 18 holes, 6444 yards. S.S.S. 71. *Green Fees:* weekdays £7.60 per round, £13.00 per day; weekends £10.00 per round, £15.00 per day. *Eating facilities:* two licensed lounges, dining room. *Visitors:* welcome any time. *Society Meetings:* book one month in advance, minimum 12, maximum 40. Secretary: Leslie Dalrymple (0592 754561).

KINCARDINE. **Tulliallan Golf Club,** Alloa Road, Kincardine, by Alloa (0259 30396). *Location:* on A908 five miles east of Alloa, one mile north of Kincardine Bridge. Parkland slightly wooded, burn winds through the course. 18 holes, 5892 yards, 5463 metres. S.S.S. 69. *Green Fees:* weekdays: round £13.00, day £17.00; weekends: round £15.00, day £21.00. Subject to amendment. *Eating facilities:* diningroom, bar 11am to 11pm. *Visitors:* no visiting parties on Fridays, Saturdays or on local holidays. *Society Meetings:* catered for with reservation, 24 limit on Sundays. Professional: Steven Kelly (0259 30798). Secretary: J.S. McDowall (0324 485420).

KINGHORN. **Kinghorn Municipal Golf Club,** Mac-Duff Crescent, Kinghorn (0592 890345/80242). *Location:* bus stop at course, railway station three minutes. 18 holes, 5217 yards. S.S.S. 67. *Green Fees:* weekdays £7.60 per round, £13.00 per day; weekends £10.00 per round, £15.00 per day. *Eating facilities:* meals at clubhouse, local hotels. *Visitors:* welcome with prior reservation if large party (up to 30). *Society Meetings:*

catered for by arrangement. Hon. Secretary: J.P. Robertson (0592 890345).

KIRKCALDY. **Dunnikier Park Golf Club,** Dunnikier Way, Kirkcaldy KY1 3LP (Kirkcaldy (0592) 261599). *Location:* one mile off A92 on the A910. Parkland course. 18 holes, 6601 yards, 6036 metres. S.S.S. 72. *Green Fees:* weekdays £8.00 per round, £11.00 per day; weekends £10.00 per round, £13.00 per day. *Eating facilities:* full dining and bar facilities. *Visitors:* welcome by arrangement with Secretary, no restrictions. Adjacent to private hotel. *Society Meetings:* catered for. Professional: Jacky Montgomery (0592 205916). Secretary: Robert A. Waddell (0592 200627).

KIRKCALDY. **Kirkcaldy Golf Club,** Balwearie, Kirkcaldy KY2 5LT (0592 260370). *Location:* west end of town adjacent to Beveridge Park. Wooded parkland with stream. 18 holes, 6004 yards. S.S.S. 70. Small practice area. *Green Fees:* weekdays £12.00 per round, £18.00 per day; weekends £15.00 per round, £21.00 per day. *Eating facilities:* full catering facilities available. *Visitors:* welcome except Saturdays, limited Tuesdays. Professional's shop. *Society Meetings:* catered for. Professional: Paul Hodgson (0592 203258). Secretary: J.I. Brodley (0592 205240).

LADYBANK. **Ladybank Golf Club,** Annsmuir, Ladybank KY7 7RA (0337 30814). *Location:* on B9129 off A91, 15 miles St. Andrews. Wooded heathland. 18 holes, 6641 yards. S.S.S. 72. Practice ground. *Green Fees:* weekdays £23.00 per round, £31.00 per day; weekends £25.00 per round, £34.00 per day. *Eating*

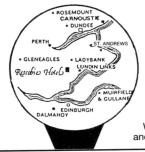

*facilities:* full catering facilities and bar. *Visitors:* welcome without reservation. Party bookings by arrangement with Secretary. *Society Meetings:* by arrangement. Professional: Martin J. Gray (0337 30725). Secretary: A.M. Dick (0337 30814).

LESLIE. **Leslie Golf Club,** Balsillie, Leslie KY6 3EZ (0592 620040). Parkland with small stream running through some fairways. 9 holes, 4940 yards. S.S.S. 64. *Green Fees:* £6.00 weekdays; £10.00 weekends. *Eating facilities:* bar open each evening 7.30pm to 11pm, weekends 12 noon to 5pm and 7.30pm to 11pm. *Visitors:* always welcome, some restrictions on competition days. Secretary: M.G. Burns (0592 741449).

LEUCHARS. **St. Michaels Golf Club,** Leuchars KY16 0DU (0334 839365). *Location:* on main road St Andrews to Dundee, north end of Leuchars village. Undulating parkland with plantation surroundings. 9 holes, 5510 yards. S.S.S. 68. *Green Fees:* £12.00 day ticket, Juniors £6.00. Five day ticket Monday to Friday £40.00. *Eating facilities:* bar facilities and meals available. *Visitors:* welcome without reservation except Sundays before 1pm. Changing rooms and showers. *Society Meetings:* by reservation with green fee deposit £2.00 per head. Secretary: Dr G.G.W. Bennet (0334 53156 home).

LEVEN. **Leven Golfing Society,** Links Road, Leven KY8 4HS (Leven (0333) 426096). *Location:* nine miles east of Kirkcaldy on the A955. Links course, flat. 18 holes, 6434 yards, 5939 metres. S.S.S. 71. *Green Fees:* weekdays £16.00 round, £22.50 day; weekends £20.00 round, £30.00 day. *Eating facilities:* full catering available. *Visitors:* welcome (except Saturdays). *Society Meetings:* by arrangement (0333 23509). Parties of under 12 persons (0333 421390). Links Secretary: Mr B. Jackson (0333 428859).

LEVEN. **Leven Thistle Golf Club,** Balfour Street, Leven (0333 426397). *Location:* eight miles east of links, top championship links used for national and international events including Open qualifying. 18 holes, 6434 yards. S.S.S. 71. *Green Fees:* weekdays £16.00 per round, £22.50 per day; weekends £20.00 per round, £30.00 per day. *Eating facilities:* full catering available, two bars, function hall. *Visitors:* welcome without reservation, except Saturdays. *Society Meetings:* for group bookings contact Leven Links Joint Committee, Promenade, Leven, Fife KY8 4HS (0333 428859). Secretary: J. Scott.

LEVEN. **Lundin Golf Club,** Golf Road, Lundin Links KY8 6BA (0333 320202). *Location:* three miles east of Leven on the A915 (Leven to St. Andrews). Seaside links. 18 holes, 6377 yards. S.S.S. 71. Practice ground. *Green Fees:* £18.00 per round, £27.00 per day weekdays; Saturdays after 2.30pm £25.00 per round. *Eating facilities:* bar and diningroom. *Visitors:* welcome Monday/Thursday 9am to 3.30pm; Friday 9am to 3pm; Saturdays no visitors before 2.30pm; Sundays no visitors. *Society Meetings:* limited numbers. Professional: David K. Webster (0333 320051). Secretary: A.C. McBride (0333 320202).

LOCHGELLY. **Lochgelly Golf Club,** Cartmore Road, Lochgelly (Lochgelly (0592) 780174). *Location:* take M90 to Junction 4 Halbeath Interchange, follow signs. Parkland. 18 holes, 5491 yards, 5063 metres. S.S.S. 67. *Green Fees:* £8.00 per round weekdays; £11.00 per round weekends. *Eating facilities:* catering available. *Visitors:* welcome, no restrictions weekdays, weekends parties limited to 24. Secretary: R.F. Stuart (0383 512238).

MARKINCH. **Balbirnie Park Golf Club,** The Clubhouse, Balbirnie Park, Markinch, Glenrothes KY7 6DD (0592 752006). *Location:* outside Markinch near the A92. Wooded parkland course. 18 holes, 6210 yards. S.S.S. 71. *Green Fees:* weekdays £18.00 per round, £25.00 per day; weekends £26.00 per round, £32.00 per day. Subject to increase. *Eating facilities:* by prior arrangement with Steward. *Visitors:* no restrictions at present other than maximum number of 24 at weekends and no visitors before 10am weekends. *Society Meetings:* welcome. Secretary: Alexander G. Grant.

ST. ANDREWS. **Balgove Course,** St. Andrews. *Location:* outskirts of St. Andrews on Dundee Road. 9 hole, beginners' course. *Green Fees:* on request. *Eating facilities:* hotels and restaurants in the vicinity. *Visitors:*

welcome without reservation. Secretary: A. Beveridge, Links Management Committee of St. Andrews (0334 75757).

ST. ANDREWS. **Eden Course,** St. Andrews (Starter – 0334 74296). *Location:* follow A91 trunk road to St. Andrews, directions to golf courses are clearly marked. Seaside links. 18 holes, 6122 yards. S.S.S. 70. Practice facilities. *Green Fees:* £12.00 per round weekdays. *Eating facilities:* hotels and restaurants in the vicinity. *Visitors:* welcome with or without reservation. *Society Meetings:* catered for except Saturday. Secretary: A. Beveridge, Links Management Committee of St. Andrews (0334 75757).

ST. ANDREWS. **Jubilee Course,** West Sands, St. Andrews KY16 9JA (Starter (0334) 73938). *Location:* follow A91 trunk road to St. Andrews, directions to golf course are clearly marked. Seaside links. 18 holes, 6805 yards. S.S.S. 73. Practice facilities available. *Green Fees:* £14.00 per round weekdays. *Eating facilities:* hotels and restaurants in the vicinity. *Visitors:* welcome with or without reservation. *Society Meetings:* catered for except Saturday. Secretary: A. Beveridge, Links Management Committee of St. Andrews (0334) 75757).

ST. ANDREWS. **New Course,** West Sands, St. Andrews (Starter (0334) 73938). 18 holes, 6604 yards, 6036 metres. S.S.S. 72. *Green Fees:* £14.00. *Eating facilities:* hotels and restaurants in vicinity. *Visitors:* welcome with or without reservation. *Society Meetings:* catered for except Saturday. Secretary: A. Beveridge, Links Management Committee of St. Andrews (0334) 75757).

ST. ANDREWS. **St. Andrews Links,** Old Course, St. Andrews KY16 9JA (0334 73190). Seaside links. 18 holes, 6566 yards. S.S.S. 72. Practice area and driving range available. *Green Fees:* £34.00 per round.

*Visitors:* welcome, Handicap Certificate required. *Society Meetings:* welcome except Saturday. Secretary: Alec Beveridge (0334 75757).

ST. ANDREWS. **The Old Course,** St. Andrews KY16 9JA (0334 73190). *Location:* follow A91 trunk road to St. Andrews – directions to golf course are clearly marked. Seaside links. 18 holes, 6566 yards, 6004 metres. S.S.S. 72. Practice facilities. *Green Fees:* £34.00 per round weekdays. *Visitors:* Handicap Certificate or letter of introduction required from recognised golf club. *Society Meetings:* welcome except Saturdays. Secretary: A. Beveridge (0334 75757).

TAYPORT. **Scotscraig Golf Club,** Tayport (Dundee (0382) 552515). *Location:* ten miles north of St Andrews. Seaside links. 18 holes, 6496 yards. S.S.S.

71. *Green Fees:* on application. *Eating facilities:* lunches and high teas, except Tuesdays. *Visitors:* welcome on weekdays or weekends by prior arrangement. *Society Meetings:* catered for subject to approval. Secretary: K. Gourlay (0382 552515).

THORNTON. **Thornton Golf Club,** Thornton KY1 4DW (Glenrothes (0592) 771111). *Location:* south east Fife located off A92, midway between Glenrothes and Kirkcaldy. Undulating, wooded, parkland. 18 holes, 6177 yards. S.S.S. 69. *Green Fees:* weekdays £10.00 per round, £15.00 per day; weekends £15.00 per round, £22.50 per day. Special rates after 5pm weekends. *Eating facilities:* full catering service and bar. *Visitors:* welcome anytime, booking advisable. *Society Meetings:* catered for. Secretary: Neil Robertson.

# Glasgow & District

GLASGOW. **Alexandra Golf Club,** Alexandra Park, Alexandra Parade, Glasgow G31 3SE (041-554 1204). *Location:* M8 off ramp to Alexandra Parade. Wooded parkland. 9 holes, 1965 yards. *Green Fees:* weekdays adults £1.60, weekends £1.90. Juniors 85p, Senior Citizens and UB40 60p. *Eating facilities:* bar, rooms available for functions. *Visitors:* welcome anytime. Blind club, Unemployed club. Professional: S. Wilson. Secretary: A. Clark.

GLASGOW. **Bearsden Golf Club,** Thorn Road, Bearsden, Glasgow G61 4BP (041-942 2351). *Location:* seven miles north-west of Glasgow. Parkland. 9 holes, 6014 yards. S.S.S. 69. *Green Fees:* information not provided. *Visitors:* welcome, but must be accompanied by member. Secretary: J.R. Mercer (041-942 2381).

SPECTACULAR SCENERY IN THE LOCH LOMOND, STIRLING & TROSSACHS AREA

40 GOLF COURSES IN 25 MILE RADIUS
ROMANTIC 700 YEAR OLD ANCESTRAL HOME OF CLAN GALBRAITH

# CULCREUCH CASTLE

**Fintry, Glasgow G63 0LW Tel: (036086) 228 Fax: (036086) 555**

Hidden away in breathtaking 1600-acre parkland grounds with salmon river and two small coarse fishing lochs. Free fishing and boating for guests. Glasgow 19 miles, Stirling and motorway 17 miles, Edinburgh 55 miles.
· 8 en-suite bedrooms including four posters & family suite · Log fires · Six foot thick walls · Battlements · 8 Scandinavian-style lodges for self-catering · Candlelit Evening Meals in the Panelled Dining Room · Dungeons Bar · Baby Listening · Squash Courts & Indoor Bowling · Colour Castle Brochure and Golfing Brochure available.

GLASGOW. **Bishopbriggs Golf Club,** Brackenbrae Road, Bishopbriggs G64 2DX (041-772 1810). Location: quarter mile from Bishopbriggs Cross off Glasgow-Kirkintilloch road. Fairly flat parkland course. 18 holes, 6041 yards. S.S.S. 69. Green Fees: £20.00 per day weekdays. Eating facilities: full service always available. Visitors: weekends/Public Holidays with member only, other times apply to Secretary. Society Meetings: catered for Tuesdays and Thursdays by applicaton to committee at least one month in advance. Secretary: John Magin (041-772 8938).

GLASGOW. **Blairbeth Golf Club,** Fernhill, Rutherglen, Glasgow (041-634 3355). Location: two miles south of Rutherglen off Stonelaw Road. Parkland. 18 holes, 5800 yards. S.S.S. 67. Green Fees: information not provided. Eating facilities: available. Visitors: welcome with reservation, by introduction. Society Meetings: not catered for. Secretary: F.T. Henderson (041-632 0604).

GLASGOW. **Bonnyton Golf Club,** Eaglesham, Glasgow G76 0QA (03553 2645). Location: B764. Moorland. 18 holes, 6252 yards. S.S.S. 71. Green Fees: £25.00 per day. Eating facilities: full diningroom and snack facilities. Visitors: welcome except weekends. Professional: Robert Crerar (03553 2256). Secretary: (03553 2781).

GLASGOW. **Bothwell Castle Golf Club,** Blantyre Road, Bothwell G71 (0698 853177). Location: adjacent to M74, three miles north of Hamilton. Parkland course. 18 holes, 6243 yards, 5606 metres. S.S.S. 70. Golf Clubs and caddy cars for hire. Practice fields. Green Fees: weekdays (8.00am to 3.30pm) £14.00 per round, £21.00 per day. (Playing times must be booked with Professional). Eating facilities: lunches, bar snacks and dinners available, bar. Visitors: welcome weekdays 9.30am to 3.30pm only. Society Meetings: catered for, courtesy granted by application on Tuesdays only. Professional: William Walker (0698 852052). Secretary: A.D.C. Watson (0698 852395).

GLASGOW. **Buchanan Castle Golf Club,** Drymen, Glasgow G63 0HY (0360 60369). Location: Glasgow/Drymen road, half a mile short of village. Flat parkland course. 18 holes, 6086 yards. S.S.S. 69. 9 hole putting area. Green Fees: weekdays £20.00. Eating facilities: full catering available. Visitors: welcome, Thursdays – official visiting day, Wednesday maximum 12. Society Meetings: welcome, maximum 12. Professional: Charles Dernie (0360 60330). Secretary: Richard Kinella (0360 60307).

GLASGOW. **Cambuslang Golf Club,** Westburn, Cambuslang (041-641 3130). Location: one mile from tation. 9 holes, 6146 yards. S.S.S. 69. Visitors: welcome Mondays, Wednesdays, Thursdays and ridays on written application to the Secretary. Society Meetings: by arrangement. Secretary: William Lilly.

GLASGOW. **Cathcart Castle Golf Club,** Mearns oad, Clarkston, Glasgow G76 7YL (041-638 0082). ocation: A77, one and a half miles from Clarkston ill. Undulating parkland course. 18 holes, 5832 yards. S.S. 68. Green Fees: information not provided. ting facilities: full catering available, lounge bar.

Visitors: welcome if playing with member. Society Meetings: on Tuesdays and Thursdays by application. Professional: David Naylor (041-638 3436). Secretary: D.A. Howe (041-638 9449).

GLASGOW. **Cathkin Braes Golf Club,** Cathkin Road, Rutherglen, Glasgow G73 4SE (041-634 6605). 18 holes, 6266 yards. S.S.S. 71. Practice ground. Green Fees: £16.00 per round, £25.00 per day. Eating facilities: available. Visitors: welcome Monday to Friday by prior arrangement. Society Meetings: catered for. Professional: Stephen Bree (041-634 0650). Secretary/Treasurer: G.L. Stevenson.

GLASGOW. **Cawder Golf Club,** Cadder Road, Bishopbriggs, Glasgow G64 3QD (041-772 7101). Location: A803 north of city. Parkland. Cawder: 18 holes, 6305 yards, 5737 metres. S.S.S. 71. Keir: 18 holes, 5891 yards, 5373 metres. S.S.S. 68. Practice area. Green Fees: £21.00. Eating facilities: lunches, high teas, dinners available. Visitors: welcome when playing with member. Society Meetings: catered for mid-week. Professional: Ken Stevely (041-772 7102). Secretary: G.T. Stoddart (041-772 5167).

GLASGOW. **Clober Golf Club,** Craigton Road, Milngavie G62 7HP (041-956 1685). Location: five minutes from Milngavie centre, seven miles from Glasgow city centre. 18 holes, 5068 yards. S.S.S. 65. Green Fees: weekdays £8.00 per round. Eating facilities: morning coffee, lunches, high teas. Visitors: welcome weekdays before 4.30pm (Fridays 4.00pm) weekends if introduced by a member. Society Meetings: catered for. Secretary: J. Anderson (041-956 2499).

GLASGOW. **Cowglen Golf Club,** 301 Barrhead Road, Glasgow G43 1AA (041-632 0556). Location: south-west Glasgow, near the Burrell Collection. Undulating parkland course. 18 holes, 6033 yards. S.S.S. 69. Practice area. Green Fees: weekdays £14.00 per round, £21.00 per day. Eating facilities: full catering facilities available. Visitors: welcome when introduced by a member. Lockers and showers available. Society Meetings: restricted numbers, apply to Secretary. Professional: John McTear (041-649 9401). Secretary: R.J.G. Jamieson, C.A. (0292 266600).

GLASGOW. **Crow Wood Golf Club,** Muirhead, Chryston, Glasgow G69 9JF (041-779 2011). Parkland. 18 holes, 6249 yards, 5875 metres. S.S.S. 70. Practice area. Green Fees: weekdays £14.00 per round, £21.00 per day. Eating facilities: bar open 11am to 11pm; catering 11am to 9pm. Visitors: welcome weekdays only by arrangement with Secretary. Professional: Stephen Forbes (041-779 1943). Secretary: Ian McInnes (041-779 4954).

GLASGOW. **Deaconsbank Golf Course,** Rouken Glen Golf Centre, Stewarton Road, Thornliebank, Glasgow G46 7UZ (041-638 7044 or 041-620 0826). Location: on Stewarton Road at Rouken Glen Park, only 250 yards from the A726. Parkland with wooded features, designed by James Braid. 18 holes, 4800 yards. S.S.S. 63 (Par 64). 15-bay floodlit driving range. Green Fees: weekdays £5.25; weekends and Public Holidays £6.50; Day Ticket £11.00. Eating facilities:

catering and bar facilities available. *Visitors:* welcome all year round. Shop, club hire, etc. *Society Meetings:* catered for all year round. Professional: (041-638 7044). Secretary: Christine Cosh (041-620 0826).

GLASGOW. **Dougalston Golf Course,** Strathblane Road, Milngavie, Glasgow G62 (041-956 5750). *Location:* A81 half a mile Milngavie. Wooded – water; three ponds. 18 holes, 6683 yards. S.S.S. 72. Practice ground. *Green Fees:* £9.00 per round, £12.00 per day weekdays; £10.00 per round, £14.00 per day weekends. *Eating facilities:* diningroom and bar meals. *Visitors:* no restrictions, open to the general public. Golf Manager: W. McInnes.

GLASGOW. **Douglas Park Golf Club,** Hillfoot, Bearsden (041-942 2220). *Location:* adjacent to railway station, Hillfoot, Bearsden, 20 yards past traffic lights at Milngavie Road/Boclair Road. 18 holes. S.S.S. 69. *Green Fees:* information not provided. *Eating facilities:* full service available. *Visitors:* must be introduced and play with member. *Society Meetings:* Mondays, Wednesdays and Thursdays on application to Secretary. Professional: David B. Scott. Secretary: D.N. Nicolson.

GLASGOW. **Dullatur Golf Club,** Dullatur, Glasgow G68 0AR (0236 723230). *Location:* 12 miles east of Glasgow, north of Cumbernauld on Kilsyth road via Dullatur. 18 holes, 6229 yards. S.S.S. 70. *Green Fees:* £18.00 per day, £10.00 per round after 1.30pm. *Visitors:* welcome weekdays. Professional: Duncan Sinclair.

GLASGOW. **East Kilbride Golf Club,** Nerston, East Kilbride G74 4PF (03552 20913). 18 holes, 6384 yards. S.S.S. 71. *Green Fees:* £14.00 per round, £20.00 per day. *Eating facilities:* full catering except Tuesdays and Thursdays. *Visitors:* welcome weekdays only on application if members of an official club. Weekends no visitors unless accompanied by a member. *Society Meetings:* catered for on application, limit of 30. Professional: A.R Taylor (03552 22192). Secretary: J.H. King (03552 47728).

GLASGOW. **East Renfrewshire Golf Club,** Pilmuir, Newton Mearns, Glasgow G77 6RT (035 55 256). *Location:* on A77, one and a half miles south of Newton Mearns. Moorland course. 18 holes, 6097 yards, 5577 metres. S.S.S. 70. *Green Fees:* weekdays £20.00 per round, £25.00 per day. *Eating facilities:* by prior arrangment with Clubmaster. *Visitors:* welcome except Saturdays but always by prior arrangement with Professional. *Society Meetings:* welcome by prior arrangement with Secretary. Professional: Gordon D. Clark (035 55 206). Secretary: A. Lindsay Gillespie (041-226 4311).

GLASGOW. **Eastwood Golf Club,** Muirshield, Loganswell, Newton Mearns, Glasgow G77 6RX (035-55 261). *Location:* on main A77 road to Kilmarnock two miles south of Newton Mearns. Parkland. 18 holes, 5864 yards. S.S.S. 68. Practice area. *Green Fees:* £16.00 per round. *Eating facilities:* snacks or full meals available. *Visitors:* welcome weekdays on application to Secretary. *Visiting parties:* welcomed on prior application. Professional: K. McWade (035-55 285). Secretary: C.B. Scouler (035-55 280).

GLASGOW. **Glasgow Golf Club,** Killermont, Bearsden, Glasgow G61 2TW (041-942 2011). *Location:* taking Maryhill Road out of Glasgow turn right at Killermont Avenue, half a mile before Canniesburn Toll. Tree-lined parkland. 18 holes, 5968 yards. S.S.S. 69. Members only. *Visitors:* only if introduced by member. *Society Meetings:* by application to Club Secretary. Professional: Jack Steven (041-942 8507). Secretary: D.W. Deas.

GLASGOW: **Haggs Castle Golf Club,** Dumbreck Road, Dumbreck, Glasgow G41 4SN (041-427 0480). *Location:* straight ahead at roundabout at end of M77 from Glasgow. Flat, tree-lined course. 18 holes, 6464 yards. S.S.S. 71. Practice area and putting green. *Green Fees:* weekdays £24.00 per round, £36.00 per day. Weekends, members only. *Eating facilities:* full catering available. *Visitors:* welcome, must book through Professional. Golf shoes must be worn. *Society Meetings:* by arrangement through Secretary. Professional: J. McAlister (041-427 3355). Secretary: I. Harvey (041-427 1157).

GLASGOW. **Hayston Golf Club,** Campsie Road, Kirkintilloch, Glasgow G66 1RN (041-775 0723). *Location:* 10 miles north-east of Glasgow and one mile north of Kirkintilloch. Undulating course with tree-lined fairways. 18 holes, 6042 yards. S.S.S. 69. Practice area. *Green Fees:* weekdays £12.20 per round, £20.00 per day. *Eating facilities:* lunches and bar snacks available; high tea or dinner if ordered in advance. *Visitors:* welcome weekdays before 4.30pm with letter of introduction from own club. Weekends only if introduced by member. *Society Meetings:* Tuesdays and Thursdays only. Professional: Steve Barnett (041-775 0882).

GLASGOW. **Hilton Park Golf Club,** Stockiemuir Road, Milngavie, Glasgow G62 7HB (041-956 5124). *Location:* on A809. Moorland courses. Allander course: 18 holes, 5374 yards. S.S.S. 67. Hilton course: 18 holes, 6007 yards. S.S.S. 70. Practice area. *Green Fees:* £18.00 per round, £24.00 per day. *Eating facilities:* full catering and bar. *Visitors:* on application to the Secretary (not at weekends). *Society Meetings:* a visitors. Professional: W. McCondichie (041-956 5125). Secretary: Mrs J.A. Dawson (041-956 4657).

GLASGOW. **Kirkhill Golf Club,** Cambuslang, Glasgow (041-641 3083 or 8499). 18 holes, 5862 yards. S.S.S. 69. *Green Fees:* £18.00 per day, £12.00 per round weekdays. *Eating facilities:* dining room and bar snacks. *Visitors:* welcome when introduced by member or on written application to the Secretary. No parties. Secretary: H.G. Marshall.

GLASGOW. **Knightswood Golf Club,** Lincoln Avenue, Glasgow G13 (041-959 2131). *Location:* close to Great Western Road, Glasgow course. 9 holes, 2717 yards. S.S.S. 66 (33). *Green Fees:* £1.75 weekdays; £1.95 weekends. Unemployed, Juniors, Senior Citizens 55p. *Visitors:* welcome anytime. Secretary: Mr Neil McCuaig (041-950 1235).

GLASGOW. **Linn Park Golf Club,** Simshill Road, Glasgow G44 (041-637 5871). *Location:* five miles south of city centre. Parkland. 18 holes, 4952 yards. S.S.S. 65. *Green Fees:* Practice nets, putting green. *Green Fees:* weekdays £3.25 adults, £1.85 Juniors; weekends £3.80. *Visitors:* welcome without restrictions. *Society Meetings:* not catered for. Secretary: Robert Flanagan.

GLASGOW. **Littlehill Golf Club,** Auchinairn Road, Bishopbriggs, Glasgow (041-772 1916). *Location:* close to Stobhill General Hospital, north of city centre. 18 holes, 6364 yards. S.S.S. 70. Golf shop. *Green Fees:* information not available. *Eating facilities:* restaurant within clubhouse. *Visitors:* welcome without reservation. *Society Meetings:* not catered for. Secretary: D.K. Hughes.

GLASGOW. **Milngavie Golf Club,** Laigh Park, Milngavie, Glasgow (041-956 1619). *Location:* situated off Glasgow to Drymen road approximately one mile past Stockiemuir Service Station, turn right at signpost. 18 holes, 5818 yards. S.S.S. 68. *Green Fees:* information not provided. *Eating facilities:* catering available. *Visitors:* welcome when introduced by member only. *Society Meetings:* catered for. Secretary: Mrs A.J.W. Ness.

GLASGOW. **Muirhill Golf Club,** Lethamhill, 1240 Cumbernauld Road, Glasgow G33 1AH (041-770 6220). *Location:* 100 yards off M8 Junction 28. Parkland, many holes with views of loch. 18 holes, 6073 yards. S.S.S. 68. Pitch and putt course (18 holes). *Green Fees:* weekdays £2.75; weekends £3.50. Passport Ticket £1.15. *Eating facilities:* snack bar. *Visitors:* welcome at all times. *Society Meetings:* official clubs, members of the Scottish Golf Union. Secretary: J. Wilson.

GLASGOW. **Pollok Golf Club,** 90 Barrhead Road, Glasgow G43 1BG (041-632 1080). *Location:* A736, four miles south of Glasgow, near end of M77. Wooded parkland. 18 holes, 6257 yards. S.S.S. 70. *Green Fees:*

£26.00 per round, £33.00 per day. *Eating facilities:* dining room and bar. *Visitors:* welcome with reservation by letter to Secretary. No visitors Saturday or Sunday. No Ladies. *Society Meetings:* catered for by letter. Secretary: A.A. Mathison Boyd (041-632 1453).

GLASGOW. **Sandyhills Golf Club,** 223 Sandyhills Road, Glasgow G32 9NA (041-778 1179). *Location:* three miles east from centre of Glasgow. 18 holes, 6253 yards. S.S.S. 70. *Green Fees:* information not provided. *Eating facilities:* lunches at club except Mondays, order in advance. *Visitors:* welcome when introduced by a member.

GLASGOW. **The Whitecraigs Golf Club,** 72 Ayr Road, Giffnock, Glasgow G46 6SW (041-639 1681). *Location:* on A77 south of city. Parkland course, 18 holes. *Green Fees:* £23.00 per round, £29.00 per day. *Eating facilities:* diningroom, lounge bar. *Visitors:* letter of introduction required. *Society Meetings:* catered for Wednesday only. Professional: William Watson (041-639 2140). Secretary: R.W. Miller (041-639 4530).

GLASGOW. **Williamwood Golf Club,** Clarkston Road, Glasgow G44 (041-637 1783). *Location:* beside Clarkston Toll on Clarkston Road. Attractive parkland course designed by James Braid. 18 holes, 5878 yards. S.S.S. 68. Practice area and putting. *Green Fees:* weekdays £3.00; weekends £5.00. *Eating facilities:* meals must be ordered. *Visitors:* must be introduced by, and play with, a member. *Society Meetings:* weekdays only by arrangement. Professional: J. Gardner (041-637 2715). Secretary: R.G. Cuthbert CA (041-226 4311).

GLASGOW. **Windyhill Golf Club,** Baljaffray Road, Bearsden, Glasgow G61 4QQ (041-942 2349). *Location:* eight miles north-west of Glasgow. Undulating parkland, moorland course. 18 holes, 6254 yards. S.S.S. 70. Practice area, caddy cars available. *Green Fees:* £15.00 weekdays; weekends with member only. *Eating facilities:* full catering and bar. *Visitors:* welcome weekdays, by prior arrangement with Secretary. *Society Meetings:* welcome weekdays by arrangement. Professional: R. Collinson (041-942 7157). Secretary: A.J. Miller (041-942 2349).

KILSYTH. **Kilsyth Lennox Golf Club,** Tak-Ma-Doon Road, Kilsyth, Glasgow G65 0RS (Kilsyth (0236) 822190). *Location:* 12 miles from Glasgow on A80. Parkland/moorland, undulating ground with superb views across central Scotland. 9 holes, 5934 yards. S.S.S. 69. (Second 9 holes currently under construction). *Green Fees:* weekdays £8.00 per round; weekends £12.00. *Eating facilities:* bar and lounge, bar snacks available. *Visitors:* welcome weekdays up to 5.00pm, Saturdays after 5.00pm, not Sundays. Professional: R. Abercrombie. Secretary: R. Hay (0236 823525).

## NOTE

All the information in this book is given in good faith in the belief that it is correct. However, the publishers cannot guarantee the facts given in these pages, neither are they responsible for changes in policy, ownership or terms that may take place after the date of going to press. Readers should always satisfy themselves that the facilities they require are available and that the terms, if quoted, still apply.

# Inverness-shire

BOAT OF GARTEN. **Boat of Garten Golf and Tennis Club,** Boat of Garten PH24 3BQ (Boat of Garten (047-983) 282). *Location:* A9 six miles north of Aviemore. Wooded birch tree-lined fairways, very scenic, overlooking Cairngorm Mountains. 18 holes, 5837 yards. S.S.S. 69. Practice net. *Green Fees:* weekdays £14.00; weekends £18.00. *Eating facilities:* catering facilities open 10am to 6pm, bar facilities open 11am to 11pm daily. *Visitors:* welcome, bookings everyday. *Society Meetings:* catered for. Secretary: J.R. Ingram.

CARRBRIDGE. **Carrbridge Golf Club,** Carrbridge (0474 984674). *Location:* eight miles north of Aviemore adjacent to A9, 23 miles south of Inverness. Moorland/parkland. 9 holes, 2630 yards. S.S.S. 66. *Green Fees:* weekdays £7.00 per day; weekends £9.00 per day. *Eating facilities:* snacks, coffee etc. No bar. *Visitors:* unrestricted except competition days (mainly Sundays). Secretary: E.G. Drayson (047984 674).

FORT AUGUSTUS. **Fort Augustus Golf Club,** Fort Augustus (Fort Augustus (0320) 6460). *Location:* new entrance 500 yards south of village on Fort William road. 9 holes, 18 tees, 5454 yards. S.S.S. 68. *Green Fees:* information not available. *Visitors:* welcome without reservation. *Society Meetings:* catered for. Secretary: I. Aitchison (0320 6460).

INVERNESS. **Inverness Golf Club,** Culcabock Road, Inverness IV2 3XQ (Inverness (0463) 233422). *Location:* one mile south of town centre. Parkland course. 18 holes, 6226 yards. S.S.S. 70. Two practice grounds. *Green Fees:* weekdays £18.00 per day, £14.00 per round; weekends and Bank Holidays £20.00 per day, £17.00 per round. *Eating facilities:* sandwiches, lunches, high teas and dinners served at club. *Visitors:* welcome except Saturdays from 25th March to 20th October. *Society Meetings;* catered for, pre-booking preferred. Professional: A.P. Thomson (0463 231989). Secretary: J. Fraser (0463 239882).

INVERNESS. **Torvean Golf Club,** Glenurquhart Road, Inverness (0463 236648). *Location:* A82 towards Fort William, approximately one mile from town centre. Parkland course. 18 holes, 5784 yards, 5288 metres. S.S.S. 69. Practice area and putting green. *Green Fees:* weekdays £7.90; weekends £9.10. *Eating facilities:* snacks and bar available in summer season 11am – 11pm. *Visitors:* booking preferred, especially at weekends – telephone 0463 237543. *Society Meetings:* welcome with advance booking through Inverness District Council. Secretary: Mrs K.M. Gray (0463 225651).

KINGUSSIE. **Kingussie Golf Club,** Gynack Road, Kingussie PH21 1JG (0540 661 374). *Location:* turn at Duke of Gordon Hotel, half a mile up road (signposted). Moorland course. 18 holes, 5555 yards, 5079 metres. S.S.S. 67. *Green Fees:* weekdays £10.00 per round, £13.00 per day; weekends £12.00 per round, £13.00 per day. *Eating facilities:* bar, catering provided. *Visitors:* welcome, tee reserved for members 8.30am – 9.30am, 12.30pm – 1.30pm and 5.30pm – 6.30pm at weekends, otherwise no restrictions. Caravan site. *Society Meetings:* welcome. Secretary: William Cook (0540 661 600).

NETHYBRIDGE.   **Abernethy Golf Club,** Nethybridge, PH25 3DE (0479 821305). *Location:* 10 miles from Aviemore lying on the B970 between Boat-of-Garten and Grantown on Spey. Delightful nine hole course close to pine woods and with commanding view of the valley of the River Spey. 9 holes, 4986 yards. S.S.S. 66. *Green Fees:* £8.00 weekdays; £12.00 weekends. *Eating facilities:* clubhouse is unlicensed but there are full catering facilities available. *Visitors:* welcome subject to short restrictions when club competitions being held. *Society Meetings:* by arrangement with the Secretary. Secretary: Bill Templeton (0479 821214).

NEWTONMORE. **Newtonmore Golf Club,** Golf Course Road, Newtonmore PH20 1AT (0540 673328). *Location:* turn off A9 at Newtonmore, course in centre of village, 45 miles south of Inverness. Mostly flat, running beside River Spey amidst beautiful scenery. 18 holes, 5880 yards. S.S.S. 68. Practice green. *Green Fees:* weekdays £12.00; weekends £15.00. *Eating facilities:* catering every day except Tuesdays, bar open 11am – 11pm April to October. *Visitors:* welcome, restrictions open competitions and society days. *Society Meetings:* welcome by appointment with Secretary. Professional: Robert Henderson (0540 673281). Secretary: Richard J. Cheyne (0540 673878).

# Kincardineshire

BANCHORY. **Banchory Golf Club,** Kinneskie Road, Banchory AB31 3TA (Banchory (03302) 2365). *Location:* 18 miles west of Aberdeen on Deeside, 100 yards south west Banchory town centre. Parkland. 18 holes, 5245 yards, 4795 metres. S.S.S. 66. *Green Fees:* weekdays £16.50; weekends £18.50. *Eating facilities:* full catering service and lounge bar. *Visitors:* welcome. *Society Meetings:* catered for except Thursdays and weekends. Professional: D.W. Smart (03302 2447). Secretary: E. Girvan (03302 2365).

STONEHAVEN. **Stonehaven Golf Club,** Cowie, Stonehaven AB3 2RH (Stonehaven (0569) 62124). *Location:* A92, one mile north of town. 18 holes, 5128 yards. S.S.S. 65. *Green Fees:* £13.00 weekdays, £18.00 weekends. *Eating facilities:* full catering including bar lunches. *Visitors:* welcome, only a few with reservation. *Society Meetings:* catered for except for Saturday and all Sundays in July and August. Secretary: E.A. Ferguson. Club Manager: R.O. Blair.

# Kinross-shire

KINNESSWOOD. **Bishopshire Golf Club,** Kinnesswood, By Kinross. *Location:* take road to Glenrothes from M90, three miles. Course has panoramic views overlooking Loch Leven. 10 holes, 4700 yards, 2151 metres. S.S.S. 64. *Green Fees:* weekdays £5.00; weekends £6.00. *Eating facilities:* by arrangement or available at the hotel 400 yards away. *Visitors:* welcome without restriction. *Society Meetings:* by arrangement. Secretary: John Proudfoot (0592 780203).

KINROSS. **Green Hotel Golf Course,** Green Hotel, The Muirs, Kinross KY13 7AS (0577 62237). *Location:* turn left in Kinross off M90 Junction 6, course 500 yards on right. Reasonably flat wooded parkland. Two courses: Blue 18 holes, 6456 yards, 5905 metres. S.S.S. TBA; Red 18 holes, 6257 yards, 5719 metres. S.S.S. TBA. Practice ground. *Green Fees:* weekdays £12.00 per round, £18.00 per day; weekends £18.00 per round, £25.00 per day. *Eating facilities:* in clubhouse and hotel. *Visitors:* welcome, booking recommended. *Society Meetings:* catered for by

arrangement. Professional: Stuart Geraghty (0577 63467). Secretary: Mrs S.M. Stewart (0577 63467).

LAURENCEKIRK. **Auchenblae Golf Club,** Auchenblae, Laurencekirk AB30 1BU. *Location:* five miles north of Laurencekirk, on A94, two miles west of Fordoun. Parkland. 9 holes, 2174 yards. S.S.S. 30. *Green Fees:* Mondays to Fridays £5.00; Saturdays £6.00, Sundays £6.50. Juniors and Senior Citizens half price at all times. *Eating facilities:* two hotels in nearby village. *Visitors:* restrictions Wednesday and Friday evenings (competitions); very busy Sundays. *Society Meetings:* small groups welcome. Secretary: A.I. Robertson (05617 8869).

MILNATHORT. **Milnathort Golf Club Ltd,** South Street, Milnathort (Kinross (0577) 64069). Parkland course. 9 holes, 5969 yards. S.S.S. 69. *Green Fees:* weekdays £10.00 per day; weekends £15.00 per day. *Eating facilities:* by arrangement. *Visitors:* welcome without reservation. *Society Meetings:* must be booked in advance. All enquiries phone Clubhouse.

# Kirkcudbrightshire

CASTLE DOUGLAS. **Castle Douglas Golf Club,** Abercromby Road, Castle Douglas (0556 2801). *Location:* in town. Parkland. 9 holes, 5408 yards. S.S.S. 66. *Green Fees:* £10.00 per round or day. *Eating facilities:* some catering may be available during season. *Visitors:* welcome without reservation, except Tuesdays or Thursdays after 4pm and competition days. *Society Meetings:* not catered for. Secretary: A.D. Millar (0556 2099).

DALBEATTIE. **Colvend Golf Club,** Sandyhills, Colvend, By Dalbeattie (0556-63 398). *Location:* six miles from Dalbeattie on the A710, Solway Coast road, between Dalbeattie and Dumfries. Picturesque seaside

course on a hill. 18 holes (visitors' tees), 4480 yards. S.S.S. 63. *Green Fees:* £10.00 per day; Juniors £5.00 (full fee Saturday and Sundays). *Eating facilities:* excellent catering available. *Visitors:* welcome almost anytime. Course must be vacated by 2pm on Tuesdays and 5.30pm on Thursdays, also some Sundays (competitions), from April to September. Secretary: J.B. Henderson (0556 610878).

GATEHOUSE OF FLEET. **Gatehouse of Fleet Golf Club,** Laurieston Road, Gatehouse of Fleet, Castle Douglas. *Location:* quarter of a mile from Gatehouse. Sloping and wooded. 9 holes, 2500 yards. S.S.S. 63. *Green Fees:* £10.00. *Visitors:* welcome at all times

### Selkirk Arms Hotel

AA ★★ RAC

**Kirkcudbright, Galloway Tel: (0557) 30402 Fax: (0557) 31639**
*Where Robert Burns wrote 'The Selkirk Grace'*

*Historic 18th century Hotel, now newly refurbished, in picturesque town. Ideal for business or family holidays. Golf, squash, sailing, fishing, sea-angling all nearby. Exciting à la carte menu prepared using finest fresh local ingredients. All rooms have private facilities. TV and telephone. Large secluded gardens.*

---

# GORDON HOUSE HOTEL
### HIGH STREET, KIRKCUDBRIGHT, DUMFRIESSHIRE DG6 4JQ

We extend a warm welcome to all visitors here at GORDON HOUSE. Local 18-hole course three minutes away with a further selection of courses at CASTLE DOUGLAS, GATEHOUSE, GLENLUCE, DUMFRIES, NEW GALLOWAY and NEWTON STEWART. Further afield there are Championship Courses at TROON, PRESTWICK, SOUTHERNESS and TURNBERRY. Special 2-night Golf Breaks: Golf, Dinner, Bed & Breakfast from £68.00 per person. Details on request.
### Telephone: (0557) 30670

---

# LEAMINGTON HOTEL
### High Street, NEW GALLOWAY, Kirkcudbrightshire

Enjoy the warmest welcome at this family-run ten bedroomed 17th century Hotel. Ideally situated for watersports, fishing, stalking, walking, golf – LOCAL SCENIC COURSE – and touring in Bonnie Galloway. Ensuite rooms, very popular licensed restaurant offering excellent fare at reasonable prices. Weekly, family and 3-day rates. BED & BREAKFAST from £14.

STB ♥♥♥ Commended                          Telephone 06442 327

---

except Sunday mornings to 11.30am. Secretary: Alan McCreath (0557 814281).

KIRKCUDBRIGHT. **Kirkcudbright Golf Club,** Stirling Crescent, Kirkcudbright (0557 30314). *Location:* signposted near centre of town. Hilly parkland. 18 holes, 5598 yards. S.S.S. 77. *Green Fees:* £12.00 per round, £15.00 per day. Reductions for parties of 20 or more. *Eating facilities:* available. *Visitors:* welcome without reservation most days. *Society Meetings:* must

have Handicap Certificates. Secretary: A. Gordon (0557 30542).

NEW GALLOWAY. **New Galloway Golf Club,** New Galloway, Castle Douglas (06443 455). *Location:* one mile off A731, Ayr to Dumfries road. Scenic with fine turf. 9 holes, 5058 yards. S.S.S. 65. *Green Fees:* £8.00 per round/day Monday to Saturdays; Sundays £10.00. *Eating facilities:* bar. *Visitors:* welcome without reservation. Accommodation and meals available in village. *Society Meetings:* by arrangement. Secretary: Alan R. Brown (06443 455).

---

# Lanarkshire

---

AIRDRIE. **Airdrie Golf Club,** Glenmavis Road, Airdrie (Airdrie (0236) 762195). *Location:* one mile north of Airdrie Cross. 18 holes, 6004 yards. S.S.S. 69. *Green Fees:* £12.00 per round, £20.00 per day (both inclusive of VAT). *Eating facilities:* available. *Visitors:* welcome on application to the Secretary. Professional: A. McCloskey (0236 754360). Secretary: D.M. Hardie.

AIRDRIE. **Easter Moffat Golf Club,** Plains, Airdrie ML6 8NP (0236 842878). *Location:* three miles east of Airdrie on old Edinburgh Road. 18 holes, 6221 yards. S.S.S. 70. Practice ground. *Green Fees:* £12.00 per round, £18.00 per day (lower rate if visited previous year). *Eating facilities:* bar and dining room. *Visitors:* welcome except weekends. *Society Meetings:* welcome. Professional: Brian Dunbar (0236 843015). Secretary: J.G. Timmons (0236 61440).

BELLSHILL. **Bellshill Golf Club,** Community Road, Orbiston, Bellshill ML4 2RZ (Bellshill (0698) 745124). *Location:* Bellshill to Motherwell road, turn right. Parkland course. 18 holes, 6604 yards, 6057 metres. S.S.S. 72. *Green Fees:* weekdays £11.00, weekends £15.00. *Visitors:* casual visitors welcome; parties by prior application (not competition days or Sundays). Secretary: A.M. Currie (03552 23101).

BIGGAR. **Biggar Golf Club,** Broughton Road, Biggar ML12 6HA (0899 20618). *Location:* from Edinburgh A702, from Glasgow A74 or M8, turn off at Newhouse. Flat, scenic parkland course. 18 holes, 5416 yards. S.S.S. 66. *Green Fees:* weekdays £8.00, weekend £10.00. Reductions for Juniors and Senior Citizens. *Eating facilities:* all day licence, full catering (no Mondays). *Visitors:* unrestricted, casual dress – r jeans. All weather tennis courts and caravan park. *Society Meetings:* welcome, early reservation essential. Secretary: W.S. Turnbull (0899 20566). Tee Reservations: (0899 20319).

CARLUKE. **Carluke Golf Club,** Maudslie Road, Hallcraig, Carluke ML8 5HG (0555 71070). *Location:* one and a quarter miles from Carluke Cross, through Clyde Street. Parkland course. 18 holes, 5800 yards. S.S.S. 68. Practice area. *Green Fees:* £10.00 per round, £15.00 per day weekdays. *Eating facilities:* available. *Visitors:* till 4pm weekdays, no visitors weekends. Tuition. *Society Meetings:* by written application to the Secretary. Professional: A. Brooks (0555 51053). Secretary: J.H. Muir (0555 70620).

COATBRIDGE. **Drumpellier Golf Club,** Drumpellier Avenue, Coatbridge ML5 1RX (Coatbridge (0236) 24139). *Location:* one mile from town centre. Parkland, wooded. 18 holes, 6227 yards. S.S.S. 70. Practice area. *Green Fees:* £16.00 per round, £22.00 per day weekdays. *Eating facilities:* catering available except Thursdays. *Visitors:* welcome with reservation. *Society Meetings:* catered for by arrangement. Professional: I. Collins (0236 32971). Secretary: W. Brownlie (0236 23065).

DOUGLAS WATER. **Douglas Water Golf Club,** Ayr Road, Rigside, Lanark (055588 361). *Location:* five miles south of Lanark on A70 – turn right at Hyndford Bridge. Hilly course, small greens. 9 holes, 2947 yards, 2694 metres. S.S.S. 69. *Green Fees:* weekdays £5.00; weekends £7.00. Subject to increase. *Eating facilities:* snacks. *Visitors:* welcome any time, with reservation on Saturdays for competitions. *Society Meetings:* contact Secretary. Secretary: Mr R.McMillan (0555 2295).

EAST KILBRIDE. **Torrance House Golf Club,** Calderglen Country Park, Strathaven Road, East Kilbride G75 0QZ (03552 49720). *Location:* East Kilbride boundary on main Strathaven road. Parkland. 18 holes, 6423 yards. S.S.S. 71. Practice area. *Green Fees:* information on request. *Eating facilities:* private clubhouse. *Visitors:* welcome mid-week only. *Society Meetings:* details on request. Secretary: Duncan A. MacIver (03552 49720). Booking Office: (03552 48636).

GARTCOSH. **Mount Ellen Golf Club,** Johnstone House, Johnstone Road, Gartcosh (Glenboig (0236) 872277). *Location:* approximately six miles north-east of Glasgow, near old Gartcosh steelworks. Flatland. 18 holes, 5525 yards. S.S.S. 68. *Green Fees:* weekdays £10.00 per round, £16 per day. *Eating facilities:* bar and excellent catering. *Visitors:* welcome weekdays, no weekend visitors. Professional: G. Reilly. Secretary: W.J. Dickson.

HAMILTON. **Hamilton Golf Club,** Riccarton, Ferniegair, Hamilton ML3 7PZ (0698 282872). *Location:* off A74 Hamilton turn-off, one and a half miles up Larkhall road. Parkland course. 18 holes, 6700 yards. S.S.S. 70. *Green Fees:* information not provided. *Eating facilities:* meals must be ordered. *Visitors:* must be accompanied by a member. *Society Meetings:* by arrangement with Secretary. Professional: M.J. Moir (0698 282324). Secretary: P.E. Soutter (0698 286131).

HAMILTON. **Strathclyde Park Golf Club,** Mote Hill, Hamilton ML3 6BY (0698 66155 ext. 154). *Location:* M74 north, Hamilton, Motherwell exit, to roundabout second exit, to roundabout second exit, pass ice rink, golf course straight ahead (about one mile from motorway turn off to course. Parkland, wooded course. 9 holes, 3147 yards. S.S.S. 70. Practice area and driving range (24 bays). *Green Fees:* adults approximately £1.90, Juniors 96p, Senior Citizens 55p. *Eating facilities:* bar and cafe available. *Visitors:* book in advance at clubhouse, or by telephone on day of play. *Society Meetings:* by arrangement with J. Rankin (0698 66155). Professional: Ken Davidson (0698 283994). Secretary: Kevin Will (0698 825363).

LANARK. **Carnwath Golf Club,** 1 Main Street, Carnwath (Carnwath (0555) 840251). Fairly hilly inland course. 18 holes, 5860 yards. S.S.S. 69. *Green Fees:* £15.00 weekdays; weekends and Bank Holidays £18.00. *Eating facilities:* lounge bar and dining room daily. *Visitors:* welcome Mondays, Wednesdays, Fridays and Sundays with prior booking. *Society Meetings:* catered for by prior arrangement. Secretary: Donald Craig (0555 4359).

LANARK. **Lanark Golf Club,** The Moor, Whitelees Road, Lanark ML11 7RX (Lanark (0555) 3219). *Location:* off A73. Tough moorland course. 18 holes, 6423 yards. S.S.S. 71. Also 9-hole course. Two practice grounds. *Green Fees:* £16.00 per round, £25.00 per day weekdays. *Eating facilities:* full catering and bar. *Visitors:* welcome daily until 4pm, no visitors weekends. *Society Meetings:* groups of 24 and over catered for Mondays and Tuesdays. Professional: Ron Wallace (0555 61456). Secretary: G.H. Cuthill.

LARKHALL. **Larkhall Golf Club,** Burnhead Road, Larkhall (0698 881113). *Location:* on A74, close to M74. Parkland. 9 holes, 6684 yards. S.S.S. 72. *Green Fees:* information not provided. *Eating facilities:* meals weekends; bar normal hours. *Visitors:* welcome, but check beforehand; every second Saturday course closed to visitors. Secretary: I. Gilmour (0698 881755).

LEADHILLS. **Leadhills Golf Club,** Leadhills, Biggar (0659 74222). *Location:* seven miles south of Abington on B797. This short but testing course is the highest in Britain. 9 holes, 2400 yards. S.S.S. 62. *Green Fees:* £4.00. *Eating facilities:* not available. *Visitors:* welcome any time. *Society Meetings:* welcome. Secretary: Harry Shaw.

LESMAHAGOW. **Hollandbush Golf Club,** Acretophead, Lesmahagow (Lesmahagow (0555) 893484). *Location:* off M74 between Lesmahagow and Coalburn. 18 holes, 6110 yards. S.S.S. 70. Practice area. *Green Fees:* £9.00 weekdays; £11.00 weekends. (Special tourist rates available). *Eating facilities:* meals at club. *Visitors:* welcome without restriction. *Society Meetings:* catered for. Professional: Ian Rae (0555 893646). Secretary: James Hamilton (055 582 222).

MOTHERWELL. **Colville Park Golf Club,** Jerviston Estate, Motherwell (0698 63017). *Location:* one mile from station (Merry Street, Motherwell). 18 holes, 6265 yards. S.S.S. 70. *Green Fees:* £14.00. *Eating facilities:* licensed and full catering facilities. *Visitors:* prior written arrangement or when accompanied by member. *Society Meetings:* by prior written arrangement. Secretary: Scott Connacher.

SHOTTS. **Shotts Golf Club,** Blairhead, Benhar Road, Shotts ML7 5BJ (Shotts (0501) 20431). *Location:* off M8 at junction B7057, one and a half miles on Benhar Road. Semi-flat moorland/wooded course. 18 holes, 6125 yards. S.S.S. 70. Practice area. *Green Fees:* weekdays £14.00 per day (off season £10.00); weekends £16.00 per day (off season £12.00). *Eating facilities:* full catering, all day licence. *Visitors:* welcome anytime except Saturdays before 4.30pm and Sundays or Public Holidays. *Society Meetings:* weekdays only. Professional: (0501 22658). Secretary: Jack McDermott (0501 20431).

STRATHAVEN. **Strathaven Golf Club,** Overton Avenue, Glasgow Road, Strathaven ML10 6NR (Strathaven (0357) 20539). *Location:* on A726 on outskirts of town. 18 holes, 6226 yards. S.S.S. 70. *Green Fees:* please contact Secretary for information. *Eating facilities:* full catering and bar. *Visitors:* welcome

weekdays, casual visitors before 4.30pm; party bookings Tuesdays only by prior arrangement. *Society Meetings:* catered for weekdays only, by prior arrangement. Professional: M.R. McCrorie (0357 21812). Secretary: A.W. Wallace (0357 20421).

UDDINGSTON. **Calderbraes Golf Club,** 57 Roundknowe Road, Uddingston (Uddingston (0698) 813425). *Location:* at end of M74, overlooking Calderpark Zoo. 9 holes, 3425 yards. S.S.S. 67. *Green Fees:* information not available. *Visitors:* welcome weekdays only. Secretary: S. McGuigan.

WISHAW. **Wishaw Golf Club,** 55 Cleland Road, Wishaw (Wishaw (0698) 372869). *Location:* centre of town, five miles from M74. Tree-lined parkland course. 18 holes, 6137 yards. S.S.S. 69. Practice area. *Green Fees:* weekdays £10.00 per round, £15.00 per day; weekends £20.00 per day. *Eating facilities:* full catering and two bars. *Visitors:* welcome before 4pm weekdays, after 11am Sundays. *Society Meetings:* by application to Secretary. Professional: J.G. Campbell (0698 358247). Secretary: D.D. Gallacher (0698 372869).

# Morayshire

ELGIN. **Elgin Golf Club,** Hardhillock, Birnie Road, Elgin IV30 3SX (Elgin (0343) 542338). *Location:* half a mile south of Elgin on Birnie Road. Undulating parkland on sandy subsoil. 18 holes, 6401 yards, 5853 metres. S.S.S. 71. Practice ground and net. *Green Fees:* weekdays £13.00 per round, £19.00 per day; weekends £18.50 per round, £26.50 per day. *Eating facilities:* bar and catering every day. *Visitors:* no restrictions but parties should book with Secretary. *Society Meetings:* by arrangement with Secretary. Early booking advised. Professional: Ian Rodger (0343 542884). Secretary: Derek J. Chambers.

ELGIN. **Hopeman Golf Club,** Hopeman, Elgin IV30 2YA (Hopeman (0343) 830578). *Location:* 7 miles north-east of Elgin on B9012. Seaside links, with spectacular 12th hole. 18 holes, 5474 yards, 5003 metres. S.S.S. 67. *Green Fees:* weekdays £10.00 per day; weekends £15.00 per day. Reductions for Senior Citizens. *Eating facilities:* bar, catering. *Visitors:* welcome, some restrictions weekends. *Society Meetings:* by arrangement. Secretary: W.H. Dumbar (0343 830687).

FOCHABERS. **Garmouth & Kingston Golf Club,** Garmouth, Fochabers (0343 87388). *Location:* west bank of River Spey, 300 yards from North Sea. Flat parkland/part links. 18 holes, 5656 yards. S.S.S. 67. *Green Fees:* weekdays £10.00 per round, £12.00 per day; weekends £14.00 per round, £18.00 per day. Reductions for parties over 20. *Eating facilities:* by arrangement, bar and snacks from 1st May to September 11am to 11pm. *Visitors:* welcome, except during local competitions. Local hotel caters for golfing holidays. *Society Meetings:* by arrangement with Secretary, very welcome. Secretary: A. Robertson (0343 87231).

FOCHABERS. **Spey Bay Golf Club,** Spey Bay Hotel, Spey Bay, Fochabers IV32 7JP (0343 820424). *Location:* four miles off A96 at Fochabers (signposted). Seaside links. 18 holes, 6059 yards. S.S.S. 69. *Green Fees:* Monday to Saturday £7.00, Sundays £8.50. *Eating facilities:* all meals available at the adjoining hotel. *Visitors:* welcome weekdays without reservation, advise prior phone call on Sundays. *Society Meetings:*

270

catered for by prior arrangement £14.00 per day. Special weekend terms including full board and golf available. Any enquiries to the Hotel Manager.

FORRES. **Forres Golf Club,** Muiryshade, Forres (Forres (0309) 72949). *Location:* one mile south from clock tower in town centre. Part parkland and wooded. 18 holes, 6141 yards, 5615 metres. S.S.S. 69. Practice ground and putting green. *Green Fees:* weekdays £12.00 per day; weekends £18.00. *Eating facilities:* excellent meals available all day every day. *Visitors:* welcome without reservation. *Society Meetings:* catered for on weekdays. Professional: Sandy Aird (0309 72250). Secretary: D.F. Black (0309 72949).

GRANTOWN-ON-SPEY. **Grantown-on-Spey Golf Club,** The Clubhouse, Golf Course Road, Grantown-on-Spey PH26 3HY (Grantown-on-Spey (0479) 2079). *Location:* situated at north end of town, A9 to A95, then turn right opposite police station. Parkland and woodland. 18 holes, 5715 yards. S.S.S. 67. Practice area and

putting green. *Green Fees:* weekdays £13.00 per day; weekends £16.00. *Eating facilities:* bar and full catering available April to December inclusive. *Visitors:* welcome weekdays, reserved for members 5.30pm – 6.30pm, Saturdays and Sundays between 8am and 10am, 1pm and 2pm, 5pm and 6pm. *Society Meetings:* catered for. Professional: W. Mitchell (0479 2398). Secretary: D. Elms (0479 2715).

LOSSIEMOUTH. **Moray Golf Club,** Stotfield Road, Lossiemouth IV31 6QS (034-381 2018). *Location:* six miles north of Elgin. Old Course 18 holes, 6643 yards, 6074 metres. S.S.S. 69. New Course 18 holes, 6005 yards, 5491 metres. S.S.S. 69. *Green Fees:* on request. *Eating facilities:* full catering and bar facilities. *Visitors:* welcome weekdays after 9.30am (except between 1-2pm). Weekends: Saturday (New Course only), Sunday not before 10.30am and not between 1-2pm. *Society Meetings:* all welcome. Handicap Certificate required. Professional: Alastair Thomson (034-381 3330). Secretary: James Hamilton (034-381 2018).

# Nairnshire

NAIRN. **Nairn Dunbar Golf Club,** Lochloy Road, Nairn IV12 5AE (Nairn (0667) 52741). *Location:* on A96, one mile east of town. Seaside links. 18 holes, 6431 yards. S.S.S. 71. *Green Fees:* weekdays £15.00; weekends £20.00. *Eating facilities:* available. *Visitors:* welcome. *Society Meetings:* catered for. Professional: B. Mason (0667 53964). Secretary: Mrs S.J. MacLennan.

NAIRN. **Nairn Golf Club,** Seabank Road, Nairn IV12 4HB (0667 52103). *Location:* Nairn West Shore, on the southern shore of the Moray Firth, 16 miles east of Inverness, five miles from Inverness Airport. Seaside links. 18 holes, 6772 yards. S.S.S. 72. Also 9 hole course (Newton Course), large practice ground. *Green Fees:* weekdays £23.00 per round, weekends £28.00. *Eating facilities:* full catering facilities. *Visitors:* welcome, no jeans in clubhouse, Handicap Certificate required. *Society Meetings:* catered for. Professional: Robin Fyfe (0667 52787). Secretary: Mr Jim Somerville (0667 53208; Fax: 0667 56328).

# Peebles-shire

PEEBLES. **Innerleithen Golf Club,** Innerleithen (0896 830951). *Location:* 25 miles south of Edinburgh, just south of Peebles. Situated in valley, easy walking but challenging. 9 holes, 5910 yards (x 2). S.S.S. 68. *Green Fees:* weekdays £7.00 per day; weekends £9.00 per day. *Eating facilities:* by prior arrangement. *Visitors:* welcome without reservation. *Society Meetings:* catered for by arrangement, limit 40. Secretary: S. Wyse (0896 830071).

PEEBLES. **Peebles Golf Club,** Kirkland Street, Peebles (0721 20197). *Location:* 51 miles from Glasgow, off A72 at west side of town, 23 miles from Edinburgh. 18 holes, 6137 yards. S.S.S. 69. *Green Fees:* weekdays £10.00 per round, £15.00 per day; weekends £16.00 per round, £22.00 per day. 10% discount to groups of 20 plus except Wednesday afternoons. *Eating facilities:* catering available to 9.30pm daily except Tuesdays. *Visitors:* welcome. *Society Meetings:* catered for subject to prior bookings, limited to 24 players in party. Secretary: R. Reeves.

WEST LINTON. **West Linton Golf Club,** West Linton EH46 7HN (0968 60463). *Location:* A702 road 17 miles south west of Edinburgh. Moorland. 18 holes, 6132 yards, 5607 metres. S.S.S. 69. Two practice areas. *Green Fees:* weekdays £13.00 per round, £18.00 per day; weekends £20.00 per round. *Eating facilities:* diningroom, lunches, high tea, morning coffee, afternoon tea and bar. *Visitors:* welcome at all times except on medal days and weekends before 1pm. *Society Meetings:* catered for weekdays except Tuesdays. Professional: Ron Tickle (0968 60256). Secretary: Grahame Scott (0968 75843).

*Please mention this guide when you write or phone to enquire about accommodation.*

# Perthshire

ABERFELDY. **Aberfeldy Golf Club,** Taybridge Road, Aberfeldy PH15 2BH (Aberfeldy (0887) 820535). *Location:* A9 to Ballinluig. Riverside course. 9 holes, 2733 yards, 2655 metres. S.S.S. 67. *Green Fees:* £10.00 per round. *Eating facilities:* snacks and bar. *Visitors:* welcome anytime. *Society Meetings:* catered for. Contact the Secretary at Aberfeldy Golf Club. Secretary: Angus M. Stewart (0887 820117).

ABERFELDY. **Kenmore Golf Course,** Mains of Taymouth, Kenmore, Aberfeldy PH15 2HN (0887 830226). *Location:* west off A9 at Ballinluig on A827, six and a half miles west of Aberfeldy through village of Kenmore on RHS. Mildly undulating natural terrain, well kept, nestled in Tay Valley. 9 holes, 6052 yards. S.S.S. 69. Practice facilities. *Green Fees:* weekdays £10.00 18 holes, £16.00 per day; weekends £11.00 18 holes, £18.00 per day. Junior rates available, rates for parties on application. *Eating facilities:* full bar and catering facilities in pleasant surroundings. *Visitors:* welcome anytime. STB 4 Crown Cottages to let and group accommodation available (self catering included). Pro shop; club and trolley hire; bowling green. *Society Meetings:* up to 35 welcome. Secretary: Robin Menzies.

ABERFELDY. **Taymouth Castle Golf Course,** Kenmore, by Aberfeldy PH15 2NT (0887 830397). *Location:* six miles west of Aberfeldy. Flat parkland set in scenic mountain terrain. 18 holes, 6066 yards. S.S.S. 69. Practice area. *Green Fees:* weekdays £14.00 per round, £22.00 per day; weekends and Bank Holidays, £18.00 per round. Half price for Juniors (under 15). *Eating facilities:* restaurant and bar. *Visitors:* welcome except competition days, tee reservations necessary (phone or letter). Tuition available, motorised buggies. *Society Meetings:* catered for by previous arrangement only. Professional: Alex Marshall (0887 820910). Director of Golf: Michael Mulcahey (0887 830228).

AUCHTERARDER. **Auchterarder Golf Club,** Orchil Road, Auchterarder PH3 1DW (Auchterarder (0764) 62804). *Location:* off A9 to south-west of town, next to Gleneagles. Flat parkland, part wooded. 18 holes, 5757 yards. S.S.S. 68. Small practice area. *Green Fees:* weekdays £12.00 per round, £17.00 per day; weekends £18.00 per round, £25.00 per day. *Eating facilities:* full catering and bar. *Visitors:* welcome without reservation except major competition days. *Society Meetings:* welcome, must book 3 months in advance. Professional: K. Salmoni (0764 63711). Secretary: W.M. Campbell (0764 62804).

AUCHTERARDER. **Gleneagles Hotel Golf Courses,** Auchterarder PH3 1NF (Auchterarder (0764) 62231; Telex 76105; Fax: 0764 62134). *Location:* A9 from Perth, 16 miles south-west: bus meets trains at Gleneagles Station. Gleneagles offers two moorland 18 hole courses. **King's Course: 6125 yards par 69; **Queen's Course: 5660 yards par 67. As well as a new 9 hole course, The Wee Course: 1481 yards par 27. *Green Fees:* on request. *Eating facilities:* at Dormy House (Bar & Restaurant) and The Gleneagles Hotel. *Visitors:* strictly Hotel residents, and members. Professional: Ian Marchbank. Hotel General Manager: Peter Lederer (0764 62231). Golf Co-ordinator: Suzanne Mailer.

BLAIR ATHOLL. **Blair Atholl Golf Club,** Blair Atholl, Pitlochry PH18 5TG (Blair Atholl (0796) 81407). *Location:* off A9, seven miles north of Pitlochry. Flat parkland. 9 holes. S.S.S. 69. Clubs for hire. *Green Fees:* weekdays £8.00 per day, weekends £9.00 per day. *Eating facilities:* bar meals and snacks. *Visitors:* welcome at all times. *Society Meetings:* by arrangement with Secretary, not Sundays. Secretary: Mr J.A. McGregor (0796 81274).

BLAIRGOWRIE. **Alyth Golf Club,** Alyth, Blairgowrie (Alyth (08283) 2268). *Location:* A926 or A927 to Alyth, B954 one mile to Club (five miles from Blairgowrie/ Coupar Angus). 18 holes, 6226 yards. S.S.S. 70. *Green Fees:* weekdays £15.00 per round, £20.00 per day; weekends £20.00 per round, £25.00 per day. *Eating facilities:* full catering facilities. *Visitors:* welcome with reservation. *Society Meetings:* catered for. Secretary: H. Sullivan.

BLAIRGOWRIE. **Blairgowrie Golf Club,** Rosemount, Blairgowrie PH10 6LG (0250 872383).*Location:* take A923 out of Perth, turn right at "Rosemount" sign. Flat wooded moorland. Rosemount Course: 18 holes, 6588 yards. S.S.S. 72. Lansdowne Course: 18 holes, 6895 yards. S.S.S. 73.

Three practice grounds. Wee Course: 9 holes, 2307 yards. S.S.S. 65. *Green Fees:* on application. No advance booking Wednesdays/Saturdays/Sundays. *Eating facilities:* full catering available. *Visitors:* advance booking Mon/Tues/Thurs/part Fri, 8.30am-4.00pm, (through Secretary). Handicap Certificate required. *Society Meetings:* catered for by application to the Secretary. (Maximum 32 without prior permission.) Professional: Gordon Kinnoch (0250 873116). Secretary/Manager: John N. Simpson (0250 872622).

BLAIRGOWRIE. **Dalmunzie Golf Course,** Spittal O' Glenshee, Blairgowrie PH10 7QG (025-085 226). *Location:* A93 Blairgowrie to Braemar road, left at Spittal O' Glenshee. A small well-kept hill course amid glorious scenery. 9 holes, 2035 yards. Practice area.

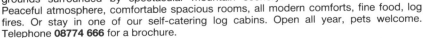

*Green Fees:* on application. Under 7 free, 7 – 14 half price (we like young golfers.) *Eating facilities:* restaurant facilities at Dalmunzie Hotel. Bar. *Visitors:* welcome without reservation. Self-catering cottages available. *Society Meetings:* catered for. Secretary: Simon Winton.

CALLANDER. **Callander Golf Club,** Aveland Road, Callander FK17 8EN (0877 30090). *Location:* M9 (Stirling) leave by Crianlarich exit on to A84 to Callander, at east end of town, just off Main Street. Parkland, partly wooded with panoramic views. 18 holes, 5125 yards. S.S.S. 66. Small practice ground. *Green Fees:* weekdays £12.00 per round, £16.00 per day; weekends £15.00 per round, £21.00 per day. *Eating facilities:* bar snacks, lunches, high teas, dinners by arrangement. *Visitors:* welcome, no restrictions. *Society Meetings:* welcome, book nine months in advance, arrange with Secretary. Professional: W. Kelly (0877 30975). Secretary: J. McClements (0877 30090). Booking Secretary: 10.00am to 2.00pm (0877 30090), 7.00pm to 9.00pm (0877 30866).

CRIEFF. **Comrie Golf Club,** Comrie (Comrie (0764) 70055). *Location:* six miles from Crieff on Crieff/Lochearnhead Road at east end of Comrie village. 9 holes, 5966 yards. S.S.S. 69. *Green Fees:* weekdays £8.00, weekends £12.00. *Eating facilities:* light refreshments during summer months. *Visitors:* welcome without reservation. *Society Meetings:* by arrangement with Secretary. Professional: Hunter Donaldson. Secretary: D.G. McGlashan (0764 70544).

CRIEFF. **Crieff Golf Club,** Perth Road, Crieff PH7 3LR (Crieff (0764) 2397). *Location:* A85 north-east outskirts of Crieff. Ferntower Course – 18 holes, 6402 yards. S.S.S. 71. Dornock Course – 9 holes, 2386 yards. S.S.S. 63. Two practice areas. *Green Fees:* Ferntower: weekdays £15.00 per round, £25.00 per day; weekends £17.00 per round. Dornock – per 18 holes: weekdays £10.00; weekends £11.00. *Eating facilities:* full restaurant facilities by arrangement (phone 0764 2397) and bar snacks. *Visitors:* welcome with reservation, prior arrangement advisable by phone. *Society Meetings:* book by phone and confirm

in writing. Senior Professional: John Stark (0764 2909). Club Professional: David Murchie. Secretary: L.J. Rundle (0764 2397).

CRIEFF. **Muthill Golf Club,** Peat Road, Muthill, Crieff PH5 2AD (076481 523). *Location:* 500 yards off main Crieff/Stirling Road at west end of village. Parkland (noted for panoramic views of Strathearn). 9 holes, 2350 yards. S.S.S. 63 for 18 holes. *Green Fees:* weekdays £7.00; weekends £10.00. *Eating facilities:* tea, coffee, soft drinks only. *Visitors:* restricted when competition and matches are being played, notice displayed at clubhouse. Changing and toilet facilities available. Secretary: W.H. Gordon (0764 3319).

CRIEFF. **St. Fillans Golf Club,** South Loch Earn Road, St. Fillans PH6 2NG (St. Fillans (0764-85) 312). *Location:* thirteen miles west of Crieff on A85 between Crieff and Lochearnhead. M9 nearest motorway. Parkland with one small hill. 9 holes, 5866 yards. S.S.S. 68 (18 holes). Practice green. *Green Fees:* weekdays £8.00 per round, £10.00 per day; weekends £12.00 per round, £14.00 per day. *Eating facilities:* light meals, teas, coffees, snacks. No bar. *Visitors:* welcome at all

times. *Society Meetings:* welcome with advance booking (not July and August). Maximum 24. Hon. Professional: J. Strait. Secretary: A.J.N. Abercrombie (0764 3643).

DUNBLANE. **Dunblane New Golf Club,** Perth Road, Dunblane FK15 0DU (Dunblane (0786) 823711). *Location:* on main Dunblane Road at Fourways Roundabout. Parkland/undulating. 18 holes, 5939 yards. S.S.S. 68. *Green Fees:* weekdays £15.00 per round. *Eating facilities:* available. *Visitors:* welcome, but restricted at weekends. *Society Meetings:* catered for Mondays and Thursdays only. Professional: R.M. Jamieson (Fax: 0786 825946). Secretary: R.S. Macrae.

DUNKELD. **Dunkeld and Birnam Golf Club,** Fungarth, Dunkeld PH8 0HU (Dunkeld (03502) 524). *Location:* turn right one mile north of Dunkeld on A9. Heathland course with panoramic views, testing. 9 holes, 5264 yards. S.S.S. 66. *Green Fees:* on application. *Eating facilities:* meals available and bar. *Visitors:* welcome. *Society Meetings:* catered for. Secretary: Mrs W.A. Sinclair (03502 564).

DUNNING. **Dunning Golf Club,** Rollo Park, Dunning. 9 holes, 4836 yards. S.S.S. 64. *Green Fees:* information not provided. *Eating facilities:* soft drinks, crisps, sweets. *Visitors:* no play before 1pm Sundays; no visitors after 5pm weekdays; no visitors before 4pm Saturday unless accompanied by a member. *Society Meetings:* welcome weekdays. Secretary: Miss C. Westwood (076484 312).

KILLIN. **Killin Golf Club,** Killin (Killin (056-72) 312). *Location:* west end of Loch Tay. Parkland with hills all around. 9 holes, 2508 yards. S.S.S. 65. Small practice area includes bunker and net. *Green Fees:* weekdays £7.50 per round, £9.00 per day; weekends £9.50 per round, £11.00 per day. Juniors £4.00. *Eating facilities:* meals and snacks all day, licensed. *Visitors:* welcome. *Society Meetings:* catered for by arrangement. Secretary: Sandy Chisholm (08383 235).

PERTH. **Craigie Hill Golf Club (1982) Ltd,** Cherrybank, Perth PH2 0NE (Perth (0738) 24377). *Location:* at west end of town, easy access from M90 and A9.

Hilly course with lovely scenery. 18 holes, 5379 yards. S.S.S. 66. Practice ground and putting green. *Green Fees:* weekdays £9.00 per round, £14.00 per day; Sundays £18.00 per day. Visitors with member £4.00, Juniors (weekdays) £3.00 per round. *Eating facilities:* full catering and bar. *Visitors:* welcome Mondays to Fridays and Sundays by arrangement. *Society Meetings:* catered for by written application in first instance. Professional: Frank L. Smith (0738 22644). Secretary: William A. Miller (0738 20829).

PERTH. **King James VI Golf Club,** Moncrieffe Island, Perth PH2 8NR (Perth (0738) 25170). Starter (0738 32460). Parkland course. 18 holes, 6026 yards. S.S.S. 68. Practice nets, green, ground. *Green Fees:* weekdays £11.50 per round, £17.00 per day; Sundays £23.00 per day. *Eating facilities:* full catering, bar. *Visitors:* welcome, phone for reservation except Saturdays. *Society Meetings:* catered for by arrangement. Fully stocked golf shop. Professional: Tony Coles (0738 32460). Secretary: Dorothy Barraclough (0738 32460).

## TIGH-NA-CLOICH HOTEL
### Larchwood Road, Pitlochry PH16 5AS

Looking for a base for your golfing holiday? The Tigh-Na-Cloich is just a par 5 away from Pitlochry Golf Course . . . and there are over 30 other courses within easy driving distance! Robin and Moira Bartrop will be happy to make advance golf bookings for you, and at the end of your day on the greens and fairways, good food, fine wines and a comfortable bed will ensure that you enjoy your stay at this Highland Victorian House. *The Tigh-Na-Cloich is a "No Smoking" hotel.*

**Telephone: (0796) 472216.**

PITLOCHRY. **Pitlochry Golf Course,** Pitlochry (Pitlochry (0796) 2792). *Location:* half mile from centre of Pitlochry on A9. 18 holes, 5811 yards, S.S.S. 68. *Green Fees:* 1st April to 31st October: weekdays £13.00 per day (£3.00 Juniors); Saturdays £16.00 per day (£5.00 Juniors); Sundays £16.00 per day. Restricted course (1st November to 31st March). Day ticket (any day) Adult £6.00, Junior £1.50. *Eating facilities:* catering and refreshments available in licensed clubhouse, except mid-October to end of March. *Visitors:* welcome. Caddy cars available for hire. *Society Meetings:* catered for. Professional: George Hampton (0796 2792). Secretary: D.C.M. McKenzie (0796 2114 for Group bookings). Fax: 0796 473599.

SCONE. **Murrayshall Golf Course,** Murrayshall, Scone PH2 7PH (0738 51171). *Location:* three miles north of Perth on Coupar Angus Road. Undulating wooded parkland. 18 holes, 6460 yards. S.S.S. 70. Golf range. *Green Fees:* £22.50 per round, £35.00 per day weekdays; £27.50 per round, £45.00 per day

weekends. *Eating facilities:* full catering service every day. *Visitors:* welcome at all times, no restrictions – advance booking advisable. Hotel. *Society Meetings:* welcome at all times by prior arrangement. Professional: Neil I.M. MacKintosh (0738 52784).

STRATHTAY. **Strathtay Golf Club,** Strathtay. *Location:* four miles west from Ballinluig on A9, four miles east from Aberfeldy. Wooded, mainly hilly course with beautiful panoramic views. 9 holes, 4082 yards. S.S.S. 63. *Green Fees:* £6.00 weekdays; £8.00 weekends. Special rates for parties of 12 or more. *Eating facilities:* coffee, snacks, soft drinks can be supplied by prior arrangement; meals arranged at adjacent hotel and cafe. *Visitors:* pre-teenagers MUST have adult supervision. NO visitors on Sundays 12 noon to 5pm. Open mixed foursomes every Tuesday evening April/ October. New changing room, toilets. *Society Meetings:* must be arranged in advance. Secretary: J.B. Armstrong-Payne (08874 367).

# FOR THE MUTUAL GUIDANCE OF GUEST AND HOST

Every year literally thousands of holidays, short-breaks and overnight stops are arranged through our guides, the vast majority without any problems at all. In a handful of cases, however, difficulties do arise about bookings, which often could have been prevented from the outset.

It is important to remember that when accommodation has been booked, both parties — guests and hosts — have entered into a form of contract. We hope that the following points will provide helpful guidance.

**GUESTS:** When enquiring about accommodation, be as precise as possible. Give exact dates, numbers in your party and the ages of any children. State the number and type of rooms wanted and also what catering you require — bed and breakfast, full board, etc. Make sure that the position about evening meals is clear — and about pets, reductions for children or any other special points.

Read our reviews carefully to ensure that the proprietors you are going to contact can supply what you want. Ask for a letter confirming all arrangements, if possible.

If you have to cancel, do so as soon as possible. Proprietors do have the right to retain deposits and under certain circumstances to charge for cancelled holidays if adequate notice is not given and they cannot re-let the accommodation.

**HOSTS:** Give details about your facilities and about any special conditions. Explain your deposit system clearly and arrangements for cancellations, charges, etc, and whether or not your terms include VAT.

If for any reason you are unable to fulfil an agreed booking without adequate notice, you may be under an obligation to arrange alternative suitable accommodation or to make some form of compensation.

While every effort is made to ensure accuracy, we regret that FHG Publications cannot accept responsibility for errors, omissions or misrepresentation in our entries or any consequences thereof. Prices in particular should be checked because we go to press early. We will follow up complaints but cannot act as arbiters or agents for either party.

# Renfrewshire

BARRHEAD. **Fereneze Golf Club,** Fereneze Avenue, Barrhead, Glasgow (041-881 1519). *Location:* nine miles south west of Glasgow. 18 holes, 5821 yards. S.S.S. 68. *Green Fees:* on application. *Eating facilities:* lunches served at club except Mondays, order in advance. *Visitors:* welcome by arrangement. *Society Meetings:* welcome, bookings arranged in advance. Professional: Gordon Graham (041-880 7058). Secretary: (041-221 6394; Fax: 041-221 0135).

BISHOPTON. **Erskine Golf Club,** Bishopton PA7 5PH (0505 862302). *Location:* north of M8, leave M8 at Bridge Toll barrier and turn left along B815 for one mile approximately. Parkland course. 18 holes, 6298 yards. S.S.S. 70. Putting green and practice area. *Green Fees:* £20.00 per round, £30.00 per day ticket. *Eating facilities:* restaurant and bar, lunches, teas and dinners served at club. *Visitors:* welcome but must play with a member or be introduced. Professional: Peter Thomson. Secretary: T.A. McKillop.

BRIDGE OF WEIR. **Ranfurly Castle Golf Club Ltd,** Golf Road, Bridge of Weir PA11 3HN (0505 612609). *Location:* M8 from Glasgow exit Junction 29, A240 and A761 to Bridge of Weir. Moorland. 18 holes, 6284 yards. S.S.S. 70. Practice ground. *Green Fees:* weekdays £20.00 per round, £25.00 day ticket. *Eating facilities:* bar snacks all day; lunches, high teas, etc by arrangement. *Visitors:*welcome weekdays, at weekends only if accompanied by member. *Society Meetings:* catered for Tuesdays only. Professional: Alastair Forrow (0505 614795). Secretary: Mr J. Walker (0505 612609).

ELDERSLIE. **Elderslie Golf Club,** 63 Main Road, Elderslie PA5 9AZ (0505 22835). *Location:* off M8 at Linwood turn-off, continue to roundabout, follow Elderslie signs A737. Club on main road. Woodland course. 18 holes, 6031 yards. S.S.S. 69. Large practice area. *Green Fees:* £15.50 per round, £21.00 per day weekdays. *Eating facilities:* diningroom, bar and bar snacks. *Visitors:* welcome weekdays, book with Professional. *Society Meetings:* welcome weekdays, book through Secretary. Professional: Andy Armstrong (0505 20032). Secretary: Mr W. Muirhead (0505 23956).

GOUROCK. **Gourock Golf Club,** Cowal View, Gourock (0475 31001). *Location:* two miles west of Gourock Station above Yacht Club. 18 holes, 6492 yards. S.S.S. 71. *Green Fees:* on application. *Eating facilities:* restaurant, full meals also bar snacks. *Visitors:* welcome with letter of introduction. *Society Meetings:* catered for on application. Professional: Robert M Collinson. Secretary: C.M. Campbell.

GREENOCK. **Greenock Golf Club,** Forsyth Street, Greenock PA16 8RE (0475 20793). *Location:* one mile from town centre. Moorland course. 18 holes, 5835 yards. S.S.S. 68. *Green Fees:* £14.00 weekdays;

£18.00 weekends. *Eating facilities:* available. *Visitors:* welcome weekdays, not Saturdays. *Society Meetings:* advance booking required. Professional: Graham Ross (0475 87236). Secretary: Eric J. Black (0475 26819).

GREENOCK. **Greenock Whinhill Golf Club,** Beith Road, Greenock (0475 24694). *Location:* 26 miles from Glasgow. Municipal course. 18 holes, 5454 yards. S.S.S. 68. *Green Fees:* information not provided. Secretary: D. McConnell.

JOHNSTONE. **Cochrane Castle Golf Club,** Craigston, Johnstone PA5 0HF (0505 22010). *Location:* A737 off Beith Road, Johnstone. Parkland course. 18 holes, 6226 yards. S.S.S. 70. Practice ground. *Green Fees:* weekdays £18.00 per day, £14.00 per round. *Eating facilities:* full catering and bar snacks. *Visitors:* welcome weekdays, maximum 32 players. *Society Meetings:* catered for by arrangement, weekdays only. Professional: Stuart H. Campbell (0505 28465). Secretary: J.C. Cowan (0505 20146).

KILMACOLM. **Kilmacolm Golf Club,** Porterfield Road, Kilmacolm PA13 4PD (Kilmacolm (050 587) 2139). *Location:* A761. Moorland course. 18 holes, 5964 yards. S.S.S. 68. Practice area. *Green Fees:* £16.50 per round, £22.00 per day. *Eating facilities:* diningroom and bar. *Visitors:* welcome on weekdays. *Society Meetings:* catered for. Professional: D. Stewart (050 587 2695). Secretary: R.F. McDonald.

LANGBANK. **Gleddoch Golf and Country Club,** Langbank PA14 6YG (047554 304). *Location:* M8 west of Glasgow, past airport to Langbank, Langbank and Gleddoch House are both signposted. Moorland, woodland and parkland. 18 holes, 6332 yards. S.S.S. 71. Practice area, indoor driving bay and putting green. *Green Fees:* £20 day ticket. Hotel residents £10.00. *Eating facilities:* bar, lounge and restaurant open all day. *Visitors:* welcome all week. Gleddoch House Hotel, 33 bedrooms. *Society Meetings:* welcome weekdays only. Professional: Keith Campbell (047554 704). Secretary: David Tierney (047554 304).

LOCHWINNOCH. **Lochwinnoch Golf Club,** Burnfoot Road, Lochwinnoch PA12 4AN (0505 842153). *Location:* between Johnstone and Beith, off A737 on Largs road A760. Parkland, extremely scenic, set in quiet country village. 18 holes, 6202 yards. S.S.S. 70. Practice area. *Green Fees:* weekdays £13.00 per day. *Eating facilities:* licensed bar and catering, except Mondays. *Visitors:* no visiting parties weekends or Public Holidays. *Society Meetings;* welcome weekdays. Professional: Gerry Reilly (0505 843029). Secretary: Mrs Evelyn McBride.

PAISLEY. **Barshaw Golf Club,** Barshaw Park, Glasgow Road, Paisley (041-889 2908). *Location:* one mile from Paisley Cross travelling east towards Glasgow (Glasgow Road). Parkland course, flat/hilly.

18 holes, 5703 yards. S.S.S. 68. Putting green. *Green Fees:* £4.50; Senior Citizens and Juniors £2.25. Unemployed £2.25 (proof to be shown). *Eating facilities:* mobile van rear of clubhouse. *Visitors:* welcome anytime, must have a bag of clubs. *Society Meetings:* apply to Superintendent Parks Department (Leisure and Recreation). Secretary: W. Collins (041-884 2533).

PAISLEY. **Paisley Golf Club,** Braehead, Paisley PA2 8TZ (041-884 2292). *Location:* up Causeyside Street, Neilston Road, turn right into Glenburn, left at roundabout. Moorland course. 18 holes, 6424 yards. S.S.S. 71. Practice area. *Green Fees:* weekdays £14.00 per round, £19.00 per day. *Eating facilities:* bar snacks and full meals. *Visitors:* welcome by prior arrangement mid-week until 4pm. Not Public Holidays or weekends. *Society Meetings:* catered for by prior arrangement. Professional: Grant Gilmour (041-884 4114). Secretary: W.J. Cunningham (041-884 3093).

PAISLEY. **Ralston Golf Club,** Strathmore Avenue, Ralston, Paisley PA1 3DT (041-882 1349). *Location:* two miles east of Paisley. *Green Fees:* information not provided. *Visitors:* welcome by introduction by members only. *Society Meetings:* catered for on application. Professional: John Scott (041-810 4925). Secretary: John W. Horne (041-883 7045).

PORT GLASGOW. **Port Glasgow Golf Club,** Devol Road, Port Glasgow PA14 5XE (0475 704181). *Location:* M8 to Newark Castle to roundabout, follow signs

for Industrial Estate. Heathland. 18 holes, 5712 yards, 5224 metres. S.S.S. 68. *Green Fees:* weekdays £10.00 per round, £15.00 per day. *Eating facilities:* meals by arrangement. *Visitors:* welcome weekdays until 4pm, weekends must be introduced. *Society Meetings:* welcome weekdays. Secretary: N.L. Mitchell (0475 706273).

RENFREW. **Renfrew Golf Club,** Blythswood Estate, Inchinnan Road, Renfrew PA4 9EG (041-886 6692). *Location:* A8 Renfrew, turn in at Stakis Normandy Hotel. Flat parkland, wooded. 18 holes, 6818 yards, 6231 metres. S.S.S. 72. *Green Fees:* weekdays £27.50. No green fees accepted at weekends. *Eating facilities:* daily restaurant facilities and bar. *Visitors:* welcome on introduction by members. Visiting parties by arrangement. *Society Meetings:* catered for on Mondays, Tuesdays and Thursdays only by written application to Secretary. Professional: Mr David Grant (041-885 1754). Secretary: Alan Brockie.

UPLAWMOOR. **Caldwell Golf Club,** Uplawmoor, Glasgow G78 (050 585 329). *Location:* five miles south of Barrhead, Glasgow on A736 Irvine Road. Parkland/ moorland. 18 holes, 6046 yards. S.S.S. 69. Practice area. *Green Fees:* £16.00 per round, £24.00 per day weekdays. *Eating facilities:* every day bar menu – filled rolls on Thursdays. *Visitors:* welcome weekdays only before 4.30pm. *Society Meetings:* weekdays only. Professional: Keith Baxter (050 585 616). Secretary: Mr Donald McLean (041-333 9770).

# Ross-shire

ALNESS. **Alness Golf Club,** Ardross Road, Alness (0349 883877). *Location:* on A9 ten miles north east of Dingwall. 9 holes, 2359 yards (twice round 4718 yards). S.S.S. 63. *Green Fees:* information not available. *Eating facilities;* licensed bar and snacks served. *Visitors:* welcome without reservation. *Society Meetings:* catered for if notice given. Secretary: J.G. Miller (0349 883877).

FEARN. **Tarbat Golf Club,** Tarbatness Road, Portmahomack, Fearn IV20 1YB (086 287 236). *Location:* 10 miles east of Tain. B9165 off A9. Seaside links course. 9 holes, 5654 yards, 1100 metres. S.S.S. 65. Practice area. *Green Fees:* weekdays £5.00; weekends £6.00. £20.00 per week. *Eating facilities:* none, local hotels. *Visitors:* welcome without reservation, restrictions Saturdays. *Society Meetings:* welcome please telephone Secretary. Secretary: D.C. Wilson (086 287 236; Fax: 0349 852131).

FORTROSE. **Fortrose and Rosemarkie Golf Club,** Ness Road East, Fortrose (Fortrose (0381) 20529). *Location:* on the Black Isle. A9 north from Inverness, across Kessock Bridge, through Munlochy, follow signs to Fortrose. Good links course, sea both sides. 18 holes,

5462 yards. S.S.S. 69. Practice area available Summer. *Green Fees:* weekdays £10.00 per round, £15.00 per day; weekends £15.00 per round. Five Day (Mon-Fri) £40.00; 10 Day (Mon-Fri) £60.00. *Eating facilities:* catering available. *Visitors:* welcome without reservation. *Society Meetings:* catered for. Professional: Graham Philp (0381 20733). Secretary: Mrs M. Collier.

GAIRLOCH. **Gairloch Golf Club,** Gairloch, IV21 2BE (Gairloch (0445) 2407). *Location:* 75 miles west of Inverness on the A832. Seaside links, extensive views. 9 holes, 2093 yards, 1770 metres. S.S.S. 63 over 18 holes. *Green Fees:* daily £10.00, £5.00 per day for Senior Citizens and Juniors; £45.00 weekly. *Visitors:* welcome without reservation. Secretary: J. Dingwall (0445 2315).

INVERGORDON. **Invergordon Golf Club,** King George Street, Invergordon (0349 852715). *Location:* two miles from A9. 9 holes, 3000 yards. S.S.S. 69 over 18 holes. *Green Fees:* information not provided. *Eating facilities:* bar lunches. New clubhouse with bar facilities. Changing rooms with showers. *Visitors:* welcome without reservation. *Society Meetings:* catered for. Secretary: Bruce Gibson.

LOCHCARRON. **Lochcarron Golf Club,** Lochcarron, Wester Ross. *Location:* one mile east of Lochcarron village. Seaside links course – very interesting 2nd hole, a short course but great accuracy required. 9 holes, 1750 yards. S.S.S. 60. *Green Fees:* £5.00. *Eating facilities:* three hotels within two miles of course. *Visitors:* welcome anytime except Saturday afternoons (club matches). Secretary: G. Weighill (05202 257).

MUIR OF ORD. **Muir of Ord Golf Club,** Great North Road, Muir of Ord IV6 7SX (0463 870825). *Location:* 15 miles north of Inverness beside A862, 12 miles north of Inverness on A9/A832. Heathland, moorland course, excellent greens. 18 holes, 5202 yards. S.S.S. 65 Medal. Practice area. *Green Fees:* October to March weekdays £9.00; weekends £10.00. Weekly tickets – six day £30.00. Monthly – seven days £100. *Eating facilities:* snacks, bar lunches; lounge and bar. *Visitors:* visiting parties welcome, weekends and times by arrangement. *Society Meetings:* catered for. Professional: J. Hamilton. Secretary: G. Reid (0463 870859). Administrator: Mrs C. Moir.

STRATHPEFFER. **Strathpeffer Spa Golf Club,** Strathpeffer IV14 9AS (0997 421219). *Location:* 20 minutes north of Inverness by A9, 5 miles west of Dingwall, quarter of a mile north of Strathpeffer Square (signposted). Upland course, panoramic views of moorland and mountain. No bunkers but plenty of natural hazards. 18 holes, 4792 yards. S.S.S. 65. Small practice area. *Green Fees:* weekdays £10.00 per round, £15.00 per day; weekends £12.00 per round, £18.00 per day. *Eating facilities:* snacks, morning coffee, lunches, high teas except Mondays. Bar open seven days. *Visitors:* welcome without reservation, but check weekends and competition days. *Society Meetings:* catered for by arrangement. Secretary: Norman Roxburgh (0997 21396).

TAIN. **Tain Golf Club,** Chapel Road, Tain IV19 1PA (Tain (0862) 892314). *Location:* off A9, 38 miles north of Inverness. Travelling north, turn right in middle of High Street – Golf Club one mile. Parkland and seaside links. 18 holes, 6238 yards. S.S.S. 70. Practice putting green. *Green Fees:* weekdays £10.00 per round, £15.00 per two rounds; weekends £12.00 per round, £20.00 per two rounds. Special rates for parties over 10. *Eating facilities:* bar and catering. *Visitors:* welcome, depending on availability. *Society Meetings:* catered for. Professional: (0862 893313). Secretary: Mrs Kathleen Ross.

# Roxburghshire

HAWICK. **Hawick Golf Club,** Vertish Hill, Hawick (0450 72293). *Location:* north along A7 from Carlisle for 40 miles or south on A7 from Edinburgh for 50 miles. Wooded parkland, 18 holes, 5929 yards. S.S.S. 69. *Green Fees:* weekdays £12.00 per round, £18.00 per day; weekends £18.00 per day only. *Eating facilities:* available all day. *Visitors:* welcome weekdays 8am to 4pm. *Society Meetings:* catered for – contact Secretary. Hon. Secretary: Mr Ian Potts (0450 76343).

HAWICK. **Minto Golf Club,** Denholm, Hawick TD9 8SH (Hawick (0450) 87220). *Location:* five miles north-east of Hawick leaving A698 at Denholm village. Parkland, trees, no bunkers. 18 holes, 5460 yards, 4992 metres. S.S.S. 68. Practice area. *Green Fees:* weekdays £10.00; weekends £15.00. *Eating facilities:* new clubhouse with full facilities, catering. *Visitors:* welcome, with prior booking. *Society Meetings:* accepted with prior booking (weekends difficult). Secretary: Mrs E. Mitchell (0450 72180).

JEDBURGH. **Jedburgh Golf Club,** Dunion Road, Jedburgh, Roxburghshire TD8 6LA (0835 63587). *Location:* three quarters of a mile south of Jedburgh on the road to Hawick. Undulating, with young trees. 9 holes, 5555 yards. S.S.S. 67. *Green Fees:* £10.00. *Eating facilities:* bar 7.30pm on May to September, meals Friday and weekend evenings. *Visitors:* welcome weekdays, weekends depending on competitions. *Society Meetings:* welcome, if notice given. Secretary: R. Strachan (0835 64175).

KELSO. **Kelso Golf Club,** Berrymoss, Kelso (0573 23009). *Location:* one mile north-east of town within Kelso Racecourse. Flat parkland within racecourse. 18 holes, 6066 yards. S.S.S. 69. Practice ground. *Green Fees:* weekdays £10.00 per round, £12.00 per day; weekends £12.00 per round, £18.00 per day. Subject to review. *Eating facilities:* catering Wednesday to Sunday. *Visitors:* welcome without reservation. *Society Meetings:* welcome with reservation. Secretary: J.P. Payne (0573 23259).

MELROSE. **Melrose Golf Club,** Dingleton, Melrose (Melrose (089682) 2855). *Location:* A68 Edinburgh – Carlisle A7/Newcastle A68 roads. Wooded/hilly course. 9 holes, 5579 yards, 5098 metres. S.S.S. 68. Practice area. *Green Fees:* £10.00. Juniors half price. *Eating facilities:* by arrangement. *Visitors:* welcome anytime when no competitions taking place. No visitor to tee off after 4pm April to October. Locker room, shower. *Society Meetings:* welcome by arrangement.

Secretary: W.G. MacRae (089682 2391; Fax: 089682 2960).

NEWCASTLETON. **Newcastleton Golf Club,** Holm Hill, Newcastleton. *Location:* A7 Carlisle to Hawick road, Newcastleton is on B6357. Hilly course with splendid views. 9 holes, 5748 yards. S.S.S. 68. *Green Fees:* £5.00. *Eating facilities:* by arrangement. *Visitors:* welcome, no restrictions except competition days. *Society Meetings:* welcome. Secretary: F.J. Ewart (03873 75257).

ST. BOSWELLS. **St. Boswells Golf Club,** St. Boswells, Melrose TD6 0AT (0835 22359). *Location:* quarter of a mile off trunk route A68 at St. Boswells Green. Flat attractive scenery along the banks of the River Tweed. 9 holes, 5250 yards. S.S.S. 65. *Green Fees:* weekdays £8.00 per round/day; weekends £10.00 per round/day. *Visitors:* no visitors after 4pm on a weekday and when competitions are being held. Secretary: G.B. Ovens (0835 22359).

# Selkirkshire

GALASHIELS. **Galashiels Golf Club,** Ladhope Recreation Ground, Galashiels TD1 2JJ (Galashiels (0896) 3724). *Location:* north east of town, approximately a quarter of a mile off A7. Parkland, hilly – municipal course. 18 holes, 5309 yards. S.S.S. 66. Practice area. *Green Fees:* weekdays £5.65; weekends £6.45. *Eating facilities:* catering, at weekends bar. *Visitors:* welcome without restriction. *Society Meetings:* catered for. Secretary: W.D. Millar (0750 21669).

GALASHIELS. **Torwoodlee Golf Club,** Edinburgh Road, Galashiels (Galashiels (0896) 2260). *Location:* leave Galashiels on A7 for Edinburgh. Entrance to course one mile on left. Parkland with wooded green alongside river and splendid par 5. Designed by Braid. 9 holes, 5720 yards. S.S.S. 68. *Green Fees:* weekday £12.00 per round, £18.00 per day; weekends £15.0 per round, £24.00 per day. *Eating facilities:* bar, dining room. *Visitors:* welcome without reservation. Restri tion Saturday and Thurday after 1pm. Showers available. *Society Meetings:* catered for weekdays, booking required. Secretary: A. Wilson (089-682 2146).

SELKIRK. **Selkirk Golf Club,** The Hill, Selkirk (Selkirk (0750) 20621). *Location:* one mile south of Selkirk on A7 road. Undulating moorland with superb views. 9 holes, 5620 yards. S.S.S. 67. *Green Fees:* £8.00 (under review). *Eating facilities:* by previous arrangement for parties only (contact Secretary). *Visitors:* restricted Mondays 2pm onwards (Ladies only) and most Saturdays and some Sundays in summer season (club competitions). *Society Meetings:* catered for by arrangement. Secretary: R. Davies (0750 20427).

# Stirlingshire

ABERFOYLE. **Aberfoyle Golf Club,** Braeval, Aberfoyle, By Stirling FK8 3UY (Aberfoyle (08772) 493). *Location:* A81 Glasgow – Stirling. Parkland. 18 holes, 5204 yards. S.S.S. 66. Practice facilities available. *Green Fees:* weekdays £10.00 per round, £15.00 per day; weekends £15.00 per round, £20.00 per day. *Eating facilities:* catering by arrangement. *Visitors:* welcome anytime but must not tee off before 10am at weekends. Secretary: Alan McDonald (08772 638).

DRYMEN. **Strathendrick Golf Club,** Glasgow Road, Drymen, Glasgow G63 (0360 40582). *Location:* one mile south of Drymen on Glasgow Road. Inland – hilly course. 9 holes, 4962 yards. S.S.S. 65. *Green Fees:* information not provided. *Visitors:* accompanied by a member welcome all week, restrictions on competition days. Secretary: Ronald H. Smith (0360 40582).

FALKIRK. **Bonnybridge Golf Club,** Larbert Road, Bonnybridge FK4 1NV (0324 812645). *Location:* five miles west of Falkirk. Parkland. 9 holes, 6060 yards. S.S.S. 69. Practice area. *Green Fees:* weekdays £8.00 per round. *Eating facilities:* catering by arrangement. *Visitors:* welcome with prior permission, no unaccompanied visitors. Secretary: C. Munn (0324 813694).

FALKIRK. **Falkirk Golf Club,** 136 Stirling Road, Camelon, Falkirk (Falkirk (0324) 611061). *Location:* one and a half miles west of town centre on A9. Parkland with streams. 18 holes, 6267 yards. S.S.S. 69. Large practice area. *Green Fees:* weekdays £9.00 per round, £16.00 per day. Sundays £12.00 per round, £20.00 per day. *Eating facilities:* full catering and bar facilities. *Visitors:* welcome Monday to Friday up to 4.00pm unaccompanied, with member only at weekends. *Society Meetings:* weekdays except Wednesdays, Sundays after 10.30am. Make arrangements with Clubmaster. Secretary: John Elliott (0324 34118).

FALKIRK. **Polmont Golf Club,** Manvelrigg, Maddiston, Falkirk FK2 0LS (Polmont (0324) 711277). *Location:* first turn to the right past Fire Brigade HQ in Maddiston. Undulating course. 9 holes, 6603 yards. S.S.S. 70. *Green Fees:* weekdays £5.00; Saturday £7.00 after 5pm, Sunday £7.00. *Eating facilities:* lunches and high teas. *Visitors:* welcome without reservation, no visitors after 5pm weekdays. *Society Meetings:* catered for. Secretary: Ian Gilchrist (0324 711253).

LARBERT **Falkirk Tryst Golf Club,** 86 Burnhead Road, Stenhousemuir, Larbert FK5 4BD (Larbert (0324) 562415). *Location:* three miles from Falkirk (M9), one mile from Larbert Station. Flat/seaside links style surface. 18 holes, 6053 yards, 5533 metres. S.S.S. 69. Practice area. *Green Fees:* weekdays £10.00 per round, £15.00 per day. *Eating facilities:* full catering – lunches, high teas, bar service. *Visitors:* welcome weekdays, not weekends. *Society Meetings:* catered for Mondays (except Bank Holidays), Tuesdays, Thursdays and Fridays only. Secretary: R.D. Wallace (0324 562054).

LARBERT. **Glenbervie Golf Club Ltd,** Stirling Road, Larbert FK5 4SJ (Larbert (0324) 562983). *Location:* one mile north of Larbert on A9 Falkirk to Stirling road. Parkland course. 18 holes, 6402 yards. S.S.S. 71. Two practice areas. *Green Fees:* £18.00 per round, £28.00 for day ticket. *Eating facilities:* lunches and high teas available, bar. *Visitors:* welcome weekdays only with reservation, letter of introduction. Weekends as members' guests only. *Society Meetings:* up to 40 competitors catered for, Tuesdays and Thursdays only. Professional: Mr John Chillas (0324 562725). Secretary: Mrs Mary Purves (0324 562605).

LENNOXTOWN. **Campsie Golf Club,** Crow Road, Lennoxtown, Glasgow G65 7HX (0360 310244). *Location:* on B822 out of Lennoxtown. Hillside course with panoramic views. 18 holes, 5517 yards, 5045 metres. S.S.S. 67. Practice fairway and putting green. *Green Fees:* weekdays £8.00 per round; weekends £12.00 per round. Reduced rates for pre-booked parties of over 12. *Eating facilities:* full catering available for parties. *Visitors:* welcome, weekdays unrestricted, weekends by prior arrangement. *Society Meetings:* catered for. Professional: Stephen D. Campbell (0360 310920). Secretary: J. M. Donaldson (0360 312249).

POLMONT. **Grangemouth Golf Club,** Polmont Hill, Polmont, Falkirk FK2 0YA (0324 711500). *Location:* quarter of a mile north of Junction 4 M9 motorway. Parkland course. 18 holes, 6314 yards. S.S.S. 71. Practice area. *Green Fees:* £6.00 per round, £9.00 per day weekdays; £8.00 per round, £11.00 per day weekends. *Eating facilities:* catering and bar facilities available. *Visitors:* welcome, bookings preferred; golf shoes must be worn. Parties at weekends limited to 40 maximum. *Society Meetings:* by arrangement through Professional. Professional: Stuart Campbell (0324 714355). Secretary: Iain Hutton (0324 712585).

STIRLING. **Bridge Of Allan Golf Club,** Sunnylaw, Bridge of Allan (Bridge of Allan (0786) 832332). *Location:* from Stirling, three miles, turn right at Bridge, keep taking the high road. Hilly course. 9 holes, 4932 yards, 4508 metres. S.S.S. 65. *Green Fees:* weekdays £7.00; weekends £10.00. *Eating facilities:* by arrangement, licensed bar. *Visitors:* welcome without reservation, no visitors on Saturdays. *Society Meetings:* catered for by arrangement. Secretary: A.M. Donoghue (0786 832007).

STIRLING. **Stirling Golf Club,** Queen's Road, Stirling FK8 2QY (Stirling (0786) 73801). *Location:* one mile from town centre, rail and bus stations; two miles from Junction 10 M9. Parkland (undulating) with superb views of mountains and castle. 18 holes, 6095 yards. S.S.S. 69. Practice area. *Green Fees:* £15.00 per round, £21.50 per day. *Eating facilities:* full bar and dining facilities. *Visitors:* welcome except at weekends but casual visitors by arrangment with Pro Shop. *Society Meetings:* welcome by arrangement. Professional: John Chillas (0786 71490). Secretary: W. McArthur (0786 64098).

STIRLING. **Tillicoultry Golf Club,** Alva Road, Tillicoultry FK13 6EB (Tillicoultry (0259) 50124). *Location:* on A91, nine miles from Stirling. Parkland. 9 holes, 5358 yards. S.S.S. 66. *Green Fees:* weekdays £7.00 per round, £10.00 after 4pm; weekends £12.00 per round. *Eating facilities:* licensed bar, snacks; meals by prior arrangement. *Visitors:* welcome at all times outwith competitions. No children under 15 weekends until 4.00pm. *Society Meetings:* catered for on application to the Secretary. Secretary: R. Whitehead (0259 51337/50124).

TORRANCE. **Balmore Golf Club,** Balmore, Torrance (041-332 0392). *Location:* A803 then A807 from Glasgow. 18 holes, 5641 yards. S.S.S. 67. *Green Fees:* information not provided. *Eating facilities:* full service available. *Visitors:* welcome if introduced by member. *Society Meetings:* catered for. Secretary: G. P. Woolard, 11 Woodside Crescent, Glasgow G3 7UL.

---

# Sutherland

BONAR BRIDGE. **Bonar Bridge-Ardgay Golf Club,** Market Stance, Migdale Road, Bonar Bridge. _Location:_ off the A9, driving north cross Bonar Bridge, straight up hill for half a mile. Wooded heathland. 9 holes, 4626 yards. S.S.S. 63. _Green Fees:_ £7.00 per day. Reduced rates for week/fortnight. _Eating facilities:_ not available. _Visitors:_ always welcome. _Society Meetings:_ limited to weekdays. Joint Secretaries: A. Turner (054-982 248) and J. Reid (08632 750).

BRORA. **Brora Golf Club,** Golf Road, Brora KW9 6QS (0408 21417). _Location:_ approximately 65 miles north of Inverness on the A9. Seaside links, 18 holes, 6110 yards. S.S.S. 69. Practice ground available. _Green Fees:_ £13.00 per day, £60.00 per week. _Eating facilities:_ lunches and snacks May to August. _Visitors:_ welcome, only restriction on tournament days. Welcome to participate in opens with Certificate of Handicap. _Society Meetings:_ catered for by arrangement. Secretary: H. Baillie (0408 21417).

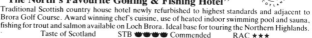

**BURGHFIELD HOUSE HOTEL**          Now ♥♥♥♥
Commended
**DORNOCH, SUTHERLAND IV25 3HN**
**Telephone: 0862 810212    Fax: 0862 810404**
If you want to enjoy golf on Royal Dornoch, stay at the Burghfield. Superb cuisine. 40 rooms. most with private facilities. Run by the Currie family since 1946. Extensively refurbished 1991. Up to 15% discount for golf parties. *Write or phone for brochure to Niall W. G. Currie.*

## CAPE WRATH HOTEL

CAPE WRATH HOTEL
& RESTAURANT

**DURNESS**
**Tel: (0971) 511212**
**Fax: (0971) 511313**

**Fishing**
*Salmon*
*Sea Trout*
*Brown Trout*

**Other activities**
*Golf*
*Bird Watching*
*Hill Walking etc.*

*Cape Wrath Hotel enjoys an envied reputation for superb food. An extensive list of quality wines, a warm and friendly atmosphere and traditional Scottish hospitality.*

DORNOCH. **Royal Dornoch Golf Club,** Golf Road, Dornoch (0862 810219; Fax: 0862 810792). *Location:* one mile from A9 to Wick. Seaside links. Championship course and Struie Course. 18 holes, 6581 yards. S.S.S. 72. Practice area. *Green Fees:* on request. *Eating facilities:* available. *Visitors:* welcome, no major restrictions other than competitions – bookings can be heavy. *Society Meetings:* must be arranged through the Secretary. Professional: W.E. Skinner (0862 810902). Secretary/Manager: I.C.R. Walker (0862 810219).

DURNESS. **Durness Golf Club,** Balnakiel, Durness. *Location:* 57 miles north-west of Lairg on A838. Links course with final hole played over deep gully. 9 greens, 18 tees, 5545 yards. S.S.S 68. *Green Fees:* £6.00 per day. Weekly ticket £24.00. *Eating facilities:* snacks available 12-5pm June to September. *Visitors:* welcome without reservation, only restriction on Sunday Mornings. Course closed during lambing season (April 20th to May 14th approximately). *Society Meetings:* by arrangement. Secretary: Lucy MacKay (097181 364).

GOLSPIE. **Golspie Golf Club,** Ferry Road, Golspie (Golspie (0408) 633266). *Location:* off A9 half a mile from Golspie. Fairly flat course, seaside links and wooded. 18 holes, 5836 yards. S.S.S. 68. Practice area available. *Green Fees:* £14.00 per day. *Eating facilities:* bar and catering service. *Visitors:* welcome, no restrictions except on competition days. *Society Meetings:* welcome by prior arrangement. Secretary: Mrs Marie MacLeod.

HELMSDALE. **Helmsdale Golf Club,** Golf Road, Helmsdale KW8 6JA (043-12 240). *Location:* on A9, 28 miles north of Dornoch. Parkland course. 9 holes, 1825 yards. S.S.S. 62 (2 x 9 holes). *Green Fees:* £3.00 per round, £5.00 per day. £15.00 weekly, £25.00 fortnightly. *Eating facilities:* Bridge Hotel, Helmsdale (04312 219). *Visitors:* welcome at all times. *Society Meetings:* welcome. Secretary: Jim Mackay (04312 240).

# Wigtownshire

NEWTON STEWART. **Newton Stewart Golf Club,** Kirroughtree Avenue, Minnigaff, Newton Stewart DG8 6PF (0671 2172). *Location:* from South leave A75 at sign to Minnigaff village. Parkland, mainly flat, set in Galloway hills and with a forest backdrop. 9 holes, 5646 yards, 5160 metres. S.S.S. 67, par 68. *Green Fees:* weekdays £8.00, weekends and Bank Holidays £12.00 per day. *Eating facilities:* bar lounge, bar snacks

and meals available. *Visitors:* welcome without restriction, but busy at weekends. *Society Meetings:* welcome. Discounts available. Secretary: D.C Matthewson (0671 3236).

NEWTON STEWART. **Wigtownshire County Go Club,** Glenluce, Newton Stewart (Glenluce (058) 420). *Location:* A75 two miles west Glenluce, eig

# SHENNANTON HOUSE

*A grand country mansion set in a 2000 acre private estate, near to around 20 golf courses and with four par 3 golf holes in the grounds.*
We also have a billiard room with a full sized antique snooker table. We offer free private river and loch fishing.
Shennanton has superb bedroom suites, many with en-suite jacuzzi baths.

**Kirkcowan, Near Newton Stewart, Wigtownshire, Scotland DG8 0EG**
**Tel: (0671) 83494 Fax: (0671) 83445**
**STB ♥♥♥♥♥ Deluxe**

We have excellent self catering accommodation suitable for family or sporting groups, or we can provide maid and meal service.

*For brochure and reservations please phone (0671) 83494.*

---

miles east Stranraer. Seaside links. 18 holes, 5716 yards. S.S.S. 68. Practice ground. *Green Fees:* weekdays £11.00 per round, £14.00 per day; weekends £13.00 per round, £16.00 per day. Weekly £45.00. *Eating facilities:* available all year round. *Visitors:* unrestricted except Wednesday evenings. *Society Meetings:* catered for. Secretary: R. McCubbin (05813 589).

PORT WILLIAM. **St. Medan Golf Club,** Monreith, Port William, Newton Stewart DG8 8NJ (09887-358). *Location:* on A747, three miles south of Port William. 9 holes, 4552 yards. S.S.S. 62. *Green Fees:* 9 holes £5.00, 18 holes £10.00. £15.00 per day. £40.00 per week. *Eating facilities:* available April to September. *Visitors:* welcome. Parties please book. Secretary: D. O'Neill (09885 555).

PORTPATRICK. **Portpatrick (Dunskey) Golf Club,** Golf Course Road, Portpatrick DG9 8TB (Portpatrick (0776 81273). *Location:* A75 or A77 to Stranraer then A77 to Portpatrick, fork right at War Memorial, then signposted on right. Cliff top links-type course. 18 holes, 5732 yards. S.S.S. 68. Also short 9 hole course, 1442 yards. S.S.S. 27. Practice ground. *Green Fees:*

weekdays £12.00 per round, £18.00 per day; weekends £15.00 per round, £22.00 per day. *Eating facilities:* lounge, bar, children's room, TV, snacks only on Mondays. *Visitors:* prior booking essential. Handicap Certificate required for 18 hole course. *Society Meetings:* catered for by prior arrangement. Hon Secretary: J.A. Horberry (0776 81273).

STRANRAER. **Stranraer Golf Club,** Creachmore, Stranraer (Leswalt (077 687) 245). *Location:* three miles from Stranraer on the Kirkcolm Road (A718). Parkland. 18 holes, 6300 yards. S.S.S. 71. Practice ground. *Green Fees:* information not provided. *Eating facilities:* meals available, order in advance. *Visitors:* welcome. No reservations for individuals but parties required to book. *Society Meetings:* catered for. Secretary: W.I. Wilson C.A. (0776 3539).

WIGTOWN. **Wigtown and Bladnoch Golf Club,** Wigtown (09884 3354). *Location:* 200 yards from square in Wigtown. Parkland course. 9 holes, 5400 yards. S.S.S. 67. *Green Fees:* weekdays £7.00; Sundays £10.00. *Eating facilities:* bar only. *Visitors:* welcome any time. *Society Meetings:* welcome by arrangement. Secretary: J. Bateman (09884 650).

---

# Scottish Islands

---

# ARRAN

---

BLACKWATERFOOT. **Shiskine Golf and Tennis Club,** Blackwaterfoot (Shiskine (077 086) 226). *Location:* off B880 at Blackwaterfoot. Seaside links with only Par 5 on island. 12 holes, 3900 yards. S.S.S. 42. Putting green. *Green Fees:* £8.00 per round, £10.00 per day except July and August. *Eating facilities:* available June to September. *Visitors:* welcome. Tennis and Bowls. Shop open Easter – October. Society Meetings: on application. Shop: Mrs Fiona W. Crown (077 086 226). Match Secretary: J. Faulkner (077 086 392). Treasurer: J. Allison (077 086 346). Secretary: Mrs Fiona Crawford (077 086 293).

BRODICK. **Brodick Golf Club,** Brodick (Brodick (0770) 2349). *Location:* one mile north of pier. Flat seaside course. 18 holes, 4404 yards. S.S.S. 62. Practice area. *Green Fees:* weekdays £7.00 per round, £10.00 per day; weekends £11.00 per day, £8.00 after 3.30pm. *Eating facilities:* bar snacks available. *Visitors:* welcome without restriction. *Society Meetings:* welcome with reservation by letter. Professional: P.S. McCalla (0770 2513). Secretary: H.M. Macrae (0770 2181).

CORRIE. **Corrie Golf Club,** Sannox, Corrie KA27 8JD (077 081 223). *Location:* seven miles north of Brodick. Hilly course. 9 holes, 1948 yards. S.S.S. 61. *Green Fees:* £5.00 daily. *Eating facilities:* meals available March to October. *Visitors:* very welcome except Saturday afternoon. *Society Meetings:* catered for. Secretary: R. Craigie Aitchison.

LAMLASH. **Lamlash Golf Club,** Lamlash KA27 8JU (Lamlash (0770) 600296). *Location:* A841 three miles south of Brodick Pier ferry terminal. Undulating heathland course. 18 holes, 4611 yards. S.S.S. 63. *Green Fees:* weekdays £8.00 per day, Senior Citizens £6.00; weekends £9.00. Three day weekend £15.00. Week £35.00. Subject to review. *Eating facilities:* tearoom, clubhouse bar. *Visitors:* welcome no restrictions. *Society Meetings:* catered for. Secretary: J. Henderson (0770 600272).

LOCHRANZA. **Lochranza Golf,** Isle of Arran KA27 8HL (077083 273). *Location:* at north end of Island of Arran in Lochranza village. Flat course surrounded by mountains and sea, superb views. New layout 1991 — well worth a visit. 9 holes (18 tees), 5500 yards, 5100 metres. S.S.S. 70. *Green Fees:* £8.00. Course closed October to March inclusive. *Eating facilities:* tearoom, meals and snacks. Home cooking. *Visitors:* singles to parties always welcome. Caravan for hire, caravan site adjacent. *Society Meetings:* catered for by arrangement, short notice if necessary. Special rates. Transport can be provided for parties leaving their cars on the mainland. Secretary: I.M. Robertson.

MACHRIE. **Machrie Bay Golf Club,** Machrie, Near Brodick. *Location:* on A841, three and a half miles north from Blackwaterfoot. Flat seaside course. 9 holes, 2082 yards. S.S.S. 32. *Green Fees:* £3.00 per day. *Eating facilities:* available Summer season. *Visitors:* welcome anytime except on club competition days. *Society Meetings:* catered for if pre-booked. Secretary: A.M. Blair (077 085 261).

WHITING BAY. **Whiting Bay Golf Club,** near Brodick (07707 487). *Location:* approximately eight miles south of Brodick. 18 holes, 4406 yards. S.S.S. 63. *Green Fees:* £5.00 per round, £6.50 per day; weekends (Friday to Sunday) £14.00; weekly £21.00; fortnightly £35.00. Juniors half price. *Visitors:* welcome, unrestricted. *Eating facilities:* available April to October. *Society Meetings:* by arrangement with Secretary. Secretary: Irene I'Anson (07707 307/326).

# BUTE

ISLE OF BUTE. **Bute Golf Club,** West Shore Sands, Stravanan, Kingarth, Rothesay. *Location:* 8 miles from Rothesay on the A845 situated on shores of Stravanan Bay. Flat seaside links in beautiful setting. 9 holes, 2497 yards, 2284 metres. S.S.S. 64 (18 holes). *Green Fees:* £5.00 adults, £1.00 Juniors. *Visitors:* welcome any day, Saturdays after 12.30pm. *Society Meetings:* catered for by arrangement. Secretary: J.M. Burnside (070 083 648).

ROTHESAY. **Port Bannatyne Golf Club,** Bannatyne Mains Road, Port Bannatyne. *Location:* two miles north of Rothesay (ferry terminal). Hill course overlooking bays and sea lochs. 13 holes, 4730 yards. S.S.S. 63. *Green Fees:* £7.00 per day, weekly £28.00, 14-day £50.00. *Eating facilities:* in village, quarter-of-a-mile

from course. *Visitors:* welcome – almost unrestricted. *Society Meetings:* very welcome. Secretary: Iain L. MacLeod (0700 502009).

ROTHESAY. **Rothesay Golf Club,** Canada Hill, Rothesay PA20 (0700 502244). *Location:* island in the Firth of Clyde, ferry terminal Wemyss Bay, 35 miles south west of Glasgow. One of Scotland's most scenic island courses, designed by James Braid and Ben Sayers. 18 holes, 5370 yards. S.S.S. 67. Practice area. *Green Fees:* on application to Professional. *Eating facilities:* full facilities at clubhouse. *Visitors:* very welcome, but at weekends by prior booking through Professional. *Society Meetings:* welcome by arrangement. PGA Professional: James M. Dougal (0700 503554). Secretary: John Barker (0700 503744).

# COLONSAY

ISLE OF COLONSAY. **Colonsay Golf Club,** Isle of Colonsay PA61 7YP. *Location:* two miles west of pier. Traditional links course, reputedly 200 years old. 18 holes, 4775 yards. *Green Fees:* information not available. *Eating facilities:* none. *Visitors:* always welcome. Secretary: Kevin Byrne (09512 316).

# CUMBRAE

MILLPORT. **Millport Golf Club,** Golf Road, Millport (Millport (0475) 530311). *Location:* Caledonian McBrayne car ferry Largs slip to Cumbrae slip (seven minutes). On hill overlooking Firth of Clyde over Bute and Arran to Mull of Kintyre. 18 holes, 5831 yards. S.S.S. 68. Large practice area. *Green Fees:* maximum charge £12.00 per day. Other charges pro rata. *Eating facilities:* full catering facilities. *Visitors:* welcome without reservation. Tee reservations available for parties Well stocked Professional's shop. Starter's telephone (0475 530305). *Society Meetings:* catered for. Special open amateur competition, Cumbrae Cup. Secretary W.D. Patrick C.A. (0475 530308).

# ISLAY

PORT ELLEN. **Machrie Golf Club,** The Machr Hotel and Golf Links, Port Ellen PA42 7AN (049 2310; Golfax: 0496 2404). *Location:* adjacent Airpo Classic links. 18 holes, 6226 yards. S.S.S. 70. *Gre Fees:* £22.50. *Eating facilities:* full service in hot *Visitors:* welcome any day without reservation. *Soci Meetings:* any number catered for. Golf packag available. Secretary: M.R. MacPherson. Propriet Murdo MacPherson.

# LEWIS

STORNOWAY. **Stornoway Golf Club,** Lady Lever Park, Stornoway, Isle of Lewis (0851 70 2240). *Location:* close proximity to town of Stornoway, in grounds of Lewis Castle. Inland course, hilly parkland, scenic. 18 holes, 5119 yards. S.S.S. 66. *Green Fees:* £7.00 per round, £10.00 per day. Weekly tickets £30.00; fortnightly ticket £50.00. Subject to alteration. *Eating facilities:* available. *Visitors:* welcome, but no Sunday golf. Car ferry daily (except Sunday) from Ullapool. British Airways service daily (except Sunday) from Glasgow and Inverness. *Society Meetings:* welcome, book through Secretary. Secretary: Mr J.D.F. Watson.

# MULL

ISLE OF MULL. **Craignure Golf Club,** Scallastle, Craignure (Craignure (06802) 370). *Location:* one mile from ferry terminal at Craignure. Seaside links. 9 holes, 2218 metres. S.S.S. 64. *Green Fees:* £6.00. *Eating facilities:* not available. *Visitors:* always welcome, no restrictions except on competition days which are usually Sundays. Hon. Secretary: Sheila M. Campbell (06802 370).

TOBERMORY. **Tobermory Golf Club,** Tobermory PA75 6PE. *Location:* situated on a hill north west of Tobermory. Clifftop course with panoramic views of Sound of Mull; testing terrain, not suitable for trolleys. 9 holes, 4921 yards, 4362 metres. S.S.S. 64. *Green Fees:* £7.50 per day, £25.00 per week, £40.00 per two weeks. *Eating facilities:* none available. *Visitors:* unrestricted except for some competition days. *Society Meetings:* welcome. Secretary: Dr W.H. Clegg (0688 2013 or 2020).

# ORKNEYS

KIRKWALL. **Orkney Golf Club Ltd,** Grainbank, Kirkwall (0856 872457). *Location:* half-a-mile west of Kirkwall. Parkland with good views over Kirkwall Bay and North Isles. 18 holes, 5406 yards. S.S.S. 68. Practice area. *Green Fees:* £8.00 per day. Weekly £30.00; Fortnightly £40.00. *Eating facilities:* available at new clubhouse. *Visitors:* welcome at all times, first tee reserved for competitions at times. *Society Meetings:* welcome, booking avoids clashing with competitions. Secretary: L. Howard (0856 874165).

TROMNESS. **Stromness Golf Club Ltd,** Ness, Stromness (0856 850772). *Location:* Stromness. Parkland/seaside links course. 18 holes, 4822 yards. S.S.S 65. *Green Fees:* £8.00 per day. £30.00 weekly ticket. *Eating facilities:* bar, and there are hotels nearby. *Visitors:* welcome, no restrictions. *Society Meetings:* by

arrangement through Secretary. Secretary: F.J. Groundwater (0856 850662).

WESTRAY. **Westray Golf Club,** Westray, Orkney Islands. *Location:* near Pierowall Village, Westray, Orkney. Seaside links course. 9 holes. *Green Fees:* £2.00 per day. £10.00 per week. *Visitors:* welcome anytime. Captain: Mr Stephen Hagan (08577 226). Secretary: Mr Michael Harcus (08577 516).

# SHETLAND

LERWICK. **Dale Golf Club,** PO Box 18, Lerwick, Shetland (Lerwick (059 584) 369). *Location:* four miles north of Lerwick on main road. Hilly, undulating course. Excellent greens. 18 holes, 5776 yards. S.S.S. 68. *Green Fees:* £5.00 per day including weekends. Juniors and Senior Citizens half-price. *Eating facilities:* bar snacks available. *Visitors:* welcome. *Society Meetings:* by arrangement with Course Manager. Course Manager: E. Groat.

# SKYE

SCONSER. **Isle of Skye Golf Club,** Sconser. *Location:* 20 miles from ferry on road to Portree. Seaside course with spectacular views. 9 holes (18 tees), 4798 yards, 4385 metres. S.S.S. 63. *Green Fees:* information not provided. *Visitors:* no restrictions. Changing and toilet facilities. Secretary: I. Stephen (0478 2000).

# SOUTH UIST

LOCHBOISDALE. **Askernish Golf Club,** Askernish, Lochboisdale. *Location:* three miles from Lochboisdale ferry terminal. Seaside links, designed by Tom Morris Senior 1891. 9 holes, 5042 yards. S.S.S. 68. *Green Fees:* £3.50. *Eating facilities:* local hotels. *Visitors:* welcome. Secretary: A.L. MacDonald (08784 541).

# TIREE

SCARINISH. **Vaul Golf Club,** Scarinish, Isle of Tiree PA77 6XH. *Location:* two miles from Scarinish and half a mile from Lodge Hotel, ferry from Oban four hours and plane from Glasgow 45 minutes. Links course with crystal white beaches to north and south. 9 holes, 5822 yards (18 holes). S.S.S. 70 (18 holes). *Green Fees:* £3.00 daily. *Eating facilities:* at the Lodge Hotel. *Visitors:* welcome, no restrictions. *Society Meetings:* catered for, arrangement with Lodge Hotel. Secretary: N.J. MacArthur (0879 2339).

# Golf in Wales

## WHERE TO PLAY • WHERE TO STAY

WHERE SCOTLAND has golf courses, Wales has castles! There are more castles per square mile in Wales than in any other country in Europe. When the two come together, as at Harlech and Royal St. Davids, then that is more than just a golfing experience.

Equally royal and equally distinguished, in South Wales, Royal Porthcawl, however, has no castle – but it has hosted the British Amateur Championship. St. Pierre near Chepstow

is another championship course in Wales also offering, like the Fairways at Porthcawl, full hotel facilities.

Good golf hotels like Coed-y-Mwstwr near Bridgend, the Wye Valley near Chepstow, the Landsdowne at Brecon and many others, compete with the self-catering opportunities found in Welsh cottages or in such complexes as Hafod at Aberdovey and Beach Holidays at Pontllyfni on Caernarfon Bay.

# Clwyd

ABERGELE. **Abergele and Pensarn Golf Club,** Tan-y-Gopa Road, Abergele LL22 8DS (Abergele (0745) 824034). *Location:* below Gwrych Castle, Abergele. Parkland in scenic setting. 18 holes, 6520 yards, 5961 metres. S.S.S. 71. Practice area. *Green Fees:* £20.00 weekdays; £24.00 weekends. *Eating facilities:* full catering facilities except Mondays, two bars. *Visitors:* welcome weekdays, Bank Holidays and weekends with official club Handicap. *Society Meetings:* catered for, by arrangment with Secretary. Professional: I. Runcie (0745 823813). Secretary: Edgar Richards.

COLWYN. **Old Colwyn Golf Club,** The Clubhouse, Woodland Avenue, Old Colwyn LL29 9NL (Colwyn Bay (0492) 515581). *Location:* signposted at main Abergele road, Old Colwyn. Parkland. 9 holes (x 2), 5268 yards. S.S.S. 66. Practice area. *Green Fees:* weekdays £10.00; weekends £12.00. Special rates for parties. *Eating facilities:* bar and meals by arrangement. *Visitors:* welcome except Saturday afternoons or Wednesday evenings. *Society Meetings:* welcome by arrangement with Secretary. Secretary: D. Jones.

DENBIGH. **Denbigh Golf Club,** Henllan Road, Denbigh (Denbigh (0745) 813888). *Location:* one mile from Denbigh town centre on the B5382 road. Parkland with excellent views. 18 holes, 5582 yards. S.S.S. 67. *Green Fees:* £15.00 weekdays, £20.00 weekends and Bank Holidays. *Eating facilities:* catering daily, bar. *Visitors:* welcome, no restrictions except Thursdays/ Saturdays after 10.30am. *Society Meetings:* by arrangement. Professional: M.D. Jones (0745 814159). Secretary: G.C. Parry (0745 816669).

DENBIGH near. **Bryn Morfydd Hotel Golf Course,** Llanrhaeadr, Near Denbigh LL16 4NP (0745 78280; Fax: 0745 78488). *Location:* south off A525 between Denbigh and Ruthin. Peter Allis designed "Par 3" course overlooking the Vale of Clwyd. Two courses. The Duchess Course – 9 holes, 1146 yards. S.S.S. 27; The Duke's Course – 9 holes, 5144 yards. S.S.S. 66. Practice area. *Green Fees:* The Duchess Course –

£4.00; The Duke's Course – £8.00. *Eating facilities:* courses attached to Country House Hotel, two restaurants and two bars. *Visitors:* welcome all year. Home of British School of Golf, Pro Shop, Hotel accommodation – 30 rooms. *Society Meetings:* welcome by arrangement all year. Professional: request transfer to Pro shop. Secretary: C. Henderson. Proprietor: D. Muirhead.

FLINT. **Flint Golf Club,** Cornist Park, Flint CH6 5HJ (0352 732327). *Location:* A548 coast road, one mile from town centre. Hilly parkland. 9 holes, 5927 yards. S.S.S. 69. Practice area. *Green Fees:* weekdays £10.00 per day, weekends with member. Special rate for golf parties numbering 12 or more. *Eating facilities:* snacks, evening meals by arrangement, bar. *Visitors:* welcome weekdays (no restrictions), weekends with member only. *Society Meetings;* catered for – advance booking (not Sundays). Secretary: A. Ryland (0352 733995).

HAWARDEN. **Hawarden Golf Club,** Groomsdale Lane, Hawarden, Deeside CH5 3EH (Hawarden (0244) 531447). *Location:* A55, first left at Hawarden Station going west. Undulating parkland. 9 holes, 5630 yards, 5200 metres. S.S.S. 67. *Green Fees:* weekdays £15.00. *Eating facilities:* full catering available. *Visitors:* weekdays by appointment with Secretary, otherwise must be playing with a member. *Society Meetings:* catered for by arrangement with Secretary. Professional: A. Davies. Secretary: T. Hinks-Edwards.

HOLYWELL. **Holywell Golf Club,** Brynford, Near Holywell CH8 8LQ (0352 710040). *Location:* turn off A55 at Springfield Hotel onto A5206 turn at traffic lights, up hill for one and a half miles, turn right at crossroads. Flat natural terrain, links type course. 18 holes, 6000 yards, 5495 metres. S.S.S. 69. Par 70. *Green Fees:* weekdays £12.00; weekends and Bank Holidays £18.00. Subject to review. *Eating facilities:* full bar facilities and catering on request. *Visitors:* welcome weekdays without reservation; Bank Holidays and weekends by prior arrangement with Secretary. Snooker table. *Society Meetings:* by arrangement. Professional: Martin Carty (0352 710040). Secretary: E.K. Carney (0352 710539).

LLANGOLLEN. **Vale of Llangollen Golf Club,** The Clubhouse, Llangollen (Llangollen (0978) 860613). *Location:* one mile east of town on the A5. 18 holes, S.S.S. 72. *Green Fees:* on application. *Eating facilities:* full catering service. *Visitors:* welcome. *Society Meetings:* welcome. Professional: D.I. Vaughan (0978 860040). Secretary: T.F. Ellis (0978 860040).

MOLD. **Mold Golf Club,** Cilcain Road, Pantymwyn, Mold CH7 1LW (Mold (0352) 740318). *Location:* three miles from Mold. Undulating course, outstanding views. 18 holes, 5548 yards. S.S.S. 67. Practice ground. *Green Fees:* weekdays £15.00; weekends and Bank Holidays £20.00. *Eating facilities:* bar and dining-room. *Visitors:* welcome at all times subject to tee availability. *Society Meetings:* written application. Professional: Martin Carty (0352 740318) (Lessons by appointment). Secretary: A. Newall (0352 741513).

MOLD. **Padeswood and Buckley Golf Club,** The Caia, Station Lane, Padeswood, Mold. *Location:* eight miles west from Chester, four miles from Mold on the A5118. 18 holes, 5823 yards. S.S.S. 68. *Green Fees:* weekdays £16.50, Saturdays and Bank Holidays £20.00. *Eating facilities:* by arrangement with Steward. *Visitors:* welcome except on Sundays. *Society Meetings:* weekdays only. Professional: David Ashton (0244 543636). Secretary: J.G. Peters (0244 550537).

PADESWOOD. **Old Padeswood Golf Club Ltd,** Station Road, Padeswood, Near Mold CH7 4JL (Buckley (0244) 547401). *Location:* off A5118 Chester to Mold road, three miles south east of Mold. Meadow-land. 18 holes, 6668 yards, 6079 metres. S.S.S. 72. Practice ground. *Green Fees:* weekdays £15.00 per round; weekends £20.00 per round. *Eating facilities:* diningroom, bar meals – two bars. *Visitors:* welcome anytime except on competition days and preferably in possession of a bona fide Handicap. *Society Meetings:* catered for weekdays only. Professional: Tony Davies (0244 547401). Secretary: Bernard Hellen (0352 770506).

PRESTATYN. **Prestatyn Golf Club,** Marine Road East, Prestatyn LL19 7HS (0745 854320). *Location:* A584, on approaching Prestatyn from Chester direction turn right at sign for Pontins Holiday Village and follow club sign. Seaside links Championship course. 18 holes, 6517 yards, 5959 metres. S.S.S. 72. Practice areas. *Green Fees:* £18.00 weekdays; £22.00 weekends and Bank Holidays. *Eating facilities:* full catering available, bar. *Visitors:* members of golf club, with Handicap Certificate. *Society Meetings:* special "all-in" arrangement for 27 holes. Professional: M. Staton (0745 854320). Secretary: Roy Woodruff (0745 888353).

PRESTATYN. **St. Melyd Golf Club,** The Paddock, Meliden Road, Prestatyn LL19 9NB (0745 854405). *Location:* beside Prestatyn to Rhuddlan main road (near Meliden village). Parkland, beautifully set. 18 holes, 5811 yards. S.S.S. 68. *Green Fees:* weekdays £14.00; weekends £18.00. *Eating facilities:* full range of catering facilities except Tuesdays. *Visitors:* welcome. *Society Meetings:* catered for by arrangement with Secretary (various golf packages). Professional: N.H. Lloyd (0745 88858). Secretary: Mr Peter M. Storey (0745 853574).

RHUDDLAN. **Rhuddlan Golf Club,** Meliden Road, Rhuddlan LL18 6LB (0745 590217). *Location:* leave A55 at St. Asaph for Rhuddlan, clubhouse 100m from roundabout on Rhyl side of Rhuddlan. Gently undulating, parkland course with natural hazards. 18 holes, 6435 yards, 5900 metres. S.S.S. 71. Extensive practice ground. *Green Fees:* £18.00 weekdays; £25.00 weekends and Bank Holidays. *Eating facilities:* available daily. *Visitors:* welcome at all times when course demand permits. Sundays with member only. No denim. Snooker table. *Society Meetings:* weekdays only, maximum 50. Professional: Ian Worsley (0745 590898). Secretary: David Morris (0745 590217).

RHYL. **Rhyl Golf Club,** Coast Road, Rhyl LL18 3RE (Rhyl (0745) 353171). *Location:* one mile east of Rhyl on A548. Seaside links. 9 holes, 6153 yards. S.S.S. 69. Practice ground. *Green Fees:* £12.00 weekdays; £15.00 weekends. Discounts for parties over 15. *Eating facilities:* bar snacks and meals available. *Visitors:* welcome any time except when competitions in progress. *Society Meetings:* catered for by prior arrangement with Secretary. Professional: Martin Carty. Secretary: W. Wilson.

RUTHIN. **Ruthin Pwllglas Golf Club,** Pwllglas, Near Ruthin (Ruthin (0824) 702296). *Location:* Corwen Road (494), two miles south of Ruthin. Hilly parkland. 10 holes, 5418 yards. S.S.S. 66. Practice area. *Green Fees:* weekdays £10.00, weekends and Bank Holidays £15.00 (with member £8.00). *Eating facilities:* none. *Visitors:* welcome without reservation except on major competition or match days. Phone call advisable in high season. *Society Meetings:* catered for midweek. Hon. Secretary: R.D. Roberts (0842 4659).

WREXHAM. **Wrexham Golf Club,** Holt Road, Wrexham LL13 9SB (0978 261033). *Location:* A543 north east of Wrexham. 18 holes, 6139 yards. S.S.S. 69. Practice facilities. *Green Fees:* weekdays £17.00, weekends £22.00. *Eating facilities:* daily, subject to functions and visiting Societies. *Visitors:* welcome subject to competitions and Society bookings. Proof of Golf Club membership and/or Handicap Certificate required. *Society Meetings:* catered for, Mondays and Fridays preferred. Professional: D.A. Larvin (097 351476). Secretary: K.B. Fisher (0978 364268).

# Dyfed

ABERYSTWYTH. **Aberystwyth Golf Club,** Brynymor Road, Aberystwyth (0970) 615104). *Location:* north end of Promenade, access near to cliff railway. Undulating meadowland. 18 holes, 5850 yards. S.S.S. 68. Practice ground. *Green Fees:* Summer: £12.00 per round, £15.00 per day weekdays; £15.00 per round, £18.00 per day weekends. *Eating facilities:* restaurant and bar. *Visitors:* welcome at all times, pre-booking helpful. *Society Meetings:* welcome, Special Deals available. Professional: Kevin Bayliss (0970 625301). Secretary: Barrie Thomas.

AMMANFORD. **Glynhir Golf Club,** Glynhir Road, Llandybie, Ammanford SA18 2TF (Llandybie (0269) 850472). *Location:* seven miles from end of M4, between Ammanford and Llandybie on the A483. Turn right up Glynhir Road and proceed for about two miles. Undulating wooded parkland course. 18 holes, 5442 metres. S.S.S. 69. *Green Fees:* £15.00 (£10.00 in Winter) weekdays; £20.00 (£12.00 in Winter) weekends and Bank Holidays. *Eating facilities:* full catering available. *Visitors:* welcome but preferably on weekdays. Not Sundays. *Society Meetings:* welcome weekdays by prior arrangement with Secretary. Accommodation available. Bed and Breakfast at clubhouse (6 to 8 persons). Professional: Ian M. Roberts (0269 851010). Secretary: E.P. Rees (0269 592345).

BORTH. **Borth and Ynyslas Golf Club Ltd,** Borth SY24 5JS (Borth (0970) 871202). *Location:* turn off A487 between Aberystwyth and Machynlleth, course is north of Borth village. Championship standard links course with natural hazards (oldest 18 hole course in Wales). 18 holes, 6116 yards. S.S.S. 70. Practice area. *Green Fees:* weekdays £15.00 except during August when weekend rates apply; weekends £20.00 per day. *Eating facilities:* full catering facilities provided advance booking made. *Visitors:* welcome at all times but should check up that tee off times are available weekends. *Society Meetings:* by arrangement with the Secretary. Professional: J.G. Lewis (0970 871557). Secretary: Ron Williams (0970 871325; Fax: 0970 871154).

CARDIGAN. **Cardigan Golf Club,** Gwbert-on-Sea, Cardigan SA43 1PR (Cardigan (0239) 612035). *Location:* three miles north-west of Cardigan. Seaside links course. 18 holes, 6641 yards. S.S.S. 72. *Green Fees:* £15.00 per day weekdays, £20.00 per day weekends and Bank Holidays. *Eating facilities:* catering and bar

facilities available. *Visitors:* welcome. Tee reserved for members 1 – 2pm. *Society Meetings:* very welcome. Professional: Colin Parsons. Hon. Secretary: J. Rhapps (0239 612035).

CARMARTHEN. **Carmarthen Golf Club,** Blaenycoed Road, Carmarthen SA33 6EH (0267 87214). *Location:* four miles north-west of town. Undulating parkland. 18 holes, 6210 yards. S.S.S. 71. Practice ground. *Green Fees:* weekdays £15.00; weekends £20.00. *Eating facilities:* full catering available. *Visitors:* welcome with reservation, Tuesday with Handicap Certificate. *Society Meetings:* catered for, 10% discount for groups of more than 20. Professional: Pat Gillis (0267 87493). Secretary: Jonathan Coe (0267 87588).

HAVERFORDWEST. **Haverfordwest Golf Club,** Arnolds Down, Haverfordwest SA61 2XQ (Haverfordwest (0437) 763565). *Location:* one mile east of Haverfordwest on A40. S.S.S. 69. Practice fairway and putting green. *Green Fees:* £14.00 weekdays (£12.00 playing with a member); £20.00 weekends (£16.00 playing with member). *Eating facilities:* bar snacks available, meals by arrangement. *Visitors:* bona fide golfers welcome. *Society Meetings:* catered for by arrangement. Professional: A.J. Pile (0437 768409). Secretary: M.A. Harding (0437 764523).

LAMPETER. **Cilgwyn Golf Club,** Llangybi, Lampeter SA48 8NN (057045 286). *Location:* five miles north-east of Lampeter, off A485 at Llangybi. Flat parkland course. 9 holes, 5318 yards, S.S.S. 67. Practice area. *Green Fees:* weekdays £8.00 per round, £12.00 per day; weekends £12.00 per round. *Eating facilities:* bar open daily; light snacks. *Visitors:* welcome without reservation. Golf shop. Caravan parking and golf for Caravan Club members. *Society Meetings:* catered for, Thursdays and Fridays. Secretary: (0570 422 793).

LLANELLI. **Ashburnham Golf Club,** Cliffe Terrace, Burry Port SA16 0HN (05546 2466). *Location:* four miles west of Llanelli – eight miles from exit 48 on M4. Seaside links with Championship status. 18 holes, 6916 yards. S.S.S. 73, Par 72. Practice area. *Green Fees:* weekdays £20.00 per round (£15.00 with member), £25.00 per day (£20.00 with member); weekends and Bank Holidays £25.00 per round (£20.00 with member), £28.00 per day (£23.00 with member). *Eating facilities:* full catering except Mondays, two bars.

*Visitors:* welcome weekdays, Wednesday ladies' day, special arrangements weekends. Certificate of Membership elsewhere needed. *Society Meetings:* catered for with advance notification to Secretary only. Professional: Robert A. Ryder (05546 3846). Secretary: David M. Llewellyn (05546 2269).

LLANRHYSTYD. **Penrhos Golf and Country Club,** Llanrhystyd SY23 5AY (0974 202999). *Location:* nine miles south of Aberystwyth on A487. Parkland and meadowland with lakes and terrific views. 18 holes, 6641 yards. S.S.S. 72. Practice ground. *Green Fees:* weekdays £12.00 per round; weekends £16.00 per round. *Eating facilities:* bar meals and à la carte restaurant. Accommodation, full leisure facilities. *Society Meetings:* welcome. Professional: Paul Diamond. Secretary: R. Rees-Evans.

MILFORD HAVEN. **Milford Haven Golf Club,** Woodbine House, Hubberston, Milford Haven (Milford Haven (0646) 692368). *Location:* one mile from Milford Haven on Dale Road. Parkland overlooking magnificent harbour. 18 holes, 6071 yards. S.S.S. 70. *Green Fees:* weekdays £12.00; weekends £15.00. *Eating facilities:* lunches, bar snacks, dinners available at clubhouse. *Visitors:* welcome at all times. *Society Meetings:* welcome, special rates depending on numbers. Professional: Stephen Adler (0646 697762). Secretary: D.G. Britton, 22 Great North Road, Milford Haven (0646 697660 evenings).

NEWPORT. **Newport (Pembs) Golf Club,** The Golf Club, Newport SA42 ONR (Newport [Dyfed] (0239) 820244). *Location:* two miles off A487 Cardigan-Fishguard at Newport, Dyfed. Flat seaside links course with mountain views. 9 holes, 5815 yards. S.S.S. 68. *Green Fees:* £10.00 per day. *Eating facilities:* full catering and bar facilities available. *Visitors:* welcome at all times, please telephone at weekends and Bank Holidays. Self-catering accommodation available adjoining clubhouse. *Society Meetings:* catered for at

any time by arrangement with the Secretary. Professional: Mr Colin Parsons. Secretary: Ron Dietrich.

PEMBROKE. **South Pembrokeshire Golf Club,** Denfensible Barracks, Pembroke Dock, Pembroke (Pembroke (0646) 683817). *Location:* on hilltop overlooking Pembroke Dock and Milford Haven waterway, near western end of A477. Parkland. 9 holes, 5804 yards. S.S.S. 69. *Green Fees:* £10.00 per day. Weekly (Mondays to Fridays) £30.00. *Eating facilities:* bar, meals by prior arrangement. *Visitors:* welcome. *Society Meetings:* catered for by arrangement. Secretary: W.D. Owen (0646 682650).

ST. DAVIDS. **St. Davids City Golf Club,** Whitesands Bay, St. Davids SA62 6QY. *Location:* left fork at Rugby Club, two miles to Whitesands Bay, turn left at sign for Whitesands Bay Hotel. Seaside links course with panoramic views of Whitesands Bay and St. Davids Head. 9 holes, 5911 yards. S.S.S. 70. *Green Fees:* £10.00 (£5.00 if playing with a member). *Eating facilities:* available at Whitesands Hotel – 200 yards from course. *Visitors:* no restrictions. No bag sharing, please. *Society Meetings:* welcome, preferably by prior arrangement with Secretary. Secretary: G.B. Lewis (0348 831607).

TENBY. **Tenby Golf Club,** The Burrows, Tenby SA70 7NP (Tenby (0834) 2787). *Location:* on A478, near Tenby Railway Station. Seaside links, Championship course, oldest club in Wales. 18 holes, 6232 yards. S.S.S. 71. Practice area. *Green Fees:* weekdays £18.00; weekends £22.50. Reduced fees in winter and for Societies booked in advance. *Eating facilities:* complete dining facilities; licensed bars, snacks. *Visitors:* always welcome, subject to club competitions. Must produce Handicap Certificate. Billiards room available. *Society Meetings:* catered for by advance booking. Professional: Terence Mountford (0834 4447). Secretary: T.R. Arnold (0834 2978).

# Mid-Glamorgan

ABERDARE. **Aberdare Golf Club,** Abernant, Aberdare (0685 871188). *Location:* half a mile from town centre. Mountain course with parkland features and view of whole Cynon Valley. 18 holes, 5845 yards. S.S.S. 69. *Green Fees:* weekdays £14.00, (with member £8.00); weekends £18.00, (with member £10.00). *Eating facilities:* bar, lounge and diningroom. *Visitors:* welcome without reservation weekdays. No casual visitors on Saturdays, with member only. Handicap Certificates required. Snooker room, ladies' lounge and changing room. *Society Meetings:* catered for by prior arrangement with Secretary. Professional: A. Palmer (0685 878735). Secretary: L. Adler (0685 872797).

BARGOED. **Bargoed Golf Club,** Heolddu, Bargoed (Bargoed (0443) 830143). *Location:* A469 to Bargoed town centre – Heolddu Road – Moorland Road. Mountain course. 18 holes, 6012 yards. S.S.S. 69. *Green Fees:* £13.00, with a member £8.00. *Eating facilities:* lunches, dinners and snacks. *Visitors:* welcome, only with member at weekends, no other restrictions. *Society Meetings:* catered for weekdays, not at weekends. Secretary: W.R. Coleman (0443 830143 or 822377).

BRIDGEND. **Southerndown Golf Club,** Ewenny, Bridgend CF35 5BT (Southerndown (0656) 880326). *Location:* three miles from Bridgend on the Ogmore Road. Downland overlooking Bristol Channel. 18 holes, 6417 yards, 5868 metres. S.S.S. 72. Practice area. *Green Fees:* £24.00 weekdays; £30.00 weekends. £18.00 after 2pm. *Eating facilities:* full

diningroom and bar facilities. *Visitors:* welcome any time except on competitions days (check with Secretary). Handicap Certificate required. *Society Meetings:* catered for on Tuesdays and Thursdays or by arrangement with Secretary. Special rates dependent on number. Professional: D. McMonagle (0656 880326). Secretary: K.R. Wilcox (0656 880476).

CAERPHILLY. **Caerphilly Golf Club,** Pencapel, Mountain Road, Caerphilly CF8 1HJ (Caerphilly (0222) 883481). *Location:* seven miles north of Cardiff on A469, 250 yards south of both railway and bus stations opposite magistrates court. Mountainside course with undulating features and areas of woodland. 14 holes, 6028 yards. S.S.S. 71. Limited practice facilities. *Green Fees:* weekdays £18.00, £9.00 with a member; weekends only if playing with a member. *Eating facilities:* men's and lounge bars, lunches; limited dining by arrangement. *Visitors:* welcome weekdays only or by arrangement. *Society Meetings:* only a limited number by arrangement. Professional: Richard Barter (0222 869104). Secretary: H.M. Matthews (0222 863441).

CAERPHILLY. **Castell Heights Public Golf Course,** Blaengwynlais CF8 1NG (0222 861128). *Location:* approximately four miles north of Cardiff on A469, two miles south of Caerphilly. 9 holes, 2688 yards. S.S.S. 66 for 18 holes. *Green Fees:* information not available. *Eating facilities:* snacks, lunches and afternoon tea available. Restaurant meals booking only (0222 886686). *Visitors:* welcome, booked times only. Professional: S. Bebb. Secretary: A.H. Godsall.

CAERPHILLY. **Mountain Lakes Golf and Country Club,** Caerphilly CF8 1NG (0222 886686). *Location:* approximately four miles north of Cardiff on A469, two miles south of Caerphilly. M4 Junction 32. Part parkland, part wooded, undulating. 20 water hazards, large penncross greens. 18 holes, 6550 yards. S.S.S. 73. 20 bay driving range. *Green Fees:* weekdays £15.00 (£10.00 with member); weekends £15.00. *Eating facilities:* full restaurant and three bars. *Visitors:* welcome at all times but must have registered handicap. *Society Meetings:* welcome at all times but must have registered handicap. Professional: Sion Bebb (0222 886666). Secretary: Jean Bull (0222 861128; Fax: 0222 869030).

HENGOED. **Bryn Meadows Golf and Country Club Hotel,** The Bryn, Near Hengoed CF8 7SM (0495 225590/224103; Fax: 0495 228272). *Location:* A472 from Ystrad Mynach to Blackwood, turn up lane at Texaco Service Station at Crown roundabout. Parkland course. 18 holes, 6200 yards. S.S.S. 69. *Green Fees:* weekdays £17.50; weekends £22.50. *Eating facilities:* restaurant, 70 covers. Functions up to 120. Conferences catered for from five to 120. Bar snacks served daily. *Visitors:* welcome, but not Sunday mornings. The "Fairways" Leisure Club including – indoor heated swimming pool, jacuzzi, sauna and steam rooms and "state of the art" multigym available. *Society Meetings:* welcome Tuesdays and Thursdays. Professional: B. Hunter (0495 221905). Secretary: B. Mayo.

KENFIG. **Pyle and Kenfig Golf Club,** Waun-y-Mer, Kenfig CF33 4PU (0656 782060). *Location:* one mile off M4 at Junction 37. Seaside links. 18 holes, 6650 yards, 6081 metres. S.S.S. 73. Five practice holes. *Green Fees:* weekdays £22.00 per round, £27.00 day; weekends only as a member's guest £13.50. *Eating facilities:* full catering and bar service (no catering Mondays). *Visitors:* welcome weekdays, proof of membership and Handicap Certificate required. *Society Meetings:* welcome by arrangement. Professional: R. Evans (0656 772446). Secretary/Manager: R.C. Thomas (0656 783093).

MAESTEG. **Maesteg Golf Club,** Mount Pleasant, Maesteg CF34 9PR (0656 732037). *Location:* half a mile out of Maesteg town centre on the Port Talbot road. Reasonably flat mountain course. 18 holes, 5900 yards. S.S.S. 69. *Green Fees:* weekdays £13.50; weekends £17.00. Special rates for Societies. *Eating facilities:* diningroom every day except Thursdays. *Visitors:* welcome without reservation, groups of more than eight by arrangement. *Society Meetings:* catered for weekdays only by arrangement. Professional: Gary Hughes (0656 735742). Secretary: W.H. Hanford (0656 734106).

MERTHYR TYDFIL. **Merthyr Tydfil (Cilsanws) Golf Club,** Cloth Hall Lane, Cefn Coed, Merthyr Tydfil (0685 723308). *Location:* off A470 two miles north of Merthyr Tydfil town centre. Mountain course in National Park area with outstanding views. 11 holes, 5957 yards. S.S.S. 69. *Green Fees:* £12.00 weekdays; £15.00 weekends. Half price playing with member. *Eating facilities:* weekends only. *Visitors:* welcome anytime except competition days (usually Sundays). *Society Meetings:* catered for by prior arrangement. Secretary: Vivian Price.

MERTHYR TYDFIL. **Morlais Castle Golf Club,** Pant, Dowlais, Merthyr Tydfil CF48 2UY (0685 722822). *Location:* near 'Heads of Valley Road', Dowlais roundabout, follow signs for Brecon Mountain Railway. Very pleasant moorland course with excellent views. 18 holes, 6320 yards, 5744 metres. S.S.S. 71. Practice area. *Green Fees:* weekdays £16.00 per day, £10.00 with member; weekends £20.00, £10.00 with a member. Subject to review. *Eating facilities:* bar meals, for other meals contact Stewardess. *Visitors:* welcome except Saturday afternoons and Sunday mornings. *Society Meetings:* please contact Secretary. Secretary: J.N. Powell.

MOUNTAIN ASH. **Mountain Ash Golf Club,** Cefn Pennar, Mountain Ash (Mountain Ash (0443) 472265). *Location:* A470 Pontypridd to Aberdare road, approximately 10 miles from Pontypridd four miles north of Abercynon. Partly wooded course. 18 holes, 5553 yards. S.S.S. 68. *Green Fees:* weekdays £14.00, £7.00 with member, weekends and Bank Holidays £14.00 only with member. *Eating facilities:* catering at club. *Visitors:* welcome any time without reservation. *Society Meetings:* catered for. Professional: Jeff Sim (0443 478770). Secretary: Geoffrey Matthews.

NELSON. **Whitehall Golf Club,** The Pavilion, Nelson CF46 6FT (0443 740245). *Location:* Abercynon, three minutes from centre. Hilly course. 9 holes, 2856 yards. S.S.S. 34. *Green Fees:* information not available. *Eating facilities:* available, meals must be ordered. *Visitors:* booking by telephone preferred. Professional: J. Sim. Secretary: V.E. Davies.

PONTYCLUN. **Llantrisant and Pontyclun Golf Club,** The Clubhouse, Talbot Green, Pontyclun (Llantrisant (0443) 222148). *Location:* 10 miles north of Cardiff, two miles north of Junction 34 M4. Parkland. 12 holes, 5712 yards. S.S.S. 68. *Green Fees:* weekdays £20.00, £8.00 with member; weekends and Bank Holidays £10.00 with member only. *Eating facilities:* by arrangement with Steward. *Visitors:* welcome with proof of membership and weekends with member only. *Society Meetings:* catered for by arrangement. Professional: Nick Watson (0443 228169). Secretary: John Williams (0443 224601).

PONTYPRIDD. **Pontypridd Golf Club,** Ty Gwyn Road, Pontypridd CF37 4DJ (Pontypridd (0443) 402359). *Location:* east side of town centre, off A470, 12 miles from Cardiff. Wooded mountain course. 18 holes, 5650 yards, 5166 metres. S.S.S. 68. *Green Fees:* information not provided. *Eating facilities:* dining facilities and bar snacks. *Visitors:* welcome weekdays without member, weekends with member only. Must be member of recognised golf club. *Society Meetings:* catered for with prior reservation. Professional: A Curtis (0443 491210). Secretary: J.G. Graham (0443 409904).

# FAIRWAYS HOTEL & THE PORTHCAWL HOTEL

**SEAFRONT, PORTHCAWL**
**MID GLAMORGAN CF36 3LS**

The Porthcawl is situated in the main shopping centre close to the seafront whilst Fairways commands a magnificent panoramic view southwards across the adjacent foreshore and over the Bristol Channel towards the Devon hills.

Both hotels have first class facilities and serve excellent food and are licensed. The Porthcawl also has a nightclub and health club. Within easy reach of Royal Porthcawl Golf Club and Pyle & Kenfig Golf Club. Brochure available.

**Telephone: (0656) 782085 or 783544. Fax: (0656) 785351.**

PORTHCAWL. **Royal Porthcawl Golf Club,** Rest Bay, Porthcawl CF36 3UW (0656 782251; Fax: 0656 771687). *Location:* 25 miles west of Cardiff off Junction 37 M4, 14 miles east of Swansea. Seaside links. 18 holes, 6691 yards. S.S.S. 74. 27 acre practice area. *Green Fees:* £30.00 weekdays, £45.00 weekends. *Eating facilities:* full catering and bar facilities. *Visitors:* playing with member only at weekends, reservations required and must have Handicap Certificate. *Society Meetings:* by arrangement. Professional: Mr Graham Poor (0656 786984). Secretary: A.W. Woolcott.

RHONDDA. **Rhondda Golf Club,** Golf House, Penrhys, Ferndale, Rhondda CF43 3PW (Tonypandy (0443) 433204). *Location:* on the Penrhys road joining Rhondda Fach and Rhondda Fawr. Mountain course. 18 holes, 6206 yards. S.S.S. 70. *Green Fees:* £15.00 weekdays; £20.00 weekends. *Eating facilities:* all facilities daily except Mondays. *Visitors:* welcome without reservation weekdays. Handicap certificate required. *Society Meetings:* welcome on written application. Professional: Rhys Davies (0443 441385). Secretary: G. Rees (0443 441384).

# South Glamorgan

BARRY. **Brynhill (Barry) Golf Club,** Port Road East, Colcot, Barry CF6 7PN (Barry (0446) 735061). *Location:* leave M4 at Junction 33 (A4232), follow signs for Barry and Cardiff (Wales) Airport onto the A4050. Club on right of road. Undulating meadowland course. 18 holes, 6077yards. S.S.S. 69. Par 71. *Green Fees:* weekdays: £20.00 per day, £9.00 with member; Saturdays and Bank Holidays: £25.00, £9.00 with member. Societies £7.00. With County Cards £9.00. Juniors £7.00. *Eating facilities:* the Steward Mr Barrie Cahill and his wife Ann extend a warm welcome, and will provide morning coffee, lunches between 12 noon and 2.00pm. Afternoon teas and dinner from 4.30 pm. Your order prior to playing is requested. *Visitors:* welcome, except Sundays; must produce membership card and Handicap Certificate. *Society Meetings:* by arrangement with Secretary – no weekends, must be members of a golf club. Professional: Peter Fountain (0446 733660). Secretary: Keith Atkinson (0446 720277).

BARRY. **RAF St. Athan Golf Club,** Barry CF6 9WA (0446 751043/798372). *Location:* first turning on right after driving through St. Athan Village, eight miles from Barry. Flat parkland, newly wooded with 2700 trees. 9 holes, 6290 yards. S.S.S. 72. Practice area and nets. *Green Fees:* £8.00/£10.00 weekdays; £10.00/£15.00 weekends with or without member. *Eating facilities:* available except Mondays. *Visitors:* green fee players welcome on display of Handicap Certificate except

Sunday mornings. *Society Meetings:* apply through the Secretary. Professional: Neil Gillette (0222 373923). Secretary: P.F. Woodhouse (0446 743025; Fax: 0446 798302).

CARDIFF. **Cardiff Golf Club,** Sherborne Avenue, Cyncoed, Cardiff (Cardiff (0222) 753067). *Location:* two miles north of city centre or M4, A48 or A48M from east to Pentwyn exit on Eastern Avenue, and take Pentwyn Industrial Road to top of hill at Cyncoed Village, turn left at Spar shop into Sherborne Avenue. Undulating parkland, all greens bunkered. 18 holes. S.S.S. 70. *Green Fees:* £25.00. Winter rate 1st October to 31st March £15.00. *Eating facilities:* catering available lunchtime and evening weekdays except Mondays. *Visitors:* welcome; Saturdays must play with a member. Professional: Terry Hanson (0222 754772). Secretary: Keith Lloyd (0222 753320).

CARDIFF. **Creigiau Golf Club,** Cardiff Road, Creigiau, Cardiff CF4 8NN (Cardiff (0222) 890263). *Location:* seven miles north-west of Cardiff, two miles Exit 34 M4. 18 holes, 5979 yards. S.S.S. 69. *Green Fees:* £21.00 per day (£10.00 with member). *Eating facilities:* meals on request. *Visitors:* welcome without reservation except weekends when with members only. *Society Meetings:* catered for by arrangement at £18.00 per head. Professional: Mark Maddison (0222 891909). Secretary/Manager: D. Bryan Jones (0222 890263).

CARDIFF. **Llanishen Golf Club,** Cwm, Lisvane, Cardiff CF4 5UD (Cardiff (0222) 752205). *Location:* five miles north of Cardiff city centre, one mile north of Llanishen village. Wooded mountain course with spectacular views. 18 holes, 5296 yards, 4844 metres. S.S.S. 66. *Green Fees:* £20.00. Special rates for County Cards or playing with member. *Eating facilities:* full bar and catering except Mondays. *Visitors:* welcome weekdays; weekends only with member. Handicap Certificate required. *Society Meetings:* catered for Thursday only on written application. Visitors must be bona fide members of a golf club. Professional: R.A. Jones (0222 755076). Secretary/Manager: Elfed Davies (0222 755078).

CARDIFF. **Radyr Golf Club,** Drysgol Road, Radyr, Cardiff CF4 8BS (Cardiff (0222) 842442). *Location:* A470, five miles north of Cardiff, turn left at Taffs Well; or Cardiff to Llandaff then Llantrisant Road, fork right past Westward Ho! Garage for Radyr. Parkland course. 18 holes, 6031 yards. S.S.S. 70. *Green Fees:* £24.00 weekdays. *Eating facilities:* snacks, lunches and evening meals. Please order in advance (0222 842735). *Visitors:* welcome except weekends, Handicap Certificate from recognised club required. *Society Meetings:* catered for Wednesdays, Thursdays and Fridays. Professional/Manager: Steve Gough (0222 842476/842408).

CARDIFF. **St. Mellons Golf Club,** St. Mellons, Cardiff CF3 8XS (Castleton (0633) 680401). *Location:* just off M4 at Junction 28 on to A48. Parkland. 18 holes, 6225 yards. S.S.S. 70. *Green Fees:* £25.00 weekdays. *Eating facilities:* available. *Visitors:* welcome with Handicap Certificates weekdays only, weekends with member only. *Society Meetings:* catered for on written application. Professional: Barry Thomas (0633 680101). Secretary: Mrs K. Newling (0633 680408).

CARDIFF. **Wenvoe Castle Golf Club Ltd,** Wenvoe, Cardiff CF5 6BE (Cardiff (0222) 591094). *Location:* exit Junction 33 M4, follow signs for Cardiff Airport. Parkland. 18 holes, 6422 yards. S.S.S. 71. *Green Fees:* weekdays £20.00; weekends £12.00 with a member only. *Eating facilities:* bar snacks and restaurant meals. *Visitors:* welcome weekdays only. *Society Meetings:*

catered for Monday to Thursday, parties of 16 or more. Professional: R. Wyer (0222 593649). Secretary: E.J. Dew (0222 594371).

CARDIFF. **Whitchurch (Cardiff) Golf Club,** Whitchurch, Cardiff CF4 6XD (Cardiff (0222) 620125). *Location:* three-and-a-half miles from Cardiff on A470 Merthyr Tydfil road. 18 holes, 6245 yards. S.S.S. 70. *Green Fees:* £21.00 weekdays, £26.00 weekends and Bank Holidays. *Eating facilities:* full catering every day. *Visitors:* welcome, if members of recognised Golf Clubs. Restricted at weekends. Please telephone Professional prior to visit. *Society Meetings:* catered for Thursdays on written application. Professional: Eddie Clark (0222 614660). Secretary/Manager: Lieutenant Commander R.G. Burley.

DINAS POWIS. **Dinas Powis Golf Club,** Golf House, Old Highwalls, Dinas Powis CF6 4AJ (Cardiff (0222) 512157). *Location:* M4 Cardiff, thereafter signposted Dinas Powis, Penarth and Barry. Mostly parkland, three holes quite hilly. 18 holes, 5151 yards. S.S.S. 66. Limited practice. *Green Fees:* weekdays £20.00; weekends £25.00. Half fee if playing with a member. Special rates for societies. *Eating facilities:* diningroom/bar snacks except Mondays. *Visitors:* welcome weekdays, weekends by arrangement. *Society Meetings:* welcome, no restrictions. Professional: G. Bennett (0222 512727). Secretary: J.D. Hughes (0222 512727).

PENARTH. **Glamorganshire Golf Club,** Lavernock Road, Penarth CF6 2UP (0222 707048). *Location:* one mile west of Penarth; M4 (Junction 33) then A4232. Parkland course overlooking Bristol Channel. 18 holes, 6150 yards. S.S.S. 70. *Green Fees:* weekdays £22.00; weekends and Bank Holidays £28.00. *Eating facilities:* full restaurant service and bar meals. Men's bar and mixed lounge bar. *Visitors:* welcome providing no competitions in progress and/or Societies on course, also must be a member of a bona fide golf club and show Handicap Certificate duly authorised by Secretary of club. *Society Meetings:* catered for with prior notice. Professional: A. Kerr Smith (0222 707401). Secretary/Manager: G.C. Crimp (0222 701185).

# West Glamorgan

CLYDACH. **Inco Golf Club,** Clydach (0792 844216). *Location:* outskirts of Swansea, easily accessible from M4. Flat, tree-lined course, with river. 12 holes, 6230 yards. S.S.S. 70. *Green Fees:* information not available. *Eating facilities:* none. Bar only. *Visitors:* welcome. *Society Meetings:* catered for by arrangement through Secretary: Mr S. Murdoch (0792 843336).

GLYNNEATH. **Glynneath Golf Club,** 'Penygraig', Pontneathvaughan, Near Glynneath SA11 5UG (Glynneath (0639) 720452). *Location:* A465 Trunk road to Glynneath onto B4242 to Pontneathvaughan. Picturesque hillside course, fairly flat – half parkland and half wooded in Brecon National Park. 18 holes, 5456

yards, 4998 metres. S.S.S. 67. *Green Fees:* weekdays £10.00; weekends £16.00. *Eating facilities:* catering available for Societies, bar snacks every day. *Visitors:* welcome without reservation. *Society Meetings:* welcomed. Secretary: R.M. Ellis (0639 720679).

NEATH. **Neath Golf Club,** Cadoxton, Neath (Neath (0639) 643615). *Location:* two miles from Neath town centre. 18 holes, 6492 yards. S.S.S. 72. *Green Fees* weekdays £15.00. *Eating facilities:* available excep Monday. *Visitors:* welcome weekdays only. Nev snooker room. *Society Meetings:* catered for b arrangement with Secretary. Professional: E.M Bennett. Secretary: D.M. Hughes Esq. (0639-632759)

NEATH. **Swansea Bay Golf Club,** Jersey Marine, Neath SA10 6JP (Skewen (0792) 812198). *Location:* on Neath to Swansea dual carriageway four miles from Neath. Seaside links. 18 holes, 6490 yards. S.S.S. 71. *Green Fees:* weekdays £15.00; weekends and Bank Holidays £20.00. *Eating facilities:* luncheons and teas available six days per week. *Visitors:* welcome without reservation. *Society Meetings:* catered for. Professional: M. Day (0792 816159). Secretary: D. Goatcher (0792 814153).

SWANSEA. **Clyne Golf Club,** 120 Owls Lodge Lane, The Mayals, Blackpyll, Swansea SA3 5DP (0792 401989). *Location:* west of Swansea, South Gower road before Mumbles. Moorland course. 18 holes, 6350 yards. S.S.S. 71. Large practice area and 9 holes putting green. *Green Fees:* weekdays £20.00; weekends £25.00. *Eating facilities:* full catering available. *Visitors:* welcome. *Society Meetings:* welcome by application. Professional: Mark Bevan (0792 402094). Secretary: B.R. Player.

SWANSEA. **Fairwood Park Golf Club Ltd,** Upper Killay, Swansea SA2 7JN (Swansea (0792) 203648). *Location:* from Swansea city centre, follow signs to 'Sketty' and 'Killay', road to club is opposite Swansea Airport. Parkland, many new trees planted and lakes being made now. Championship course. 18 holes, 6606 yards. S.S.S. 72. Ample practice area and nets. *Green Fees:* £20.00 weekdays; £25.00 weekends and Bank Holidays. *Eating facilities:* full range, from bar snacks to three course meals. (Order full meals before playing). *Visitors:* welcome, large parties by appointment. If playing with a member £1.00 reduction. *Society Meetings:* welcome all through the year. Apply to Professional. Professional: Mark Evans (0792 299194). Secretary: Jim Beer (0792 386293). Administrator: Bryn Morgan (0792 297849). Steward: J. Pettifer (0792 203648).

SWANSEA. **Langland Bay Golf Club,** Langland Road, Langland, Swansea (Swansea (0792) 366023). *Location:* Swansea main road to Mumbles, followed by Langland Bay. 18 holes, 5830 yards. S.S.S. 69. *Green Fees:* weekdays £24.00; weekends and Bank Holidays £26.00. *Eating facilities:* lunches, teas and supper, also bar snacks. *Visitors:* welcome without reservation. *Society Meetings:* restricted, by arrangement, £18.00, 12 or more in number. Professional: T. Lynch (0792 366186). Secretary: T.J. Jenkins (0792 361721).

SWANSEA. **Morriston Golf Club,** 160 Clasemont Road, Morriston, Swansea SA6 6AJ (Swansea (0792) 771079). *Location:* half a mile east of Junction 46 on M4, three miles north of Swansea on A48. Leave M4 at Junction 45, 46 or 47 (DVLA Tower overlooks). Parkland course, rather difficult. 18 holes, 5773 yards. S.S.S. 68. *Green Fees:* weekdays £18.00; weekends and Bank Holidays £25.00. £12.00 with member. Special rates for parties of 10 or over with prior notice. *Eating facilities:* catering by arrangement with caterer (0792 700310). *Visitors:* welcome without reservation any weekday. Only with member at weekends. *Society Meetings:* catered for weekdays by arrangement with Secretary. Professional: Deryl Rees (0792 772335). Secretary: Leonard T. Lewis (0792 796528).

SWANSEA. **Palleg Golf Club,** Lower Cwmtwrch, Swansea SA9 2QQ (Glantawe (0639) 842193). *Location:* off A4067 (A4068) north of Swansea 14 miles, 25 miles Brecon. 9 holes, 6510 yards. S.S.S. 72. *Green Fees:* weekdays £10.00; weekends £15.00. *Eating facilities:* evening bar meals Tuesday, Thursday, weekend lunches. *Visitors:* welcome, restrictions Saturday (Summer) and Sunday mornings (Winter). *Society Meetings:* welcome if arranged. Secretary: Mr D.W. Moses (0792 862303).

SWANSEA. **Pennard Golf Club,** 2 Southgate Road, Southgate, Swansea SA3 2BT (044128 3131). *Location:* eight miles west of Swansea A4067, B4436. Seaside links. 18 holes, 6289 yards. S.S.S. 71. Practice areas. *Green Fees:* weekdays £16.00, with a member £12.00; weekends £20.00, with a member £15.00. *Eating facilities:* dining room and two bars. *Visitors:* welcome at any time. Squash courts. *Society Meetings:* catered for weekdays only. Professional: M.V. Bennett (044128 3451). Secretary: J.D. Eccles (044128 3131).

SWANSEA. **Pontardawe Golf Club,** Cefn Llan, Pontardawe, Swansea SA8 4SH (0792 863118). *Location:* four miles north of M4 Junction 45 on A4067 Swansea-Brecon road. Wooded course. 18 holes, 6162 yards. S.S.S. 70. *Green Fees:* £16.50 weekdays; £25.00 weekends. *Eating facilities:* restaurant open daily except Mondays. *Visitors:* welcome, weekends by prior arrangement only. Handicap Certificate required. *Society Meetings:* catered for by application/appointment. Professional: G. Hopkins (0792 830977). Secretary: Lyn Jones (0792 830041).

# Gwent

ABERGAVENNY. **Monmouthshire Golf Club,** Llanfoist, Abergavenny NP7 9HE (Abergavenny (0873) 3171). *Location:* two miles out of Abergavenny on Llanellen to Llanellen Road. Parkland with scenic mountain views. 18 holes, 6045 yards. S.S.S. 69. Practice ground. *Green Fees:* weekdays £21.00, weekends and Bank Holidays £26.00. *Eating facilities:* full meals except Tuesdays (order in advance). *Visitors:* welcome. Proof of membership of recognised golf club required. *Society Meetings:* catered for. Booking to be confirmed before Jan. 31st each year. Professional: P.

Worthing (0873 2532). Secretary: G.J. Swayne (0873 2606).

BLACKWOOD. **Blackwood Golf Club,** Cwmgelli, Blackwood (0495 223152). *Location:* one mile north of Blackwood on Tredegar road A494. 9 holes, 5350 yards. S.S.S. 66. *Green Fees:* weekdays £12.50; weekends and Bank Holidays £15.00. *Visitors:* welcome weekdays only. *Society Meetings:* by arrangement. Secretary: A.M. Reed-Gibbs.

CAERLEON. **Caerleon Public Golf Course,** The Broadway, Caerleon, Newport (Caerleon (0633) 420342). *Location:* three miles off M4 at turnoff for Caerleon. Flat parkland. 9 holes, 3000 yards. S.S.S. 68. Driving range. *Green Fees:* weekdays £2.80; weekends £3.60. Senior Citizens and Juniors £2.00. *Eating facilities:* cafe and bar. *Visitors:* welcome. *Society Meetings:* welcome. Professional: Alex Campbell. Secretary: Ray Evans.

CHEPSTOW. **St. Pierre Hotel Golf and Country Club Ltd,** St. Pierre Park, Chepstow NP6 6YA (0291 625261). *Location:* five minutes from M4/Severn Bridge on A48 to Newport. Old course 18 holes, Championship/Medal 6700 yards, S.S.S. 73; standard tees 6285 yards, S.S.S. 71. Mathern course 18 holes, 5762 yards, S.S.S. 68. *Green Fees:* Old Course – weekdays £40.00, weekends £50.00; Mathern Course weekdays £25.00, weekends £30.00. *Eating facilities:* restaurant, coffee shop. *Visitors:* welcome with current membership of a bona fide golf club. *Society Meetings:* weekdays only, except when resident in hotel which has 150 bedrooms with bathrooms, including 42 executive lodge bedrooms, conference rooms and extensive leisure facilities. Professional: Renton Doig. Secretary: T.J. Cleary.

CWMBRAN. **Greenmeadow Golf and Country Club,** Treherbert Road, Croesyceiliog, Cwmbran NP44 2BZ (0633 869321). *Location:* M4 Junction 26 north on A4042. Turn right off Croesyceiliog by-pass. Next to Gwent Crematorium. Parkland course. 18 holes, 5606 yards. S.S.S. 69. Practice green and putting area. *Green Fees:* weekdays £14.00; weekends £19.00. *Eating facilities:* diningroom with 80 covers, patio restaurant 50 covers. *Visitors:* welcome weekdays, weekends by prior notice. No jeans allowed and golf shoes must be worn. *Society Meetings:* always welcome, bookings via our Professional. Package deals with meals available. Professional: C. Coombs (0633 862626). Secretary: Peter Richardson.

CWMBRAN. **Pontnewydd Golf Club,** West Pontnewydd, Cwmbran (Cwmbran (0633) 482170). *Location:* two miles north of Cwmbran on B4244. 9 holes, 5403 yards. S.S.S. 67. *Green Fees:* £15.00, £6.00 with a member. *Visitors:* welcome all week, must play with member at weekends. *Society Meetings:* not catered for. Secretary: H. R. Gabe.

LLANWERN. **Llanwern Golf Club,** Tennyson Avenue, Llanwern NP6 2DY (Newport (0633) 412380). *Location:* four miles east of Newport, one mile from M4 Junction 24. Parkland. 18 holes, 6202 yards, S.S.S. 70. 9 holes, 5674 yards, 5186 metres. S.S.S. 69. Small practice area. *Green Fees:* £20.00 weekdays. *Eating facilities:* full catering and bar. *Visitors:* welcome weekdays and Thursdays

especially, must have Handicap Certificate. No casual visitors at weekends. *Society Meetings:* catered for by arrangement. Professional: S. Price (0633 413233). Secretary: D.J. Peak (0633 412029).

MONMOUTH. **Monmouth Golf Club,** Leasbrook Lane, Monmouth (Monmouth (0600) 712212). *Location:* turn left (signposted) one mile along A40 (Monmouth to Ross road). Undulating parkland. 18 holes, 5900 yards. *Green Fees:* weekdays £10.00; weekends and Bank Holidays £15.00 (inclusive of VAT). Weekly ticket (Monday/Friday inclusive) £35.00. *Eating facilities:* Clubhouse every day (except Mondays). *Visitors:* welcome, except weekends and Bank Holidays. *Society Meetings:* catered for upon application. Secretary: P.C. Harris (0600 712941).

MONMOUTH. **The Rolls of Monmouth Golf Club,** The Hendre, Monmouth NP5 4HG (0600 715353; Fax: 0600 713115). *Location:* four miles west of Monmouth on the B4233 Monmouth/Abergavenny road. Wooded, hilly parkland course on private estate. 18 holes, 6723 yards. S.S.S. 72. Practice area, practice net, putting green. *Green Fees:* on request. *Eating facilities:* full catering. *Visitors:* welcome any day. *Society Meetings:* welcome on any day including weekends. Secretary: J.D. Ross.

NANTYGLO. **West Monmouthshire Golf Club,** Pond Road, Nantyglo NP3 4YX (Brynmawr (0495) 310233). *Location:* Heads of the Valleys Road to Brynmawr, roundabout to Nantyglo, signposted. Mountain and heathland course. 18 holes, 6118 yards. S.S.S. 69. *Green Fees:* weekdays £10.00; Saturdays £12.00; Sundays £17.00; £2.00 reduction if playing with member except Saturdays. *Eating facilities:* 24 hours notice required. *Visitors:* welcome weekdays; by appointment Saturdays and Sundays. *Society Meetings:* catered for by appointment only. Secretary: Allan L. Offers (0495 303663).

NEWPORT. **Newport Golf Club,** Great Oak, Rogerstone, Newport NP1 9FX (Newport (0633) 892683). *Location:* four miles west of Newport, one and a half miles west of exit 27 of M4 (signposted Highcross), on B4591. Parkland. 18 holes, 6314 yards, 5830 metres. S.S.S. 71. Two practice areas. *Green Fees:* £30.00 weekdays, £40.00 weekends. *Eating facilities:* full dining facilities at club. *Visitors:* welcome weekdays without reservation. *Society Meetings:* catered for weekdays (except Tuesdays). Professional: Roy Skuse (0633 893271). Hon. Secretary: Allen David Jones (0633 892643 and 896794).

NEWPORT. **Tredegar Park Golf Club Ltd,** Bassaleg Road, Newport NP9 3PX (Newport (0633) 895219). *Location:* exit 27 M4, then via Western Avenue and Bassaleg Road. Parkland. 18 holes, 6097 yards, 5575

# FOR THE MUTUAL GUIDANCE OF GUEST AND HOST

Every year literally thousands of holidays, short-breaks and overnight stops are arranged through our guides, the vast majority without any problems at all. In a handful of cases, however, difficulties do arise about bookings, which often could have been prevented from the outset.

It is important to remember that when accommodation has been booked, both parties — guests and hosts — have entered into a form of contract. We hope that the following points will provide helpful guidance.

**GUESTS:** When enquiring about accommodation, be as precise as possible. Give exact dates, numbers in your party and the ages of any children. State the number and type of rooms wanted and also what catering you require — bed and breakfast, full board, etc. Make sure that the position about evening meals is clear — and about pets, reductions for children or any other special points.

Read our reviews carefully to ensure that the proprietors you are going to contact can supply what you want. Ask for a letter confirming all arrangements, if possible.

If you have to cancel, do so as soon as possible. Proprietors do have the right to retain deposits and under certain circumstances to charge for cancelled holidays if adequate notice is not given and they cannot re-let the accommodation.

**HOSTS:** Give details about your facilities and about any special conditions. Explain your deposit system clearly and arrangements for cancellations, charges, etc, and whether or not your terms include VAT.

If for any reason you are unable to fulfil an agreed booking without adequate notice, you may be under an obligation to arrange alternative suitable accommodation or to make some form of compensation.

While every effort is made to ensure accuracy, we regret that FHG Publications cannot accept responsibility for errors, omissions or misrepresentation in our entries or any consequences thereof. Prices in particular should be checked because we go to press early. We will follow up complaints but cannot act as arbiters or agents for either party.

metres. S.S.S. 70. Two practice holes. *Green Fees:* weekdays £22.00; weekends and Bank Holidays £27.50. *Eating facilities:* lounge bar – 19th hole – and restaurant. *Visitors:* welcome with letter of introduction or membership card. *Society Meetings:* bona fide members of golf clubs catered for. Professional: M.L. Morgan (0633 894517). Secretary: Mr R.T. Howell (0633 894433).

PONTYPOOL. **Pontypool Golf Club,** Lasgarn Lane, Trevethin, Pontypool NP4 8TR (Pontypool (0495) 763655). *Location:* Pontypool A4042 to St. Cadoc's Church, Trevethin. Undulating hillside course, with mountain turf and fine views. 18 holes, 6046 yards. S.S.S. 69. Practice area. *Green Fees:* £13.00 weekdays, £20.00 weekends and Bank Holidays.

*Eating facilities:* diningroom and bar snacks. *Visitors:* welcome with Handicap Certificates. *Society Meetings:* catered for by arrangement. Professional: Jim Howard (0495 755544). Secretary: Mrs E. Wilce (0495 763655).

RHYMNEY. **Tredegar and Rhymney Golf Club,** Cwmtysswg, Rhymney NP2 3BQ (0685 840743). *Location:* junction of A4048 and A465 Heads of the Valley road. Mountain course. 9 holes, 5564 yards. S.S.S. 68. *Green Fees:* weekdays £10.00 (with member £7.50); weekends and Bank Holidays £12.50 (with member £10.00). *Eating facilities:* bar snacks. *Visitors:* welcome without reservation. *Society Meetings:* catered for without reservation. Secretary: V. Davies (049525 6096).

# Gwynedd

ABERDOVEY. **Aberdovey Golf Club,** Aberdovey LL35 0RT (0654 767210). *Location:* west end of Aberdovey on A493, adjacent to railway station. Championship links. 18 holes, 6445 yards. S.S.S. 71. Practice area. *Green Fees:* on application. *Eating facilities:* restaurant and bar. *Visitors:* welcome on production of Handicap Certificate. *Society Meetings:* catered for by prior arrangement (not August or Bank Holidays). Professional: J. Davies (0654 767602). Secretary: J.M. Griffiths (0654 767493).

ANGLESEY. **Baron Hill Golf Club,** Beaumaris, Anglesey (Beaumaris (0248) 810231). *Location:* turn left on approach to Beaumaris from Menai Bridge on A545. Parkland. 9 holes, 5062 metres. S.S.S. 67. *Green Fees:* weekdays £10.00, £5.00 with a member. Weekly £40.00. *Eating facilities:* clubhous destroyed by fire – hope to resume full facility in near future. *Visitors:*

welcome, competitions most Sundays, tee reserved for ladies on Tuesdays 10.30 – 12.30. *Society Meetings:* welcome, prior arrangement with secretary. Secretary: A. Pleming.

ANGLESEY. **Bull Bay Golf Club Ltd,** Bull Bay, Amlwch, Anglesey LL68 9RY (Amlwch (0407) 830213). *Location:* A5025 coast road north west of Amlwch. Seaside links. 18 holes, 6160 yards. S.S.S. 70. Practice ground and putting green. *Green Fees:* £15.00 per day weekdays, £20.00 per day weekends (including Fridays). Discount for parties of 12 and over. *Eating facilities:* bar and bar snacks, dining room. *Visitors:* welcome, competitions permitting. *Society Meetings:* catered for by arrangement. Professional: Neil Dunroe (0407 831188). Secretary: Rennie Tickle (0407 830960).

BALA. **Bala Golf Club,** Penlan, Bala (0678 520359). *Location:* turn right before coming to Bala Lake on the main Bala-Dolgellau road. Upland course with superb views in the Snowdonia National Park. 10 holes, 4970 yards, 4512 metres. S.S.S. 64. *Green Fees:* weekdays £10.00; weekends and Bank Holidays £10.00 per day. Weekly tickets £30.00. *Eating facilities:* bar with snacks available. *Visitors:* welcome all year, some restrictions on Bank Holidays and weekends. Snooker table and small golf shop. *Society Meetings:* very welcome by prior arrangement. Professional: David Larvin (visiting). Secretary: Martin Wright (0678 520057 evenings).

BANGOR. **St. Deiniol Golf Club,** Penybryn, Bangor LL57 1PX (Bangor (0248) 353098). *Location:* at A5/A55 intersection, follow A5122 for one mile to eastern outskirts of Bangor. Parkland course with magnificent views. 18 holes, 5545 yards, 5068 metres. S.S.S. 67. *Green Fees:* £10.00 per day weekdays; £15.00 weekends and Bank Holidays. *Eating facilities:* two bars; full catering Mondays excepted. *Visitors:* welcome without reservation, restrictions at weekends. *Society Meetings:* welcome by prior arrangement. Secretary: J.R. Harries.

BETWS-Y-COED. **Betws-y-Coed Golf Club,** Betws-y-Coed (Betws-y-Coed (06902) 710556). *Location:* turn north off A5 in village. Parkland course on valley floor of River Conwy. 9 holes, 4996 yards. S.S.S. 64. *Green Fees:* £12.50 weekdays, £17.50 weekends. *Eating facilities:* catering, bar 12 – 2pm and from 4.30pm. *Visitors:* no restrictions provided there are no club competitions. *Society Meetings:* catered for. Secretary: G.B. Archer (069-03 202).

CAERNARFON. **Caernarfon Golf Club,** Aberforeshore, Llanfaglan, Caernarfon (0286 3783). *Location:* two miles from town along the Menai Straits. Parkland course in superb sea and mountain setting. 18 holes, 5869 yards. S.S.S. 69. *Green Fees:* weekdays £15.00; weekends £18.00. Special rates for visiting parties, weekdays only. *Eating facilities:* excellent catering and bar facilities. *Visitors:* welcome Monday to Friday. *Society Meetings:* welcome, subject to pre-arranged bookings. Secretary: J.O. Morgan (0286 78359).

CONWY. **Conwy (Caernarvonshire) Golf Club,** Morfa, Conwy LL32 8ER (Aberconwy (0492) 593400). *Location:* quarter-of-a-mile west of Conwy off A55. Seaside links. 18 holes, 6901 yards. S.S.S. 73. Practice facilities. *Green Fees:* weekdays £18.00; weekends and Bank Holidays £23.00. Weekly ticket £72.00 (Monday to Friday). *Eating facilities:* available except Monday evening and all day Tuesday. *Visitors:* welcome with reservation, restrictions at weekends. *Society Meetings:* catered for on application to Secretary. Professional: Peter Lees (0492 593225). Secretary: E.C. Roberts (0492 592423).

CRICCIETH. **Criccieth Golf Club,** Ednyfed Hill, Criccieth (Criccieth (0766) 522154). *Location:* in High Street (A497) turn right past Memorial Hall, keep going up lane to Club. 18 holes, 5755 yards. S.S.S. 68. *Green Fees:* £8.00 weekdays; £10.00 weekends. *Eating facili-*

*ties:* light meals available April to September. *Visitors:* welcome without reservation. *Society Meetings:* catered for with prior reservation. Secretary: M.G. Hamilton (0766 522697).

DOLGELLAU. **Dolgellau Golf Club,** Ffordd Pencefn, Dolgellau (0341 422603). *Location:* half-a-mile from town centre. 9 holes, 4671 yards. S.S.S. 63. *Green Fees:* weekdays £12.00; weekends £14.00. *Eating facilities:* bar and catering facilities available. *Visitors:* welcome without reservation. *Society Meetings:* catered for. Secretary: H.M. Edwards (0341 422603).

FFESTINIOG. **Ffestiniog Golf Club,** Y Cefn, Ffestiniog (0766 762637). *Location:* located on B4391, one mile from Ffestiniog village. Upland course. 9 holes, 5032 yards. S.S.S. 66. *Green Fees:* approximately £6.00. *Eating facilities:* available by prior arrangement. *Visitors:* welcome at any time, some restrictions mainly at weekends during club competitions. *Society Meetings:* by prior arrangement. Secretary: Andrew M. Roberts (0766 831829).

HARLECH. **The Royal St. David's Golf Club,** Harlech LL46 2UB (0766 780203). *Location:* A496 lower Harlech road. Seaside links. Championship course. 18 holes, 6427 yards. S.S.S. 71. Large practice ground. *Green Fees:* weekdays £20.00 per day; weekends £25.00 per day. *Eating facilities:* full catering and bar facilities available. *Visitors:* must be members of bona fide golf clubs with handicap – booking advisable. *Society Meetings:* catered for by prior arrangement. Professional: John Barnett (0766 780857). Secretary: R.I. Jones (0766 780361).

LLANDUDNO. **Llandudno Golf Club (Maesdu) Ltd,** Hospital Road, Llandudno LL30 1HU (0492 76016). *Location:* OLlandudno General Hospital. A55 and then A470. Parkland. 18 holes, 6513 yards. S.S.S. 72. *Green Fees:* weekdays £18.00 per day; weekends and Bank Holidays £24.00 per day. *Eating facilities:* full catering, bar (large) available. *Visitors:* welcome everyday, tee reservations for members. *Society Meetings:* must be booked, catered for. Professional: S. Boulden (0492 75195). Secretary: George Dean (0492 76450).

# ESPLANADE HOTEL

### Glan-y-Mor Parade, Promenade, Llandudno
### Tel: (0492) 860300 (5 lines) Fax: (0492) 860418

SPECIAL ATTENTION GIVEN TO GOLFING PARTIES
MEMBERSHIPS FOR NORTH WALES GOLF CLUB

Premier seafront position. Ideally situated for town and leisure facilities. 60 rooms all with bathroom and toilet en-suite, tea/coffee making facilities, colour TV, radio, intercom and baby listening service, direct dial telephones. Central heating throughout. Car Park. Fully licensed. Lift. Small ballroom. Open all year. Christmas and New Year festivities. Spring and Autumn breaks.

---

AA ★★★ RAC

## The *'Risboro'* Hotel
### Clement Avenue, LLANDUDNO, Gwynedd LL30 2ED
### Telephone: (0492) 876343 Fax: (0492) 879881
### *EXCELLENT GOLFING WEEKEND OR MIDWEEK BREAKS*

Privately owned 65 bedroom Hotel with large HEATED INDOOR SWIMMING POOL AND HEALTH COMPLEX INCLUDING MULTI GYM. PERFECT base for four 18 HOLE GOLF COURSES – OTHERS ONLY HALF AN HOUR. The Hotel has every requirement for your comfort with our well known Chef Cuisine. Reduction in green fees will be made available from Hotel for ALL COURSES. Please phone for brochure. Play ALL the courses and enjoy magnificent scenery. Enjoy our leisure amenities and have a healthy break.

### *"AFTER GOLF WHAT SHALL WE DO?!!!"*
Swim, play snooker, dance, relax in comfortable bar lounges, wine and dine the night away, work out in the gym, an hour in the health complex, watch satellite TV.
### *"ALL THE ABOVE AVAILABLE TO YOU IN THE RISBORO"*

---

WTB
Commended

AA ***
RAC ***

# GOGARTH ABBEY HOTEL
### West Shore, Llandudno, Gwynedd LL30 2QY

The Hotel itself is situated on the quieter West Shore of Llandudno. Luxuriously appointed, the Gogarth Abbey offers all facilities and amenities for your comfort. The Hotel has its own indoor heated swimming pool, solarium, sauna and games area, and there is ample private parking in the Hotel grounds. Three Championship Courses – MAES DU, NORTH WALES and CONWY – are all within a radius of three miles from the Gogarth Abbey.

**Fax: (0492) 879881**          **Telephone: (0492) 876211**

---

All bedrooms are en-suite with direct dial telephone, radio, satellite TV and beverage tray. Guests have use of our Health and Fitness Centre during their stay, which we are certain you will find welcoming after a day's Golf. The centre has swimming pool, sauna, steam room, solarium, cardio-vascular gym, snooker room and physiotherapy unit. Special breaks all year round. Call for details and a brochure.

*The Imperial Hotel* Llandudno

WTB
Commended
AA ★★★ RAC

The Promenade, Llandudno, Gwynedd, North Wales LL30 1AP
Telephone: 0492 877466 Fax: 0492 878043

LLANDUDNO. **North Wales Golf Club Ltd,** 72 Bryniau Road, West Shore, Llandudno LL30 2DZ (Llandudno (0492) 875325). *Location:* one-and-a-half miles from Llandudno town centre on West Shore. Seaside links. 18 holes, 6132 yards, 5580 metres. S.S.S. 69. *Green Fees:* weekdays £17.00 per day, weekends and Bank Holidays £22.00 per day. Inclusive package available November to March. *Eating facilities:* full bar and catering facilities. *Visitors:* welcome with reservation after 9.45am. Some other time restrictions. Current Handicap Certificate required. *Society Meetings:* catered for by arrangement. Professional: R.A. Bradbury (0492 876878). Secretary: G.D. Harwood (0492 875325).

LLANDUDNO. **Rhos-on-Sea Residential Golf Club,** Penrhyn Bay, Llandudno LL30 3PU (Llandudno (0492) 549100). *Location:* A55 to Colwyn Bay follow signs to Rhos-on-Sea, one mile past Rhos-on-Sea on coast road in Penrhyn Bay. Flat seaside parkland course. 18 holes, 6064 yards, S.S.S. 69. *Green Fees:* £15.00 weekdays; £20.00 weekends. *Eating facilities:* available, bar meals 12 – 2pm, teas, coffees, snacks available all day. Evening meals by arrangement. Licensed bar open 11am – 3pm lunch, 5.30pm – 11pm evenings; Sundays 12 – 2pm lunch, 7pm – 10.30pm evenings. *Visitors:* all welcome any time, prior booking required particularly weekends. 18 bedrooms, two full size snooker tables, small TV lounge. Two £100 jackpot fruit machines. *Society Meetings:* catered for. Professional: Mr Mike Greenough (0492 548115). Secretary: Mr Graham J. Robinson (0492 544551). New Stewards: Mr and Mrs J. John.

LLANFAIRFECHAN. **Llanfairfechan Golf Club,** Llannerch Road, Llanfairfechan LL33 0EB (0248 680144). *Location:* signposted off old A55, 300 yards west of traffic lights. Hillside parkland. 9 holes, 3119 yards. S.S.S. 57. *Green Fees:* weekdays £6.00; weekends £10.00. *Eating facilities:* no eating facilities, bar open weekends and weekday evenings. *Visitors:* welcome anytime except Sundays. *Society Meetings:* by arrangement, weekdays only in Summer. Secretary: M.J. Charlesworth (0248 680524).

LLANGEFNI. **Llangefni Public Golf Course,** Llangefni, Isle of Anglesey. Short, parkland course. 9 holes, 1467 yards, 1342 metres. S.S.S. 28. Practice net. *Green Fees:* information not provided. Reduced rates

Juniors and OAP's. *Eating facilities:* light refreshments only. *Visitors:* welcome at all times, no booking. Golf equipment available for hire. Professional: Paul Lovell (0248 722193).

MORFA BYCHAN. **Porthmadog Golf Club,** Morfa Bychan, Porthmadog LL49 9UU (0766 512037). *Location:* turn in Porthmadog High Street at Woolworths towards Black Rock Sands, club on left hand side of road one mile west. Part parkland, part seaside links. 18 holes, 6240 yards. S.S.S. 70. Practice area. *Green Fees:* £15.00 weekdays, £20.00 weekends, £25.00 Bank Holidays. *Eating facilities:* new clubhouse with much enlarged dining facilities. Restaurant lunches, teas and evening meals by arrangement. Bar snacks. *Visitors:* welcome, no restrictions except for competitions. *Society Meetings:* catered for by prior arrangement. Bookings via Match Secretary. Professional: Peter Bright (0766 513828). Secretary: Glyn Humphreys. Match Secretary: Dennis Morrow (0766 514286 evenings).

NEFYN. **Nefyn and District Golf Club,** Golf Road, Morfa Nefyn, Pwllheli LL53 6DA (Nefyn (0758) 720218). *Location:* north coast Lleyn Peninsula, two miles west of Nefyn, 20 miles west of Caernarfon. Seaside course. 18 holes, 6335 yards. S.S.S. 71. Practice area. *Green Fees:* weekdays £16.00 per round, £20.00 per day; weekends and Bank Holidays £22.50 per round, £30.00 per day. Reduction for parties over eight. *Eating facilities:* full restaurant facilities and two bars. *Visitors:* welcome without reservation, except club competition days. Billiards room available. *Society Meetings:* catered for by arrangement with Secretary. Professional: J.R. Pilkington (0758 720218). Secretary: Lt Col R.W. Parry (0758 720966).

PENMAENMAWR. **Penmaenmawr Golf Club,** Cae Maen Pavilion, Conwy Old Road, Penmaenmawr LL34 6RD (Penmaenmawr (0492) 623330). *Location:* situated at the foot of Sychnant Pass between Conwy and Penmaenmawr (A55). Undulating parkland with panoramic views. 9 holes (alternate tees), 5223 yards. S.S.S. 66. Practice putting green. *Green Fees:* £12.00 weekdays, £16.00 weekends. *Eating facilities:* available by arrangement; bar open daily. *Visitors:* welcome subject to availability of tees. *Society Meetings:* welcome except Saturdays and by arrangement. Secretary: Mrs J.E. Jones (0492 623330).

PWLLHELI. **Abersoch Golf Club,** Golf Road, Abersoch, Pwllheli (0758 812622). *Location:* on left beyond village along the shore. Parkland and seaside links course. 18 holes, 5881 yards. S.S.S. 69. *Green Fees:* £15.00. *Eating facilities:* catering, bar. *Visitors:* welcome, booking required. Shop. *Society Meetings:* catered for. Secretary: Brian Guest.

PWLLHELI. **Pwllheli Golf Club,** Golf Road, Pwllheli LL53 5PS. *Location:* A499 from Caernarvon (20 miles). Parkland/seaside links. 18 holes, 6091 yards, 5571 metres. S.S.S. 69. Two practice areas and putting green. *Green Fees:* £16.00 weekdays; £18.00 weekends. Reductions for parties. *Eating facilities:* two large lounge bars and diningroom. Steward: (0758 612520). *Visitors:* welcome without reservation. *Society Meetings:* catered for by prior arrangement. Professional: G.D. Verity (0758 612520). Secretary: R. Eric Williams (0758 612520).

RHOSNEIGR. **Anglesey Golf Club Ltd,** Station Road, Rhosneigr, Anglesey (Rhosneigr (0407) 810219). *Location:* turn south off A5 between Gwalchmai and Bryngwram onto A4080. In about three miles turn right at Hanfaelog church about one mile from course. Links course. 18 holes, 5713 yards. S.S.S. 68. *Green Fees:* £10.50 weekdays, £12.50 weekends. *Eating facilities:* bar meals and restaurant. *Visitors:* no restriction – preferably after 10am and 1.30pm. *Society Meetings:* catered for, reservation advised. Professional: Paul Lovell (0407 811202). Manager: Mr Arfon Jones (0407 811202).

TREARDDUR BAY. **Holyhead Golf Club,** Lom Carreg Fawr, Trearddur Bay, Anglesey (0204 762119). *Location:* near Holyhead. 18 holes, 6058 yards. S.S.S. 70. *Green Fees:* weekdays £17.00; weekends £20.00. Five day ticket £68.00 (Monday-Friday). *Eating facilities:* all catering facilities provided. *Visitors:* welcome, must be members of recognised golf clubs. *Society Meetings:* catered for if members of bona fide golf clubs. Dormy house accommodation available for up to 12. Professional: Paul Capper (0407 762022). Secretary: D. Entwistle (0204 763279).

# Powys

BRECON. **Brecon Golf Club,** Newton Park, Brecon (Brecon (0874) 2004). *Location:* on A40 west of town, half a mile from centre. 9 holes, 5218 yards. S.S.S. 66. *Green Fees:* £8.00 at all times. *Visitors:* welcome without reservation. *Society Meetings:* catered for. Secretary: D.H.E. Roderick.

BUILTH WELLS. **Builth Wells Golf Club,** Golf Club Lane, Builth Wells LD2 3NF (Builth Wells (0982) 552737). *Location:* off A483, Builth Wells. Parkland. 18 holes, 5376 yards. S.S.S. 67. Practice area. *Green Fees:* £14.00 weekdays, £18.00 weekends and Bank Holidays. Five day ticket £50.00, seven day ticket £60.00. *Eating facilities:* restaurant (not Mondays), bar. *Visitors:* limited only by tournaments. Handicap Certificate required. *Society Meetings:* size limited by catering facilities. Professional: Bill Evans (0982 553293). Secretary: R.A. Jones (0982 553296).

BUILTH WELLS. **Rhosgoch Golf Club,** Rhosgoch, Builth Wells LD2 3JY (0497 851251). *Location:* near Hay-on-Wye. Parkland course. 9 holes 4842 yards. S.S.S. 64. *Green Fees:* £7.00 weekdays, £10.00 weekends. *Eating facilities:* bar/restaurant meals, two bars. *Visitors:* welcome anytime. Accommodation available. *Society Meetings:* anytime. Secretary: C. Dance (054422 286).

CRADOC. **Cradoc Golf Club,** Penoyre Park, Cradoc, Brecon LD3 9LP (Brecon (0874) 623658). *Location:* about two miles north of the market town of Brecon, off B4520 Upper Chapel Road (signposted) past Brecon Cathedral. Attractive parkland course situated in the Brecon Beacons National Park. 18 holes, 6301 yards. S.S.S. 71. Separate practice ground. *Green Fees:* £15.00 weekdays, £18.00 weekends. *Eating facilities:* full catering facilities daily except Mondays. *Visitors:* welcome daily but restricted on Sundays when must be playing with a member. *Society Meetings:* welcome during weekdays. Professional: Douglas Beattie (0874 625524). Secretary: G.S.W. Davies. Host of 1982 Welsh Stroke Play Championships. Home of the Welsh Brewers Champion of Champions Tournament.

CRICKHOWELL. **Old Rectory Hotel and Golf Club,** Llangattock, Crickhowell NP8 1PH (Crickhowell (0873) 810373). *Location:* Crickhowell is between Abergavenny and Brecon. Course is on a hill with spectacular views. 9 holes, 2878 yards. S.S.S. 54. *Green Fees:* information not provided. *Eating facilities:* restaurant, bar meals, two bars. *Visitors:* welcome at all times. Accommodation available, outdoor swimming pool.

KNIGHTON. **Knighton Golf Club,** Ffryd Wood, Knighton LD7 1DG (Knighton (0547) 528646). *Location:* on ring road of town, turn left off Ffryd Road. Hill course, wooded. 9 holes, 5320 yards, 5014 metres. S.S.S. 66. *Green Fees:* weekdays £8.00; weekends £10.00. *Eating facilities:* bar open in evenings, Saturday and Sunday lunch hour. *Visitors:* welcome every day except Saturday and Sunday afternoons. *Society Meetings:* catered for by arrangement. Secretary: E.J.P. Bright (0547 528684).

LLANDRINDOD WELLS. **Llandrindod Wells Golf Club,** Llandrindod Wells (Llandrindod Wells (0597) 822010). *Location:* well signposted from A483 and centre of town. Hill top course with beautiful views. 18 holes, 5687 yards. S.S.S. 68. *Green Fees:* £15.00 weekdays, £18.00 weekends. *Eating facilities:* every day (except Tuesday), order in advance. *Visitors:* welcome, occasional restrictions when course is closed for special functions. *Society Meetings:* catered for, three months' notice required for weekends. Secretary/Manager: Mr F.T. James (0597 823873).

LLANIDLOES. **St. Idloes Golf Club,** Pen-yr-Rhallt, Llanidloes (05512 2559). *Location:* take Trefeglwys Road from Llanidloes – one mile – turn left at cottage on top of hill. Slightly undulating terrain. 9 holes, 5300 yards. S.S.S. 66. *Green Fees:* information not provided. *Eating facilities:* full menu available. *Visitors:* welcome without reservation. *Society Meetings:* available Monday to Friday throughout the year. Secretary: D.N. Jones, "Hillcrest", 40 Caegwyn, Llanidloes (05512 3459).

# PUBLISHER'S NOTE

While every effort is made to ensure accuracy, we regret that FHG Publications cannot accept responsibility for errors, omissions or misrepresentation in our entries or any consequences thereof. Prices in particular should be checked because we go to press early. We will follow up complaints, but cannot act as arbiters or agents for either party.

MACHYNLLETH. **Machynlleth Golf Club,** Ffordd Drenewydd, Machynlleth SY20 8UH (0654 702000). *Location:* A489 from Newtown, left hand turn before the speed restriction sign on entering Machynlleth. Undulating meadowland course. 9 holes, 5726 yards, 5285 metres. S.S.S. 67. Small practice area. *Green Fees:* weekdays £12.00; weekends £15.00. £7.00 with a member. *Eating facilities:* by arrangement. Bar. *Visitors:* welcome except during competition days. *Society Meetings:* welcome. Secretary: Gary Holdsworth (0654 703264).

NEWTOWN. **St. Giles Golf Club,** Pool Road, Newtown (Newtown (0686) 625844). *Location:* convenient to town centre, quarter-of-a-mile on Welshpool Road from Newtown. Pleasant riverside course. 9 holes, 5864 yards. S.S.S. 68. *Green Fees:* weekdays £10.00 per day, weekends and Bank Holidays £12.50 per day.

£50.00 per week. *Eating facilities:* bar and catering facilities, no catering on Mondays except Bank Holidays. *Visitors:* welcome, with reservation Saturday afternoons and Sunday mornings. Handicap Certificate required. Golf shop and Professional. *Society Meetings:* catered for. Secretary: Mr T.A. Hall.

WELSHPOOL. **Welshpool Golf Club,** Golfa Hill, Welshpool (Castle Caereinion (093 883) 249). *Location:* A458 West from Welshpool 4 miles signpost on right at junction with main road. Rather hilly but very beautiful scenery. 18 holes, 5708 yards. S.S.S. 69. *Green Fees:* £10.00 weekdays, £15.00 weekends. Half price when playing with member. *Eating facilities:* open most of the day for food and drink. *Visitors:* welcome, booking advisable for weekend golf. *Society Meetings:* by arrangement. Secretary: D.B. Pritchard (0938 552215).

# Golf in Northern Ireland

## Antrim

ANTRIM. **Massereene Golf Club,** 51 Lough Road, Antrim BT41 4DQ (Antrim (08494) 29293). *Location:* one mile S.W. of town, 3 miles from Aldergrove Airport, situated alongside the shores of Lough Neagh. 18 holes, 6440 yards. S.S.S. 72. *Green Fees:* weekdays £16.00; weekends £20.00. *Eating facilities:* Full catering facilities 12 noon till 9.00pm. *Visitors:* welcome. *Society Meetings:* catered for. Secretary: Mrs Marie Agnew (08494 28096). Professional: Jim Smyth (08494 64074).

BALLYCASTLE. **Ballycastle Golf Club,** Cushendall Road, Ballycastle (Ballycastle (02657) 62536). *Location:* approximately 50 miles along the coast road west of Larne Harbour. Seaside links/undulating. 18 holes, 5662 yards, 5177 metres. S.S.S. 68. *Green Fees:* (1992) weekdays £11.00 (with member £6.00),

weekends and Public Holidays £16.00 (with member £8.00). *Eating facilities:* catering by arrangement. *Visitors:* welcome, best days during the week, no particular restrictions. *Society Meetings:* by arrangement. Professional: T. Stewart (02657 62506). Hon. Secretaries: T.J. Sheehan and M.E. Page (02657 62536).

BALLYCLARE. **Ballyclare Golf Club,** 25 Springvale Road, Ballyclare BT39 9JW (Ballyclare (09603) 42352). *Location:* two miles north of Ballyclare. Parkland, lakes and river. 18 holes, 5840 metres. S.S.S. 71. *Green Fees:* weekdays £12.00; weekends £18.00. *Eating facilities:* catering available. *Visitors:* welcome weekdays except Thursday. *Society Meetings:* catered for. Secretary: Harry McConnell (09603 22696).

BALLYMENA. **Ballymena Golf Club,** 128 Raceview Road, Ballymena (Ballymena (0266) 861207). *Location:* two miles east of town on A42. Flat/parkland. 18 holes, 5068 metres. S.S.S. 67. *Green Fees:* weekday £11.00 (£7.00 with a member); weekends £13.50 (£8.50 with a member). *Eating facilities:* restaurant and bar snacks. *Visitors:* welcome at all times, however Saturdays are usually extremely busy (club competitions). *Society Meetings:* catered for except Tuesdays and Saturdays. Professional: J. Gallagher (0266 861652). Secretary: M.J. MacCrory (0266 861487).

BELFAST. **Cliftonville Golf Club,** 44 Westland Road, Belfast BT14 6NH (Belfast (0232) 744158). Parkland with rivers bisecting three fairways. 9 holes, 6210 yards, 5672 metres. S.S.S. 70. Practice fairway and nets. *Green Fees:* weekdays £12.00, playing with a member £8.00; weekends £15.00, playing with a member £10.00. Special rates – 25% discount for parties of 20 or over. *Eating facilities:* bars, catering on request. *Visitors:* no visitors after 5pm weekdays, until 6pm Saturdays and after 12 noon Sundays. *Society Meetings:* very welcome, especially by arrangement. Hon. Secretary: Martin Henderson (0232 746595).

BELFAST. **Dunmurry Golf Club,** 91 Dunmurry Lane, Dunmurry, Belfast BT17 9JS (Belfast (0232) 621402). *Location:* one mile off M1 (Dunmurry cut-off). Parkland – partially wooded. 18 holes, 5333 metres. S.S.S. 68. Practice area. *Green Fees:* weekdays £13.00; weekends £17.00. *Eating facilities:* restaurant and bar snacks, every day. *Visitors:* welcome except Friday and Saturday. *Society Meetings:* catered for. Professional: Paul Leonard (0232 621314). Secretary: Mr C. Mackerell (0232 610834).

BELFAST. **Fortwilliam Golf Club,** Downview Avenue, Belfast BT15 4EZ (0232 776798). *Location:* one mile Fortwilliam Junction M2. Parkland. 18 holes, 5933 yards. S.S.S. 68. *Green Fees:* £12.00 weekdays, £17.00 weekends and Public Holidays. *Eating facilities:* available. *Visitors:* welcome most days. *Society Meetings:* catered for Tuesdays and Thursdays. Professional: Peter Hanna (0232 770980). Secretary: R.J. Campbell (0232 370770).

BELFAST. **Gilnahirk Golf Club,** Manns Corner, Upper Braniel Road, Castlereagh, Belfast (0232 448351). *Location:* two miles from city centre, east Belfast. Parkland. 9 holes, 2699 metres. S.S.S. 68. Putting green. *Green Fees:* £3.30 weekdays for 9 holes; £4.15 weekends for 9 holes. *Visitors:* welcome, municipal course. Professional: Mr K. Gray (0232 448477). Secretary: Mr H. Moore (0232 659653).

BELFAST. **Malone Golf Club,** 240 Upper Malone Road, Dunmurry, Belfast BT17 9LB (Belfast (0232) 612695). Parkland, wooded course with large lake. 18 holes, 6476 yards. S.S.S. 71. 9 holes, 2895 yards. S.S.S. 72. Two practice grounds. *Green Fees:* £22.00 weekdays (except Wednesday when fee is £25.00); £25.00 weekends and Bank Holidays. *Visitors:* welcome weekdays except Wednesdays. After 5pm Saturdays and time sheet on Sundays. Dress code observed on course and in clubhouse. *Society Meetings:* Mondays and Thursdays. Professional: Peter O'Hagan (0232 614917). Secretary: Mr T. Aitken (0232 612758).

BUSHMILLS. **Bushmills Golf Club,** Bushfoot Road, Portballintrae, Bushmills BT57 8RR (Bushmills (02657) 31969). *Location:* one mile north of Bushmills. Seaside course. 9 holes, 5812 yards. S.S.S. 67. Pitch and putt. *Green Fees:* £10.00 weekdays (£6.00 playing with a

member). *Eating facilities:* bar and restaurant available. *Visitors:* welcome weekdays, but must be with members at weekends. *Society Meetings:* welcome weekdays, not weekends. Secretary/Manager: J. Knox Thompson.

CARRICKFERGUS. **Carrickfergus Golf Club,** 35 North Road, Carrickfergus BT38 8LP (Carrickfergus (09603) 51203). *Location:* north road, one mile from main shore road. Fairly flat parkland course, partially wooded. 18 holes, 5752 yards. S.S.S. 68. *Green Fees:* weekdays £12.00; weekends £17.00. *Eating facilities:* full catering and bar facilities. *Visitors:* welcome weekdays. *Society Meetings:* catered for on weekdays but not after 1pm on Fridays. Professional: Ray Stevenson (09603 51803). Hon. Secretary: I.D. Jardine (09603 63713).

CARRICKFERGUS. **Greenisland Golf Club,** 156 Upper Road, Greenisland, Carrickfergus BT38 8RW (Whiteabbey (0232) 862236). 9 holes, 5596 metres. S.S.S. 69. *Green Fees:* weekdays £10.00, Sundays £12.00. *Eating facilities:* lunches at club, order in advance. *Visitors:* welcome except before 5.30pm Saturdays. Secretary: J. Wyness.

CARRICKFERGUS. **Whitehead Golf Club,** McCrae's Brae, Whitehead, Carrickfergus (Whitehead (09603) 53792). *Location:* Whitehead 15 miles from Belfast, 10 miles from Larne. 18 holes, 6362 yards. S.S.S. 71. *Green Fees:* information not provided. *Eating facilities:* by arrangement with Steward. *Visitors:* welcome Monday to Friday, weekends with a member only. *Society Meetings:* by prior arrangement. Secretary/Manager: J.M. Niblock (09603 53631 9am – 1pm).

CUSHENDALL. **Cushendall Golf Club,** Shore Road, Cushendall (Cushendall (02667) 71318). *Location:* 25 miles north on Antrim coast road from Larne Harbour. Seaside – wooded. River comes into play in seven out of nine holes. 9 holes, 4678 yards, 4030 metres. S.S.S. 63. *Green Fees:* weekdays £9.00 per day, weekends and Bank Holidays £11.00; £3.00 concession if playing with member. *Eating facilities:* normal bar hours – by arrangement with caterers. *Visitors:* welcome without reservation, time sheet in operation on Sundays. *Society Meetings:* by arrangement. Hon. Secretary: Shaun McLaughlin (0266 73366).

LARNE. **Cairndhu Golf Club Ltd,** 192 Coast Road, Ballygally, Larne BT40 2QG (0574 583248). *Location:* four miles north of Larne. Parkland course. 18 holes, 6112 yards, 5598 metres. S.S.S. 69. Practice area. *Green Fees:* £11.00 weekdays; £17.00 weekends. *Eating facilities:* dining and bar facilities available. *Visitors:* welcome except Saturdays. *Society Meetings:* welcome. Professional: R. Walker (0574 583417). Secretary: Mrs Josephine Robinson (0574 583324).

LARNE. **Larne Golf Club,** 54 Ferris Bay Road, Islandmagee, Larne BT40 3RT (Islandmagee (09603) 82228). *Location:* six miles north of Whitehead on Browns Bay Road. Part links, part parkland. 9 holes, 6066 yards. S.S.S. 69. Practice ground. *Green Fees:* weekdays £8.00; weekends £12.00. With a member

50% off. *Eating facilities:* two lounges, diningroom. *Visitors:* welcome Mondays to Thursdays, avoid Fridays and Saturdays, Sundays by application. *Society Meetings:* welcome on application. Secretary: J.B. Stewart.

LISBURN. **Lisburn Golf Club,** Blaris Lodge, 68 Eglantine Road, Lisburn BT27 5QR (0846 677216; Fax: 0846 603608). *Location:* three miles south of Lisburn on A1. Parkland. 18 holes, 6101 metres. S.S.S. 72. Practice area. *Green Fees:* £18.00 weekdays; weekends with members only. *Eating facilities:* bar and restaurant. *Visitors:* welcome weekdays, Tuesdays Ladies have preference. Saturday after 5.30pm only, Sundays with member only. Snooker room. *Society Meetings:* catered for Mondays, Thursdays and Fridays. Professional: B.R. Campbell (0846 677217). Secretary: G. Graham (0846 677216).

NEWTOWNABBEY. **Ballyearl Golf and Leisure Centre,** 585 Doagh Road, Newtownabbey BT36 8RZ (0232 848287). *Location:* six miles north of Belfast on M2, then main road to Larne, first right onto Doagh Road. Parkland. 9 holes, 2402 yards, 2196 metres. Par 3. 36 bay floodlit driving range. *Green Fees:* weekdays adult £3.00, Junior £2.00, Senior Citizen £1.50; weekends adult £4.00, Junior £3.00, Senior Citizen £2.00. *Eating facilities:* private bar, can be signed in. *Visitors:* no restrictions – pay and play. Professionals: Jim Robinson and Karl O'Donnell (0232 840899). Secretary: Alan Bevan.

PORTRUSH. **Rathmore Golf Club,** Bushmills Road, Portrush BT56 8JG (0265 822285). *Location:* north east coast – six miles from Coleraine, beside roundabout on road to Bushmills. Flat seaside links. 18 holes, 6273 yards. S.S.S. 71. *Green Fees:* £12.00 weekdays; £16.00 weekends. *Eating facilities:* bar but no eating facilities. *Visitors:* Saturday and Sunday 1.30 to 2.30pm, Monday to Friday no restrictions except Tuesday after 11am September to March. *Society Meetings:* must register at Royal Portrush Golf Club and green fees paid before commencement of play. Professional: Dai Stevenson (R.P.G.C.) (0265 823335). Secretary: Derek Ross Williamson (0265 822996).

PORTRUSH. **Royal Portrush Golf Club,** Bushmills Road, Portrush BT56 8JQ (Portrush (0265) 822311). *Location:* one mile from Portrush on the main Portrush/Bushmills Road. Natural seaside links. 18 holes, 6772 yards. S.S.S. 73. Two practice grounds. *Green Fees:* £30.00 per day weekdays; £35.00 per day weekends. *Eating facilities:* three bars, restaurant with snacks and à la carte. *Visitors:* must contact Secretary prior to visit. Restrictions Wednesday and Friday afternoons and Saturday and Sunday mornings. *Society Meetings:* accepted with prior booking. Professional: Dai Stevenson (0265 823335). Secretary: Miss W. Erskine (0265 822311; Fax: 0265 823139).

# Armagh

ARMAGH. **County Armagh Golf Club,** The Demesne, Newry Road, Armagh (Armagh (0861) 522501). *Location:* Newry Road out of Armagh. Parkland. 18 holes, 6150 yards. S.S.S. 69. Practice area and putting. *Green Fees:* £10.00 weekdays, £15.00 weekends. *Eating facilities:* bar and restaurant, no catering Mondays. *Visitors:* welcome by arrangement. Not Saturdays or Thursdays. *Society Meetings:* welcome by arrangement except Saturdays or Thursdays. Professional: Alan Rankin (0861 525864). Secretary: June McParland (0861 525861).

CRAIGAVON. **Craigavon Golf and Ski Club,** Turmoyra Lane, Lurgan, Craigavon (Lurgan (0762) 326606). *Location:* half a mile from motorway, one mile from town centre, adjacent to ski slope. Parkland/ wooded. 18 holes, 5901 metres. S.S.S. 72. 9 hole Par 3; 12 hole pitch and putt. Driving range. *Green Fees:* weekdays £7.00; weekends £10.00. *Eating facilities:* full restaurant facilities. *Visitors:* open to everyone. Modern clubhouse, showers and lockers. *Society Meetings:* welcome – book beforehand. Manager: Mr V. McCorry.

LURGAN. **Lurgan Golf Club,** The Demesne, Lurgan, Craigavon BT67 9BN (Lurgan (0762) 322087). *Location:* one mile from motorway, half a mile from Town Centre. Parkland. 18 holes, 5561 metres. S.S.S. 70. Small practice area. *Green Fees:* weekdays £12.50; weekends £15.00. Reductions if playing with a member. *Eating facilities:* restaurant and lounge bar. Caterer: (0762 322337). *Visitors:* welcome Mondays, Thursdays, Friday mornings and Sundays. *Society Meetings:* welcome as per visitors. Weekdays £10.00; weekends £15.00. Professional: D. Paul (0762 321068). Secretary: Mrs G. Turkington.

PORTADOWN. **Portadown Golf Club,** 192 Gilford Road, Portadown, Craigavon BT63 5LF (Portadown (0762) 355356). *Location:* A59 south east of Portadown for two miles, entrance on right. Parkland. 18 holes, 5621 metres. S.S.S. 70 off white tees; 68 off green tees, 67 off yellow tees. Practice net. *Green Fees:* weekdays £12.00 (men), £10 (ladies); weekends and Bank Holidays £15.00 (men), £12.00 (ladies). Eating facilities: bar snacks, restaurant, members bar and lounge. *Visitors:* welcome at all times except Tuesdays and Saturdays. Squash, indoor bowling and snooker. *Society Meetings:* catered for. Professional: Paul Stevenson (0762 334655). Secretary: Mrs Lily Holloway (0762 355356).

TANDRAGEE. **Tandragee Golf Club,** Markethill Road, Tandragee, Craigavon BT62 2GR (0762 840727). *Location:* approximately five miles from Portadown on road to Newry and Dublin. Hilly parkland and wooded. 18 holes, 5519 metres. S.S.S. 69. Practice area and net. *Green Fees:* £10.00 weekdays; £15.00 weekends. Societies (parties over 20) £9.00 and £14.00. *Eating facilities:* full catering and bars. *Visitors:* welcome all days except Thursdays (Ladies Day) and Saturdays (competition day). *Society Meetings:* welcome by arrangement, except Saturdays. Professional: John Black (0762 841761). Secretary: H. McCready (0762 841272).

# Down

ARDGLASS. **Ardglass Golf Club,** 4 Castle Place, Ardglass (Ardglass (0396) 841219). *Location:* nearest town – Downpatrick. Situated on the coast 30 miles due south of Belfast. Seaside links. 18 holes, 5515 metres. S.S.S. 69. *Green Fees:* weekdays £13.00; weekends £16.00. *Eating facilities:* bar and diningroom. *Visitors:* welcome. *Society Meetings:* catered for. Advance booking necessary. Professional: Kevin Dorrian (0396 841022). Secretary: Alan Cannon (0396 841219).

BALLYNAHINCH. **Spa Golf Club,** 20 Grove Road, Ballynahinch BT24 8PN (Ballynahinch (0232) 562365). *Location:* Ballynahinch half mile, Belfast 11 miles. Parkland, wooded. 18 holes, 5938 yards. S.S.S. 72. Practice area. *Green Fees:* weekdays £11.00.

Playing with member £8.00; weekends £14.00. Societies £8.50 weekdays, £14.00 Sundays. *Eating facilities:* bar snacks. *Visitors:* welcome Mondays, Tuesdays and Thursdays. Sundays with member only and Wednesdays not after 3.00pm. *Society Meetings:* welcome Monday, Tuesday, Thursday;, Sunday 10.00 to 11.45am. Secretary: John M. Glass (0232 812340).

BANBRIDGE. **Banbridge Golf Club,** Huntly Road, Banbridge (Banbridge (08206) 62342). *Location:* half-a-mile out of Banbridge on Huntly Road. Parkland. 18 holes, 5453 yards, 5003 metres. S.S.S. 67. Practice ground. *Green Fees:* weekdays £6.00, weekends £10.00. Reduction if playing with a member. *Eating facilities:* bar snacks. Meals for Societies by arrangement. *Visitors:* welcome. Restrictions on Ladies' Day (Tuesday) and Men's Competition (Saturday). *Society Meetings:* catered for. Arrange with Secretary/Manager: Secretary/Manager: Thomas F. Fee (08206 23831).

BANGOR. **Bangor Golf Club,** Bangor BT20 4RH (Bangor (0247) 465133). *Location:* one mile from town centre off Donaghadee Road. Parkland. 18 holes, 6424 yards. S.S.S. 71. Practice facilities. *Green Fees:* weekdays £15.00; weekends £21.00. *Eating facilities:* diningroom (booking essential), lunches and evening meals, bar snacks. *Visitors:* welcome Monday and Wednesday, weekends after 6pm. Tuesdays Ladies Day. *Society Meetings:* advance booking necessary. Professional: Norman Drew (0247 462164). Secretary: Tom Russell (0247 270922).

BANGOR. **Carnalea Golf Club,** Station Road, Bangor BT19 1EZ (Bangor (0247) 465004). *Location:* one minute walk from Carnalea Railway Station. Seaside parkland. 18 holes, 5564 yards. S.S.S. 67. *Green Fees:* weekdays £9.00, weekends £12.00. *Eating facilities:* full restaurant and two bars. *Visitors:* welcome without reservation. *Society Meetings:* catered for. Parties over 20 persons – £8.00 each. Professional: M. McGee (0247 270122). Secretary: J.H. Crozier (0247 270368).

BANGOR. **Helen's Bay Golf Club,** Golf Road, Helen's Bay, Bangor BT19 1TL (Helen's Bay (0247) 852601). *Location:* A2 from Belfast – 9 miles. 9 holes, 5154 yards. S.S.S. 67. *Green Fees:* information not provided. *Eating facilities:* available. *Visitors:* welcome. *Society Meetings:* catered for. Secretary: John H. Ward.

BELFAST. **Balmoral Golf Club Ltd,** 518 Lisburn Road, Belfast BT9 6GX (Belfast (0232) 668540). *Location:* two miles south of Belfast City Centre, Lisburn Road, next to King's Hall. Parkland course. 18 holes, 5702 yards. S.S.S. 70. *Green Fees:* weekdays £12.00 (Wednesdays £14.50); weekends £18.00. *Eating facilities:* full restaurant facilities and bars. *Visitors:* Mondays and Thursdays only. *Society Meetings:* Mondays and Thursdays. Professional: G. Bleakley (0232 667747). General Manager: Robert McConkey (0232 381514).

BELFAST. **Belvoir Park Golf Club,** 73 Church Road, Newtownbreda, Belfast BT8 4AN (Belfast (0232) 641159 or 692817). *Location:* three miles from city centre on road to Newcastle. Parkland – well wooded. 18 holes, 6501 yards, 5943 metres. S.S.S. 71. Practice area. *Green Fees:* weekdays (excluding Wednesday) £25.00, weekends and Wednesdays £30.00. *Eating facilities:* dining and snack meals – bar. *Visitors:* welcome except Saturday. *Society Meetings:* by prior booking only. Professional: M. Kelly (0232 646714). Secretary: W.I. Davidson (0232 491693 and 646113).

BELFAST. **Knock Golf Club,** Summerfield, Dundonald, Belfast BT16 0QX (0232 482249). *Location:* four miles east of Belfast. 18 holes, 5845 metres. S.S.S. 71. *Green Fees:* weekdays £17.00, weekends and Bank Holidays £22.00. Parties over 25 or more (must book in advance) £15.00 per player. *Eating facilities:* catering and bar facilities available. *Visitors:* welcome. *Society Meetings:* catered for Mondays and Thursdays. Professional: G. Fairweather (0232 483825). Secretary/Manager: S.G. Managh (0232 483251).

BELFAST. **Knockbracken Golf and Country Club,** 10 Ballymaconaghy Road, Knockbracken, Belfast BT8 4SB (0232 792100). *Location:* south from the centre of Belfast on the Ormeau Road to "Four Winds" public house and restaurant, half a mile out on Ballymaconaghy Road, on left by ski slopes. Parkland on undulating ground. 18 holes, 5391 yards. S.S.S. 68. *Green Fees:* £7.75 weekdays, £8.00 with member; £11.00 weekends and Public Holidays, £7.00 with member. *Eating facilities:* full meals and snacks served from 1100-2200hrs seven days a week. *Visitors:* welcome weekdays, no restrictions except weekend mornings. *Society Meetings:* by prior arrangement. Professional: David Jones (0232 701648). Secretary: M. Grose (0232 401811).

BELFAST. **Mahee Island Golf Club,** Comber, Newtownards, Belfast (Killinchy (0238) 541234). *Location:* take Comber to Killyleagh Road and turn left a mile from Comber signposted "Ardmillan". Bear left for six miles and arrive on the island (no through road). Parkland/seaside. 9 holes, 5588 yards, 5108 metres. S.S.S. 67. Par 68 over 18 holes. Practice net, green and chipping area. *Green Fees:* weekdays £8.00, weekends £12.00. Half fees playing with member. *Eating facilities:* by arrangement (no bar). *Visitors:* welcome, restricted Wednesdays after 4.00pm and Saturdays until 4.00pm. *Society Meetings:* welcome, booking by letter. 50p reduction when 16 or more. Professional: F. Marshall. Hon. Secretary: T. Reid.

BELFAST. **Ormeau Golf Club,** 50 Park Road, Belfast BT7 (Belfast (0232) 641069). *Location:* Belfast south/east. Parkland course. 9 holes, 2653 yards, 2425 metres. S.S.S. 65. *Green Fees:* £7.00 weekdays, £9.00 weekends. *Eating facilities:* bar and restaurant. *Visitors:* welcome Tuesdays and Saturdays. *Society Meetings:* on application. Professional: M. Kelly. Secretary: G. McVeigh. Hon. Secretary: R. Burnett.

BELFAST. **Shandon Park Golf Club,** 73 Shandon Park, Belfast BT5 6NY (Belfast (0232) 793730). Parkland. 18 holes, 5714 metres. S.S.S. 70. *Green Fees:* weekdays £16.00 per round; weekends £20.00 per round. *Eating facilities:* restaurant facilities, bar snacks. *Visitors:* welcome everyday subject to advance clearance by Professional. *Society Meetings:* Mondays

and Fridays only. Professional: Barry Wilson (0232 797859). General Manager: H. Wallace (0232 401856).

DONAGHADEE. **Donaghadee Golf Club,** Warren Road, Donaghadee BT21 0PQ (Donaghadee (0247) 882519). *Location:* take Bangor road from Belfast through Bangor, five miles on coast road (21 miles). Seaside and parkland. Magnificent sea views to Scottish coast. 18 holes, 6100 yards. S.S.S. 69. *Green Fees:* weekdays £11.50; weekends £15.50. On Saturdays and Public Holidays visitors must be accompanied by a member. *Eating facilities:* first class restaurant, snacks, lunches, dinner. *Visitors:* welcome any day except on Saturdays. *Society Meetings:* welcome, special society rates (24 plus). Professional: Gordon Drew (0247 882921). Hon. Secretary: J.G. Partridge (0247 883624).

DOWNPATRICK. **Bright Castle Golf Club,** 14 Coniamstown Road, Bright, Downpatrick BT30 8LU (0396 841319). *Location:* off the main Downpatrick Killough Road approximately two and a half miles off main road. Parkland – excellent fairways and greens, plenty trees. 18 holes, 7143 yards. S.S.S. 74. Putting green. *Green Fees:* £7.00 weekdays, £8.00 weekends. Summer evenings weekdays only £4.00 after 6pm. *Eating facilities:* snacks available. *Visitors:* very welcome, no restrictions. *Society Meetings:* very welcome, tee must be reserved. Secretary: Raymond Reid.

DOWNPATRICK. **Downpatrick Golf Club,** 43 Saul Road, Downpatrick BT30 6PA (Downpatrick (0396) 612152). *Location:* one and a half miles from town centre, south-east direction. Parkland, challenging upland course. 18 holes, 6424 yards. S.S.S. 69. Putting area. *Green Fees:* weekdays £13.00; weekends £16.00. 20 per cent discount on weekdays for groups of 20 plus. *Eating facilities:* two lounges, diningroom and snack bar. *Visitors:* welcome. Snooker room. *Society Meetings:* catered for by prior arrangement. Secretary: Daniel McGreevy (0396 615947).

HOLYWOOD. **Holywood Golf Club,** Demesne Road, Holywood (Holywood (023 17) 2138). 18 holes, 5885 yards. *Green Fees:* information not provided. *Eating facilities:* bars and restaurant. *Visitors:* welcome. Professional: Michael Bannon. Secretary/Manager: Gerald R. Magennis.

KILKEEL. **Kilkeel Golf Club,** Mourne Park, Kilkeel (Kilkeel (069-37) 62296). *Location:* 16 miles from Newcastle and three miles from Kilkeel on main road to Newry. Parkland, wooded, undulating. 18 holes, 5657 metres. S.S.S. 69. Practice area available. *Green Fees:* weekdays £12.00 for 18 holes, weekends £15.00 for 18 holes. *Eating facilities:* full catering services on application, bar facilities. *Visitors:* welcome all days of the week except Tuesdays and Saturdays. *Society Meetings:* catered for. Secretary: S.C. McBride (06937 63787).

LISBURN. **Down Royal Park,** Dunygarton Road, Maze, Lisburn BT27 5RT (0846 621339). *Location:* inside Maze Racecourse. Heathland. 18 holes, 6824 yards. *Green Fees:* weekdays £10.00; Saturdays £12.00; Sundays £15.00. *Eating facilities:* licensed restaurant. *Visitors:* welcome at all times. *Society Meetings:* welcome. Secretary: N.F. Ewing (acting).

NEWCASTLE. **Royal County Down Golf Club,** Newcastle BT33 0AN. *Location:* adjacent to north side of Newcastle, approach from town centre. Championship Course: 18 holes, 6968 yards. Course: 18 holes, 4100 yards. S.S.S. 63. *Green Fees:* weekdays Summer £35.00, Winter £25.00; weekends Summer £40.00, Winter £30.00. *Eating facilities:* light lunches and bar, weekdays only, April to September. *Visitors:* welcome with prior reservation. *Society Meetings:* catered for. Professional: Kevan J. Whitson (03967 22419). Secretary: P.E. Rolph (03967 23314).

NEWTOWNARDS. **Clandeboye Golf Club,** Tower Road, Conlig, Newtownards BT23 3PN (0247 271767). *Location:* Conlig village off A21 between Bangor and Newtownards. Wooded, undulating parkland/heathland. 18 holes, 5915 metres, S.S.S. 72. 18 holes, 5172 metres, S.S.S. 67. Practice ground. *Green Fees:* weekdays £16.00 and £13.00; weekends £21.00 and £16.00. *Eating facilities:* full catering and bar. *Visitors:* welcome weekdays; Saturdays and certain times on Sundays must be accompanied by member. (Thursday ladies' day). *Society Meetings:* welcome weekdays except Thursdays (in winter Mondays and Wednesdays only). Reduced rates for parties over 20. Professional: Peter Gregory (0247 271750). Secretary/Manager: Ian Marks (0247 271767).

NEWTOWNARDS. **Kirkistown Castle Golf Club,** 142 Main Road, Cloughey, Newtownards (02477 71353). *Location:* A20 west of Belfast then B173. Seaside links. 18 holes, 6176 yards. S.S.S. 70. *Green Fees:* £10.00 weekdays; £17.00 weekends and Public Holidays. Subject to review. *Eating facilities:* full catering and snacks. *Visitors:* welcome. *Society Meetings:* catered for. Professional: Jonathan Peden (02477 71004). Secretary: D.J. Ryan (02477 71233).

NEWTOWNARDS. **Scrabo Golf Club,** 233 Scrabo Road, Newtownards BT23 4SL (Newtownards (0247) 815048). *Location:* approximately 10 miles from Belfast off main Belfast to Newtownards road. Upland course. 18 holes, 5699 metres, S.S.S. 71. *Green Fees:* weekdays £10.50; weekends £15.00. Societies weekdays £8.50, weekends £12.00. *Eating facilities:* full facilities available except Mondays. *Visitors:* welcome except Saturdays. *Society Meetings:* over 20 players, welcome. Professional: (0247 817848) Secretary: Ken Graham (0247 812355).

WARRENPOINT. **Warrenpoint Golf Club,** Lower Dromore Road, Warrenpoint (Warrenpoint (06937) 52219). *Location:* five miles south of Newry on coast road. Parkland. 18 holes. 5640 yards. S.S.S. 70. *Green Fees:* weekdays £12.00, weekends £18.00. *Eating facilities:* full catering and bar facilities. *Visitors:* welcome Sunday, Monday, Thursday, Friday. Squash, snooker facilities available. *Society Meetings:* catered for by prior arrangement. Professional: Nigel Shaw (06937 52371). Secretary: John McMahon (06937 53695; Fax: 06937 52918).

# Fermanagh

ENNISKILLEN. **Enniskillen Golf Club,** Castlecoole, Enniskillen BT74 6HZ (0365 325250). *Location:* one mile north east of Enniskillen (off Tempo Road) on Castlecoole Estate. Parkland. 18 holes, 5990 yards, 5574 metres. S.S.S. 70. *Green Fees:* weekdays and weekends £8.50, £6.00 for Societies or visitors playing with member. *Eating facilities:* bar snacks daily – full catering by arrangement. *Visitors:* welcome without restriction. *Society Meetings:* welcome. Secretary: Billy Hamilton (0365 323206).

# Londonderry

CASTLEROCK. **Castlerock Golf Club,** 65 Circular Road, Castlerock, Coleraine BT51 4TJ (Coleraine (0265) 848215). *Location:* A2, six miles west of Coleraine, one mile Coleraine side of Mussenden Temple. Links, testing course. 18 holes, 6687 yards. S.S.S. 72. Large practice area. *Green Fees:* weekdays £13.00 per round; weekends £25.00. *Eating facilities:* full restaurant facilities, two bars. *Visitors:* Monday to Thursday no restrictions. *Society Meetings:* welcome Monday to Thursday. Professional: R. Kelly (0265 848314). Secretary: R.G. McBride (0265 848314).

COLERAINE. **Brown Trout Golf and Country Club,** 209 Agivey Road, Aghadowey, near Coleraine (0265 868209). *Location:* eight miles south of Coleraine in A54. Parkland course heavily wooded, crossing water seven times in nine holes. 9 holes, 2519 metres. S.S.S. 68. *Green Fees:* weekdays £6.00; weekends £8.50. *Eating facilities:* à la carte restaurant, bar snacks, barbecues. *Visitors:* always welcome. 4 bedrooms available. *Society Meetings:* welcome except Wednesday and Thursday after 5pm. Professional: Ken Revie. Secretary/Manager: Bill O'Hara.

MAGHERAFELT. **Moyola Park Golf Club,** Shanemullagh, Castledawson, Magherafelt BT45 8DG (0648 68468). *Location:* 40 miles north of Belfast on M2. Wooded parkland course with large, mature trees. 18 holes, 6517 yards. S.S.S. 71. *Green Fees:* £12.00 weekdays; £16.00 weekends. *Eating facilities:* full bar and catering facilities. *Visitors:* always welcome mid-week, weekends (restricted) by prior arrangement. Snooker. *Society Meetings:* mid-week and Sundays by arrangement. Professional: V. Teague (0648 68830).

PORTSTEWART. **Portstewart Golf Club,** Strand Head, Portstewart (Portstewart (026583) 2015). Coastal links. Strand (No. 1) course 18 holes. Town (No. 2) course 18 holes. Strand 6784 yards, S.S.S. 72; Town 4733 yards, S.S.S. 63. *Green Fees:* information not available. *Eating facilities:* meals available –

advance orders. *Visitors:* welcome Mondays to Fridays with reservation. *Society Meetings:* catered for. Professional: A. Hunter (026583 2601). Secretary: Michael Moss.

PREHEN. **City of Derry Golf Club,** 49 Victoria Road, Prehen BT47 2PU (0504 311610). *Location:* three miles from city centre on the road to Strabane – follow the River Foyle. Parkland, wooded. 18 holes, 6362 yards. S.S.S. 71. Also 9 hole course, 4708 yards. S.S.S. 63. Practice area. *Green Fees:* information not provided. *Eating facilities:* catering and bar facilities available. *Visitors:* welcome on weekdays up to 4.30pm, weekends please contact Professional. Convenient for hotel and guest houses. *Society Meetings:* welcome please contact Secretary. Professional: M. Doherty (0504 46496). Secretary: P.J. Doherty (0504 46369).

# Tyrone

COOKSTOWN. **Killymoon Golf Club,** Killymoon Road, Cookstown (Cookstown (06487) 62254). *Location:* private road off A29. Signposted at Dungannon end of town opposite Drum Road. Mainly flat parkland. 18 holes, 5513 metres. S.S.S. 69. Practice area. *Green Fees:* weekdays £11.50; weekends and Bank Holidays £15.50, not Saturday afternoons. *Eating facilities:* full catering at club (large groups please book). *Visitors:* welcome except Saturday afternoons. *Society Meetings:* Sundays limit 20, Saturdays none, weekdays welcome but ladies have priority Thursdays. Societies of 20 or more £10.50 weekdays. Professional: Barry Hamill (06487 63460). Secretary: Les Hodgett (06487 63762).

DUNGANNON. **Dungannon Golf Club,** 34 Springfield Lane, Dungannon BT70 1QX (Dungannon (08687) 22098). *Location:* one mile west of Dungannon. 18 holes, 5904 yards. S.S.S. 68. *Green Fees:* £8.00 weekdays, £10.00 weekends and Bank Holidays. *Visitors:* welcome. Hon. Secretary: L.R.P Agnew (08687-27338/22602/22098).

*Castlerock Club, Co. Londonderry.*

FINTONA. **Fintona Golf Club,** Kiln Street, Ecclesville, Demesne, Fintona (0662 841480). *Location:* eight miles south of Omagh, county town of Tyrone. Parkland with a river running through the course. 9 holes, 5716 metres. S.S.S. 70. *Green Fees:* information not provided. *Eating facilities:* bar food. *Visitors:* welcome daily but check by telephoning at weekends. Snooker tables. *Society Meetings:* catered for by advance booking. Secretary: G. McNulty (0662 841514).

NEWTOWNSTEWART. **Newtownstewart Golf Club,** 38 Golf Course Road, Newtownstewart, Omagh BT78 4HH (Newtownstewart (06626) 61466). *Location:* signposted from Strabane Road (A57) at Newtownstewart, two miles west of Newtownstewart on B84. Parkland and wooded course. 18 holes, 5982 yards, 5468 metres. S.S.S. 69. Practice ground adjacent to clubhouse. *Green Fees:* weekdays £8.00; weekends £10.00. Weekly £25.00. *Eating facilities:* available. *Visitors:* welcome at all times except during club competitions. Accommodation available in chalets beside clubhouse. *Society Meetings:* catered for. Hon. Secretary: Mr J.E. Mackin. Secretary/Manageress: Miss D. Magee.

OMAGH. **Omagh Golf Club,** 83a Dublin Road, Omagh BT78 1HQ (Omagh (0662) 243160). *Location:* one mile from Omagh centre on Belfast/Dublin Road. Parkland. 18 holes, 4972 metres. S.S.S. 67. *Green Fees:* weekdays £10.00; weekends and Bank Holidays £12.00. £2.00 reduction if playing with a member, Senior Citizens half price. *Eating facilities:* snacks and bar facilities. *Visitors:* welcome any day except Tuesday and Saturday. Special arrangements with Royal Arms Hotel for guests. *Society Meetings:* welcome. Hon. Secretary: Joseph A. McElholm. Secretary: Florence E.A. Caldwell (0662 241442).

STRABANE. **Strabane Golf Club,** Ballycolman Road, Strabane (0504 382271). *Location:* Omagh – Strabane main road. Parkland. 18 holes, 5552 metres. S.S.S. 69. *Green Fees:* weekdays £8.00, £6.00 with a member; weekends £12.00, £8.00 with a member. *Eating facilities:* two bars, catering by arrangement. *Visitors:* welcome weekdays only. *Society Meetings:* by arrangement with Secretary. Secretary: Terry Doherty (0504 883109).

# Republic of Ireland

## COUNTY CARLOW

CARLOW. **Carlow Golf Club,** Deer Park, Carlow (0503 31695). *Location:* 52 miles south of Dublin, two miles north of Carlow town on N9. Parkland. 18 holes, 5844 metres. S.S.S. 70. *Green Fees:* weekdays £16.00; weekends £20.00. Weekly ticket £60.00, fortnightly ticket £100. *Eating facilities:* restaurant open all day, bar open from 9.30am – 12 midnight. *Visitors:* welcome Monday to Friday, avoid Tuesday (Ladies Day), Saturdays difficult, Sundays impossible – pre booking advisable. *Society Meetings:* must be pre booked with Secretary. Professional: Andrew Gilbert (0503 31545). Secretary: Margaret Meaney (0503 31695; Fax: 0503 40065).

## COUNTY CAVAN

DRUMELIS. **County Cavan Golf Club,** Aranmore House, Drumelis (049 312 83). *Location:* county town of Cavan. Parkland course. 18 holes, 5519 metres. S.S.S 69. *Green Fees:* £10.00 weekdays; £12.00 weekends. *Eating facilities:* available. *Visitors:* welcome throughout the year. *Society Meetings:* welcome with pre-booking. Secretary: Donal Crotty (049 31643).

SLIGO via. **Black Lion Golf Club,** Toam, Black Lion, via Sligo (072 53024; from the UK 010 353 72 53024). *Location:* Black Lion/Belcoo on Enniskillen to Sligo Road. Flat parkland, wooded copses, lake partially in play, scenic. 9 holes, 6175 yards, 5614 metres. S.S.S. 69. *Green Fees:* IR£5.00 weekdays; IR£8.00 weekends. Group rates by prior arrangement. *Eating facilities:* bar with bar snacks. *Visitors:* welcome weekdays, Sundays after 4pm. *Society Meetings:* by arrangement. Hon. Secretary: Robert Thompson.

## COUNTY CLARE

LAHINCH. **Lahinch Golf Club,** Lahinch (065 81003; Fax: 065 81592). *Location:* 30 miles north-west of Shannon Airport, 200 yards from Lahinch village on Lisconner Road. Links Course. Old Course, 18 holes, 6699 yards. S.S.S. 67. *Green Fees:* on application. *Visitors:* weekdays only, by arrangement. *Society Meetings:* catered for by arrangement. Professional: R. McCavery (065 81408). Secretary: M. Murphy.

## COUNTY CORK

CARRIGROHANE. **Muskerry Golf Club,** Carrigrohane (021 385104). *Location:* seven and a half miles north west of Cork City. Parkland/wooded. 18 holes, 5786 metres. S.S.S. 70. *Green Fees:* weekdays £17.00. *Eating facilities:* available. *Visitors:* welcome weekdays – Monday and Tuesday all day, Wednesday up to 11.30am, Thursday after 12.30pm to 3.30pm. *Society Meetings:* welcome. Professional: W.M. Lehane (021 385104). Secretary: J.J. Moynihan (021 385297).

CASTLETOWNBERE. **Berehaven Golf Club,** Castletownbere. *Location:* by the main Castletownbere – Glengarriff Road. Seaside links. 9 holes, 4748 metres. S.S.S. 64. *Green Fees:* £7.00. *Visitors:* welcome at all times. Tennis and swimming facilities. *Society Meetings:* all welcome – £6. Secretary: A. Hanley (027 70039 or 70164).

CHARLEVILLE. **Charleville Golf Club,** Charleville (063 81274). *Location:* main road from Limerick to Cork, 25 miles from Limerick. Parkland, very wooded. 18 holes, 6430 yards. S.S.S. 70. *Green Fees:* £10.00. *Eating facilities:* full eating facilities and bar. *Visitors:* welcome except weekends. *Society Meetings:* welcomed except weekends. Secretary: James Murphy (063 81257).

DOUGLAS. **Douglas Golf Club,** Douglas (021 891086; Fax: 021 895297). *Location:* in Douglas Village, three miles to the south of Cork City. Parkland course – very flat. 18 holes, 5664 yards. S.S.S. 69. *Green Fees:* weekdays £15.00; weekends £16.00. *Eating facilities:* full restaurant and bar available. *Visitors:* Monday, Wednesday, Thursday, Friday mornings, preferably mid-morning; Saturday and Sunday after 2pm. Advisable to check in advance. *Society Meetings:* welcome but bookings are made in January each year. Professional: Gary Nicholson (021 362055). Secretary: Brian Barrett (021 895297).

LITTLE ISLAND. **Cork Golf Club**, Little Island (021 353263). *Location:* five miles east of Cork, half-mile off Cork/Cobh road. Parkland, very scenic championship course. 18 holes, 6065 metres. S.S.S. 72. Practice ground. *Green Fees:* weekdays £22.00; weekends £25.00. Special rates for groups of 20 or more, £17.00. *Eating facilities:* full catering facilities, bar. *Visitors:* welcome Mondays, Tuesdays, Wednesdays and Fridays except 12.30 to 2pm; weekends ring in advance. *Society Meetings:* catered for, arrange with Secretary/Manager. Professional: David Higgins (021 353421). Secretary: Matt Sands (021 353451; Fax: 021 353410).

LITTLE ISLAND. **Harbour Point Golf Club**, Little Island (021 353094; Fax: 021 354408). *Location:* enter Little Island by taking a right off the main Cork/Rosslare Road, then take your next left and then right. Parkland course by banks of River Lee. 18 holes, 6630 yards, 6063 metres. S.S.S. 72. 21 bay floodlit driving range. *Green Fees:* weekdays £20.00; weekends £22.00. *Eating facilities:* full bar and restaurant licence. *Visitors:* welcome every day by appointment. *Society Meetings:* welcome every day. Professional available on request.

TIVOLI. **Silver Springs Golf Club**, Tivoli (021 507533). *Location:* five minutes from Cork city centre. 9 holes, 4680 yards. S.S.S. 62 for 18 holes, Par 34 (68). *Green Fees:* information not provided. Special rates for groups of 20 or more. *Eating facilities:* full catering facilities, bar. *Visitors:* welcome, ring beforehand. Hotel on site, accommodation available. Full sports centre, indoor pool, squash, indoor tennis, sauna & steam bath, gym. Manager: Ian Foulger.

YOUGHAL. **Youghal Golf Club**, Knockaverry, Youghal (024 92787). *Location:* N25 main road from Rosslare to Cork. Seaside course with panoramic views of Youghal Bay/Blackwater Estuary. 18 holes, 6300 yards. S.S.S. 69. *Green Fees:* £(I)14.00. *Eating facilities:* full kitchen facilities. *Visitors:* phone re weekends and Wednesdays (ladies day). *Society Meetings:* welcome, please phone. Special rates available. Professional: Ciaran Carroll (024 92590). Secretary: Kieran Quill.

# COUNTY DONEGAL

BUNDORAN. **Bundoran Golf Club**, Great Northern Hotel, Bundoran (072 41302). *Location:* 25 miles west of Enniskillen, 25 miles north of Sligo (on coast). Undulating seaside and parkland (no trees). 18 holes, 6328 yards, 5785 metres (blue tees), 5434 metres (yellow tees). S.S.S. 71 and 69 respectively. *Green*

*Fees:* weekdays £11, weekends £13. *Eating facilities:* snacks in bar. Hotel on course. *Visitors:* welcome by appointment. Weekends busy, advance booking necessary. Most weekend competitions from Easter to end October are open. *Society Meetings:* very welcome if can be accommodated. Professionals: Leslie and David Robinson (072 41302). Secretary: Liam M. Devitt.

LETTERKENNY. **Dunfanaghy Golf Club**, Dunfanaghy, Letterkenny (074 36335). *Location:* on main Letterkenny to Dunfanaghy Road – N56. Seaside links. 18 holes, 5066 metres. S.S.S. 66. *Green Fees:* £8.00 weekdays; £10.00 weekends. *Eating facilities:* bar snacks – soup, tea and sandwiches. *Visitors:* welcome at all times. *Society Meetings:* welcome most days by booking. Club Secretary: Mary Quinn.

LETTERKENNY. **Portsalon Golf Club**, Portsalon, Letterkenny (074 59459). *Location:* 20 miles north of Letterkenny. Seaside links. 18 holes, 5878 yards, 5379 metres. S.S.S. 68. *Green Fees:* £10.00. Weekly ticket £50.00. *Eating facilities:* diningroom and bar in clubhouse. *Visitors:* welcome. *Society Meetings:* welcome weekdays. Secretary: Michael Kerr (074 59102).

# COUNTY DUBLIN

BALBRIGGAN. **Balbriggan Golf Club**, Blackhall, Balbriggan (8412173). *Location:* quarter of a mile south of Balbriggan on main Belfast/Dublin Road. Parkland course with fine views of Cooley Peninsula and Mourne Mountains. 18 holes, 2968 metres. S.S.S. 71. *Green Fees:* £12.00 weekdays; £16.00 weekends. *Eating facilities:* full restaurant and snacks. *Visitors:* welcome, Tuesday Ladies Day, Saturdays and Sundays not good as club competitions take place. *Society Meetings:* catered for Mondays, Wednesdays, Thursdays and Fridays. Secretary: Leslie Cashell (8412229).

DONABATE. **Corballis Public Golf Club**, Donabate (436583). *Location:* main Dublin to Belfast Road. Links course. 18 holes, 4600 yards, 4543 metres. S.S.S. 64. *Green Fees:* £6.00 weekdays; £7.00 weekends. Half price weekdays Senior Citizens and Students. *Eating facilities:* snack foods. *Visitors:* welcome anytime. *Society Meetings:* welcome. Secretary: P.J. Boylan.

DUBLIN. **Elm Park Golf and Sports Club**, Nutley House, Donnybrook, Dublin 4 (0001 2693438; Fax: 2694505). *Location:* between R.T.E. and St. Vincent's Hospital. Flat parkland course. 18 holes, 5929 yards, 5422 metres. S.S.S. 68. *Green Fees:* £27.00 weekdays; £30.00 weekends. *Eating facilities:* full bar and dining facilities. *Visitors:* welcome but must telephone t arrange times with Professional. *Society Meetings:* by special arrangement. Professional: S. Green (0001 2692650). Secretary: A. McCormack.

DUBLIN. **The Royal Dublin Golf Club,** North Bull Island, Dollymount, Dublin 3 (0001 337153). *Location:* three and a half miles north east of city centre on coast road to Howth. Seaside links. 18 holes, 6850 yards, 6262 metres. S.S.S. 71. Large practice ground. *Green Fees:* weekdays £35.00 IR; weekends £45.00 IR. *Eating facilities:* grill room, restaurant, two bars. *Visitors:* Monday, Tuesday, Thursday, Friday and Sunday 10.30 to 12.30 or after 3pm. *Society Meetings:* catered for, written application must be made. Tournament Professional: Christy O'Connor. Professional: Leonard Owens (0001 336477). Secretary: J.A. Lambe (0001 336346; Fax: 0001 336504).

DUN LAOGHAIRE. **Dun Laoghaire Golf Club,** Eglinton Park, Tivoli Road, Dun Laoghaire (01 2805116). *Location:* half a mile from town centre. Parkland. 18 holes, 5495 metres. S.S.S. 69. *Green Fees:* weekdays IR£20.00. *Eating facilities:* bars, restaurant, snacks. *Visitors:* welcome weekdays. *Society Meetings:* welcome. Professional: Owen Mulhall (01 2801694). Secretary: Terry Stewart (01 2803916).

FOXROCK. **Leopardstown Golf Course,** Foxrock (01 895341). *Location:* five miles south of Dublin city centre, situated in Leopardstown race course. 9 holes, 5516 yards. Par 34 (68). *Green Fees:* information not provided. Special rates for societies and groups. *Eating facilities:* restaurant. *Visitors:* welcome. Manager: Michael Hoey.

HOWTH. **Deer Park Hotel and Golf Courses,** Howth (010 3531 322624). *Location:* follow coast road via Fairview, Clontarf to Howth, nine miles from city centre. Parkland course set in the grounds of Howth Castle, spectacular views of the coast. 18 holes, 6647 yards, 6078 metres. S.S.S. 72. *Green Fees:* on application. *Eating facilities:* light meals available all day; lounge bar; restaurant. *Visitors:* welcome seven days, non residents must expect delays. Residents may book the tee. 48 bedroomed hotel. *Society Meetings:* welcome. Managers: David and Antoinette Tighe.

PORTMARNOCK. **Portmarnock Golf Club,** Portmarnock (0001 323082). *Location:* 8 miles NE of Dublin along north coast, four miles from Airport. Seaside links – winds. Three courses: 'A' – 27 holes, 7097 yards. S.S.S. 75. 'B' – 7047 yards. S.S.S. 75. 'C' – 6596 yards. S.S.S. 74. Practice area. *Green Fees:* IR£35.00 weekdays (Ladies IR£25.00); IR£45.00 weekends. *Eating facilities:* available. *Visitors:* by arrangement, restriction weekends and Bank Holidays. *Society Meetings:* on application, 12 or more Mondays, Tuesdays and Fridays only. Professional: J. Purcell (0001 8462634). Secretary: W. Bornemann (0001 462968).

T. MARGARETS. **St. Margarets Golf Club,** St. Margarets (Tel & Fax: 361897). *Location:* one mile east of Ashbourne Road at the Ward; eight miles north of Dublin City centre; three miles to Dublin Airport. Parkland, ultra-modern design by Craddock and Ruddy. 18 holes, 6900 yards. Extensive practice areas.

Green Fees: £25.00 weekdays; £30.00 weekends. *Eating facilities:* full range of services. *Visitors:* welcome to all golfers. *Society Meetings:* welcome. Secretary: Denis Kane.

SUTTON. **Howth Golf Club,** St. Fintan's, Carrickbrack Road, Sutton (01 323055). *Location:* one and a half miles from Sutton Cross on city side of hill of Howth. Moorland course with scenic views of Dublin Bay – very hilly. 18 holes, 5419 metres. S.S.S. 68. *Green Fees:* weekdays £15.00. *Eating facilities:* bar snacks from 11am. *Visitors:* welcome weekdays except Wednesdays. *Society Meetings:* bookings accepted by arrangement with Secretary. Professional: John McGuirk (01 322844). Secretary: Mrs Ann MacNeice.

# COUNTY GALWAY

CLIFDEN. **Connemara Golf Club,** Aillebrack, Ballyconneely, Near Clifden (095 23502; Fax 095 23662). *Location:* nine miles south of Clifden. Seaside links. Championship course: 18 holes, 6611 metres. S.S.S. 75. Medal course: 18 holes, 6173 metres. S.S.S. 73. Practice fairway. *Green Fees:* £16.00 per round. *Eating facilities:* à la carte restaurant and bar. *Visitors:* Monday to Saturday preferable, booking in advance advised particularly during Summer. *Society Meetings:* groups of 20 or more £9.00 per person (rate does not apply from June to September inclusive). Secretary: Matt Killilea.

LOUGHREA. **Loughrea Golf Club,** Loughrea (091 41049). *Location:* one and a half miles north east of town, on New Inn Road. Parkland, undulating, with beautiful views of town and Sl. Aughty Mountains in background. 18 holes, 5613 yards. Par 69. Practice area. *Green Fees:* £10.00. *Eating facilities:* light snacks and bar. *Visitors:* welcome weekdays and open days. *Society Meetings:* welcome, please telephone. Secretary: Brendan Blake (091 41339).

# COUNTY KERRY

BALLYBUNION. **Ballybunion Golf Club,** Ballybunion (068 27146). *Location:* nearest town Ballybunion. Seaside links. Old Course – 18 holes, 6542 yards. S.S.S. 72. New Course – 18 holes, 6278 yards. S.S.S. 73. *Green Fees:* information not available. *Eating facilities:* full bar and catering facilities. *Visitors:* there are no restrictions on visitors but weekends are extremely busy – to be avoided when possible. *Society Meetings:* catered for from 1st October to 1st April, no societies on Old Course at weekends. Professional: E. Higgins (068 27209). Secretary: S. Walsh (068 27611).

BALLYFERRITER. **Ceann Sibeal (Dingle) Golf Club,** Ballyferriter (066 56255; Fax: 066 56255). *Location:* turn right quarter of a mile after Ballyferriter. Traditional links, most westerly golf course in Europe. 18 holes, 6550 yards. S.S.S. 71. Practice ground. *Green Fees:* £15.00 per round, £20.00 per day. *Eating facilities:* full facilities for 1993 season. *Visitors:* welcome at all times, book in advance. Hotel adjacent. *Society Meetings:* all welcome. Professional: Dermot O'Connor. Secretary: Garry Partington.

KILLARNEY. **Killarney Golf and Fishing Club,** Mahony's Point, Killarney (064 31034/31242; Fax: 064 33065). *Location:* Killarney town, two miles west on Ring of Kerry road. Undulating parkland courses – lakeside. Mahony's Point: 18 holes, 6152 metres. S.S.S. 72. Killeen: 18 holes, 6457 yards. S.S.S. 73. Practice area. *Green Fees:* £22(IRL) per round. Reduced rates for groups of 20 or more. *Eating facilities:* available all day. *Visitors:* welcome at all times, reservations in advance required. *Society Meetings:* welcome. Professional: T. Coveney (064 31615). Secretary: T. Prendergast (064 31242).

SNEEM. **Parknasilla Golf Club,** Parknasilla, Sneem (064 45122). *Location:* on the Ring of Kerry route, two miles east of Sneem Village. Hilly seaside course, wooded. 9 holes, 4894 yards. S.S.S. 65. *Green Fees:* £9.00. *Eating facilities:* available at Great Southern hotel, 10 minutes' walk. *Visitors:* welcome, no restrictions. *Society Meetings:* contact 064 45122. Professional: Charlie McCarthy. Secretary: Maurice Walsh (064 45233).

TRALEE. **Tralee Golf Club,** West Barrow, Ardfert, Tralee (066 36379). *Location:* Tralee to barrow via the Spa and Churchill. Seaside links. 18 holes, 6252 metres. S.S.S. 72. *Green Fees:* £25.00 weekdays, £30.00 weekends. *Eating facilities:* bar and restaurant. *Visitors:* unrestricted except Wednesdays and weekends. *Society Meetings:* catered for with advance bookings. Secretary: Peter Colleran (066 36379; Fax: 36008).

# KILDARE

CURRAGH. **Curragh Golf Club,** Curragh (045 41238). *Location:* three miles south of Newbridge. Parkland. 18 holes, 6003 metres. S.S.S. 71. Practice grounds. *Green Fees:* weekdays £13.00; weekends and Bank Holidays £16.00. *Eating facilities:* full catering. *Visitors:* restricted, please check in advance for course availability. *Society Meetings:* by appointment. Professional: by appointment (045 41896). Secretary: Ann Culleton (045 41714).

DONADEA. **Knockanally Golf and Country Club,** Donadea, North Kildare (Tel & Fax: 045 69322). *Location:* three miles off N4 between Enfield and Kilcock. Parkland. 18 holes, 6495 yards. S.S.S. 72. *Green Fees:* £13.00 weekdays; £16.00 Saturdays, £14.00 Sundays. *Eating facilities:* available. *Visitors:* welcome, no restrictions. *Society Meetings:* by arrangement. Professional: Peter Hickey. Secretary: Noel A. Lyons (045 69322/6287716).

# COUNTY KILKENNY

THOMASTOWN. **Mount Juliet Golf Club,** Thomastown (056 24725; Fax: 056 24828). *Location:* Thomastown – on main Dublin to Waterford Road. Parkland, designed by Jack Nicklaus featuring specimen trees, water hazards and bunkers. 18 holes, 7142 yards, 6493 metres. S.S.S. 74. 3 hole teaching academy and practice range. *Green Fees:* £55.00. Hotel residents £30.00. *Eating facilities:* full catering and bar facilities. *Visitors:* welcome, no restrictions but please book in advance. 32 bedroom de luxe Hotel. *Society Meetings:* welcome everyday except weekends before 12 noon. Professional: Keith Morgan. Director of Golf: Katherine MacCann.

# COUNTY LAOIS

PORTLAOISE. **The Heath Golf Club,** Portlaoise, Co Laois (0502 46533). *Location:* three and a half miles north east of Portlaoise. Relatively flat with furze and gorse. 18 holes, 5721 metres. S.S.S. 70 white, 69 green. 10 bay floodlit driving range. *Green Fees:* weekdays £10.00; weekends £14.00. *Eating facilities:* full bar and catering facilities available. *Visitors:* welcome at all times but advance booking required for weekends and Public Holidays. *Society Meetings:* welcome by prior arrangement. Professional: Eddie Doyle (0502 46622). Secretary: Frank Conway (0502 21034).

# THE ABBEY TAVERN
## Abbeydorney, Tralee

Situated at the Village Inn in Abbeydorney, these self catering flats are ideally placed for touring County Kerry. Both Tralee and Banna Beach are five miles away and Ballyheigue, Killarney, Dingle and the Ring of Kerry are also within easy reach. Near Tralee, Killarney and Ballybunion Golf Courses. Clean and reasonably priced, the flats have shower, toilet; living room; kitchenette with electric cooker, fridge, heater etc. Electricity by 50p meter. Linen and towels supplied. Cot on request. A car is essential and there is ample parking. Overnight stops welcome. Evening meal available for self catering guests. Bed and Breakfast and Partial Board also available. Meals served all day. A four bedroom house is also available.

*Further details from Mrs Mary O'Connor (010-353-6635145).*

# LIMERICK

CASTLEROY. **Castleroy Golf Club,** Castleroy, Co. Limerick (061 335261; Fax: 061 335373). *Location:* three miles from Limerick City on N7 (Dublin Road). Parkland with numerous trees. 18 holes, 6330 yards. S.S.S. 71. *Green Fees:* weekdays £20.00; weekends with a member only, £12.00. *Eating facilities:* full catering service, bar. *Visitors:* welcome, most weekdays, restrictions weekends and Thursday afternoons, Tuesday is Ladies' Day – advisable to phone. *Society Meetings:* welcome Mondays, Wednesdays and Fridays, group rates available. Professional: M. Cassidy (061 338283). Secretary: Laurence Hayes (061 335753).

# LOUTH

DROGHEDA. **County Louth Golf Club,** Baltray, Drogheda (041 22327). *Location:* Drogheda, five miles north east. Championship links course. 18 holes, 6783 yards. S.S.S. 72. *Green Fees:* weekday £24.00; weekends £30.00. *Eating facilities:* restaurant, coffee shop and bar. *Visitors:* welcome weekdays except Tuesdays on application, weekends restricted. Accommodation available for 20 persons. *Society Meetings:* on application. Professional: Paddy McGuirk (041 22444). Secretary: Michael Delany (041 22329; Fax: 041 22969).

DUNDALK, **Dundalk Golf Club,** Blackrock, Dundalk (042 21379). *Location:* Dundalk coast road to Blackrock, three miles. Parkland. 18 holes, 5504 yards, 6115 metres. S.S.S. 72 (Par 72). Six acre field practice ground. *Green Fees:* weekdays £15.00; weekends £18.00. *Eating facilities:* full restaurant and bar. *Visitors:* welcome Mondays, Wednesdays, Thursdays and Fridays, restrictions Tuesdays and weekends. *Society Meetings:* welcome except Tuesdays and Sundays. Professional: James Cassidy. Secretary: Joe Carroll (042 21731).

# COUNTY MAYO

ACHILL. **Achill Golf Club,** Keel, Achill. *Location:* Achill to Keel main road. Flat seaside links course. 9 holes, 2723 yards, 2489 metres. S.S.S. 66. *Green Fees:* on application. *Visitors:* welcome at all times, no restrictions. *Society Meetings:* by prior arrangement. Secretary: Patrick Lavelle.

BALLINROBE. **Ballinrobe 'Golf Club,** Castleton Road, Ballinrobe (092 41448). *Location:* Ballinrobe on the Castleton Road. Flatland in the middle of a racecourse. 9 holes, 5540 metres. S.S.S. 68. Practice ground. *Green Fees:* £7.00. *Eating facilities:* bar and restaurant during the Summer. *Visitors:* welcome at all times except Tuesday evenings and Sundays. *Society Meetings:* welcome. Secretary: Pat Holian (092 659).

# COUNTY MEATH

NAVAN. **Royal Tara Golf Club,** Bellinter, Navan (046 25244). *Location:* 25 miles north of Dublin off National Primary Route N3. Parkland, private course. 18 holes, 5757 yards. S.S.S. 70. 9 hole course, 3184 yards. S.S.S. 35. *Green Fees:* £12.00 weekdays; £15.00 weekends. *Eating facilities:* bar and full catering facilities. *Visitors:* welcome, Tuesday Ladies Day, please check with club in advance. *Society Meetings:* welcomed Monday, Thursday, Friday and Saturday. Professional: Mr Adam Whiston. Secretary: Mr Paddy O'Brien (046 25508).

# COUNTY MONAGHAN

CASTLEBLAYNEY. **Castleblayney Golf Club,** Onomy, Castleblayney (042 46194). *Location:* Hope Castle Estate, 500 yards from town centre. Scenic parkland course with lakes and forest in centre of Leisure Park. 9 holes, 5345 yards. S.S.S. 66. *Green Fees:* £5.00 weekdays; £8.00 weekends. *Eating facilities:* restaurant and bar. *Visitors:* welcome at all times except during major competitions. *Society Meetings:* welcome. Secretary: Des McGlynn.

# COUNTY ROSCOMMON

ROSCOMMON. **Roscommon Golf Club,** Mote Park, Roscommon (0903 26382). *Location:* half a mile from Roscommon town. Parkland. 9 holes, 5784 metres. S.S.S. 70. *Green Fees:* £8.00, Saturdays only by arrangement. £5.00 for Societies. *Eating facilities:* light snacks, tea, coffee, etc. *Visitors:* welcome all year round, but not Sundays except on open days. *Society Meetings:* as Visitors. Secretary: Cathal McConn (0903 26062).

# COUNTY SLIGO

ENNISCRONE. **Enniscrone Golf Club,** Enniscrone (096 36657). *Location:* on coast road from Sligo to Ballina, about nine miles from Ballina. Championship links course - host to the Irish Close Championship 1993. 18 holes, 6570 yards. S.S.S. 72. Practice area and putting green. *Green Fees:* £15.00 per day weekdays; £15.00 per round weekends. *Eating facilities:* bar and full catering facilities. *Visitors:* welcome. *Society Meetings:* groups of 12 or more, Green Fee £10.00. Professional: Charlie McGoldrick. Secretary: John Fleming.

## COUNTY TIPPERARY

CARRICK-ON-SUIR. **Carrick-on-Suir Golf Club,** Garravoone, Carrick-on-Suir (051 40047). *Location:* one mile from Carrick-on-Suir on Dungarvan Road. Scenic 9 hole course on elevated ground close to town. 9 holes, 5948 yards. S.S.S. 68. *Green Fees:* £10.00. *Eating facilities:* full meals and bar snacks available by prior arrangement. *Visitors:* welcome Monday to Saturday, avoid Tuesday and Wednesday evenings in summer (competitions). Special rates for groups. *Society Meetings:* all welcome by prior arrangement. Secretary: Michael Guiry (Tel & Fax: 051 46078).

CLONMEL. **Clonmel Golf Club,** Mountain Road, Clonmel (052 21138). *Location:* set in the scenic slopes of the Comeragh Mountains, just a short distance from the town of Clonmel. 18 holes, 5785 metres. S.S.S. 70. Driving range. *Green Fees:* £12.00 weekdays; £15.00 weekends. *Eating facilities:* full catering, soup, sandwiches, four course meals and bar. *Visitors:* always welcome. *Society Meetings:* welcomed. Professional: Robert Hayes (052 24050). Secretary: William O'Sullivan (052 24050).

## COUNTY WATERFORD

LISMORE. **Lismore Golf Club,** Ballyin, Lismore (058 54026). *Location:* one kilometre north of Lismore Heritage Town, just off the N72. Undulating parkland with mature trees, course surrounded by woodlands. 9 holes, 5196 metres. S.S.S. 67. *Green Fees:* £8.00 weekdays; £10.00 weekends and Bank Holidays. Reductions for Societies. *Eating facilities:* tea, coffee, snacks. *Visitors:* welcome weekdays, restriction may apply on Wednesday (ladies day). *Society Meetings:* welcome weekday except Wednesday. Secretary: Patrick Norris.

## COUNTY WICKLOW

BRITTAS BAY. **The European Club,** Brittas Bay (Dublin 2808459; Fax: 2808457). *Location:* one mile south of main Brittas Bay beach on coast road, 40 miles south of Dublin City Centre. Rolling linksland overlooking Arklow Bay, designed and owned by Pat Ruddy. 18 holes, 6900 yards. Extensive practice areas. *Green Fees:* £20.00 weekdays; £25.00 weekends. *Eating facilities:* full services. *Visitors:* welcome to all golfers. *Society Meetings:* welcome. Secretary: Pat Ruddy.

# FOR THE MUTUAL GUIDANCE OF GUEST AND HOST

Every year literally thousands of holidays, short-breaks and overnight stops are arranged through our guides, the vast majority without any problems at all. In a handful of cases, however, difficulties do arise about bookings, which often could have been prevented from the outset.

It is important to remember that when accommodation has been booked, both parties — guests and hosts — have entered into a form of contract. We hope that the following points will provide helpful guidance.

**GUESTS:** When enquiring about accommodation, be as precise as possible. Give exact dates, numbers in your party and the ages of any children. State the number and type of rooms wanted and also what catering you require — bed and breakfast, full board, etc. Make sure that the position about evening meals is clear — and about pets, reductions for children or any other special points.

Read our reviews carefully to ensure that the proprietors you are going to contact can supply what you want. Ask for a letter confirming all arrangements, if possible.

If you have to cancel, do so as soon as possible. Proprietors do have the right to retain deposits and under certain circumstances to charge for cancelled holidays if adequate notice is not given and they cannot re-let the accommodation.

**HOSTS:** Give details about your facilities and about any special conditions. Explain your deposit system clearly and arrangements for cancellations, charges, etc, and whether or not your terms include VAT.

If for any reason you are unable to fulfil an agreed booking without adequate notice, you may be under an obligation to arrange alternative suitable accommodation or to make some form of compensation.

While every effort is made to ensure accuracy, we regret that FHG Publications cannot accept responsibility for errors, omissions or misrepresentation in our entries or any consequences thereof. Prices in particular should be checked because we go to press early. We will follow up complaints but cannot act as arbiters or agents for either party.

# Isle of Man

DOUGLAS. **Douglas Golf Club (playing over Municipal Course)**, Pulrose Golf Course, Pulrose Road, Douglas (0624 75952). *Location:* one mile from Douglas Pier, near to large Cooling Tower landmark. Buses every 15 minutes. Parkland – testing course, often venue for Manx Championship. 18 holes, 5922 yards. S.S.S. 68. *Green Fees:* information not provided. *Eating facilities:* light meals available in licensed clubhouse. *Visitors:* welcome without reservation. *Society Meetings:* catered for after prior notification. Professional: K. Parry. Hon. Secretary: G. Allen.

DOUGLAS. **Pulrose Golf Course**, Douglas. *Location:* one mile from town centre, next to power station. Undulating parkland with memorable 17th hole. 18 holes, 5922 yards. S.S.S. 68. Putting and practice area. *Green Fees:* information not provided. *Eating facilities:* bar; meals available at all times. *Visitors:* welcome, no restrictions. *Society Meetings:* by arrangement with Professional. Professional: K. Parry (0624 75952). Secretary: G. Allen.

FORT ISLAND. **Castletown Golf Club**, Castletown Golf Links Hotel, Fort Island, Derbyhaven (Castletown (0624) 822201). *Location:* 12 miles from Douglas. Three miles from Ronaldsway airport. Seaside links course. 18 holes, 6731 yards. S.S.S. 73. *Green Fees:* weekdays £19.00 per person per day; weekends £25.00 per person per day. *Eating facilities:* table d'hôte/à la carte restaurant, daytime and evening bistro snacks. *Visitors:* welcome without reservation. Accommodation available, plus sauna, sunbeds, swimming pool, changing rooms. *Society Meetings:* catered for. Professional: Murray S. Crowe (0624 822211). General Manager: Miss J.M. Mitchell (0624 822201). Hon. Secretary: Mr A. Karran.

ONCHAN. **King Edward Bay Golf and Country Club**, Groudle Road, Howstrake, Onchan (0624 620430). *Location:* north headland of Douglas Bay. Stunning views from Headland links course. Watered greens, excellent fairways. 18 holes, 5450 yards. S.S.S. 57. Practice area. *Green Fees:* weekdays £8.00;

weekends £10.00. *Eating facilities:* full catering available, three bars. *Visitors:* welcome without reservation except not before 9.30am Sundays. *Society Meetings:* most welcome by arrangement. Professional: Donald Jones (0624 620430 extension 25). Secretary: Miss K. Nightingale (0624 676794).

PEEL. **Peel Golf Club**, Rheast Lane, Peel (0624 842227). *Location:* outskirts of Peel on main Douglas Road. Heathland links. 18 holes, 5914 yards. S.S.S. 68. Practice ground. *Green Fees:* weekdays £12.00; weekends £16.00. *Eating facilities:* full bar service and meals. *Visitors:* welcome, but check in advance for weekend availability. *Society Meetings:* catered for, check in advance. Pro Shop: R. Garrard (0624 844232). Secretary: P. Kissack (0624 843456).

PORT ERIN. **Rowany Golf Club**, Rowany Drive, Port Erin (0624 824108). *Location:* off the Promenade. Hilly setting by the seaside. 18 holes, 5480 yards. S.S.S. 68. Driving range. *Green Fees:* £10.00 weekdays; £15.00 weekends. 25% discount for societies. *Eating facilities:* restaurant and bar. *Visitors:* welcome by arrangement. Accommodation can be arranged. *Society Meetings:* welcome. Professional: Callum Wilson. Secretary: R.D. Humphreys-Jones.

PORT ST. MARY. **Port St. Mary Golf Club**, Point Road, Port St. Mary (0624 834932). *Location:* clearly signposted after entering Port St. Mary. Seaside links with beautiful panoramic views. 9 holes, 2754 yards. S.S.S. 66. *Green Fees:* weekdays £7.00; weekends £10.00. Parties of 10 or more 10% discount. *Eating facilities:* restaurant and bar open all day. *Visitors:* welcome at all times only restrictions weekends between 8am to 10.30am. Secretary: (0624 832274).

RAMSEY. **Ramsey Golf Club**, Brookfield (0624 813365). *Location:* west boundary of Ramsey. Parkland. 18 holes, 6019 yards. S.S.S. 69. Practice ground. *Green Fees:* weekdays £10.00 winter, £15.00 summer; weekends £12.00 winter, £18.00 summer. *Eating facilities:* bar snacks and lunches available every day, à la carte restaurant available Thursday, Friday and Saturday. *Visitors:* welcome, teeing off between 10am – 12 noon and 2pm – 4pm only. *Society Meetings:* welcome weekdays only. Professional: Mr Peter Lowey (0624 814736). Secretary: Mrs S.J. Birchall (0624 812244).

# Channel Islands

ALDERNEY. **Alderney Golf Club,** Route des Carrieres, Alderney (0481 822835). *Location:* one mile east of St. Anne. Seaside links with sea views from every hole. 9 holes, 2528 yards. S.S.S. 65. Putting and practice area. *Green Fees:* weekdays £12.00; weekends £18.00 (half these rates if playing with member). *Eating facilities:* bar and meals. *Visitors:* welcome all year. Parties over 4 must contact Club for availability. *Society Meetings:* welcome by arrangement. Secretary: Nigel Soane-Sands (0481 822835).

GUERNSEY. **Royal Guernsey Golf Club,** L'Ancresse, Vale, Guernsey (0481 47022). *Location:* three miles north of St. Peter Port. Seaside links. 18 holes, 6206 yards. S.S.S. 70. Practice ground. *Green Fees:* weekdays £23.00 per day; weekends £23.00 per day or round. £15.00 playing with a member. *Eating facilities:* restaurant and bar. *Visitors:* welcome except Thursday and Saturday afternoons and Sundays unless playing with a member. Must have Handicap Certificate. *Society Meetings:* October to March only, by prior arrangement. Professional: Norman Wood (0481 45070). Secretary: M. De Laune (0481 46523).

GUERNSEY. **St. Pierre Park Golf Club,** Rohais, St. Peter Port, Guernsey (0481 728282 ext 564). *Location:* 10 minutes from St. Peter Port. Wooded parkland with numerous lakes. 9 holes, 2511 yards. S.S.S. 27. Driving range, putting green. *Green Fees:* weekdays £15.00 (£5.00 if resident at hotel), weekends £17.00 (£7.50 if resident at hotel). Weekly rate for residents of Hotel £35.00. *Eating facilities:* two restaurants and two bars in hotel. *Visitors:* welcome subject to rules and regulations on display. Hotel accommodation 135 luxurious rooms and suites. Pro shop. Shop Manager: R. Corbet.

JERSEY. **Jersey Recreation Grounds,** Greve D'Azette, St. Clement, Jersey (0534 21938). *Location:* inner coast road near St. Helier. Flat course with some water hazards. 9 holes, 2244 yards. S.S.S. 30. Practice range and putting green. *Green Fees:* information not provided. *Eating facilities:* licensed buffet. *Visitors:* welcome at all times. *Society Meetings:* welcome. Managing Director: P.A.O. Graham.

JERSEY. **La Moye Golf Club,** St. Brelade, Jersey
(0534 42701). *Location:* on road to Corbiere Lighthouse at La Moye, St. Brelade. Turn right at airport
crossroads, right again at crossroads traffic lights.
Seaside links championship course. 18 holes, 6512
yards. S.S.S. 72. Practice ground. *Green Fees:* on
application. *Eating facilities:* full restaurant/snack facilities, three bars. *Visitors:* weekdays 9.30-11am and
2-3.30pm, weekends 2.30pm onwards. Must have
Handicap Certificate. *Society Meetings:* by prior
appointment only. Professional: Mr David Melville
(0534 43130). Secretary: Mr Pat Clash (0534 43401).

JERSEY. **Royal Jersey Golf Club,** Grouville, Jersey
(0534 51042). *Location:* four miles east of St. Helier

(follow coast road). Links course. 18 holes, 6051 yards.
S.S.S. 70. *Green Fees:* weekdays £30.00 per round;
weekends and Bank Holidays £35.00 per round (after
2.30pm). *Eating facilities:* restaurant and two bars.
*Visitors:* welcome if member of recognised club. Handicap Certificate required. *Society Meetings:* welcome by
prior arrangement. Professional: Tommy A. Horton
(0534 52234). Secretary: R.C. Leader (0534 54416).

ST. OUEN'S. **Les Mielles Golf Course,** The Mount,
Val de la Mare, St. Ouen's, Jersey JE3 2PQ (0534
82787; Fax 83739). *Location:* centre of St. Ouen's Bay.
12 holes (extending to 18 holes in the near future).
Driving range. *Green Fees:* information not provided.
Secretary: J.E. Hurley.

# Golf in France
## WHERE TO PLAY • WHERE TO STAY
*by Michael Gedye*

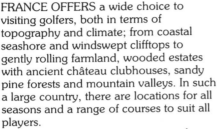

FRANCE OFFERS a wide choice to visiting golfers, both in terms of topography and climate; from coastal seashore and windswept clifftops to gently rolling farmland, wooded estates with ancient château clubhouses, sandy pine forests and mountain valleys. In such a large country, there are locations for all seasons and a range of courses to suit all players.

From the 450-plus courses spread over twenty sub-regions, we have selected some of the best for the travelling visitor. Courses in interesting locations, in good condition, with full facilities and a guaranteed welcome. For convenience, these are grouped under seven regional headings.

The NORTH comprises those areas closest to Britain, just across the Channel, which formed one of the holiday golfing playgrounds in the early part of the century. Nord Pas-de-Calais, Picardy and Normandy can offer historic golfing gems such as Wimereux, Granville, Le Touquet, Hardelot and Deauville alongside more recent additions such as Champ de Bataille and Omaha Beach.

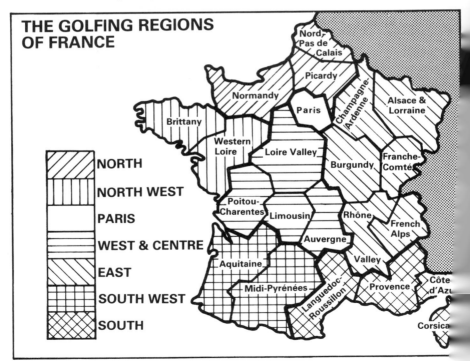

THE GOLFING REGIONS OF FRANCE

NORTH
NORTH WEST
PARIS
WEST & CENTRE
EAST
SOUTH WEST
SOUTH

Nord, Pas de Calais
Picardy
Normandy
Brittany
Paris
Champagne-Ardenne
Alsace & Lorraine
Western Loire
Loire Valley
Burgundy
Franche-Comté
Poitou-Charentes
Limousin
Rhône
French Alps
Auvergne
Valley
Aquitaine
Midi-Pyrénées
Languedoc-Roussillon
Provence
Côte d'Azur
Corsica

The NORTH WEST area of Brittany and the Western Loire has long been a golfing favourite for its ease of access by ferry and car and its timeless ambience. In its southern reaches, it also enjoys a unique micro-climate. Golf in Brittany tends to follow the coast, with such treats as St. Malo Le Tronchet, Brest Iroise, L'Odet and St. Laurent. Inland, Rennes has two courses, of which La Freslonnière is well worth a detour for its understated charm. The château and wine regions of the Western Loire yield further rich bounty, notably La Baule and La Bretesche near the coast in the north, St. Jean de Monts and La Domangère similarly further south plus the Anjou Country Club and Golf de Sablé inland near Angers.

For those visiting the capital, PARIS can offer golf to the visitor, often of very high quality. Tigers will want to flex their skills on the fairways of Golf National, home of the French Open. Lesser lights will enjoy the wooded beauty of Yvelines.

The WEST & CENTRE region includes the Loire Valley, Poitou-Charente, Limousin and Auvergne. For a real test, try Les Bordes with its many hazards or for sheer magnificence, tackle the plunging fairways of Royan near the sea.

The largest geographic region is undoubtedly the EAST, which includes Champagne-Ardennes, Lorraine, Alsace, Burgundy, Franche-Comte, French Alps and the Rhone Valley. Players at Chamonix hole out under the eternal snows of Mont Blanc while those embraced in the luxuries of Evian have the vista of Lake Leman.

Golf began, as far as Europe is concerned, in the SOUTH WEST and the coast from Bordeaux to Biarritz is sprinkled with attractions. Golf du Medoc offers vinified style, Pessac and Gujan pure holiday enjoyment while down the coast the litany of old and new delights includes Moliets, Seignosse, Hossegor, Chiberta, Biarritz, Arcangues and Nivelle – a golfer's paradise along the seashore.

Finally, in the SOUTH, one can discover the sun-splashed greens of Languedoc-Roussillon, Provence and the Côte d'Azur, where natural beauty and elegance go hand in hand. Contrast the rugged slopes of Cap d'Agde and Les Baux with the manicured excellence of Cannes and St. Raphael or, for a real examination, visit the trilogy of Massane, La Grande Motte and Nîmes, fine championship courses that have tested the best. A final flourish in a selection to suit all tastes and talents.

# NORTH

BAYEUX. **Golf de Bayeux,** Omaha Beach, 14520 Port-en-Bessin (31.21.72.94; Fax: 31.22.36.77). *Location:* towards the coast approximately eight km north-west of Bayeux. Cliff top course with fine views. 18 holes, 6234 metres, Par 72. 9 holes, 2875 metres, Par 5. Practice ground, putting green. *Eating facilities:* clubhouse bar and restaurant. Pro Shop; cart, club and trolley hire. Hôtel Altea nearby.

BOULOGNE. **Golf de Wimereux,** Route Ambleteuse, 62930 Wimereux (21.32.43.20). *Location:* north of Wimereux on the D940 approximately seven km north of Boulogne. Venerable Scottish-style links course with broad fairways between sea and dunes. 18 holes, 6150 metres, Par 72. Practice ground, putting green. *Eating facilities:* clubhouse, bar and restaurant. Trolley and club hire.

CAEN. **Golf de Caen,** Le Vallon, 14112 Biéville-Beauville (31.94.72.09; Fax: 31.84.76.19). *Location:* three km north of Caen towards the sea. A relatively new course over undulating land with mature trees and some densely wooded areas. 18 holes, 6135 metres, Par 72. Driving range, putting green. *Eating facilities:* bar and restaurant in clubhouse. Pro shop; trolley and club hire.

DEAUVILLE. **Golf de St Gatien Deauville,** Le Mont Saint Jean, 14130 Saint-Gatien-des-Bois (31.65.19.99; Fax: 31.65.11.24). *Location:* about eight km inland and eight km east of Deauville. An interesting course with 9 holes, sloping steeply through woodland, plenty of sand and strategic water. 18 holes, 6200 metres, Par 72. 9 holes 3035 metres, Par 36. Driving range, putting green. *Eating facilities:* bar and restaurant in rustic 18th century clubhouse. Pro shop; cart, trolley and club hire.

DEAUVILLE. **New Golf Lucien Barriere Deauville,** 14800 Deauville, Saint-Arnoult (31.88.20.53; Fax: 31.88.75.99). *Location:* on the south-western side of Deauville with the sea to the north. A scenic and varied course, hilly in part with fast greens. 18 holes, 5934 metres, Par 71. 9 holes, 3033 metres, Par 36. Practice ground and putting green. *Eating facilities:* bar and restaurant in clubhouse; all facilities at the adjoining Golf Hôtel. Pro shop; club, cart and trolley hire.

GRANVILLE. **Golf de Granville,** Bréville-sur-Mer, 50290 Bréhal (33.50.23.06). *Location:* just north of Granville on the coast. A well established natural links course running through the "green dunes" by the sea; playable all year. 18 holes, 5854 metres, Par 72. 9 holes, 2323 metres, Par 36. Driving range, putting green. *Eating facilities:* bar and restaurant in clubhouse. Pro shop; trolley and club hire.

HARDELOT. **Golf d'Hardelot "Les Dunes",** Allée des Fauvettes, 62152 Hardelot Plage (21.91.90.90; Fax: 21.83.24.33). *Location:* at Hardelot Plage, 15km south of Boulogne. A spectacular course across lakes and wooded dunes with coastal views. 18 holes, 6095 metres, Par 73. Practice ground, putting green. *Eating facilities:* clubhouse bar and restaurant. Pro shop; club and trolley hire.

HARDELOT. **Golf d'Hardelot "Les Pins",** 3 Avenue du Golf, 62152 Hardelot Plage (21.83.73.10; Fax: 21.83.24.33). *Location:* the beach-resort of Hardelot Plage is 15 km south of Boulogne. Attractive course carved through a pine forest. 18 holes, 5870 metres, Par 72. Practice ground, putting green. *Eating facilities:* clubhouse with bar and fine restaurant. Pro shop; club and trolley hire.

LAON. **Golf de l'Ailette,** 02860 Cerny-en-Laonnois (23.24.83.99; Fax: 23.24.84.66). *Location:* about 10km south of Laon. An interesting course laid out on the edge of a forest flanked by large areas of water. 18 holes, 6127 metres, Par 72. 9 holes, 1165 metres, Par 28. Driving range, putting green. *Eating facilities:* bar and restaurant in clubhouse. Pro shop; trolley and club hire.

LE TOUQUET. **Golf du Touquet,** Avenue du Golf, 62520 Le Touquet (21.05.68.47). *Location:* on the coast, two km south of Le Touquet. The Forest Course – in the heart of an old pine forest. 18 holes, 5912 metres, Par 71. The Sea Course – a championship links course bordered by sand dunes. 18 holes, 6082 metres, Par 72. Also a 9 hole beginners' course. Practice ground and putting green. *Eating facilities:* bar and restaurant in clubhouse. Pro shop; trolley and club hire.

LILLE. **Golf de Bondues,** Château de la Vigne, 59910 Bondues (20.23.20.62; Fax: 20.23.24.11). *Location:* about 10km north of Lille, west of the N17. In the grounds of an 18th century château, the courses have well protected greens with deep bunkers and several water hazards. 18 holes, 6261 metres, Par 73. 18 holes, 6000 metres, Par 72. Driving range, putting green. *Eating facilities:* bar and restaurant in clubhouse. Pro shop.

NEUBOURG. **Golf Club du Champ de Bataille,** 27110 Le Neubourg (32.35.03.72; Fax: 32.35.83.10).

*Location:* south-west of Rouen, about 28km north-west of Evreux. A fine test of golf attractively laid out through the wooded estate of the elegant château. 18 holes, 5983 metres, Par 72. Driving range, putting green. *Eating facilities:* bar and restaurant in château clubhouse. Pro shop; cart, trolley and club hire.

ST OMER. **AA Saint-Omer Golf Club,** Chemin des Bois, Acquin-Westbecourt, 62380 Lumbres (21.38.59.90; Fax: 21.38.59.90). *Location:* off the A26 approximately 40km south of Calais and 10 km west of St. Omer. Undulating parkland and mature trees overlooking the valley of the River Aa. 18 holes, 6400 metres, Par 72. 9 holes, 2003 metres, Par 31. Practice ground and putting green. *Eating facilities:* clubhouse bar and restaurant. Pro shop; trolley and club hire.

# NORTH WEST

ANGERS. **Anjou Golf and Country Club,** Route de Cheffes, 49330 Champigné (41.42.01.01; Fax: 41.42.04.37). *Location:* about 20km north of Angers, west of the D768. A pleasant layout over former farmland surrounding a château. Recently opened 18 hole course, 6195 metres, Par 72. Short 6 hole course, 710 metres, Par 19. *Eating facilities:* bar and restaurant in clubhouse. Pro shop; cart, trolley and club hire.

ANGERS. **Golf de Sablé-Solesmes,** Domaine de l'Outinière, Route de Pincé, 72300 Sablé-sur-Sarthe (43.95.28.78; Fax: 43.92.39.05). *Location:* east of the A11, about 40km north of Angers, south-east of Le Mans. Three totally different 9's – Forest and River: 18 holes, 6207 metres, Par 72; Waterfall: 9 holes, 3069 metres, Par 36, radiate from the large clubhouse. Testing and spectacular with park, woodland and lakeside holes. Driving range, putting green. *Eating facilities:* bar and restaurant in clubhouse. Pro shop; cart, trolley and club hire.

AURAY. **Golf de Baden,** Kernic, 56870 Baden (97.57.18.96; Fax: 97.57.22.05). *Location:* between the village of Baden and the sea, south of the RN 165 a Auray exit. Undulating course partly through pine woods and around lakes. 18 holes, 6112 metres, Par 72. 3 hole, 535 metre pitch and putt course. *Eating facilities:* bar and restaurant in clubhouse. Pro shop; trolley and club hire. Neighbouring hotels "L Gavrinis" and "du Loch" offer year-round golfing breaks.

AURAY. **Golf de Saint Laurent,** 56400 Auray Ploemel (97.56.85.18; Fax: 97.56.89.99). *Location* about five km west of Auray and not far from Car with its ancient standing stones. High quality cha pionship course, undulating through mature trees. holes, 6112 metres, Par 72. 9 hole course, 26 metres, Par 35. *Eating facilities:* bar and restaurant on-course Fairway Hôtel St. Laurent; also on-cou "Maeve" self catering cottages available. Pro she cart, trolley and club hire.

BENODET. **Golf de l'Odet,** Menez Groas, Clohars-Fouesnant, 29950 Bénodet (98.54.87.88; Fax: 98.54.61.40). *Location:* south of Quimper, towards the sea at Bénodet. An undulating partly wooded course. 18 holes, 6235 metres, Par 72. 9 holes, 1100 metres, Par 27. Driving range and putting green. *Eating facilities:* bar, restaurant and on-site Hôtel Eurogreen, whose residents have reduced green fees. Other accommodation nearby. Pro shop; cart, trolley and club hire.

BREST. **Golf de Brest Iroise,** Parc de Loisirs de Lann Rohou, 29800 Landerneau (98.85.16.17; Fax: 98.21.52.08). *Location:* east of Brest, five km south of Landerneau. A tough course, open to the breeze in a beautiful natural setting. 18 holes, 5885 metres, Par 72. 9 holes, 3329 metres, Par 37. Driving range, putting green. *Eating facilities:* bar and restaurant and all facilities at the Golf Hôtel d'Iroise. Pro shop; cart, trolley and club hire.

LA BAULE. **Golf de la Baule,** Domaine de St. Denac, 44117 St. André-des-Eaux (40.60.46.18; Fax: 04.60.89.21). *Location:* just outside La Baule, to the north-east. A parkland course winding through mature trees with hills and a large lake affecting the back nine. 18 holes, 6157 metres, Par 72. Practice ground and putting greens. *Eating facilities:* attractive thatched clubhouse with bar and restaurant. Pro shop; cart, club and trolley hire.

LA BAULE. **Golf de la Bretesche,** Domaine de la Bretesche, 44780 Missillac (40.88.30.03; Fax: 40.88.36.28). *Location:* 20km north-east of La Baule; 50km north-west of Nantes on the N165. In peaceful wooded parkland surrounding a magnificent château and lake. 18 holes, 6080 metres, Par 72. *Eating facilities:* bar and restaurant in club. Self catering cottages next to the course. Pro shop; cart, trolley and club hire.

LA ROCHE-SUR-YON. **Golf Club de la Domangère,** Route de Nesmy, 85310 Nesmy (51.07.60.15; Fax: 51.07.64.09). *Location:* approximately 10km south of La Roche-sur-Yon east of the D747. A long and majestic course with plenty of strategic water, mature trees and bordered by the River 'on. 18 holes, 6480 metres, Par 72. 4 hole practice course, driving range, putting green. *Eating facilities:* bar, grill-room and restaurant in the on-site Hôtel de la Domangère. Club, cart and trolley hire.

LORIENT. **Golf de Ploemeur Ocean,** Saint Jude/erham, 56270 Ploemeur (97.32.81.82; Fax: 7.32.80.90). *Location:* on the coast at Ploemeur close to Lorient. Undulating links, overlooking the sea, with water hazards. 18 holes, 5957 metres, Par 72. Driving range. *Eating facilities:* clubhouse with bar and grill-room. Hotels in Ploemeur. Pro shop; trolley and club hire, golf school.

LORIENT. **Golf du Val Quéven,** Kerrousseau RD 6, 56530 Quéven (97.05.17.96: Fax: 97.05.19.18). *Location:* at Pont Scorff near Quéven off the RN 165 shortly after Lorient. A varied course, wooded and with water hazards. 18 holes, 6140 metres, Par 72. Driving range, putting green. *Eating facilities:* bar and restaurant. Pro shop; club and trolley hire.

RENNES. **Golf de la Freslonnière,** 35650 Le Rheu (99.60.84.09; Fax: 99.60.94.98). *Location:* three km from Rennes towards Lorient. Well watered and level, winding through attractive woodland. 18 holes, 5671 metres, Par 71. Practice ground and putting green. *Eating facilities:* clubhouse, restaurant and bar. Golf holiday packages from nearby Novotel Rennes. Pro shop; club, cart and trolley hire.

RENNES. **Golf de Rennes,** St. Jacques de la Lande, 35136 Rennes (99.64.24.18; Fax: 99.60.37.37). *Location:* eight km south of Rennes, off the D177 to Redon. Set amongst mature woodland with several water hazards; a new course to enjoy. 18 holes, 6150 metres, Par 72. 9 holes, 2068 metres, Par 32. Short 9 hole course. *Eating facilities:* bar and restaurant in clubhouse. Pro shop; trolley and club hire.

ST. MALO. **Golf de St-Malo-le-Tronchet,** Le Tronchet, 35540 Miniac Morvan (99.58.96.69). *Location:* 23km south of St. Malo, 12km east of Dinan, south of the N176. Rolling parkland designed on a grand scale with vast greens and sand traps, strategic water. 18 holes, 6049 metres. S.S.S. 72. 9 holes, 2684 metres, Par 36. Driving range, putting green. *Eating facilities:* clubhouse bar and restaurant. "Hostellerie Abbatiale" close by the course with all hotel facilities and golf holiday packages. Pro shop; trolley and club hire.

ST.-JEAN-DE-MONTS. **Golf Club de St. Jean-de-Monts,** Avenue des Pays de Monts, 85160 St. Jean-de-Monts (51.58.82.73; Fax: 51.59.18.32). *Location:* a partly links-style course along the seaside with pine trees and dunes. On the Atlantic coast some 60/70km south-west of Nantes. 18 holes, 5962 metres, Par 72. Short 5 hole course. Practice ground and putting greens. *Eating facilities:* clubhouse with bar and restaurant. The Hôtel de la Plage in nearby Notre Dame de Monts offers golfing breaks. Pro shop; cart, club and trolley hire.

# PARIS

**PARIS. Golf de Forges-les-Bains,** Rue de Général Leclerc, 91470 Forges-les-Bains (64.91.48.18; Fax: 64.91.40.52). *Location:* about 35km south-west of Paris, near the A10. Undulating layout with holes sloping through mature woodland. 18 holes, 6207 metres, Par 72. Driving range, putting green. *Eating facilities:* bar and restaurant in clubhouse. Pro shop; trolley and club hire.

**PARIS. Golf de la Vaucouleurs,** 78910 Civry-la-Forêt (34.87.62.69; Fax: 34.87.70.09). *Location:* off the A13 at the Mantes interchange, then south off the road to Houdan. Two 18 hole courses. "The River" – very varied with trees, water and hills, 6298 metres, Par 73; "The Little Valley" – a links-type course, 5638 metres, Par 70. Practice ground, putting green. *Eating facilities:* bar and restaurant in clubhouse; also at nearby Hôtel la Dousseine at Anet. Pro shop; club and trolley hire.

**PARIS. Golf de St. Quentin-en-Yvelines,** RD 912, 78190 Trappes (30.50.86.40; Fax: 34.82.88.82). *Location:* about 20km west of Paris off the D912. A very popular public facility of 36 holes. White Course – 18 holes, 6048 metres, Par 72; Red Course – 18 holes, 5969 metres, Par 70. Also 3 hole compact course, driving range, putting green. *Eating facilities:* bar and restaurant in clubhouse. Pro shop; trolley and club hire.

**PARIS. Golf des Yvelines,** Château de la Couharde, 78940 La Queue-les-Yvelines (34.86.48.89). *Location:* about 45km from Paris, south of the N12 near Montfort-l'Amaury. Built around the elegant château, with fairways cut through thick woods. 18 holes, 6390 metres, Par 72. 9 holes, 2040 metres, Par 31. Practice ground, putting green. *Eating facilities:* the château is the clubhouse with excellent facilities. Club and trolley hire.

**PARIS. Golf National,** 2 Avenue de Golf, 78280 Guyancourt (30.43.36.00; Fax: 34.43.85.58). *Location:* about 25km south-west of Paris off the D91. A public facility of 45 holes laid out in four courses. "The Albatross" – 18 holes, 6500 metres championship course with severe water hazards and winding fairways, Par 72; "The Eagle" – 18 holes, 6000 metres Par 72 for experienced players; "The Birdie" – 9 hole, 2100 metres beginners' course, Par 32 and driving range; "The Par" – a warm-up, practice course. Putting greens. *Eating facilities:* on-site Hôtel Novotel. Cart, club and trolley hire.

# WEST & CENTRE

**CHEVERNY. Golf du Château de Cheverny,** La Rousselière, 41700 Coutres (54.79.24.70). *Location:* on the south of the Cheverny 15km south of Blois. Built over the former hunting grounds of the Château with large well-kept greens. 18 holes, 6272 metres, Par 71. 3

hole practice course, driving range and putting green. *Eating facilities:* bar and restaurant in clubhouse. Pro shop; club and trolley hire.

**COGNAC. Golf du Cognac,** Saint-Brice, 16100 Cognac (45.32.18.17). *Location:* five km east of Cognac, north of the N141 across the River Charente. Undulating fairways with views of vineyards and the river; some water hazards. 18 holes, 6122 metres, Par 72. 4 hole practice course, putting green and driving range. *Eating facilities:* clubhouse with restaurant and bar. Pro shop; cart, club and trolley hire.

**LOUDUN. Golf Public Saint-Hilaire,** 86120 Roiffe (49.98.78.06; Fax: 49.98.72.57). *Location:* 15km north of Loudun towards Saumur on the D147. An attractive woodland course with water hazards. 18 holes, 6280 metres, Par 72. 6 hole practice course, driving range and putting green. *Eating facilities:* clubhouse with restaurant and bar. Pro shop; trolley and club hire.

**ORLEANS. "Les Bordes" Golf International,** 41220 St-Laurent Nouan (54.87.72.13; Fax: 54.87.78.61). *Location:* about 30km south-west of Orléans, near the south bank of the Loire. Laid out over the former hunting park, this spectacular and difficult course has many large bunkers and severe water hazards. 18 holes, 6412 metres, Par 72. Driving range, putting green. *Eating facilities:* bar and restaurant in clubhouse. Pro shop; carts, trolley and clubs for hire.

**POITIERS. Golf de Haut-Poitou,** Parc de Loisirs de St.Cyr, 86130 Jaunay-Clan (49.62.53.62). *Location:* just east of the N10 20km north of Poitiers and 15km south of Chatellerault. Undulating course with wooded hills and a lake. 18 holes, 6590 metres, Par 73. 9 holes, 1800 metres, Par 31. Practice ground, driving range, putting greens. *Eating facilities:* clubhouse with restaurant and bar. Pro shop and equipment hire.

**ROYAN. Golf de Royan,** Miane-Gaudin, La Palud, 17420 St.-Palais-sur-Mer (46.23.16.24). *Location:* on the D25 coast road, six km north-west of Royan. An exciting course with narrow fairways undulating through tall pines. 18 holes, 6033 metres, Par 71. 6 hole pitch and putt, practice ground with driving range, putting green. *Eating facilities:* restaurant and bar in clubhouse. Pro shop with equipment hire.

**TOURS. Golf d'Ardrée,** B P 1, 37360 St.-Antoine du-Rocher (47.56.77.38; Fax: 47.56.79.96). *Location:* 10km north of Tours. An attractive parkland course with strategic water and sand. 18 holes, 5804 metres, Par 71. Practice ground and putting green. *Eating facilities:* restaurant and bar in clubhouse. Pro shop; club and trolley hire.

**TOURS. Golf du Château des Sept Tours,** 3733 Courcelles de Tourraine (47.24.91.34; Fax: 47.24.97.22). *Location:* about 30km from Tours along the Loire to Langeais then north towards Château-la Valière. A long demanding course with attractive trees and water. 18 holes, 6312 metres, Par 72. Practice ground and putting green. *Eating facilities:* bar and restaurant in on-site Hôtel Château des Sept Tours. Pro shop; club and trolley hire.

## GOLF IN THE DOMAINE

There is a special haven of peace overlooking Lake Leman at Evian. Tucked away in 40 private acres, the recently renovated Royal Golf Club offers a challenging 18 holes with superb greens & Alpine views. Guests at the luxury resort Hotels within The Domaine – Hotel Royal and Hotel Ermitage – enjoy free green fees, reserved starting times and transport as well as a range of other complimentary sports, activities and services. *See also colour display page 38.*
**Domaine du Royal Club Evian, Rive sud du Lac de Génève, 74500 Evian Les Bains, France**
**Tel: 50.26.85.00 Fax: 50.75.61.00**

# EAST

AIX-LES-BAINS. **Golf Club d'Aix-les-Bains,** Avenue de Golf, 73100 Aix-les-Bains (79.61.23.35; Fax: 79.34.06.01). *Location:* three km south of Aix by the Lac du Bourget. An attractive parkland course on sloping land surrounded by wooded hills. 18 holes, 5595 metres, Par 71. Driving range, putting green. *Eating facilities:* bar and restaurant in clubhouse. Pro shop; trolley and club hire.

CHAMONIX. **Golf de Chamonix,** Route des Praz, 74400 Chamonix (50.53.06.28; Fax: 50.53.15.85). *Location:* on the N506 three km north of Chamonix. Green fairways follow the valley floor with streams and trees. Spectacular mountain views including Mont Blanc. 18 holes, 6076 metres, Par 72. Driving range, putting green. *Eating facilities:* bar and restaurant in clubhouse. Pro shop; cart, trolley and club hire.

EVIAN. **Royal Golf Club d'Evian,** Rive Sud du Lac de Genève, 74500 Evian-les-Bains (50.26.85.00; Fax: 50.75.61.00). *Location:* overlooking Lac Leman (de Genève) on the south side, two km west of Evian. A beautiful course, hilly with fine views and recently remodelled greens. 18 holes, 6006 metres, Par 72. Practice ground, putting green. *Eating facilities:* new

clubhouse with bar and restaurant. The Hôtel Royal also has pitch and putt and a putting green. Pro shop; cart, club and trolley hire.

GRENOBLE. **Golf International de Grenoble,** Route de Montavie, 38320 Eybens (76.73.65.00). *Location:* five km south of Grenoble. A long course with winding fairways, small lakes, trees. 18 holes, 6410 metres, Par 72. Practice ground and putting green. *Eating facilities:* clubhouse and nearby hotel. Pro shop; cart, trolley and club hire.

LYON. **Golf de Lyon Vilette d'Anthon,** 38280 Vilette d'Anthon (78.31.11.33). *Location:* bordered by the River Rhône about 20km east of Lyons. Sheltered, wooded and rather flat. 27 holes: Red Course – 18 holes, 6415 metres, Par 73; Green Course – 18 holes, 6140 metres, Par 72; Blue Course – 18 holes, 6345 metres, Par 73. Practice ground, putting green. *Eating facilities:* bar and restaurant in clubhouse. Pro shop; equipment hire.

ST. JULIEN (Geneva). **Golf and Country Club de Bossey,** Château de Crevin, Bossey, 74160 St.-Julien-en-Genèvois (50.43.75.25). *Location:* just in France on the southern outskirts of Geneva. Challenging mountain golf with fine views. Well wooded with water hazards. 18 holes, 6022 metres, Par 71. Driving range, putting green. *Eating facilities:* bar and restaurant in château clubhouse. Pro shop; cart, trolley and club hire.

# SOUTH WEST

ANGLET. **Golf de Chiberta,** 104 Boulevard des Plages, 64600 Anglet (59.63.83.20; Fax: 59.63.30.56). *Location:* three km north-east of Biarritz. A well-established combination of seashore and wooded parkland. 18 holes, 5650 metres, Par 70. Driving range, putting green. *Eating facilities:* bar and restaurant in clubhouse. Pro shop; trolley and club hire.

RCACHON. **Golf de Gujan Mestras,** B P 74, Route e Sanguinet, 33470 Gujan Mestras (56.66.86.36; Fax: 5.66.10.93). *Location:* a spectacular course with ell-located water obstacles. 12 km east of Arcachon, Jkm west of Bordeaux, north of the A66. 18 holes, 225 metres, Par 72. 9 holes, 2630 metres, Par 35. ting facilities: restaurant, clubhouse and at nearby tel. Pro shop; equipment and trolley hire.

BAYONNE. **Golf de la Côte d'Argent,** 40660 Moliets (58.48.54.65; Fax: 58.48.54.88). *Location:* about 30km north of Bayonne on the Atlantic coast at Moliets. Part of a leisure seaside complex with links and wooded inland holes. 18 holes, 6164 metres, Par 72. 9 holes, 1905 metres, Par 31. Practice ground, putting green. *Eating facilities:* bar and restaurant in clubhouse and in on-site hotels. Pro shop; cart, club and trolley hire.

BAYONNE. **Golf de Seignosse,** Carrefour Bocau, 40510 Seignosse (58.43.17.32; Fax: 58.43.16.67). *Location:* about 25km north of Bayonne on the D79 north of Hossegor. A testing championship course with much water, sand and many trees; very scenic. 18 holes, 6124 metres, Par 72. Practice ground, putting green. *Eating facilities:* bar and restaurant in clubhouse. Pro shop; cart, club and trolley hire.

BIARRITZ. **Golf d'Arcangues,** Argelous, 64200 Arcangues (59.43.10.56; Fax: 59.41.12.60). *Location:* three km south-east of Biarritz. A fine rolling test in modern but natural style. Mounded bunkers and strategic water. 18 holes, 6142 metres, Par 72. *Eating facilities:* bar and restaurant in clubhouse. Pro shop and equipment hire.

BIARRITZ. **Golf de Biarritz Le Phare,** 21 Avenue Edith Cavell, 64200 Biarritz (59.03.71.80; Fax: 59.03.26.74). *Location:* in Biarritz, facing the ocean with cooling breezes. A historic course (1888) with fast greens, level, many bunkers. 18 holes, 5379 metres, Par 69. Practice ground, putting green. *Eating facilities:* bar and restaurant in clubhouse, the nearby Hôtel du Palais and other hotels. Pro shop; club and trolley hire.

BORDEAUX. **Golf de Bordeaux Cameyrac,** St.-Sulpice et Cameyrac, 33450 St. Loubès (56.72.96.79). *Location:* 15km from Bordeaux on the N89 close to the famous vineyards of St. Emilion and Pomerol. Fairways run through forest, alongside ponds and vineyards. 18 holes, 5972 metres, Par 72. 9 holes, 1188 metres, Par 28. Practice ground, putting green. *Eating facilities:* bar and restaurant in clubhouse. Pro shop; equipment hire.

BORDEAUX. **Golf de Pessac,** Rue de la Princesse, 33600 Pessac (56.36.24.47; Fax: 56.36.52.89). *Location:* on the western outskirts of Bordeaux, four km from the city and close to the airport. A level course with large bunkers and some water. 27 holes providing alternative 9 hole layouts plus 9 hole practice course. 18 holes, 6123-6242 metres, all Par 72. Driving range, putting green. *Eating facilities:* clubhouse with restaurant and fine "Bordeaux" wine list. Pro shop; cart, club and trolley hire.

BORDEAUX. **Golf du Médoc,** Chemin de Courmateau, 33290 Le Pian Médoc (56.72.01.10; Fax: 56.72.03.44). *Location:* 15km to the north-west of Bordeaux by the River Garonne. Two courses, the original with widespread fairways, water and banks; 18 holes, 6316 metres. S.S.S. 71. The newer course "Des Vignes" winding through lakes and pine trees, has each of its 18 holes named after a Médoc wine château:

6291 metres, Par 70. Practice ground, pitching and putting greens. *Eating facilities:* clubhouse with bar and quality restaurant. Pro shop; cart, club and trolley hire.

CASTELJALOUX. **Golf de Casteljaloux,** Route de Mont-de-Marsan, 47700 Casteljaloux (53.93.51.60; Fax: 53.93.04.10). *Location:* 12km south of the A62 on the D933. A modern, sporting course built around Lake Clarens; gentle slopes and some difficult greens. 18 holes, 5916 metres, Par 72. Practice holes, bunkers and tees, driving range and putting green. *Eating facilities:* bar and restaurant in clubhouse with fine views. Pro shop; club and trolley hire.

HOSSEGOR. **Golf d'Hossegor,** Avenue du Golf, 40150 Hossegor (58.43.56.99; Fax: 58.43.98.52). *Location:* about 15km north of Bayonne just west of the A63. Fine classic test of golf over gently undulating, heavily wooded land. 18 holes, 5867 metres, Par 71. Driving range, putting green. *Eating facilities:* bar and restaurant in clubhouse. Pro shop; trolley and club hire.

PAU. **Golf de Pau Billère,** Rue du Golf, 64140 Billère (59.32.02.33). *Location:* two km south of Pau, off the A64. The first course in continental Europe (1856). Level parkland in good condition by a winding river. 18 holes, 5389 metres, Par 69. Driving range, putting green. *Eating facilities:* bar and restaurant in clubhouse. Pro shop; trolley and club hire.

SAINT-JEAN-DE-LUZ. **Golf de la Nivelle,** Place William Sharp, 64500 Ciboure (59.47.18.99; Fax: 59.47.21.16). *Location:* two km south of Saint-Jean, on the banks of the River Nivelle. A "town" course; classic parkland with mature trees and harbour views. 18 holes, 5513 metres, Par 69. Practice ground, putting green. *Eating facilities:* bar and restaurant in clubhouse. Self catering flats on golf course. Pro shop; equipment hire.

TOULOUSE. **Golf International de Toulouse Seilh,** Route de Grenade, 31840 Seilh (61.42.59.30; Fax: 61.42.34.17). *Location:* about 12km north-west of Toulouse near the A62. "Yellow" Course of moderate difficulty, 18 holes, 4202 metres, Par 64; "Red" Course of competition standard, 18 holes, 6200 metres, Par 72.

Extensive practice and training facilities. *Eating facilities:* bar and restaurant in clubhouse. Pro shop; club, cart and trolley hire.

VILLENEUVE-SUR-LOT. **Golf de Castelnaud,** "La Menuisière", 47290 Castelnaud de Gratecambe (53.01.74.64; Fax: 53.01.78.99). *Location:* on the N21 10km north of Villeneuve, between the scenic valleys of the Lot and the Dordogne. Inland course with water and many trees. 18 holes, 6322 metres, Par 72. 9 hole practice course, 1092 metres, Par 27. Practice ground, putting green. *Eating facilities:* the clubhouse is an 18th century manor house with what is reputed to be the best golf course restaurant in France. Pro shop; equipment hire.

# SOUTH

AIX-EN-PROVENCE. **Golf International de Château L'Arc,** Domaine de Château L'Arc, 13710 Fuveau (42.53.28.38; Fax: 42.29.08.41). *Location:* about 15km south-east of Aix-en-Provence just south of the A8. A challenging course of varying terrain through rivers, sloping fairways and water hazards. 18 holes, 6300 metres, Par 73. Driving range, putting green. *Eating facilities:* bar and restaurant in clubhouse. Pro shop; cart, trolley and club hire.

AVIGNON. **Golf des Baux de Provence,** Domaine de Manville, 13520 Les Baux de Provence (90.54.37.02; Fax: 90.54.40.93). *Location:* south of Avignon about one km north-east of Arles on the D5. Exhilarating golf course carved from the wooded foothills of Les Alpilles. 9 holes, 2820 metres, Par 36. Driving range, putting green, compact 9 hole course. *Eating facilities:* bar and restaurant in clubhouse. Pro shop; cart, club and trolley hire.

BEZIERS. **Golf de Cap d'Agde,** Avenue des Alizes, 34300 Cap d'Agde (67.26.54.40; Fax: 67.26.97.00). *Location:* on the coast, about 60km south-west of Montpelier and 20km east of Béziers. A quality course of rolling craggy heathland. 18 holes, 6160 metres, Par 72. Practice ground, putting green. *Eating facilities:* bar and restaurant in clubhouse. Club, trolley and cart hire.

CANNES. **Golf Club de Cannes-Mandelieu,** Route de Golf, 06210 Mandelieu-la-Napoule (93.49.55.39; Fax: 93.49.92.90). *Location:* across the mouth of the small River Siagne, abouth seven km west of Cannes, south of the A8. A short, level course, third oldest and most popular in France. 18 holes, 5867 metres, Par 71. 9 holes, 2409 metres, Par 34. Practice ground, putting green. *Eating facilities:* bar and restaurant in attractive clubhouse. Pro shop; club, cart and trolley hire.

CANNES. **Golf Country Club Cannes-Mougins,** 175 Route d'Antibes, 06250 Mougins (93.75.79.13; Fax: 93.75.27.60). *Location:* about eight km behind Cannes, north of the A8. A high-class private course, undulating through wooded hills, part of the annual Volvo Tour. 18 holes, 6304 metres, Par 72. Driving range, putting green. *Eating facilities:* bar and restaurant in clubhouse. Pro shop; cart, trolley and club hire.

CANNES. **Riviera Golf Club,** Avenue des Amazones, 06210 Mandelieu (92.97.66.33). *Location:* less than five km west of Cannes, just south of the A8. A new 18 hole course by American master Robert Trent Jones; mostly level, some hills and lakes. 18 holes, 6080 metres, Par 72. Driving range, putting green. *Eating facilities:* in clubhouse. Pro shop; equipment hire.

CORSICA. **Golf de Sperone,** Domaine de Sperone, 20169 Bonifacio (95.73.17.13; Fax: 95.73.17.85). *Location:* at the southern tip of Corsica, south of Bonifacio. Another new Trent Jones creation, part on rocky maquis inland, part overlooking the Mediterranean. 18 holes, 6130 metres, Par 72. Driving range, putting green. *Eating facilities:* clubhouse and La Caravelle nearby. Pro shop; cart, trolley and club hire.

FREJUS. **Golf de Roquebrune,** CD 7, 83520 Roquebrune-sur-Argens (94.82.92.91; Fax: 94.82.94.74). *Location:* inland, midway between Cannes and St. Tropez. A natural and attractive course, with water traps. 18 holes, 6241 metres, Par 71. Large 3 hole practice area, driving range and putting green. *Eating facilities:* bar and restaurant in clubhouse. Pro shop; club and trolley hire.

GRASSE. **Golf de la Grande Bastide,** Chemin des Picholines, 06740 Chateauneuf de Grasse (92.94.48.32). *Location:* just north-east of Grasse about 12km from coast. Gently rolling, of equal challenge to all grades of player. A new 18 hole course, 6105 metres, Par 72. Driving range, putting green. *Eating facilities:* bar and restaurant in clubhouse. Trolley and club hire.

MARSEILLES. **Golf d'Aix Marseilles,** Domaine de Riquetti, 13290 Les Milles (42.24.20.41). *Location:* between Marseilles and Aix-en-Provence, west of the A51. A mature parkland course in a natural setting with a wealth of established trees. 18 holes, 6289 metres, Par 72. Driving range, putting green. *Eating facilities:* bar and restaurant in clubhouse. Pro shop; trolley and club hire.

MONTE CARLO. **Monte Carlo Golf Club,** Route du Mont Agel, La Turbie, 06320 Cap d'Ail (93.41.09.11). *Location:* by the A8, three km north of Monte Carlo. Set on an elevated plain high abouve town and sea with superb views. 18 holes, 5667 metres, Par 71. Driving range, putting green. *Eating facilities:* bar and restaurant in clubhouse. Pro shop; cart, trolley and club hire.

MONTPELIER. **Golf Club de Fontcaude,** Domaine de Fontcaude, 34990 Juvignac (67.03.34.30; Fax: 67.03.34.51). *Location:* at Juvignac, six km west of Montpelier. Undulating over a rolling, scrub-covered landscape, this course provides a fair and interesting challenge. 18 holes, 6292 metres, Par 72. Driving range, putting green. *Eating facilities:* bar and restaurant in clubhouse. Pro shop; cart, trolley and club hire.

MONTPELIER. **Golf de la Grande-Motte,** BP16, 34280 La Grande-Motte (67.56.05.00; Fax: 67.29.18.84). *Location:* on the coast, east of Montpelier. Former marshland, now a 42 hole complex with fast greens, water, trees and bunkers. "The Pink Flamingos" – 18 competition class holes, 6161 metres, Par 72; "The Seagulls" – 3220 metres, Par 58; and 9 hole practice, 560 metres, Par 19. Practice ground, putting green. *Eating facilities:* bar and restaurant in clubhouse and on-course Golf Hôtel. Pro shop; trolley and cart hire.

MONTPELIER. **Golf de Massane,** Domaine de Massane, 34670 Baillargues (67.87.87.87; Fax: 67.87.87.90). Tough championship layout which hosts the annual Volvo Tour qualifying. Elevated greens protected by sand and water. 18 holes, 6375 metres, Par 72. 9 hole compact course. Extensive teaching school with large driving range, pitching and putting greens. *Eating facilities:* bar and restaurant in clubhouse, hotel on course. Pro shop; cart, trolley and club hire.

NIMES. **Golf de Nîmes-Campagne,** Route de Saint-Gilles, 30900 Nîmes (66.70.17.37). *Location:* about three km south of Nîmes, by the airport. A classic parkland course of championship calibre built around a hill. 18 holes, 6135 metres, Par 72. Driving range, putting green. *Eating facilities:* bar and excellent restaurant in imposing hilltop clubhouse. Pro shop; cart, trolley and club hire.

NIMES. **Golf des Hauts de Nîmes,** Vacquerolles, Route de Sauve, 30900 Nîmes (66.23.33.33). *Location:* on the north-west outskirts of Nîmes. New course running up a valley and over steeply wooded hills. 18 holes, 6286 metres, Par 72. Driving range, putting green. *Eating facilities:* bar and restaurant in clubhouse. Pro shop; trolley and club hire.

ST. RAPHAËL. **Golf de l'Estérel,** Avenue du Golf, 83700 St. Raphaël (94.82.47.88; Fax: 94.44.61.37). *Location:* inland just a few metres north of St. Raphaël, close to Golf de Valescure. Not long but rated difficult; many trees, narrow fairways and water hazards protecting beautiful greens. 18 holes, 1400 metres, Par 29. Practice area, putting green. *Eating facilities:* bar and restaurant in clubhouse and on-site Hôtel Latitides-Valescure. Pro shop; club, cart and trolley hire.

ST. RAPHAËL. **Golf et Tennis Club de Valescure,** BP451, Route de Golf, 83700 St.-Raphaël (94.82.40.46; Fax: 94.82.41.42). *Location:* about five km east of St.-Raphaël. An established course (1896), winding attractively through the umbrella pine trees. 18 holes, 5607 metres, Par 70. Driving range, putting green. *Eating facilities:* bar and restaurant in period clubhouse. Also at golf hotel nearby. Pro shop; trolley and club hire.

# Golf in Portugal
## WHERE TO PLAY • WHERE TO STAY
*by Michael Gedye*

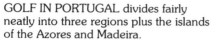

GOLF IN PORTUGAL divides fairly neatly into three regions plus the islands of the Azores and Madeira.

In the north, the COSTA VERDE has three courses – Oporto Golf Club (where Portuguese golf was born in 1890), Miramar and the latest seashore test of Estela, near Povoa da Varzim. Inland at Vidago, a pleasant 9-hole course complements the spa hotel.

Centrally, the COSTA DE LISBOA has traditionally drawn the tourist to its elegant urban sophistication, historical relics and appealing beach resorts. There are three 18-hole and three 9-hole courses west of the capital, the best undoubtedly being the Estoril Palacio Golf Club, a fine design by Mackenzie Ross of Turnberry fame, which exerts its subtle strategic charms through an undulating chain of eucalyptus and pine, backed by birdsong and the heady scent of mimosa – an aficionado's treat.

Across the Tagus river bridge south of Lisbon are two of the finest courses in the country. The Portuguese Country Club at Aroeira is an unheralded masterpiece by English architect Frank Pennink. Carved through a natural pine forest carpeted with wild flowers, it represents fine golf for all levels and a haven of peace only a short drive from the city. Farther south at Troia, Robert Trent Jones built a demanding examination on a sand bar – exhilarating and tough. A further course, Montado, has also recently opened for play.

Down in the sunny ALGARVE, nearly half the country's courses are situated along a coast of stunning white beaches, sheer cliffs and rolling orchards. Tourist golf has been available here since 1966, designed for the holiday market and with many new courses still to come. The coast can be separated into three regions. The western end has six golfing locations, from the challenge of Parque da Floresta to the popular slopes of Palmares and the famous international examination of Penina. Newcomers include the Alto

*On the tee at Quinta do Lago.*

Club and Quinta do Gramacho, near Carvoeiro.

Centrally, near Albufeira, are three golfing locations, the largest being the extensive complex of Vilamoura with three separate courses and a total of 63 holes in play. Near neighbours are Vila Sol, venue for the 1992 Portuguese Open and a great course in excellent condition, and Pine Cliffs with its dramatic tee shot across the seaside escarpment.

Nearer Faro, one finds the best collection of courses in the Algarve. Vale do Lobo, Quinta do Lago, San Lorenzo and now Pinheiros Altos – a total of 90 holes laid out over rolling, sandy, pine-encrusted land with sparkling sea views and more to come. Golfing treasure indeed.

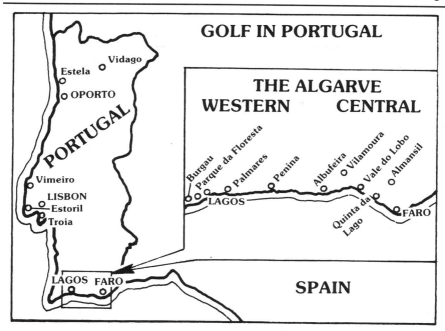

## ALGARVE

ALBUFEIRA. **Pine Cliffs Golf and Country Club,** Pinhal do Concelho, Albufeira (010 351 89 50884). *Location:* about seven km west of Vilamoura. A seaside course with some spectacular tee shots. 9 holes, 2320 metres, Par (equivalent) 67. *Visitors:* course reserved for Pine Cliffs and Sheraton Hotel residents.

ALMANSIL. **San Lorenzo Golf Club,** Quinta do Lago, 8315 Almansil, Loule 8100 (010 351 89 396534). *Location:* located within the Quinta Do Lago estate. Parkland, wooded course. Seaside view. 18 holes, 6238 metres. S.S.S. 73. Practice range. *Green Fees:* 2500,00 esc. *Eating facilities:* bar and restaurant. *Visitors:* welcome, please reserve a day before wishing to play. Accommodation available at Dona Fizipa Hotel. *Society Meetings:* always through the Dona Filipa Hotel. Professional: B. Evans and A. Rodrigues. Secretary: Antonio Santos (010 351 89 396522).

ALMANSIL. **Sociedade do Golfe da Quinta do Lago,** Quinta do Lago, 8135 Almansil (089 396002/3; Fax: 089 394013). *Location:* 15 minutes west of Faro Airport, nearest town Almansil. Gently undulating sandy land covered with umbrella pines, wild flowers and lakes. 4 courses – A,B,C,D. A/D 6850 yards, A/C 7040 yards, B/C 7137 yards, B/D 6915 yards. S.S.S. A/D 73, A/C 73, B/D 73, B/C 73. Driving range. *Green Fees:* Visitors: 10,000 esc; Residents: 7,500 esc. *Eating facilities:* clubhouse restaurant and bar; snack bar on

course. *Visitors:* welcome subject to availability. Pro Shop, boutique and golf academy. Professional: Domingos Silva (089 394529). Secretary: Jose A. Capela (089 394529).

ALMANSIL. **Vale do Lobo Golf Club,** Vale do Lobo, Almansil, Loule 8100 (089 393939; Fax: 089 394713. Telex: 56842). *Location:* on the cliff edge, overlooking the sea, 15 minutes' drive west from Faro. 27 holes, three loops of 9; average 18-hole length 6600 yards. S.S.S. 72. *Facilities:* clubhouse with restaurant, bar and shop. Nearby the 5 star Dona Filipa Hotel and luxury villa estate with leisure complexes. Secretary: J.A. Walker.

ALVOR. **Alto Golf Club,** Quinto do Alto do Poco, Alvor, 8500 Portimao (082 416913; Fax: 082 458557). *Location:* in Alvor, just behind the coastline of the Bay of Lagos. A new course originally designed by Sir Henry Cotton over two compact valley areas. Narrow and steeply undulating. 18 holes, 6125 metres, Par 72. Driving range, putting green. *Eating facilities:* bar and restaurant in temporary clubhouse. Pro shop; cart, trolley and club hire.

BUDENS/SALEMA. **Parque da Floresta Golf and Country Club,** Vale do Poco, Budens, 8650 Vila do Bispo (082 65333/4 Fax: 082 65196). *Location:* follow N125 west through Lagos, following signs to Sagres. Located just past Budens on right. Undulating course. 18 holes, 6020 metres. S.S.S. 72. Large practice ground, driving range, putting green. *Green Fees:* on application. *Eating facilities:* restaurant and bar. *Visitors:* most welcome with no restrictions. Advisable to book starting times by phone. Pro shop. *Society Meetings:* catered for by arrangement with Golf Manager. Golf Manager: Thomas A. Pidd.

LAGOA. **Quinta do Gramacho,** Carvoeiro Golfe, Apartado 24, 8400 Lagoa (082 52610; Fax: 082 341459). *Location:* just inland from Carvoeiro. An innovative course on an attractive compact site, with 18 greens and a selection of different tees linking with 9 fairways. Interesting and highly playable. 18 holes, 5919 metres, Par 72. Driving range, putting green. *Eating facilities:* in timber clubhouse. Pro shop; trolley and club hire.

LAGOS. **Palmares Golf Club,** Meia Praia, Lagos 8600 (082 762961; Fax: 082 762534). *Location:* five kilometres from centre of Lagos on main Meia Praia beach. Part hilly, part alongside beach. 18 holes, 5961 metres. S.S.S. 72. Practice driving range, pitch and putt. *Green Fess:* 7,000.00 escudos. *Eating facilities:* restaurant and bar. *Visitors:* always welcome. *Society Meetings:* by prior arrangement. Professional: Luis Espadinha. Secretary: Dennis Garvey (082 762953).

PORTIMAO/PENINA. **Penina Golf Club,** Penina Golf Resort Hotel, Penina, PO Box 146, Penina, 8502 Portimao (082 415415; Fax: 082 415000). *Location:* five km from Portimao, 12km from Lagos. Long, flat course with lakes, trees and bunkers. 18 holes (plus two 9 holes), 7041 yards, 6439 metres. S.S.S. 73. Also Monchique Course 9 holes, 3268 yards, 2987 metres. S.S.S. 35 and Quinta Course 9 holes, 2035 yards, 1851 metres. S.S.S. 31. Driving range, putting green. *Green Fees:* Championship course 9.500esc; Monchique course 6.000esc; Quinta 5.000esc. Special tickets June, July, August. *Eating facilities:* clubhouse with bar and snack-bar. Restaurant and leisure facilities at Hotel Penina (5 star).*Visitors:* welcome, Handicap Certificate required. Professional: Jose Lourenco and Robin Liddle. Secretary: Leonel Rio.

VILAMOURA. **Golf Vila Sol,** Vila Sol, Alto do Semino (089 302144; Fax: 089 302147). *Location:* just east of Vilamoura off the road leading down to Quarteira. An excellent natural course undulating through umbrella pines with good water hazards and superb greens. 18 holes, 6183 metres, Par 72. Driving range, putting green. *Eating facilities:* bar and restaurant in clubhouse. Pro shop; cart, trolley and club hire.

VILAMOURA. **Vilamoura One (The Old Course),** Vilamoura, Quarteira 8125 (089 321652; Telex: 56914 LUGOLF). *Location:* 20 kms from Faro Airport, 25 kms from Faro. Narrow fairways through wild pine woods. Sea views. 18 holes, 6331 metres. S.S.S. 72. Practice and putting greens. *Green Fees:* information on request. *Eating facilities:* restaurant and bar. *Visitors:* course open to all players with Handicap Certificate. Pro shop, hire of trolleys. Professional: Joaquim Catarino (089 321652). Secretary: Jorge Marcelo (089 389908).

VILAMOURA. **Vilamoura Two (The New Course),** as Vilamoura One (089 314470). *Location:* as Vilamoura One. Pinewood setting, sea views. 18 holes, 6256 metres. S.S.S 71. Driving range, putting green. *Green Fees:* on request. *Eating facilities:* bar and restaurant. *Visitors:* open to players with Handicap

Certificate. Professional: Manuel Pardal (089 321562). Secretary: Eduard Sousa (089 322704).

VILAMOURA. **Vilamoura Three and Four,** Vilamoura – 8125 Quarteira (089 380724; Telex: 56018 VIGOLF; Fax: 089 380726). *Location:* 20 kms from Faro Airport – 25 kms from Faro. 27 challenging holes set up overlooking the sea; although not particularly long for a modern layout; its 10 different lakes being the principal hazards. 3 x 9-holes. Driving range, putting green. *Eating facilities:* on request. *Eating facilities:* restaurant and bar. *Visitors:* Vilamoura Three is open to players with Handicap Certificate, Vilamoura Four is open to beginners. Professional: Abilio Coelho (089 380724). Secretary: Susete Calado (089 380722/ 380723).

# LISBON

ARDEIRA. **Clube de Campo de Portugal,** Herdade de Aroeira, Fonte da Telha, 2825 Monte de Caparica, Aroeira, Costa Lisboa (01 2263244; Fax: 01 2261358). *Location:* just 20 minutes south of Lisbon behind the cliffs running down from the seaside resort of Caparica. This well-established course remains one of Portugal's best kept secrets. A superb test through a floral pine forest by Frank Pennink; one for purists to savour. 18 holes, 6040 metres, Par 72. Driving range, putting green. *Eating facilities:* bar and restaurant in clubhouse. Pro shop; cart, trolley and club hire.

ESTORIL. **Estoril Palacio Golf Course,** Estoril (4680400). *Location:* an undulating links course with views of the Atlantic, north west of Lisbon. Pine trees and natural hazards. 27 holes including 18-hole championship course, 5700 yards. S.S.S. 69. *Facilities:* clubhouse with restaurant, bar and swimming pool. The 5 star Estoril Palacio Hotel one mile away with superb amenities. Hotel's guests are entitled to special privileges at the Estoril Golf Course. General Manager: Manuel Quintas.

ESTORIL. **International Golf Academy,** Estoril Sol Golf Club, Quinta do Outeiro, Linho, Sintra 2710 (351-1-9232461). *Location:* take the main Cascas-Sintra road and turn left at the village of Linho towards Lagos Azul. 18 holes, 3341 metres. S.S.S. 62. Purpose-built golf academy – practice facility, chipping greens, putting green. *Green Fees:* 3.600 esc. *Eating facilities:* restaurant and bar. *Visitors:* no restrictions. *Society Meetings:* welcome. Professionals: Tom Lister/Antonio Dantas Jr. Secretary: Nuno Texeira Bastos.

ESTORIL. **Penha Longa Golf Club,** Lagoa Azul, Linho, 2710 Sintra (01 9240320; Fax: 01 9240388). *Location:* half an hour west of Lisbon, just north of Estoril on the main road to Sintra. A new course of quality laid out over craggy hills, wooded slopes and valleys surrounding an ancient royal palace. 18 holes, 6170 metres, Par 72. Driving range, three putting greens. *Eating facilities:* bar and restaurant in palatial new clubhouse. Pro shop; cart, trolley and club hire.

ESTORIL. **Quinta da Marinha Golf Club,** Casa 36, Quinta da Marinha, Cascais 2750 (4869881). *Location:*

30 km north west of Lisbon, close to Estoril and Cascais. Championship golf course designed by Robert Trent Jones. Open sandy course with pine trees, lakes and spectacular views over the mountains and ocean. 18 holes, 6684 yards. S.S.S. 71. *Green Fees:* 5800esc. *Eating facilities:* clubhouse with bar and restaurant. Accommodation in luxury villas and townhouses surrounding the golf course. Professional: Antonio Damtas. Secretary: Numo Texeira Bastos.

LISBON. **Lisbon Sports Club,** Casal da Carregueira, Belas, Queluz 2745 (01 4310077). *Location:* 25 km from Lisbon. Parkland. 18 holes, 5216 metres. S.S.S. 68. *Green Fees:* 4,000esc weekdays, 5,000esc weekends. *Facilities:* clubhouse with restaurant, bar and swimming pool. *Visitors:* Handicap required. Professional: Jose Baltazar. Secretary: Mrs Manuela De Sousa (01 4312482).

TROIA. **Troia Golf Club,** Troia, Setubal 2900 (065 4412; Fax: 065 44162; Telex: 18138). *Location:* on the Troia Peninsula, 42 km south of Lisbon by motorway. Seaside links, small greens, long fairways and sandy roughs. 18 holes. S.S.S. 74. Two putting areas and driving range. *Green Fees:* 6,000 esc. Special rates for Hotel Magnoliamar guests. *Eating facilities:* clubhouse with bar/restaurant. *Visitors:* welcome, no restrictions all year round. Golf/Hotel Special Packages available. *Society Meetings:* welcome, special rates. Secretaries: Madalena O'Neil, Pinheiro de Mello (065 44151).

VIMEIRO. **Vimeiro Golf Club,** Praia do Porto Novo, Vimeiro, Torres Vedras 25600 (98157; Telex: 43353). *Location:* approximately 70 km north of Lisbon, overlooking the sea. A level course, divided by a river and sheltered by rocky cliffs. 9 holes with 18 tees, 5228 yards. S.S.S. 67. *Facilities:* the neighbouring Hotel Golf Mar offers all facilities.

# OPORTO

ESPINHO. **Oporto Golf Club,** Lugar do Sisto, Paramos, Espinho 4500 (351 02 722008; Fax: 351 02 726895). *Location:* 18 miles south of Oporto, one mile south of Espinho. Seaside links, few trees, founded in 1890. 18 holes, 6500 yards. S.S.S. 70. Practice ground. *Green Fees:* 6,000 esc per round, half price for guests of hotels mentioned below. *Eating facilities:* bar with snacks (restaurant – members only). *Visitors:* welcome

Tuesdays to Fridays (closed Mondays); weekend and Bank Holidays till 10am. Handicap Certificate required. Beach, hotels – Hotel Solverde, Hotel Praia – Golf, casino nearby. Professional: Eduardo Maganinho. Secretary: Margarida Moreira.

ESTELA. **Estela Golf Club,** Rio Alto-Estela, 4490 Povoa de Varzim (52 601567/612400; Fax: 52 612701; Telex: 25654). *Location:* 30 km north of Oporto, 24 km from the international airport. Seaside links. 18 holes, 6095 metres. S.S.S. 73. *Green Fees:* 3.500esc (£14.00). *Eating facilities:* full bar and catering facilities. *Visitors:* welcome anytime when no competitions taking place. Sopete Hotel guests entitled to special privileges. *Society Meetings:* by arrangement. Professionals: Carlos Alberto, Geoff Hutchinson, Carlos Henrique. Secretary/Manager: Francisco Pinheiro.

PRAIA DE MIRAMAR. **Clube de Golf de Miramar,** Av. Sacadura Cabral, Miramar, Valadares 4405 (02 7622067. Fax: 02 7627859). *Location:* approximately 13 km south of Oporto. Flat coastal course amongst dunes alongside the beach. 9 holes, 5146 metres. S.S.S. 67. *Green Fees:* 8.000esc. *Eating facilities:* clubhouse with restaurant and bar. Hotels, restaurants and casino nearby. Professional: Manuel Ribeiro/Geoff Hutchinson. Secretary: Manuela Pinto Leite.

VIDAGO. **Vidago Golf Club,** Vidago 5425 (97106; Telex: 238888). *Location:* mountain valley course, in spa/resort area well inland, only 25 km from Spanish border. Short 9-hole course, 1000ft high, 2678 yards. S.S.S. 63 (18 holes). *Facilities:* Vidago Palace Hotel.

# MADEIRA

MADEIRA. **Madeira Golf Course,** Santo Antonio da Serra, 9100 Santa Cruz (091 552345; Fax: 091 552367). *Location:* on high ground at the eastern end of the island, 25km from Funchal. Recently opened, this challenging course is laid out across and down the volcanic mountainside at Santo Antonio da Serra. Three 9 hole loops offer great natural beauty, breathtaking views and fine golf. 27 holes (Desertas, Machico and Serras courses), with 18 hole combinations from 5797 to 6082 metres, all Par 72. Driving range, putting green. *Eating facilities:* bar and restaurant in clubhouse. Pro shop; cart, trolley and club hire.

# GOLF IN MAJORCA

THE climate of Majorca, like its Balearic neighbours Minorca and Ibiza, is ideal for golf. Play is possible every day in the year. Little wonder that Majorca attracts short- and long-stay visitors for its golfing opportunities as well as the island's attractions as a year-round resort.

## MAJORCA

CALA D'OR. **Vall D'Or Golf Club,** Apartado 23, 07660 Cala D'Or (971 837001; Fax: 971 837299). *Location:* approximately 60km east of Palma on the road from Porto Colom to Cala D'Or. Undulating, winding course, with trees. 18 holes, 5881 metres. S.S.S. 71. Driving range., club hire. *Green Fees:* 5900ptas. 10% discount if player comes with a card from hotel. *Eating facilities:* clubhouse, bar and restaurant. *Visitors:* welcome with Handicap. Nearby hotels include Cala D'Or, Rocador, Rocador Playa. Professional: Antonio Gonzalez (971 837001). Secretary: Celestino Padial (971 837068).

MAGALLUF. **Poniente Golf Club,** Crta. Cala Figuera S/N, Costa de Calvia (03471 130148). *Location:* 18km west of Palma, one km from Magalluf on the Andraix Road. The course is considered long and difficult surrounded by trees and water, with large and fast greens. 18 holes, 6430 metres. S.S.S. 72. Driving range, putting green. *Green Fees:* information not provided. *Eating facilities:* clubhouse, restaurant and bar. Nearby hotels include Son Callu, Club Galatzo.

PALMA. **Real Golf de Bendinat,** Campoamor S/N, 07015 Calvia, Baleares (3471 405200; Fax: 3471 700786). *Location:* five km west from Palma centre. A short, hilly but interesting course. 9 holes, 4988 metres. S.S.S. 67. Driving range, putting green. *Green Fees:* 5000ptas. *Eating facilities:* restaurant and coffee shop "Hoyo 10". *Visitors:* welcome, 20% discount for large groups. Please reserve tee-off times through our Fax

No: (3471 700786). Professional: Ricardo Galiano (3471 405450). Secretary: Beatriz Arnau (3471 405200).

PALMA. **Son Vida Golf,** Urb. Son Vida, 07013 Palma de Mallorca (0034-(9)71-79.12.10; Fax: 79.11.27). *Location:* five km north-west of Palma. Majorca's first course (1964) winding through trees and estate villas with lakes and gentle slopes. 18 holes, 6276 yards. S.S.S. 71. Driving range, Pro Shops, car, trolley and club rental. *Green Fees:* 6.200pts (1.9.92 – 30.6.93); 4500pts (1.7.93 – 31.8.93). *Eating facilities:* snacks and lunches in the comfortable clubhouse, excellent restaurant El Pato (The Duck) overlooking 18th hole. *Visitors:* welcome. Nearby hotels (20% discount on green fees) include Arabella Golf Hotel (5 stars), Hotel Son Vida (5 stars) on the course, Victoria Sol (5 stars) Palma, Bonanza Playa Illestas, Son Caliu. Manager: Peter Haider.

POLLENSA. **Pollensa Golf Club,** Ctra. Palma Pollensa, 07460 Pollensa (00-34-71 533216; Fax: 00-34-71 533265). *Location:* in the north of the Island of Mallorca, 45 km from Palma Airport and 2 km from Pollensa. On the south side of a hill with smooth and beautiful undulations and sea views. 9 holes, 5304 metres. S.S.S. 70. Driving range. *Green Fees:* 4800pts; Juniors 2500pts. *Eating facilities:* available. *Visitors:* welcome, tee reservation recommended. Pro Shop, swimming pool, sauna. Professional: Carlos Insua.

SANTA PONSA. **Santa Ponsa Golf Club One,** Santa Ponsa, 07184 Calvia (690211; Fax: 693361). *Location:* 18km on motorway from Palma to Andraitx, turn off roundabout Santa Ponsa. Gently sloping fairways with water hazzards. 18 holes, 6170 metres. S.S.S. 72. Practice range, two putting greens. *Green Fees:* 5900pts. *Eating facilities:* restaurant and bar in clubhouse, one bar on golf course. *Visitors:* welcome, maximum Handicaps – 28 men, 36 ladies. Accommodation available, swimming pool, paddling pool, tennis. *Society Meetings:* welcome. Professionals: Diego Lopez/George Oosterlynck. Secretary: Jose M. Comez.

SANTA PONSA. **Santa Ponsa Golf Club Two,** Santa Ponza, Calvia (690211/102732; Fax: 693364/102732). *Location:* as Santa Ponza One. A very interesting and enjoyable course, it has a mixture of holes some with very tight fairways and others with many water hazards. Designed by Jose Gancedo. White Stakes – 6036 metres, Par 72; Yellow Stakes – 5672 metres, Par 70; Blue Stakes – 5144 metres, Par 72; Red Stakes – 4883 metres, Par 70. S.S.S. 72. Practice range, putting green. *Green Fees:* on request. *Eating facilities:* as Santa Ponza One. *Visitors:* at moment only open for shareholders.

SON SERVERA. **Son Servera Golf Club,** Costa de los Pinos, 07550 Son Servera (56.78.02). *Location:* on Majorca's east coast, north of the Caves of Drach and approximately 60km east from Palma. Flattish and narrow course, set among pine trees. 9 holes, 2978 metres. S.S.S. 36. Driving range. *Green Fees:* 5000pts. *Eating facilities:* club, bar and restaurant. *Visitors:* welcome, no restrictions. Nearby hotels include Eurotel Golf Punta Roja, Rotja, Flamenco, Royal Mediterranea, Gran Sol. Professional: Santiago Sota.

# Driving Ranges

## LONDON

CHINGFORD. **Chingford Golf Range,** Waltham Way, Chingford E4 8AQ (081-529 2409). *Location:* two miles south of Junction 26 M25. 23 bay two tier driving range. *Fees:* information not provided. *Opening hours:* 9.30am to 9.30pm. Practice putting green, practice bunker; new multi-level practice mat; video, tuition available at all times. Professional: Gordon Goldie.

LONDON. **Ealing Golf Range,** Rowdell Road, Northolt, Middlesex UB5 6AG (081-845 4967). *Location:* A40 Target roundabout, Northolt. Golf range with 40 floodlit bays – 36 covered and 4 open. *Fees:* £1.00 for 28 balls. *Eating facilities:* bar and catering. *Opening hours:* 10am to 10pm. Four teaching professionals. Shop open 10am to 10pm weekdays, 10am to 8pm weekends. Squash club, gymnasium and function room. Head Professional: David Elliot (081-845 4967).

information not provided. *Opening hours:* 8am to 10pm daily. *Eating facilities:* "Racecourse Restaurant" and Golfers' bar and terrace.

WOKINGHAM. **Downshire Driving Range,** Easthampstead Park, Wokingham RG11 3DH (0344 302030). *Location:* between Bracknell and Wokingham, off the Nine Mile Ride. 30 bay covered floodlit driving range. *Fees:* £1.50 bucket. *Eating facilities:* bar and restaurant, bar snacks available. *Opening hours:* 7.30am to 10pm. PGA Professionals, golf teaching academy, 18 hole course and 9 hole pitch and putt course. Membership available.

WOKINGHAM. **Sindlesham Driving Range,** Mole Road, Wokingham RG11 5DJ (0734 788494). *Location:* two minutes from M4 Junction 11. 25 covered, floodlit bays. Professional tuition available. *Fees:* £1.00 per bucket. *Opening hours:* 7am to 10pm. *Eating facilities:* restaurant and bar. *Visitors:* open to the public. Health club and squash club. Professional: Andrew R. Wild (0734 788494).

## BEDFORDSHIRE

DUNSTABLE. **Tilsworth Golf Centre,** Dunstable Road, Tilsworth, Near Leighton Buzzard (0525 210721/2). *Location:* take A5 north from Dunstable for approximately one and a half miles, turn left, golf centre immediately on right. 30 bay covered floodlit driving range. *Fees:* £1.35 50 balls; £2.25 100 balls. *Opening hours:* 10am – 10pm. *Eating facilities:* restaurant and bar (extensive menu), function suite. Large Pro shop, repairs, tuition and group lessons. 18 hole golf course open to public.

LEIGHTON BUZZARD. **Aylesbury Vale Golf Club,** Wing, Leighton Buzzard LU7 0UJ (0525 240196). *Location:* four miles west of Leighton Buzzard and half a mile south of Stewkley Village. 10 covered, lit bays, Astroturf, 90 compression balls. *Fees:* £2.00 for 65 balls. *Eating facilities:* restaurant and bar open all day; from snacks to Sunday roast catered for. *Opening hours:* 7am to 10pm. Indoor golf available – play "Pebble Beach". Tuition given, well stocked shop. Professional: Lee Scarbrow (0525 240197). Secretary/Manager: Chris Wright (0525 240196).

## BERKSHIRE

MAIDENHEAD. **Hawthorn Hill Golf Centre,** Drift Road, Hawthorn Hill, Near Maidenhead SL6 3ST (0344 75588/26035). *Location:* on A330 Ascot to Maidenhead road. 36 covered, floodlit bays. 18 hole 'pay and play' course. Professionals. Tuition. *Fees:*

## BUCKINGHAMSHIRE

COLNBROOK. **Colnbrook Golf Range,** Galleymead Road, Colnbrook SL3 0EN (0753 682670). *Location:* one mile from Junction 5 M4, one mile Junction 14 M25. 27 bay covered floodlit grassed range. *Fees:* £1.00 for 35 balls. *Opening Hours:* 9am to 10.30pm. *Eating facilities:* fully licensed bar 11am to 11pm six days a week, catering anything from snacks to full à la carte – excellent resident chef. Professional: Graham Hepsworth; Assistant: Paul Laycock. Very well equipped golf shop. Full tuition, video assisted lessons given.

MILTON KEYNES. **Windmill Hill Golf Range,** Tattenhoe Lane, Bletchley, Milton Keynes MK3 7RB (0908 378623). *Location:* off A421 at Bletchley. 23 bay covered floodlit driving range. *Fees:* half bucket (46 balls) £1.60; 92 balls £3.00. *Eating facilities:* public bar and catering. *Opening hours:* 9am to 9pm weekdays, 8am to 8pm weekends. Professional, tuition, public course – 18 holes, Par 73.

## CAMBRIDGESHIRE

ST. NEOTS. **Abbotsley Golf and Squash Club,** Eynesbury, Hardwicke, St Neots PE19 4XN (0480 215153/474000). *Location:* A45 St. Neots bypass to Abbotsley, south east of St. Neots Junction 13 M11. 21 bay range and grass. *Fees:* £2.00 per bucket (80 balls). *Opening hours:* 9am to 10pm. *Eating facilities:* bar and food available all day. Two courses (36 holes), residential golf school, shop, tuition. 15 bedroom hotel, 6 squash courts, snooker, 2 sun beds, sauna.

# CHESHIRE

STOCKPORT. **Cranford Golf Driving Range,** Harwood Road, Heaton Mersey, Stockport SK4 3AW (061-432 8242). *Location:* five minutes from M63 and M56 motorways. 30 all weather covered tees, fully floodlit, open seven days a week. *Fees:* £2.50 per bucket (50 balls). No booking or membership required. *Eating facilities:* bar available weekends and evenings. Professional: available.

# CORNWALL

REDRUTH. **Radnor Golf and Ski Centre,** Radnor Road, Redruth TR16 5EL (0209 211059). *Location:* follow signs from Old Redruth by-pass (A3047) or cross roads at north country. 18 bay covered floodlit driving range. *Fees:* £1.40 for 50 balls. Subject to review. *Eating facilities:* bar available. *Opening hours:* weekdays 8.30am to 9pm; weekends and Bank Holidays 8.30am to 6pm. PGA Approved. Teaching, club repairs, shop. Indoor ski machine, snooker. 9 hole Par 3 course.

TRURO. **Killiow Golf Club Driving Range,** Killiow Golf Park, Kea, Truro (0872 70246). *Location:* take A39 from Truro directed to Falmouth, 2.75 miles. Large sign on right into park. All weather floodlit driving range with bunker and putting facilities. *Fees:* information on request. *Visitors:* some restrictions – check with Reception. Secretary: John Crowson (0872 72768).

# ESSEX

BRAINTREE. **Towerlands Driving Range,** Panfield Road, Braintree CM7 5BJ (0376 326802). *Location:* off A120 in Braintree. 6 grassed bays. *Fees:* £1.25 for 50 balls. *Opening hours:* 8.30am till dark. *Eating facilities:* full bar and restaurant. 9 hole course, professional tuition, indoor bowls, squash, full sports hall and equestrian facilities.

COLCHESTER. **Colchester Golf Range,** Old Ipswich Road, Ardleigh, Colchester (0206 230974). *Location:* next to the Crown Inn, Old Ipswich Road. Covered, floodlit range, 12 bays. Professional tuition available. Putting green. *Fees:* on request. *Opening hours:* weekdays 10am to 9pm, weekends 10am to 5pm. *Eating facilities:* The Crown Inn, 50 yards from course.

COLCHESTER. **Earls Colne Golf and Leisure Centre,** Earls Colne, Colchester CO6 2NS (0787 224466; Fax: 0787 224410). *Location:* B1024 between A120 and A606 Earls Colne. 20 bay covered floodlit driving range. *Fees:* £1.75 for 50 balls. *Eating*

*facilities:* full restaurant and bar facilities. *Opening hours:* 9am to 10pm seven days a week. Tuition available. 18 hole and 9 hole courses, 4 hole teaching course. Leisure centre – swimming pool, gym, sun beds, beauty parlour, spa bath. Creche. Professional: Owen McKenna.

ILFORD. **Fairlop Waters,** Forest Road, Barkingside, Ilford IG6 3JA (081-500 9911). *Location:* two miles north of Ilford, half a mile from A12, one and a half miles from southern end of M11. Covered, floodlit range, 36 bays. 18 hole golf course, 9 hole Par 3 course. Individual or group tuition available. *Fees:* information not provided. *Opening hours:* 9am to 10pm. *Eating facilities:* three bars and restaurant. Banqueting facilities and conferences. 38 acre sailing lake, 25 acre country park, children's play area. Professional: Tony Bowers (081-501 1881). Manager: John Topping.

# GLOUCESTERSHIRE

GLOUCESTER. **Gloucester Hotel and Country Club,** Robinswood Hill, Matson Lane, Gloucester GL4 9EA (0452 525653). 12 bays covered and floodlit. *Fees:* £2.00 per basket of balls for driving range. *Opening hours:* 9am to 9.30pm. *Eating facilities:* available. Five professional instructors, private and group tuition available. Sebastian Coe Health Park, dry ski slope, 27 hole golf course, indoor swimming pool, sauna, solarium, gymnasium, 6 squash courts, two tennis courts, snooker, pool, skittles etc.

# HAMPSHIRE

BORDON near. **Kingsley Golf Club,** Main Road, Kingsley, Near Bordon GU35 9NG (04203 88195). *Location:* B3004 off A325 Farnham to Petersfield road. *Fees:* information not provided. Indoor computerised driving bay, equipment store, golf school for tuition. Professional/Acting Secretary: Richard Adams.

# HEREFORD & WORCESTER

LEOMINSTER. **The Grove Golf Centre,** Fordbridge, Leominster HR6 0LE (0568 611804). *Location:* adjacent to Leominster Golf Club, three miles south of Leominster on A49. 18 bay range (four of the 18 outdoor). *Fees:* £1.50 per 50 balls. *Opening hours:* 8am to 10pm. Also 9 hole putting green, practice bunker, club hire, tuition available. Professional: Gareth Bebb.

# HERTFORDSHIRE

ROYSTON. **Whaddon Golf Centre,** Whaddon, Royston SG8 5RX (0223 207325). *Location:* four miles north of Royston, nine miles south of Cambridge off A14. 9 open bays, 14 bays – 14 covered, floodlit and grassed. *Fees:* £1.00 for 50 balls. *Opening hours:* 9am to 9pm weekdays, 8am to dusk weekends. Three Professionals – coaching by appointment. Putting and Par 3 approach course.

WARE. **Whitehill Golf Centre,** Dane End, Ware SG12 0JS (0920 438495). *Location:* turn at Happy Eater, High Cross on A10 north of Ware. 25 bays covered, floodlit, grassed. *Fees:* £1.30 45 balls, £2.50 90 balls. *Eating facilities:* bar and food. *Opening hours:* Wednesday to Friday 7am to 10pm, Tuesday 10am to 10pm, Monday 7am to 10pm, weekends and Bank Holidays 7am to dusk. Professional tuition, 18 hole golf course, practice bunkers.

WELWYN GARDEN CITY. **Gosling Stadium,** Stanborough Road, Welwyn Garden City AL8 6XE (0707 331056). *Location:* aim Welwyn Garden City exit follow signs, one mile. 24 bays covered, floodlit driving range. *Fees:* to be arranged. *Opening hours:* 9am to 11pm. *Eating facilities:* extensive. Resident Professional, tuition and shop. Extensive facilities with ski-ing, tennis, athletics, bowls, cycling, badminton. Health suite, etc.

# HUMBERSIDE

SCUNTHORPE. **Grange Park Golf Range,** Butterwick Road, Messingham, Scunthorpe DN17 3PP (0724 764478). *Location:* five miles south of Scunthorpe between Messingham and East Butterwick, four miles south of Junction 3 of M180. 20 bay covered floodlit driving range. *Fees:* £1.25 for 50 balls. *Opening hours:* 9am to 10pm weekdays, 9am to 9pm weekends. Large Pro shop and exclusive golf ladies' wear shop. Professional available. 9 hole pay and play course on site.

# KENT

CHATHAM. **Chatham Golf Centre,** Street End Road, Chatham ME5 0BG. *Location:* five minutes' drive from Rochester Airport. Covered, floodlit range, 30 bays. Tuition available. *Fees:* £1.80 per 55 balls. *Opening hours:* 10am to 10pm. *Eating facilities:* licensed snack bar. Fully stocked Pro Shop. Competitive prices. Professional: Colin Bentley (0634 848925). Secretary: R. Burden (0634 848907).

EDENBRIDGE. **Tony Noble Professional Golf Management,** Edenbridge Golf Driving Range, Crouch House Road, Edenbridge TN8 6LQ (0732 865202). *Location:* one mile from B2026. 14 covered floodlit bays. *Fees:* information not provided. *Opening*

*hours:* 8am to 10pm, last balls sold 9.30pm. *Eating facilities:* available at clubhouse. Three teaching Professionals in attendance. Also two 18 hole courses and a 9 hole beginners' course.

MAIDSTONE. **Langley Park Driving Range,** Sutton Road, Langley, Maidstone ME17 3NQ (0622 863163). *Location:* south of Maidstone on A274, first turning after Park Wood Industrial Estate. 26 covered, floodlit bays. *Fees:* £1.40 for 42 balls. *Eating facilities:* fully licensed bar, snacks available. *Opening hours:* 10am to 9pm. Practice putting green opening soon.

ORPINGTON. **Ruxley Park Golf Centre,** Sandy Lane, St. Pauls Cray, Orpington BR5 3HY (0689 871490; Fax: 0689 891428). *Location:* off old A20 at Ruxley Corner. 24 bays, covered, floodlit, grassed. *Fees:* large basket £4.00, small basket £2.50. *Opening hours:* 9am to 10.30pm. *Eating facilities:* breakfast, lunch available, bar open all day. 18 hole Par 71 golf course.

# LANCASHIRE

KEARSLEY. **Kearsley Golf Driving Range,** Moss Lane, Kearsley, Bolton BL4 8SF (Farnworth (0204) 75726). *Location:* Manchester to Bolton A666. Small 9 hole pitch and putt attached. *Fees:* £1.40 for multiples of 25 balls. *Opening hours:* weekdays 11am to 9.30pm; weekends 11am to 4.30pm. *Eating facilities:* bar and snack bar. *Visitors:* welcome. Professional: E. Raymond Warburton.

# NORTHAMPTONSHIRE

NORTHAMPTON. **Delapre Golf Complex,** Eagle Drive, Nene Valley Way, Northampton NN4 0DU (0604 763957 or 764036). *Location:* three miles from M1 Junction 15 towards Wellingborough. 40 covered, floodlit bays plus 30 grassed areas. *Fees:* practice balls dispensed at £2.00 per unit. *Opening hours:* 7am to 10.30pm. *Eating facilities:* cooked meals served. PGA qualified teaching professionals available, 18 and 9 hole golf courses and 9 hole pitch and putt.

# NOTTINGHAMSHIRE

NOTTINGHAM. **Carlton Forum Leisure Centre (South),** Foxhill Road, Carlton, Nottingham NG4 1RL (0602 612949). *Location:* east side of Nottingham. 28 bay covered, floodlit range. *Fees:* £2.20 per basket (approximately 75 balls). *Eating facilities:* bar, restaurant, function suite. *Opening hours:* Monday noon to 10.30pm, Tuesday-Sunday 9.30am to 10.30pm. Resident Professional, private tuition and courses, all standards, latest teaching and video aids. Dry ski slope and 32 acres of pitches, golf shop.

## STAFFORDSHIRE

BURTON-ON-TRENT. **Craythorne Golf Centre,** Craythorne Road, Stretton, Burton-on-Trent DE13 0AZ (0283 64329). *Location:* Stretton, one and a half miles north of Burton – A5121/A38 Junction. 14 bay covered floodlit driving range. *Fees:* £1.50 per bucket. *Opening hours:* weekdays 9am to 9pm; weekends 9am to dusk.

## EAST SUSSEX

HORAM. **Horam Park Golf Course and Floodlit Driving Range,** Chiddingly Road, Horam TN21 0JJ (04353 3477, Fax: 04353 3677). *Location:* 13 miles north of Eastbourne, 7 miles east of Uckfield. Covered, floodlit, Astroturf range. 16 bays. 5 PGA golf Professionals, lessons and tuition available. Golf shop. *Fees:* £1.75 per large bucket; £1.00 after 9pm, 6pm weekends. *Opening hours:* weekdays 8am to 10.30pm. *Eating facilities:* restaurant bar and spike bar.

## SURREY

CHESSINGTON. **Chessington Golf Centre,** Garrison Lane, Chessington KT9 2LW (081-391 0948). *Location:* as Chessington Course entry. Covered, floodlit range, 18 bays. 9 hole course. Private and group tuition available. *Fees:* £1.00 per 35 balls. *Opening hours:* 9am to 10pm. *Eating facilities:* available.

COBHAM. **Silvermere Driving Range,** Redhill Road, Cobham KT11 1EF (0932 867275). *Location:* half a mile from Junction 10 on M25, take B366. Covered, floodlit range, 34 bays. 18 hole course. Teaching available. *Fees:* £2.00 per bucket. *Opening hours:* 9am to 10pm. *Eating facilities:* full facilities.

CROYDON. **Croydon Driving Range,** 175 Long Lane, Addiscombe, Croydon CR0 7TE (081-654 7859). *Location:* on A222 about two miles east of Croydon. 24-bay driving range. *Fees:* information not provided. *Eating facilities:* licensed bar and snacks available. *Visitors:* very welcome at all times, open to the public. Professional: Nick Parfrement (081-656 1690).

ESHER. **Sandown Golf Centre,** More Lane, Esher KT10 8AN (0372 463340). *Location:* centre of Sandown Park Racecourse. 33 bay covered floodlit range plus grassed area. *Fees:* £2.00 for 70 balls. *Eating facilities:* coffee shop and bar. *Opening hours:* 10am to 10pm weekdays; 10am to 9pm weekends. Three PGA Professionals. Snooker club.

OLD WOKING. **Hoebridge Golf Centre,** Old Woking Road, Old Woking GU22 8JH (0483 722611). Covered, floodlit range. 25 bays. Two 18 hole courses and 9 hole course. *Fees:* information not provided. *Opening hours:* dawn to dusk in summer, 8am to 11pm in winter. *Eating facilities:* available.

RICHMOND. **Richmond Golf Range,** The Athletic Ground, Kew Foot Road, Richmond TW9 2SS (081-940 5570). *Location:* next to Richmond swimming pool on the 316 road. Covered, floodlit driving range, 23 bay and grassed area. *Fees:* £1.50 40 balls, 75 balls £2.20. *Opening hours:* 9.30am to 9.30pm. *Eating facilities:* some catering. Professional tuition available.

## WEST SUSSEX

CRAWLEY. **Gatwick Manor Golf Club,** Gatwick Manor Hotel, London Road, Lowfield Heath, Crawley RH10 2ST (0293 26301). *Location:* A23 Crawley to Gatwick airport on London Road on right. 9 grassed tees. *Fees:* information available on request. *Eating facilities:* hotel facilities at Gatwick Manor. *Opening hours:* 9am to 8.00pm seven days a week.

LITTLEHAMPTON near. **Rustington Golf Centre,** Golfers Lane, Rustington, Near Littlehampton BN16 4NB (0903 850786/850790). *Location:* A259 towards Littlehampton. 30 bay range. *Fees:* £2.95 bucket of balls, £1 club hire. *Eating facilities:* coffee shop. *Opening hours:* 9am to 9pm seven days. Teaching Professional, well stocked golf shop.

## TYNE AND WEAR

NEWCASTLE-UPON-TYNE. **Gosforth Park Golfing Complex Ltd,** High Gosforth Park, Newcastle-Upon-Tyne NE3 5HQ (091-2364480). *Location:* off A1 for Gosforth Park. Covered, floodlit range, 30 bays. 18 hole golf course and 9 hole pitch and putt. Professional tuition available. *Fees:* information not provided. *Opening hours:* 8am to 10.30pm. *Eating facilities:* bar and restaurant.

WASHINGTON. **Washington Moat House Golf Club,** Stone Cellar Road, High Usworth, District 12 Washington NE37 1PH (091-417 2626). *Location:* just off A1(m), take A194 then exit A195 Washington. 24 bay floodlit grassed range. 18 hole pitch and putt. *Fees:* information on request. *Eating facilities:* Bunkers Bar, 9am to 11pm, serves snacks. Buffets etc by arrangement. *Opening hours:* 9.30am to 10pm. Golf professional, tuition available. Snooker club, leisure club with sauna, pool, solarium, multi gym, spa.

# WARWICKSHIRE

COVENTRY. **John Reay Golf Centres,** Sandpits Lane, Keresley, Coventry CV7 8NJ (0203 333920). *Location:* three miles from Coventry city centre along A51 Tamworth Road. Covered, floodlit driving range. 30 bays. Golf club repair facility. Teaching professionals using latest video techniques. *Fees:* 45 balls £1. *Opening hours:* weekdays 9am to 10pm. *Eating facilities:* Hogan's Bar & Bistro open every day. *Visitors:* open to the public. Large Golf Shop with all the leading brands of golf equipment. Professional: John Reay (0203 333920/3333405).

WARWICK. **Warwick Golf Centre,** The Racecourse, Warwick CV34 6HW (0926 494316). *Location:* Racecourse, Warwick. 28 bay covered, floodlit range. *Fees:* large basket £2.30, medium basket £2.00 and small basket £1.30. *Opening hours:* 10am to 9pm. *Eating facilities:* bar only. Professional tuition, 9 hole golf course open to the public.

# WEST MIDLANDS

DUDLEY near. **Swindon Ridge Golf Driving Range,** Bridgnorth Road, Swindon, Near Dudley DY3 4PU (0902 896191). *Location:* B4176 Bridgnorth/ Dudley Road, three miles from Himley A449 Junction. 27 bay floodlit range (22 covered). *Fees:* £1.40 for small bucket, £2.20 for large bucket, £3.50 for extra-large bucket. Tuition £8.00 per half hour with large bucket free. *Opening hours:* 9am to 9.30pm weekdays, 8.30am to 6pm weekends. *Eating facilities:* licensed bar and restaurant. 18 hole private golf club on site plus 9 hole Par 3. Two snooker tables in bar.

WOLVERHAMPTON. **Three Hammers Golf Complex,** Old Stafford Road, Coven, Wolverhampton WV10 7PP (0902 790428). *Location:* Junction 2 M54 north on A449, one mile on right. 24 covered floodlit bays. *Fees:* balls from £1.00. *Eating facilities:* bookings taken from 10.30am, details on (0902 791917). *Opening hours:* weekdays 9.30am to 10pm, Saturdays 9.30am to 6pm, Sundays 9.30am to 5.30pm. 18 hole Par 3 course, two teaching Professionals.

# WILTSHIRE

WINDON. **Broome Manor Golf Complex,** Pipers Way, Swindon SN3 1RG (0793 532403/495761). *Location:* two miles from Junction 15 on M4, follow signs for Golf Complex. 35 bays, 30 covered, five covered, floodlit range. *Fees:* large basket £2.65, standard £1.90. *Eating facilities:* full service available. *Opening hours:* 8am to 9pm. 18 hole course, 9 hole course, short game practice area, pitch and putt. Professional tuition available.

# NORTH YORKSHIRE

BRADFORD. **Shay Grange Golf Centre,** Long Lane, off Bingley Road, Heaton, Bradford BD9 6RX (0274 483955). *Location:* take the A650 Bradford to Bingley road, turn left at Cottingley lights, the Centre will be found on the left after two miles. 32 bay covered, floodlit, grassed range. *Fees:* £2.00 for 60 balls. *Eating facilities:* coffee shop. *Opening hours:* weekdays 9am to 10pm, weekends 7.30am to 9pm. Golf instruction school, all weather putting green, sand bunker. Professional: Steve Dixon.

# CHANNEL ISLANDS

ST. OUEN'S. **Les Mielles Golf Course,** St. Ouen's Bay, Jersey (0534 482787). *Location:* centre of St. Ouen's Bay. 36 bay grassed driving range. *Fees:* 21 balls 50p, clubs 30p. 12 hole course £5.00, clubs £2.50. *Opening hours:* dawn 'till dusk. *Eating facilities:* kiosk. Grade A PGA Professional Terry Le Brocq. Crazy golf, public golf facility. Manager: J.A. Le Brun.

---

# SCOTLAND

# ABERDEENSHIRE

ABERDEEN. **Kings Links Golf Centre,** Golf Road, Aberdeen AB2 1RZ (0224 641577; Fax: 0224 639410). *Location:* behind Pittodrie Stadium, on the Kings Links, by the beach. 34 bay covered, floodlit range. *Fees:* £1.50 for 48 balls. *Eating facilities:* sandwiches at lunchtime, vended drinks and snacks. *Opening hours:* 8.30am to 9pm weekdays, 8am to 5pm weekends. Adjoins Kings Links Golf Course, PGA qualified Professionals for tuition and club repair. Short game area (bunkers and putting) and putting green. Concessions available for Senior Citizens, Unemployed and beginners.

# EDINBURGH & LOTHIANS

EDINBURGH. **Port Royal Golf Range,** Eastfield Road, Ingliston, Edinburgh EH28 8TR (031-333 4377). *Location:* follow signs to Edinburgh Airport, on slip road approximately 100 yards from airport entrance. Five miles from centre of Edinburgh. 36 bays, 24 covered, floodlit and 12 grassed. Pro shop, Professional and tuition. *Fees:* £1.40 per basket of 50 balls. *Eating facilities;* bar and lounge area, bar meals all day. *Opening hours:* 10am to 10pm. 1000 square yard putting green and 9 hole, par 3 golf course. Open all year.

THE GOLF GUIDE 1993

LASSWADE. **Melville Golf Range,** South Melville, Lasswade EH18 1AN (031-663 8038). *Location:* direct access, off Edinburgh City Bypass on NEW A7 (Galashiels); on number 8 LRT bus route. 22 covered bays plus 12 outdoor mats. Floodlit. *Fees:* top quality balls from £1.60, various concessions. *Eating facilities:* hot and cold beverages available. *Opening hours:* weekdays 9am to 10pm; weekends 9am to 8pm. Club hire and repairs, golf shop, ladies equipment and golf ware, trial clubs, synthetic grass mats.

# GLASGOW & DISTRICT

UDDINGSTON. **Clydeway Golf Centre,** Blantyre Farm Road, Uddingston G71 7RR (041-641 9201). *Location:* B758 off Main Street, Uddingston, near Glasgow Zoo. 25 covered floodlit bays. *Fees:* £1.50 for 60 balls. *Opening hours:* 10am to 9pm weekdays, 10am to 5.30pm weekends. Tuition and repairs, very large modern shop including ladies department.

# RENFREWSHIRE

RENFREW. **Normandy Golf Range,** Inchinnan Road, Renfrew PA4 9EG (041-886 7477). *Location:* take M8; turn-off Glasgow Airport turn off; take Renfrew Road one mile away. 25 bays covered, floodlit. *Fees:* £1.00 coin for 40 balls. *Opening hours:* 9.30am to 10.00pm seven days. *Eating facilities:* full hotel facilities. Professional, assistants, tuition anytime. Adjacent to Renfrew Golf Club. Large comprehensive stock of all leading golf equipment.

# WALES

# WEST GLAMORGAN

SWANSEA. **Birchgrove Golf Driving Range,** Gwernllwynchwyth Road, Birchgrove, Swansea SA7 9PL. *Location:* M4 Junction 44 take A48 to Morriston, turn right at first lights, approximately half a mile on right. 20 covered, floodlit bays. *Fees:* information available on request. *Opening hours:* 9am to 9pm weekdays, 9am to 7pm weekends. Professional: John Burns (0792 796164).

# IRELAND

# ANTRIM

NEWTOWNABBEY. **Ballyearl Golf and Leisure Centre,** 585 Doagh Road, Newtownabbey BT36 8RZ (0232 848287). *Location:* six miles north of Belfast on M2 then first right onto Doagh Road from Belfast to Larne Road. 32 bay covered, floodlit range, 20 grassed bays. *Fees:* £2.00 small bucket (70 balls), £2.70 large bucket (110 balls). *Eating facilities:* bar – may be signed in. *Opening hours:* 9am to 10.15pm. Professionals: Jim Robinson and Karl O'Donnell. Five squash courts, sunbed, theatre, golf, fitness suite and art classes. Various courses available.

# ARMAGH

CRAIGAVON. **Craigavon Golf and Ski Centre,** Turmoyra Lane, Silverwood, Lurgan, Craigavon BT66 6NE (0762 326606). *Location:* A76 off M1 motorway. Floodlit driving range with 10 covered and 10 grassed bays. *Fees:* £1.60 per bucket. *Eating facilities:* full restuarant. *Opening hours:* 9am to 9pm. Professional, equipment hire, ski slope.

# COUNTY DOWN

KNOCKBRACKEN. **Knockbracken Golf Centre,** 24 Ballymaconaghy Road, Knockbracken, Belfast BT8 4SB (0232 792108). *Location:* outskirts of Belfast, approximately three miles from centre along Ormeau Road near "Four Winds" Restaurant and Public House. 36 bays covered, floodlit and grassed. *Fees:* £2.20 for 100 balls, £1.80 for 70 balls, £1.25 for 40 balls. *Opening hours:* 9am to 11pm. *Eating facilities:* bar open seven days a week during normal opening hours, catering available seven days a week 11am to 10pm. Tuition available at Golf Academy by PGA Professionals. Snooker, playing machines, ski slope in season, equipment hire available, bowling (indoors).

# COUNTY DUBLIN

FOXROCK. **Leopardstown Driving Range,** Foxrock (01 895341). *Location:* five miles south of Dublin city, centre situated in Leopardstown race course. 38 indoor, 38 outdoor floodlit bays. *Fees:* information no[t] provided. *Opening hours:* 9am to 10pm. *Eating facil[i]ties:* restaurant. Professional tuition – practice green. [ ] hole golf course and 18 hole par 3.

# Index

# Index to Advertisers

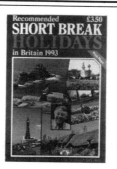

# ONE FOR YOUR FRIEND 1993

FHG Publications have a large range of attractive holiday accommodation guides for all kinds of holiday opportunities throughout Britain. They also make useful gifts at any time of year. Our guides are available in most bookshops and larger newsagents but we will be happy to post you a copy direct if you have any difficulty. We will also post abroad but have to charge separately for post or freight.

The inclusive cost of posting and packing the guides to you or your friends in the UK is as follows:

**Farm Holiday Guide**
**ENGLAND, WALES and IRELAND**
Board, Self-catering, Caravans/Camping, Activity Holidays. Over 400 pages. **£4.00**

**Farm Holiday Guide SCOTLAND**
All kinds of holiday accommodation. **£3.00**

**SELF-CATERING & FURNISHED HOLIDAYS**
Over 1000 addresses throughout for Self-catering and caravans in Britain. **£3.50**

**BRITAIN'S BEST HOLIDAYS**
A quick-reference general guide for all kinds of holidays. **£3.00**

**The FHG Guide to CARAVAN & CAMPING HOLIDAYS**
Caravans for hire, sites and holiday parks and centres. **£3.00**

**BED AND BREAKFAST STOPS**
Over 1000 friendly and comfortable overnight stops. Non-smoking, The Disabled and Special Diets Supplements. **£3.50**

**CHILDREN WELCOME! FAMILY HOLIDAY GUIDE**
Family holidays with details of amenities for children and babies. **£4.00**

**Recommended SHORT BREAK HOLIDAYS IN BRITAIN**
'Approved' accommodation for quality bargain breaks. Introduced by John Carter. **£4.00**

**Recommended COUNTRY HOTELS OF BRITAIN**
Including Country Houses, for the discriminating. **£4.00**

**Recommended WAYSIDE INNS OF BRITAIN**
Pubs, Inns and small hotels. **£4.00**

**PGA GOLF GUIDE**
**Where to play and where to stay**
Over 2000 golf courses in Britain with convenient accommodation. Endorsed by the PGA. Holiday Golf in France, Portugal and Majorca. **£8.50**

**PETS WELCOME!**
The unique guide for holidays for pet owners and their pets. **£4.00**

**BED AND BREAKFAST IN BRITAIN**
Over 1000 choices for touring and holidays throughout Britain. Airports and Ferries Supplement. **£3.00**

**THE FRENCH FARM AND VILLAGE HOLIDAY GUIDE**
The official guide to self-catering holidays in the 'Gîtes de France'. **£8.50**

Tick your choice and send your order and payment to FHG PUBLICATIONS, ABBEY MILL BUSINESS CENTRE, SEEDHILL, PAISLEY PA1 1TJ (TEL: 041-887 0428. FAX: 041-889 7204). **Deduct** 10% for 2/3 titles or copies; 20% for 4 or more.

**Send to:** NAME ........................................................................................

ADDRESS ................................................................................

................................................................................................

........................................................... POST CODE ..............

I enclose Cheque/Postal Order for £ ...............................................

SIGNATURE ......................................................... DATE ........................

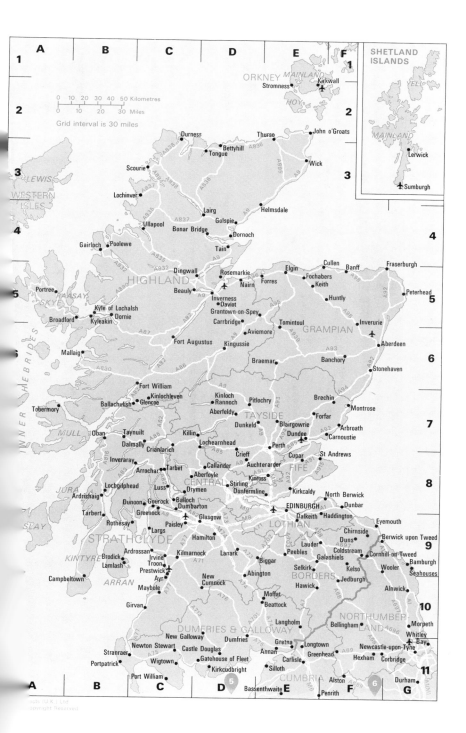

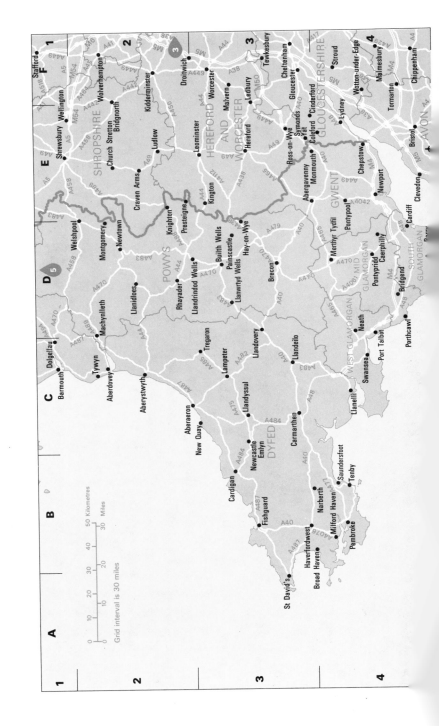

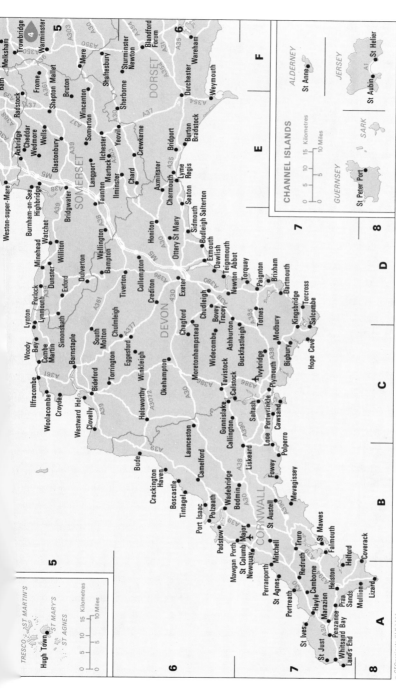

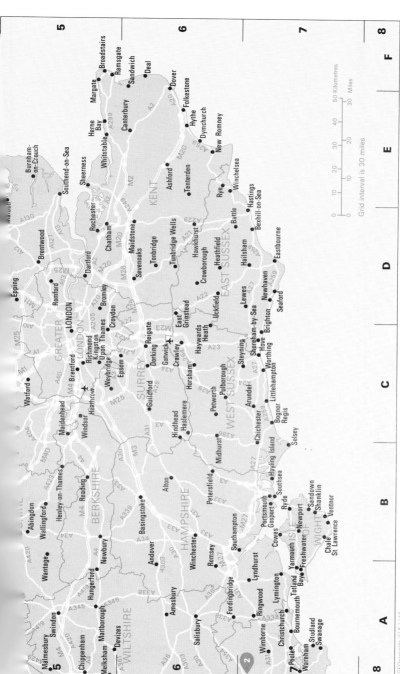

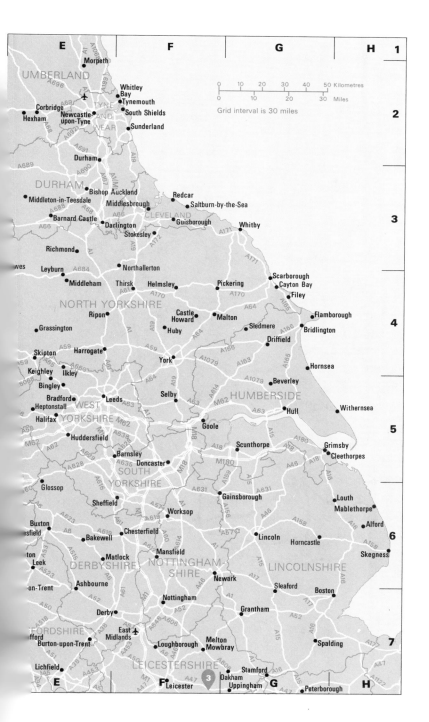

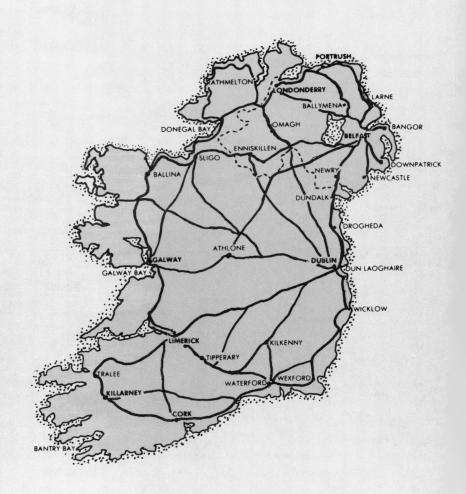